HANDBOOK OF
STATES OF
CONSCIOUSNESS

HANDBOOK OF STATES OF CONSCIOUSNESS

Edited by

Benjamin B. Wolman
and
Montague Ullman

VNR VAN NOSTRAND REINHOLD COMPANY

New York

Manufactured in the United States of America

Published by Van Nostrand Reinhold Company Inc.
115 Fifth Avenue
New York, New York 10003

Van Nostrand Reinhold Company Limited
Molly Millars Lane
Wokingham, Berkshire RG11 2PY, England

Van Nostrand Reinhold
480 La Trobe Street
Melbourne, Victoria 3000, Australia

Macmillan of Canada
Division of Canada Publishing Corporation
164 Commander Boulevard
Agincourt, Ontario M1S 3C7, Canada

15 14 13 12 11 10 9 8 7 6 5 4 3 2

Library of Congress Cataloging in Publication Data

Main entry under title:

Handbook of states of consciousness.

Includes index.
1. Consciousness—Addresses, essays, lectures.
I. Wolman, Benjamin B.   II. Ullman, Montague,
BF311.H335 1984   154   85-7432
ISBN 0-442-29456-5

Contributors

Roger Broughton Department of Medicine (Neurology), University of Ottawa, Ottawa, Canada

Thomas H. Budzynski Behavioral Medicine Associates, Englewood, Colorado

Patricia Carrington Princeton University, Princeton, New Jersey

Roland Fischer Johns Hopkins and Georgetown University Medical Schools, Baltimore, Maryland and Washington, D.C.

Jayne Gackenbach University of Northern Iowa, Department of Psychology, Cedar Falls, Iowa

Leonard George University of Western Ontario, London, Ontario, Canada

Alyce M. Green Menninger Foundation, Topeka, Kansas

Elmer E. Green Menninger Foundation, Topeka, Kansas

Francis Jeffrey Alive Systems Group, Big Sur, California

Joel Kahan Department of Psychiatry, Medical College of Georgia, Augusta, Georgia

Stanley Krippner Center for Consciousness Studies, Saybrook Institute, San Francisco, California

Stephen LaBerge Sleep Research Center, School of Medicine, Stanford, California

Judith R. Malamud Brooklyn Community Counseling Center, Brooklyn, New York

Samuel C. McLaughlin Department of Psychology, Tufts University, Medford, Massachusetts

Claudio Naranjo Department of Psychiatry, University of California, Berkeley, California

E. Mansell Pattison Department of Psychiatry, Medical College of Georgia, Augusta, Georgia

Ernest Lawrence Rossi Department of Psychology, University of California, Los Angeles, California

Jon Tolaas Eiol Vidg. Skule, Nordfjordeid, Norway

Montague Ullman Department of Psychiatry, Albert Einstein College of Medicine, New York, New York

Helen H. Watkins Department of Psychology, University of Montana, Missoula, Montana

John G. Watkins Department of Psychology, University of Montana, Missoula, Montana

J. H. Michael Whiteman Department of Mathematics, University of Capetown, Capetown, South Africa

Benjamin B. Wolman International Encyclopedia of Psychology, Psychiatry, Psychoanalysis and Neurology, New York, New York

Preface

Consciousness or conscious (I am using these two terms interchangeably) has always been the focal issue in psychological studies. One hundred years ago Wundt maintained that psychology is the science of human consciousness. Then came Pavlov and Watson, who presented psychology as a study of conditioned reflexes and overt behavior. Dilthey introduced the concept of understanding psychology, and his approach inspired the Gestalt, field theory, and humanistic psychologists. Freud must be credited with a depth analysis of the concept of consciousness, for he introduced the topographic theory of conscious, preconscious, and unconscious.

And yet, the issues of states of consciousness are far from being solved. The more research continues and the more knowledge is acquired, the more complex are the problems to be dealt with. Parapsychology has opened new vistas, and the current research in meditation, dreams, hypnosis, mysticism, drug addiction, sensory deprivation, biofeedback, and other fields has pointed to new and hitherto unknown areas of the human mind.

The present book is an effort to do justice to these rapidly expanding fields of knowledge. It was not an easy task to put together what is now known about the various states of consciousness. This book deals with three major areas of states of consciousness, namely, theory, manifestations, and applications, their neurological corollaries, and the immense wealth of related issues.

The twenty chapters of the *Handbook* do not represent identical or even similar views. They reflect diverse approaches and different viewpoints. Every chapter is a sort of monograph that bears witness to the high caliber of intellectual work of its author, and the *Handbook* as a whole faithfully represents the *entire field*, its diverse ramifications, and thought-provoking issues.

I was fortunate to obtain the cooperation of more than twenty leading authorities who have made original contributions to this volume. Dr. Broughton's chapter is the only previously published one, and we are grateful to him for allowing us to reprint his work.

This book is a joint effort of Dr. Montagu Ullman and myself. Frankly, it is more Ullman than Wolman, for Dr. Ullman's knowledge of the field certainly surpasses my own. We have also frequently turned to Dr. Roland Fischer for his competent advice.

We are also immensely grateful to Eugene Falken, Vice-President, and Susan Munger, Editor, of Van Nostrand Reinhold for their most friendly and unswerving cooperation.

BENJAMIN B. WOLMAN
MONTAGUE ULLMAN

Contents

Preface vii

Part One: Theory

1 Toward a Neuroscience of Self-Experience and States of Self-Awareness and Interpreting Interpretations, *Roland Fischer* / 3
2 Transformatory Framework: Pictorial to Verbal, *Jon Tolaas* / 31
3 Dimensionality and States of Consciousness, *Samuel C. McLaughlin* / 68
4 Altered States of Consciousness in Everyday Life: Ultradian Rhythms, *Ernest L. Rossi* / 97
5 Hypnosis, Multiple Personality, and Ego States as Altered States of Consciousness, *John G. Watkins and Helen H. Watkins* / 133
6 Lucid Dreaming, *Stephen LaBerge and Jayne Gackenbach* / 159
7 Personal Experience as a Conceptual Tool for Modes of Consciousness, *E. Mansell Pattison and Joel Kahan* / 199

Part Two: Manifestations

8 Working in Isolation: States That Alter Consensus, *Francis Jeffrey* / 249
9 Trance and Possession States, *E. Mansell Pattison, Joel Kahan and Gary S. Hurd* / 286
10 Protoconscious and Psychopathology, *Benjamin B. Wolman* / 311

11 Psi Phenomena as Related to Altered States of Consciousness, *Stanley Krippner and Leonard George* / 332
12 Drug-Induced States, *Claudio Naranjo* / 365
13 On the Remembrance of Things Present: The Flashback, *Roland Fischer* / 395
14 Clinical Applications of Non-Drug-Induced States, *Thomas H. Budzynski* / 428
15 Human Consciousness and Sleep/Waking Rhythms, *Roger Broughton* / 461

Part Three: Accessibility

16 Meditation as an Access to Altered States of Consciousness, *Patricia Carrington* / 487
17 Access to Dreams, *Montague Ullman* / 524
18 Biofeedback and States of Consciousness, *Elmer E. Green and Alyce M. Green* / 553
19 Becoming Lucid in Dreams and Waking Life, *Judith R. Malamud* / 590
20 The Mystical Way and Habitualization of Mystical States, *J. H. M. Whiteman* / 613

Name Index / 661

Subject Index / 669

HANDBOOK OF
STATES OF
CONSCIOUSNESS

Part One
Theory

1. Toward a Neuroscience of Self-Experience and States of Self-Awareness and Interpreting Interpretations

Roland Fischer

The mind and the world—as conceived by the mind—make themselves up together. The observer embodies the world within his mind, while the world does not mind to include its observer. The mind and the world are like lover and beloved. "They asked the Lover, 'What is the world?' He answered, 'It is a book for those who can read in which is revealed my Beloved.' They asked him, 'Is your Beloved in the world then?' He answered, 'Yes, just as the writer is in his book.' 'And in what does this book consist?' 'In my Beloved, since my Beloved contains all, and therefore the world is in my Beloved, rather than my Beloved in the world.'" (Ramon Lull /1232–1316/, 1978, p. 111).

And Paul de Mann (1971) reaffirms the "absolute dependence of the interpretation on the text and the text on the interpretation" (p. 141).

THE EXPERIENCE OF MOVING AS A MOVING EXPERIENCE

If you happen to be a living organism that is capable of intentional, goal-directed movements (and not a plant that is rooted in the earth), then you have to have consciousness. Without consciousness, or self-reflexive "knowing," you would be unable to make decisions about "the next move" and could not survive. Consciousness is a domain of internalized motion, an insight into oneself as a moving experience. Mental activities hence may be "thought of" as muscular acts, since relaxation of striated (voluntary) muscle activity results in an experience of the void—with electromyographic (EMG) recording registering less than one millionth of a volt, that is, zero

3

potential (McGuigan, 1978). Note that EMG activity may be elicited irrespective of whether the willed motor activity is actually performed or just experienced in cognitive space (or imagination). This points to a continous mapping of transformation between external and internal spaces. Attneave and Pierce (1978) report experimental evidence that indeed demonstrates a functional continuity of physical space with imagined space. Such a unity of information ("what") and its utilization ("how") (Konorski, 1962) is impressively illustrated by Evarts (1967), who has shown that neuronal firing in the motor cortex of monkeys is not proportional to the lengthening or shortening of the muscles involved in depressing a lever. Instead, firing is proportional to the weight attached to the lever, that is, the force necessary to move the lever. It is not the muscle or its contraction but the logic of the goal-directed use to which the muscle is put, the "next move" to be achieved (teleologic), that is reflected in the activity of the cortical cells. Piaget and Morf (1958) were correct in locating the roots of logical structures in sensory-motor schemes.

Psychopharmacological evidence supports and strengthens the thought-movement relationship. The sympathomimetic drug amphetamine and related central nervous system stimulants of the "speed" type increase restlessness, and hence *motor* activity, while at the same time mental clarity is improved and *thinking* speeded up. Furthermore, all major tranquilizers that ameliorate schizophrenic *thought* disorder are capable of producing *motor* disorders, and Feinberg (1978) wonders whether these extrapyramidal syndromes might result from alterations of internal feedback in striatal pathways. Could it be that antischizophrenia drugs alter the feedback systems of thought by opening disordered feedback loops and thus alleviating schizophrenic symptoms? It is assumed then that conscious thought shares some properties of simpler motor acts, including internal feedback or corollary discharge. The subjective experience of these discharges should correspond to the experience of will or intention.

Moreover, the minor tranquilizers Librium and Valium, the most frequently prescribed antianxiety drugs of the Western world, are as strong *muscle relaxants* in nonsedative doses as the major tranquilizers (Sternbach, 1979; Costa et al., 1978). By relaxing the muscles, Librium and Valium provide relief from anxiety-arousing thoughts. Note also how neuromuscular disorders, for instance those of old age, or even certain neuromuscular behavior patterns or styles (a particular gait or other mannerisms of movement) reflect either disorders of thinking or unusual mannerisms in thought formation.

Consciousness is an introspectively accessible self-referential aspect of nervous system functioning: the integrating domain of internalized motion.

If conscious thought did not share some properties of simpler motor acts, including internal feedback or corollary discharge, the logical structure of descriptions would not reflect the logical structure of movements. The two phases of elementary motor behavior, "approach" and "withdrawal," the precursors of "yes" and "no," establish the operational origin of the two fundamental axioms of two-valued (Aristotelean) logic, namely, the "law of the excluded contradiction" ("not : x *and* not-x") and the law of the excluded middle" ("x *or* not-x"). Moreover, the logical structure of descriptions as well as their truth values are coupled to movement (v. Foerster, 1981). Willed motor activity is clearly a logically necessary condition of consciousness, that is, a *sine qua non* of organismic self-regulation and "knowing-how."

The threefold meaning of consciousness derives from the Latin 'con-*scio*,' that is, to cut or make a distinction and hence to *know* (the difference); it refers to 'con-*scientia*,' a personal, self-reflexive "knowing for oneself," while the third meaning reveals a socially, consensually validated 'con-scientia,' or "knowing with others." Whenever we perform the magic ritual of drawing a sensory distinction and validating it through willed movement, what emerges in response to such sensory/motor closure is the sensible world of everyday reality.

But not each and every sensory pudding may be validated through motor eating! Only those perceptions that make sense, that is, those for which we have an appropriate behavior, are allowed to actualize. A baby boy castrated at birth, for example, will not perceive women as sexually desirable twenty years later because he has no appropriate behavior for such a perception. Behavioral control of perception (Powers, 1973, and Walls, 1974, in my Chapter 13 on the flashback in this book) implies that perceptions with no corresponding appropriate behavior will not be actualized and, in fact, will be denied, misperceived, repressed, condensed, distorted, and/or sublimated—in accordance with one's personal defense style.

THE EMERGENCE OF THE SENSIBLE WORLD THROUGH SENSORY-MOTOR CLOSURE

What is meant by a sensory/motor (S/M) closure? Every change in activity in the motor domain of an organism triggers a change in activity in the sensory domain of the same organism and vice versa (Maturana, 1978). This relationship is labeled "the relative independence of voluntary movement and sensory processing" (Roland, 1979, p. 310). Or, in the words of von Foerster (1981), whenever changes in a self-referential creature's *sensations* are accounted for by its voluntary *movements*—and vice versa—an S/M closure ensues, and "recursion" enters the picture. By recursion is meant that at a certain point of a process or processing, a function is substituted for its own argument (or "the medium becomes the message"), as, for example, in "this sentence has thirty-three letters." The reentrant form is the meaning of this specific kind of internal coherence or eigenbehavior (Varela, 1977). Making an S/M closure by halving or doubling the string of a harp, for example, as Pythagoras did long ago, and registering the change in pitch by an octave, is (in my definition) *self-tuning*. This self-tuning is experienced as "the sensible world" or "environment"—with the sound of a higher or lower octave (seemingly from "out there")—although "environment" for Maturana is but a means for closure.

During the survival routine of the waking hours—in our "normal" state of consciousness—the universe (i.e., ourself) becomes sensible (and makes sense) as a consequence of our intention and ability to perform an approximately 1:1 S/M closure. But most of us do not "realize" that in this "normophrenic" state (Bader, 1969) the actual image of a tree, the smell of a flower, and harmony of music are sensations experienced within the body; yet we "locate" them "out there" and not on the retina, the nose, and the cochlea. These externalizations are real "out-of-the-body" experiences, while those reported during fever, in response to the ingestion of hallucinogenic drugs, and in certain psychoses are hallucinated projections or depersonalizations.

What are hallucinations? They may best be characterized by a prevalence of the subjective sensory component of self-awareness at the expense of the objective motor component, that is, a high S/M ratio.

When do we make closures with a high S/M ratio? When sensory perception and willed motor activity, in particular, become inhibited. This occurs, for example, during the highly aroused (paradoxical or rapid eye movement—REM) dreaming sleep or during hallucinogenic drug-induced, hyperaroused waking dream states. In these dreamy (or hallucinated) states of consciousness, the sensible world, that is, the reality of touchy experiences, loses dimensions and gradually becomes dematerialized into appearances of things. Strangely, by being able to create a sensible world we also have a solid base for leaving it, while riding high on rising levels of arousal. The high sensory involvement with concomitant loss of (willed motor) freedom—high S/M ratio—carries us into another hallucinatory or dreamy world, from the new vantage point of which the sensible world of daily routine may be seen as just one of the varieties of states of consciousness.

In an earlier report we gave a quantitative meaning to the S/M ratio by measuring the components of a (psychomotor) S/M performance—specifically, handwriting area (measured in square centimeters) and handwriting pressure (in 10^4 dynes averaged over time)—and found a 31 percent hallucinogenic drug-induced increase in mean S/M ratio from pre-drug to drug-peak in a sample of forty-seven college-age volunteers. In these studies, the drug psilocybin was administered in a dosage range of 160–250 micrograms per kilogram body weight (Fischer et al., 1970; Thatcher et al., 1970; Fischer, 1971).

WE ARE A CLOSED ("INFORMATION-TIGHT") SYSTEM

The nervous system—while switching from one state of consciousness to another (e.g., approximately every 90 minutes during the night from slow wave sleep into the dreamy rapid eye movement state)—operates as a *closed system* and generates only states of relative activity between its component neurons and sensory and motor elements. The nervous system does not generate input and output relations. These relations are *ex post facto* in the eye of the "outside" observer, since "organization is in the eye of the beholder" (Beer, 1966, p. 350). Let me illustrate this with an example. The bacteria in the vagina and intestines of humans are but aware of the "ultimate reality" of their universe and unaware of their role as subsystems that maintain an ecological balance, that is, an optimal pH in the respective tissues that are part of a larger host system. Clearly, the insight of an "ecologically balanced organization" exists only in the eye of the beholder! (What would bacteria do if they were made to evolve to the awareness of their own organization? Living in a vagina of "chance and necessity," would they yearn for interaction with an extravaginal intelligence?)

We are a closed system, comparable to a pilot in a cockpit whose instrumental flight at zero visibility consists only in maintaining and adjusting certain dial readings (Maturana, 1978). In no sense is there environmental information being processed. "For what takes place in the operation of the nervous system is always the same kind of process: distinction of relations of relative neuronal activities through relations of relative neuronal activities, and so on recursively" (p. 35). What does Maturana's pilot do while busy adjusting dial readings during instrumental flight? Each perceptual–behavioral performance, that is, each S/M closure, is analogous to an adjustment of a dial reading. For example, walking toward or away from a particular point in space-time, kissing your beloved one, drinking a glass of water are all adjustments on dial readings in order to maintain the organization of the system "person." What our particular system attempts and succeeds at maintaining is not the constancy of the *milieu interieur* but self-organization brought about thermodynamically in and by dissipative structures under conditions (not too) far from equilibrium (Nicolis and Prigogine, 1976). In fact, the system is open to energy but (nearly) closed to information (Ashby, 1956). The paradoxical nature of such "information-tightness," that is, the double-blind, double-bind nature of what "I am observing," becomes evident, for example, during "instrumental flights" or sensory-motor closures, when one considers that the "I" of the observation and the goal-seeking observer who proposes it are self-reflecting. Analogously, in the Epimenedean, or Cretan, paradox "I am lying" and its Gödelian abbreviated version "some true statements are not decidable," the subject of both the proposition and of the goal-seeking subsystem that proposes it is identical (Wilden and Wilson, 1976).

BEYOND THE 6TH SYNAPSE: CIRCUITS
OF EXPERIENCED SELF-REFLECTIVITY

In the current theory of perception, inputs of the sensory channel are subject to "sensory information processing." The inputs are described in terms of information theory, but the processes are described in terms of old-fashioned mental acts: recognition, interpretation, inference, concepts, ideas, and storage and retrieval of ideas. These are still the operations of the mind upon the deliverances of the senses. This theory, says Gibson (1979), will not do.

The plight of the "information-processing" neurophysiologist concerned with inputs and outputs is further elaborated by Haber (1979). "A visual stimulus initiates a predictable chain of events in the nervous system. We understand a fair amount about the early events and processes of this sequence and can describe them in terms of neurophysiological [in my terms "brain"] function. But by the 5th or 6th synapse we have to switch our descriptive language abruptly to various conceptual terms. We then talk about recognition, identification or perseveration of information and the like [in my terms "mind," self-reflexive "mind" function] without making any serious attempt to specify these processes in terms of anatomy or physiology" (Haber, 1979, p. 263).

Let me unify these processes in a cybernetic framework by emphasizing the existence in neural tissue of self-adjusting feedback systems with built-in criteria of expected (goal-directed) performance. They are the circuits of experienced self-reflexivity, a very common property of neural tissue. For example, some of the outputs of the somatosensory cortical receiving area are nerve fibers that modulate the activity of their own sources of input (Towe, 1973; Gordon, 1978).

Could it be that differentiation into brain functions (neurophysiology) and mind functions (psychology) is mainly due to an increase in self-reflexive feedback systems operating after the 5th or 6th synapse? Such a reasonable assumption could also help to explain other related puzzles. Penfield (1968), when applying electrical stimulation to certain areas of the brain, caused his patient's hand to move, but the patient did not feel that he was willing the movement ("you made me move it"). So where is the

"I" that did not wish the arm to move? It would not be remarkable to find—comments Glassman (1983)—that a patient can sense the extrinsic origin of a movement elicited by electrical stimulation of the motor cortex pyramidal cells that are only *two* synapses away from the muscles. But there are areas of the brain *farther removed* from motor outputs or sensory inputs, where stimulation yields effects that might easily be interpreted as tampering with the (self-reflective) will. It appears that within a hierarchically organized (nervous) system an *increase* in the number of firing synaptic circuits and functioning feedback subsystems allows *quantity* to change into *quality*—reflex to become self-reflexivity—and thus mind emerges from brain-function. It is also probable that, in certain cases, what we call a "stimulus" is already a perceived "response" of the nervous system (as an "individual," to begin with, is a product of society).

"Determinism" and "free will" may be, at least to some extent, functions of the amount of interconnected reflexive (feedback) circuitry involved. In this sense, free will may be regarded as an awareness of one's goal-directed, self-reflective "now." We are free to make decisions while choices present themselves "now"; but with the termination of the present, *determinism* accounts for past causative behavior.

If no decisions are to be made with respect to the "next move," we do not need feedback for assessing the details of subsequent choices, and hence we do not have to be conscious of what we are doing. Driving a car while solving a mathematical problem, for example, may result from switching off reflexive circuits pertinent to car driving and thus switching the function of driving the car (in the brain) on "automatic." Consciousness is, after all, a process by which "non-dominant action systems" are prevented from becoming active (Shallice, 1972).

Apparently we seem to know that lower level distinctions, represented by a causal-structural "reflex" network of the brain, (up to the 5th or 6th synapse) differ in character from the higher level (reflexive feedback) functioning of the mind that knows that the lower level distinctions are represented by a causal-structural (deterministic) network. . . . There is an "operation bootstrap" involved here—a reflection of reflexive circuits) that should remind us that the brain is the only organ that has unfinished embryogenesis and is programmed to develop registering its interactions as an *experience of itself*. The brain changes its structure, triples its mass between birth and maturity, and goes on differentiating and changing until it collapses, and even then it has not finished (Trevarthen, 1979). The tastes and smells, the moving experiences, the visible and audible realities of conscious states are spatio-temporal as well as temporary, interactional constructs, a living brain's and mind's self-perceptions.

If what we believe to be the world is only self-perception, then we have a good case of "mistaken identity." It is easier now to understand why brain and mind cannot explain themselves. A knife cannot cut itself! Our mind makes us believe that it explains the world, but that world is a self-reflexive "knowing of oneself." For Ramon Lull, "the mind and the world" were "like lover and beloved" (see the beginning of this chapter), but if Lull could take a second and closer look today, and see with our eyes, he might realize that *the mind and the world are like Narcissus looking into the mirror.*

Narcissus, in fact, sees himself as an object in a mirror while holding another mirror that reflects him as a subject looking into a mirror, still seeing himself as an object. These mirrors stand for the varieties of objective and subjective reflections; the subjective reflections are based on internal feedback loops, and the objective reflections on *external* feedback loops, that is, *motor, acts* actively performed "out there." Making the closure between these two domains results in "being in the world," or a recursive reflection of the self-referential subject in the mirrors of a universe that is himself.

The very act of observation (or measurement) on the part of Narcissus—whether on a quantum level or on that of a living organism (Norwich, 1983)—changes the outcome of what is to be observed (or measured). We cannot, therefore, regard the world as an objective reality with a given structure conceptually separable from us as observers. Instead, as Stent (1979) paraphrases Niels Bohr, the world is simply there, with us in it as an integral and inseparable part. Thus, there must be limits to the depth of understanding that we can hope to gain of the world, because of our joint role as spectators and actors in the drama of existence, a drama—without both author and plot—that proceeds by enacting and reenacting itself. . . .

MODELING THE EXPERIENCE OF BEING ONE'S SELF

A few years ago I critically examined a variety of models of brain function and put forward a novel socio-biological model (Fischer, 1981). The social behavior of ant colonies, and particularly that of the desert ant *Cataglyphis bicolor,* it was proposed, embodies a set of principles that account for the plasticity of the young human brain and follow both the law of mass action and the law of equipotentiality (Lashley, 1929).

There is another, lesser known, theory of "what's in a brain that ink may character" (108th sonnet of Shakespeare). It is based on a series of papers by Baird and Noma (1975), whose subjects had to (but could not) generate numbers at random. To account for this observation, the not particularly original but supreme possibility was considered that nervous system functioning may be governed by "fundamental mathematical laws." The speculation was forwarded that the preferred numbers obtained from Baird's subjects represented a preferred state (that can be described mathematically as a power function), and, hence, the psychophysical power function of Stevens may be merely an outward manifestation of perceptual transformations involved in the human system's creation of preferred states (Fischer, 1974, 1984).

The quest for "fundamental mathematical laws" can be traced to a mentality that matured in the Gutenberg era of printing (around 1500) and, specifically, to the notion of "places" that in Lefèvre d'Etaples' tables commonly take the form of quasi-algebraic, or arithmetical, displays (Ong, 1958, p. 77). Related attempts by Celaya to model brain function through the geometrization of logic culminated in his "geometry of the mind" (Ong, 1958, p. 81).

Nearly 500 years later Pellionisz and Llinás also considered the central nervous system (CNS) function *geometrico modo,* assuming that the sensory and motor subsystems use different natural coordinate systems. Motor coordination is then a translation of "self"-knowledge from CNS-hyperspace into "universal knowledge" in three-dimensional (3-D) Cartesian space. Neuronal networks, such as loops and reflexes, are regarded as tensors, and the function of the cerebellum may be explained by the available tensor theory. Sensory information is resolved into *covariant* vectorial components, while motor execution is composed of *contravariant* components. Thus coordination is defined as a geometrical transformation of the motor vector from covariant to contravariant expression; the first featuring intention, the latter allowing execution. The scheme is a unification of the notion on temporal lookahead by Taylor expansion and the notion of cerebellar function as a metric tensor. The covariant, distributed space–time components are first extrapolated by a lookahead, and then transformed by the space–time metric tensor (Pellionisz and Llinás, 1979, 1980).

A neocortical operation based on a *mathematical function* to couple the sensory and motor domains may be another conceptual scheme that links the onlooker to a stage that it creates. Von Foerster (1976) proposed that it may be more economical for the CNS to process functions in preference to processing data. The processing of functions as a coherent pattern of activity may be dynamically maintained by indefinite recursion. A recursive loop unfolds (like its topological equivalent, the Moebius strip) according to an algorithm that repeats information from a previous state in subsequent iterations. This "strange loop" copies itself as it goes along by reembedding, and sometimes inverting, the lower levels of the twist in higher patterns of organization (Hofstadter, 1979). Analogously, at fixed points in the semantics of computer programs, patterns of indefinite recursion result, for instance, in the emergence of eigenbehaviors (Varela, 1977). Within functions that compute functions, the computing functions of the brain would require less logical depth—or sequential complexity—than the functions that are computed (von Neumann, 1958).

What is the "text and context" of consciousness? Consciousness is said to have a content. But the (self-deconstructing) antithesis of the above statement also makes sense: all that there is, exists in consciousness. Is consciousness the experiencing of one's self while making the "next move" in a "sensible world," that is, the cognitive (cortical) interpretation of a particular level of (subcortical) arousal? One may further specify a state of consciousness in terms of processed signals that are *re*entered at the processing path of the next internally generated cycle. The reentered phase—like a moving Moebius strip—displays its internal nature as if it were an external one, and the actualizing recursion is experienced as meaning, or self-interpretation, within the continuing frame of spatio-temporal stability. The role of arousal is to modulate the phasic nature of the reentry operations, with higher levels of arousal intensifying the meaning of meaning.

The minimal set of features required for awareness according to the reentrant-signal model (Edelman and Mountcastle, 1978, pp. 82–85) are degenerate selection, reflexive recognition of neuronal groups by each other, the processing of activation and signals in a coordinate fashion, rhythmic activity with phased states, and appropriate signal-holding networks allowing reentrant processing over a multidimensional store.

The need for a "thinking homunculus" is removed by the ties between phasic reentrant processing and the abstract multidimensional store, defining "self" as a world model in terms of past S/M closures. The need for an infinite regress is also removed, and no causal requirements are placed on input signals.

In paraphrasing and amplifying Edelman and Mountcastle (1978, p. 95), consciousness may be considered a form of associative recollection with updating, based on present reentrant processing (cognition becoming *re*cognition) that continually confirms or alters the meaning of a "world model" or "self-concept" by means of parallel sensory-motor closures. Changes in the level of arousal alter the S/M ratio of closures, and, hence, the prevailing state of consciousness.

COMPLEMENTARITY OF EXCITATION AND EXPECTATION

The capability of recursive convergence on some expected function may create the psychic phenomenology of intentional states and associative causality. That this, indeed, may well be the case is supported by what Freeman (1981) has to say:

The cortical signal is presumed to be based as much on the expectant function as on the excitation function. The animal perceives the stimulus it models or expects to receive, unless the received input differs from expectation so that the input is rejected. "The definition of perception is 'the integration of sensory impressions . . . as a function of . . . expectation . . . and serving as a basis for . . . (expectant) action'" (p. 578).

Freeman's insightful and most important remarks about what I would christen the "complementary equivalence of expectation and excitation," are fully in line with the already mentioned "information-tightness" of living systems (Ashby, 1956) and with the original observations of Norwich (1982) that "One cannot perceive something about which one is perfectly certain; in fact, if a steady sensory input is maintained the awareness of it will fade away." Only those external events are perceived about which one is initially uncertain. The uncertainty arises at the sensory receptor level. It is the *rate* of impulse transmission along the primary afferent neuron issuing from the sensory receptor that relays to the brain the rate at which the eye becomes more certain that a steady light is shining. An organism cannot perceive certainty; perception is always relative to the expectation of the organism (Norwich, 1983).

Uncertainty and *expectations* refer to the domain of past experiences, that is, evolutionary (genetic and epigenetic) learning as well as individually acquired *interpretive* behaviors; whereas central excitation, or *arousal,* is the "component" that is to be *interpreted.* The following example should illustrate the vicarious, or complementary, role of expectation and arousal, the two cardinal pillars of "knowing."

It is well known that wearing distorting prism spectacles results in a variety of visual distortions that gradually disappear, since the world is apparently rethought (cortically) to be seen "as it should be" in accordance with past experience, and in spite of the distorted image on the (subcortical) retina (Fischer, 1969a; Kohler, 1964). The visual cortical (perceptual) rethinking—in line with one's *expectations*—is conceptualized as the result of a recalibration of target-directed orientation of head and limb. Each of the two types of effects is produced by re-afferent information related to the control of the appropriate S/M system (Mikaelian and Malatesta, 1974). Moreover, the rethinking, or conceptualization, of more than one world is possible in squirrel monkeys as well as in humans (McGonigle and Flook, 1978). Perceptual thinking need not be a transient phenomenon; both monkeys and student volunteers can rethink the effects of two prisms displacing in equal and opposite directions and eventually conserve the validity or expectation of both world concepts ("adaptations") together with their normal reaching behavior.

Excitation ("presentation") and *expectation* (compensatory "adaptation") are separable aspects of brain space (Bossom, 1965): excitation is vulnerable to the effects of posterior lesions, while expectation is impaired by lesions that lie far anteriorly, that is, subcortical lesions involving the head of the caudate nucleus.

One of the preconditions of compensatory adaptation for making the correct "next move" is the low (approximately 1:1) S/M ratio of daily routine. But when voluntary motor activity is inhibited, and the S/M ratio consequently is raised (for instance, through the ingestion of *arousal*-inducing hallucinogenic drugs such as LSD, psilocybin, and mescaline, or through the hypnotically induced hallucinogenic experience (Gwynne et al., 1969)), cortical *expectations* or interpretive behavior recedes, and the subject is compelled to perceive the world distorted as it appears on the excited (subcortical) retina (Fischer and Hill, 1971).

The interpretive (hermeneutic) aspect of perceptual processes is complementary to the teleological aspect of willed motor acts, and, analogously, expectation is complementary to excitation. What Freeman (1981) refers to on the neural level of olfaction we have established on the perceptual level of vision (Fischer, 1969b; Gwynne et al., 1969; Hill and Fischer, 1970; Fischer and Hill, 1971). Our psychopharmacological studies with college-age volunteers implement the problem in *quantitative* terms: 4.5 prism diopters of visual distortion are needed in the normal state of daily routine to just noticeably bend a straight line. In other words, the visual cortical *expectation* of the continuing straightness of a line is so strong that it can only be broken down through 4.5 diopters of subcortical (retinal) *excitation*. Under the influence of 160–200 micrograms/kilogram of the arousal-inducing drug psilocybin, however, subcortical excitation—leading to the reality of the distorted (bent) line on the retina—becomes so prominent that the cortical expectation of straightness is being relinquished already under the impact of 2 prism diopters of optically distorting excitation.

From "where" can we expect expectation to have originated? Routtenberg's (1968) animal studies led him to conclude that there exist two kinds of arousal, one being "drive" arousal and the other being "motivational" arousal. Nelsen and Goldstein (1972) could show that not only are the two types of arousal separable, but one can shift from the one to the other by administration of certain pharmacological agents in widespread use by humans (e.g., nicotine). It is conceivable, therefore, that expectation in humans is excitatory in origin and that motivational arousal in animals is equivalent to human expectant (interpretive) behavior, that is, a comparing of the image of a figure (against its ground) with figures already experienced before.

The complementary relation between excitation and expectation not only prevails on the neural and perceptual levels, but can be easily put to test in the behavioral domain, for example, through the power of prayer. Strong religious belief, and persistent prayer in particular, may change what is a potentially stressful event. *Expectations* based on strong religious belief can alleviate or even inhibit the stress response, that is, the process of adrenal cortical and medullary activation, and reduce *excitation,* that is, peripheral responsiveness to secreted noradrenaline (Benson, 1983).

SUMMING UP AND PREVIEW
OF "INTERPRETING INTERPRETATIONS"

Being (a) human (system) means being both actor and spectator in an experiential drama that is enacted on a stage of subjective and objective reflections. Effecting a closure between these self-reflexive sensory (S) and motor (M) domains results in recursive reflections of the self-referential subject in the mirror of a universe that is himself. An approximately 1:1 S/M ratio reflects the normal state of daily routine materializing "out there," whereas higher S/M ratios, that is, a prevalence of the subjective component, are the main feature of nonordinary hyper- and hypo-aroused states of consciousness that are actualized in dematerialized inner space.

The two complementary aspects of self-experience are CNS-*excitation,* that is, (subcortical) arousal, and (cortical or cognitive) expectation, that is, *interpretive* behavior.

In the following pages we shall cartograph a continuum of nonordinary or altered states of consciousness; each state of "knowing" is discernible as and defined by a particular level of hyper- and hypo*arousal*. Levels of arousal are *interpreted* according to specific plots (scripts or scenarios) based on past dialogues between genes and history as recorded in myth, fairy tale, and narrative fiction—the codified human interpretive repertoire. Narrative fiction embodies all human desires and expectations, and asserts the rhetorical status of psychic manifestations. Nonordinary states of consciousness represent plots and scenarios that make the distinction between fact and fiction illusory.

Our view of the universe holds that it is self-perception and self-interpretation. Other points of view could include the possibility that the universe becomes conscious by being reflected in our self-experience. According to an intermediate position: the analysis of the physical world will lead back in some now-hidden way to man himself, to conscious mind, tied through the very act of observation and participation to partnership in the foundation of the universe (Wheeler, 1974). Lastly there is a proposition—unpalatable to believer and unbeliever alike—that is the provocative central premise of Olaf Stapledon's (1983) work: mankind is irrelevant to the purposes of the universe.

Let me conclude this section by invoking the spirit of John Locke (1690). According to Locke: "If God placed a man at the edge of the Universe, he could not stretch his hands beyond his body" (p. 150). And that reminds me of a story told by Russ Hanson (Gregory, 1981, p. 543) of an Oxford undergraduate who staggered his tutor by asking, "What is the external world external to?" I would have replied by quoting two lines from *Dejection: An Ode,* by Coleridge (Bloom, 1961, p. 221):

> for "we receive but what we give,
> And in our life alone does Nature live."

Interpreting Interpretations

A CARTOGRAPHY OF NONORDINARY STATES OF CONSCIOUSNESS

Our voyage along a circular continuum of nonordinary states of consciousness (Figure 1) proceeds within the complementarity of central nervous system excitation or *arousal* and its expectant *interpretation.* Conscious experience is posited to emerge from the cognitive interpretation of (subcortical) arousal. The meaning of "to arouse" is: to stir up, to rise, arise, wake, awake (Onions, 1966), and to excite to action (Webster, 1958). To "excite" may refer, for example, to electrons, single neurons, a nervous network, an organism, a person or masses of people. By using the term "arousal," we wish to emphasize the unity of a person, since "arousal" stands for both physiological *and* psychological excitation and thus refers to one and the same common function. In short, "arousal" is a holistic, organismic concept that denotes generalized reticular activity contributing to the waking state (Moruzzi and Magoun, 1949). Specific types of arousal, for example, the aroused emotion of anxiety, are meant to be a feeling of threat and danger *and* a physiological reaction of alarm and defense (Grace and Graham, 1958). There is no separate body and mind to be studied; it is rather the domain of interest and specialized technical competence of the

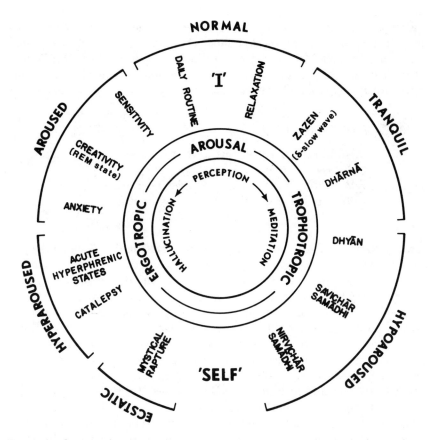

Figure 1. States of consciousness are mapped on a perception–hallucination continuum of increasing central (ergotropic) or hyperarousal (left) and a perception–meditation continuum of increasing central (trophotropic) or hypoarousal (right).

A labeling in terms of psychopathology has been omitted from this map. It is perfectly normal to be hyperphrenic and ultimately ecstatic in response to increasing levels of hyperarousal. Only when a person gets stuck in a particular (including the normal) state, should he be labeled a patient. The capability to "rebound," therefore, is an indication of health.

The hyperaroused rapid eye movement stage of dreaming sleep may be placed between creativity and anxiety (on the left side), whereas the delta or slow-wave EEG sleep is on the horizontally corresponding right side of the map (i.e., between zazen and dhārnā). Hence, each night during sleep we repeatedly travel through a revolving excited and tranquil stage set and become actor and audience of creative or stereotyped scenarios, the dialogues between the "I" (or the world) and the "Self."

investigator (observer) that determines whether arousal is referred to as somatic aspect or an aspect of psychological inquiry. Arousal always excites, and is accompanied by increased catecholamine output (Levy, 1965), irrespective of whether the interpretation of arousal (involving also the set and setting of the experience) is unpleasant or pleasurable (bad or good).

A MAP OF INNER SPACE

> And in the midst of this wide quietness
> A rosy sanctuary will I dress
> With the wreath'd trellis of a working brain,
> With buds, and bells, and stars without a name,
> (*Ode to Psyche,* by John Keats)

Two voyages are charted on the map (Figure 1). The first is along the perception–hallucination continuum of increasing ergotropic arousal, an inner, central sympathetic excitation or hyperarousal; and the second is along the perception–meditation continuum of increasing trophotropic arousal, a tranquil relaxation, or central hypoarousal. A voyage along the path of hyperarousal is experienced by Western travelers as normal, creative, and hyperphrenic (including manic and schizophrenic as well as cataleptic and ecstatic) states. The voyage along the path of hypoarousal is a succession of meditative experiences referred to by Eastern travelers as *zazen, dhārnā, dhyān, savichār,* and *nirvichār samādhi* (Fischer, 1978).

The starting point of both voyages is the "I" or the "world," at the top of Figure 1, the objectified universe of normal daily routine, a "normophrenic" state of mind (Bader, 1969), containing all that which is *known* and *seen* in the world. The "I" is related to Freud's *ego* (1953, p. 17) which he defined as "a coherent organization of mental process" controlling "the approaches to motility—that is to the discharge of excitation into the external world." The "Self," at the bottom of our circular diagram, is the destination of both voyages, a destination that can only be approached but never reached. Being the subjective *knower* and *seeer*, the "Self" cannot fully know and see itself.

THE PERCEPTION-HALLUCINATION CONTINUUM

On the perception–hallucination continuum (left half of Figure 1) normality (or "normophrenia"), creativity, and hyperphrenic states, including mystical rapture, are identified as states of increasing ergotropic arousal (for a definition of "ergotropic," see Fischer, 1975b, p. 237). A state of consciousness refers to a particular cerebral connectivity and sensory/motor ratio, both of which are stabilized through the prevailing level of arousal. Above a critical level, or change, in general, destabilization occurs first, followed by stabilization on another level of connectivity, sensory/motor ratio, and level of arousal. One can conceptualize states of consciousness as the ledges of cybernetic step function within a dynamic, ultrastable system.

Creativity is an excited-exalted state of arousal with a characteristic increase in both data content ("space") and rate of data processing ("time"). The acute schizophrenic state—"exhaustion" in response to what is experienced as stress—is marked by an even higher level of arousal, but the increase in data content cannot be matched by a corresponding increase in data processing. This "jammed computer state" may be further specified: "only the controlled serial information processing system seems disordered, whereas the automatic parallel process is intact or may appear even supernormal" (Callaway and Naghdi, 1982, p. 340).

Hyperaroused states may arise naturally or be elicited experimentally. Increasing amounts of the hallucinogenic drugs psilocybin, LSD, and mescaline can induce central excitation and move a subject through anxious, creative, and hyperphrenic states. Such a "trip" is accompanied by a reduction in the modulation of sensory input and intensification of the experience of meaning. The simultaneously proceeding desynchronized-hypersynchronous electroencephalographic (EEG) activity is associated with hallucinatory behavior and an increase in nor-adrenergic, sympathetic discharge ascending from the *locus coeruleus*. Hofmann (1968) characterizes this state as an *excitation syndrome* and does not fail to mention that motor activity is strangely damped. Translating Hofmann in our terminology: hyperaroused states are marked by a rising sensory/motor (S/M) ratio, and, we may add that there is a simultaneously decreasing expectation/excitation (E/e) ratio. There is an increase in muscle tone and a decrease in skin resistance, fast habituation to alpha-blocking, mydriasis, hyperthermia, pyloerection, hyperglycemia, and tachycardia. The stimulation of synapses in the reticular formation results in an increased sensitivity to sensory stimuli in "minimizers"—that is, subjects who at the peak of a drug-induced arousal state prefer to reduce sensory input ("reducers")—and decreased sensitivity in "maximizers" (or "augmenters") (for a review see, e.g., Fischer, 1980; about catalepsy and mystical rapture, see Fischer, 1971, 1975b, 1978).

THE PERCEPTION-MEDITATION CONTINUUM

On the perception–meditation continuum (right half of Figure 1) the path of increasing hypoarousal: zazen, the dhārnā and dhyān states, as well as the Christian Prayer of Simplicity, are all states of increasingly restful inner alertness. Trophotropic arousal (see Fischer, 1971, p. 897) and in the initial phase EEG synchronization, an increase in alpha-rhythm amplitude and decrease in frequency, are characteristic features of meditative states, including TM or transcendental meditation, a standardized, transcultural, contemporary variety of mantra-meditation.

Meditation or prayer decreases muscle tone and induces a hypometabolic state of decreased oxygen consumption, carbon dioxide production, and respiratory rate. There is an increase in skin resistance, discharges to the sweat glands are diminished, and a decline of blood lactate levels is noted (no anxiety). Relaxation of the striated muscles is another important feature of meditation, whether achieved through religious practices or through autogenic training and related approaches implicit in "progressive relaxation."

The ceremonial renunciation of the world through Zen and Yogic practices culminates in the dissolution of all thought processes, that is *nirvichār samādhi,* a state of pure self-reference without content; this state is marked by extremely low levels of arousal and metabolic rate. (For more information about both the perception–hallucination and perception–meditation continua, see Fischer, 1975a,b, 1976a, b.)

THE INTERPRETIVE REPERTOIRE OF PLOTS AND SCENARIOS

Let us now close our eyes and transfigure metaphorically the circular cartography (in Figure 1) to an immense experiential theater. The revolving stages form another circle, one "whose center is everywhere and its circumference nowhere" (Mahnke, 1937, pp. 21, 25). The "inner space" of each segment or stage set corresponds to a hyperaroused and hypoaroused state of consciousness, each being concerned with particular "knowing," that is, archetypal or stereotyped scripts and scenarios. Each "knowing," whether artistic, literary, religious, or esoteric, is considered to be programmed (Fischer, 1978, p. 25), innate or "already there" (Plato, 398 B.C., 1956, p. 138), and as the stage is set by a particular level of hyperarousal or hypoarousal, the pertaining scenario is being reexperienced or flashed back. Thus, the cognitive manifestation of experience is arousal-state-bound as well as (Western or Eastern) stage-bound (Fischer, 1978).

The repertoire of each revolving stage set is limited to a few plots or scripts. The *themata* consist largely of wish-fulfilling self-interpretations that are the warp and woof of narrative fiction. The nature of fiction and our fictitious nature are revealed through the revolving transformations of consciousness.

The themes of scripts and stories are constantly rewritten, repainted, and recomposed for each generation with but slight variations within a change in style begun by others. In music, Meyer (1980) contends, few of the greatest artists have been promulgators of new principles. Most of the great masters have transcended no limits; rather they have been inventive strategists, imaginative and resourceful in exploiting and extending existing limits (e.g., Haydn, Mozart, Schubert, Chopin, Brahms, Verdi, Berlioz, and so on).

In literature, and particularly in narrative fiction, after allowance has been made for the influence of literary tradition in creating a stereotyped form, one example should illustrate the repetitive nature of the human interpretive repertoire, our "knowing" expectations—based on philogenetically and ontogenetically learned past experience. Heliodorus is one of the three great epic poets of Greek antiquity (in company with Homer and Virgil). His voluminous novel *Ethiopica* was revived and in vogue around 1590, and such authors as Tasso, Cervantes, Lope de Vega, Calderón, and Racine were influenced by Heliodorus' model of the novel; they adapted, imitated, and dramatized it. Although few people know Heliodorus today, plot and topic of his novel are still mirrored in Verdi's *Aida* (Hägg, 1983, p. 206).

Narrative fiction embodies the whole range of human expectations and hence may be viewed as codification of the interpretive repertoire of our species. The greatest freedom of interpretation—based on a large variety of plots and scenarios—prevails in those states of consciousness that cluster around the "I" state of daily routine. In these states, characterized by high expectations (E) and moderate excitation (e) or arousal (*high E/e* ratio) as well as a *low* to moderate sensory/motor (*S/M*) ratio, we are free to vary the "content" of consciousness, a content directed toward action in the sensible world "out there."

As we move away from the "I" state toward the "Self" (Figure 1), we leave behind the material constructs of physical (4 dimensional) space–time (Fischer, 1969b) and slowly descend into the reaches of dematerialized ($n-1$ dimensional) timeless inner space. The universe that appears in these states of consciousness has to be interpreted in a "less-action"-minded and more stereotyped and predictable manner; in other words, the loss of freedom of hallucinatory or dreamy states is accompanied by a *low E/e* and *high S/M* ratio. In the most hyperaroused states the experienced loss of freedom is interpreted as "being under a spell," "manipulated," "possessed by invisible powers," and so forth. Indeed, hyperaroused consciousness becomes the stage of a puppet theater with a restricted range of hyperphrenic scenarios that are imbued with a vaguely numinous quality. A magnificent passage from a narrative fiction of Gérard de Nerval, "the mad poet," should illuminate the compulsive magic of such hyperphrenic states:

Immense circles traced themselves in the infinite like the orbs that troubled water will form after the fall of a body; every region, peopled by radiant figures, was colored, moved, and mingled one by one, and a divinity, always the same, smilingly refused the furtive masks of its diverse incarnations, finally to take refuge, unseizable, in the mystic splendors of the Asian sky. (Quoted from Poulet, 1966, p. 175)

Hence being creatively inspired, and, on an even higher level of arousal, being possessed (Fischer, 1969c), may be varieties of self-possession or self-actualization, depending on the intellectual and spiritual sophistication of the persona. Novalis, the eighteenth-century German romantic master, is said to have believed that, indeed, the greatest magician would be the one who could cast a spell on himself so that his own magic would appear to him strange and from without (Novalis, 1968, p. 323). Nerval's prose reveals the "case history" of such a strange magician.

THE INTERPRETIVE REPERTOIRE OF AROUSED STATES AND ITS RULES OF REWRITING

If myth, fairy tale, and the "poems" of narrative fiction constitute the interpretive repertoir of human consciousness, then the "stories" that are constantly rewritten by and for each generation with *slight variations* represent the codification of that repertoir. Each and every reader is also programmed as a potential author of these "stories."

What is the nature of these variations or the rules of rewriting in terms of intra-poetic influences and relationships? Harold Bloom offers an account of how one poet helps to form another, by asserting that "poetic history is indistinguishable from poetic influence, since strong poets make that history by *misreading* one another, so as to clear imaginative space for themselves" (Bloom, 1973a, p. 5). There are six revisionary ratios or tropes of poetic influence, the first of which we have just mentioned, namely:

- *Clinamen,* which is poetic misreading or misprision.
- *Tessera,* which is completion and antithesis.
- *Kenosis,* the movement toward discontinuity with the precursor.
- *Daemonization,* or generalizing away the uniqueness of the earlier work.
- *Askesis,* or a movement of self-purgation.
- *Apophrades,* or the return of the dead: creation of the appearance that the later poet himself had written the precursor's characteristic work. (Bloom, 1973a, pp. 14–16)

By trope we mean the linguistic manifestation of (not literal) meaning by which poetic meaning is established or "the word becomes flesh," for example.

But what topics (*topoi,* in Greek) are troped in these varied texts? And can one clearly separate *tropos* from *topos*? *Topos* is a technical term from Greek rhetoric for a traditional image; insofar as it refers to the world "out there," it is a *motive* (e.g., the hero's descent down to the underworld). With reference to ideas and concepts the meaning of *topos* is a *theme,* such as the search for wisdom (Scholes and Kellogg, 1966). Walter J. Ong (1958) regards *topoi* as informational structures and conceptualizations characteristic of an oral culture; they are means of amplification: "topics of invention." The Homeric *topoi,* like those of the Germanic oral poetic tradition, were at one time closely associated with religious ritual, and their thematic content still displays a "vaguely sacred" quality (Scholes and Kellogg, 1966, p. 27). The cultic aspect of Greek tragedy is a reflection of this sacred quality, and Wheeler (1982) argues that

> the narrative structure of Plato's *Republic* exploited the dramaturgical structure of the great playwrights, moving the reader, as surrogate initiate, from the lesser to the greater mysteries.
>
> The raw materials Plato used were ready at hand and he made them into an analogue-in-rhetoric of the process of persuasion that had come out of Eleusianian ritual to turn into the plot structure of Greek drama: affective dramaturgical alchemy was converted into cognitive dialectical invention. The rhetorical *drōmenon,* the thing to be analyzed, was drawn out of the dramaturgical *legomenon,* the thing to be experienced. (Wheeler, 1982, p. 228)

Bloom (1973b), in his *Preface to Plato,* refers to Eric Havelock's fine speculation that Empedocles was Plato's precursor in trying to wrest language from the image-thinking of the poets to the concept-thinking of the philosophers. Yet, though Plato tries to move the trope from Homer's figures of will to a figure of knowing, rhetoric remains incurably poetic, a drive toward will-to-identify rather than toward a knower/known dualism.

Between rhetoric as persuasion and rhetoric as a system of tropes there falls always an *aporia,* a figuration of doubt. This uncertainty marks the limit where persuasion yields to a dance or interplay of tropes. The evolution of the "content" of consciousness, that is, narrative fiction, appears to run parallel with the evolution of cognitive wisdom. Both developments, the invention of fiction and the invention of fact, are rooted in the dialectic between topic and trope, the struggle between uncertainty of utterance and uncertainty of signification. Norwich posits that uncertainty arises because we perceive only that about which we are uncertain. With complete certainty comes unperceivability or adaptation. Perception as uncertainty becomes then a model of perception; and the establishment of uncertainty by active participation of the perceiving system becomes a model of the generation of uncertainty (Norwich, 1983). The paradoxical nature of perception is anchored to the uncertain *realization* of (fictitious) expectations that are in the eye of the perceiver.

No clear separation is therefore possible between tropes and *topoi;* and for analogous reasons "representative figures" in narrative fiction have multiple meaning: they "refer to human figures within a novel, a figure of the writer itself and to 'figure of speech', i.e., the characteristic tropes of the generation" (Lewis, 1959, p. 9).

Cabbalistic rhetorical theory, as formulated particularly by Cordovero in the figuration he called *behinot,* anticipated the uncertainties of meaning and interpretation and accordingly "considered texts not as linguistic structures but as instances of the will to utter within a tradition of uttering" (Bloom, 1973b, p. 393). The *behinots,* as composite tropes, are magical devices for gaining the power that lies beyond the literal or proper truth. Such devices are dangerously close to wishes, equivocations, or, in psychoanalytical terms, repressed and masked material—or lies told to the self by the self.

TOPICS AND THEMES OF SELF-KNOWLEDGE

When scripts and scenarios of *narrative fiction* (the "severe poems" of Bloom) are regarded as representations of the human cognitive repertoire, then, *literary criticism,* and particularly its most advanced form, "deconstruction," could open the way to a commentary on the processes that culminate in "states of consciousness." Deconstruction is the examination of what is repressed. The main tenet of deconstructive thought is that writing requires an act of suppression in order to come into being. What the text "says"—the "lies told to the self by the self"—is based upon what its author had to suppress in order to say it. If this is the case, then, altered states of consciousness refer to a particular variety or patterns of cerebral connectance that display a high form to content ratio. A voyage into the inner space of altered states of consciousness is a departure from the realm of content (message) into the realm of form (medium, representing rule, norm, and structure). The abstract geometric hallucinatory form constants (Fischer, 1975a) that accompany such a voyage may be form-al manifestations of a content one had to suppress in the normal state of daily routine. Or, the mind suppresses the secrets of its functioning from itself in order to function. Narrative fiction and cerebral networks are homologous structures that reveal and conceal. Bloom contends (1973b, p. 387) that for a deconstructive critic, a trope is a figure of knowing and not a figure of willing, and therefore such a critic seeks to find a cognitive moment in a poem. But what can a cognitive or epistemological moment in a poem be? How can we speak of knowing in the blind world of the wish and desire where the truth is always elsewhere, always uncertain, and desire often overrides the role of the self (as perception alters the very thing that is perceived)? Bloom (1961), therefore, postulates an analogical relation between tropes and psychic defenses, whereby tropes are defined as necessary errors about language defending against the deadly danger of literal meaning.

Strangely, the deconstructive critic may also be a constructive one. If every poem is a misinterpretation of a parent poem, there are no interpretations but only misinterpretations, and so all criticism is prose poetry. Each new reinterpretation may be a potentially creative misinterpretation of the original misinterpretation, and hence a meta-misinterpretation. Analogously, Gödel's celebrated statement (in abbreviated form) "some true statements are not provable within the system" is, itself, a meta-statement and should remind us that each new and potentially creative misinterpretation prevents us from getting stuck in a system of the original (dogmatic) misinterpretation.

We have attempted to follow the story of story-making, that is, the evolution of a circuitry of fiction as a constantly reinterpreted misinterpretation: the "content" of consciousness.

Scientific "poems" or themes also follow the very same, constantly reformulating path. The themes (or *themata*) of science (Holton, 1973) that are constantly reformulated like the stories of narrative fiction are persistent ideas: Einstein's "longing for preestablished harmony" is an unusual conscious reference to the Pythagorean theme of mathematical harmony ("characterized by supreme purity, clarity and certainty" and capable of providing "the theory of every natural process, including life, by pure deduction . . . "). The "longing for preestablished harmony" is as manifest in the concern of modern physics for symmetry as it was in the Greek preoccupation with circularity-sphericity in the heavens (Durham and Purrington, 1983, p. 240). Quantum cosmology articulates symmetry and harmony as "gauge invariance," which—coupled with what is called "spontaneous symmetry breaking"—leads to the symmetry principles of modern fundamental particle theory.

The world as organism, the preference for teleological explanations, the macrocosmos–microcosmos correspondence, the continuum and its opposite, atomicity, all have persisted since Democritus. The theme of continuity versus discreteness continues to cause difficulties in our present quantum-theoretical era; matter is still unwilling to conform to either discreteness or continuity.

> At the most fundamental and general level it is not certain whether physical systems are atomic, and in what precise sense. . . . What does it mean to "divide" a quantized-field-particle which extends to infinity but may vanish at any moment?

concludes Lancelot Law-Whyte (1961, pp. 102 and 21).

A systematic description of the troping of scientific *themata* would require a separate study. The recurring themes of science appear to be embedded in tropes that in time evolve in complexity and sophistication; not the themes but the compelling nature of the tropes makes us believe that the solution of a problem is imminent.

The evolution of mathematical troping appears like a clear line running from the Pythagoreans through Plato and Aristotle to Kepler, Galileo, and Newton (with matter and time already existing). One aspect of the contemporary quantum description of matter tropes that static description closer to the imagery, and myth, of creation. There are some contemporary theorists who go, indeed, "far out" in speculating that the physical laws themselves somehow "condense," perhaps statistically, at the same moment that matter emerges. "This admittedly remote language is reminiscent of Anaximander's dynamic principle, the separation of opposites from the Infinite, which itself echoes the Middle Eastern creation myths" (Durham and Purrington, 1983, p. 241).

Hence, an attempt to clearly separate *themata* from embedding tropes would encounter similar difficulties to the separation of *topos* from *tropos* in the poetry of narrative fiction.

If the Egyptian pyramid texts of Heliopolis are correct, the universe should be open and infinite. But for those of us who prefer the belief in a closed but unbounded and cyclic universe, the myth of the "eternal return" appears as recursion or the reentrant form of an eigenbehavior that refers to "eternally returning" stories and *themata* that are constantly rewritten, reformulated, and retroped by and for passing generations. The meaning of these stories and *themata* is that they are being rewritten, reformulated, and retroped. Their nature and meaning mark the limits of self-knowledge, the self-knowledge of a universe that can have nothing in mind but itself.

ACKNOWLEDGMENT

The kind and sophisticated assistance of Dr. Thomas E. Hanlon, Baltimore, and Drs. Ruth von Brunn, Werner Brönnimann, and Tommy Pughe, Basel, is gratefully acknowledged.

REFERENCES

Ashby, W. R. *An introduction to cybernetics.* London: Chapman & Hall, 1956.

Attneave, F. and Pierce, C. R. Accuracy of extrapolating a pointer into perceived and imagined space. *American Journal of Psychology,* 1978, *91,* 371-387.

Bader, A., suggested the term "normophrenic" in a personal communication, 1969.

Baird, J. C. and Noma, E. Psychophysical study of numbers, I-V. *Psychological Research,* 1975, *37,* 281-297; *38,* 81-95; *38,* 97-115; *38,* 175-187; *38,* 189-207.

Beer, S. *Decision and control.* London: Wiley, 1966.

Benson, H. The relaxation response. *Trends in Neurosciences,* 1983, *6,* 281-284.

Bloom, H. *The visionary company; a reading of English romantic poetry.* New York: Doubleday, 1961.

Bloom, H. *The anxiety of influence; a theory of poetry.* London: Oxford University Press, 1973a.

Bloom, H. *Wallace Stevens.* Ithaca: Cornell University Press, 1973b.

Bossom, J. The effect of brain lesions on prism adaptation in monkeys. *Psychonomic Science,* 1965, *2,* 45-46.

Callaway, E. and Haghdi, S. An information processing model for schizophrenia. *Archives of General Psychiatry,* 1982, *39,* 339-348.

Costa, E., Guidotti, A., and Toffano, A. Molecular mechanisms mediating the action of Diazepam on GABA receptors. *British Journal of Psychiatry,* 1978, *133,* 239-248.

Durham, F. and Purrington, R. D. *Frame of the universe; a history of physical cosmology.* New York: Columbia University Press, 1983.

Edelman, G. and Mountcastle, V. B. *The mindful brain.* Cambridge, Mass.: M. I. T. Press, 1978.

Evarts, E. V. Relation of pyramidal tract activity to force exerted during movement. *Journal of Neurophysiology,* 1968, *31,* 14-27.

Feinberg, I. Efference copy and corollary discharge: implications for thinking and its disorders. *Schizophrenia Bulletin,* 1978, *4,* 636-640.

Fischer, R. Out on a (phantom) limb; variations on the theme: stability of body image and the golden section. *Perspectives in Biology and Medicine,* 1969a, *12,* 259-273.

Fischer, R. Psychotomimetic drug induced changes in space and time. *Proceedings of the 4th International Congress on Pharmacology.* Basel: Schwabe Publ., 1969b, *3,* 28-77.

Fischer, R. The perception-hallucination continuum. *Diseases of the Nervous System,* 1969c, *30,* 161-171.

Fischer, R. A cartography of the ecstatic and meditative states. *Science,* 1971, *174,* 897-904.

Fischer, R. On symmetries and the structure of our own nature. *Leonardo,* 1974, *7,* 147-148.

Fischer, R. Cartography of inner space. In R. Siegel and J. West (Eds.), *Hallucinations: behavior, experience, theory.* New York: Wiley, 1975a.

Fischer, R. Transformations of consciousness. A cartography I. The perception-hallucination continuum. *Confinia Psychiatrica,* 1975b, *18,* 221-244.

Fischer, R. Transformations of consciousness. A cartography II. The perception-meditation continuum. *Confinia Psychiatrica,* 1976a, *19,* 1-23.

Fischer, R. Consciousness as role and knowledge. In L. Allman and D. Jaffe (Eds.), *Readings in abnormal psychology: contemporary perspectives.* New York: Harper & Row, 1976b.

Fischer, R. Cartography of conscious states: Integration of East and West. In A. A. Sugerman and R. Tarter (Eds.), *Expanding dimensions of consciousness.* New York: Springer, 1978, pp. 24-57.

Fischer, R. On the arousing effect of hallucinogens or who is who under psilocybin. *Journal of Altered States of Consciousness,* 1980, *5,* 321-324.

Fischer, R. Matter's mastermind: the model-making brain. *Diogenes,* 1981, No. 116, 18-39.

Fischer, R. The structure of ancient wisdom; comments. *Journal of Social and Biological Structures,* 1984, *7,* 387–389.

Fischer, R. and Hill, R. M. Psychotropic drug-induced transformation of visual space. *International Pharmacopsychiatry,* 1971, *6,* 28–37.

Fischer, R., et al. Personality trait-dependent performance under psilocybin I. *Diseases of the Nervous System,* 1970, *31,* 91–101.

Foerster, H. v. Notes on an epistemology for living things. In E. Morin and M. Piatelli-Palmerini (Eds.), *L'Unité de l'homme; invariants biologiques et universaux culturals.* Paris: Seuil, 1974.

Foerster, H. v. Formalisation de certains aspects de l'équilibration des structures cognitives. In B. Inhelder (Ed.), *Epistemologie génétique et équilibration* (Hommage à Jean Piaget). Neuchatel: Delachaux et Nestlé, 1976.

Foerster, H. v. *Observing systems.* Seaside, California: Intersystems Publ., 1981, pp. 232–255.

Freeman, W. J. A physiological hypothesis of perception. *Perspectives Biol. and Med.,* 1981, *16,* 561–592.

Freud, S. *The ego and the id,* The Standard Edition, J. Strachey (Ed.). London: Hogarth Press, 1953–1974, *19.*

Gibson, J. *An ecological approach to perception.* Boston: Houghton-Mifflin, 1979.

Glassman, R. B. Free will has a neural substrate: critique of Joseph F. Rychlak. *Zygon,* 1983, *18,* 67–82.

Gordon, G. (Ed.) *Active touch.* New York: Pergamon, 1978.

Grace, W. I. and Graham, D. T. Relationship of specific attitudes and emotions to certain bodily diseases. In L. A. Gottschalk et al. (Eds.), *Psychosomatic classics.* Basel: Karger, 1958, pp. 225–242.

Gregory, R. L. *Mind in science.* London: Weidenfeld and Nicholson, 1981.

Gwynne, P. H., Fischer, R., and Hill, R. M. Hypnotic induction of the interference of psilocybin with optically induced spatial distortion. *Pharmakopsychiatrie Neuro-Psychopharmakologie,* 1969, *2,* 223–234.

Haber, R. N. Absolute timing of mental activity; commentary. *Behavioral and Brain Sciences,* 1979, *2,* 263.

Hägg, T. *The novel in antiquity.* Oxford: Blackwell, 1983.

Hill, R. M. and Fischer, R. Psilocybin-induced transformations of visual space. *Pharmakopsychiatrie, Neuro-Psychopharmakologie,* 1970, *3,* 256–267.

Hofmann, A. Psychotomimetic agents. In A. Burger (Ed.), *Chemical constitution and pharmacodynamic action 2.* New Yorker: Dekker, 1968.

Hofstadter, D. R. *Goedel, Escher, Bach: an eternal golden braid.* New York: Basic Books, 1979.

Holton, G. *Thematic origin of scientific thought.* Cambridge, Mass.: Harvard University Press, 1973.

Kohler, I. The formation and transformation of the perceptual world. *Psychological Issues 3,* (No. 4) Monograph 12. New York: International Universities Press, 1964.

Konorski, J. The role of central factors in differentiation. In R. W. Gerard and J. W. Duyff (Eds.), *Information processing in the nervous system.* Amsterdam: Excerpta Medica Foundation, 1962, pp. 318–329.

Lashley, K. S. *Brain mechanisms in intelligence.* Chicago: University of Chicago Press, 1929; reprinted New York: Dover, 1962.

Law-Whyte, L. *Essay on atomism.* Middletown, Connecticut: Wesleyan University Press, 1961.

Levy, L. The urinary output of adrenaline and noradrenaline during pleasant and unpleasant emotional states. *Psychosomatic Medicine,* 1965, *27,* 80–85.

Lewis, R. W. B. *The picaresque saint:representative figures in contemporary fiction.* New York: Horizon Press, 1959.

Locke, J. Essay concerning human understanding. 1690, Chapter XIV, paragraph 21.

Lull, R. *The book of the lover and loved.* Allison Peers, E. (transl.), Leech, K. (Ed.), New York: Paulist Press, 1978.

Mahnke, D. *Unendliche Sphaere und Allmittelpunkt,* Halle: F. Frommann Verl. (Guenther Holzboog).

de Mann, P. *Blindness and insight.* Oxford: University Press, 1971.

Maturana, H. Cognition. In *Wahrnehmung und Kommunikation,* Hejl, P. J., *et al.* (Eds.), Frankfurt A. M.: Peter Lang, 1978.

McGonigle, B. O. and Flook, J. Long term retention of single and multistate prismatic adaptation. *Nature,* 1978, *272,* 364–366.

McGuigan, F. J. Interview with Edmund Jacobson. *Biofeedback & Selfregulation,* 1978, *3,* 287–300.

Meyer, L. B. Exploiting limits: creation, archetypes and style change. *Daedalus,* 1980, *109,* 177–205.

Mikaelian, H. H. and Malatesta, V. Specialized adaptation to displaced vision. *Perception,* 1974, *3,* 135–139.

Moruzzi, G. and Magoun, H. W. Brain stem reticular formation and activation of the EEG. *Electroencephalography & Clinical Neurophysiology,* 1949, *1,* 455–473.

Nelsen, J. M. and Goldstein, L. Improvement of performance on an attention task with chronic nicotine treatment in rats. *Psychopharmacology,* 1972, *26,* 347–360.

Neumann, J. v. *The computer and the brain.* New Haven: Yale University Press, 1958.

Nicolis, G. and Prigogine, I. *Self-organization in non-equilibrium systems.* New York: Wiley, 1976.

Norwich, K. E. The magical number seven: making a "bit" of sense. *Perception and Psychophysics,* 1982, *29,* 409–422.

Norwich, K. E. To perceive is to doubt: the relativity of perception. *Journal of Theoretical Biology,* 1983, *102,* 175–190.

Novalis (Hardenberg) F. v. *Werke und Briefe.* Muenchen: Winkler Verlag, 1968.

Ong, W. J. *Ramus—method, and the decay of dialogue.* Cambridge, Mass.: Harvard University Press, 1958.

Onions, C. T. *Oxford dictionary of English etymology.* Oxford: Clarendon Press, 1966.

Pellionisz, A. and Llinás, R. Brain modeling by tensor network theory and computer simulation. *Neuroscience,* 1979, *4,* 323–348.

Pellionisz, A. and Llinás, R. Tensorial representation of space–time in CNS: sensory-motor coordination via distributed cerebellar space–time metric. *Abstracts, Society of Neuroscience,* 10th Annual Meeting, 1980, p. 510.

Penfield, W. Engrams in the human brain. *Proceedings Royal Society of Medicine* (Canada) 1968, *61,* 831–841.

Piaget, J. and Morf, A., et al. *Logique et perception; études d'epistemologi génétique* VI. Paris: Presses Univ. de France, 1958.

Plato, *Protagoras and Meno.* Guthrie, W. K. C. (transl.) Baltimore: Penguin Books, 1956.

Poulet, G. *The metamorphosis of the circle,* C. Dawson and E. Coleman (transl.) Baltimore: The Johns Hopkins Press, 1966.

Roland, P. E. Sensory feedback to the cerebral cortex during voluntary movement in man. Commentary. *Behavioral and Brain Sciences,* 1979, *2,* 305–312.

Routtenberg, A. The two-arousal hypothesis: reticular formation and limbic system. *Psychological Review,* 1968, *75,* 51–80.

Scholes, R. and Kellogg, R. *The nature of narrative.* London: Oxford University Press, 1966.

Shallice, T. Dual functions of consciousness. *Psychological Review,* 1972, *79,* 383, 393.

Stapledon, O. *A man divided.* London: Oxford University Press, 1983.

Stent, G. S. Does god play dice? *The Sciences,* 1979, *19,* 18–23.

Sternbach, L. H. The benzodiazepine story. *Journal of Medicinal Chemistry,*1979, *22,* 1–7.

Thatcher, K. et al. Personality trait-dependent performance under psilocybin II. *Diseases of the Nervous System,* 1970, *31,* 181–192.

Towe, A. L. Somatosensory cortex: descending influences on ascending systems. In A. Iggo (Ed.), *Handbook of sensory physiology; somatosensory system.* New York: Springer, 1973.

Trevarthen, C. Comment. In discussion of Creutzfeld, O. D., Neurophysiological mechanisms and consciousness. In *Brain and mind,* Ciba Foundation (New) Series 69. Amsterdam: Elsevier Excerpta Medica, 1979.

Valera, F. J. The nervous system as a closed network. *Brain Theory Newsletter,* 1977, *2,* 66–67.

Webster's new collegiate dictionary, 2nd ed. Springfield, Mass.: Merriam Co. Publ., 1958.

Wheeler, H. The structure of ancient wisdom. *J. Social Biol. Struct.,* 1982, *5,* 223–232.

Wheeler, J. A. The universe as home for man. *American Scientist,* 1974, *62,* 683–691.

Wilden, A. and Wilson, T. The double bind: logic, magic, and economics. In C. E. Sluzki (Ed.), *Double bind: the foundation of the communicational approach to the family.* New York: Grune & Stratton, 1976, pp. 263–286.

2. Transformatory Framework: Pictorial to Verbal

Jon Tolaas

Altered states of consciousness are typically experienced as mental imagery but are generally mediated in the form of a verbal report. This transfiguration of the imaging mode into the discursive, verbal mode is bound to have consequences for all our thinking about altered states of consciousness. In this chapter we will take a close look at the transformatory framework with a view to mapping and elucidating the consequences of the mode shift from pictorial experience to verbal report. Consider the following extract from the hypnotic dream of a hysteric young woman who was told simply "to have a dream":

> I'm in a hospital bed . . . I like the room . . . it's not an ordinary hospital . . . it's way up high with a beautiful view . . . the walls are tinted pale green . . . I see the nurse's face or something . . . and it ought to startle me because her tips are gone . . . on the first two fingers, down to the second joint . . . and I was going to interrupt and tell the nurse . . . if it is a nurse. . . . (Brenman, 1967, p. 132)

What is being communicated by the hypnotic subject is a predominantly visual experience that cannot be "televised" or mediated directly in its full richness and dynamic unfolding through any channel or in any known code. The experience that is being detailed in the course of happening is a "process-in-itself" that we can only infer and generalize through introspection and share through natural language or possibly through some other semiotic code such as drawings and paintings. In cases such as this we had rather speak of the verbal report as simultaneous transformation rather than

31

as simultaneous translation. The same is true of reports of experiences during guided mental imagery or waking dreams (Desoille, 1961; Daudet, 1926; Frétigny and Virel, 1968; Godel, 1952; Leuner, 1969; Assagioli, 1975) and waking fantasy (Klinger, 1971), techniques that require the subject to make a verbal report of a predominantly visual experience. The following spontaneous dream was told to me by a young woman who had just been visiting with her parents:

> I stood there with a naked baby in my arms. It was in B. It was my baby that was going to be weighed on a kind of scale. Around me there were many people who were looking critically at the scene. I don't remember who they were.

In this case the verbal report is based on the dreamer's more or less fragmentary memories of the subjective experience, as night dreams always are. Laboratory experiments aimed at teaching dreaming subjects to report their ongoing (REM) dreams have not been successful, just as if nature had not meant us to speak about them there and then (Cartwright, 1977). Furthermore, the experience has been through secondary elaboration and is shaped by the dynamic interplay and demand characteristics of the reporting situation. More important perhaps, the experience that we recognize at once as a visual one, is constrained through the inescapable tool of waking consciousness: natural language, and more specifically by this particular dreamer's verbal capacity and idiosyncracies.

Most of the illustrative examples in this chapter will be chosen from spontaneous and EEG-monitored dreams because dreaming appears to be the pictorial experience par excellence and one that is typically mediated in words. Besides, it is ontogenetically primitive (Roffwarg et al., 1966), functionally normal, and fairly well known with regard to physiological as well as psychological parameters (for recent surveys, see Arkin et al., 1978; Drucker-Colin et al., 1979; Wolman, 1979).

The question we are going to discuss is this: Can we detect and analyze basic transformatory rules or consequences of the mode shift from pictorial experience to verbal report? This problem will be viewed in the ontological perspective and from a psychological as well as a physiological point of view. Pedagogical implications are also discussed.

VISUAL EXPERIENCE-VERBAL REPORTS

We map or model our experience of the world by using different more or less valued representational systems: vision, audition, kinesthetics, olfaction, and gustation. Quite possibly, we also receive and represent information through as yet little-known channels in addition to the five well-known ones, for example, weak bioelectrical fields and what we presently term extrasensory phenomena. Information received through one of these input channels may be stored in a map or model that is different from the input channel; for example, visually received information may be represented in the form of natural language (for discussion, see Grinder and Bandler, 1975 and 1976). Through language we are able to present our experience of any of the other representational systems. For example, the visual experience of the hypnotic dream cited at the beginning of this chapter, is described in words such as "way up high," "beautiful view," "tinted pale green," "I see the face," and so on. Similarly, auditory experiences may be described in terms such as "crumbling," "silent," "cry," "explode," and so on (see Grinder and Bandler, 1976). Thus we create a language map of our visual and auditory maps. But just as the territory is not the map, one map (e.g., visually received and represented information), is not another one (e.g., natural language). Presenting the experience of one representational system through language implies transformation. In the typical dreaming state, REM sleep, activity in the visual representational system is aroused internally so that all information drawn from memory, regardless of input channel during the waking state, tends to be given visual representation. Similarly, admitted external and proprioceptive input is generally transformed into visual imagery (for discussion, see Arkin et al., 1978; Tolaas, 1979–80). What this means is that in reporting our dreams we impose one mode of being (waking consciousness) and one representational system (language) on another mode of being (dreaming) and another representational system (a sensory mode that is predominantly visual).

MENTAL IMAGERY
AND VERBAL/PROPOSITIONAL REPRESENTATION

Foulkes (1978) claims that dreams are highly structured, meaningful sequences that may easily be translated into words. As he sees it, "Words are the form in which dream images originated, and verbal/propositional structures mold the way in which images are expressed" (p. 15). If I read Foulkes correctly, this means that he does not consider a separate nonpropositional image system, human cognition being exclusively based on verbal/ propositional representation. Opinions are divided on this question. Some researchers posit two different representational systems, imagery and verbal/propositional representation, with different roles in ontogeny. Thus the development of symbolic processes may be described as a shift from imaginal to verbal modes of representation (Bruner, 1964; Bruner et al., 1966; Piaget and Inhelder, 1971; Werner and Kaplan, 1963). Kosslyn (1980) takes issue with the followers of Piaget on the so-called representation-development hypothesis. Based on extensive experimentation, he concludes that young children do not tend to use imagery in their thinking more than adults do, nor do they use imagery more efficiently (as measured in time used to see specific image properties). But young children do use imagery, and Kosslyn (1980) does not consider it to be verbal/propositional.

The ontogenetic problem is of particular interest for our topic, as REM sleep is ontogenetically primitive, accounting for more than 50 percent of total sleep time in newborn babies (Roffwarg et al., 1966). Can we infer that a preverbal infant who wakes up from REM sleep crying and showing all external signs of fear has had a nightmare or a fear-inspiring dream? If so, is it likely that it was experienced as visual imagery based on verbal/propositional structures? Evidently this is an open question, but a significant one that has to be considered. In my view the imagery/proposition controversy (for discussion, see Kosslyn, 1980) seems to hinge on a failure to understand or attempt analysis of the basic nature of mental imagery. I am not thinking of a definition in the dictionary sense of the word, which would imply much more understanding of what we call mind and its relationship with the brain than is presently available. What I have in mind is an operational definition of the basic properties and characteristics of mental imagery and image formation ("image-consciousness").

THE NATURE OF MENTAL IMAGERY

Mental images are not pictures. From introspection we know that they are unframed, occupying the field of vision. Besides, they are typically dynamic rather than static. In that respect the pictures that they resemble most are cinematographic pictures, but unlike them they are three-dimensional. We may say that they are extended in mental space, their space being gravitational, that is, balanced around an invisible horizontal and vertical axis. Analyzing dream images, for example, we may divide their space into quadrants, thus describing (in words) spatial relationships between characters, objects, movements, and so on. For our topic the important point is that mental images and all pictures share one characteristic in common, which I refer to as the basic nature of imagery: they represent what they represent by exhibiting their form. They make visible through form, their structure being determined by the fact that their primary function is to represent, no matter whether the information relates to objects, living beings, actions, or ideas. There is no need to distinguish between different categories of mental images such as hallucinations and images induced by a verbal suggestion or drugs or biologically triggered dream images because we have to do with a basic, generalizable fact.

Language, on the other hand, describes and explains by words ordered in structural patterns. Images code relationships, for example, *A is pictured as hitting B,* and relationships may be translated into words, for example, *A hits B,* but still there is an unbridgeable gap between the organic image providing a wealth of information all at once, for example, relating to facial expressions, appearance, and surroundings, and the simple verbal statement. Verbally more information can only be provided by more statements while the total, immediate representation of the image remains unattainable. In current theorizing we distinguish between serial processing of information (discursive language) and parallel processing (imagery) (for discussion, see Kosslyn, 1980; Neisser, 1967; Paivio, 1971).

Mental images are in a deep sense organic, representing a pattern of relations between the tensions existing in a living being. Their function is itself a living process, and therefore as complex as all living processes are. Philippe (1903) called the mental image the living cell of mental life and considered it as complex as the physiological cell. Such patterns of tensions cannot be satisfactorily translated into discursive or linear language. Researchers relying solely on a propositional representational system (Pylyshyn, 1973), and not on a separate image system, are faced with the problem of parsimony. An infinite number of propositions would be needed to describe even simple scenes. This becomes particularly clear in Pylyshyn's hierarchical model in which information on different levels is represented at the same time. Commenting on this question, Kosslyn (1980) writes: "If limited encoding or memory capacity is an important factor to internal representation, then it is advantageous to encode and store as little as possible and deduce as much as possible when more detailed information is required" (p. 25). This is what might be done through a separate image system. Again to quote Kosslyn (1980): "Information about an object is inherent in the pattern of the representation itself, is 'worn on its sleeve', as it were" (p. 23). This is another way of saying that images exhibit their information through form. As soon as this becomes clear, it seems to me that we have to postulate separate image and verbal/propositional systems. In this connection it is worth noting that language is not always discursive or the tool of a binary, analytic logic. Language may be poetic or "analog," that is, preoccupied with concrete iconic representation through metaphors, similes, rhythm, and so on. This topic is taken up in a later section.

"IMAGE-CONSCIOUSNESS"

Among the people who have contributed most to our understanding of the topic of mental imagery, I would give a place apart to phenomenologists such as Husserl, Heidegger, and Sartre. Here I will use some aspects of

Sartre's work on mental imagery (Sartre, 1947), presented in summary form, as a basis for a discussion of "image-consciousness."

Following Husserl, Sartre speaks of consciousness as intentional, meaning that consciousness is always directed toward something, always an awareness of something. In his major philosophical work, *Being and Nothingness* (1956), he develops his thesis of consciousness as prereflective, maintaining that consciousness-of-something lies beneath the reflective act of self-knowledge. Rather than Descartes' formula "I am conscious of myself, consequently I am," the starting point of Sartre's philosophy is "I am a consciousness," which can only become aware of itself as *not* the thing toward which it is directed by a secondary self-reflective act. This basic distinction lies behind Sartre's analysis of mental imagery. These characteristics of consciousness are true of any consciousness, voluntarily directed in the waking state, drug-induced, biologically triggered in sleep, and so forth, and, of course, they are found in young and old alike. Consider the following example: I wake up in the morning, and out of an infinite number of things I direct my consciousness toward a cup of coffee. Then it becomes cup-of-coffee consciousness. When I produce the image of cup of coffee in me, it is the real cup (the one with bluebells around the rim) that is the object of my actual consciousness, and as long as this consciousness remains unaltered, I can give a description of the object as it appears to me, but not of *the image as such* (see Sartre, 1947, p. 13). This takes a secondary, self-reflective act. The knowledge that I "have an image" is given to me with absolute certainty. Such considerations form the starting-point of a phenomenology of imagery. Reflecting on the image of the cup, we can describe the following four main characteristics of mental images:

1. Image-Consciousness

The cup I am conscious of is not *in* my consciousness, or *in* the image. The idea that it may be so is referred to as the illusion of immanence. On the contrary, the cup is a special kind of image-consciousness, no matter whether I perceive (whether my consciousness "meets" it) or imagine it. The cup that I imagine is referred to as an analogon. It is a synthetic organization, a special relationship between the object and consciousness. Thus, in the synthetic acts of consciousness certain structures that we call images sometimes appear. "They are born, develop and disappear according to laws that are proper to them . . . " (Sartre, 1947, p. 17).

2. Perceiving and Imagining

Perceiving, I observe the objects that I may touch, measure, and so on. But they are never given to me from more than a certain side at a time (as a series of profiles). The object itself may be described as the total of these profiles. But when we have a mental image of an object, it is immediately given for what it is: a cup is a cup. In other words, an image is a *synthetic act.* We may zoom in on a part of a perceived object and learn more about it *gradually,* for example, about the bluebells on the cup in front of me. A mental image, on the other hand, never reveals more than the consciousness we have of it. It gives itself en bloc immediately. If I find more in the image I have after a few seconds, as frequently happens, it has nothing to do with pure and simple observation; according to Sartre, it is given at once. Sartre calls our attitude to the object of the image quasi-observation. Many readers may have had the experience of reading a book page in a dream. Did you gather more and more information as you were following the lines down the page (as you do when you are reading a "real" book), or was it given to you immediately?

3. The Image as Nothingness

Consciousness is always consciousness of something and can only be described through a reflective act. But the two levels of consciousness are closely interwoven. If this were not so, cup-consciousness, for example, would at the irreflective level be unconscious of itself, which would be a contradiction in terms. How does irreflective image-consciousness give its object? Sartre answers that it "gives its object as a nothingness" (*comme un néant d'être*) (Sartre, 1947, p. 25). At the irreflective level saying that "I have an image of the cup with bluebells around the rim," for example, means that "I do not see that cup," or rather "I see nothing at all." The image-consciousness of that particular cup is "an intentional synthesis" of a number of memories I have of it. I direct my consciousness to that particular cup, but in my doing so it is not there, "it is given as absent to intuition" (Sartre, 1947, p. 25). This is no hindrance for our subsequent reaction to the image as if its object were present.

4. Spontaneity

The reflective level of consciousness is an undefinable quality of consciousness to direct itself to itself. As image-consciousness at the irreflective level gives its object as a "nothingness," we experience it through reflective consciousness as spontaneous and creative. It produces and maintains its object as image "but without posing as object this creative aspect" (Sartre, 1947, p. 26). Perceptual consciousness is constituted by an indefinite number of possible facts to be revealed, whereas the object of image-consciousness is never more than the consciousness we have of it. It is there as we say, "out of the blue," "fully created," a synthetic form that appears at a certain moment of a temporal synthesis and integrates itself (*s'organise*) with other kinds of consciousness preceding and following it . . . " (Sartre, 1947, p. 27).

From this summary of Sartre's analysis of image-consciousness, we may learn to steer clear of the illusion of immanence, or the illusion that the object we direct our consciousness to is *in* the consciousness or *in* the image. Moreover, we may see why mental images presented to irreflective consciousness as a "nothingness" appear to reflective consciousness as spontaneous and creative. The essential "nothingness" of the imagined object also distinguishes it radically from the perceived ("real") object. His analysis is of special interest for our topic because altered states of consciousness are known as states where image-consciousness predominates, and dreaming, in particular, is probably the purest state of image-consciousness a human being can experience. We *are* our spontaneously created images, and existing as images we do not suddenly slide into another kind of consciousness, as is usually the case in the waking state. This is not to say that dreaming is a kind of irreflective, regressive state. Image-consciousness is always made up of two inseparable, closely interwoven levels, irreflective and reflective consciousness. We are all the time giving ourselves new images (irreflective level) and reflecting upon them at the same time. Thus the person who appears in the dream "out of the blue" is immediately recognized as a crook we have to avoid, so we make up a good excuse and leave him. A knife is there "fully created," and as we *know* that it is meant as a surprise we carefully hide it in a safe place where nobody will look, and so on. The point is that we remain image-conscious for as long as we are dreaming and do not look at or reflect on our being "image" from outside. This notion comes close to Rechtschaffen's (1978) description of dreaming as a state of single-mindedness. There are, of course, lucid dreams, or dreams where we dream that we dream (see Tolaas, 1980). Lucid dreams may be seen as dreams where we are standing with one foot, or perhaps more aptly, with one brain half in the waking state, a fragile double-mindedness where image-consciousness may crumble at any moment. Image-consciousness is a functionally normal alternative mode of being in the world, having its own "laws" and its own language based on the exhibition of information through form. Waking consciousness is another universe of discourse mainly based on discursive language and linear logic. We are now ready to approach the consequences of the transformation from the pictorial experience of image-consciousness to the verbal report of what we recall of it in the waking state.

FROM VISUAL EXPERIENCE AND PARALLEL PROCESSING
TO VERBAL REPORT
AND SERIAL PROCESSING

Time Distortion

In the waking state when we recall and record what we remember of a night dream or a hypnotic dream, we will likely feel that a lot of information was presented or made visible in a very short time and that recording or describing orally even a "glimpse" may be a time-consuming business. Still we feel that there was more to it than our pile of verbal statements reflects. As imagery does allow processing of more information in shorter intervals of chronological time (as measured by some "event counter" such as a stopwatch or EEG recordings), the "subjective feeling" may be said to be a product of the mode shift and not only, as is often said, of unconscious material welling up in this state.

Cooper and Erickson (1954) give an example of a thirty-year-old woman hospitalized for recurrent episodes of hysterical amnesia, who, after a hypnotic dream of 20 seconds, spent several hours telling about the past traumatic memories. Her dream reads like a picture strip of related memories. Here is an excerpt:

> My dress is pink. It's my birthday. I'm sitting in a high chair. I'm going to eat my cake. My daddy is going to kiss me. He falled down. That's what happened. My father died of heart failure. I was three years old. Pink dress. When Deborah (her daughter) wanted a pink birthday dress I forgot everything and I went to the hospital. I couldn't think. My head ached . . . I'm going on a train ride. Mammie is taking me. It's fun. See the pretty trees. There's cows, too. Mammie is coughing. She's sick. Her handkerchief is all red. . . . (Cooper and Erickson, 1954, p. 172)

Our concern here is not the method used to elicit these images from an amnesic patient, nor the phenomenon of condensation (which is discussed later), but the fact that a 20-second mental "picture strip" of personal memories may contain "frames" enough to be turned into a long story once you wake up and change processing mode from parallel to sequential. Therefore it may feel like a "time grain" exploding.

Experimental work shows that (REM) dreams are not instantaneous (for surveys, see Arkin et al., 1978; Wolman, 1979), but the question of the objective time of a dream is an extremely complex one. This becomes clear when we ask such questions as: How long does it take to "hate someone intensely" or to imagine "going from Bergen to New York on roller skates"? Measuring image-consciousness with some event counter or other device is likely to be a frustrating business.

The "All-of-a-sudden Effect"

To my knowledge no statistics are available on the frequency of words and expressions such as "suddenly," "all of a sudden," "abruptly," "out of the blue," "I had scarcely . . . when," "no sooner had I . . . when," and so on, in dream reports. Still I would guess that these are among the most common expressions in dreams, as they are a natural and predictable consequence of the mode shift. Constrained through discursive language and linear logic, the dynamic, concrete experience of images giving their information all at once and as a "nothingness" is likely to be characterized as vivid and quick with unpredictable shifts in time and place. As mentioned above, all mental images have spatial dimensions being extended in what we may call mental space. Spatiality implies *concrete* depiction. (The word "concrete" is derived from the Latin *concretus,* meaning "what is grown together.") In my view the question of concreteness is of vital importance for the understanding of pictorial language (which consists in presentation of "what is grown together") in general, and the nature of the shift from visual to verbal presentation in particular. It may be useful to approach this problem by an example, a short spontaneous dream reported by a male dreamer. Henceforth it will be referred to as the "butterfly dream":

I was walking along a road with another man.
We were walking side by side.
All of a sudden, and for no apparent reason, he turned on me and threw a matchbox at me.
When it hit me, I was immediately transformed into butterflies and there were prostitutes all around.

Teaching dreams to young students, I usually tell a dream such as this one slowly, and sometimes twice. I then invite them to take part in a guided visualization of the dream. It is immediately clear that the visual experience is much more vivid (colors, motion, movement) and much richer in descriptive detail than the verbal report. More important, the concrete, organic images with all kinds of individual variations are experienced as in motion, much like the "inner film" we associate with dreaming. Visualizing the sequence, we notice that there are no stop-gaps or hesitations between the images, no slow building up of premises; each image is being born out of the other swiftly and apparently effortlessly, or, as Sartre might put it, giving itself as a "nothingness." This dynamic experience is, so to speak, frozen in a static, verbal reification in the waking state.

Not only is it possible to predict the "all-of-a-sudden effect"; it is also possible to say something about where in a verbal report we are most likely to find sudden, inexplicable "jumps." We may proceed by dividing the verbal report into what have been variously termed *segments* or *situations* (Moser et al., 1980), and *acts* and *scenes* (or *episodes*) (see, e.g., Baylor and Deslauriers, 1983; Ullman, 1969). Deslauriers and Baylor (1982) emphasize that there are no hard and fast rules for the division of a report into acts and scenes. Generally, the shift from one episode to another is accompanied by a change of location, the arrival of a new dream character, or the termination of a series of actions and the dreamer's turning toward a new goal. According to Moser et al. (1980), a dream segment or situation "contains the cognition of parts of the time–space environment of the individual. The situation is determined exactly by those cognitive elements which are mentioned by the subject . . . " (p. 12). They describe the transition between segments or situations as caused by interrupts (Moser et al., 1974), which are often characterized by cognitive elaborations "in which the dreamer reflects his affective state as well as those aspects of the situation that might have generated this state" (Moser et al., 1980, p. 12). To judge from the authors' segmented dream examples, the segment and the act/scene concepts are closely related.

Our butterfly dream may be segmented the following way:

Act I:	I was walking along a road with another man.
(One scene)	We were walking side by side.
Act II, Scene I:	All of a sudden, and for no apparent reason,
Act II, Scene II:	he turned on me and threw a matchbox at me.
Act III, Scene I:	When it hit me, I was immediately transformed into butterflies
Act III, Scene II:	and there were prostitutes all around.

As we see from this example, the "all-of-a-sudden effect" crops up as an act shifts, which is what we might expect as one act follows the other spontaneously and without any explantion as we are used to in the waking state. On the basis of the mode shift, we can predict five rather well-defined categories of act shifts where we are likely to find one of the expressions cited above or a similar one in verbal reports:

a. *Time shifts* (excerpts from my collection of dreams): "Suddenly I was in the Middle Ages in front of a church. . . . "
b. *Location shifts:* "I was in Oslo discussing a grant. Then the scene

suddenly shifted and I was in a New York office. . . . " "It was dark and I was in the kindergarten. Then all of a sudden I was in the bathroom where I saw the mouse. . . . "

  c. *Metamorphosis:* "Before I could say knife, he got old and grey. . . . "
  d. *Personification:* "I was taken by surprise as the picture suddenly started talking."
  e. *Unexplained actions:* "Suddenly he threw himself from the mountaintop. . . . "

Two or more of the shifts, for example, time and location, may appear together. In the butterfly dream we see an instance of unexplained actions: "All of a sudden . . . he turned on me. . . . " Unexplained actions such as this are predictable in dreams, since images do not explain but exhibit their information. We also witness an instance of sudden metamorphosis (dreamer–butterflies) Metamorphosis and personification are logical consequences, or natural syntactical categories in concrete, pictorial language (discussed below).

Metamorphosis and Personification

Metamorphosis is bound to be an important syntactical device in dreams as in fairy tales and myths and wherever language becomes concrete. As we do not "see" such transformations in the waking state, we tend to describe them in such words as "strange," "bizarre," "curious," "implausible," and so on. In actual fact they are perfectly logical consequences of concrete syntax. Anyone who has had any experience with dreams or guided fantasy will have a lot of examples: When you reach out for your lover's head, it may turn into a big, cold pearl. The "childish" secretary may turn into a tot, and the boy who feels like an ant may become one. The "strangeness" of such transformations is a product of the mode shift, a point I would spend much time emphasizing in teaching dreams. In concrete, pictorial language to "become" means a visualized change of state (for example, alive–dead, old–young, sober–drunk) or partial or complete metamorphosis (change of form, shape, or structure).

Turning to the butterfly dream, it might be interesting to throw a matchbox at someone asking him how he would show that he has *become* a butterfly, a difficult but instructive task. Or one might ask a dream student to mime to the other participants of a group that he has *become sick* because he has drunk some polluted liquid, or that he will become sick if he drinks it. Then the role of body language, particularly facial expression and body posture, in metamorphosis will become clear. The relationship with play activities (see Piaget, 1962; Bateson, 1973) and drama (see, e.g., Perls, 1969; Shands, 1966; Tolaas, 1980) is also obvious.

In a sense it may be said that all the elements of a dream are personifications or parts of the dreamer created by him and for him, like the matchbox and the butterfly in our dream. However, personification in the more narrow, literary sense of the word (i.e., inanimate objects or abstract notions being imbued with life and action or the attributes of living beings) is another predictable consequence of pictorial concreteness. Thus the "life-like" photograph may start talking, the new car may run wild like a horse, the swamp may drag you down with its "hands," and the politician's plane may open its mouth to let you see a glimpse of a big, cleft serpent's tongue. Personifications may be difficult to demonstrate, but a few tasks may help familiarize dream students with this device. For example, how could an armchair show its "friendliness"? How could a fence be "hostile" and actively hinder one from entering a house?

Enactment of Feelings

Hall and Van De Castle (1966) draw attention to the low number of expressed feelings in their stratistical studies of manifest dream content. The number of expressed feelings is low viewed in the light of the nature of the actions and interactions described in the reports, for example, aggressive, friendly, or sexual acts. This finding reflects the shift of representational system from visual imagery to discursive language. Dream language demonstrates feelings: we *are* hate, fear, love, and so forth. Consequently, when we record our dreams, we tend to describe the actions and take the feelings for granted. The role of demand characteristics shows this clearly. If we ask someone to record his/her dreams for some time and discuss them with him/her drawing attention to the low number of expressed feelings, we are likely to get many more such expressions in subsequent dreams. Similarly, we are likely to get more expressions of color in dreams if we draw attention to such expressions in dream reports. It is taken for granted that the grass is green and a handball round. If the grass happens to be red, however, the ball square, it is likely to be mentioned in the verbal report. Similarly, you need not tell yourself that you are afraid if you are running to escape a murderer.

As Sartre (1947) sees it, image-consciousness gives itself an object that it already knows in its full richness including feelings (affects). Knowledge and feelings are indissolubly linked to the intentionality of consciousness. As dreaming is almost pure image-consciousness giving itself objects it already knows affectively and cognitively, we tend to take the feelings for granted in the waking state. As the Gestaltists claim (see, e.g., Perls, 1969) one way of getting behind the words and back to the emotional experience is to act out the dream or go back to concrete visualization.

For anyone working with dreams, there is a very great difference between reading a dream report and having the dreamer in front of you so that you can listen to the fine inflections of voice, facial expressions, and body language in general, what we may call "the contours of emotions." In spite of the fact that emotions are not frequently expressed in verbal dream reports, dreams are often described as exaggerating emotions (see, e.g., Hadfield, 1954). This is, of course, an observation we make in the waking state where similar experiences to those of the dream would be characterized as highly emotional and dramatic. The boy who is threatened at school by another boy yelling at him "I'll kill you," dreams that he is alone in the dark shouting "Help me, help me!" But no one comes to his rescue, and he tries to escape from his persecutor, who has many of the traits of the boy who threatened him at school. Nearly exhausted, he climbs first one fence, then another; but seeing a third one, which is very high, he just turns his back to it, stretching out his arms like Christ on the cross and stands still waiting for the hangman who is approaching. Then he wakes up in a sweat, slowly calming himself down in the "cold light of reason." The dream demonstrates what feelings there are, and the demonstrator is the dreamer acting or living through it for his own self-knowledge. Image-consciousness is on target, precise and unequivocal, occupying the whole field of "inner vision" without any artificial split between "intellect" and "affect": you are going through the act of being killed. To waking consciousness expressing itself in discursive language within the constraints of waking, "real" existence, the dreamt experience is bound to appear "exaggerated" and "highly dramatic"; still it is only "saying" "I'll kill you" in its own idiom (see also Tolaas, 1979–80).

The Problem of Negation

Freud (1957) claimed that the dream neglected the logical category of opposition and contradiction so that the concept No did not exist in dreams. Let us consider this statement in the light of what has already been said about concrete, pictorial language. It follows from the nature of concreteness that a dream would not *say* no; it would use its own idiom and *act* the negation. If the concept No exists at all, it would be demonstrated. How would you demonstrate to your daughter (in the waking state) that she should not touch alcohol? Individual possibilities are legion, but you might, for example, give her a drink and, just at the moment her lips are touching the glass, rap her over the fingers, or you just look at her with an expression of disgust and sadness. How would the little boy who does not want to eat his soup demonstrate his no? He might, for example, spill it on the floor, taste it and spit, and so on. This is the kind of negation we find in dreams. We find negated actions, but this does not mean that the concept No does not exist. In this connection it is well to bear in mind that a spoken or written no in everyday language may mean a lot of different things, from an absolute no (as in binary logic) to a no that "is a door rather than a wall." It cannot be understood out of context and reduced to the flip/flop of the computer (see Dreyfus, 1972).

Bateson (1973) draws attention to the fact that in what he calls iconic communication, which is what we find in dreams, organisms are often forced into "saying the opposite of what they mean in order to get across the proposition that they mean the opposite of what they say" (p. 114). For example, how would two dogs (or two boys using pictorial language as in a dream) tell each other thay they want to "play a fight"? The one who takes the initiative would have to fight first and then signal through body language that he wants to play. This is the kind of opposition one might find in dreams. Stripped down to fundamentals, we may say that in concrete language a thing/idea (as an idea is demonstrated) or an action is generally negated by another thing or action, which is negative relative to the first one, and sometimes its opposite, insofar as it is possible to speak of something as opposite to something else.

The claim that the concept No does not exist in dreams is a product of the mode shift from what we might call exhibited logic to discursive explanation.

Condensation and Displacement

In Freudian (1953) metapsychology, condensation and displacement are the names given to two of the disguising techniques of the dream work, that is, the unconscious transformation from latent into manifest content used to elude censorship and render the dream content, which obeys and is guided by the pleasure principle, more acceptable to the dreamer. Condensation refers to the reduction, or compression of the latent content into denser form by omission of certain elements and combination or fusion of different latent elements into composite images. Displacement refers to the shifting or transformation of affective stress from one important dream element to another less important and less objectionable one, in order to elude censorship.

Piaget (1962) has pointed out that condensation and displacement are inseparable, "since it is impossible to combine in a single image features borrowed from several objects, without displacing the affective stress" (p.

192). This seems to be a reasonable hypothesis. Besides, he shows that there are strong reasons to doubt that displacement is the result of unconscious censorship and disguise mechanisms. For example, the content of dream symbols sometimes "corresponds to thoughts or desires which are perfectly conscious and which the subject recognizes when he is awake" (p. 192). Transparent dreams, or dreams whose symbolism is immediately understood on awakening, are a case in point.

While I am in accord with Piaget, I will try to show that condensation and displacement are predictable and necessary consequences of pictorial representation regardless of metapsychological predilections. As noted earlier, Sartre describes a mental image as a synthetic act that never reveals more than the consciousness we have of it. I am trying to imagine Sylvette, who was in Oslo last year but is now living in London. The image, which appears to me as a "nothingness," is a synthesis of the Sylvette I knew in Oslo and even earlier but who is now living in London, and perhaps of other "Sylvettes" I have known. She has a mouth I remember from the trip we took on the fjord and is wearing the sweater of some other girl I know. She is in Oslo, but at the same time in London. The image gives all its information, cognitive and affective, at once. Consider the photograph of Sylvette you have in front of you, a perceived object you can scrutinize and learn more and more about gradually. Then consider the caricature of Sylvette you have on the wall. It makes you smile in recognition. It is more "like" her than the photograph; it is a kind of synthesis of the bits that set her apart from other girls and/or make you associate her with someone else (who also had a pointed nose). The mental image is not observed like the photo or the caricature; it is a synthesis giving all its information en bloc. In its synthetic nature, it is more like the caricature than the photo, but unlike it, it is not static but dynamic, spontaneous, and creative. Another way of saying it is that "everything" that is Sylvette to me at a given point of time, including both cognitive and affective aspects, is "compressed," "condensed," or synthetized into the mental image. In this sense a mental image is a condensation regardless of any such postulates as a censor.

In the waking state image-consciousness tends to appear at a certain point of time integrating itself with other kinds of consciousness (for discussion, see Sartre, 1947, p. 27). Dreaming is the state of image-consciousness par excellence. In this state we are, so to speak, images existing as a series of synthetic acts. Therefore dreaming, and any other state where image-consciousness predominates, such as guided waking dreams (see, e.g., Frétigny and Virel, 1968), will likely be felt as outstanding with regard to such phenomena as condensation and displacement. Piaget (1962) suggests that condensation and displacement may be viewed as functional equivalents of the generalization and abstraction involved in concepts, a point of view consistent with the one presented here. I would emphasize that we are faced with predictable characteristics of a mode of being where image-consciousness, itself a conceptualizing process, predominates.

"Illogical" Dream Narratives

So far we have been concerned with single images making up scenes and acts, and not with the way images are linked in a narrative. As this question is of crucial importance for the understanding of dreams and other pictorial experiences, we will discuss it at some length. Kretschmer (quoted from Koestler, 1977), who studied Bushman language, illustrates their way of thinking and speaking by the following story told by a Bushman:

> "Bushman-there-go, here-run-to-Whites, White-give-tobacco, Bushman-go-smoke, go-fill-tobcco sack, White-given-meat-Bushman, Bushman-go-eat-meat, get-up-go-home, go-merry, go-sit, graze-sheep Whites, White-go-strike-Bushman, Bushman-cry-much-pain, Bushman-go-run-away-Whites, White-run-after-Bushman, Bushman-there-other-this-graze-sheep, Bushman-all-away." (p.323)

The Bushman who told this story was hired by a white man as a shepherd, but was ill-treated and ran away. The white man then hired another Bushman who was treated the same way. Kretschmer comments that the story reads like a picture roll, each visual image dominating the scene throughout. Logical connections are tenuous and loose. On a slightly lower level still, language would be completely asyntactical, writes Kretschmer. The story refers to a perceived, memorized experience that is unfolding in discrete "word pictures." Compare it with the hypnotic dream and it will be seen that they have much in common. The hypnotic subject is also commenting on unfolding, memorized events.

In ordinary verbal narratives causal and conditional conjunctions generally link sentences explaining the actions and interactions of the characters. Such conjunctions as "as," "since," "because," and "if" are missing here as they also are in the butterfly dream; still we conceive the word strips as narratives or coherent accounts. Why? The obvious answer is the chronology, one event following after the other. Causality is assumed between one thing that happens after another. This is said to be typical of "primitive" thinking, the thinking of children, and the kind of thinking we find in dreams (see Freud, 1953; Jung, 1956; Hadfield, 1954). But chronology is present in sophisticated verbal narratives as well as in picture strip accounts, and then there are highly sophisticated narratives that are almost completely lacking in causal and conditional conjunctions, such as the Norse sagas and many of the short stories of Hemingway. Assumed causality based on time sequence does not account for the fact that we conceive of such strips as narratives. The most likely reason why we are able to understand the meaning of narrative is that the ability to understand human actions/interactions is epistemologically primitive (for discussion, see, e.g., Husserl, 1950; Weber, 1947). Skjervheim (1953) likens it to the ability of perceiving color, which is given, whereas the name of special colors (special meanings) is the result of cultural conditioning. A is kicking the cat and B is laughing. Did the cat spill his milk? Puke in his bed? Does he compensate for being passed over for promotion? Is B laughing because she thinks he is behaving childishly? Is she a sadist? We do not know, but we are able to perceive the episode as meaningful.

The more we know of the context in which the action takes place, the better our chance to understand the special meaning. We do have the ability to understand the meaning of such pictorial narratives as dreams and reveries, but it is difficult. Why? There are probably three main reasons:

1. We fail to grasp the consequences of the mode shift from a state where causality is explained to a state where it is made visible in condensed images, only to be couched in discursive language where we start looking for conjunctions and explanations (see also metamorphosis and personification). In my experience, this is particularly true with regard to *actions*.
2. Cultural conditioning, at least in verbo-centric Western countries, is working against concrete, pictorial language; it is for children and old ladies.
3. The nature of the content is often painful and unsettling and therefore subject to selective forgetting.

For the two latter reasons we do not even try to understand our own images. To train young students in concrete syntax, I may begin by pinning three or four art prints by the same painter on the wall, asking them to tell me how they can be linked in a narrative. They will then realize that "link" between pictures is equivalent to "similarity," successive images, mental or plastic, being linked by analogy. The next question is then: What can similarity between images consist in? An image is an organic whole that ought to be compared with another whole, avoiding any kind of atomization. But as soon as we move from visualization and parallel processing to verbalization and sequential processing, we have to divide the images into components such as settings, objects, characters, activities, actions and interactions, and colors (see, e.g., Hall and Van De Castle, 1966). Thus we can say that scene A resembles scene B with regard to certain well-defined tracer elements. This analysis can be performed through purely statistical techniques counting numbers and frequencies of predefined elements. Analyzing the acts of a dream or several dreams this way, we may observe the recurrence of the same or similar elements in all or several acts, for example, tools and girls belonging to a certain ethnic minority. I call this kind of similarity *categorical analogy.*

However, categorical analogy itself does not throw more light on the nature of pictorial narrative. We may for example recognize the same weapons used in two aggressive actions involving similar characters in two successive acts, but how are they connected? Obviously we need to understand the *special meaning* of the elements, and as dreaming is an act of self-communication, this is equivalent to "meaning of the elements for the dreamer." I refer to the special meanings as *semantic analogy.* Let us say that we have succeeded in mapping most of the morphological and semantic analogies of a dream and look at it again trying to understand the nature of pictorial narrative. We are then faced with two alternatives:

1. The observed analogies between images (scenes, acts) are a kind of "freewheeling"; that is, they follow each other in an asyntactical sequence, an automatic reeling off of related memory bits that do not form a narrative in the sense that they are not stretched out along a visible plot line.
2. The analogies are linked in a meaningful way; that is, as the plot is unfolding they provide accumulating information relating to the dreamer's self-knowledge.

If we settle for the second alternative, the question is: How can a succession of self-generated images related through analogies be said to provide accumulating information, and what is the precise meaning of information in this context?

Information may be defined as news of a difference (Bateson, 1973, 1979). "To produce news of difference, i.e. *information,* there must be two entities (real or imagined) such that the difference between them can be immanent in their mutual relationship; and the whole affair must be such that news of their difference can be represented as a difference inside some information-processing entity, such as a brain or, perhaps, a computer" (Bateson, 1979, p. 68). These conditions are met by the dream narrative, which may be characterized as a succession of (mainly) visualized differences centering around main themes. We may characterize the shift from scene to scene and act to act as *information leaps.* The maximal leap, which does not necessarily provide more information than a "smaller" one, is reversal, perceived as the unity of opposites. Understanding the nature of picturized concreteness, we could predict reversals to emphasize and clarify. Thus the calculating woman may have cold hands and the loving woman warm hands; the sinner (at least in most Western countries) may be dressed in black, the innocent in white; and so on. The minimal information leap is repetition or the succession of two or more scenes perceived by the dreamer as "alike," for example, in recurrent dreams. To quote Bateson (1973): "In the world of mind nothing—that which is *not*—can be a cause. . . . Zero is different from one, and because zero is different from one, zero can be a cause in the psychological world, the world of communication" (p. 427). In fact, repetition, like reversal, is a concrete means of emphasizing the importance of something. In between reversal and repetition we may postulate all kinds of mappable information leaps.

To be meaningful the analogic search through memory storage must result in synthetic images composed of the traits that the personal experiences they are derived from share in common. They may be said to make up a kind of personal identity kit, fusing and clustering related bits instead of placing them side by side with all kinds of superfluous details and digressive components. Still, two human experiences will never be exactly alike; there will always be a difference. The fusing and clustering of analogous bits into composite images will likely lead to such expressions in verbal reports as: "It was Mr./Mrs. X, but at the same time it was my old teacher . . . "; "I was here, but at the same time I was also in B. . . . " In other words, condensation and displacement, used in a general non-Freudian sense, are predictable, natural consequences of narratives made up of synthetic images. In the Freudian metapsychology manifest dream elements are said to be overdetermined as they are derived from a number of latent thoughts (Freud, 1953). However, there is no need to postulate manifest and latent dream levels to understand the phenomenon of overdetermination as a syntactical tool. It is inherent in the nature of pictorial narrative.

Analogy presupposes a first image to which the other images are similar, as a basis for comparison. One could argue that this basis is the total life context of the dreamer, as any image in a dream is a reified part process woven together with that individual's total life experience. In both the waking and the dreaming "states" the organism is the carrier of an accumulating record of gene–environment interaction that we may dip into through, for example, a blood test or a dream report. Blood, like dreams, is the product of the same record of ongoing growth. As Grotstein (1979) puts it: "What we commonly call the "dream" is the visual transformation of a never-ending pageant of events in the internal world" (p. 15). But if we study dream reports closely, we see that besides this more general level of continuity, concrete, locatable events from the day before are incorporated in the dream material (for survey, see Tolaas, 1979–80) and that these events seem to trigger the analogic narrative. In other words, some perceived, felt, and stored event from our waking existence is transformed into (predominantly) visual imagery entering the stage at recurrent intervals of high brain arousal (REM periods).

In the literature, no one else has insisted so strongly and consequently on the importance of these events for the appreciation of dreams as Ullman (Ullman, 1973, 1969; Ullman and Zimmerman, 1979). In his formulation these events share in common the qualities of novelty, unexpectedness, and unpreparedness. The event may be novel in the sense that it catches the person off guard, as there are no immediately available ways of coping with it at the time it is encountered. The intrusiveness of the event is then due to its being linked with unsolved issues in the experient's past history. Alternatively, the event is novel in the sense that it is experienced for the first time, in which case the experient is also understandably unprepared for it. In this connection it is reasonable to hypothesize that small children are likely to incorporate more events of the second category than adults with a richer past history (Tolaas, 1979–80). Thus it is the fact that such events are unsettling and intrusive that accounts for their being woven into our dreams. Their relative intrusiveness may be defined in terms of their ability to challenge our value system, social status, and psychological mechanisms of defense (Ullman, 1973). This formulation has much in common with Klinger's "current concern" (Klinger, 1971) and presupposes that behavior may be organized around affective responses (Klinger, 1971).

REM sleep is biologically triggered, presumably by brain stem mechanisms (Jouvet, 1969; Hobson and McCarley, 1979), and one of the main characteristics of this sleep stage is a high degree of brain activation. Vigilance (Ullman, 1973) is a prerequisite for perceiving and processing the novel, unsettling, and ambiguous, the "news of a difference" that challenges our psychological well-being. In the waking state we are able to neglect, rationalize, deny, push away, or repress our feelings. In the dream state, however, we have to confront and assess the feelings stirred up by the recent event, as dreaming is an involuntary act. This is the fuse of the analogic narrative and the polarizing instrument of relevant bits. "Relevant" then refers to "emotionally contiguous experiences." Unsettling events need not be negative; for example, your coming into a lot of unexpected money may be the precipitating event of a dream, but negative feelings such as anxiety are likely to predominate. In that connection, and also for what has been said earlier about the enactment of feelings, it is of interest to note that the REM state may contain a physiological mechanism "for controlling, modulating, and muting the anxiety response, perhaps involving the fact that the REM state is physiologically activated to begin with, constituting a preparation for 'fright' . . . " (Fisher et al., 1974, p.

393). Thus we may go on sleeping after even "strong" dreams, just as if we were made for this alternative mode of existence, removing drama (Greek: action) from the outer verbo-centric stage to the inner imago-centered stage where we communicate with ourselves about our connections and disconnections with others, which is essentially what emotions are about (for discussion, see Bateson, 1973; Sartre, 1947).

Consider again the buttefly dream. So far nothing has been revealed about a possible recent event reflected in this dream, nor of the dreamer's biography. But no dream originates *in vacuo*. In cases where you have only a verbal report and do not know the dreamer, there is only one approach to an understanding of the dream if you do not choose to resort to any specific metapsychology, namely, a phenomenological analysis of the dream report itself. This is taken up later. Time is ripe for revealing the background of the dreamer and the context from which the butterfly dream sprang. The dreamer is a highly educated, fifty-year-old bachelor who was brought up to believe in the ideals of puritanical Christianity. In particular, he was taught to look upon premarital sex as sinful and immoral. The day before he had the dream, he was on a visit to his native village where he met a life-long acquaintance, also an unmarried man of about fifty. This man, however, was in the habit of saving up money for drinking sprees and prostitutes in town. On this occasion he asked the dreamer to come with him. The dreamer considers him a tempter, as he admits to having certain problems in living up to his ideals with regard to sex. To begin with the dreamer did not know the identity of the other man in the dream, but he soon saw the connection with the events of the previous day.

Now we see the dreamer living through his doubts and conflicts triggered by the encounter with the friend. The recent event transformed into imagery is the bridge into the dream, just as the pictorial narrative transformed into a verbal report is the bridge out of it. The moment we learn to walk the bridge, our lives can come full circle. Is the kind of thinking we see in this and other dreams "primitive" (Freud, 1953; Jung, 1956), "prelogical" (Piaget, 1962), "childish" (Hadfield, 1954)? If so, why? Because we are estranged from our own metaphors (Ullman, 1979; Fromm, 1951; Bastide, 1972)? Could discursive language offer more relevant and precise information in a shorter time interval? Could a discursively related report given in the waking state have a stronger and more clarifying impact on the dreamer than this pictorial narrative? Ullman (1969) writes of the dream as a major metaphorical statement, a very sensitive conceptualizing process that is in no way regressive or primitive. This seems to me to be on target: the dream informs, or gives form to, what threatens to disturb our psychological well-being by holding up all our analogic resources in a seamless, synthesized narrative.

It is interesting to view the analogic search we see in dreaming in the light of Hobson and McCarley's activation–synthesis hypothesis (Hobson and McCarley, 1979). Assuming mind–body isomorphism, they postulate that the main elements of dreams are produced by a synthesis of information generated by activation of motor pattern generators and of sensory systems. Thus they argue that "part of the stuff of dreams is internally generated sensory activation . . . " (p. 15). One of their examples is quoted in full:

I was spinning, my body was spinning around. The circus performers put the bit in their horses and they spin around. The trapeze was spinning like that. Hands at my sides and yet there was nothing touching me. I was as nature made me and I was revolving at 45 rpm record (speed). Had a big hole in the center of my head. Spinning, spinning, and spinning. At the same time, orbiting. Orbiting what, I don't know. I'd stop for a second, stop this orbit and spinning (Dream 1651). (p. 115).

They comment that this dream is probably "a relatively pure form of inclusion of an internally generated vestibular sensory experience . . . " (p. 115) and that it "appears unlikely to reflect a memory of the day's events" (p. 115). Why is this dream unlikely to reflect a recent event from the preceding day? I am thinking in particular of the concrete reference to circus performers and the theme of the dream: "spinning around in the world, naked and with a big hole in the center of the head orbiting God knows what." Was the dreamer asked about such events? Was he asked to keep a diary? The authors offer many other examples that seem to me to be analogic chain reactions that might very well be triggered by recent events. There are good reasons to believe that any dream, be it spontaneous or derived from REM awakenings, contains an intrusive event (for discussion, see Tolaas, 1979–80). Viewed within the continuity framework, Hobson and McCarley's work acquires new importance: they seem to be carefully mapping the physiology of the similarity network without as yet including the relevancy pointer.

The REM dreams of a night are probably thematically related (Dement and Wolpert, 1958; Trosman et al., 1960; Kuper, 1983), and this also appears to be the case with dreams from a clinical setting (for discussion, see Hadfield, 1954). Though much remains to be said about this question, particularly with regard to the role of instigating events, we may postulate an analogic network spread out through all the related REM dreams of the night. A similarity network of this kind may also be postulated for other image-based states, such as reverie states and hypnotic dreams (see, e.g., the hypnotic dream on p. 10). In summary, when the intrusive novelty enters dream space, we may conceive of it as triggering a similarity network based on concrete material that lends itself to visual presentation and developing along vectors or plot lines. The outer boundaries of this similarity network are the mental universe or the totality of stored information/experience of the dreamer. Within this similarity network we may postulate individual preference patterns (favorite themes) with subpatterns (unified motifs) explainable in terms of the dreamer's past history, style, and personality makeup. Furthermore, within the preference pattern there would be nodes (acts) synthesized from minor nodes (scenes/images) within the subpatterns. The similarity network may be seen as bound together by the nodes by interwoven categorical and semantic analogies linked in information leaps—jumps between nodes—and stretched out longitudinally through long-term and short-term memory. In that sense the dream may be described in chronological time though the analogies do not have tense. They all exist in the tenseless field set up by the intrusive novelty. Following this model, a "good" dreamer might be described as someone who is unusually good at locating and retrieving appropriate analogies from memory and confronting them in a creative effort at assimilation. The intrusive novelty is then "put to rest," or in computer language "referred to terminal assignment." What happens when the threat to the self-image becomes so intense that the dreamer wakes up might be that: no relevant analogy is found, no older analogy can be modified so as to provide helpful information, or, simply, no useful analogy is available using known strategies.

Potentially, we might feed into a computer information about a dreamer's preference patterns and infrapatterns joined in a similarity network based on emotional contiguity and triggered by an intrusive novelty. Through careful analysis of a large number of dreams including recent events, we might be able to create a large data base with fairly sensitive pointers between the nodes of the preference structures, somewhat like the programs used for computer vision (Winston, 1975). The result might be a bleak, artificial replica of a rudiment of a dream. Even though we might be able to convey some idea of the way concrete language works, which I think is possible, we would not be able to simulate the main characteristic of image-consciousness: the inexhaustible, spontaneous creativity. An average person will have approximately 150,000 (REM) dreams in his/her life, and all of them are original, emotionally relevant, precise, and highly sophisticated creations (for computer models, see Evans and Newman, 1964; Moser et al., 1974, 1980).

METAPHOR BLINDNESS

It follows from what has already been said about semantic analogy that the dream images are metaphors. Metaphors are symbolic statements, but I prefer "metaphor" to "symbol" as the latter term is generally used in reference to specific metapsychological systems—so that, for example, "teeth falling out" may represent "loss of semen" to a Freudian and possibly "parturition" to a Jungian, and so forth (for discussion and comparison, see Fosshage and Loew, 1978). If we approach the dream from the point of view of a particular metapsychology, we may speak of dream interpretation. If, however, we choose to approach the dream phenomena as private metaphors, we instead speak of dream appreciation (for discussion, see Ullman and Zimmerman, 1979). Dream metaphors come close to poetic metaphors, which may be described as propositions equating two terms or images known as the *vehicle,* that is, the metaphoric word or image, and the *tenor,* that is, the subject to which the word or image is applied (Richards, 1965). Dream metaphors are implicit or unlabeled, which means that the specific tenor is unknown. (In a more general sense, the dreamer's life and personality are always the tenor.) If the specific tenor were to be known, it would have to be *shown* through other images, which would make nonsense of the metaphoric process.

Dreamers often ask why dreams express themselves in this language. My answer is that imagery is a natural medium for self-communication, and visual metaphors are perfectly suited for capturing the tension of an emotional field set up by a recent intrusive event. They are synthetic acts organizing and visualizing the emotional structures on the basis of all available memory resources. Saying that metaphors are private does not mean that people living in the same cultural setting and having similar backgrounds do not share metaphoric meanings. But metaphors always have private connotations. In the butterfly dream one of the vehicles we have to creep into (or onto) is the butterfly, riding to the tenor in this particular dreamer's life. In fact, the dreamer, whom I know personally and who has made it a habit to share his dreams with me, has quoted a love poem by Ibsen on more than one occasion: "Agnes, my beautiful butterfly. . . . " He also laughingly did so when we were talking about the dream. Besides the dreamer knows much about butterflies.

We could go on "riding" from metaphor to metaphor, but the point is that many dreamers never arrive at the destination; they are metaphor-blind, seeing only words where things are revealed in their original concreteness. Fromm (1951) suggested that this "forgotten" language ought to be taught in schools. I have tried teaching metaphors to young students in introductory psychology classes using the following method:

1. Going from things to words using well-known metaphors. For example, I may bring with me a deck of cards, shuffle it and "put the cards on the table," asking them what I am doing. Or I may fasten a small plastic heart on my sleeve to demonstrate the original concreteness of the expression "wearing one's heart on one's sleeve." Be-

sides, I ask them about the connotations of "plastic" heart. Or I may take up some coins and "put money aside." There are numerous possibilities for the interested teacher; you can have a bee in your bonnet (if you are able to catch one), or an ace up your sleeve, put all your eggs in one basket, and so on.

2. Going from words to visualization, drawing their attention to four basic sources of metaphoric raw material that are likely to be found in any sociocultural setting (with varying frequencies and all kinds of individual differences): (a) The body and body posture, (b) gravitational space and spacial relationships, (c) natural phenomena, and (d) clothes, tools, and implements.

- We speak of an *arm*chair, the *foot* of the mountain, a whiskey that puts *hair on the chest*. An *upright* may may be *bent with* sorrow.
- Even *down-to-earth* people may have their *ups and downs*. You may *rise* or *come down* in the world. Someone may be *above* meanness, and so on.
- Politicians are sometimes *caught with the pants down*. Even dream researchers may *cross swords;* they may even be at it *hammer and tongs*.

These and numerous other metaphoric expressions have become part and parcel of everyday language and are no longer felt as metaphors; they are dead. I believe it may be useful to try to resuscitate them in an effort to understand the nature of metaphoric process. Therefore I would ask dream students to make a list of such expressions and try to visualize them so as to sense their concreteness and original impact. They will then likely see that metaphors arise out of a need and a wish to capture the unknown, novel, and surprising. The original vehicle makes us see the tenor in a new light. When I was a boy I once saw a lady with a very big mouth. When I said so to my uncle, he said, "It isn't a mouth, boy, it's a waffle iron." The metaphor is etched in my mind.

3. Sensitizing them to their own metaphoric potential, for example, by having them plot in Osgood's Semantic Potential (Osgood, 1952) to some key words such as home, knife, baby, loss, love, and so on, or words of their own choice. They then exchange sheets to see how different our metaphoric worlds are.

4. Exploring the metaphors of one of their own dreams. If anyone offers his/her dream (anonymously), we use it for discussion in class. I generally offer one or more of mine.

This simple method works, but there are *always* a few who are so *deeply rooted* in words that they are unable to get into *contact* with things as they are immediately *revealed* in dreams. They seem to me to be able to turn things into words but not words into things, a sad *state of things*.

"Anything may be anything" or "Everything is what it is"

Working with metaphors, one is likely to hear the comment that in a dream anything may be anything; there are no generalizable facts so that the approach is not scientific—it is an art. My answer to this is that a dream originates in a context and cannot be understood out of that context. As the context is the dreamer's life and personality, the observation is correct. It is an art, and you cannot "master" it as something definitive or "authorized"; you can (I do not say only) experience and respond to a series of revelatory states of mind. But a dream report may also be viewed as a semantically autonomous document and subjected to phenomenological analysis according to the scientific method brought to its perfection by Heidegger (1962) and applied to dreams by, for example, Binswanger (1947), Boss (1974, 1975), and Kelman (1950, 1967). The metaphoric search described above and phenomenological analysis are in no way mutually exclusive. On the contrary, they may be said to supplement each other.

To illustrate the method we again return to the butterfly dream. Holding up a matchbox I ask my students: What is a matchbox? We will likely end up with something like: a container for matches, a tool for lighting things. I may then throw it at someone, asking him what I am doing. They will then likely "see" that I am "igniting him" not by giving or handing the box to him, but by throwing it at him in order to hit him. It might be interesting to ask them how they would "set someone on fire" having only concrete, pictorial language at their disposal. Answers might be: You might use a flame-thrower, push him into a fire, use the lenses of your glasses as a burning glass, sprinkle self-igniting liquid on his clothes, and so on. Imagination is the only limit as in dreams, but you always have to rely on some *thing*. The dreamer turns into butterflies and is surrounded by prostitutes. What is a butterfly? A beautiful, light insect fluttering from flower to flower transporting pollen. It does not soar like a bird, but moves near the earth from flower to flower during its short life. What kind of a metamorphosis do we witness? What is the significance of prostitutes in this connection? I would leave these questions for the students to answer without any comments. It will be seen that throughout we proceed by logical analysis of the phenomena themselves without resorting to any metapsychology or biographical data. The dream is treated much like a literary text whose meaning may be discovered through granting it semantic autonomy (for discussion, see McQuarrie, 1979). We go back to the phenomena in an attempt to unearth their basic or essential meaning.

In the Western tradition, science is inextricably linked to quanitification. We look at things without trying to "see" their essential meaning. In a basic sense we are "removed" from the immediacy of revealed meaning through abstraction and verbalization. One of the most obvious aspects of the phenomena, *spatiality,* deserves special mention. When language becomes pictorial and concrete, emotions are demonstrated as an inherent part of space just as space is an inherent part of emotions. We may speak of the spatiality of emotions and the emotionality of space. Prepositions we use in verbal language become what they are: concrete indicators of positions relative to other persons or objects in mental–emotional–gravitational space. Basically an emotion is a relationship (Tolaas, 1980). The two men in the butterfly dream "walk along" "side by side" "close" to each other in the full spatial–emotional sense of that word. They walk the same direction and obviously toward the same goal. Then the other man "turns against" the dreamer, that is, toward, so as to meet in an adverse or hostile act. We have to see through the words and place the men in space, make them move in mental space. This is the catch for many students and a kind of deconditioning process may be needed.

Adler (1959) explored the dimensions "up" and "down" (superiority–inferiority) in dreams, but the most comprehensive analysis of the topic is probably by Bachelard (1942, 1943) in his work on poetry and dreams. There is a fine passage about pure form and motion in dreams in May's book *Courage to Create* (1976). May, who is both a therapist and a painter, suggests turning dreams into series of spatial forms, an abstract painting. One of his examples is a female dreamer "who would move onto the stage of the dream; then another female would enter; a male would appear; the females would exit together. This kind of movement in space occurred in the Lesbian period of this particular person's analysis" (May, 1976, p. 128). Then he began to observe a progression of spatial forms corresponding to the progress of her analysis, and he concludes by stating that: "Perhaps the meaning of her dreams, and the progress of her analysis could be better understood by how she constructed these forms moving in space—of which she was quite unaware—than in what she verbalized about her dreams" (p. 129). Using a broad felt-tip pen, I have often drawn the spatial forms that appear in verbal reports (e.g., triangles, dyadic relations, up and down movements, etc.) to sensitize dreamers to the way they order chaos. This sometimes has an almost magical effect. They see as for the first time that preference structures or favorite themes also are a "preference space." Movements, motions, shifting positions, levels, and constellations that may seem "bizarre," "implausible," and "unpredictable" to waking consciousness may well be the basic fabric that holds the tapistries we make about our deepest concerns.

THE NEUROPHYSIOLOGY OF THE TRANSFORMATORY
FRAMEWORK: PICTORIAL TO VERBAL

Neurophysiological research on the differential function of the cerebral hemispheres suggests a number of global dichotomies such as verbal (left) versus spatial (right) (for survey, see Galin, 1974), analytic versus synthetic (Levy, 1969), propositional or logical, convergent versus appositional or intuitive, divergent, gestalt (Bogen, 1969), serial versus parallel (Cohen, 1973), and logical and rational versus holistic and intuitive (Ornstein, 1972). As Gur and Gur (1977) suggest, none of these dichotomies are mutually exclusive, but rather they reflect differences in emphasis and perspective. The left hemisphere is frequently described as "dominant" due to its superiority for language processes and mathematical ability. Recent research suggests that we ought to view cerebral dominance as a continuous process evolving throughout life (Brown and Jaffe, 1975). Thus Brown and Jaffe (1975) argue that the right hemisphere may be dominant in infancy "for the type of visual and acoustic communication which is relevant to the prelinguistic child" (p. 108). Visual recognition of caring figures, for example, would be important for the developing child. The lateralization process generally ends up with left hemisphere dominance for the deductive aspects of language and analytic thinking, with exception for "pure" left-handers where the right "minor" hemisphere tends to take over the functions of the left "dominant" hemisphere (see, e.g., Bogen and Bogen, 1969).

Three lines of evidence indicate genetic programming for left-brain language specialization:

1. Hemispherectomy of either hemisphere within the two first years of life (Basser, 1962; Krynauw, 1950; McFie, 1961) appears to delay language development in proportion to mental retardation. At this early stage of development, language function can be taken over by either hemisphere. But by the age of five, left hemispheric lesion generally leads to aphasia involving mutism and agrammatism, whereas this is unusual after right hemispheric lesion (Guttman, 1942). Thus the left brain seems to have developed language specialization by this time.
2. The EEG response from the left hemisphere of newborn babies is relatively stronger than from the right hemisphere after speech sounds. However, this effect is reversed after nonspeech stimuli (Molfese et al., 1976).
3. The functional asymmetry of the human brain appears to be paralleled by morphological asymmetry, observed both in the fetal brain and in the adult brain. The most striking asymmetry is in the temporal lobe cortex in the region *planum temporale* of the left brain, containing

part of Wernicke's speech and language area. Geschwind and Levitsky (1968) found that this region was more extensive in the left hemisphere in 65 out of 100 adult human brains. A similar asymmetry has been reported in fetal brains (Witelson and Pallie, 1973) from the gestational age of the 29th week (Wada et al., 1975). Interestingly, this is the age at which it becomes possible to distinguish between REM and NREM (Bakan, 1975).

In summary, lateralization ought to be viewed as a process. There is some evidence that the left hemisphere is genetically superior with regard to language (see also Turkewitz, 1977), and that left-brain language specialization may be established at the age of five. In adults there is a clear tendency for the right hemisphere to specialize in pictorial–spatial thinking (parallel processing) and for the left brain to specialize in verbal thinking (serial processing). One consequence of this dichotomy is that the right brain is more creative if we think of the ability to generate new ideas in visual images and suddenly recognizing unrelated principles (Shepard, 1978; Blakslee, 1980). Obviously it takes synergistic collaboration between both halves to evaluate and hammer out the product; so the creative enterprise is an "all brain" affair (Zangwill, 1976; see also Corbalis, 1980). Besides, right-brain mentation is described as "affective," "concrete," and "metaphoric" (Bakan, 1975; Nebes, 1978).

Not surprisingly, a number of altered states of consciousness (e.g., trance states, hypnosis, mediation, and dreaming) have been associated with right-brain functions such as visual imagery and recognition of emotional overtones of external stimuli (Stone, 1977; Studdert-Kennedy, 1975). The similarities between functions attributed to the right brain and dreaming, as described earlier, are striking. Bakan (1975) discusses several lines of evidence suggesting the right hemisphere as "the dreamer." In addition to the facts that pictorial thinking, "emotionality," and body imagery functions are associated with the right hemisphere, some of the main findings he lists are:

1. Greater EEG activation of the right hemisphere during REM sleep.
2. Reduced callosal communication during REM sleep, indicating greater independence of the hemispheres.
3. Right hemisphere injury accompanied by reduced ability to recall dreams and to produce imagery in the waking state.
4. Evidence for a right hemisphere hormonal system linking penile erections, REM sleep and the right hemisphere.

In addition to these findings, several researchers (Bertini et al., 1983; Gordon et al., 1982) have reported better performance on tests associated with the right hemisphere following awakening from REM sleep. On the basis of this suggestive evidence, I believe that the thesis is sound (for critical comments, see Hobson and McCarley, 1979), though I do not want to overemphasize the duality of mind. Somewhat simplified, we may then say that when we wake up, our left hemisphere (verbal consciousness) starts thinking or speaking about the recalled pictorial–emotional experience that presumably took place in the right brain to which it has access, and with which it interacts in a complex manner through the corpus callosum. The right brain is often said to be "unconscious" because split-brain patients cannot verbally explain right-brain activities (see, e.g., Popper and Eccles, 1977; Blakslee, 1980), so that in recalling and recording dreams and other image-based experiences we are really speaking about our unconscious. This is a tenuous thesis considering the fact that these patients understand speech and show through pointing and other bodily signals that they are capable of responding correctly to verbal commands (Corbalis, 1980; Nebes, 1978). The problem is that they cannot produce articulate speech.

People with undamaged brains do have access to the right brain and can speak about typical right-brain experiences transforming them according to "rules" we have tried to trace in this chapter. Perhaps we are closer to this forgotten language also during the day than we realize. Rather than the waking state, we ought to speak about waking "states," or abstracted spatio-temporal constellations of interlacing and interacting physiological–psychological variables. Among these states there appear to be cyclical shifts with periods resembling REM sleep (Broughton, 1975). Thus we may have to do with a basic rest–activity cycle running through the 24 hours (Kleitman, 1963, 1968) and involving shifts in relative right- and left-brain hemispheric dominance. This cycle has been observed in the cat (Sterman, 1970) and in humans (Globus, 1966; Friedman and Fisher, 1967; Othmer et al., 1969) with REM-like periods about every 90 minutes. Similarly, an approximate 90-minute fantasy cycle has been reported (Kripke and Sonnenschein, 1973).

Commenting on the distinction between the "private and the public" in connection with dream reflection seminars, Jones (1979) writes: "What I conclude from this as a psychologist is embarrassing. It is that human mentality is indeed bifocal, as every major student of it has concluded from Freud to Maslow. Primary process–secondary process, assimilation–accommodation, presentational symbolization–discursive symbolization, trans-schematic symbols–conventional symbols, divergent thinking–convergent thinking, subsidiary awareness–focal awareness, B cognition–A cognition"

(p. 73). I would like to add to his list the thought processes associated with Pavlov's 1st and 2nd signal systems (Pavlov, 1957), Angyal's homonomy-autonomy (Angyal, 1941), and Deikman's reception and action modes (Deikman, 1971). In recent thinking we may recognize the two poles of the cognitive continuums described above in their "pure" forms as analog and digital processes (Bateson, 1973, 1979; Wilden, 1972; Watzlawick, 1978). Digital processes, brought to their context-free, nonhuman (Dreyfus, 1972) perfection in the on–off of the digital computer, center around binary, analytic logic associated with the goal-directed, language-accompanied action mode. Digital processes are preoccupied with discrete elements used to map boundaries or "either–or's" precisely, so the language associated with them must be discursive. Analog processes, on the other hand, are preoccupied with wholes and relations, with concrete, iconic representation proceeding by similarity and contiguity. The language associated with such processes is imagery, or, if verbal, highly context-dependent poetic and metaphoric language. There are no impenetrable partition walls between these thought processes, and there are no a priori reasons for calling one mode regressive in any pejorative sense. They are different, useful for different purposes, and interwoven like the neurons of the corpus callosum.

In technological societies we may have been suppressing and neglecting this "inefficient" image-language until whole generations have come to suffer from the deficiency disease I have called metaphor blindness. The fact that dreaming is a universal phenomenon and an involuntary act points to its basic biological significance. Perhaps nature also wants us to "stand and stare" and "to go off into a reverie" at certain intervals during the day because we need to probe into the invisible emotional field linking us to others.

I will conclude this chapter by a few lines on verbal language in dreams. Dream characters talk and converse with each other, crack jokes, sing, write letters, and read books. From lab studies we know that such verbal activity increases significantly in prominence in late-night REM dreams, probably reflecting more left-brain activity as the night progresses and we approach awakening (Cohen, 1977; Bakan, 1975). The point I want to make is that verbal language in dreams is subordinate to the dominant sensory mode, and often when we wake up and write down the remarks and conversations, and so forth, that we have dreamed, they turn out to have a surrealist, poetic ring including assonances, alliterations, and puns. This is what we might expect given the metaphoric similarity search described earlier. In fact, an assonance may be described as an auditive metaphor (for examples, see Berger, 1963). I have myself awakened from dreams spontaneously and under lab conditions with fragments of sentences, sometimes poetic lines, on the tip of the tongue, such as: "Ask the flower to make fire seeds," when the sunflowers my son and I had planted were broken in a storm. As I was speaking the words in the dream, or so it seemed to me, they "materialized" in a big beautiful flower with a heart of deep-red seeds. They were "word-things" just as written words in a dream may become graphic "things" that image-consciousness directs itself toward and shows itself. There are also dreams where conversations and remarks, spoken or written, seem exactly like waking verbalization. Still, the framework in which they appear is sensory and predominantly visual. Image-consciousness knows what it shows itself, turning everything into concrete building blocks of our relief tableaus. Verbalization proper is a waking concern, a wonderful tool for the one-step-a-time approach to the world, and an inescapable tool of transformation of visualized "togetherness."

REFERENCES

Adler, A. *The practice and theory of individual psychology.* Paterson: Littlefield, Adams, 1959.

Angyal, A. *Foundations for a science of personality.* New York: The Commonwealth Fund, 1941.

Arkin, A. M., Antrobus, J. S. and Ellman, S. J. *The mind in sleep: Psychology and psychophysiology.* Hillsdale, N.J.: Erlbaum, 1978.

Assagioli, R. *Psychosynthesis.* New York: Turnstone Books, 1975.

Bachelard, G. *L'eau et les revês.* Paris: Librairie José Corti, 1942.

Bachelard, G. *L'air et les songes.* Paris: Librairie José Corti, 1943.

Bakan, P. Dreaming, REM sleep and the right hemisphere. A theoretical integration. Paper presented at the *Second International Congress of Sleep Research,* Edinburgh, Scotland, June 30, 1975.

Basser, L. Hemiplegia of early onset and the faculty of speech with special reference to the effects of hemispherectomy. *Brain,* 1962, *85,* 427–447.

Bastide, R. *Le rêve, la transe et la folie.* Paris: Flammarion, 1972.

Bateson, G. *Steps to an ecology of mind.* St. Albans, Herts.: Paladin, 1973.

Bateson, G. *Mind and nature. A necessary unity.* New York: E. P. Dutton, 1979.

Baylor, G. W. and Deslauriers, D. Dream understanding exercise. Université de Montréal, 1983. Unpublished manuscript.

Berger, R. J. Experimental modification of dream content by meaningful verbal stimuli. *British Journal of Psychiatry,* 1963, *109,* 722–740.

Bertini, M., Violani, C., Zoccolotti, P., Antonelli, A., Di Stefano, L. Performance on a unilateral tactile test during waking and upon awakening from REM and NREM sleep. In W. Koella (Ed.), *Sleep 1982.* Basel: Karger, 1983, pp. 383–385.

Binswanger, L. *Ausgewählte Vorträge und Aufsätze. Zur phänomenologischen Anthropologie. Band I.* Bern: Francke Verlag, 1947.

Blakslee, T. R. *The right brain.* London: Macmillan, 1980.

Bogen, J. E. The other side of the brain II: An appositional mind. *Bulletin of the Los Angeles Neurological Societies,* 1969, *34,* 135–162.

Bogen, J. E. and Bogen, A. The other side of the brain III: The corpus callosum and creativity. *Bulletin of the Los Angeles Neurological Society,* 1969, *34,* 191–220.

Boss, M. *Der Traum and seine Auslegung.* Munich: Kindler-Verlag, 1974.

Boss, M. *Es traümte mir vergangene Nacht.* Bern: Verlag Hans Huber, 1975.

Brenman, M. Dreams and hypnosis. In C. S. Moss (Ed.), *Hypnotic investigation of dreams.* New York: Wiley, 1967, pp. 127–136.

Broughton, R. Biorhythmic variations in consciousness and psychological functions. *Canadian Psychological Revue,* 1975, *16,* 217–239.

Brown, J. W. and Jaffe, J. Hypothesis on cerebral dominance. *Neuropsychologia,* 1975, *13,* 107–110.

Bruner, J. S. The course of cognitive growth. *American Psychologist,* 1964, *19,* 1–15.

Bruner, J. S., Olver, R. R., and Greenfield, P. M. *Studies in cognitive growth.* New York: Wiley, 1966.

Cartwright, R. D. *Nightlife.* Englewood Cliffs, N.J.: Prentice-Hall, 1977.

Cohen, D. B. Changes in REM dream content during the night: implications for a hypothesis about changes in cerebral dominance across REM periods. *Perceptual and Motor Skills,* 1977, *44,* 1267–1277.

Cohen, G. Hemispheric differences in serial versus parallel processing. *Journal of Experimental Psychology,* 1973, *97,* 349–356.

Cooper, L. F. and Erickson, M. H. *Time distortion in hypnosis.* Baltimore: Williams & Wilkins, 1954.

Corbalis, M. C. Laterality and myth. *American Psychologist,* 1980, *35(3),* 284–295.

Daudet, L. *Le rêve éveillé.* Paris: Ed. Bernard Grasset, 1926.

Deikman, A. Bimodal consciousness. *Archives of General Psychiatry,* 1971, *25,* 481–489.

Dement, W. and Wolpert, E. Relationships in the manifest content of dreams occurring on the same night. *Journal of Nervous and Mental Disease,* 1958, *126,* 568–578.

Deslauriers, D. and Baylor, G. W. Manuel d'analyse des rêves selon la méthode de graphique de résolution de problème: l'éclosion d'un rêve. Université de Montréal, 1982. Unpublished paper.

Desoille, R. *Théorie et pratique du rêve eveillé dirigé.* Genève: Collection Action et Pensée, Editions du Mont-Blanc, 1961.

Dreyfus, H. L. *What computers can't do.* New York: Harper and Row, 1972.

Drucker-Colin, R., Shkurovich, M., and Sterman, M. B. (Eds.). *The function of sleep.* New York: Academic Press, 1979.

Evans, C. R. and Newman, E. A. Dreaming: An analogy from computers, *New Scientist,* 1964, *419,* 577–579.

Fisher, C., Kahn, E., Edwards, A., and Davis, D. A psychophysiological study of nightmares and night terrors. *Psychoanalysis and Contemporary Science,* 1974, *3,* 317–398.

Foulkes, D. *A grammar of dreams.* Hassocks: The Harvester Press, 1978.

Fosshage, J. L. and Loew, C. A. *Dream interpretation: A comparative study.* New York: SP Medical & Scientific Books, 1978.

Frétigny, R. and Virel, A. *L'imagerie mentale.* Genève: Editions du Mont-Blanc, 1968.

Freud, S. The antithetical meaning of primal words. In J. Strachey (Ed.), *Standard edition of the complete works of Sigmund Freud.* London: Hogarth Press, 1957, vol. 2, pp. 156–158.

Freud, S. The interpretation of dreams. In J. Strachey (Ed.), *Standard edition of the complete works of Sigmund Freud.* London: Hogarth Press, 1953, vol. 4.

Friedman, S. and Fisher, C. On the presence of a rhythmic, diurnal, oral instinctual drive cycle in man: A preliminary report. *Journal of the American Psychoanalytical Association,* 1967, *15,* 317.

Fromm, E. *The forgotten language.* New York: Rinehart, 1951.

Galin, D. Implications for psychiatry of left and right cerebral specialization. A neurophysiological context for unconscious process. *Archives of General Psychiatry,* 1974, *31,* 572–583.

Geschwind, N. and Levitsky, W. Human brain: Left–right asymmetries in temporal speech region, *Science,* 1968, *161,* 186–187.

Globus, G. Rapid eye movement cycle in real time: Implications for a theory of the D-state. *Archives of General Psychiatry,* 1966, *15,* 654.

Godel, R. *Essais sur l'experience liberatrice.* Paris: Gallimard, 1952.

Gordon, H. W., Frooman, B., and Lavie, P. Shift in cognitive asymmetry between waking from REM and NREM sleep. *Neuropsychologia,* 1982, *20,* 99–103.

Grinder, J. and Bandler, R. *The structure of magic I and II.* Palo Alto: Science and Behavior Books, 1975 and 1976.

Grotstein, J. S. Who is the dreamer who dreams the dream and who is the dreamer who understands it. *Contemporary Psychoanalysis,* 1979, *15,* 110–169.

Gur, R. and Gur, R. Correlates of conjugate lateral eye movements in man. In S. Harnad, R. W. Doty, L. Goldstein, J. Jaynes, and G. Krauthamer (Eds.), *Lateralization in the nervous system.* New York: Academic Press, 1977, pp. 261–281.

Guttman, E. Aphasia in children. *Brain,* 1942, *65,* 205–219.

Hadfield, J. *Dreams and nightmares.* Baltimore: Penguin, 1954.

Hall, C. and Van De Castle, R. *The content analysis of dreams.* New York: Appleton-Century-Crofts, 1966.

Heidegger, M. *Being and time.* London: SGM Press, 1962.

Hobson, A. and McCarley, R. The form of dreams and the biology of sleep. In B. Wolman (Ed.), *Handbook of Dreams.* New York: Van Nostrand Reinhold, 1979.

Husserl, E. *Cartesianische meditationen. Husserliana I.* Haag: Martinus Nijhoff, 1950.

Jones, R. *The dream poet.* Cambridge, Mass.: Schenkman, 1979.

Jouvet, M. Biogenic amines and the states of sleep. *Science,* 1969, *163,* 32–41.

Jung, C. G. *Two essays on analytical psychology.* New York: Meridian Books, 1956.

Kelman, H. Movement in dreams. Abstract author. *American Journal of Psychoanalysis,* 1950, *10(1),* 77–79.

Kelman, H. A phenomenological approach to dream interpretation, Part II: Clinical examples. *American Journal of Psychoanalysis,* 1967, *27(1),* 5–94.

Kleitman, N. *Sleep and wakefulness.* Chicago: University of Chicago Press, 1963.

Kleitman, N. Basic rest–activity cycle in relation to sleep and wakefulness. In A. Kales (Ed.), *Sleep: physiology and pathology.* Philadelphia: J. P. Lippincott, 1968, pp. 33–38.

Klinger, E. *Structure and functions of fantasy.* New York: Wiley, 1971.

Koestler, A. *The act of creation.* London: The Picador Pan Books, 1977.

Kosslyn, S. M. *Image and mind.* Cambridge, Mass.: Harvard University Press, 1980.

Kripke, D. F. and Sonnenschein, D. A 90-minute daydream cycle. Paper presented at the *Meeting of the Association for the Psychophysiological Study of Sleep,* San Diego, May, 1973.

Krynauw, R. Infantile hemiplegia treated by removing one cerebral hemisphere. *Journal of Neurological and Neurosurgical Psychiatry,* 1950, *13,* 243–267.

Kuper, A. The structure of dream sequences. Institute of Cultural and Social Studies, 2300 RA Leiden, The Netherlands. Unpublished paper, 1983.

Leuner, H. Guided affective imagery (GAI): A method of intensive psychotherapy, *American Journal of Psychotherapy,* 1969, *23,* 4–22.

Levy, J. Possible basis for the evolution of lateral specialization of the human brain. *Nature,* 1969, *224,* 614–615.

May, R. *Courage to create.* London: Collins, 1976.

McFie, J. The effects of hemispherectomy on intellectual functioning in cases of infantile hemiplegia. *Journal of Neurological and Neurosurgical Psychiatry,* 1961, *24,* 240–259.

McQuarrie, E. Dreams as poetry. Evergreen State College, 1979. Unpublished manuscript.

Molfese, D., Nung, V., Seibert, S., and Ramanaiah, N. Cerebral asymmetry: changes in factors affecting its development. *Annals of the New York Academy of Sciences,* 1976, *280,* 821–833.

Moser, U., Pfeifer, R., Schneider, W., and Zepelin, I. *Zwischenbericht über das Projekt "Simulation von Traumprozessen" für die Zeit vom I. November 1973 bis 31. Oktober, 1974.* Zürich: Interdisziplinäre Konfliktforschungsstelle, Soziologisches Institut der Universität Zürich, 1974.

Moser, U., Pfeifer, R., Schneider, W., and Zepelin, I., in collaboration with Schneider, H. *Computer simulation of dream process.* Zürich: Soziologisches Institut, Psychologisches Institut, 1980.

Nebes, R. D. Direct examination of cognitive function in the right and left hemispheres. In M. Kinsbourne (Ed.), *Asymmetrical function in the brain.* London: Cambridge University Press, 1978.

Neisser, U. *Cognitive psychology.* New York: Appleton-Century-Crofts, 1967.

Ornstein, R. E. *The psychology of consciousness.* San Francisco: W. E. Freeman, 1972.

Osgood, C. E. The nature and measurement of meaning, *Psychological Bulletin,* 1952, *49,* 197–237.

Othmer, E., Hayden, M. P., and Segelbaum, R. Encephalic cycles during sleep and wakefulness in humans: a 24 hour pattern. *Science,* 1969, *164,* 447–449.

Paivio, A. *Imagery and verbal processes.* New York: Holt, Rinehart and Winston, 1971.

Pavlov, I. P. *Experimental psychology and other essays.* New York: Philosophical Library, 1957.

Perls, F. *Gestalt therapy verbatim.* Lafayette, Calif.: Real People Press, 1969.

Philippe, J. *L'image mentale (evolution et dissolution).* Paris: Alcan, 1903.

Piaget, J. *Play, dreams, and imitation in childhood.* London: Routledge and Kegan Paul, 1962.

Piaget, J. and Inhelder, B. *Mental imagery in the child.* New York: Basic Books, 1971.

Popper, K. and Eccles, J. C. *The self and its brain.* Berlin: Springer, 1977.

Pylyshyn, Z. W. What the mind's eye tells the mind's brain: a critique of mental imagery. *Psychological Bulletin,* 1973, *80,* 1–24.

Richards, I. *The philosophy of rhetoric.* New York: Oxford University Press, 1965.

Rechtschaffen, A. The singlemindedness and isolation of dreams. *Sleep,* 1978, *1,* 97–109.

Roffwarg, H., Muzio, J., and Dement, W. Ontogenetic development of the human sleep-dream cycle. *Science,* 1966, *152,* 604–618.

Sartre, J. P. *L'imaginaire: psychologie phénoménologique.* -aris: Gallimard, 1947.

Sartre, J. P. *Being and nothingness.* New York: Philosophical Library, 1956.

Shands, H. Dreams as drama. In J. Masserman (Ed.), *Science and Psychoanalysis.* New York: Grune & Stratton, 1966, pp. 174–178.

Shepard, R. N. The mental image. *American Psychologist,* 1978, *33,* 125–137.

Skjervheim. H. *Objectivism and the study of man.* Oslo: University Press, 1959.

Sterman, M. The REM state: evidence for its continued manifestation as a basic physiological rhythm during wakefulness in the cat. *Psychophysiology,* 1970, *7,* 308.

Stone, M. H. Dreams, free association, and the non-dominant hemisphere: An integration of psychoanalytical, neurophysiological, and historical data. *Journal of the American Academy of Psychoanalysis,* 1977, *5(2),* 255–284.

Studdert-Kennedy, M. Dichotic studies. *Brain and Language,* 1975, *2,* 123–130.

Tolaas, J. Dreams, dreaming and recent intrusive events. *Journal of Altered States of Consciousness,* 1979–80, *5(3),* 183–210.

Tolaas, J. The magic theater and the ordinary theater: A comparison. *Journal of Mental Imagery,* 1980, *4,* 115–127.

Trosman, H., Rechtschaffen, A., Offenkrantz, W., and Wolpert, E. Studies in the psychophysiology of dreaming: relations among dreams in a sequence. *Archives of General Psychiatry,* 1960, *3,* 602–607.

Turkewitz, G. The development of lateral differentiation in the human infant. *Annals of the New York Academy of Sciences,* 1977, *299,* 309–318.

Ullman, M. Dreaming as metaphor in motion. *Archives of General Psychiatry,* 1969, *21,* 696–703.

Ullman, M. A theory of vigilance and dreaming. In V. Zigmind (Ed.), *The oculomotor system and brain function.* London: Butterworth, 1973, pp. 455–465.

Ullman, M. and Zimmerman, N. *Working with dreams.* New York: Delacorte, 1979.

Wada, J. A., Clark, R., and Hamm, A. Asymmetry of temporal and fronta speech zones in 800 adult and 100 infant brains. *Archives of Neurology,* 1975, *32,* 239–246.

Watzlawick, P. *The language of change.* New York: Basic Books, 1978.

Weber, M. *The theory of social and economic organization.* New York: Oxford University Press, 1947.

Werner, H. and Kaplan, B. *Symbol formation: An organismic developmental approach to the psychology of language and the expression of thought.* New York: Wiley, 1963.

Wilden, A. *System and structure. Essays in communication and exchange.* London: Tavistock, 1972.

Winston, P. H. (Ed.). *The psychology of computer vision.* New York: McGraw-Hill, 1975.

Witelson, S. F. and Pallie, W. Left hemisphere specialization for language in the newborn: Neuroanatomical evidence of asymmetry. *Brain,* 1973, *96,* 641–647.

Wolman, B. (Ed.) *Handbook of dreams.* New York: Van Nostrand Reinhold, 1979.

Zangwill, O. L. Thought and the brain. *British Journal of Psychology,* 1976, *67,* 301–314.

3. Dimensionality and States of Consciousness

Samuel C. McLaughlin

It has often been suggested that the higher dimensions are related to higher consciousness. (For examples, see Zöllner, 1888; Hinton, 1904; Bragdon, 1913; Ouspensky, 1922, 1931; Nicoll, 1952; Govinda, 1960; McLaughlin, 1978, 1979. For reviews, see Schubert, 1903, pp. 66–111; and Rucker, 1977, pp. 119–133.) These suggestions, however, have never been taken seriously by physical scientists and mathematicians, for whom dimensionality is a complex and multifaceted mathematical concept having no relation whatever to consciousness and its states. In this chapter, I shall try to reconcile these conflicting views by distinguishing between (a) the dimensional structure of the physical universe and (b) geometric and mathematical models of that structure. Only the former is related to states of consciousness. This distinction leads to a more exact and rigorous description of the relationship than has previously been possible, and throws new light on the characteristics, significance, and classification of the states of human consciousness.

THE SEQUENCE OF DIMENSIONS

In this section, I specify what I mean by a "dimension." For those who are familiar with technical uses of the term, I also discuss (in an appendix to this chapter) dimension theory, dimensional analysis, and the Minkowski–Einstein interpretation of dimensionality.

Nonmetric Dimensions

The Oxford English Dictionary (1933) gives several meanings for the noun "dimension." Only one of these is of interest here:

3. *Math.* a. *Geom.* A mode of linear measurement, magnitude, or extension, in a particular direction; usually as co-existing with similar measurements or magnitudes in other directions.

The three dimensions of a body, or of ordinary space, are length, breadth, and thickness (or depth); a surface has only two dimensions (length and breadth); a line only one (length). Here the notion of *measurements* or *magnitude* is commonly lost, and the word denotes merely a particular mode of spatial extension.

Even though these two paragraphs are parts of a single definition, they express two fundamentally different concepts. The first is probably found in all languages and cultures, for it refers to the operation of comparing two lengths. The second denotes a visual intuition linking form to number, and is not found in any pre- or extra-Hellenic culture (not, at any rate, in Egyptian, Babylonian, Hindu, Chinese, Hebrew, Aztec, Mayan, or Hopi). To distinguish between these two meanings, I call the first metric ("having to do with measurement or magnitude") and the second nonmetric. Throughout this chapter, I use the word "dimension" in the nonmetric sense.

Real-World Dimensions

One more semantic distinction is necessary before we can arrive at a satisfactory definition of "dimension" in the nonmetric sense, for the definition we now have—the second paragraph of the *OED* definition—is ambiguous. Its meaning depends on whether the three "modes of extension" are assumed to be (a) identical and interchangeable, or (b) different from one another, the first being linear, the second surface-like, and the third spatial or solid. (The ambiguity is not resolved by identifying the three with length, breadth, and thickness or depth; for the terms "breadth," "thickness," and "depth" are themselves ambiguous, each denoting a linear measurement but also implying surface-like or spatial extensiveness.)

It is at this point—in resolving the ambiguity between these two assumptions—that we distinguish between the dimensional structure of the real world and geometric–mathematical models of that structure. In geometry, and in certain branches of mathematics (those having to do with coordinates, vectors, tensors, and spinors), it is convenient to think of a "dimension" as one of several more or less identical elements, and of the dimensional sequence (point–line–surface–solid) as formed by the repeated addition of identical and interchangeable elements ("dimensions"). But in the real world each dimension represents a different kind or quality of extensiveness, and the dimensional sequence is a series of qualitative changes

(Plato called it a series of "transformations"; see Burkert, 1972, p. 26). That is, there is nothing in the point (a location in space) to suggest the quality of extensiveness that we find in a line of sight, nothing in the line that enables us to predict the new and unique kind of extensiveness that is present in the surface of an object, and nothing in the surface that points the way toward the solid or spatial kind of extensiveness. Each new dimension is a whole new ball game, and each gives new meanings to the words "extension" and "dimension." (E. A. Abbott, in a science-fiction classic of the last century, dramatized this property of the dimensional sequence by recounting the difficulties that might arise in trying to explain spatial extensiveness to a surface-bound intelligence [1884/1952, pp. 59–64], or surface-like extensiveness to a line-bound intelligence [pp. 68–72]. Also see LeShan and Margeneau, 1982, pp. 99–100.)

So, with the aim of getting at the intuitive substrate of the mathematics of dimensions, we define the first dimension as the dimension of lines and curves in the real world (lines of sight, boundaries, and the edges of things), the second as the dimension of the surfaces of material objects, and the third as the dimension of material objects and the space they occupy—or, as Socrates put it, "the dimension of everything that has depth."

HIGHER DIMENSIONS

The Fourth Dimension

These definitions imply a sequence in which each dimension introduces a new quality of extensiveness, and each includes (in the logical sense; see under "The Classification of States of Consciousness," below) and infinitely exceeds its predecessor. So, to identify the fourth dimension (to discover its distinctive quality), we turn not to geometry or mathematics but to direct observation of the objects we see around us, and we ask what quality of extensiveness we can discern there that includes and infinitely exceeds spatial extensiveness. The answer is embodied in the "four-dimensional space–time continuum" of relativistic physics, which has as its physical referent a universe that extends in time as well as space (H. Minkowski, 1908/1952; Einstein, 1916/1952; Gödel, 1966; Williams, 1968; Eddington, 1958, pp. 42, 52; Goodman, 1964; Quine, 1964; Smart, 1964; McVittie, 1965, p. 60). We therefore define the fourth dimension as the dimension of material objects and of space, conceived as extensive in time; and to the traditional sequence of point, line, surface, and solid we add one more element, the enduring solid.

To visualize the fourth dimension, let us imagine some object—say, a tree—as it exists over time. We imagine the tree first as a tiny seedling, then as a young sapling, then as a full-grown tree, and finally as a decaying log; and we fill in the gaps as best we can, so that the result is a long series of images, each one corresponding to a moment in the life of the tree. We then allow all these images to coalesce into a single composite figure, spread out in time. This composite figure is of the fourth dimension, for it extends in time as well as space; we may think of it as the "fourth-dimensional figure" of the tree.

The Fifth Dimension

The fourth dimension provides a more accurate model of physical reality than the third, for the universe obviously does extend in time as well as space. But the fourth-dimensional model has a serious defect that can only be corrected by postulating a fifth dimension. The defect has to do with the fact that anything conceived as being of the fourth dimension is permanent and enduring in a way that far exceeds our usual understanding of those terms. The tree as fourth-dimensional figure does not age or change, for it contains all its ages and changes; and fourth-dimensional figures in general do not grow or diminish, wax or wane, come into existence or pass out of existence, flow or move or come to pass. Anything conceived as being of the fourth dimension possesses a kind of permanence that is qualitatively different from ordinary permanence; thus conceived, the flutter of a leaf in the breeze is as enduring as the pyramid at Gizeh, for both have their existence beyond the flow of time and so both have always existed and will continue to exist forever.

This means that the universe conceived as fourth-dimensional is rigidly deterministic: an unchanging and unchangeable array of static phenomena that is totally unaffected by anything we do, a universe in which there is and can be no spontaneity, no chance, no creativity, no free will, no quantum indeterminacy, nothing that might serve to alter the predestined course of events. By contrast, the world as we experience it is, to use Whitehead's phrase, "a creative advance of nature," a world of constant becoming in which each moment contains an infinite variety of possibilities for the future, and in which our conscious decisions and actions may sometimes play a crucial role.

In order to see how another dimension can provide a more realistic model of the universe, let us first imagine the ultimate fourth-dimensional figure: the entire universe, extensive in time as well as space, conceived as a unit. This figure is integral and indivisible, and cannot be divided into different "dimensions"; but in imagination we separate out the first three dimensions (the "spatial" dimensions) and set them aside temporarily. The result resembles a line in that it has only one dimension, extensive in time: we call it the "time line" of the universe.

Next, we assume that the universe is not rigidly deterministic but contains an element of free will (or quantum indeterminacy, or creativity, or spontaneity). On this assumption, there exist at any moment a large number of alternative possibilities, any one of which may come to pass in the immediate future. If these alternative possibilities really exist, then they exist as fourth-dimensional figures, for no lower-dimensional form of existence is possible. Let us therefore imagine each of them as a fourth-dimensional figure, and each reduced to a time line.

We now have, as the schematic representation of a nondeterministic universe, an array of parallel time lines (parallel in the sense that they all correspond to the same time segment). We restrict our attention to a particular group of these time lines—say, those in which it will snow here in Limerick this afternoon—and we imagine all these "snow" time lines lying in, or forming, a single surface.

Just as an ordinary surface is of higher dimensionality than an ordinary line, so this higher-dimensional surface is of higher dimensionality than each of the time lines of which it is composed. The "surface" is therefore of the fifth dimension, and is a skeletal representation of the fifth-dimensional figure of the universe. To flesh out the skeleton, we retrieve the three dimensions that we set aside a moment ago. Each point of the surface then becomes a complete spatially extensive universe. We call each of these an "event," and we call the surface the "event surface."

Any surface has two qualities of extensiveness. In the case of the event surface, the two are time and alternativity. Thus, by visualizing the array of possible events as a surface, we are able to grasp the sense in which alternativity, like time or space, is a mode of extension.

The fifth dimension, then, is the dimension of a single well-defined group of alternative possibilities, or, to put it another way, it is the first dimension of alternative possibilities.

The Sixth Dimension

In order to construct the event surface, we restricted our attention to a single well-defined group of time lines (the snow group). If we now remove that restriction, we have a figure made up of time lines that do not all lie in the same plane. This figure is of the sixth dimension; we call it the "event solid." Again, by retrieving the first three dimensions, so that each point of the solid becomes a spatially extended universe, we obtain the sixth-dimensional figure of the universe. The sixth dimension, then, is the second dimension of alternative possibilities; or, to put it another way, it is the dimension of an array of well-defined groups of alternative possibilities.

The Endless Sequence of Dimensions

The division of the sixth-dimensional array into fifth-dimensional groups, like the division of a third-dimensional solid into surfaces, is arbitrary. That is, different physical cuts in a third-dimensional object will lead to different conclusions as to which portions of the object are to be classified together as constituting a single surface; and, in the same way, different definitions of a "well-defined group" lead to different conclusions as to which events from the sixth-dimensional array will be classified together as constituting a single fifth-dimensional event surface.

Not only the way in which events are classified, but also the number of categories (the number of dimensions) is arbitrary. For example, if we consider the fifth-dimensional "snow" group to be a portion of the sixth-dimensional array "sun not shining," then we are free to consider the latter as a portion of a still more comprehensive array, "cloudy or partly cloudy"; and this last would represent a universe of the seventh dimension. By considering increased numbers of groups of possibilities, we can conceive the universe as being of the eighth, ninth, tenth, or any higher dimension. Thus, a statement that the universe has some specific number of dimensions, or corresponds to some particular dimension, has no meaning in terms of the physical properties of the universe, but merely represents one way of categorizing the alternative possibilities inherent in a particular moment or situation.

Except that they are informed by the fundamental distinction between geometric and qualitative dimensions, the conceptions of the fifth and sixth dimensions presented here are not new. Both were expressed by Ouspensky (1931/1971, pp. 374–376), and the former was proposed also by Einstein and Bergmann (1938), who "ascribe physical reality to the fifth dimension" (p. 683). Bergmann later explained that the 1938 paper had been a response to the rigid determinacy of the fourth-dimensional model:

> Physical considerations motivated the development of this theory. It appeared impossible for an ironclad four-dimensional theory ever to account for the results of quantum theory, in particular, for Heisenberg's indeterminacy relation. (Bergmann, 1942, p. 272)

Dimensional Levels of Reality

It is not difficult to think of reality in dimensional terms, for our usual criterion of reality is a substantive, material object—an object of the third dimension—and we recognize that the surface-like and linear features of such an object have no physical reality except that which they borrow from the object itself. Furthermore, even among these features we can discern a gradation in substantiality, and hence in reality, as Proclus pointed out in his fifth-century commentary on Euclid:

> [Matter] partakes more of the principle of the body than of the plane, of the plane more than of the form of the line, and of the line more than of the point. (Morrow, 1970, p. 73)

This relationship between dimensionality and reality holds all the way up the dimensional scale. An object of the third dimension—which only a moment ago we took as our criterion of reality—is itself unreal in relation to an enduring object of the fourth dimension, for an object with no duration cannot exist. But the enduring object in turn is unreal in relation to an "object" of the fifth dimension, for the latter incorporates, as any real object must, alternative possibilities for the future. The fifth-dimensional object, however, contains only an artificially restricted set of possibilities, and so is artificial (unreal) in relation to the sixth-dimensional "object"; and so on up the dimensional scale. Reality, in short, is a dimensional phenomenon; never absolute, but always relative to dimensional level.

Between Three and Four Dimensions

Imagine a line that extends indefinitely at both ends, changes direction frequently, and is confined to a surface—say, the surface of this page. In the limit, the line will tend to fill up the entire surface, and so we may think of it as having some of the quality of the second dimension. On the basis of this observation, we say that this irregular line is of fractional dimensionality between one and two. The greater its degree of irregularity (the more frequent and erratic its changes in direction), the more closely its dimensionality will approach two. This link between irregularity and fractional dimensionality is well established in mathematical physics. For example, the dimensionality of an irregular coastline may be 1.25 rather than 1 (Mandelbrot, 1977, p. 365).

To extend this idea to the next higher dimension, we imagine a surface (say, the surface of this page) confined to a bounded volume (this book). To complete the analogy with the irregular line, we imagine the surface extending indefinitely at all its edges, changing direction more or less frequently, doubling back on itself, and eventually filling up the volume of the book. Such a surface would have some of the quality of the third dimension, and would be assigned a fractional dimensionality between two and three. Again, the more irregular the surface, the more closely its dimensionality will approach three. A pulmonary membrane, for example, may have dimensionality of 2.90 rather than 2 (Mandelbrot, 1977, p. 365).

To summarize: a line, nominally of the first dimension, is said to be of dimensionality between one and two when it possesses in finite degree the distinctive quality of the second dimension (surface-like extensiveness); and a surface, nominally of the second dimension, is said to be of dimensionality between two and three when it possesses in finite degree the distinctive quality of the third dimension (spatial extensiveness). It is irregular lines and surfaces that have this property of lying between dimensions, but the irregularity is incidental. The underlying principle is *possession in finite degree of the distinctive quality of the next higher dimension.*

Having grasped this underlying principle, we are ready to extend this line of reasoning to the next higher dimension: we shall say that a material object (nominally of the third dimension) is of dimensionality between three and four when it possesses in finite degree the distinctive quality of the fourth dimension—that is, when it is of finite duration. Since all objects in the real world are of finite duration, all are of dimensionality between three and four.

The mathematical formulae that have been devised for calculating fractional dimensions (Mandelbrot, 1967, 1977, 1982) are not applicable to dimensions higher than the third. So, to specify the dimensionality of any material object we shall simply use the raw datum, the duration of the object. This procedure has the disadvantage that it is mathematically inelegant (it does not give us a convenient number such as 3.12 or 3½), but it has the advantage that it reduces the concept of fractional dimensionality—initially somewhat difficult and counterintuitive—to a simple matter of duration. Thus, the dimensional specification for a flash of lightning might be a few milliseconds; for a raindrop, several minutes; and for a human body, usually less than a century.

(In mathematical physics, fractional dimensions are often called "fractals," a term coined by Mandelbrot [1977, pp. 2–3]. I have avoided that term here because the fractal concept is an outgrowth of dimension theory [see appendix to this chapter] and therefore does not recognize any qualitative distinctions among the dimensions. As a result, the rationale for fractional dimensions [possession in finite degree of the distinctive quality of the next higher dimension] is not applicable to fractals. The term "fractal" also obscures the distinction—which I wish to preserve—between whole-number and fractional dimensions [Mandelbrot, 1977, p. 21.])

AWARENESS AS A DIMENSIONAL PHENOMENON

The apparent dimensionality of the universe, in contrast to its intrinsic dimensionality, depends not on any property of the universe itself but on a characteristic of the observer. I call this characteristic the "dimensional level of observation." This introduces no new idea, but is simply a matter of terminology: to say that a (hypothetical) observer has a dimensional level of observation of three (or four) is to say that, to this observer, the world appears to consist of third-dimensional forms (or fourth-dimensional figures).

Sense-Impressions

Our usual assumption is that the world as shown to us by our senses is of the third dimension, but this assumption is inaccurate, for it implies a world without duration; so the third-dimensional level of observation is not possible for human observers. Fourth-dimensional sensory observation is also outside the human range, for it implies direct sensory observation of the eternal sequence of events as a unit, whereas the world as shown to us by our senses is of finite duration. A human observer, then, is like a passenger in a moving vehicle who looks out at the passing scene through a narrow vertical slit. The passenger sees at any moment only a segment of the total scene; and in the same way we look out through the window of our senses (our "sensory time window"), seeing at any moment only a narrow time segment of the time-extended world.

To a good approximation, the width of the human sensory time window is .1 sec (Stroud, 1955, p. 179; Burr, 1980). That is, when we look at an object we see not its third-dimensional form but a tenth-of-a-second time segment of its fourth-dimensional figure; or, to put it another way, we see the integrated sum of all the third-dimensional forms that the object has during an interval of .1 sec. This datum corresponds to a specific fractional dimension between three and four, and the dimensionality thus specified is the dimensional level of our sense-impressions. This dimensional specification plays an important role in the physical sciences, for what we are trying to describe when we speak of "sensory," "empirical," "objective," "detached," "unbiased," or "scientific" observation is observation at the dimensional level corresponding to .1 sec.

If we let U stand for the universe, and subscripts denote dimensionality, then U_3 represents the universe as third-dimensional form at time t_0. We denote by 3s the fractional dimensional level that corresponds to a time interval of .1 sec; then U_{3s} represents the universe in its sensory-material aspect. Noting that any symbol with the subscript 3 is an infinitesimal, we then write:

$$S = U_{3s} = \int_{t=0}^{.1 \ sec} U_3 \ dt \qquad (1)$$

S being the total sensory input for a particular observer over the time interval specified. That is, .1 sec is the width, and S the content, of the sensory time window.

The Time-Integration of Sense-Impressions

Whenever we see or hear or touch something, we combine the immediate sensory impression with others that have preceded it or are anticipated as likely to follow it. When we listen to music, for example, we unconsciously combine the elements of the auditory stimulus into notes, phrases, melodies, movements, and other musical units; and it is from these relatively long temporal sequences, comprising both elements heard and elements not yet heard, that each note of the composition takes, in the instant that it is heard, its distinctive emotional tone and aesthetic quality. When we watch a movie or walk or chop wood or carry on a conversation, we perceive and respond to the action as a whole, the completed action, comprising elements accumulated as well as elements anticipated; and it is only in this way that we can make sense of the flow of events and act in a coordinated fashion.

In other words, every act of awareness reaches out into the past and future for related sensory impressions which are then brought into the on-going act of awareness and made an integral part of it. The "reaching out" may be primarily into the past (as when we recognize an old friend), or into the future (as when a child sees and touches a new toy); from the past we may dredge up fantasies and dreams and inaccurate recollections, and from the future hopes and fears never to be realized; but we reach into the past and future because there is nowhere else to reach. In the present tenth of a second there is only this bare and meaningless sensory impression, and if it is to be enriched by connotations and associations, these can only come from elsewhere in time. As William James put it, "The knowledge of some other part of the stream, past or future, remote or near, is always mixed with our knowledge of the present thing" (1890/1981, Vol. I, p. 571).

(Whitehead: "The past and future meet and mingle in the ill-defined present" [1920, p. 73].)

Perception may therefore be thought of as a process in which the temporal extension of events is compressed, so that past and future enter our experience not in their original (time-extended) form, but by subtly transforming the immediate sensory impression, perfusing it with nonsensory qualities. Whenever anything appears to us as beautiful or ugly, friendly or unfriendly, alive or dead, useful or useless, strange or familiar, sacred or profane, desirable or repugnant, interesting or dull, moving or stationary—in short, whenever we perceive in any object qualities that are not intrinsic to it as an instantaneous stimulus—then we are time-integrating the momentary sensory impression. Pure sensory awareness—seeing or hearing or feeling only the immediate stimulus—is a hypothetical situation that never occurs in real life, for we always time-integrate, projecting onto the immediate stimulus our hopes, fears, desires, regrets, and other things having to do with the past and future rather than with the moment of awareness. Thus do memory and anticipation become threads in the seamless fabric of perception.

Dimensional Levels of Awareness

In the metaphor of the moving vehicle, let us represent the time-integration of sense-impressions by adding, on each side of the narrow slit, a section of translucent glass through which portions of the landscape already past, and other portions not yet lined up with the slit, can be discerned indistinctly, like events that are remembered or expected. I call this wider window, which allows past and future events to affect the momentary sense-impression, the time window.

The time-integration of sense-impressions is a complex physiological process: the choice of sense-impressions from the storehouses of memory and anticipation may be dictated by a variety of factors, state of arousal and unconscious motivation among them; sense-impressions from the immediate past and future may be ignored in favor of others more remote in time; and, as I have already suggested, the process may be asymmetrical with respect to past and future. None of these deviations from simple time-integration is insignificant, and in particular situations one or another of them may be the controlling factor; but they represent, in general, relatively minor irregularities in the primary pattern, which is a bidirectional temporal spread from the moment of perception. We therefore take as our quantitative measure of this complex physiological process a single number, namely, the time span over which integration takes place—that is, the width of the time window, which we denote by w.

From the point of view of our sense-based experience, the width of the *sensory* time window (.1 sec) is the irreducible unit of time. (For example, two brief stimuli presented within .1 sec are perceived as one; and even a microsecond stimulus, if it is perceived, seems to last for .1 sec.) Therefore, in order to write an expression for the time-integration of sense-impressions, we treat S (which corresponds to a duration of .1 sec) as an infinitesimal (cf. Stroud, 1955, p. 201; Duhem, 1976, p. 186). Then, using the conventions of equation (1), we have:

$$A = U_{3w} = \int_{t=0}^{w} U_{3s}\, dt = \int_{t=0}^{w} S\, dt \qquad (2)$$

where A denotes the content of conscious awareness, 3w the dimensional level of awareness, and S all sense-impressions (past, present, and future) incorporated into conscious awareness during the time interval w.

The Light of Conscious Awareness

We have been ignoring the fifth and higher dimensions. To reintroduce them, let us imagine that we are looking down on the event surface (see under "The Fifth Dimension," above), and that our gaze, like the beam of a flashlight, illuminates a portion of the surface. We call this illumination "the light of conscious awareness," and we imagine it moving around on the surface, tracing out a path in time, among alternatives. There is nothing hypothetical or esoteric about this; it is simply a dimensional metaphor for what we do with our lives.

If we move closer to the surface, becoming more enmeshed in the moment-by-moment sequence of events, our awareness (the illuminated portion of the surface) contracts; and it we move farther back, becoming "detached" in the Buddhist sense, it expands. These "motions"—which take place in "space" of the sixth and higher dimensions—represent, respectively, the lowering and raising of the dimensional level of consciousness (the narrowing and widening of the time window).

This metaphor, like any other visualization of the higher dimensions, is imperfect (its most obvious defect is the false implication that expansion of awareness lessens our ability to discern details of the event surface), but it serves to portray certain essential features of the relation between awareness and dimensionality: awareness has no object except the multidimensioned universe, its primary and principal mode of variation is dimensional, and a widening of the time window (an increase in the illuminated area) augments not only the temporal span of awareness but also its probability span. That is, as our dimensional level of awareness increases, we integrate with the immediate sense-impression not only more elements from the past and future, but also more of the probabilities that are inherent in the object and moment of perception.

This metaphor also illustrates another important implication of the relation between awareness and dimensionality: the act of awareness coincides with the actualizing of events—that is, with the selection from the unmanifest matrix of possible events (represented in the metaphor by the event surface) of that particular sequence of events that comes to pass in our experience (cf. Grünbaum, 1963, p. 324).

Dimensionality and Time

It is usual to distinguish between two meanings of the word "time." The first is the linear variable t, in which past and future are differentiated only by numerical value or algebraic sign, the present moment having no existence except as an infinitesimal (instantaneous) dividing mark between the two. The second is time as experienced, "that shifting, mysterious, imposing, and mighty ocean that I see everywhere around me when I think about time" (E. Minkowski, 1970, p. 18), in which the only reality is the present moment, and the past and future have no existence except as they are manifested in the present: the past as "that which is to be surpassed" and the future as the living source of direction, purpose, and *élan vital* (E. Minkowski, 1970, pp. 38–43, 157–168). "To me," says Whitman, "the converging objects of the universe perpetually flow."

Time in the latter sense is the stuff of conscious awareness; it represents the gradual precipitation into our awareness of elements from the higher-dimensional matrix of events, and is therefore multidimensional, its exact (fractional) dimensionality varying with the width of the time window. The linear variable t is a one-dimensional abstraction from the multidimensioned reality. We identify this linear variable not with the fourth dimension but with a fourth linear coordinate (H. Minkowski, 1908/1952, pp. 79–80).

This dimensional interpretation enables us to confirm E. Minkowski's intuition that there are "phenomena that slip in between and are spaced out between these two extreme aspects of time" (1970, p. 24), for the variable t is appropriate only at the dimensional level U_3, where the "moment" (the irreducible unit) is a mathematical infinitesimal. U_{3s} corresponds to a phenomenally different time, for which a moment is .1 sec; at U_{3w} the moment has a duration of w, and at U_4 the moment is of infinite duration. At U_5, the idea of "duration" must be replaced by a concept orthogonal to duration, and a similar orthogonal transformation in the meaning of time takes place at each successive integral dimensional level.

The Experience of Higher-Dimensional Consciousness

We integrate our sense-impressions sometimes over a short time span and sometimes over a longer one. When our time window is narrow, we add relatively little to the immediate sense-impression, and so we tend to perceive the world around us in a relatively neutral way, as devoid of nonsensory qualities such as emotional tone, meaning, and aesthetic quality; and we ourselves therefore feel unemotional, preoccupied with the moment-by-moment flow of events. At such times we tend to be "objective" in the narrow scientific sense, "practical" in the short-term economic sense, our attention sharply focused on the concerns of the present moment and on our individual needs and desires.

As our time window widens, we find ourselves living in a very different world, in which even the most ordinary objects are endowed with profound meanings and extremes of aesthetic quality. It is through a wide time window that Aldous Huxley sees "a bunch of flowers shining with their own inner light and all but quivering under the pressure of the significance with which they were charged" (1954, p. 17), and William Blake finds "a world in a grain of Sand/And a Heaven in a Wild Flower" (1977, p. 506). In a world thus transformed, it is only natural that our values and interests should change in a fundamental way, so that we become more concerned with insight and wisdom than with syllogistic logic, more with natural beauty than with economics, more with long-term significance than with immediate practicalities and short-term gain.

A simple way to measure the width of the time window is to ask oneself, "What am I doing?" Right now, for example, I am writing a word, putting together a sentence, composing a chapter, developing a system of ideas concerning the dimensional structure of human awareness, and experiencing the events of a lifetime. Which of these actions I choose as my answer to the question will be determined not by what I am observed to be doing, but by the time-interval over which I am integrating my sensory impressions— that is, by my dimensional level of awareness.

To illustrate the way in which a widening of the time window can bring about profound changes in perception with no change in the objective stimulus, let us imagine that we are looking at an unfamiliar abstract painting, and that we see at first only a meaningless jumble of lines, colors, and textures. After a few seconds, however, we discern the outlines of a face: eyes, nose, and mouth emerge from the canvas, and we *see* a grin or a frown, an expression of wonder or disdain. This is a widening of the time window, for now our perception incorporates new elements from the past (faces remembered) and from the future (the element of intent or anticipation that is the essence of facial expression). If the painting happens to be that of an old friend, then, as recognition dawns, there is a further widening of the time window, for now the painting elicits, and seems to embody, the memory of shared pleasures and the anticipation of future meetings.

To illustrate a more extreme case, imagine that the viewer of the painting is a person of deep religious faith, and that the portrait is that of a great spiritual leader, painted with such skill and insight as to convey the feeling of a living and immanent presence, the embodiment of divinity. Now the momentary act of awareness may reach infinitely far into the past and future, as the face in the painting becomes the image of timeless being.

Unity

So far we have approached the higher dimensional levels of consciousness from below, starting with "normal waking consciousness" and gradually expanding the time window. Now let us approach them from above, so to speak, by starting with four-dimensional awareness.

The world as we ordinarily experience it has first of all certain fundamental dichotomies—matter and spirit, good and evil, earlier and later—and then a descending heirarchy of categories, divisions, and distinctions, leading to an infinite multiplicity and variety of objects and events. But the world in its fourth-dimensional aspect is, before all its other qualities and characteristics, unitary. When we constructed the fourth-dimensional figure of the tree, we arbitrarily chose as its starting-point a tiny seedling, and as its end-point a decaying log. But these artificial discontinuities had no basis in reality; they had to do only with the word "tree." In the world as it exists apart from the names we give to things, the existence of the tree is not a separate phenomenon but an integral part of a continuous process that is without beginning or end. In reality (a higher-*dimensional* reality), the fourth-dimensional figure of the tree extends indefinitely far into the past and future. In the world conceived as fourth-dimensional, there are no points in time where one thing leaves off and something else begins.

As in time, so in space. Birds nest in the tree, animals climb it, vines grow on it; it draws substance from earth and air and sun; and all these "non-tree" elements are integral parts of the fourth-dimensional figure of the tree. The list can be extended indefinitely: the fourth-dimensional figure of anything includes, in the final analysis, everything. The world in its fourth-dimensional aspect is an all-encompassing unity, and an observer who became aware of the world in its fourth-dimensional aspect could hardly fail to become aware of that fact.

One might expect that such a pervasive sense of unity would impair one's ability to distinguish among various objects and events; but there is no reason to expect any sensory impairment or deficit at the higher dimensional levels of consciousness, because the width of the *sensory* time window remains constant at .1 sec. What is to be expected is that the differences among objects, among events, and among people will seem trivial and superficial in contrast to the fundamental interrelatedness of all things. "All things by immortal power," says the poet Francis Thompson,

> Near or far,
> Hiddenly,
> To each other linkéd are
> That thou canst not stir a flower
> Without troubling of a star.

There is no logical basis for excluding the observer from the oneness of the fourth-dimensional universe. On the contrary, from the fourth-dimensional point of view subject and object are one. An observer of the world in its fourth-dimensional aspect could not be a "detached" observer, could not regard anything as "other" or "alien" with respect to himself or herself. It is this feature of the higher-dimensional levels of consciousness that gives rise to the sensations and emotions that we group together under the heading of "love." From the dimensional point of view, there are degrees of love, and they differ not primarily in intensity but in scope: love that is directed primarily or exclusively toward a single individual or object is of lower dimensionality than that which encompasses all that is, for the latter represents a more inclusive state of awareness.

The Perception of Time

In quoting Huxley, Blake, and Thompson, and in drawing analogies to mystical-religious experience, I am anticipating my conclusion, that the higher-dimensional levels of consciousness are to be identified with the states of consciousness ordinarily called "higher." However, let us now distinguish between the two, so that we can ignore the complex and diverse factors that affect time perception in the higher states of consciousness (characteristics of the observer, balance between sympathetic and parasympathetic activity, body temperature, the particular psychophysical method by which the perceived rate of flow of events is measured, etc.), and confine our attention to those factors that are associated with dimensionality. (For a fuller account of time perception in the higher states of consciousness, see Fischer, 1975, and in Chapter 13 of this book.) We imagine, then, a situation in which nothing changes except the width of the time window.

In this situation, a narrow time window will give rise to a sensation of events following one another in rapid succession (suggestive of Fischer's chronosystole), but also, paradoxically, to a sensation of time passing slowly (Fischer's chronodiastole). The passenger in the moving vehicle, looking out through the narrow window, will see objects suddenly appearing and as suddenly disappearing, events that are past before there has been time to respond to them, and phenomena that come into view piecemeal and therefore seem unrelated and confusing. Trying to make sense of the passing scene, the passenger will feel overwhelmed by the unceasing pressure of new and unpredictable stimuli, and will find it impossible to focus attention on one object for any appreciable length of time. The net result will be a sensation of great speed; but time will seem to pass slowly as measured by the clock because, with a narrow time window, the amount of time encompassed by a single moment will be small, and there will be many such moments in a single minute of clock time. Shakespeare's Juliet says,

I must hear from thee every minute in th' hour
For in a minute there are many days.

An unusually wide time window gives rise to the contrary paradox: the present moment being of long duration, there will be few such moments in a minute, so that time will seem to pass quickly as measured by the clock, and the observer might report that only a few seconds have passed in a single minute of clock time; but the accompanying sensation is one of events passing in leisurely fashion, with plenty of time for each to unfold at its own pace. In the moving vehicle, a wide window allows the passenger a broad panoramic view in which each object is seen for a prolonged period and in context, so that the relations among different objects are more clearly discerned, and attention can easily remain focused on one object for a long period of time.

In the extreme case, at the fourth-dimensional level of observation, the apparent flow of events ceases altogether. Here the lower-dimensional metaphor of the moving vehicle is no longer appropriate, for we would have to postulate something other than "motion" to describe the relation between the vehicle and its surroundings. Again, the perception is paradoxical, for, despite the absence of any sensation of the flow or passage of events, these events continue to succeed one another in the normal fashion, and the observer has no difficulty in making fine temporal discriminations. Events still happen in the present moment, and, indeed, consciousness is centered in the present moment far more acutely than usual; but the moment is eternal.

These considerations, however, have to do with only one aspect of our experience of time, namely, the perceived rate of flow of events. We also experience changes in the richness or fullness of the present moment; and here the time-window metaphor is even more direct and appropriate, for the primary effect of a narrow time window will be to diminish, and of a wide time window to enlarge, the content of conscious awareness (A in equation 2). Hence the feeling, in the state of mystical transcendence, that our conscious awareness is coexistent with all that is.

Negative and Positive Affect

We tend to suppress those impulses, fears, and desires that are most heavily charged with emotional content—that is, those that are most *real* to us. Repression also tends to be nonspecific: when we repress one strong emotion (anger), we tend to repress them all (including, say, joy). Putting together these two characteristics of repression—its strong emotional content and its nonspecificity—we see that repression can be defined, in dimensional terms, as the exclusion from conscious awareness of higher-dimensional perceptions.

Consider now the situation of an individual who is not familiar with the higher-dimensional levels of awareness, and who has repressed certain painful memories for many years. Such an individual, on first becoming aware of the world in its higher-dimensional aspects, is likely to be overwhelmed by an avalanche of traumatic effects: the dissolution of spatial and temporal frames of reference, the withdrawal of customary criteria of what is real, the threatened loss of personal identity and independence, and the sudden emergence of repressed material. To such an individual, the higher-dimensional levels of awareness will seem not "higher" in any sense, but an abyss of anguish and disorientation. Clearly, adequate preparation and guidance are desirable for an initial approach to the higher-dimensional levels of consciousness, and any technique or substance that facilitates such awareness should be used with care.

However, when these initial obstacles have been overcome—when the repressed material has been dealt with, and when reality, space, time, and individuality are understood in dimensional terms, then a widening of the time window results in a deep and comforting sense of oneness with all that is. The feeling that "each of us is alone" (Snow, 1969, p. 6) "vanishes into an all-embracing unity, and there is knowledge that at the heart of the universe is Joy and Beauty" (Johnson, 1953, p. 320). Paradoxically, the loss of separateness becomes an enrichment of individuality, for we become that with which we merge. Anxiety and guilt vanish, for one is associated with past time and the other with future time, and both are seen to be illusory. Furthermore, these aspects of higher-dimensional awareness appear not (as in the present discussion) as logical deductions from the properties of the dimensional sequence, but as direct and immanent perceptions. To re-create the experience of higher-dimensional awareness, we must think of it not as an altered state of consciousness, but as being in a different environment (one of higher *dimensionality*) where we can look around and see, as a matter of direct observation, that all things are one and that life and consciousness are everywhere. We can then begin to appreciate what would be obvious to a fourth-dimensional observer, namely, that the universe as it stands, without the addition of man-made theological concepts or religious institutions, is worthy of the most profound reverence.

The states of consciousness that we associate with the trancendence of space and time are often described as states of bliss, joy, and ecstasy; but the higher-dimensional levels contain all of human experience, and there is nothing in the dimensional structure of the universe, or in the nature of human consciousness, that might lead to a separating-out of the particular experiences that lower-dimensional judgments classify as "good" or "pleasant." An episode of higher-dimensional consciousness that lacked sensitivity to the suffering and evil in the world would be like a Bach mass with all minor chords and bass notes deleted, or an El Greco painting with no somber tones. The result might be "pretty," but would be shallow and unimpressive, lacking in artistic power and emotional substance. As Emerson puts it:

> In the hour of vision, there is nothing that can be called gratitude, nor properly joy. The soul raised over passion beholds identity and eternal causation, perceives the self-existence of Truth and Right, and calms itself with knowing that all things go well. . . . Long intervals of time, years, centuries, are of no account. (1883, p. 69)

Paradoxicality and Ineffability

Higher-dimensional consciousness is relatively easy to describe when, as in the present discussion, it is recognized for what it is, and its properties are related to the physical properties of the fourth-dimensional universe. But consider the situation of an observer who, following an episode of higher-dimensional consciousness, tries to describe that experience to listeners who have not had, or cannot recall, a similar experience. Let us make the reasonable assumption that neither observer nor listeners have any knowledge of the concept of dimensional levels of consciousness. In this situation, the observer must appear to speak in paradoxes and riddles, and to use terms (such as "outside of time") that to his listeners are cryptic. He must try to describe not a different place or a different form of existence, but a different aspect of ordinary existence. He must assert that all things are one, but that objects are nevertheless distinguishable from one another; that events succeed one another, but that the flow of time is an illusion; and that the world of ordinary experience is somehow less real than this other aspect of the world—all without using the word "dimension" or its variants, except perhaps in poetic metaphor. Clearly, both observer and listeners will be forced to conclude that the experience is in principle not amenable to verbal description, and so the word "ineffable" enters the vocabulary of altered states of consciousness (James, 1902/1958, p. 292).

We should also expect to find, among observers who are familiar with the world in its higher-dimensional aspects, an acceptance of paradox that is foreign and suspect to the narrow skepticism of the sensory-material point of view. Such observers would have no difficulty, for example, in accepting the obvious paradoxes enumerated in the preceding paragraph. On the realistic assumption of a society in which higher-dimensional observers are a small minority, and in which higher-dimensional observation is regarded as an abnormal condition rather than a superior form of perception, we would expect to find higher-dimensional observers regarded as gullible, illogical, and out of touch with "reality."

The White Light

Throughout this discussion, I have emphasized that our sensory faculties remain unimpaired during a shift to higher-dimensional consciousness. But we must now take account of the fact that what we see and hear is affected by what we know. When we viewed the abstract painting, our knowledge of faces, and of particular persons, enabled us to see on the canvas things to which we might otherwise have been blind; and when we listen to a Mozart concerto, familiarity with other musical compositions, and with instrumental technique, can enable us to hear things to which we might otherwise be deaf.

At the very high dimensional levels of awareness, there is an enormous disparity between what our senses reveal to us and what we know to be there. We have only this present moment, but we know that it is eternal; around us are ordinary objects, but we recognize each as an embodiment of the All; and so we become acutely aware that what we see and hear and touch is but a vanishingly small portion of a reality so vast that it seems as if our minds would "burst and perish from a single contact with the infinite actualization" (Ouspensky, 1931/1971, p. 124). The physiological substrate of human perception being what it is, this knowledge must somehow be reflected in what we see, and it commonly takes a form that mimics the effect of electromagnetic radiation and appears as a "light" or "glow," a visual-sensory metaphor for the unlimited substantive and energetic content of the world that lies behind the shallow illusion of the senses. In its milder forms, it is the glow that lights up the smiling face of a child; in its more extreme forms, it is the golden light—and, finally, the White Light—that seems to illuminate the entire universe in a "lightning flash of Brahmic splendor" (Bucke, 1901, p. vi).

The White Light, like every other feature of higher consciousness, is paradoxical: so bright that it seems as if it should incapacitate the visual mechanism, it does not interfere with vision in the least, but merely shows the world in its true light (cf. Fischer, 1978).

EMPIRICAL CONFIRMATION

The characteristics of fourth-dimensional consciousness as I have derived them from the physical properties of the world in its fourth-dimensional aspect—the pervasive sense of undifferentiated unity, the sensation of a higher (more real) reality, the transcendence of time and space, the incidence of extreme negative and positive emotions, the sense of sacredness, the perception and acceptance of paradox, the feeling of ineffability—all are equally characteristic of mystical or transcendent experience (James, 1902/1958, pp. 292–328; Stace, 1960; Pahnke and Richards, 1969; Friedlander, 1969, pp. 59–84). The identity is complete: except for the specific link to the dimensional structure of the extended universe, there is no characteristic of fourth-dimensional consciousness that has not also been described in scholarly and personal accounts of mystical experience, and no characteristic of mystical transcendence that cannot be described in dimensional terms. I conclude, therefore, that fourth-dimensional and mystical consciousness are identical, and that the dimensional levels of consciousness intermediate between the sensory-material level and the fourth-dimensional level correspond to the states of consciousness that are—as in Fischer's "cartography" (1971)—intermediate between ordinary and mystical consciousness.

THE CLASSIFICATION OF STATES OF CONSCIOUSNESS

The prime difficulty in classifying the states of human consciousness is that of applying lower-dimensional judgments and criteria to higher-dimensional phenomena. It is for this reason that the condition of mystical transcendence, obviously "higher" to those who have experienced it, is often regarded as a state of confusion by those who have not; and the term "higher" in this context is used only in a literary or figurative sense ("more exalted; more complex in development").

The only way to give the word "higher" a logically defensible meaning (in any nongravitational sense) is by way of the logical relation of inclusion (Birkhoff and MacLane, 1953, p. 335). This relation is the logical basis of all ordering, including specifically that of the natural numbers. In terms of this relation, the higher is that which includes the lower, and the lower exists only as an aspect or feature, a subset, a special case, a restricted category, a limited version, a particular instance or manifestation, in relation to the higher.

In geometry and mathematics, we conceive of lines and surfaces as existing in their own right, without necessarily being attached to (included in) any higher-dimensional structures; but in the real world there are no surfaces except the surfaces of objects, no lines except those that extend in space of the third dimension (and hence along some surface included in that space), no spaces that are not part of a fourth-dimensional universe, no space–time universes not included in a fifth-dimensional event surface, and so on up the dimensional scale. In short, the relation of each dimension to its predecessor is the logical relation of inclusion.

This relation holds also between higher and lower fractional dimensions in the range between three and four, for any longer time interval includes any shorter time interval in the same sense that 3 includes 2; and the higher-dimensional levels of consciousness are therefore higher than the lower in the same sense that 3 is higher than 2.

The system of classification that is suggested by this relationship corresponds closely to our intuitive judgment as to what constitutes a "higher" state of consciousness, and leaves us with many of the same problems. For example, an observer who is lost in mystical exaltation ("spaced-out") may fail to respond to inquiries as to date, place, and time of day, and may fail to keep appointments; and the guide or experimenter must still decide in each instance whether these failures result from impairment of function or preoccupation with more important matters. Despite these difficulties, however, this system of classification, when used in conjunction with other systems that take other factors into account (e.g., Fischer, 1971), places the idea of *levels* of consciousness on a firm logical basis, and provides an answer to those who argue that the "higher" levels of consciousness are not higher in any meaningful sense.

THE RANGE OF HUMAN CONSCIOUSNESS

The dimensional model as I have so far described it might be construed as implying that the fourth dimension constitutes an upper limit for human consciousness, and that beyond it lie realms of consciousness not accessible to us. This false implication results from representing a higher-dimensional phenomenon by a lower-dimensional model. For a more realistic model, imagine an infinite series in which the first member is the time window (varying only in time) and the second the illuminated area of the event surface (varying in time and alternativity). The "final" member of this series— a "time window" of infinite dimensionality—corresponds to the reality of the situation. We therefore conceive all the nonintegral dimensional ranges as being, in a sense, parallel, so that a widening time window traverses, so to speak, all of them simultaneously. The fourth dimension does not mark a limit except in the sense that it represents the infinite expansion of awareness. We use it as a marker or name for the infinite expansion of consciousness only because it is the upper limit of the dimensional range in which we communicate; and we communicate in this range because time, sense-based experience, individual identity, and conscious awareness all exist (in the forms familiar to us) only within this range.

We may find it easier to discuss these matters if we follow our previous convention of allowing subscripts to denote dimensionality, and let C_{34} represent consciousness in the dimensional range between three and four, and U_{34} the universe in the corresponding dimensional aspect. (C and U are one, but we consider them separately in order to arrive at a better understanding of their unity.) We can then summarize the preceding paragraph by noting that C_{23}, C_{34}, C_{45}, C_{56}, and so on, are parallel realms representing qualitatively different aspects of our awareness, each including (in the logical sense) and infinitely exceeding its predecessor. There is nothing arbitrary, obscure, or esoteric about this; it is merely a way of expressing the observation (which follows directly from the fact that the universe has an integral dimensional structure) that there are not higher-dimensional entities than ourselves; rather, there are higher-dimensional aspects of the consciousness and existence of which we are lower-dimensional aspects or manifestations, and anything we do—particularly in the way of raising or lowering our dimensional level of consciousness—affects all consciousness and all existence, at all dimensional levels.

Nevertheless, this aspect of higher consciousness, like all others, is paradoxical; and there is an important sense in which dimensional levels higher than the fourth are discontinuous with the C_{34} range, and inaccessible to (incompatible with) what we know as "conscious awareness." To the C_{34} type of consciousness, an "object" appears as a succession of more or less three-dimensional forms (forms having the dimensional structure U_{34}). C_{45}, then, would be a type of consciousness in which an "object" appears as a temporal succession of more or less four-dimensional figures (figures having the dimensional structure U_{45}). An object having the dimensional structure U_{34} is (at any moment) fully extensive in space but only partially extensive in time; an object having the dimensional structure U_{45} would be (at any "moment" of C_{45} time) fully extensive in both space and C_{34} time but only partially extensive in the first dimension of alternativity. To put it another way, the "border" between time and space, which for C_{34} lies between the third and fourth dimension, is shifted upward for C_{45}, so that what was the "extension in time" dimension has become another "spatial" dimension, the fifth dimension is now associated with temporal extensiveness, and the sixth is the first dimension of alternative universes. A moment, for C_{45}, is our eternity. We can imagine how our form of awareness might appear from the C_{45} point of view if we try to imagine C_{23}, for whom eternity is a brief instant of our time. But then, having grasped the triviality of our form of awareness from the C_{45} point of view, we must again remind ourselves that this higher consciousness is not anything "other" or "foreign" in relation to ourselves, but is merely another aspect of our own being.

So, having previously noted the sense in which C_{34}, C_{45}, and so on, are parallel, we now note the sense in which they are successive: they constitute an endless sequence of modes of transcendence, each related to its predecessor as eternity to the instant, and all accessible to us by virtue of the fact that we, like everything else in the universe, are infinitely dimensioned. At each level, the transformation of consciousness is so profound that everything we ordinarily think of as absolute—time, space, unity, transcendence, divinity, truth, infinity, eternity, awareness, reality, existence, knowledge— takes on an entirely new meaning, not predictable from any lower-dimensional level of awareness and "ineffable" in the modes of communication that are operative at lower levels. Furthermore, all events that happen during C_{34} eternity happen simultaneously at the C_{45} level; so that, if it be assumed that we shall all transcend before the end of time, then it follows that we shall discover, when we get there, that we all transcended simultaneously. (For this insight, I am indebted to Paul Horvat.)

Thus, an understanding of the dimensional structure of the universe allows us to see beyond the narrow confines of sense-bound experience, and to glimpse the broad sweep of the infinitely dimensioned Creation. The glimpse reveals that at the level of real transcendence we are indissolubly one, and so we must "return," as the Boddhisatva did, to lead others along the path that leads beyond time and hence beyond death, which is an event in time.

APPENDIX

Dimension Theory

Mathematical dimension theory is a branch of point-set mathematics, which means that its "objects" (and its lines, surfaces, and spaces as well) are point-set "objects," each consisting of nothing more than an imaginary collection (a "set") of dimensionless point-elements (Cantor, 1915/1955; Menger, 1943; Pears, 1975). These mathematical entities, like the "solids" of geometry, are not to be confused with the physical objects of which they are models. This is not to suggest that there is no relation at all between real-world dimensionality and the mathematics of dimensions. On the contrary, the qualitative interpretation of dimensionality is the candle of intuition that illuminates, from however great a distance, the most recondite developments in dimension theory; and each of these developments, in turn, throws new light on one or another aspect of the intuitive concept. But in mathematics, as in geometry, the word "dimension" refers to a system of classification for abstract concepts, and not to real-world extensiveness. Nobody has ever been struck by a mathematical set, whatever its dimension number.

Dimensional Analysis

Dimensional analysis is the branch of mathematical physics that is concerned with the analysis of physical problems in terms of fundamental physical parameters ("dimensions") such as mass, length, time, temperature, and electrical charge (Bridgman, 1931; Bender, 1958). Following Bochner (1966, p. 211), I refer to the dimensions of dimensional analysis as "physical dimensions."

From the point of view of the present inquiry, the most important fact about physical dimensions is that they do not refer to the spatial-extensive structure of the extended universe. An apparent exception to this generalization arises in the case of length (L) as a physical dimension. Here linear, areal, and volumetric extensiveness are represented by L, L^2, and L^3, respectively; and the representation is nonmetric, so that these particular physical dimensions might easily be confused with qualitative dimensions. But the arithmetic operations of squaring and cubing have to do only with the calculation of areas and volumes, and not with the transformations from linear to surface-like to solid extensiveness. That is, there is no basis for assuming that the multiplying of linear elements, any more than their addition, can produce the higher qualities of extensiveness. A parameter of physical dimension L^2 is qualitatively different from one of physical dimension L; but this difference is not accounted for by the operation of squaring, and is therefore not represented in dimensional analysis. If it were, then L^4 would be equivalent to the physical dimension T (time), and this is not the case.

The Minkowski–Einstein Continuum

As I have emphasized (see under "Higher Dimensions," above), the four-dimensional space–time continuum of Minkowski and Einstein is based on the same intuitive concept as the fourth qualitative dimension. But, as the word "continuum" reveals, it is a geometric–mathematical interpretation of dimensionality, and assumes that the four dimensions can be identified with, or defined in terms of, four linear-extensive elements (coordinates). This "coordinate" interpretation of dimensionality has long since been abandoned by mathematicians (Poincaré, 1913/1963, p. 28); Hurewicz and Wallman, 1941, p. 4; Kline, 1972, p. 1021). The Minkowski-

Einstein conception of dimensionality has no place in mathematical dimension theory, and it has been noted that Einstein's interpretation of dimensionality is "far from unambiguous" (Capek, 1976, p. xlv).

Despite its incompatibility with mathematical dimension theory, the Minkowski–Einstein interpretation of dimensionality is the cornerstone of modern relativistic physics; it is the only way of accounting for certain physical phenomena (the finite velocity of light and of all physical phenomena, the principle of nonsimultaneity, and the constancy of physical laws in all inertial frames of reference) that are important for describing and predicting phenomena that are very large (on the astronomical scale) or very small (on the atomic or subatomic scale). But the Minkowski–Einstein equations have little relevance to phenomena on the human scale, and unless the space–time continuum is conceived in nonmathematical terms, and thus identified with the fourth qualitative dimension, it provides no conception of the fourth dimension that the mind can grasp and that makes sense in terms of our ordinary experience.

The essential difference between the Minkowskian and qualitative conceptions of dimensional structure is revealed by the way each deals with the idea of extension. To illustrate this difference, imagine two observers, one on the earth and the other on the moon. Since any information-carrying signal (light, radio) requires more than a second to travel from one observer to the other, the idea of any event being exactly simultaneous for the two observers is, for all practical purposes, meaningless; and in this sense there is (in the astronomical scale) no such thing as simultaneity. But the idea of simultaneity is prerequisite to the idea of extensiveness; that is, when we say that a line segment is extensive, we mean that it exists simultaneously at its two ends and everywhere in between. The Minkowskian four-coordinate equations take account of the lack of simultaneity in astronomical observations, and in so doing abandon the ordinary conception of extensiveness; the qualitative interpretation of dimensionality assigns a primary and fundamental role to the idea of extensiveness, and therefore cannot incorporate the principle of nonsimultaneity.

So, if we are to think of the world as having a nonmetric dimensional structure, we must think in terms of two coexisting universes: one extensive in the sense that all its parts exist simultaneously, the other "light-structured," and therefore having a kind of nonsimultaneous extensiveness that is difficult to conceive in nonmathematical terms. Both are essential, the former to provide the extensional framework within which the latter can exist, the latter to account for observed physical phenomena. The qualitative dimensional sequence describes the first of these universes; the four-coordinate equations of Minkowski and Einstein describe the second.

The light-structured universe, as Bergson and others have pointed out, is not fourth-dimensional. The fact that it exists in time is enough to tell us that it is of fractional dimensionality between three and four. Taking the age of the light-structured universe as its duration (since we cannot know its terminal date), its dimensional specification is between 10^{10} and 2×10^{10} years (Harrison, 1976).

The relation between these two universes is that which obtains between any two phenomena of different dimensional level, namely, the logical relation of inclusion (see under "The Classification of States of Consciousness," above). That is, the physical (light-structured) universe is a particular manifestation (a manifestation in time) of the infinitely dimensioned universe. There is nothing esoteric or counterintuitive about this conclusion; we could have arrived at it without discussing dimensionality, for the fact that the manifest (light-structured) universe came into existence at some particular time in the past—now widely accepted by cosmologists—implies the existence of a larger and more enduring framework within which and from which it emerged and continues to emerge.

REFERENCES

Abbott, E. A. *Flatland,* 2nd ed. New York: Dover, 1952. (Originally published in 1884.)

Bender, W. *Introduction to scale coordinate physics.* Minneapolis, Minn.: Burgess Publ. Co., 1958.

Bergmann, P. *Introduction to the theory of relativity.* New York: Dover, 1942.

Birkhoff, G. and MacLane, S. *A survey of modern algebra.* New York: Macmillan, 1953.

Blake, W. *The complete poems.* A. Ostriker (Ed.). New York: Penguin Books, 1977.

Bochner, S. *The role of mathematics in the rise of science.* Princeton, N.J.: Princeton University Press, 1966.

Bragdon, C. *A primer of higher space.* Tucson, Ariz.: Omen Press, 1972. (Originally published in 1913.)

Bridgman, P. W. *Dimensional analysis.* New Haven, Conn.: Yale University Press, 1931.

Bucke, R. M. *Cosmic consciousness.* New York: E. P. Dutton Co., 1901.

Burkert, W. *Lore and science in ancient Pythagoreanism,* E. L. Minar, Jr. (transl). Cambridge, Mass.: Harvard University Press, 1972.

Burr, D. Motion smear. *Nature,* 1980, *284,* 164–165.

Cantor, G. *Contributions to the founding of the theory of transfinite numbers,* translated, with introduction and commentary, by P. E. B. Jourdain. N. Y.: Dover, 1955. (Originally published in 1915.)

Capek, M. (Ed.) *The concepts of space and time.* Boston: Reidel, 1976.

Duhem, P. The problem of the absolute clock. In M. Capek (Ed.), *The concepts of space and time.* Boston: Reidel, 1976, pp. 185–186.

Eddington, A. *The nature of the physical world.* Ann Arbor, Mich.: The University of Michigan Press, 1958.

Einstein, A. The foundation of the general theory of relativity. *Annalen der Physik, 49.* In W. Perrett and G. B. Jeffrey (transl.), *The principle of relativity.* New York: Dover, 1952.

Einstein, A. and Bergmann, P. On a generalization of Kaluza's theory of electricity. *Annals of Mathematics,* 1938, *39,* 683–701.

Emerson, R. W. *Essays.* Boston: Houghton-Mifflin, 1883.

Fischer, R. A cartography of the ecstatic and meditative states. *Science,* 1971, *174,* 897–904.

Fischer, R. Manipulation of space and time through hallucinogenic drugs. In D. V. Silva-Sankar (Ed.), *LSD: a total study.* Westbury, N.Y.: PJD Publications, 1975, pp. 362–394.

Fischer, R. On images and pure light: integration of east and west. *Journal of Altered States of Consciousness,* 1978, *3,* 205–212.

Freidlander, P. *Plato, VOl. I.* H. Meyerhoff (transl.). Princeton, N.J.: The Bollingen Foundation, 1969.

Gödel, K. Static interpretation of space-time. In M. Capek (Ed.), *The concepts of space and time.* Boston: Reidel, 1966.

Goodman, N. Time and language, and the passage of time. In J. J. C. Smart (Ed.), *Problems of space and time.* New York: Macmillan, 1964, pp. 356–359.

Govinda, L. The ecstasy of breaking-through in the experience of meditation. In J. White (ED.), *The highest state of consciousness.* Garden City, N.Y.: Doubleday, 1952.

Grunbaum, A. *Philosophical problems of space and time.* New York: Knopf, 1963.

Harrison, R. Entry under "Universe" in *Encyclopedia Brittanica,* 1976 ed. Macropedia, vol. 18, p. 1007.

Hinton, C. H. *The fourth dimension.* London: Sonnenschein, 1904.

Hurewicz, W. and Wallman, H. *Dimension theory.* Princeton, N.J.: Princeton University Press, 1941.

Huxley, A. *The doors of perception and heaven and hell.* New York: Harper & Row, 1954.

James, W. *The principles of psychology.* Cambridge, Mass.: Harvard University Press, 1981. (Originally published in 1890.)

James, W. *The varieties of religious experience.* New York: New American Library, 1958. (Originally published in 1902.)

Johnson, R. C. *The imprisoned splendour.* New York: Harper, 1953.

Kline, M. *Mathematical thought from ancient to modern times.* Oxford, 1972.

LeShan, L. and Margeneau, H. *Einstein's space and Van Gogh's sky.* New York: Macmillan, 1982.

Mandelbrot, B. How long is the coast of Britain? Self-similarity and fractional dimension. *Science,* 1967, *155,* 636–638.

Mandelbrot, B. *Fractals: form, chance, and dimension.* San Francisco: Freeman, 1977.

Mandelbrot, B. *The fractal geometry of nature.* San Francisco: Freeman, 1982.

McLaughlin, S. *On feeling good.* Brookline, Mass.: Autumn Press, 1978.

McLaughlin, S. The relation between physical dimensions and higher consciousness. *Journal of Altered States of Consciousness,* 1979, *5,* 65–82.

McVittie, G. C. *General relativity and cosmology.* Urbana: University of Illinois Press, 1965.

Menger, K. What is dimension? *American Mathematical Monthly,* 1943, *50,* 2–7.

Minkowski, E. *Lived time.* N. Metzel (transl.). Evanston, Ill.: Northwestern University Press, 1970.

Minkowski, H. Space and time. In W. Perrett and G. B. Jeffrey (transl.), *The principle of relativity.* New York: Dover, 1952. (Originally published in 1908.)

Morrow, G. *Proclus: a commentary on the first book of Euclid's Elements.* Princeton, N.J.: Princeton University Press, 1970.

Nicoll, M. *Living time.* London: Vincent Stuart, 1952.

Ouspensky, P. *Tertium organum.* New York: Random House, 1970. (Originally published in 1922.)

Ouspensky, P. *A new model of the universe.* New York: Random House, 1971. (Originally published in 1931.)

Pahnke, W. and W. Richards. Implications of LSD and experimental mysticism. In C. Tart (Ed), *Altered states of consciousness.* New York: Wiley, 1969, pp. 399–428.

Pears, A. R. *Dimension theory of general spaces.* Cambridge: Cambridge University Press, 1975.

Poincare, H. *Mathematics and science: last essays* J. Bolduc (transl.). New York: Dover, 1963. (Originally published in 1913.)

Quine, W. V. Time. In J. J. C. Smart (Ed.), *Problems in space and time.* New York: Macmillan, 1964, pp. 370–374.

Rucker, R. *Geometry, relativity, and the fourth dimension.* New York: Dover, 1977.

Schubert, H. *Mathematical essays and recreations.* Chicago: Open Court Publ. Co., 1903.

Smart, J. J. C. *Problems in space and time.* New York: Macmillan, 1964.

Snow, C. P. *The two cultures and A second look.* Cambridge: Cambridge University Press, 1969.

Stace, W. T. *Mysticism and philosophy.* New York: Macmillan, 1960.

Stroud, J. M. The fine structure of psychological time. In H. Quastler (Ed.), *Information theory in psychology.* New York: Free Press, 1955.

The Oxford English Dictionary. Oxford: The Clarendon Press, 1933.

Whitehead, A. N. *The concept of nature.* Cambridge University Press, 1920.

Williams, D. The myth of passage. In R. M. Gale (Ed.), *The philosophy of time.* New York: Humanities Press, 1968, pp. 98–116.

Zöllner, J. K. F. *Transcendental physics,* C. C. Massey (transl.). Boston: Colby & Rich, 1888.

4. Altered States of Consciousness in Everyday Life: The Ultradian Rhythms

Ernest Lawrence Rossi

It is a curious but undeniable fact that consciousness, the essence of knowing, does not know itself very well. Evolution has favored the development of consciousness with an outer focus while the capacity of consciousness to turn inward and see itself—self-reflection—is poorly developed (Rossi, 1972a,b). The most peculiar blind spot of consciousness is its inability to recognize its own limitations and altered states when it is experiencing them; consciousness seems committed to maintaining a fixed, stable view of itself. How little does the average consciousness recognize that it is dreaming rather than awake; that it is altered in ways that it does not totally understand by its own past and currently changing experiences and motivations? Even gross alterations in its functioning induced by emotions, drugs, shock, fatigue, and general psychophysiological desynchronization (Wever, 1982) are frequently misunderstood and underestimated. Thus the average person in the course of a normal day does not recognize the many subtle alterations that are constantly taking place in his/her own consciousness.

While this unawareness seems to be the more common condition of consciousness, sensitive observers throughout human history have continually struggled to express the subjective sense of change or alteration in their own states of consciousness (Bucke, 1901; Krishna, 1975; Wilber, 1977; Tart, 1983a and b). What has been lacking in these fascinating but essentially anecdotal accounts is a systematic, empirical approach that could provide the verifiable, objective type of experimental data required of scientific knowledge. In this chapter we will explore the possibility that very recent developments in psychophysiological research in the previously unrelated areas of the sleep–dream cycle, hypnosis, ultradian rhythms, psychosomatic illness, and state-dependent memory and learning may be coalescing into one broadly integrated area—an area that can provide new approaches to the study of altered states of consciousness.

Everyday alterations of mood, work efficiency, and consciousness have been studied as manifestations of the 24-hour circadian (L., *circa* + *dies,* about a day) cycle. Ultradian rhythms are much shorter psychophysiological processes involving alternating autonomic and brain functions that have a 90- to 120-minute periodicity within the 24-hour circadian cycle. In this chapter we will explore some of the issues researchers have raised recently regarding the interaction between ultradian rhythms and the phenomenology of mind and behavior.

In the first section we will review the process of serendipitous discovery that led the author to hypothesize a relation between altered states in everyday life, the common everyday trance, hypnosis, and the psychophysiological ultradian rhythms (Rossi, 1982). This review will include an outline reflecting the basic areas of ultradian research, with particular emphasis upon the behavioral correlates and subtle altered states of consciousness in everyday life that have been associated with them.

In the second section we will explore the general hypothesis that ultradian rhythms are one of the major psychophysiological bases of altered states of consciousness and behavior in everyday life. We will review the three-phase history of ultradian research from the original formulation of the *Basic Rest-Activity Cycle* (BRAC) by Kleitman to current research, illustrating its clinical and transpersonal significance.

In the third section we will study in greater detail one specific area of recent ultradian research that has introduced a new technique that may be of seminal significance for future studies of altered states of consciousness. This is the so-called *nasal cycle,* which offers an easily accessible and non-invasive method for assessing and altering the psychophysiology of the autonomic nervous system, the cerebral hemispheres, and subjective states of mind. The potential contributions of this approach in integrating different areas from psychosomatic medicine and state-dependent learning to transpersonal psychology will be touched upon.

In the final sections we will review the implications of these studies and outline the types of experimental research that are now needed to consolidate and further expand the new research frontier of ultradian rhythms and altered states of consciousness.

THE COMMON EVERYDAY TRANCE, THE NATURALISTIC APPROACH TO HYPNOSIS, AND ULTRADIAN RHYTHMS

Twelve years of intensive observation, recording, and analysis of the therapeutic sessions of Milton H. Erickson (MHE)—generally regarded as the

founder of our current permissive and naturalistic approaches to hypnotherapy (Erickson, 1980)—revealed a number of unique characteristics:

1. MHE was an acute observer whose ideal was to impose nothing of
   himself upon patients; rather he sought to indirectly *utilize* patients'
   own mental mechanisms, frames of reference, personality characteristics, motivations, and behaviors to induce altered states that would
   facilitate therapeutic change.
2. His patients frequently did not recognize that they had experienced
   hypnosis, or any sort of altered state, even when they manifested dramatic hypnotic behaviors and therapeutic changes.
3. Unlike the typical 50-minute hour of most therapists, MHE's sessions
   usually ranged between 90 and 120 minutes, or more.

In his later years MHE would usually facilitate therapeutic trance after
he had observed that the patient's physical and mental processes had "qui-
eted down." MHE would explain to this observer that he was *utilizing natural periods* of quietness and expectation during which time the patient's
receptivity was optimal for experiencing trance. We soon began to call these
periods of quiet receptivity the "common everyday trance" because it appeared to be a normal feature of most individual's daily life experience:

> The housewife staring vacantly over a cup of coffee, the student with
> a faraway look in his eyes during the middle of a lecture, and the driver
> who automatically reaches his destination with no memory of the details
> of his route, are all varieties of the common everyday trance. (Rossi,
> 1982, p. 22)

Over a number of years the author carefully compiled lists of the behavioral features associated with the common everyday trance (Erickson et al.,
1976; Erickson and Rossi, 1979, 1981; Rossi et al., 1983) in an effort to
improve his own powers of observation and enhance the probability of selecting the correct moment to facilitate therapeutic trance. He gradually felt
himself becoming privy to the traditional fraternity of experienced hypnotherapists, who would wink or smile knowingly at one another when they
recognized that another colleague or audience member was drifting into a
light state of somnambulism (with various behavioral manifestations of the
common everyday trance) without quite knowing it. Yet no one seemed to
write about these observations—often they appeared to be nothing more
than a social joke. But the wise seemed to take them seriously. Once capable
of making these observations, the author began to feel a deepening appreciation for those old yet ever new philosophical and metaphysical writers

who insisted that the average man was "unawakened," "sleepwalking," "unaware of his trance condition," "lost in maya," and so on (Ouspensky, 1920; Shankara, 1947; Goleman, 1977; Merrell-Wolff, 1983a,b).

Characteristics of the Common Everyday Trance

Table 1 delineates the many possible spontaneous behavioral characteristics of the common everyday trance. No one individual manifests all these behaviors; rather, each person has his/her own individual style that exhibits the behaviors in different amounts and combinations. It is an acquired skill to learn to recognize the unique way in which these individual patterns of the common everyday trance are manifested.

Erickson, for example, trained himself from youth to spot those barely discernible pulse movements that may appear on the face, neck, wrist, or ankles where arteries are close to the skin surface. He taught the author to recognize subtle manifestations of the common everyday trance by focusing attention on minimal behavioral cues. Thus the author learned to study

---

TABLE 1. CHARACTERISTICS OF AUTONOMOUS ALTERATIONS IN PSYCHOPHYSIOLOGICAL STATES DURING THE COMMON EVERYDAY TRANCE (EXPANDED FROM ROSSI, 1982).

Hypnotherapeutic Periodicity
  90-120-minute length of Erickson's hypnotic sessions
Hemispheric Laterality
  Shift to right-hemispheric dominance
Psychophysiological Processes (shift to parasympathetic dominance)
  Gastrointestinal activation
  Genito-urinary activation
  Heart rate (pulse slowing)
  Peripheral blood flow
    (blush and warmth vs. blanch and coolness)
  Psychosomatic responses
  Respiration
    (respiratory shift: yawn, sigh)
  Sweating
    (shine on face vs. dryness)
Eye Behavior
  Eyeball
    (active vs. fixed staring)
  Eyeblink
    (eyelid droops vs. wide-eyed expectation)
  Pupillary responses
    (dilation or contraction; vacant, faraway look)

TABLE 1. CONTINUED.

Sclera (reddening)
Tears
Motor Behavior
  Body activity
    (economy of movement; accident-prone)
  Muscle tonicity
    (cataplexy or catalepsy, face flaccid, tics, tremors)
  Response latency
    (slowing of reflexes, startle response)
Sensory–Perceptual Behavior
  Auditory alterations
    ("stopped hearing," or delayed response)
  Visual alterations
    (afterimages, fog, clouds)
    (depth perception changes)
    (illusions and hallucinatory phenomena)
    ("stopped vision," or delayed response)
  Tactile alterations
    (anesthesias and paresthesias)
Cognitive Behavior
  Age regression
  Amnesias and dissociations
  Autonomous ideation
    (fantasy and mind wandering)
  Confusion
    (open, questioning attitude)
  Process shift
    (easy intuition vs. defensive rationalization)
  Time distortion
    (time lag in conceptual response)
Affective Behavior
  Comfort and relaxation
  Distance and dissociation
  Sense of objectivity or impersonality
Transpersonal Sense
  Blissful, objective sense
  Dissolution of subject–object dichotomy
  Noncognitive
Social Behavior
  "Take-a-break"
  "Take-a-break" periodicity (90 minutes)
    (interest in and need of a "change of pace")
  Response attentiveness versus defensive withdrawal
    (easy eye contact and smiling when secure)
    (open and receptive body language)
    (suggestible when secure)
    (tendency toward introversion)

people's faces, noting when a particular topic of conversation was associated with either a blanching or blushing, with or without a just barely discernible sweating evidenced by a slight shine on the forehead, cheeks, or nose. Psychophysiological reflexes such as swallowing and eyeblinking slow down during the common everyday trance, and there is a noticeable shift in respiratory rhythm. This respiratory shift is manifested in a variety of subtle ways: a deeper breath (or two or three), a yawn, or a seemingly involuntary sigh may occur as the definite shift in attention from outer to inner takes place. There may be an embarrassing hiccup, burp, or sound from the gastrointestinal tract; and, alas, now it seems that the moment has come for a bit of flatus, a delayed bowel movement, or an annoying urinary urgency. These are not forms of psychological resistance, however. They are simple signs of the shift toward parasympathetic dominance that takes place in the common everyday trance, along with relaxation and the potential for mild sexual arousal.

Erickson readily utilized the eyes as a window of hypnotic receptivity. He frequently noted that pupillary dilation occurred at the moment of entering trance, or at the moment an item of en*tranc*ing interest and fascination was experienced (Erickson, 1967). In general, eyeblinking becomes less frequent in the common everyday trance, and the eyeballs themselves move less. This occurs as the person tends to stare off into space, or to spontaneously fix his focus on one particular spot. Sometimes the upper eyelids droop with the need for rest. This may then shift to its reverse of wide-eyed expectancy as subjects experience a mild sense of confusion or surprise at the subjectively recognizable change of state that occurs as they enter trance. At such moments they tend to look to the hypnotherapist for support and/or further suggestion. Shiny eyes due to a tendency toward tearing and a reddening of the sclera are not uncommon.

The common everyday trance is perhaps most easily noted in audiences and public places by the general body immobility that is so characteristic of those who have obviously tuned out their surrounding world in favor of a semi-napping state: crossing the arms or legs, leaning the head or body to one side (or forward or backward), or wiggling the neck, legs, or thumbs may all be characteristic, outer manifestations of this special inward turning. There is usually a generalized economy of movement at this time (nothing moves unless absolutely necessary). There is a greater response latency to questions—questions are answered more slowly, or with a clearing of the throat and with a slightly deeper vocal quality. Very mild (subclinical) forms of cataplexy may be present (loss of muscle tonus with the preservation of consciousness), as well as its reverse of catalepsy (muscular hypertonus with a seeming loss of consciousness as evidenced by an amnesia for what one was thinking about). These mild cataplexies and catalepsies can be recognized by an awkward positioning of a finger, arm, leg, head, or entire body as the individual closes his eyes or stares vacantly for a few moments.

Altered states of consciousness usually accompany these body alterations, but we do not comment on them because of the amnesias that so characteristically mask the common everyday trance. In fact, these are the moments when perfectly "normal" people experience illusions and split-second hallucinations—which, however, are then quickly dismissed as unusually vivid thoughts (auditory) or the flash of an internal image (visual) that "just seemed to be out there for a moment" (Rossi, 1972b). Some people will readily admit that the world had a slightly brighter look and a deeper, three-dimensional perspective that felt good as they stared vacantly for those few moments; others may report a world that seemed flat and two-dimensional—which did not feel so good. Also common are paresthesias (an itch or mild changes in skin sensations), alterations in the subjective sense of warmth or coolness, or an anesthesia experienced as a loss of sensation in any part of the body (hypnotic subjects will say, "I seemed to lose feeling in my hand [foot, finger, elbow, etc.]").

A phenomenon called "stopped hearing" may occur whereby subjects simply do not hear what is said. They do not realize they are being addressed, or they belatedly respond with a mildly confused, "Huh?" Not seeing is evidenced by people bumping into things, stubbing their toes, stumbling, or accidentally knocking something over. More rare are reports of "stopped vision" during somnambulistic states, in which individuals see just so far and no further, although there is nothing material blocking their vision (Erickson, 1967). Sometimes afterimages will persist with changing colors, and spots or a fog will clutter the visual field. A little fog or "a white, cloud-like form" may seem to hover in space when children are awakening from their naps, thus evoking pleading questions about whether ghosts are real.

The mind seems to wander during the common everyday trance. Memories flow easily, and we even experience spontaneous bits of socially acceptable age regression: a business executive will burst into a boyhood whistle; a scholar will attempt to "make a basket" with a wadded piece of paper. At this point we may momentarily forget what we were doing. We make mistakes in our work as needed abstract attitudes are temporarily blurred by an unfamiliar literalism and an overall slowing down in the conceptualizing processes. Minor amnesias (such as the "it's-on-the-tip-of-my-tongue" phenomenon) and temporary dissociations are very characteristic during these periods, particularly when we are engaged in highly linear, verbal, or abstract tasks. After 20 or 30 minutes we are surprised to discover how much time we have "wasted," and we dutifully snap ourselves back to an alert, work state. In actual fact, we have experienced a bit of time distortion during the common everyday trance.

All of these "disturbances" in linear work suggest that the common everyday trance involves a shift to right-hemispheric dominance and parasympathetic activation that is subject to many varied states, moods, and emotions. Indeed what is relaxation, comfort, and even bliss to one person may be experienced as depression and discomfort to another who is unwilling to accept the personal truths that come unbidden during these naturally unguarded periods. For yet others these quiet times may be host to a kind of impersonal—or, better, a *transpersonal*—sense of wisdom: momentarily transcending some of their typical ego preoccupations, they catch fleeting, musing glimpses of the "big picture." For these individuals, such times can be creative periods during which deeper insight is intuited.

If all goes well during the common everyday trance, we are in a state of "response attentiveness" (Erickson and Rossi, 1979): we enjoy taking a break and relaxing socially; eye contact may be easier (if we are not overly fatigued); body language is open and receptive; we are interested in matters other than work; and we are more open to accepting suggestions, provided the environment is permissive and supportive. We want and need support during these times. If the environment is demanding or threatening, however, we may become irritated and find ourselves preferring to be alone, to lie down, to take a nap—in short, "to get away from it all." In summary, then, *the common everyday trance can be viewed as a natural period of introversion* or, at most, of nondemanding social relatedness.

The Ultradian Hypothesis

Initially the author conceptualized the characteristics of the common everyday trance listed in Table 1 as a spontaneous and generalized shift toward parasympathetic and right-hemispheric dominance that occurred randomly throughout the day (Erickson et al., 1976; Erickson and Rossi, 1981). The behavioral alterations associated with the common everyday trance were deemed worthy of careful study because it was hypothesized that they might signal the optimum psychophysiological periods during which hypnosis could be most readily induced. They likewise signaled the periods during which autohypnosis and posthypnotic suggestion might be most effective, particularly for the healing of psychosomatic problems.

It then came as a total and welcome surprise when the author accidentally stumbled upon the growing research literature on ultradian rhythms and found an almost exact correspondence between the manifestations of the common everyday trance and the behaviors studied in ultradian research.

(Table 2 organizes ultradian research in a manner that corresponds to Table 1 so that the relationship between the common everyday trance and the ultradian behaviors would be clear.)

In studying this correspondence how could any investigator not leap immediately to the obvious inductive hunch and hypothesize that Milton H. Erickson's *naturalistic approach* to hypnosis, with its 90–120 minute sessions, was an unwitting utilization of ultradian rhythms with their similar periodicity? Further, perhaps ultradian rhythms are themselves one of the long-sought psychophysiological bases of hypnotic phenomena.

The remainder of this chapter will be devoted to bringing together information from a variety of sources that will be needed to formulate scientifically valid tests of these hypothesis and others that naturally arise in relation to them. These tests of the common everyday trance and hypnosis will be of central significance for the basic controversy in modern hypnosis research: the so-called *special-state-non-special-state* issue. We will thus turn our attention to that issue because it is of fundamental importance in understanding our basic concept of altered states in everyday life, and in planning research in this area.

The State–Nonstate Controversy in Hypnosis

There is a long history of evidence for the fact that all so-called hypnotic phenomena can be experienced while the subject is apparently awake (Barber, 1972; Sarbin and Coe, 1972). This fact has given rise to the state-nonstate controversy, with the nonstate (or "alternative paradigm") theorists using it as a centerpiece for their view that hypnosis does not involve a special or altered state of consciousness. Special-state theorists (mostly clinicians) with their own national society (The American Society of Clinical Hypnosis) and journal (*The American Journal of Clinical Hypnosis*) and nonstate theorists (mostly academic researchers) with their own national society (The Society of Clinical & Experimental Hypnosis) and journal (*The Journal of Clinical and Experimental Hypnosis*) remain steadfastly separate as two subcultures even today (Coe, 1983).

If it can be established, however, that most classical hypnotic phenomena are more readily experienced during those periods of the ultradian rhythms when they are most available (primarily during the common everyday trance), we may have a resolution of the state–nonstate controversy. The state theorists would be correct in part with the validation that there are real alterations in a broad range of psychophysiological processes relevant for experiencing what has been traditionally called "hypnosis." The nonstate theorists would be correct in part with the validation that there is nothing really unique about the "hypnotic state": it does not have a separate

and discrete reality outside the normal range of psychophysiological fluctuations in ultradian rhythms we all experience throughout the 24-hour day.
Hypnosis (or trance) does not exist as a mysterious special state. Rather,
the experience we have traditionally called "hypnosis" is a ritually induced
way of enhancing and vivifying certain naturally occurring ultradian behaviors.

As we learn more about the parameters of ultradian rhythms, we should
be able to use real knowledge (rather than traditional but now meaningless
ritual) of how these ultradian behaviors interact, of how they can be po-
tentiated even further ("deepening hypnosis"), and of how they can be neu-
tralized so that people can be "dehypnotized" from unwanted beliefs, states,
and behaviors. A review of the current status of ultradian research is now
needed to probe for the information required in designing the studies that
could resolve this state–nonstate controversy. To this research in ultradian
rhythms, we now turn our attention.

ULTRADIAN RHYTHM RESEARCH: A THREE-PHASE HISTORY

Phase One: Kleitman's Formulation of the BRAC Hypothesis

In historical perspective there now appear to be three phases in the discovery and investigation of ultradian rhythms. The first phase involved a long
period of sporadic and unrelated studies by investigators who reported periodicities in various physiological processes and human performance capacities as far back as one hundred years ago (Table 2). Kleitman (1969,
1970) summarized this first phase by formulating the concept of a "Basic
Rest–Activity Cycle" in relation to sleep and wakefulness (the BRAC hypothesis). Because this BRAC hypothesis is the foundation upon which all
subsequent theorists constructed their views, we will quote some of the essential features of Kleitman's original formulation (1969, 1970):

> Manifestations of a basic rest–activity cycle (BRAC) in the functioning
> of the nervous system were amply established by recording EEGs of
> sleepers. There is an alternation of phases of high voltage, low frequency
> activity (stages 3 and 4) and low voltage, mixed frequency activity (stage
> REM); the latter phases are accompanied by certain visceral and somatic
> changes: variations in heart rate and respiration, contractions of small
> muscles about the head—especially rapid eye movements (REMS)—and
> simultaneous relaxation of other muscle groups. . . .
> The operation of the BRAC in wakefulness is not as obvious as it is

TABLE 2. ALTERED STATES AND BEHAVIORAL/PSYCHOPHYSIOLOGICAL
PROCESSES THAT HAVE BEEN STUDIED FOR ULTRADIAN RHYTHM RESEARCH.

Psychophysiological Periodicity

90-minute sleep–dream rhythm	Dement and Kleitman, 1957; Kleitman, 1963; Kripke, 1974, 1982; Jouvet, 1973; Kales et al., 1964
Waking BRAC: 90–120-minute ultradian cycles throughout 24-hour day	Globus, 1966; Hartmann, 1968a,b; Kleitman, 1969, 1970; Kripke, 1982; Marquis, 1941; Wada, 1922
Hemispheric Laterality	Goldstein et al., 1972; Gordon et al., 1982; Klein and Armitage, 1979; Kripke, 1982; Werntz, 1981; Werntz et al., 1981, 1982
Psychophysiological Processes	
Gastrointestinal activation	Friedman and Fischer, 1967; Hiatt and Kripke, 1975; Kripke, 1972; Lewis et al., 1977; Marquis, 1941; Oswald et al., 1970; Reinberg et al., 1979; Wada, 1922
Oral activities (smoking, etc.)	Friedman, 1972; Friedman and Fischer, 1967
Genito-urinary activation	
Sexual arousal	Ohlmeyer et al., 1944
Urinary output	Lavie and Kripke, 1977; Lavie et al., 1980; Luboshitsky et al., 1978
Heart rate	Anch et al., 1976; Broughton and Baron, 1978; Friedell, 1948; Hymes and Nurenberger, 1980; Lovett, 1980; Orr et al., 1974, 1976; Wilson et al., 1977
Peripheral blood flow	Lovett, 1980
Body temperature	Hunsaker et al., 1977; Romano and Gizdulish, 1980; Wilkenson, 1982
Psychosomatic responses	Friedman, 1978; Friedman et al., 1978; Poirel, 1982; Rossi, 1982; Wehr, 1982
Respiration	Horne and Whitehead, 1976
Nasal cycle	Alexiev and Roth, 1978; Eccles, 1978; Funk and Clarke, 1980; Hasagawa and Kem, 1978; Kayser, 1895; Keuning, 1963; Malcomson, 1959; Malm, 1973; Rao and Potdar, 1970; Singh-Khalsa and Singh-Khalsa, 1976; Vinekar, 1966; Werntz, 1983; Werntz et al., 1981, 1982
Eye Behavior	
Eyeblink and eyeball motility	Krynicki, 1975; Othmer et al., 1969; Ullner, 1974
Pupillary response	Lavie and Schulz, 1978; Stevens et al., 1971
Motor Behavior	Luce, 1970; Naitoh, 1982
Body activity	Clements et al., 1976
Muscle tonicity	Katz, 1980; Lovett et al., 1978; Rasmussen and Malven, 1981; Tierney et al., 1978

(Continued)

TABLE 2. CONTINUED

Response latency	Globus et al., 1970; Kripke, 1972; Kripke et al., 1978; Lovett and Podnieks, 1975; Meier-Koll et al., 1978; Orr et al., 1974; Podnieks and Lovett, 1975
Sensory–Perceptual Behavior	Lavie, 1976, 1977; Lavie et al., 1974; Lavie et al., 1900; Lovett, 1976; Lovett and Podnieks, 1975
Rorschach alterations	Globus, 1966, 1968
Visual illusions	Gopher and Lavie, 1980
Cognitive Behavior	
Cognitive style	Klein and Armitage, 1979
Fantasy	Cartwright and Monroe, 1968; Kripke and Sonnenschein, 1978
Memory	Folkard, 1982; Graeber, 1982; Orr et al., 1974
Observing response	Globus, 1972; Kripke, 1972
Response latency (time sense)	Meier-Koll et al., 1978
Affective Behavior	Friedman, 1978; Friedman, S. et al., 1978; Poirel, 1982; Wehr, 1982; Stroebel, 1969
Transpersonal Sense	Broughton, 1975; Eccles, 1978; Funk and Clarke, 1980; Rao and Potdar, 1970; Vinekar, 1966; Werntz, 1981; Werntz et al., 1981, 1982
Social Behavior	Bowden et al., 1978; Delgado-Garcia et al., 1976; Lavie and Kripke, 1981; Maxim et al., 1976
"Take-a-break" periodicity (90 minutes) napping time	Lavie and Scherson, 1981
Hormonal Behavior and neuroendocrinal functions	Bykov and Katinas, 1979; Eriksson et al., 1980; Filicori et al., 1979; Friedman, A. and Piepho, 1978; Kripke, 1982; Levin et al., 1978; Millard et al., 1981; Quabbee et al., 1981; Shiotsuka et al., 1974; Simon and George, 1975; Steiner et al., 1980; Tannenbaum and Martin, 1976; Tannenbaum et al., 1976; Ullner, 1974; Weitzman, 1974; Yen et al., 1974
Psychoactive Drug Sensitivity	Naber et al., 1980

---

in sleep; there are too many external influences that tend to disrupt or obscure the cycle. . . . [Nevertheless], everyday observations support the view that the BRAC operates during the waking hours as well as in sleep. The now common "coffee-break" at 10:30 A.M. divides the three-hour office stint from 9:00 A.M. to noon into two 90-minute fractions. The relief obtained by some individuals from brief 10 to 15 minute catnaps perhaps represents a "riding over" the low phase of a BRAC, and postprandial drowsiness may be an accentuation of the same phase. (1969, pp. 34–47)

Phase Two: Extension and Criticism of the BRAC Hypothesis

The second phase of ultradian research, during the 1970s, was heavily supported by the U.S. Department of Health, Education and Welfare, by the military, and by Veterans Administration contracts concerned with investigating a variety of problems. Some of these problems included periodicities of human efficiency on vigilance tasks with changing work schedules (Luce, 1970; Naitoh, 1982), periods of continuous and sustained work performance (West et al., 1962; Kripke, 1982), and the chronobiology of transmeridian flight (Graeber, 1982). Much of this research had relevance as a series of tests involving the BRAC hypothesis, and thus constituted a series of additions, modifications, and criticisms of Kleitman's original formulation.

Table 2 presents these major areas of ultradian research in a manner that demonstrates their similarity to the characteristic areas of the common everyday trance listed in Table 1.

In a recent review of this area, Kripke (1982) summarized the situation as follows:

> The wealth of phenomena that have been uncovered in pursuit of the BRAC hypothesis should console any investigator troubled that the hypothesis remains controversial. Dramatic behavioral cycles have been discovered, both in man and lower primates, and perhaps these cycles have important ethologic functions. Cycles in fantasy, hemispheric dominance, and perceptual processing have been described. The significance of these cycles in both normal and pathologic functioning deserves our attention. Episodic hormone secretion seems to be a fundamental property of endocrine metabolism, and it is somehow related to the REM cycle. The suggestion that the pituitary is only responsive to intermittent releasing hormone stimulation is particularly exciting, for it suggests one way in which ultradian cycles may be a functional necessity. The early stages of research for cycles must now give way to more analytic studies that explore the mechanisms and functional implications of each ultradian cyclic process. (p. 336)

Figure 1 outlines five interrelated levels for conceptualizing our current understanding of the alterations of consciousness in everyday life. These range from the anatomical and physiological to the psychological–behavioral and socio-cultural. Because of the current uncertainty regarding the

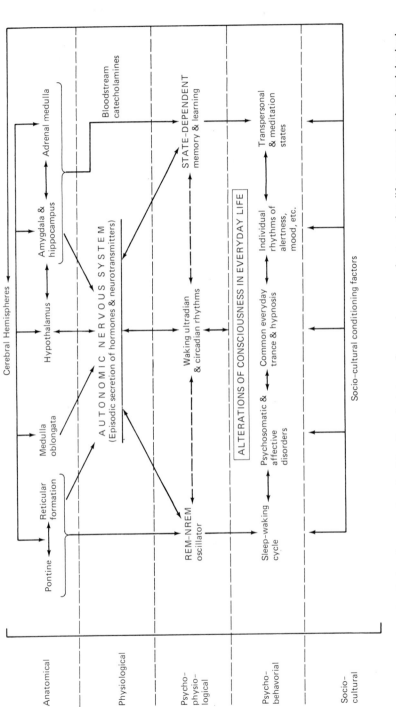

Figure 1. Five basic levels associated with altered states of consciousness in everyday life: anatomical, physiological, psychophysiological, psychological-behavioral, and social-cultural—together with a few of their interrelationships.

actual neurophysiological mechanisms between the REM–NREM cycle and the waking ultradian rhythms, we have placed a question mark and only a dash-line connecting them on the psychophysiological level in Figure 1. It is worthwhile noting that the REM–NREM oscillation, the ultradian–circadian rhythms, and state-dependent memory and learning processes are the three major psychophysiological determinants of altered states of consciousness receiving the greatest amount of research and attention at this time. However, we would certainly expect that as the interrelations between them are explored further, many more equally fundamental psychophysiological sources of altered states would be found.

The other uncertainty in Figure 1 is the question mark and dash-line connection between ultradian rhythms and the processes of state-dependent memory and learning (McGaugh, 1983). (See also Roland Fischer's Chapter 1 in this book.) The author (Erickson and Rossi, 1974) has previously conceptualized how state-dependent memory and learning processes are related to hypnotic phenomena and possibly constitute the fundamental nature of phenomenological experience and consciousness:

> Taken together these clinical and naturalistic investigations strongly suggest that hypnotic trance is an altered *state* of consciousness and amnesia, in particular, is a natural consequence of this altered state. Recent research in "state-dependent learning" lends experimental support to the general view of all amnesias as being "state-bound." We can now understand hypnotic amnesia as only one of a general class of verifiable phenomenon rather than a special case.
>
> . . . We would submit that hypnotic trance itself can be most usefully conceptualized as but one vivid example of *the fundamental nature of all phenomenological experience as "state-bound."* The apparent continuity of consciousness that exists in everyday normal awareness is in fact a precarious illusion that is only made possible by the associative connections that exist between related bits of conversation, task orientation, etc. (Quoted from Erickson, 1981, Vol. III, pp. 87–88)

In the final section of this chapter a number of experimental approaches to this hypothesized relationship between state-dependent memory and learning, ultradian rhythms, and the phenomenology of consciousness will be suggested.

Phase Three: The Clinical and Transpersonal Significance of the BRAC Hypothesis and Ultradian Rhythms

Clinical Significance.   The third phase of ultradian research partially overlaps the second phase in time, but its clinical and transpersonal focus is very different: the third phase is characterized by the search for reliable indices of ultradian rhythms and an integrated theory of their psychophysiological relationships that could be used for therapeutic purposes. This current phase is typified by the author's work described above (Rossi, 1982) in searching for the correlates between the common everyday trance, hypnosis, and ultradian rhythms; by the work of Friedman and his associates (Friedman, 1978; Friedman, S., et al., 1978) on the possible relation between ultradian rhythms, instinctual drives, and psychosomatic problems; by the work of Wehr (1982) in seeking the clinical relevance of circadian rhythms for depression and mania in man; and by the work of Poirel (1982) on the relations between circadian rhythms and experimental psychopathology in animals.

An excellent example of the clinical implications of ultradian rhythms can be found in the work of Friedman (1978), who first formulated and tested "a theoretical model proposing that 'desynchronized' forms of this cycle are a precondition for the outbreak of a psychosomatic disease, and that control of such malfunction should lead to improvement or remission of a reversible psychosomatic disorder" (p. 110). During this same time period the author was independently formulating a very similar concept but from an entirely different background of research and practice. When the author finally published his views (Erickson and Rossi, 1981; Rossi, 1981a, b), he had not yet heard of Friedman's previous work. The author hypothesized the relatedness between ultradian rhythms, psychosomatic illness, hypnosis, and cerebral-hemispheric dominance as follows:

The implications of this association between disruptions of the ultradian cycle by stress and psychosomatic illness are profound. If the major proposal of this section is correct—that therapeutic hypnosis involving physiological processes is actually a utilization of ultradian cycles—then we can finally understand in psychophysiological terms why hypnosis traditionally has been found to be an effective therapeutic approach to psychosomatic problems: *Individuals who override and disrupt their own ultradian cycles (by ignoring their natural periodic needs for rest in any extended performance situation, for example) are thereby setting in motion the basic physiological mechanisms of psychosomatic illness.* Most of this self-induced stress could be conceptualized as left-hemispheric processes overriding their ideal balance with right-hemispheric processes and associated parasympathetic functions. *Naturalistic therapeutic hypnosis provides a comfortable state wherein these ultradian cycles can simply normalize themselves and thus undercut the processes of psychosomatic illnesses at their psychophysiological source.* (Rossi, 1982, p. 26)

Friedman and his associates (1978) took the next step and attempted to validate their desynchronization model by proposing a testable clinical hypothesis concerning the treatment of neurodermatitis. Twenty-three out of 24 expected results were obtained in support of their hypothesis. The authors properly cautioned, however, that this rather remarkable set of results could not be taken as crucial experimental support for their hypothesis; there was no way of establishing that their drug intervention had achieved its therapeutic results entirely as a result of its proposed effect on the ultradian rhythms of sleep. In the final section of this chapter, further experimental studies relevant for this ultradian desynchronization hypothesis of psychosomatic illness will be proposed.

Transpersonal Significance. The significance of ultradian rhythms for the altered states associated with "higher consciousness" or transpersonal psychology was first introduced and reviewed by Broughton (1975). The recent seminal work of Werntz et al. (Werntz, 1981; Werntz et al., 1981, 1982), which utilized the nasal cycle as the most conveniently available ultradian "window" of alterations in the autonomic system and CNS activity (particularly the cerebral hemispheres), however, may finally prove to be the Rosetta stone of research in this area. Because of the particular methodological significance of the work of Werntz and her associates on the nasal cycle as a foundation for further research on altered states of consciousness, we will now present it in some detail.

THE NASAL CYCLE: ITS HISTORY, DYNAMICS, AND MEASUREMENT

If one considers the ancient yoga science of *pranayama* (controlled breathing) to have relevance, then one must admit that the manual manipulation of the nasal cycle during meditation (dhyana) is the most thoroughly documented of techniques for altering consciousness. For thousands of years these techniques for the subtle alterations of nasal breathing have been gradually codified into classical texts. Some of these are the *Hatha Yoga Pradipika* (II, 6-9, 19-20), *Siva Samhita* (III, 24, 25), *Gheranda Samhita* (V, 49-52), and *Yoga Chudamani Upsanisad* (V, 98-100). These ancient texts of instructions, poetry, and ecstatic exhortation are difficult to locate and often make difficult and tedious reading for modern consciousness. Fortunately their essence has been admirably condensed and carefully summarized in detail for Westerners by the meditation Master, B. K. S. Iyengar (Iyengar, 1981).

A new tradition of psychophysiological and experimental research exploring these ancient techniques has been developing during the past few decades, (Hasegawa and Kem, 1978). The work of Vinekar (1966), Rao and Potdar (1970), Eccles (1978), and Funk and Clarke (1980) also provides a broad background of independent studies using Western laboratory methods in studying the relationship of this nasal cycle to the ancient yogic tradition of *pranayama* in achieving psychosomatic health and the transpersonal states of *dhyāna* and *samādhi*. This research has been carried on more or less independently of the modern ultradian research summarized above. Recently, however, there has been a very fruitful interaction between them, culminating in the work of Werntz, Bickford, Bloom, and Singh-Khulsa (1981, 1982). Before we can fully appreciate the significance of this work, however, it is necessary first to overview the pertinent neurophysiology involved in the nasal cycle, and the methods used in measuring it.

The History and Physiological Dynamics of the Nasal Cycle

The German rhinologist R. Kayser (1895) is usually credited with observing and naming the "nasal cycle." He carefully described the dynamic process by which the nasal mucosa of the left and right nasal chambers periodically alternate in their size and shape, causing a change in the degree to which the breath flows in and out easily. Thus when the left nostril is open to permit the easy passage of air, the right nostril is congested, and vice versa. This alternation in the size of the nostril opening is accomplished by a layer of spongy "erectile" tissue that lines the inside of each nostril right under the mucous membrane. When the erectile tissue of one nostril fills with blood, it expands and thereby cuts off the flow of air in that nostril; simultaneously in the other nostril blood is draining out of the erectile tissue so that it contracts and opens that nostril to the free flow of air. This type of erectile tissue is found only in a few areas of the body: the nose, the breasts, and the genitals. Interestingly, one of Sigmund Freud's earliest colleagues was the German rhinologist, Wilhelm Fleiss (Jones, 1961). Fleiss's early theories of the cyclic alternations of these erectile tissues and their purported relationship to illness and sexuality are credited with having had a significant role in Freud's earliest formulation of the sexual etiology of psychoneurosis.

The beginning of the modern era of research on the nasal cycle in the United States is credited to Lillie (1923), who made careful observations of the alternating activity of the nasal chambers; he observed that as the erectile tissue of one nostril constricts, its mucosal glands increase their secretion to facilitate the filtration of air by the microscopic cilia on the surface of the mucosa. Meanwhile the opposite nasal chamber becomes engorged with blood; the erectile tissue expands, and the mucosal gland secretion diminishes as the airflow is cut off (Table 3). Heetderks (1927), a research fellow at the Mayo Clinic, confirmed these observations with a study of sixty normal individuals. The central regulation of the nasal cycle by the medulla, which controls respiration and/or the hypothalamus, was first proposed by Stoksted in 1953. The latter view received its initial experimental documentation by Malcomson in 1959, who found that electrical stimulation of the cat hypothalamus resulted in nasal vasoconstriction. The autonomic innervation and control of the nasal blood vessels, with the consequent expansion and contraction of the nasal erectile tissues, was confirmed and gradually clarified by three separate research projects: Drettner (1961) studied the vascular reactions of the human nasal mucosa to cold; Malm (1973) studied the reactions of cat noses to sympathetic nerve stimulation; Eccles and Wilson (1974) demonstrated sympathetic and autonomic innervation of the nasal blood vessel in cats; Dallimore and Eccles (1977) and Eccles (1978) studied the changes in nasal resistance associated with exercise and hyperventilation, confirming the central regulation of the nasal cycle in humans.

An outline of the physiological dynamics of the nasal cycle is presented in Table 3.

Table 4 summarizes some of the results of the most interesting studies on the duration of the nasal cycle conducted in the past half century. As with all other ultradian behaviors, the range is wide—from 1/2 to 8 hours—but the average duration is around the typical ultradian mean of $1\frac{1}{2}$ to 2 hours. It seems likely that this wide range in the duration of the nasal cycle, together with the wide range of subjects exhibiting the cycle (38–100%), is due to a number of significant methodological variables: the frequency of measurements, the duration of measurements, and the method of measurements may all be factors. It is to this latter variable of methodology that we now turn our attention.

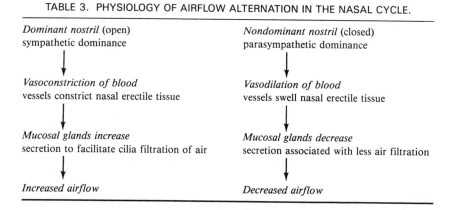

TABLE 3. PHYSIOLOGY OF AIRFLOW ALTERNATION IN THE NASAL CYCLE.

Dominant nostril (open)	*Nondominant nostril* (closed)
sympathetic dominance	parasympathetic dominance
↓	↓
Vasoconstriction of blood vessels constrict nasal erectile tissue	*Vasodilation of blood* vessels swell nasal erectile tissue
↓	↓
Mucosal glands increase secretion to facilitate cilia filtration of air	*Mucosal glands decrease* secretion associated with less air filtration
↓	↓
Increased airflow	*Decreased airflow*

TABLE 4. FIFTY YEARS OF RESEARCH ON THE DURATION OF THE NASAL CYCLE.*

Authors	No. of Ss	Frequency of measurements	Duration of measurements	% of Ss with nasal cycle	Range of cycle	Average duration of cycle	Method of measurement
Heetderks, 1927	60	10 minutes	2 hours +	80	1–4 hours	≈2½ hours	Direct observation
Stoksted, 1952, 1970	26	30 minutes	3–4 hours	38	1½–5 hours	2½ hours	Rhinomanometer with rate meters
Soubeyrand, 1964	50	15 minutes	NA	100	80%: 2–5 hours; 20%: 5–8 hours	3½ hours	Anterior rhinomanometry
Keuning, 1968	17	15 minutes	3–4 hours	71	2–7 hours	4½ hours	—
Hasegawa & Kem, 1978	50	15 minutes	7 hours	72	1–6 hours	2.9 hours	Pneumotachograph mask flowmeter with gas transducer
Eccles, 1978	2	30 minutes	3–7 days	100	1–2½ hours	≈ 2 hours	Pneumotachograph with storage oscilloscope
Clarke, 1980 Funk & Clarke, 1980	5	30 minutes	30 days	100	1½–6 hours	4 hours	Mirror condensation
Werntz, 1981 Werntz et al., 1981 Werntz et al., 1982	43	15 minutes	0.66–3.6 hours	51	0.5–3.3 hours	NA	Thermistors with polygraph & magnetic tape storage

*Expanded from Funk, 1980.

Methods for Measuring the Nasal Cycle

A major reason for the more detailed examination of the nasal cycle as an example of research on the ultradian rhythms lies in the all-important area of measurement. The variety of noninvasive measurement techniques developed over the past fifty years in laboratory research—together with centuries of yogic experience—suggests that the nasal cycle can become one of the most valuable and easily available approaches to the study and alteration of consciousness. Moreover, these noninvasive measurement techniques can be utilized in three distinct settings, each yielding its own valuable contribution. There is the experimental setting, in which research is conducted in a laboratory where very exact control and measurement is made possible by highly sophisticated electronic monitoring; there is the clinical setting, which provides a more relaxed but scientifically valid arena for field experimentation; and there is the everyday setting of daily life, where simple but reliable methods of measurement can be accomplished with nothing more than a small pocket mirror—or, indeed, with no devices at all once subjects are trained.

The current laboratory methods of electronic monitoring with air strain gauge transducers, pneumotachographs and storage oscilloscope, and thermistors have been adequately described in the literature (Connell, undated mimeograph; Hasegawa and Kem, 1978; Eccles, 1978; Werntz, 1980; Werntz et al., 1981, 1982); and Hey and Price (1982) have investigated methods of expressing these measures mathematically. Here we will focus on the simpler methods most suitable for a variety of long-term (days, weeks, months) field-type experiments that are now needed, and which are outlined in the final section of this chapter.

The Mirror-Condensation Method.   This is a very simple but reliable measurement method used by yoga breathing experts in studying their own nasal cycles. A small pocket mirror is held under the nose perpendicular to the nasal flow, and a natural, gentle, two- to three-second exhalation is allowed to condense a pattern of moisture under each nostril. Funk and Clarke (1980) have determined that subjects are able to examine which nostril produces the greater blot of condensation and make a subjective appraisal of nostril dominance (the nostril exhaling the most air and producing the greatest condensation) that agrees with laboratory rhinomanometric determinations 92 percent of the time (114 accurate judgments out of 123 tests).

The Sound of Exhalation Method.   Requiring slightly more training but no devices is the method of comparing the sound of the breath exhaled through each nostril. One nostril is closed by applying gentle thumb pressure to the opening, and then a short, sharp exhalation is made through the other, open nostril. The greater the congestion (erectile tissue swelling) in the exhalation nostril, the higher will be the pitch of the exhaling sound. One can alternate a few of these exhalations back and forth between each nostril to confirm which nostril is giving the higher pitch and is thus more blocked. *The nostril giving the lower pitch* is allowing air to flow through more freely and *is thus the dominant nostril at that time.*

Tactile Sensations Method. With a bit more practice most subjects quickly learn to determine nasal dominance by becoming more aware of their nose sensations while taking a slow, steady inhalation. However, greater individual differences in sensitivity have been found with this method. Sometimes a short, sharp inhalation is more effective in making the determination. If the determination of dominance cannot be made with this technique, the mirror-condensation measurement often confirms that in fact both nostrils are about equal in their openness or congestion. This condition of equal air flow occurs because the nasal cycle is in the midst of its shift from one side to the other.

Testing five subjects with the mirror-condensation method, Clarke (1980) made careful comparisons of the laterality of nasal dominance and the condition of equal nasal flow between them. He found that in four subjects the nostril dominance was almost equal over a 30-day period (measured every 30 minutes). In one subject the right nostril was dominant two to five times more than the left. For all subjects there was an equal airflow in both nostrils about 10 percent of the time.

Methods of Changing Nostril Dominance

A fascinating aspect of the nasal cycle is that it can be brought under voluntary control. This factor becomes particularly significant for the use of the nasal cycle in (1) altering states of consciousness and changing aspects of (2) autonomic functioning and (3) cerebral-hemispheric dominance. Iyengar (1981) has detailed the manual methods used by yogis to block one nostril and alternate the quantity and quality of the nasal cycle in a great variety of patterns. Rao and Potdar (1970) have documented how nostril dominance can be shifted by body position in the sitting and lying positions: in general it is found that when lying on one's side, the nostril on the down side (resting on a bed, for instance) becomes rapidly congested, thus shifting nasal openness and dominance to the nostril on the upper side. In preliminary studies on himself, this author has found that simply lying flat on his back and quietly meditating or resting after intellectual activity shifts a dominant (open) right nostril to a dominant (open) left nostril. The relevance of this observation for cerebral-hemispheric dominance will become clear when we examine the work of Werntz and her associates in the next section.

THE NASAL CYCLE: "WINDOW" OF AUTONOMIC NERVOUS SYSTEM AND CEREBRAL HEMISPHERIC DOMINANCE

The concept of hemispheric dominance, following the original work of Sperry and Gazzangia (1967) on cerebral commissurotomy, presumed that specific functions such as verbal skills or pattern recognition were localized in each hemisphere and that these functions remained in a fixed, unvarying relationship to one another. In a series of unrelated studies, however, it gradually became clear that a spontaneous alternation in dominance over time took place between the left and right cerebral hemisphere. Goldstein et al. (1972) reported changes in interhemispheric amplitude relationships in the EEG during sleep, and this was confirmed by Gordon et al. (1982). This natural alternation in cerebral hemispheric dominance was dramatically confirmed in normal waking subjects by Klein and Armitage (1979), who found 1½-hour oscillations in cognitive style.

Taking her clue from this work, Werntz (1981) measured the relative airflow through the nostrils of forty-three subjects. She used identically matched thermistors (with a response range including the span 21–38°) and at the same time recorded their EEGs (Alpha, Beta, Delta, and Theta) on both cerebral hemispheres. Her results indicated that there was "a direct relationship of cerebral hemispheric activity (EEG) and the ultradian rhythm of the nasal cycle. Relatively greater integrated EEG values in one hemisphere is positively correlated with a predominant airflow in the contralateral nostril" (Werntz et al., 1982, p. 226).

In a follow-up study, Werntz et al. (1981) took the next logical, experimental step and found that they could change nasal dominance by forced uninostril breathing through the nondominant (closed) nostril. Further, *this experimentally induced shift in nasal dominance resulted in an accompanying shift in cerebral hemispheric dominance to the contralateral hemisphere!* Not only was the ultradian nasal cycle a window on cerebral hemispheric activity, but voluntarily induced changes in nasal airflow could be used to change the relative locus of activity in the highest centers of the brain and thereby influence the all-pervasive autonomic system that regulates practically every major function of the body. Objective, Western science had finally validated the basic principles that underlay thousands of years of subjective, empirical experience by Eastern adepts! Werntz et al. (1981) summarize their work as follows:

We feel that the correlation of the nasal cycle with the alternation of cerebral hemispheric activity is consistent with a model for a single ultradian oscillator system* and imposes a new conceptual understanding for the nervous system. . . . We propose an even more complete and integrated theoretical framework which incorporates an organization for all ultradian rhythms and their regulation by the autonomic nervous system most specifically the integration of autonomic and cerebral hemispheric activity. It could be suggested at this point that there might be some basis to believe that the "separate forms of intelligence" localized in each hemisphere require an increased metabolic support of the contralateral side of the body in terms of the overall bias they might serve. *In this context, the nasal cycle can be viewed as an easily measureable indicator or "window" for this framework.*

. . . Thus the whole body goes through the Rest/Activity or Parasympathetic/Sympathetic oscillation while simultaneously going through the "Left Body–Right Brain/Right Body–Left Brain" shift. This then produces ultradian rhythms at all levels of organization from pupil size to higher cortical functions and behavior. . . . It is important to note that this represents an extensive integration of autonomic and cerebral cortical activity, a relationship not previously defined or studied. We propose that as the nasal cycle probably is regulated via a centrally controlled mechanism, possibly the hypothalamus, altering the sympathetic/parasympathetic balance, this occurs throughout the body including the brain and is the mechanism by which vasomotor tone regulates the control of blood flow through the cerebral vessels thereby altering cerebral hemispheric activity. (pp. 4–6)

THE PSYCHOPHYSIOLOGY OF TRANSPERSONAL STATES

In Figure 1 (above) transpersonal states are placed on the psychological-behavioral level because they apparently share the same sources on the anatomical and physiological levels as do the other altered-state phenomena on this level (Fischer, 1971). That is, both ancient and modern sources on the psychophysiology of transpersonal states implicate the autonomic nervous system on the physiological level and the cerebral cortex, the medulla oblongata, the hypothalamus, and the glandular system (particularly the adrenals) on the anatomical level (White, 1979). As our survey in this chapter indicates, these are also the sources for the more "ordinary" alterations of consciousness in everyday life: sleeping, dreaming, meditation, ultradian

---

*Note the divergence from Kripke's (1982) views quoted earlier where he, apparently without the knowledge of Werntz's work reviewed here, finds a *multi*oscillator system to be more consistent with the total mass of ultradian data.

rhythms, and the common everyday trance (Timmons and Kamiya, 1970; Timmons and Kanellakos, 1974).

Indeed Gopi Krishna (1975) considers alterations such as psychosomatic symptoms, mental illness, and the spontaneous trances of everyday life to be malformations of a natural process whereby "normal everyday consciousness" breaks down in its ongoing evolution toward higher transpersonal states (Bucke, 1901). According to this view, the transformative process is supposedly the next step in the evolution of human consciousness, but unfortunately most of humanity just does not know how to do it yet. Only the geniuses, great spiritual leaders, and mystics have successfully tapped into it. Gopi Krishna therefore calls for a concerted research effort to explore how this transformative process can be facilitated in all of humanity. It is in this spirit of search that the author now proposes the sixty-four research projects comprising the next and final section of this chapter.

SIXTY-FOUR RESEARCH PROJECTS IN SEARCH OF A GRADUATE STUDENT

1. Replicate Werntz (1981) as closely as possible on all methodological, measurement, and subject-selection parameters for an all-important confirmation of her basic findings.

2–3. Replicate Werntz (1981) using the simpler mirror and nasal pitch methods of measuring nasal cycles to determine how reliable these techniques can be for studies of altered states of consciousness and behavior outside of the laboratory.

4–5. Replicate Werntz (1981) for very significant developmental studies on the relations between the nasal cycle and the autonomic system and cerebral hemispheric activity from infancy through old age. This can then be used as a basis for studying developmental shifts in altered states of consciousness, cognitive style, mood, and so on (London, 1963).

6–8. Replicate Werntz (1981) on any carefully selected clinical population with measurable alterations in autonomic system function or disease and/or cerebral hemispheric activity to (a) critically assess Werntz's new view of an integrated system of autonomic and cerebral hemispheric activity, and (b) gain further insights into the implications of this new view for the various phases of altered states in normal functioning and the variations introduced via clinical pathology (Flor-Henry, 1976; Passouant, 1974).

9–10. Replicate Werntz et al. (1981) on the use of forced shifts in nasal dominance to influence autonomic nervous function and shifts in consciousness and cognitive style via changes in hemispheric dominance.

11–12. Explore the use of forced shifts in nasal dominance to replicate the classical left–right hemispheric specialization studies that have been developed since Sperry's discovery of altered states of consciousness in patients with surgically separated cerebral hemispheres. To what extent can forced nasal dominance be used to study altered states of consciousness as a noninvasive substitute for the surgical separation of the cerebral hemispheres?

13–14. Explore the relation of nasal dominance to virtually all the other ultradian rhythms associated with altered states of cognition and affect reported in Table 2 of this chapter.

15–17. Explore the relationship of nasal dominance to mental set and attitude in sports performance, sexual activity, meditation, hypnosis, and the common everyday trance; explore the variations, if any, produced by forced shifts in nasal dominance on these activities.

18. The author speculates that people with habitual head tilts to the right or left side may be influencing their nasal and cerebral hemispheric dominance, just as they do when lying down on their right or left sides. This leads to the testable hypothesis that subjects with habitual head tilts to the right are exhibiting a preferential use of their right hemisphere. This could be measured by EEG recordings, by increased levels in hypnotizability, and by better performance on holistic-synthetic versus analytic tasks. (The reverse would be hypothesized for subjects with habitual left-side tilts.)

19. Using the same line of reasoning as above, the author has isolated a dozen facial characteristics that may be associated with left- and right-cerebral hemispheric dominance (Rossi, 1985). This association between facial laterality and hemispheric dominance could be tested by the same EEG, hypnotizability, and task performance tests as described above.

20. Is nasal dominance or forced changes in it associated with moods and clinically defined groups of mental disorders such as the alterations of manic depression? Will self-report mood scales correlate with shifts in nasal dominance (Tart, 1972)?

21–23. Are shifts in nasal dominance associated with the altered states of consciousness induced by psychedelics, alcohol, tranquilizers, and so forth? Can forced nasal dominance via uninostril breathing be used to potentiate, block, or otherwise modify psychedelic effects?

24–26. Is the nasal cycle related to the manifestations of the common everyday trance as listed in Table 1? Can forced shifts in nasal dominance change these manifestations?

27–28. Is nasal dominance shift during sleep associated with turning over and changing the side of the body one is sleeping on? Is this related to the REM–NREM cycle?

Ultradian Rhythms, the Sleep–Dream Cycle, and State-Dependent Memory and Learning

29–31. Figure 1 suggests that ultradian rhythms, the sleep–dream cycle, and state-dependent memory and learning are the basic psychophysiological processes so far isolated for studies on altered states of consciousness in everyday life. How are they related to one another? Review Kripke (1982), Werntz (1981), and McGaugh (1983) as a background for designing studies to determine how the anatomical and physiological processes of the dream cycle, ultradian rhythms, and state-dependent memory and learning interact to produce altered states of consciousness in everyday life, in mental illness, and in transpersonal states.

32. Will surgical excision or drug blockage of the function of the *pontine reticular neurones* and the *locus coeruleus* (which regulate the REM–NREM sleep cycle) also interfere with the periodicity of other ultradian rhythms? This has implications for the multioscillator (Kripke, 1982) versus the unioscillator (Werntz et al.) hypotheses of ultradian rhythms.

33–34. What vigilance and performance tasks will be maximized by structuring regular ultradian rest breaks throughout work periods? How long do these rest breaks need to be?

35–36. Is the continual override of the ultradian rest period the cause of stress and stress-induced psychosomatic problems? Determine the ultradian rhythms most likely associated with each of the major psychosomatic disorders, and determine if the disorder can be varied by the degree of desynchrony of this rhythm.

37. Will experimental desynchrony of ultradian rhythms result in the typical neurohormonal changes associated with stress? Which of the ultradian rhythm desynchronies is most potent in inducing stress and altered states?

38. Will experimental desynchrony of ultradian rhythms disrupt state-dependent memory and learning? Which ultradian rhythms are most influential?

39. Personal communication with Pir Vilayat Inayat Khan, the present head of the Sufi Order in the West and leader of hundreds of meditation groups around the world, confirms that a 90-minute verbally guided meditation is about optimum. Zazen practioners report that 45 minutes (one-half ultradian cycle) is optimal for their more strenuous meditation (Kapleau, 1980). Do other meditation leaders from other backgrounds confirm this ultradian rhythm in meditation? Do ashrams and monasteries tend to have a full 90- to 120-minute ultradian periodicity, or a 45-minute half cycle in their daily activities?

State-Dependent Memory/Learning and Altered States of Consciousness

40. Run the classical state-dependent memory and learning experiments during different phases of the different ultradian rhythms. Which phase of which rhythms gives the most striking results for altered states?

41. Is the nasal cycle particularly significant in state-dependent learning

and memory? Will forced shifts in nasal dominance result in the expected differences in the state-dependent learning of nonsense syllables, music, poetry, prose?

42. Will the selective activation of the cerebral hemispheres by forced uninostril breathing have measurable effects on the types of memory, affect, and cognition associated with each cerebral hemisphere?

The Common Everyday Trance and Hypnosis

43–46. Construct a scale from the list of manifestations listed in Table 1 to measure the common everyday trance and report on its various validity and reliability coefficients with different subject populations and age groups.

47–48. Will subjects with high scores on this Common Everyday Trance Scale (associated with the rest or parasympathetic phase of their ultradian rhythms) score higher on standard scales of hypnotic susceptibility?

49. Will the correlation attempted above be complicated by the fact that some hypnotic phenomena require sympathetic system activation rather than the parasympathetic activation assumed present in the common everyday trance?

50. Will subjects high on the Common Everyday Trance Scale score higher on waking suggestions as defined by Weitzenhoffer (1957)?

51. Will subjects who have a talent for a particular hypnotic phenomenon more easily and completely experience it when they are in a high-score phase of the Common Everyday Trance Scale?

52–53. Will posthypnotic suggestion be more effective when it is administered during a high-score phase of the Common Everyday Trance Scale and when its future execution is limited to similar phases of the common everyday trance?

54–55. Will hypnotic amnesia be more effective in the high-score phase of the Common Everyday Trance Scale? What would be the implications of positive results for our theories of memory and our concept of altered states of consciousness in everyday life?

56. Run a number of classical memory and learning experiments (nonsense syllables, prose, poetry, etc.) during different phases of the common everyday trance. Does the phase account for a significant portion of the variance usually associated with such studies?

57. Do patients with psychosomatic disorders tend to experience more acute disturbances when they attempt to override the rest phase of their common everyday trance? Can psychosomatic symptomatology be ameliorated by training such patients to recognize reliable signs of their own common everyday trances and rest during these periods?

Ultradian Rhythms and Transpersonal States
of Consciousness

58. *Pranayama* training that shifts nasal dominance via forced changes in nostril breathing patterns means that yogis "presumably . . . have developed conscious control over their autonomic nasal center" (Eccles, 1978) and related autonomic functions. What shifts in autonomic functioning are measurable with such training?

59-61. Study the effects of different forms of meditation on the nasal cycle. Do the results suggest how some forms of meditative practice lead to the altered states and psychophysiological benefits claimed? Do more highly experienced meditators evidence shifts in the nasal cycle sooner than beginners in meditation?

62. What other ultradian rhythms are found associated with transpersonal states (*samadhi, satori,* cosmic consciousness)? An unexpected breakthrough of kundalini is said to be associated with gross malfunctions of many autonomic system activities. Review the available literature to determine what autonomic functions are thrown into desynchrony.

63. Personal accounts of transpersonal states suggest that there may be two general classes: those dependent on a high sympathetic innervation (the kundalini experience) versus those associated with high parasympathetic activity (*samadhi*). This suggests a Bipolar Theory of Transpersonal States. The Zen practice of using "transpersonal double binds" called *koans* to bind the rational mind so that it can be transcended (giving rise to the enlightenment experience of *kensho* and *satori*) appears to use both. First there is an activation of the sympathetic system ("exert yourself to the utmost"), and suddenly that is reversed into its opposite with a flooding parasympathetic response (tears, "dissolving of the ego"). Can nasal dynamics be used as a window or facilitator of these experiences?

64. How can more effective double binds be formulated to facilitate the altered states of therapeutic and transpersonal experience (Erickson and Rossi, 1975; Jickakw, 1983)? Are these experiences more likely to occur during definite phases of certain ultradian cycles?

REFERENCES

Alexiev, A. and Roth, B. Some peculiar changes in the pattern of respiration connected with REM sleep: A preliminary report. *Electroencephalography and Clinical Neurophysiology,* 1978, *44,* 108-111.

Anch, M., Orr, W., and Karacan, I. Stress, cardiac activity and sleep. *Journal of Human Stress,* Sept. 1976, 15-22.

Barber, T. Suggested ("hypnotic") behavior: The trance paradigm versus an alternative paradigm. In E. Fromm and R. Shor (Eds.), *Hypnosis: Research developments and perspectives.* Chicago: Aldine-Atherton, 1972, pp. 115-182.

Bowden, D., Kripke, D., and Wyborney, V. Ultradian rhythms in waking behavior of rhesus monkeys. *Physiology and Behavior,* 1978, *21,* 929-933.

Broughton, R. Biorhythmic variations in consciousness and psychological functions. *Canadian Psychological Review,* 1975, *16,* 217-239.

Broughton, R. and Baron, R. Sleep patterns in the intensive care unit and on the ward after acute myocardinal infarction. *Electroencephalography and Clinical Neurophysiology,* 1978, *45,* 348-360.

Bucke, M. *Cosmic consciousness.* New York: Innes & Son, 1901; republished, New York: Dutton, 1967.

Bykov, V. and Katinas, G. Temporal organization of the thyroid in the A/He mice (morphometric investigation). *Biol. Bull. Acad. Sci. USSR,* 1979, *6,* 247-249.

Cartwright, R. and Monroe, L. Relation of dreaming and REM sleep: The effects of REM deprivation under two conditions. *Journal of Personality and Social Personality,* 1968, *10,* 69-74.

Clarke, J. The nasal cycle II: A quantitative analysis of nostril dominance. *Research Bulletin of the Himalayan International Institute,* 1980, *2,* 3-7.

Clements, P., Hafer, M., and Vermillion, M. Psychometric, diurnal, and electrophysiological correlates of activation. *Journal of Personality,* 1976, *33,* 387-394.

Coe, W. Trance: A problematic metaphor for hypnosis. Invited Address, *91st Annual Conference of American Psychological Association,* Anaheim, Calif., 1983.

Connell, J. Rhinometry: Description of a method and instrument. Undated, unpublished mimeograph available from the author, 575 Jones Road, Englewood, N.J.

Dallimore, N. and Eccles, R. Changes in human nasal resistance associated with exercise, hyperventilation, and rebreathing. *Acta Otolaryngol,* 1977, *84,* 416-421.

Delgado-Garcia, J., Grau, C., DeFeudis, P., Del Pozo, F., Jimenez, J., and Delgado, J. Ultradian rhythms in the mobility and behavior of rhesus monkeys. *Experimental Brain Research,* 1976, *25,* 79-91.

Dement, W. and Kleitman, N. Cyclic variations in EEG during sleep and their relation to eye movements, body motility, and dreaming. *Electroencephalography and Clinical Neurophysiology,* 1957, *9,* 673-690.

Drettner, B. Vascular reactions of the human nasal mucosa on exposure to cold. *Acta Otolaryngol Supplement,* 1961, 166.

Eccles, R. The central rhythm of the nasal cycle. *Acta Otolaryngol,* 1978, *86,* 464-468.

Eccles, R. and Wilson, H. The autonomic innervation of the nasal blood vessels of the cat, *J. Physiol.* 1974, *238,* 549-560.

Erickson, M. Further experimental investigation of hypnosis: Hypnotic and nonhypnotic realities. Originally published by *The American Journal of Clinical Hypnosis,* 1967, *10,* 87-135. Republished in vol. I of *The collected papers of Milton H. Erickson on hypnosis,* Ernest L. Rossi (Ed.). New York: Irvington, 1980, pp. 18-82.

Erickson, M. *The collected papers of Milton H. Erickson on hypnosis,* Ernest L. Rossi (Ed.). New York: Irvington, 1980.

Erickson, M. and Rossi, E. Varieties of hypnotic amnesia. *The American Journal of Clinical Hypnosis,* 1974, *16,* 225-239.

Erickson, M. and Rossi, E. Varieties of double bind. *The American Journal of Clinical Hypnosis,* 1975, *17,* 143-157.

Erickson, M. and Rossi, E. *Hypnotherapy: An exploratory casebook.* New York: Irvington, 1979.

Erickson, M. and Rossi, E. *Experiencing hypnosis.* New York: Irvington, 1981.

Erickson, M., Rossi, E., and Rossi, I. *Hypnotic realities.* New York: Irvington, 1976.

Eriksson, E., Edén, S., Modigh, K., and Häggendal, H. Ultradian rhythm in rat hypothalamic dopamine levels. *Journal of Neural Transmission,* 1980, *48,* 305–310.

Filicori, M., Bolelli, G., Franceschetti, F., and Lafisca, S. The ultradian pulsatile release of gonadotropins in normal female subjects. *Acta Europaea Fertilitatis,* 1979, *10,* 29–33.

Fischer, R. A cartography of ecstatic and meditative states. *Science,* 1971, *174,* 897–904.

Flor-Henry, P. Lateralized temporal-limbic dysfunction and psychopathology. *Annals of the New York Academy of Sciences, Neurological Parallels and Continuities (II).* New York: Academy of Sciences, 1976, *280,* 777–797.

Folkard, S. Circadian rhythms and human memory. In F. Brown and R. Graeber (Eds.), *Rhythmic aspects of behavior.* Hillsdale, N.J.: Erlbaum Associates, 1982, 313–344.

Friedell, A. Automatic attentive breathing in angina pectoris. *Minnesota Medicine,* 1948, *31,* 875–881.

Friedman, A. and Piepho, R. Effect of photo period reversal on patterns for GABA levels in rat brain. *International Journal of Chronobiology,* 1978, *5,* 445–458.

Friedman, S. On the presence of a variant form of instinctual regression: Oral drive cycles in obesity–bulimia. *Psychoanalytic Quarterly,* 1972, *41,* 364–383.

Friedman, S. A psychophysiological model for the chemotherapy of psychosomatic illness. *The Journal of Nervous and Mental Diseases,* 1978, *166,* 110–116.

Friedman, S. and Fischer, C. On the presence of a rhythmic diurnal, oral instinctual drive cycle in man: A preliminary report. *Journal of the American Psychoanalytic Association,* 1967, *15,* 317–343.

Friedman, S., Kantor, I., Sobel, S., and Miller, R. On the treatment of neurodermatitis with a monomine oxidase inhibitor. *The Journal of Nervous and Mental Diseases,* 1978, *166,* 117–125.

Funk, E. Biorhythms and the breath: The nasal cycle. *Research Bulletin of the Himalayan International Institute,* Winter 1980, 5–8.

Funk, F. and Clarke, J. The nasal cycle observations over prolonged periods of time. *Research Bulletin of the Himalayan International Institute,* Winter 1980, 1–4.

Globus, G. Rapid eye movement cycle in real time. *Archives of General Psychophysiology,* 1966, *15,* 654–659.

Globus, G. Observations on sub-circadian rhythms. *Psychophysiology,* 1968, *4,* 366.

Globus, G. In "Periodicity in sleep and in waking states," D. Weizman (chapter ed.), in M. Chase (Ed.), *The sleeping brain.* Los Angeles: Brain Research Institute, UCLA, 1972.

Globus, G., Phoebus, E., and Moore, C. REM "sleep" manifestations during waking. *Psychophysiology,* 1970, *7,* 308.

Goldstein, L., Stoltzfus, N., and Gardocki, J. Changes in interhemispheric amplitude relationships in the EEG during sleep. *Physiology and Behavior,* 1972, *8,* 811–815.

Goleman, D. *The varieties of meditative experience.* New York: Dutton, 1977.

Gopher, D. and Lavie, P. Short-term rhythms in the performance of a simple motor task. *Journal of Motor Behavior,* 1980, *12,* 207–221.

Gordon, H., Frooman, B., and Lavie, P. Shift in cognitive asymmetries between wakings from REM and NREM sleep. *Neuropsychologia,* 1982, *20,* 99–103.

Graeber, R. Alterations in performance following rapid transmeridian flight. In F. Brown and R. Graeber (Eds.), *Rhythmic aspects of behavior.* Hillsdale, N.J.: Erlbaum Associates, 1982, pp. 173–212.

Hartmann, E. Dauerschlaf: A polygraphic study. *Archives of Psychiatry,* 1968a, *18,* 99.

Hartmann, E. The 90-minute sleep–dream cycle. *Archives of General Psychiatry,* 1968b, *18,* 280.

Hasegawa, M. and Kem, E. Variations in nasal resistance in man: A rhinomanometric study of the nasal cycle in 50 human subjects. *Rhinology,* 1978, *16,* 19–29.

Heetderks, D. Observations on the reaction of normal nasal mucous membrane. *American Journal of Medical Science*, 1927, *174*, 231–244.

Hey, E. and Price, J. Nasal conductance and effective airway diameter. *Journal of Physiology*, 1982, *330*, 429–437.

Hiatt, J. and Kripke, D. Ultradian rhythms in waking gastric activity. *Psychosomatic Medicine*, 1975, *37*, 320–325.

Hilgard, E. *Divided consciousness: Multiple controls in human thought and action*. New York: Wiley, 1977.

Horne, J. and Whitehead, M. Ultradian and other rhythms in human respiration rate. *Experientia*, 1976, *32*, 1165–1167.

Hunsaker, W., Reiser, B., and Wolynetz, M. Vaginal temperature rhythms in sheep. *International Journal of Chronobiology*, 1977, *4*, 151–162.

Hymes, A. and Nuernberger, P. Breathing patterns found in heart attack patients. *Research Bulletin of the Himalayan International Institute*, 1980, *2*, 10–12.

Iyengar, B. *Light on Pranayama: The yogic art of breathing*. New York: Crossroads, 1981.

Jichakw, P., Fujita, G., and Shapiro, S. The double bind and koan Zen. *The Journal of Mind and Behavior*, 1984, *5*, 2, 211–222.

Jones, E. *The life and work of Sigmund Freud*, L. Trilling and S. Marcus (Eds.). New York: Basic Books, 1961.

Jouvet, M. Essai sur le rêve. *Archives Italiennes de Biologie*, 1973, *3*, 564–576.

Kales, A., Hoedemaker, F., and Jacogson, A. Dream deprivation: An experimental reappraisal. *Nature*, 1964, *204*, 1337.

Kapleau, P. *The three pillars of Zen*. New York: Anchor, 1980.

Katz, R. The temporal structure of motivation, III: Identification and ecological significance of ultradian rhythms of intracranial reinforcement. *Behavioral and Neural Biology*, 1980, *30*, 148–159.

Kayser, R. Die exacte Messung der Luftdurchgangigkeit der Nase. *Archiv fuer Laryngologie und Rhinologie*, 1895, *3*, 101–120.

Keuning, J. Rhythmic conchal volume changes. *International Rhinology*, 1963, *2*, 57.

Klein, R. and Armitage, R. Rhythms in human performance: 1-1/2-hour oscillations in cognitive style. *Science*, 1979, *204*, 1326–1328.

Kleitman, N. *Sleep and wakefulness*, 2nd ed. Chicago: University of Chicago Press, 1963.

Kleitman, N. Basic rest–activity cycle in relation to sleep and wakefulness. In Kales (Ed.), Sleep: *Physiology and pathology*. Philadelphia: Lippincott, 1969.

Kleitman, N. Phylogenetic, ontogenetic and environmental determinants in the evolution of sleep–wakefulness cycles. In S. Kety, E. Evarts, and H. Williams (Eds.), *Sleep and altered states of consciousness*. Baltimore: Williams & Wilkins, 1967, *45*, 30.

Kleitman, N. Implications of the rest–activity cycle: Implications for organizing activity. In E. Hartmann (Ed.), *Sleep and dreaming*. Boston: Little, Brown, 1970.

Kripke, D. An ultradian biological rhythm associated with perceptual deprivation and REM sleep. *Psychosomatic Medicine*, 1972, *34*, 221–234.

Kripke, D. Ultradian rhythms in sleep and wakefulness. In E. Weitzman (Ed.), *Advances in sleep research*, vol. I. New York: Spectrum, 1974, pp. 305–325.

Kripke, D. Ultradian rhythms in behavior and physiology. In F. Brown and R. Graeber (Eds.), *Rhythmic aspects of behavior*. Hillsdale, N.J.: Erlbaum Associates, 1982.

Kripke, D. and Sonnenschein, D. A biologic rhythm in waking fantasy. In K. Pope and J. Stringer (Eds.), *The stream of consciousness*. New York: Plenum, 1978, pp. 321–332.

Kripke, D., Mullaney, D., Wyborney, V., and Messin, S. There's no basic rest-activity cycle. In F. Stott et al. (Eds.), *ISAM 1977: Proceedings of the Second International Symposium on ambulatory monitoring*. London: Academic Press, 1978, 105–113.

Krishna, G. *The awakening of kundalini*. New York: Dutton, 1975.

Rossi, E. *Dreams and the growth of personality.* New York: Pergamon, 1972a.

Rossi, E. Self-reflection in dreams. *Psychotherapy: Theory, Research, and Practice,* 1972b, *9,* 290–298.

Rossi, E. Hypnosis and ultradian rhythms. Advanced Training Seminar of the Southern California Society of Clinical Hypnosis, Feb. 1981a.

Rossi, E. Hypnotist describes natural rhythm of trance readiness. *Brain–Mind Bulletin,* Mar. 1981b, *6*(7), 1.

Rossi, E. Hypnosis and ultradian cycles: A new state(s) theory of hypnosis? *The American Journal of Clinical Hypnosis,* 1982, *1,* 21–32.

Rossi, E. Ericksonian Hypnotherapy now and in the future. In Zeig, J. (Ed.), *Ericksonian Psychotherapy, Vol. 1, Structures.* New York, Brunner/Mazel, 1985.

Rossi, E., Ryan, M., and Sharp, F. (Eds.). *Healing and hypnosis: The lectures, workshops, and seminars of Milton H. Erickson,* vol. 1 New York: Irvington, 1983.

Sarbin, T. and Coe, W. *Hypnosis: A social psychological analysis of influence communication.* New York: Holt, Rinehart & Winston, 1972.

Shankara. *Crest-jewel of discrimination,* S. Prabhavananda and C. Irsherwood (trans.). Hollywood, Calif.: Vedanta Press, 1947.

Shiotsuka, R., Jovonovich, J., and Jovonovich, J. In vitro data on drug sensitivity: circadian and ultradian corticosterone rhythms in adrenal organ cultures. In J. Aschoff et al. (Eds.), *Chronobiological aspects of endocrinology.* Stuttgart: Schattauer, 1974, pp. 225–267.

Simon, M. and George, R. Diurnal variations in plasma corticosterone and growth hormone as correlated with regional variations in norepinephrine, dopamine and serotonin content of rat brain. *Neuroendocrinology,* 1975, *17,* 125–138.

Singh-Khalsa, G. and Singh-Khalsa, S. Kundalini energy. *Kundalini Quarterly,* Fall 1976. Republished in J. White (Ed.), *Kundalini, evolution, and enlightenment.* New York: Anchor Books, 1979, pp., 254–290.

Sperry, R. and Gazzangia. M. Language following disconnection of the hemispheres. In C. Millikan and F. Darley (Eds.), *Brain mechanisms underlying speech and language.* New York: Grune & Stratton, 1967, pp. 177–184.

Steiner, R., Peterson, A., Yu, J., Conner, H., Gilbert, M., terPenning, B., and Bremner, W. Ultradian luteinizing hormone and testosterone rhythms in the adult male monkey, *macaca fascicularis. Endocrinology,* 1980, *107,* 1489–1493.

Stevens, J., Kodama, H., Lonsbury, B., and Mills, L. Ultradian characteristics of spontaneous seizure discharges recorded by radio telemetry in man. *Electroencephalography and Clinical Neurophysiology,* 1971, *31,* 313–325.

Stoksted, P. Rhinometric measurements for determination of the nasal cycle. *Acta Otolaryngol Supplement,* 1953, *109,* 159–175.

Stroebel, C. Biological rhythm correlates of disturbed behavior in rhesus monkeys. In F. Rohles (Ed.), *Circadian rhythms in non-human primates. New York: S. Karger, 1969.*

Stoksted, P., The physiologic cycle of the nose under normal and pathologic conditions. *Acta Oto-Laryngol,* 1952, 42:175–179.

Soubeyrand, L., Action des medicaments vasomoteurs sur le cycle nasal et la fonction ciliare, *Revue de Laryngologie Oto-Rhonologie,* 1964, 85:43–113.

Tannenbaum, G. and Martin, J. Evidence for an endogenous growth hormone secretion in the rat. *Endocrinology,* 1976, *98,* 562–570.

Tannenbaum, G., Martin, J., and Colle, E. Ultradian growth hormone rhythm in the rat: effects of feeding, hyperglycemia, and insulin-induced hypoglycemia. *Endocrinology,* 1976, *99,* 720–727.

Tart, C. Measuring the depth of an altered state of consciousness, with particular reference to self-report scales of hypnotic depth. In E. Fromm and R. Shor (Eds.), *Hypnosis: Research development and perspectives.* Chicago: Aldine-Atherton, 1972, pp. 445–477.

Tart, C. *Transpersonal psychologies.* El Cerrito, Calif.: Psychological Processes, Inc., 1983a.

Tart, C. *States of consciousness.* El Cerrito, Calif.: Psychological Processes, Inc., 1983b.

Tierney, I., McGuire, R., and Walton, H. Distributions of body-rocking manifested by severely mentally deficient adults in ward environments. *Journal of Mental Deficiency Research,* 1978, *22,* 243-254.

Timmons, B. and Kamiya, J. The psychology and physiology of meditation and related phenomena: A bibliography, I. *Journal of Transpersonal Psychology,* 1970, *2,* 41-59.

Timmons, B. and Kanellakos, D. The psychology and physiology of meditation and related phenomena: A bibliography, II. *Journal of Transpersonal Psychology,* 1974, *6,* 32-38.

Ullner, R. On the development of ultradian rhythms: The rapid eye movement activity in premature children. In L. Scheving et al. (Eds.), *Chronobiology.* Tokyo: Igaku Shoin, 1974, 478-481.

Vinekar, S. Electro-nasagraphy. *Neurology India,* 1966, *14*(2), 75-79.

Wada, T. An experimental study of hunger and its relation to activity. *Archives of Psychological Monographs,* 1922, *8,* 1.

Wehr, T. Circadian rhythm disturbances in depression and mania. In F. Brown and R. Graeber (Eds.), *Rhythmic aspects of behavior.* Hillsdale, N.J.: Erlbaum Associates, 1982, pp. 339-428.

Weitzenhoffer, A. *General techniques of hypnotism.* New York: Grune & Stratton, 1957.

Weitzman, E. Temporal organization of neuroendocrinal function in relation to the sleep-waking cycle in man. In *Recent studies of hypothalamic function,* International Symposium, Calgary, 1973. Basel: S. Karger, 1974, 26-38.

Werntz, D. Cerebral hemispheric activity and autonomic nervous function. Doctoral dissertation, University of California, San Diego, 1981.

Werntz, D., Bickford, R., Bloom, F., and Singh-Khulsa, S. Selective cortical activation by alternating autonomic function. Paper presented the Western EEG Society, Feb. 21, 1981.

Werntz, D., Bickford, R., Bloom, F., and Singh-Khulsa, S. Alternating cerebral hemispheric activity and lateralization of autonomic nervous function. *Neurobiology,* 1982, *4,* 225-229.

West, L., Janszen, H., Lester, B., and Cornelisoon, F., Jr. The psychosis of sleep deprivation. *Annals of the New York Academy of Sciences,* 1962, *96,* 66-70.

Wever, R. Behavioral aspects of circadian rhythmicity. In F. Brown and R. Graeber (Eds.), *Rhythmic aspects of behavior.* Hillsdale, N.J.: Erlbaum Associates, 1982, pp. 105-171.

White, J. (Ed.) *Kundalini, evolution and enlightenment.* New York: Anchor Books, 1979.

Wilber, K. *The spectrum of consciousness.* Wheaton, Ill.: Quest, 1977.

Wilkinson, R. The relationship between body temperature and performance across circadian phase shifts. In F. Brown and R. Graeber (Eds.), *Rhythmic aspects of behavior.* Hillsdale, N.J.: Erlbaum Associates, 1982, pp. 213-240.

Wilson, D., Kripke, D., McClure, D., and Greenburg, A. Ultradian cardiac rhythms in surgical intensive care unit patients. *Psychosomatic Medicine,* 1977, *39,* 432-435.

Yen, S., Vandenberg, G., Tsai, C., and Parker, D. Ultradian fluctuations of gonadotropins. In M. Ferin et al. (Eds.), *Biorhythms and Human Reproduction.* New York: Wiley, 1974, pp. 203-218.

5. Hypnosis, Multiple Personality, and Ego States as Altered States of Consciousness

John G. Watkins and Helen H. Watkins

Hypnosis has historically been considered an altered state of consciousness, often called "trance." Most textbooks in the field (Crasilneck and Hall, 1985; Edelstien, 1981; Kroger, 1977; Meares, 1961) speak of it as an altered state that is initiated by a set of procedures called "induction techniques." When this altered state has been achieved, then various therapeutic maneuvers in the form of suggestions or other psychological interventions are performed and are called the practice of "hynotherapy." This altered state is characterized by increased suggestibility and enhanced imagery and imagination, including the availability of visual memories from the past. There is also a lowering of the planning function and a reduction in reality testing (Hilgard, 1977, pp. 163–165). Most early writers regarded it that way (Bernheim, 1964; Bramwell, 1956; Liebeault, 1892), and probably the majority today still view hypnosis within such a theoretical framework.

This trance or altered state, has not only been considered a necessary prerequisite for the most efficacious implantation of therapeutic suggestions, but it has also been described along a continuum of "depth" (Shor, 1979).

Scales of hypnotic depth have been developed (Tart, 1972) and also scales of hypnotic susceptibility, such as the Harvard (Shor and Orne, 1962) and the Stanford (Weitzenhoffer and Hilgard, 1959) scales. These show considerable validity in distinguishing individuals who are capable of attaining a "deep" hypnotic state from those who achieve only "light" or "medium" states. Many research studies have used these scales on the assumption that high-scoring individuals will constitute a population capable of manifesting the phenomena associated with deep hypnosis. By studying differences between low-scoring and high-scoring subjects in laboratories, we have learned much about the modality of hypnosis, its possibilities, and its limitations.

Most practitioners of hypnotherapy have felt that the deeper this depth, the more likely it is that suggestions will be acted upon. While hypnotic susceptibility is not necessarily equated with hypnotic depth, those who achieve high scores on the susceptibility tests are generally able to manifest the more complex phenomena of anesthesia, regression, posthypnotic hallucinations, and so on, that are classically associated with a deeper trance.

This view has been modified by some contributors (Conn, 1959), who have called attention to the fact that excellent results can often be achieved when patients are only in a light or relaxed state. However, it has generally been found true that total anesthesia, for example, in an individual suffering severe pain is seldom achieved when the trance state is light (Hilgard and Hilgard, 1975). Accordingly, practitioners are stimulated to deepen the state following initial induction (Kroger, 1977, pp. 76–79; J. Watkins, 1984a, Chap. 7 "Deepening").

The majority of hypnosis research studies have been conducted within a theoretical conception that concedes the existence of trance or an "altered state of consciousness." Nevertheless, during the past two decades a number of investigators, such as Sarbin and Coe (1972) and Barber (1969, 1979), have challenged the trance concept.

Barber has consistently maintained that hypnosis is simply a form of "task motivation," and the concept of an altered state is neither necessary nor sufficient to account for its phenomena. Using a series of suggestions to subjects presumably in a normal conscious state, he has been able to induce many "hypnotic" phenomena in some individuals. He argues that he does not first initiate a "trance state," but that with adequate instruction and motivation, subjects can manifest anesthesia, hypermnesia, and so on, behaviors usually considered possible only after induction of a "deep" hypnotic trance.

Barber's "induction" procedures seem to be somewhat stereotyped. (He sometimes used taped techniques.) His laboratory technique relies greatly on traditional "relaxation" methods, which have, in general, not proved so effective as fantasy procedures. One might also wonder whether or not his "non-hypnotized" subjects, those who were given only "task motivation" instructions and not an induction procedure, were hypnotized. Barber's laboratory, by its very abundance of studies and journal publications, is well known as a place for the investigation of hypnosis. Subjects volunteering and coming to this laboratory are hardly unaware that hypnosis will be the topic studied. They may thus be already programmed to become hypnotized in spite of the absence of a formal induction and instructions to the contrary.

WHAT IS HYPNOSIS?

All this focuses attention on the questions of just what is hypnosis, and just when is an individual hypnotized. Both research and observation indicate that many individuals apparently slip in and out of trance with little external intervention. A low score on a standard hypnotic susceptibility test does not guarantee that a subject may not slip into hypnosis during a different situation.

Another factor is that hypnotized subjects apparently are very sensitive to subtle cues coming from their therapist or experimenter. Orne (1979) has called attention to the fact that inadvertently hypnotists can transmit their expectations to their subjects, who then give back to the hypnotist the desired behavior. It is not surprising that investigators often report contradictory results. Very little seems to have been done in controlling the beliefs, theories, and expectations of researchers.

Hypnosis, like a chameleon, seems to take on the beliefs and characteristics of the particular experimenter or laboratory in which it is being studied. While most of the major controversies in the field have been extensively studied, to date few of them have been completely and satisfactorily resolved. The controversy as to whether antisocial behavior can be initiated in hypnotized individuals has raged for many years (Conn, 1972; Kline, 1972; Orne, 1972; J. Watkins, 1972).

The controversy as to whether hypnosis should be viewed as an altered state of consciousness or can be better conceptualized within a different framework is just such a situation. The hypnotized subject does behave in many different and apparently "nonnormal" ways, or at least is capable of so behaving. He/she is more responsive to suggestion, can "remember" much more material, although a number of studies (Hilgard and Loftus, 1979; Orne, 1979; Putnam, 1979) show that such "memories" may be confabulated and contaminated. In fact, the verity or reality of hypermnesia and regression is today a topic of discussion. Clinicians who work hypnoanalytically use such memories in their treatment and believe that valuable therapeutic changes are achieved thereby. Forensic examiners, who employ hypnotists to enhance recall in witnesses, have found that even though a larger quantity of data has been secured, a greater amount of false information has also been elicited. As a consequence certain states (Arizona, California) have refused to accept hypnotically secured testimony as valid and credible. Other researchers (Eiblmayr, 1980; Sturm, 1982) have pointed out that unhypnotized subjects who score high on hypnotic susceptibility scales may make as many or even more mistakes in memory compared to unhypnotized witnesses. These investigators would hold that the errors are characteristic of the investigative process with all interviewees, and do not inhere only in a subject who is hypnotized. It has also been maintained that witnesses who score high on susceptibility tests, but who are not hypnotized by a formal induction, may become so spontaneously. Hence, the court never knows whether or not a given witness was or was not questioned while in a "state of hypnosis."

Numerous attempts have been made to determine just what the essential characteristics of hypnosis are. Pavlov (1923) defined hypnosis as partial cortical inhibition, and he also called it partial sleep, a view that has been dispelled by electroencephalographic studies (Evans, 1979). Schneck (1963) described it as a primitive psychophysiological state in which consciousness was eliminated. Kline (1958) felt that it was a state characterized by a lowered criticality. Early writers (Braid, 1960; Liebeault, 1892; Bernheim, 1964) described it as a state that was most characterized by hypersuggestibility.

Psychoanalytic writers have noted a close relationship of hypnosis with the concept of transference (Ferenczi, 1926; Gill and Brenman, 1959; J. Watkins, 1954, 1963). Gill and Brenman have also described hypnosis as a form of "regression in the service of the ego." Meares (1961) considered it as a regression, but one of an atavistic type, wherein the individual returns to a mode of mental functioning that probably characterized the early development of the human species during its evolution from simpler life forms. Sarbin and Coe (1972) held that it was a form of role-playing.

Janet (1907) seems to have been the first who focused on its dissociative aspects. Multifactor theories of hypnosis have been proposed. Thus, Shor (1962) held that it represented a composite of three separate dimensions: trance, role-taking, and archaic involvement, by which he meant regression.

An attempt to define the essential ingredient in hypnosis has been that of Orne (1959, 1979). He held that the "essence" of hypnosis, that which distinguishes a truly hypnotized individual from one who is only simulating hypnosis, is the ability of a hypnotized subject to freely mix his perceptions derived from reality with those that stem from his imagination. He termed this characteristic "trance logic."

Double Hallucination Test

A study performed by Orne to illustrate this point was the "double hallucination" test. A hypnotized subject is given the posthypnotic suggestion that he will perceive an acquaintance sitting in a chair across from him. The subject is brought out of hypnosis and then reports seeing the acquaintance. He behaves in every way as if this hallucination were real. His attention is then directed to the real acquaintance who has been stationed on the other side and perhaps slightly behind the subject, and the question is asked, "Then who is this?" Having committed himself to the statement that the hallucinated individual in front was the acquaintance, simulators (individuals instructed to fake hypnosis) often deny seeing the real acquaintance, since perceiving both would be inconsistent. "Reals," truly hypnotized subjects, manifest "trance logic" by accepting both perceptions, and according to Orne, do so without a great show of surprise. J. Watkins (1985) agrees that truly hypnotized subjects perceive both images (the real one and the hallucinated one) but may indeed manifest surprise behavior. Other investigators of this phenomenon (Blum and Graef, 1971; Orne, 1979) have reported that reals tend to look back and forth at the two images in an attempt to resolve the inconsistency. There seems little doubt that trance logic does often characterize hypnotized subjects. It has been compared (Watkins, 1985) to the primary process thinking that is typical of dreaming and psychotic behavior.

Even though trance logic seems to be a significant characteristic of many hypnotized subjects, the claim that it is the "essence" of hypnosis and a sine qua non has yet to be substantiated. Eiblmayr (1980), using a circle-touch test, found that other mechanisms than trance logic accounted for the fact that subjects who had been instructed to respond with "yes" when touched outside of an anesthetized spot on the hand and "no" when touched within, produced contradictory behaviors. Orne had argued that hypnotized individuals would fail to recognize the inconsistency of responding with "no" when touched inside, thus manifesting trance logic. Many of Eiblmayr's subjects continued to respond "yes" when touched in the presumably anesthetized zone. In a subsequent inquiry they reported that they had experienced the point of contact as the boundary between the two zones, thus utilizing displacement rather than trance logic in resolving the inconsistency. There were almost oppposite patterns of response between lightly hypnotized subjects (those who scored in the intermediate range of 4 to 8 on the Harvard Hypnotic Susceptibility Scale) and the more deeply hypnotized ones (those who scored 9 to 12 on the scale). This latter finding argues for a qualitative difference between levels of hypnotic susceptibility, rather than a continuum in which "deep" hypnosis is simply more of whatever inheres in a lightly hypnotized individual. To maintain a "state" concept of hypnosis in the light of such findings one would have to posit that a "deep" state of hypnosis was something qualitatively different from an "intermediate" state of hypnosis. That hypnotic "depth" is not simply a continuum from an alert condition has also been found in other investigations (Sturm, 1982).

Tart (1969) has defined an altered state of consciousness as one in which an individual "clearly feels a qualitative shift in his pattern of mental functioning." If this is so, and if there is a qualitative shift felt between being deeply hypnotized and being lightly unconscious, then perhaps we should speak of hypnosis as altered *states* of hypnosis rather than as a unitary state. Since the studies of Eiblmayr and Sturm were made with different individuals who were tested as having different levels of hypnotic susceptibility rather than as single individuals moving through different "depths," we do not yet have the data to conclude that there is more than one hypnotic "state."

A more recent development has been moving many investigators away from the concept of hypnosis as an altered state, namely, the studies on neo-dissociation performed by the Hilgards at Stanford University (Hilgard, 1977; Hilgard and Hilgard, 1975).

Once when hypnotic deafness was being induced in a volunteer before a class, a student asked Hilgard if it was possible that the subject (who was apparently unresponsive to sound) could hear "at some level." Hilgard then said to the subject, "Although you are hypnotically deaf perhaps some part of you is hearing and processing the data at some level. If this is the case lift the index finger of the right hand." The finger rose. Hilgard discovered that even though unresponsive to a stimulus within normal conscious awareness, some hypnotized subjects indicated an underlying or "unconscious" awareness.

He repeated these studies using pain stimuli, achieved either by putting the subject's hand into circulating ice water or through ischemic pain, which occurs when circulation is restricted for a brief period by a tourniquet. Again some subjects indicated an awareness of the pain during hypnosis in spite of not manifesting any in the nonhypnotic state. He described this phenomenon as a "cognitive structural system" and termed it "the hidden observer." The reality of this hidden observer phenomenon has been challenged by some investigators (Spanos and Hewitt, 1980), who maintain that it is only a suggested artifact.

From these hidden observer studies Hilgard moved increasingly to emphasize the "dissociative" aspects of hypnosis rather than those related to a "trance" concept. In this respect he revived the long-neglected views of Janet (1907) into a "neo-dissociation" theory of hypnosis. In this theory, emphasis is placed on the discreteness of hypnotic phemomena and the degree to which irrational behavior can be induced, which seems to be untouched by the usual censoring processes of the individual. The fact that a highly hypnotized individual can perceive a hallucinated person while at the same time seeing the real person seated nearby demonstrates the extent to which true perception and rational cognition are "dissociated" from the suggested hallucination. Or, again, the removal of the sensation of pain in an injured limb through hypnotic suggestion indicates that the individual is capable of processing simultaneously two streams of data that are not compatible with one another. It is as if there are two separate but coexisting experiential-cognitive structures within the organism functioning independently of one another, and hence dissociated.

This parallel processing is illustrated also by the emergence, in creative individuals, of full-blown and completed compositions, writings, and inventions. Prior to the moment of its emergence the creative person apparently is not aware of working on the creation; but at some covert or unconscious level much cognitive processing must take place for the product that emerges to consciousness to be so completely constructed.

Executive and Monitoring Functions

As a consequence of his hidden-observer experiments, Hilgard described two functions, the "executive" and the "monitoring." These were related to the concept of "central control" as manifested by two separate "subsystems." In the normal individual these subsystems are assumed to be under a central control. However, once activated each of them may continue with a measure of autonomy. This process might be compared to the withdrawal of all alertness from behaviors that have become habits. The concept of subsystems has previously been proposed by such writers as Gill and Brenman (1959) and Blum et al. (1967). Hebb (1975) suggested that "cell assemblies" may provide a neurological stratum for such cognitive systems.

Executive functions include planning for goals, initiating appropriate action for achieving them, and maintaining action for overcoming intervening obstacles. The monitoring function represents a kind of feedback that keeps track of what is taking place. The monitor is selective in its perception, such as choosing an interest in certain situations to the exclusion of others. It also includes a critical or judgmental role.

The two functions cannot be sharply differentiated because initiated action is also monitored when the individual is functioning harmoniously. However, sometimes the two functions are not balanced, with resultant cognitive dissonance and maladjustment. In such cases the monitoring function may be in conflict with the executive function. Then the individual may manifest "dissociation" wherein the "right and left hand" do not know just what the other is doing.

The hypnotic experience is characterized by a greater ease when there is dissociation, thus permitting cognitive processing to take place at different levels simultaneously and in different directions. There is a greater separation of the monitoring function from the executive one. This experience occurs in an interpersonal relationship between therapist and patient or experimenter and subject, which Hilgard (1977, p. 224) calls "the hypnotic contract." The subject "agrees" to suspend close monitoring of various executive-initiated behaviors. This emphasis on the *relationship* in hypnosis, rather than its *trance* aspects, deemphasizes its concept as an altered state of consciousness and is more in line with the arguments presented by Barber (1979). Some hypnotherapists (J. Watkins, 1978) have attempted to combine the relationship and the trance positions by calling hypnosis a "state-relationship."

Modern-day hypnotists conceive of the hypnotic contract as one of mutual responsibility, hence, as a sharing of the executive function. This is contrasted with an older (and more popular) view of hypnosis as the imposition of the hypnotist's will on that of the subject. During hypnosis some of the independent initiating by the subject's executive is removed; he "cooperates" with the hypnotist. Once the individual has accepted the hypnotic contract, that is, has agreed to relinquish some of the control, the activity of the monitor is reduced, thus making possible separate and parallel processing of data that may be cognitively inconsistent with each other in the fully conscious or alert condition. This situation exists within a hypnotic relationship. It fails to exist when a trance not involving a hypnotist–subject dyad has been induced merely by eye fixation alone or through monotonous stimulation, such as the ticking of a metronome. This argues against the concept of hypnosis as simply an altered state of consciousness.

ALTERED STATES OF CONSCIOUSNESS

Some of the controversy regarding hypnosis as an altered state of consciousness has been discussed. However, when we consider two other areas, "multiple personalities" and "ego states," different criteria must be applied. Ludwig (1969), who provides a keynote introductory chapter to Tart's (1969) symposium on altered states of consciousness, defines these conditions as follows: "I shall regard altered state(s) of consciousness hereafter referred to as ASC(s) as any mental state(s), induced by various physiological, psychological or pharmacological maneuvers or agents, which can be recognized subjectively by the individual himself (or by an objective observer of the individual) as representing a sufficient deviation in subjective experience or psychological functioning from certain general norms for that individual during alert, waking consciousness."

By such a definition both "multiple personalities" and "ego states" (a more recent conception that will be explained further) deserve to be considered as altered states (ASCs). They do meet the above criteria. However, a definite distinction needs to be made between them and such other "states" as "hypnosis," "dreams," "psychedelic drugs," "ecstasy," and "meditation," topics reviewed in Tart's significant work (1969).

Most ASCs are considered to be generalized experiences changing or altering the entire area of behavior, emotion, perception, and cognition. This is analogous to saying "The U.S. is in a *state* of economic depression," "The country is in a *state* of war," and so on. This kind of "state" results in an alteration of all functions within the nation, even as an ASC results in an alteration of all functions within the individual.

In multiple personalities and "ego states" we are confronted with a *division* in consciousness (which is certainly an alteration from the normal). Thus, Hilgard (1977), in discussing these phenomena ("amnesia," "fugue," "multiple personality," "hidden observers," and "hypnosis,") used the term *divided consciousness*. In such conditions consciousness is focused on only a segment of the repertory of behaviors and experiences "normally' available to an individual. The analogy here is employment of the word "state" as used to label the "*state* of Montana" or the "*state* of California." In the conditions of multiple personality and ego states we are concerned with an alteration of consciousness by separating it into segments that are more or less distinct from one another. These conditions limit the range of experiences and responses that the individual can manifest at any given moment. Such an alteration of awareness through division is (as in the case of multiple personalities) often maladaptive. However, "ego states" (as will be apparent when we pursue this topic further) can be both adaptive or maladaptive, and when activated through hypnosis or other psychological interventions can add to an individual's conscious behavior and experiences.

MULTIPLE PERSONALITIES

Although once thought to be "extremely rare" this diagnosis (though still "uncommon") is now recognized as much more frequent, and there is considerable renewed interest in the phenomenon. There are today over 200 clinical reports on this condition. Classical cases include (Prince, 1906), Thigpen and Cleckley (1957), and Schreiber (1974). The April 1984 issue of the *International Journal of Clinical and Experimental Hypnosis* is a monograph devoted to papers on multiple personality. Legal battles over whether or not a defendant is a multiple personality, and if so, to what extent this should mitigate guilt, have raged in a number of courts (Orne et al., 1984; J. Watkins, 1984). Since so much material on this issue is available elsewhere, and it has not been planned to make "multiple personality" the main thrust of this paper, we will confine our discussion of it as an "altered state of consciousness" to pointing out wherein it meets previously published criteria for ASC.

Ludwig (1969, pp. 13–18) lists the following "common denominators or features" of ASCs, indicating which ones "tend to be characteristic of most ASC's" to a greater or lesser degree: "Alterations in thinking," "Disturbed time sense," "Loss of control," "Change in emotional expression," "Body image change," "Perceptual distortions," "Change in meaning of significance," "Sense of the ineffable," "Feelings of rejuvenation," and "Hypersuggestibility."

Most of these conditions can be found in multiple personalities. These cases manifest significant "alterations in thinking," from one personality to the next. Steve, the secondary personality that this writer (JGW) found in Kenneth Bianchi, the Los Angeles "Hillside Strangler," confessed to the murders using language and thinking quite opposite to the normal or "Ken" personality. Videotape recordings of the interactions between Bianchi's various personalities (Ken, Steve, Billy) plus Rorschach tests and samples of handwriting exhibited strikingly different patterns of perception, emotion, behavior, and cognition. The Los Angeles Court did not accept the diagnosis of multiple personality, and the matter is still very controversial among specialists in this disorder (Orne et al., 1984; J. Watkins, 1984).

Battles between different personalities (often manifested by "migraine" headaches) ensue over control, hence, which one is to come out or be "executive." Each personality fears a "loss of control" to other personalities (Watkins and Johnson, 1982). A major personality may suffer from "perceptual distortions" in the form of auditory hallucinations. It is interesting to note that psychiatric evaluations of hallucinating psychotic patients often report the hearing of voices but seldom indicate any interest in trying to find out just "who is doing the talking." Inquiries into this matter may result in the activation of secondary personalities, in which case the diagnosis should be changed from "schizophrenia" to "dissociative reaction."

"Change in meaning or significance" is also found from one personality to another, each placing a quite different interpretation on "significance" or meaning for an external event or person. Individuals viewed as friendly or benign by one personality may be regarded as hostile enemies by a different personality.

Finally, "hypersuggestibility" seems to be a characteristic of hypnosis and of multiple personalities (who are always quite hypnotizable). In fact, legal controversies over the reality of a multiple personality diagnosis may hinge on the extent to which an examiner might or might not have "suggested" the simulating of this condition to a defendant in order to secure a defense of not guilty by reason of insanity. When different personalities emerge, they experience themselves as quite different from each other. Each personality feels itself as subject ("I") and regards the other personalities as objects ("he," "she," or "them"). This is certainly an alteration of normal consciousness and supports the contention that a *division* of consciousness is another form of consciousness alteration.

At this point let us move to the consideration of a much broader concept of divided consciousness, one that includes multiple personalities and other "ego states." The "ego psychology" developed by Paul Federn (1952) has provided us with a significant initial formulation.

THE EGO PSYCHOLOGY OF PAUL FEDERN

Federn (1952), a close associate of Freud, developed theories of personality that were not in the mainstream of psychoanalysis, and, accordingly, did not become well known. His two major contributions were the concepts of "ego cathexis" and "ego states." The following is an exposition of his views, which have been modified and extended by J. Watkins (1978).

It will be recalled that Freud's early theories centered around a psychic energy, which he termed "libido" and which he felt was erotic in nature. The term "libido" has been employed as a sexual energy, an integrating energy, and a life energy. Federn believed that a single energy system could not account for many psychological manifestations. He used the term "cathexis," that is, an investment of energy for the purpose of stimulating a psychological process. A "cathexis" is a quantum of energy that activates a psychological process, much like a motor is made to turn when it is invested or "cathected" with electricity.

Federn believed that there were two kinds of such energy, not merely one, a subject or "ego cathexis" and an "object cathexis." Although initially he used the term "ego libido" to represent the first, he gradually discarded the word "libido" to avoid confusion with Freud's concept.

Ego cathexis was a self energy. It was not merely the energy of the self; it *was* the self. To Federn, self was an energy, and when that energy was invested into any physical or psychological item, the individual experienced that item as "I" or "my." For example, I experience my hand as "my" hand because it has ego cathexis invested in it. When the hand becomes paralyzed (perhaps through hypnosis), it is no longer felt as a part of my self, no longer experienced as being within my body ego. This happens because the "ego cathexis" has been withdrawn from it. If a hysterically paralyzed limb is invested with ego cathexis, normal feeling and movement are returned. It ceases to be an "it" and becomes part of the "me."

Object cathexis is an "it" energy. Processes that are invested or "cathected" with this energy are experienced as object, as "it" or "not-me." Any part of the body and any mental process can be changed from subject to object or vice versa by moving object or ego cathexis into or out of it. For example, if an idea such as "I am thinking about my dead mother" becomes conscious, but its activating energy is *object* cathexis, then it is experienced as a perception, as if it were an object. The thought becomes a hallucination. The individual reports "seeing" his mother, not thinking about her, and we diagnose him as psychotic. If the idea of the dead mother then has its object cathexis removed and replaced with ego cathexis, the individual tells us simply that he is "thinking" about his mother—and we no longer regard him as psychotic. Changes in subject (ego) and object (it) energies determine what is experienced as a part of one's self and what is not.

Consciousness, on the other hand, is determined by the amount or quantum of energy in a process, not the nature of that energy. If the energy is minimal, then the experience may fall below the threshold necessary to activate the experience of being conscious or aware. Thus, if the type of energy in the "dead mother" concept is object cathexis, but is less than a certain amount, it will not impact another part of the self (which has been ego-cathected) sufficiently to set off the experiences of conscious awareness. It can be compared to an earthquake below 2 on the Richter Scale, which is not generally noticeable. However, if the ego boundary on which this internal object lightly impacts is sufficiently ego-cathected (highly energized), then the individual may become conscious of it. We might compare this to the "third ear" (Reik, 1948) of an exceedingly sensitive psychotherapist who picks up tiny nuances of unconscious behavior overlooked by the average person. Existence is the impact of object on subject. Conscious awareness occurs when the impact is "loud" enough, either because the energy of the impacting object is strong enough or because the ego cathexis of the impacted boundary is sufficient. Weak eyes require strong lighting; a highly sensitive retina can discern a dimly lit object. The magnitude of the *experienced* impact must be above a minimal threshold for consciousness to take place (J. Watkins, 1978).

A psychotherapist is attempting to alter balances of object and ego cathexes within the patient so as to bring subliminal process to consciousness (e.g., lifting repressions), improving reality testing and relieving symptoms. He/she is a manipulator of energies.

Such energies can be redirected more expeditiously if first a "state of hypnosis" is induced. The hypnotherapist, after inducing a trance in the patient may say, "Feeling and movement will now return to your paralyzed arm." Ego cathexis is being directed into the arm. If the suggestion is successful, the patient begins to move his arm. He reports that he can now feel it. He is aware it is a part of himself again.

While the accepting of Federn's theories of ego and object cathexes is not essential to the practice of "ego-state therapy," the concepts do provide a rationale to account for many psychological phenomena such as dissociation, hallucinations, hysterical symptoms, and so on. This formulation also provides psychotherapists with a rationale for what they are doing with their patients (J. Watkins, 1978).

Ego States

The second conception of Federn that has contributed to our understanding of multiple personalities and other dissociations is that of "ego states." According to Federn, an ego state represented an organization or pattern of mental elements that were ego-cathected, hence invested with self energies. It constituted a kind of "sub-self," with its own discrete consciousness, which would be partially or completely separate in its awareness depending on the permeability of its boundary with the primary or "executive" state.

Since ego patterns seemed to include object elements (items experienced as perceptions as well as thoughts), J. Watkins (1978) modified Federn's original conception of ego states to include both object and subject items, provided they were organized into experiential and behavioral patterns or segments. We (Watkins and Watkins, 1979, 1981, 1982) define these segments as follows: An ego state is an organized system of behavior and experience whose elements are bound together by some common principle but which is separated from other such states by boundaries that are more or less permeable. (See also H. Watkins, 1984.) By this definition multiple personalities are ego states. However, they are ego states that are characterized by a high degree of organization, are highly energized, and are separated by ego boundaries that are very rigid and impermeable. Not only may their boundaries be so impermeable that items (feelings, ideas, etc.) cannot slip from one to another, but when one of these ego states is "executive," it shows no awareness of the contents of other states. We prefer to reserve the term "multiple personalities" not only to those individuals whose ego states have the above characteristics (have well-organized patterns of behavior and experience, are highly energized and enclosed within rigid boundaries) but also to individuals in whom the alternation of the ego states occurs spontaneously because of inner dynamic needs, not through hypnotic manipulations. We use the more general term "ego states" for those *covert* personality patterns that seldom come to full conscious awareness spontaneously, but which exist as underlying sources of "unconscious" influence on the normally overt personality. They can usually (and more easily) be activated through hypnosis.

Between the two extremes of minor mood changes and true multiple personalities lies an area of *covert* ego states that manifest varying degrees of awareness of one another on the continuum of dissociation. One can regard them as "covert personalities." To understand the origin and function of ego states, let us consider the basic processes by which a human personality comes into being and grows.

THE ORIGIN AND FUNCTION OF EGO STATES

The human organism develops a personality by the operation of two basic processes: integration and differentiation. Through conditioning the child learns to "integrate" separate concepts into a broader generalization. Experiences with cat, dog, horse, and so on, are developed into the concept "animal." By putting things together the developing person builds increasingly complex patterns of thought and behavior. We say he is "learning."

Simultaneously, with the "putting together" is another process, a "taking-apart." The child learns to "differentiate." He comes to distinguish a white dog from a brown dog. He learns that some cats scratch; others do not. He distinguishes between objects that taste good when put into the mouth and those that do not. Both integration and differentiation are normal developmental processes that are adaptive. They permit him to make differential responses to different situations.

However, differentiation, a separating and splitting-off process, can be carried to pathological lengths. We then call it "dissociation," and it becomes maladaptive. When an individual finds one set of his motivations so cognitively dissonant with another that great conflict and painful anxiety result when they are in contact with each other, he may use the differentiation–dissociation process to separate them. When his behaviors and experiencing become so contradictory that he claims to be a different person at one time from that of another, and when such a split in his personality also appears to outside observers, we diagnose him as having a multiple personality. His efforts to protect himself from extreme inner conflict have resulted in inconsistent and maladaptive behavior in his external world and within his own self.

At what point adaptive differentiation becomes maladaptive dissociation it is difficult to say; but this separating process, whether termed "differentiation" or "dissociation," appears to lie on a continuum. At one end of this continuum are individuals whose behavior is fairly consistent and predictable, demonstrating only minor changes in moods from time to time. At the other end of the continuum are those more rare individuals such as *Sybil* (Schreiber, 1974) or "Rhonda–Mary" in *We the Divided Self* (Watkins and Johnson, 1982) whose personalities were fragmented into warring segments that threatened both their own lives and others, and which were diagnosed as multiple personalities.

Personality has usually been conceptualized as organized into a oneness (the vast majority of individuals) or in perhaps a very few instances as "dissociated," and as manifested by cases of amnesia, fugue states, or multiple personalities. But when we look at most psychological processes—anxiety, depression, phobias, and so on—we seldom find one that shows an "either-or." Rather, they exist on continuums, and we are confronted not merely with whether a person has anxiety or depression, but with how much, how severe the process. Mild anxiety may even be adaptive in situations where extreme complacency would be dangerous, yet in some mentally ill patients it can be almost completely incapacitating. It is becoming increasingly apparent that the process of dissociation, like almost all other psychological processes, is not an "either-or," but rather exists to varying degrees.

From the definition of ego states as patterns of behavior and experience organized around a common principle, it is possible for an almost infinite number of such organized systems to exist, since there can be any number of common principles. For example, if through hypnotic regression we were to "activate" the experience of being six years old, the six-year-old ego state should contain the various thoughts, motivations, attitudes, feelings, and behaviors that characterized the individual at that age. (We are mindful of the "contaminations" found in the memories of regressed witnesses as referred to earlier in this chapter, and we anticipate some "leakage" of items from other areas of the individual's life if the ego state's boundaries are partially permeable.) In this case being six years old would constitute the "common principle" around which the various psychological items comprising the state would be organized. If we use hypnosis to create such entities by suggesting that we wish to be in contact with a "part" of an individual "which concerns your relationship with your sister," we may well construct only a temporary artifact of personality organization—an accusation that has been made about our studies. To minimize the creation of such artifacts we are very nondirective in our instructions to subjects and patients. We wait to see if they themselves will manifest ego states, which they then name and whose contents (origin, motivations, attitudes, feelings, etc.) they describe.

Although it is possible to temporarily "create" an artifact ego state through suggestion, there are also present relatively permanent states that have already been organized around some "common principle" in response to a real and long-term need, as, for example, a fear or distrust of father figures. Such an ego state would contain those elements of behavior and feeling related to the individual's early experience with father and later with father figures, such as his teacher, boss, commanding officer, and so on. The items within this ego state would be relatively consonant with one another. Contradictory experiences (such as favorable impacts with father) may have been excluded or "dissociated" into other ego states. The ego state thus tends to be "purified" rather than to be completely "true" and represent only "reality." By such a process a multiple personality is able to dissociate all favorable behaviors and experiences related to another individual, perhaps a parent, into one segment of consciousness, and all angry ones into another. One personality loves, and the other hates.

The point wherein ego-state theory differs from previous conceptions of multiple personality is that an ego state may be *partially* dissociated and function like a *covert* multiple personality. Nevertheless, it can act as a whole, have its own attitudes, motivations, needs, and so forth, and be relatively autonomous from other states and from the entire personality—or primary ego state. Because it is not highly energized, and because its limiting boundary is somewhat permeable, it does not emerge consciously and become totally executive over the individual's body, behavior, and self-perception as is the case in a true, overt multiple personality.

Our findings regarding ego states come primarily from treating a broad spectrum of dissociated conditions plus experimentation with "normal" hypnotic subjects. We do find the theories of Paul Federn helpful in conceptualizing our cases. For example, in one multiple personality case (Watkins and Johnson, 1982) when "Rhonda" was "out" (hence the Rhonda ego state was executive), "Mary," another personality, was regarded as object ("she"). Rhonda experienced her own feelings, needs, and behaviors as subject, a part of "me." Those belonging to Mary were referred to as object, or "hers." Rhonda prior to her integration termed her own behaviors as "what I do," and Mary's behaviors as "what she did." Mary's behaviors, although performed by the same body were not experienced by Rhonda as part of her own self. Federn's theories of object and ego cathexes provide a rationale to account for such a division of consciousness. Moreover, although Mary could emerge spontaneously, hypnosis became a procedure for manipulating the various cathexes by her therapist to activate either Rhonda or Mary when desired for purposes of the therapy.

The existence of ego states became increasingly apparent to us when performing hypnotherapy. Patients in whom there was no suspicion of multiple personality, but who were referred for such lesser problems as depression, anxiety, phobias, being overweight, and smoking, manifested various ego states spontaneously when hypnotized.

Until recently the diagnosis of multiple personality was considered to be quite rare. We believe it is more common than previously thought, but we deplore the fact that many practitioners are now activating covert ego states in the course of hypnotherapy and announcing they have discovered another multiple personality. The diagnosis of multiple personality should not be made for these lesser and partially dissociated systems in relatively normal individuals. It should be used only when the ego states are highly energized, have extremely rigid boundaries, and emerge spontaneously without hypnotic intervention. In the extreme forms the respective personalities are often not even aware of the existence of the other ones. The patient's primary personality experiences periods of amnesia when other states are executive. Therapeutic intervention, generally through hypnosis, may bring an awareness of the existence of the other personalities to the primary state. The patient is then conscious of these other personalities but as *objects,* and refers to them as "he," "she," "it," or "them." This is the first step in reducing the permeability of their separating boundaries and moving toward an "integration."

These more covert entities, which are separated by lesser degrees of dissociation, more permeable boundaries, and which we are calling "ego states" as distinct from "multiple personalities," still have many of the characteristics of true multiple personalities. Some are highly organized, act like "part-persons," and possess well-defined motivations, needs, feelings, attitudes, perceptions, and so on. They may give themselves names—"George," "Mary," "Dark One," "Love," "The Little One"—almost like complete persons. They show likes, dislikes, affections, and hatreds. They may be cooperative with one another, and the individual is adaptive and well adjusted. Or they may be competitive with one another, and as a consequence the individual has anxiety, psychosomatic symptoms, and maladaptive behaviors.

Many true multiple personality cases describe their experience of a conflict between a secondary personality that wishes to emerge and the present executive one that has been trying to maintain its control of consciousness, as a "migraine" headache. In a similar way, conflicts between covert ego states can be experienced by the individual as painful even though he/she is unaware of the existence of these states.

EGO-STATE THERAPY

Ego-state therapy is the utilization of family and group treatment techniques for the resolution of conflicts between the different ego states that constitute a "family of self" within a single individual. It brings to the field of psychotherapeutic treatment concepts analogous to those of multivariate analysis in the field of research. In experimental studies we are concerned with how much of an observed behavioral variance is due to each of several factors, and how much to their covariance with one another. In ego-state therapy we are concerned with which of the total behaviors of an individual are due to each of several ego states, and which are due to their interaction with one another.

In achieving the therapeutic goal many different forms of therapeutic interventions might be employed, such as suggestion, motivation, diplomacy, advice, reinforcements, free association, dream interpretation, and analysis of the transferences. These may be employed with any directive, behavioral, cognitive, humanistic, or psychoanalytic treatment strategy. However, they are directed at the various ego segments rather than at the whole body that sits in front of the therapist. The goal is to reduce internal conflict between the various ego states by internal diplomacy aimed at making more permeable their separating boundaries and bringing them into a more cooperative arrangement within the personality structure. This is best accomplished in the hypnotic modality. H. Watkins (Watkins and Watkins, 1982) has also developed techniques that can activate ego states without the need of a formal induction.

One of the therapeutic tactics in ego-state therapy is the utilization of one ego state as a co-therapist in the treatment of another. One may serve as a kind of internal diagnostician, alerting the therapist to needs, the location of conflicts, and the reaction of the patient's primary or other ego states to the various treatment techniques used.

A patient, Ed (Watkins and Watkins, 1980), reported being unable to study. As a consequence he was failing his foreign language course. An underlying ego state, "Old One," when activated hypnotically, was greatly distressed since he (Old One) had been trying to force Ed to spend all his time studying. A four-year-old ego state, "Sandy," spontaneously emerged and claimed that he was the one who was interfering with the studying. If he (Sandy) were not permitted to play, he would not allow Ed to study. The therapist (Helen Watkins) made friends with the child state and induced it to "play at night," thus permitting Ed to study during the day. A week later Ed returned in great delight reporting that he had studied well during the past week and had gotten an A on his foreign language examination. He wondered, though, why he was having such vivid dreams and "in technicolor" every night. When Sandy was hypnotically activated he reported that he had kept his agreement, was playing at night and permitting Ed to study during the day time. Old One was not even aware of this child state until he was informed about Sandy's existence by the therapist.

In another case (H. Watkins, 1978) the patient was unable to lose weight because of an underlying ego state (the Dark One) that perceived its role as protecting her (the patient) from men who might hurt her if she lost weight and became more attractive. Dark One was originally created as the result of a trauma when the patient as a child was sexually molested. In the course of the treatment this ego state was changed from a liability into an asset and converted into a therapeutic ally. Dark One was taught Wolpian desensitization techniques (Wolpe, 1961), and given the task of desensitizing a phobia in another, child ego state—which it did most successfully. Here one segment of consciousness within a patient was mobilized for the treatment of another symptom-ridden one. The "treatment" was continued throughout the week between the regular sessions with the psychotherapist, and at each subsequent regular meeting of patient and therapist, Dark One reported his progress in a kind of internal "case conference" and received further guidance and supervision.

A young woman (a former WAC) suffering from intermittent bouts of "stinging back pains" was referred (to J. Watkins) by her orthopedic physician with the note that no organic pathology could be found. She mentioned that she was reared by a cruel grandmother who used to whip her "on the back," and that Grandma often threw Grandpa out of the house, and then locked the door on him for several days. She discussed her own marriage, mentioning that after a quarrel with her husband he would go to the local bar, and she would lock him out for a day or two. She was asked to keep a diary of just when she experienced the back pains and when she fought with her husband. As anticipated they alternated. When the back pains occurred on Monday and Tuesday, the fights with her husband occurred on a Friday and Saturday.

From an ego-state viewpoint this makes much sense; her introjected grandmother ego state (object-cathected) in psychosomatic memory "whips" her on the back. It is like a stone in the stomach, within but not part of the self. The patient is object to the grandmother's psychic repetition of the whipping. The patient solves the problem by withdrawing the object cathexis from the grandmother ego state and investing it instead with ego cathexis, with selfness. She is no longer the object of the grandmother, and the back pains cease. However, now she *is* the grandmother. The grandmother ego state becomes executive, and she behaves like the grandmother. She quarrels with her husband and locks him out of the house. Later, she is lonely for a relationship with her husband. She removes the ego cathexis from the grandmother, returning it to her "adolescent ego state," and invests the grandmother state with object cathexis. She can now have a good relationship with her husband but must bear the psychosomatic (hysterical?) pain of the grandmother ego state whipping the adolescent ego state, as experienced in the back. This is another example of how ego-state theory provides a rationale for such alterations in consciousness and helps in the formulation of appropriate treatment strategies.

The main focus of this chapter is on hypnosis and ego states as altered states of consciousness, not on the techniques of hypnotherapy or ego-state therapy. Those readers primarily interested in therapy are referred to our books, papers, and tapes on treatment (H. Watkins, 1978; J. Watkins, 1978; Watkins and Johnson 1982; Watkins and Watkins, 1979, 1979–1980, 1980, 1981, 1982).

We have also given courses in ego-state therapy at the University of Montana, as well as various workshops and institutes sponsored by other universities, professional societies, and institutions. We are concerned here with the ego-state theory rather than practice. So let us now consider the theory further.

EGO-STATE THEORY

Differentiation–dissociation appears to be a much more widely employed adaptive mechanism than previously thought. There is a definite limit to the amount of mental material that can be held within consciousness at any given time. Accordingly, we believe that ego states are developed in the growing child as a part of normal differentiation for the purpose of an efficient psychic economy. In our psychological department store it is simply not feasible to have all our goods in the front display window at the same time. Some must be diverted to the warehouse (unconscious) until they are appropriately needed. The child learns to avoid overload by banishing from his stream of consciousness not only single wishes, impulses, feelings, and so on, but organized systems of these entities, and to bring such "packages" forth into awareness at other times when the respective demands of home, play, companions, and school call for them.

In the normal adult this is manifested when we activate one ego state during a party Saturday night (a playing state) and another Monday at the office (a working state). It would be quite inefficient to spoil one's fun at the party by worrying about uncompleted papers on one's desk, even as it would be inefficient to re-enjoy the party when one should be completing a work project. Behavior and experience are thus segmented normally as a human develops. This is the first way in which we feel that ego states come into being.

As we grow, we come into contact with other people—parents, siblings, friends, teachers, and others—some of whom make a significant impact upon us. The more significant influencers may be internalized as objects—or "introjected," as the pschoanalysts put it. The perceiving child erects an internal "image" of the significant person, often a parent. This "image" consists not merely of a visual replica (as may appear in dreams), but incorporates also the attitudes, values, motivations, and behaviors of that individual as they are *perceived* by the child. There may now be created a "mother ego state" or a "father ego state." This establishes within the child's self (but not as a part of it, since the introject is object, not subject) an organized entity that may act with varying degrees of autonomy. Children introject not merely the images of their parents but also the *drama* between them. For example, if mother and father used to fight when the patient was a child, and if the child has introjected both of them, he/she may now have two warring objects within. A conflict can occur between these two covert ego states, neither of which is conscious. As a result the patient may suffer severe headaches but does not know their cause. After a hypnotic activation and internal diplomatic resolution of the argument, the headaches may cease. The second method whereby ego states are created, therefore, is their origin and development around the introjects of significant others. They behave according to the *child's perception* of them, not necessarily the way parents perceived themselves or others perceived them.

Removing the object cathexis from an introject and cathecting it with ego energy changes it into subject. It becomes a part of the self. If the original person who was introjected was a nurturing person, then the "identofact" of the individual (object turned into subject by the investment of ego cathexis) will make the self of the person into a more kindly and nurturing one, resulting, for example, in a likable and well-regarded personality. However, if the introjected person was cruel or harmful, its change from object to subject, from not-self into self, will result in the creation of a more antisocial and perhaps criminal ego state.

Finally, dissociation also takes place as a consequence of severe trauma. Multiple personalities in general show a history of child abuse, molestation, and physical or psychological cruelty. The child finds itself incapable of adapting. No matter what it does, it is wrong, and it is made to suffer. In its effort to be "good" and perhaps win parental love, it splits off a segment of the self that contains fear, anger, and needs for revenge. Sometimes this first appears as an imaginary playmate that has been created only for the purpose of having an "object relationship" with an "outside person." Existence is the impact between self and not-self, between subject and object. The child validates the existence of its own self by turning part of the self into an object. It invests this segment with object cathexis, and it now has a friend, an "outsider" with whom it can talk, play, and interact. The child is no longer alone. This suggests the macabre story of the child who, having one angleworm, cut it in two pieces "so it would not be alone." Lonely and abused children often do something like this (J. Watkins, 1984; Watkins and Johnson, 1982). The imaginary playmate in most children becomes unnecessary and is discarded when the child goes to school or develops other friends. In a few, however, the playmate is simply repressed for several years. It becomes a covert ego state, and later reappears after it has become highly energized as a full-blown multiple personality, angry, suicidal, or homocidal. It takes over the body and controls behavior. The boundary separating it from the more normal, primary ego state is now so impermeable that the person may not be aware of its existence, experiencing times in the secondary state as simply amnesic periods. Not only do true, overt multiple personalities stem from childhood traumas, but lesser dissociations in the form of covert ego states may also be created as a result of such experiences. These usually become the more maladaptive or malevolent ego states that we discover in individuals coming for treatment. We have found that such ego states were originally created for defensive purposes, that is, to help the person cope with an overwhelming emotional experience. They may later become maladaptive and dispose the patient to depression, suicide, or homocide.

Ego states can seldom be eliminated by therapeutic pressures or suggestions. Being semiautonomous they struggle to maintain their identity, and the therapist who tries to eliminate them or to force their "integration" will have about the same success as he would have trying to force the Israelis and Arabs to "integrate" into one single, large Middle Eastern nation. This holds equally true in treating multiple personalities or other ego-state problems. Ego-state conflicts can be resolved only if the therapist maintains a sympathetic neutrality toward all parties and reduces the cognitive dissonance between them. An angry ego state can destroy all therapeutic efforts if antagonized by the therapist.

An interesting experience with one "integrated" multiple personality clearly demonstrated the relationship between ego states throughout the range of the dissociative continuum, and the fact that dissociation is not simply an "either–or."

A former multiple personality patient had apparently been successfully treated. She was now "integrated," and her various secondary personalities no longer emerged. She was hypnotized once again simply to check on what her internal state of affairs was. To our surprise one of her former alter-personalities emerged and said, "We are no longer separate persons; we are just parts of her." With this "ego state" now merely a "covert" entity that could be elicited only by hypnosis, the patient was quite similar to the many normal subjects (volunteers for hypnosis research from our introductory psychology classes) who have spontaneously brought forth different ego states when under hypnosis.

Ego states often have overlapping content. Thus, an ego state constructed about experiences with a father figure, and one built around the "principle" of being six years old, will both contain experiences with father at the age of six. If during treatment a patient has been regressed to the six-year-old level (hence, his six-year-old ego state has been activated), and the experiences with father have become the focus of attention, it is possible, either spontaneously or by therapist focusing, for energy to be directed into the father ego state. This latter one now becomes "executive" and the center of consciousness. The "self in the now" relives a range of father-experiences extending over many years and becomes the center of therapeutic attention. Ego states, as organizational patterns of the personality, can be large or small, overlapping, existing in one time period, or crossing time lines.

When given the opportunity under hypnosis (but not specifically suggested) we often find several of these ego-state entities emerging in both patients and in normal subjects who volunteer for experiments in hypnosis. These structural systems seem to have been in existence continuously over long periods, although old ones can become inactive, or absorbed by others, and new ones can appear as an adaptation to changed circumstances.

In practical work the number of ego states is limited, perhaps three to ten. Such organized entities can account for 90 percent or more of the total variance of behaviors and experiences in a single person. They represent the major segments of the personality, and psychotherapy can usually resolve a patient's major conflicts by dealing with them. Smaller or splinter patterns play very minor roles in the individual's adjustment.

Hidden Observers

The hidden observer phenomenon (Hilgard, 1977) was described earlier. It occurred to us that Hilgard's hidden observer might be the same type of cognitive structural system as our ego states. We performed an experiment to test this as follows (Watkins and Watkins, 1979–1980, 1980):

Five former ego-state patients treated by Helen Watkins volunteered as experimental subjects. The therapy for three of them had been completed over a year earlier, and the other two were being seen very infrequently. Each had from six to eight well-developed and thoroughly studied ego states, identified by self-given names. Each subject was hypnotized, the left hand was placed in ice water, and he/she was asked to keep it there as long as possible. Immersion time was noted.

Then the subject was hypnotized, the right hand was made analgesic to pain posthypnotically, and thrust into the ice water with the same suggestions. It was removed only after the subject had left it there for at least five times as long a period as he had the left hand. The hidden observer was activated using the same verbalizations as reported by Hilgard. When the now hypnotized patient indicated (by a finger signal) that the pain was felt by some "part" at some level, we asked to talk to that "part." One or more of the ego states with which we had dealt a year earlier emerged, often complaining of the pain.

The experiment was repeated using hypnotic deafness. The results were similar. Hidden observers proved to be previously studied ego states. Certain ones of them responded to the pain study, certain ones responded to the deafness study, and some to both. Some ego states that we had seen a year earlier responded to neither, and in several cases entirely new ego states emerged. However, the general thesis that hidden observers are the same covert cognitive structural systems as ego states was supported.

When considering the many forms that altered states of consciousness take, we are constantly reminded of the fact that the abnormal may only be normal processes carried to an extreme degree. Their original aim was defensive adaptation to threatening circumstances and to enhance life. The more we learn about the human mind, the more questions we can answer about its functioning, the greater becomes our wonderment at its complexity—and the more new questions arise that impel us to seek further answers. Altered states of consciousness are among nature's most fascinating enigmas.

REFERENCES

Barber, T. X. *Hypnosis: A scientific approach.* New York: Van Nostrand Reinhold, 1969.

Barber, T. X. Suggested ("hypnotic") behavior: The trance paradigm versus an alternative paradigm. Chap. 8 in E. Fromm and R. E. Shor (Eds.), *Hypnosis: Developments in research and new perspectives.* New York: Aldine, 1979.

Bernheim, H. *Hypnosis and suggestion in psychotherapy.* New Hyde Park, N.Y.: University Books, 1964. (Originally published in 1886 under the title *Suggestive therapeutics.*)

Blum, G. S. and Graef, J. R. The detection over time of subjects simulating hypnosis. *International Journal of Clinical and Experimental Hypnosis,* 1971, *19,* 211–224.

Blum, G. S., Geiwitz, P. J. and Stewart, C. G. Cognitive arousal: The evolution of a model. *Journal of Personality and Social Psychology,* 1967, *5,* 138–151.

Braid, J. *Braid on hypnotism: The beginning of modern hypnosis* (rev. ed. by A. E. Waite). New York: Julian Press, 1960.

Bramwell, J. M. *Hypnosis: Its history, practice and theory.* New York: The Institute for Research in Hypnosis and the Julian Press, 1956. (Originally published in 1903 by Grant Richards, England.)

Conn, J. H. Cultural and clinical aspects of suggestion. *International Journal of Clinical and Experimental Hypnosis,* 1959, *7,* 175–185.

Conn, J. H. Is hypnosis really dangerous? *International Journal of Clinical and Experimental Hypnosis,* 1972, *20,* 61–79.

Crasilneck, H. B. and Hall, J. A. *Clinical hypnosis: Principles and applications.* New York: Grune & Stratton, 2nd ed. 1985.

Edelstien, M. G. *Trauma, trance, and transformation: A clinical guide to therapy.* New York: Brunner/Mazel, 1981.

Eiblmayr, K. An examination of the phenomenon of trance logic using objective measurement and limiting the hypnotist/subject relationship. Unpublished master's thesis, Missoula, Mont.: University of Montana, 1980.

Evans, F. J. Hypnosis and sleep: Techniques for exploring cognitive activity during sleep. Chap. 6 in E. Fromm and R. E. Shor (Eds.), *Hypnosis: Developments in research and new perspectives.* New York: Aldine, 1979, pp. 139–193.

Federn, P. *Ego psychology and the pschoses,* E Weiss (Ed.). New York: Basic Books, 1952.

Ferenczi, S. *Further contributions to the theory and technique of psychoanalysis.* London: Hogarth, 1926.

Gill, M. M. and Brenman, M. *Hypnosis and related states.* New York: International Universities Press, 1959.

Hebb, D. O. Science and the world of imagination. *Canadian Psychological Review,* 1975, *16,* 4–11.

Hilgard, E. R. *Divided consciousness: Multiple controls in human thought and actions.* New York: Wiley, 1977.

Hilgard, E. R. and Hilgard, J. R. *Hypnosis in the relief of pain.* Los Altos, Calif.: William Kaufmann, 1975.

Hilgard, E. R. and Loftus, E. F. Effective interrogation of the eyewitness. *International Journal of Clinical and Experimental Hypnosis,* 1979, *27,* 342–357.

Janet, P. *The major symptoms of hysteria.* New York: Macmillan, 1907.

Kline, M. V. *Freud and hypnosis: The interaction of psychodynamics and hypnosis.* New York: Julian Press, 1958.

Kline, M. V. The production of antisocial behavior through hypnosis: New clinical data. *International Journal of Clinical and Experimental Hypnosis,* 1972, *20,* 80–81.

Kroger, W. S. *Clinical and experimental hypnosis,* 2d ed. Philadelphia: Lippincott, 1977.

Liebeault, A. *Du sommeil et des états analogues considérés surtout au point de vue de l'action moral sur le physique.* Vienna: Deuticke, 1892.

Ludwig, A. M. Altered states of consciousness. In C. T. Tart (Ed.), *Altered states of consciousness.* New York: Wiley, 1969, pp. 9–22.

Meares, A. *A system of medical hypnosis.* Philadelphia: Saunders, 1961.

Orne, M. T. The nature of hypnosis: Artifact and essence. *Journal of Abnormal and Social Psychology,* 1959, *58,* 277–299.

Orne, M. T. Can a hypnotized subject be compelled to carry out otherwise unacceptable behavior? A discussion. *International Journal of Clinical and Experimental Hypnosis,* 1972, *20,* 101–117.

Orne, M. T. On the simulating subject as a quasi-control group in hypnosis research: What, why, and how. Chap. 16 in E. Fromm and R. E. Shor (Eds.), *Hypnosis: Developments in research and new perspectives.* New York: Aldine, 1979, pp. 518–565.

Orne, M. T., Dinges, D. F., and Orne, E. C. On the differential diagnosis of multiple personality in the forensic context. *International Journal of Clinical and Experimental Hypnosis,* 1984, *32,* 118–169.

Pavlov, I. P. The identity of inhibition with sleep and hypnosis. *Scientific Monthly,* 1923, *17,* 603–608.

Prince, M. *The dissociation of a personality.* New York: Longmans-Green, 1906.

Putnam, W. H. Hypnosis and distortions in eyewitness memory. *International Journal of Clinical and Experimental Hypnosis.* 1979, *27,* 437–448.

Reik, T. *Listening with the third ear.* New York: Farrar, 1948.

Sarbin, T. R. and Coe, W. C. *Hypnosis: A social psychological analysis of influence communication.* New York: Holt, Rinehart & Winston, 1972.

Schneck, J. M. *Hypnosis in modern medicine.* Springfield, Ill.: Thomas, 1963.

Schreiber, F. R. *Sybil.* New York: Warner Paperback Library, 1974.

Shor, R. E. Three dimensions of hypnotic depth. *International Journal of Clinical and Experimental Hypnosis,* 1962, *10,* 23–38.

Shor, R. E. A phenomenological method for the measurement of variables important to an understanding of the nature of hypnosis. In E. Fromm and R. E. Shor (Eds.), *Hypnosis: Developments in research and new perspectives.* Chicago: Aldine, 1979, pp. 105–135.

Shor, R. E. and Orne, E. C. *The Harvard Group Scale of Hypnotic Susceptibility, Form A.* Palo Alto, Calif.: Consulting Psychologists Press, 1962.

Spanos, N. P. and Hewitt, E. C. The hidden observer in hypnotic analgesia: Discovery or experimental creation? *Journal of Personality and Social Psychology,* 1980, *39,* 1201–1214.

Sturm, C. Eyewitness memory: A comparison of guided memory and hypnotic hypermnesia techniques. Unpublished doctoral dissertation, University of Montana, 1982.

Tart, C. T. (Ed.). *Altered states of consciousness: A book of readings.* New York: Wiley, 1969.

Tart, C. T. Measuring the depth of an altered state of consciousness with particular reference to self-report scales of hypnotic depth. In E. Fromm and R. E. Shor (Eds.), *Hypnosis: Research developments and perspectives.* Chicago: Aldine, 1972.

Thigpen, C. H. and Cleckley, H. M. *Three faces of Eve.* New York: McGraw-Hill, 1957.

Watkins, H. H. Ego-state therapy. Chap. 22 in J. Watkins (Ed.), *The therapeutic self.* New York: Human Sciences Press, 1978.

Watkins, H. H. Ego-state theory and therapy. In R. Corsini (Ed.), *Encyclopedia of psychology.* New York: Wiley, 1984, Vol. 1, pp. 420–421.

Watkins, J. G. Trance and transference. *Journal of Clinical and Experimental Hypnosis.* 1954, *2,* 284–290.

Watkins, J. G. Transference aspects of the hypnotic relationship. Chap. 1 in M. V. Kline (Ed.), *Clinical correlations of experimental hypnosis.* Springfield, Ill.: Thomas, 1963.

Watkins, J. G. Antisocial behavior under hypnosis: Possible or impossible? *International Journal of Clinical and Experimental Hypnosis,* 1972, *20,* 95–100.

Watkins, J. G. *The therapeutic self.* New York: Human Sciences Press, 1978.

Watkins, J. G. The Bianchi (Los Angeles "Hillside Strangler") case: Sociopath or multiple personality. *International Journal of Clinical and Experimental Hypnosis,* 1984, *32,* 67–101.

Watkins, J. G. *Clinical hypnosis: Vol. I. Hypnotherapeutic technique.* New York: Irvington Publishers (in press 1985).

Watkins, J. G. and Johnson, R. J. *We, the divided self.* New York: Irvington Publishers, 1982.

Watkins, J. G. and Watkins, H. H. The theory and practice of ego-state therapy. In H. Grayson (Ed.), *Short term approaches to psychotherapy.* New York: National Institute for the Psychotherapies and Human Sciences Press, 1979.

Watkins, J. G. and Watkins, H. H. Ego states and hidden observers. *Journal of Altered States of Consciousness,* 1979–1980, *5,* 3–18.

Watkins, J. G. and Watkins, H. H. *I. Ego states and hidden observers. II. Ego-state therapy: The woman in black and the lady in white* (audio tape and transcript). New York: Jeffrey Norton, 1980.

Watkins, J. G. and Watkins, H. H. Ego-state therapy. In R. J. Corsini (Ed.), *Handbook of innovative psychotherapies.* New York: Wiley, 1981, pp. 252–270.

Watkins, J. G. and Watkins, H. H. Ego-state therapy. In L. E. Abt and I. R. Stuart (Eds.), *The newer therapies: A sourcebook.* New York: Van Nostrand Reinhold, 1982.

Weitzenhoffer, A. M. and Hilgard, E. R. *Stanford Hypnotic Susceptibility Scale, Forms A & B.* Palo Alto, Calif.: Consulting Psychologists Press, 1959.

Wolpe, J. The systematic desensitization of neuroses. *Journal of Nervous and Mental Disease,* 1961, *132,* 189–203.

6. Lucid Dreaming

Stephen LaBerge and Jayne Gackenbach

"Lucid dreaming," as the phenomenon of dreaming while knowing that one is dreaming is commonly termed, is arguably one of the most remarkable states of consciousness a normal person is likely to experience. The case for this assertion can be seen by considering that the lucid dreamer can apparently be in full possession of his or her waking faculties (this is the meaning of "lucid") being able to " . . . reason clearly, remember freely, and act volitionally upon reflection, all while continuing to dream vividly" (LaBerge, 1980a). Both lucid dreamers' subjective reports and the physiological evidence to be reviewed below indicate that these experiences take place during sound sleep. Taken together, these facts make lucid dreaming seem something of a paradox: while lucid dreamers are fully asleep to the external reality of the physical world, they are at the same time fully awake to the inner reality of their dream worlds.

We deal here with four general areas: first, with a descriptive phenomenology of the lucid dream itself; second, with individual differences and general charcteristics of frequent lucid dreamers; third, with physiological aspects of the phenomenon; and fourth, with some of the applications and implications of lucid dreaming for research on altered states of consciousness.

THE PHENOMENOLOGY OF LUCID DREAMING

Let the experience speak for itself; here are three lucid dream reports:

> I am crossing a bridge over an abyss. When I look into the depths I am afraid to continue. My companion, behind me, says, "You know, you

don't *have* to go this way. You can go back the way you came," and points back down an immense distance. But then it occurs to me that if I became lucid I would not need to fear the height. As I realize that I *am* dreaming, I'm able to master my fear—I cross the bridge and awaken. (LaBerge, 1981)

In the dream, she was informed that she could choose either to have intercourse with a fantastic dream lover and be strangled by him afterward, or never to have sex again. Her growing desire for a life lived to the full rather than a living death led her to choose the former, and as she was being led into the arena she suddenly became lucid. Instead of waking herself up or changing the scene, she decided to trick them all and go along with the game; and as she laughed to herself as how she would get up and walk away at the end, the environment expanded, the colors deepened, and she was high. Then the scene changed and she found herself flying in an extraordinarily high state, going through walls and windows without difficulty, and although she had been looking forward to the sex, now her deprivation did not seem to matter because she was enjoying other even more exhilarating experiences. (Faraday, 1974, p. 339)

[During a lucid dream] eventually we left the carnival and fire behind us and came to a yellow path, leading across a desolate moor. As we stood at the foot of this path it suddenly rose up before us and became a roadway of golden light stretching from earth to zenith.

Now in this amber-tinted shining haze there appeared countless coloured forms of men and beasts, representing man's upward evolution through different stages of civilization. These forms faded away; the pathway lost its golden tint and became a mass of vibrating circles of globules (like frog's eggs), a purplish-blue in colour. These in their turn changed to "peacock's eyes"; and then suddenly there came a culminating vision of a gigantic peacock, whose outspread tail filled the heavens. I exclaimed to my wife, "The Vision of the Universal Peacock!" Moved by the splendor of the sight, I recite in a loud voice a mantra. Then the dream ended. (Fox, 1962, p. 90)

The three very different accounts just quoted above illustrate something of the diversity of form and content shown by lucid dreams. Although lucid dreams can differ in particulars as much as lucid dreamers, they nevertheless possess a variety of common features allowing for a degree of generalization regarding what happens in them. Let us first consider how the lucid dreaming state of consciousness is initiated and terminated.

Initiations

The lucid dreamer can be metaphorically viewed as a compound composed of two constituents, dreaming and lucid consciousness (LaBerge, 1980b). The lucid dreaming state can therefore, in principle, be initiated in two general ways: either when the person is already dreaming and lucidity is added, or when the person is already conscious and dreaming is added. In the two cases, the initial states are respectively ordinary, nonlucid dreaming and vigilant wakefulness.

In what is by all accounts (cf. LaBerge, 1980b) the most common form of lucid dream initiation, the dreamer realizes in some way during an on-going dream that he or she is dreaming. One of the ways in which this typically happens involves the perception of inconsistencies in dream content *as anomalous,* followed by the critical recognition that the explanation for the bizarre events is that *it is all a dream.*

Anomalous dream content is not in most cases fully recognized as such. Depending upon the degree to which reality is tested, the dreamer will attain corresponding degrees of lucidity. Fox (1962) believed critical thinking to be the key to lucid dreaming and has provided an unexcelled account of the range of reality testing and perception of anomaly that may occur:

Let us suppose, for example, that in my dream I am in a cafe. At a table near mine is a lady who would be very attractive—only, she has four eyes. Here are some illustrations of those degrees of activity of the critical faculty.

1. In the dream it is practically dormant, but on waking I have the feeling that there was something peculiar about this lady. Suddenly I get it—"Why, of course, she had four eyes!"

2. In the dream I exhibit mild surprise and say, "How curious, that girl has four eyes! It spoils her." But only in the same way that I might remark, "What a pity she has broken her nose! I wonder how she did it."

3. The critical faculty is more awake and the four eyes are regarded as abnormal; but the phenomenon is not fully appreciated. I exclaim "Good Lord!" and then reassure myself by adding, "There must be a freak show or a circus in the town." Thus I hover on the brink of realization, but do not quite get there.

4. My critical faculty is now fully awake and fully refuses to be satisfied by this explanation. I continue my train of thought, "But there never was such a freak! An adult with four eyes—it's *impossible.* I am dreaming." (p. 35)

As a result of inadequate reality testing, a dreamer for whom the question arises as to whether or not he is dreaming, will sometimes mistakenly decide that he is in fact awake and *not* dreaming as in Fox's third example above. A dream in which the dreamer has at one point raised this question without arriving at the correct conclusion is commonly termed "pre-lucid" (Green, 1968).

Dreamers who suspect that they could be dreaming may test their state in a variety of ways. However, few of these tests are reliably effective in distinguishing dreaming from waking. For example, pre-lucid dreamers too often conclude that they could not possibly be dreaming because everything seems so solid and vividly real. Or they may pinch themselves, following along with the classical test. This most often has the result not of awakening the dreamer, but of merely producing the convincing sensation of a pinch and the mistaken conviction that he or she is awake.

A better test used by many lucid dreamers seems to be trying to fly (Brown, 1936). Attempted reading may be a still more reliable test. LaBerge (1985) reports that some degree of dyslexia is extremely characteristic of lucid dreams (see also Moers-Messmer, 1939, and discussion below). LaBerge (ibid.) has argued that dreams are more readily distinguishable from waking perceptions on the basis of the relative instability of dream content rather than any necessary differences in vividness. But the last word in reality testing has been provided by McCreery (1973), who pointed out that while awake we almost never doubt whether we are awake or not. Therefore, whenever we find ourselves wondering whether or not we are dreaming, we probably are.

Returning to the content accompanying the emergence of lucidity, it was formerly thought that in the general population lucidity was most likely to emerge as a result of a nightmare or anxiety dream (Green, 1968). However, recent research has shown that although this occurs, it is not the most frequently reported reason (LaBerge, 1980b; Hearne, 1983; Gackenbach, 1978, 1982). Hearne (1983) noted that the majority (53%) of his adult sample cited dream inconsistencies, such as seeing people whom the dreamer knows to be dead, as the apparent cause of lucidity. In contrast, only 19 percent of the more than 300 students in Gackenbach's (1982) sample reported their lucid dreams were due to inconsistencies. In an adult sample, Gackenbach (1978) found that dream inconsistency the least likely way in which individuals reported attaining lucidity.

According to Gackenbach (1978, 1982), the reason most often reported by both her samples as the cause of lucidity was a sense of the "dream-likeness" of the dream. The precise meaning of such reports is problematic. One might suspect that subjects describing the cause of their lucidity in such global terms are just being vague. Perhaps they did not notice or forgot exactly which features of their dreams made them seem "dreamlike." It seems reasonable to suppose that these anomalies were the actual descriminative stimuli. It may be that what causes some lucid dreams to be attributed to perception of the "dreamlikeness" and others to be attributed to recognition of incongruities is cognitive differences in the lucid dreamers. These could perhaps be explained by reference to the familiar division of mental processes into two levels: preattentive process versus focal attention (Neisser, 1967). The study of individual cognitive differences in relation to these two styles of lucidity initiation would seem a productive direction for future research.

Gackenbach (1982) has reported content and situational differences accompanying lucid dreams initiated in the three ways just described. The day before nightmare-initiated lucids, subjects reported more depressed feelings and more hostile feelings, feelings of lack of attention, and insecure feelings than on days before lucid dreams that were initiated by the dreamlike quality of the dream. Likewise, on the day after these two types of lucid dreams, nightmare-initiated lucid dreams were followed by more anxiety, hostility, depression, insecurity, and lack of attention than dreamlike-initiated lucids. Not surprisingly, nightmare-initiated lucids were viewed as having fewer positive and more negative emotions than dreamlike-initiated lucids. Finally, lucid nightmares were reported as having less of a sense of dream control than the dreamlike lucids. Incongruent-element-initiated lucid dreams were similar to both other types. For instance, incongruent lucids were reported as having as much positive emotion as nightmare-initiated lucids, but significantly less negative emotion than lucid nightmares. In sum, dreamlike-initiated lucids represent the most experientially positive lucid dream experience. They are preceded by "good days" and result in the same.

In factor analytic work with her adult sample, Gackenbach (1978) reported that lucid dreams emerging from nightmares were loaded with experiencing lucidity as a child. This supports the notion that children most typically learn lucid dreaming as a means of coping with nightmares (LaBerge, 1985). The other two dream causes of lucidity (i.e., dreamlikeness and incongruence) were loaded with dream lucidity occurring directly upon awakening or upon falling back to sleep after having awakened in the morning.

In summary, the three major ways dreamers recognize they are dreaming are: (1) perception and rational interpretation of inconsistencies; (2) emotional arousal, especially anxiety; and (3) direct recognition of the dreamlike nature of the experience. It should be unnecessary to add that although these are the most frequent triggers of consciousness during the dream state, they are not the only ones (see LaBerge, 1980b; Gackenbach and LaBerge, in press). Moreover, dream consciousness can also arise from the waking state, which brings us to the other general class of lucid dream initiations—those beginning in wakefulness rather than in sleep.

It is possible to maintain continuous reflective consciousness while falling asleep and hence to enter a lucid dream directly from the waking state. It seems that this mode of entry to the lucid dream state is a skill that improves with motivation (LaBerge, 1980b) and also with practice. Indeed, its cultivation was described hundreds of years ago by Tibetan yogis (Evans-Wentz, 1960) and more recently by a number of others (Ouspensky, 1931; Rapport, 1948; Rajneesh, 1974; Tulku, 1978; LaBerge, 1980a, 1985; Tholey, 1983).

Most mental techniques claiming to enhance the frequency of lucid dreaming are pre-sleep exercises aimed at developing appropriate cognitive sets that it is hoped will persist into the dream state and there favor the emergence of the critical attitude of lucid consciousness. For example, it is frequently recommended (Narayana, 1922; Evans-Wentz, 1960; Rajneesh, 1974; Tulku, 1978; Malamud, 1980; Tholey, 1983; LaBerge, 1985) that would-be lucid dreamers ask themselves during the day, "Is this a dream?" All agree that this should be practiced as often as possible: indeed, Rajneesh (1974) specifies doing this "for three weeks continuously!" The basis of this method is, of course, that following sufficient daily practice, habit will carry the tendency to ask the critical question over into our dreams.

The other major class of mental techniques for inducing lucid dreams focuses on intention. For example, the classical Tibetan instruction manual for the Yoga of the dream-state (Evans-Wentz, 1960) exhorts the would-be lucid dreamer to "firmly resolve to comprehend the dream state," making no fewer than twenty-one efforts each morning. The importance of intention is insisted upon by most writers (e.g., Narayana, 1922; Garfield, 1974a, 1979; LaBerge, 1980a,b, 1985), although not all (e.g., Tholey, 1983). Others sometimes suggest a form of paradoxical intention such as Sparrow's (1976) claim that meditation in the early morning hours frequently resulted in lucid dreams during subsequent sleep as long as he was careful not to meditate for the specific purpose of having lucid dreams. Others have also suggested that meditation favors lucid dreaming (Banquet, 1973; Reed, 1978; McLeod and Hunt, 1983). In a related approach, Ogilvie et al. (1982) reported alpha feedback training prior to sleep onset was without effect on subsequent lucid dreaming frequency.

Garfield tested an autosuggestion method (1974a) over an eight-month period, reporting that she obtained a "classical learning curve, increasing the frequency of prolonged lucid dreams from a baseline of zero to a high of three per week" (1975). During the first nine months of her study, she had only four lucid dreams (1974b), which illustrates the necessity of patience at the outset. At last report, after five or six years of practicing autosuggestion, Garfield was having an average of four to five lucid dreams per month (1979, p. 120).

LaBerge (1980a,b) undertook a personal study investigating whether it was possible to learn to dream lucidly at will. Starting with an autosuggestion method similar to Garfield's (1974b), over the course of three years LaBerge recorded a total of 389 lucid dreams and developed a mnemonic method for the induction of lucid dreams (MILD), with which he was able to volitionally induce lucid dreams. He reported that MILD yielded eighteen to twenty-six lucid dreams per month, with as many as four in a single night. Although the efficiency of MILD has been clearly demonstrated for a single subject, we have as yet little definitive information on how effective it is for others. LaBerge (1980b) suggested that the two essential requirements for learning the technique were high motivation and excellent dream recall (i.e., two or three dreams per night). Tholey (1983) has described a similar method, as well as a "combined technique" borrowing elements from most of the preceding procedures. Although Tholey reports this combination to be most effective, he provides no supporting evidence in the form of quantitative data allowing statistical evaluation of the performance of any of these approaches. This criticism unfortunately also applies to most other accounts of techniques put forward as facilitating lucid dreaming.

Hypnosis is another promising but little-researched approach to lucid dream induction (LaBerge, 1980a). Tart (1979) has also reported pilot data indicating "that posthypnotic suggestions may have some potential in inducing lucid dreaming." Relatedly, Dane (1984) found high hypnotic susceptibility to facilitate successful induction of lucid dreams while using MILD (LaBerge, 1980b). Another major approach to lucid dream induction is based on the idea of providing an external cue to remind a dreamer that he or she is dreaming. A number of efforts to put this idea into practice have been attempted with various degrees of limited success. Most studies have utilized auditory cues (LaBerge, 1980a; LaBerge et al., 1981c; Ogilvie et al., 1983; Tholey, 1983), while the remainder have focused on tactile stimuli (Hearne, 1983; Tholey, 1983).

How effective are these various methods of external cuing? The most data is available on the study taking the most direct approach: testing whether a direct verbal suggestion (i.e., "this is a dream") applied to a prepared subject during REM could be used to induce lucidity. A pilot study by LaBerge (1980a) yielded promising results, suggesting the feasibility of such a technique. Thus encouraged, LaBerge, Owens, Nagel, and Dement (1981) recorded four subjects (two experienced lucid dreamers and two inexperienced) for one to two nights each. A tape recording repeating the phrase "this is a dream" was played at gradually increasing volume, 5 to

10 minutes after the beginning of each REM period. The subjects were instructed to signal by means of a pair of left and right eye movements whenever they heard the tape or realized they were dreaming. The technician turned off the tape recorder immediately upon observing this eye movement signal on the polygraph. LaBerge et al. reported that the tape stimulus was applied fifteen times, producing lucidity in 33 percent of the cases, although not all of these lucid dreams lasted more than a few seconds.

In a similar study, Ogilvie et al. (1983) used a buzzer to cue lucid dreamers after 15 minutes of REM sleep from epochs with high or low alpha activity. Subjects were to signal immediately after the cue and 30 seconds later if in a lucid dream; 30 to 60 seconds later, they were awakened to allow dream reports to be collected. The thirty-one cue applications apparently resulted in six persistent lucid dreams (20%) with no difference in number between the two alpha conditions.

In a tactile variation on the REM reminder theme, Hearne (1983) tested the effectiveness of electric shocks to the wrist. Of fifteen female subjects who spent one night each in the sleep laboratory, six had lucid dreams stimulated by this method. Hearne does not report the total number of cue applications, making evaluation difficult. Other studies have reported this procedure to be relatively ineffective (Hearne, 1978; Venus, 1982).

Having dealt with techniques aimed at intentionally inducing lucid dreams, let us ask whether or not there are any pre-sleep activities or circumstances that favor the occurrence of spontaneous lucid dreams. Both Garfield (1975) and Hearne (1978) reported that lucid dreams occur most frequently on nights following days of high-level arousal and activity. Although Gackenbach (1978) was unable to demonstrate such a relationship, in a more comprehensive follow-up study, she found that both women and men were more likely to have lucid dreams on nights following unpleasant social interactions (Gackenbach, Curren, and Cutler, 1983). Additionally, pre-sleep negative emotions favored lucid dreaming for women only; while for men only, high activity was favorable. Faraday (1974) believed her own lucid dreams to result from "an actual coming together of head and heart somewhere in waking life during the course of the day" (p. 57). A variety of other waking activities, especially during the night or early morning have been said to promote lucid dreaming. Sparrow (1976), as mentioned above, reported that early morning meditation favors lucid dreaming. Garfield (1975), on the other hand, wrote that "sexual intercourse in the middle of the night was often followed by a lucid dream." LaBerge cites anecdotal evidence implicating early morning reading, writing, or even being sick in the middle of the night, concluding that "the diversity of the proposed activities suggests that it is not the particular activity, but the alert wakefulness that facilitates lucid dreaming during subsequent sleep" (1980b).

A final factor affecting lucid dreaming frequency is the extent to which a person is familiar with what is dreamlike about his or her dreams. The more intimately one knows the typical idiosyncracies of one's dreams, the more easily will they be recognized as dreams. This probably partially accounts for the positive correlations between lucid dreaming and high overall dream recall (Belicki et al., 1978; Gackenbach, 1978). As part of his lucidity training programs, LaBerge (1985) has students classify the anomalies occurring in the content of their own dreams to develop this useful skill. Malamud (1980) has extensively developed a similar approach; see her Chapter 19 (this book) for details. This completes our survey of how lucid dreams are initiated; having dealt with how they begin, let us now turn to how they end.

Terminations

Returning to the concept described above, treating the lucid dream as a compound of lucidity and the dream state, just as there were in principle two ways of initiating it, likewise there are two general possibilities for terminating it. Either lucidity is lost while the dream continues, or the dream ends with an awakening, with a degree of lucidity presumably remaining.

The first mode of termination is probably the more common in less experienced lucid dreamers. Neophytes are more likely to lose their lucidity, once they have it. Accordingly, after having become at least momentarily lucid, the inexperienced dreamer will frequently become reabsorbed by the dream, forgetting that it is a dream and continuing to dream nonlucidly. This forgetfulness can be countered by repeating to oneself "this is a dream" while dreaming, just as we use speech to organize behavior during the early stages of learning. However, later such talk is unnecessary. For more experienced lucid dreamers, the second mode of termination, awakening, becomes more common than the loss of lucidity characteristic of beginners. For example, LaBerge (1980b) reported that in his own case, lucidity was lost in at least 18 percent of the lucid dreams he recorded during the first year of his study; during the next two years, he retained lucidity until awakening in 99 percent of his lucid dreams.

There are two other possible forms of lucid dream termination, involving the loss of lucidity. One possibility is that the lucid dreamer might enter non-REM sleep, thereby losing lucidity and perhaps also dreaming. If awakened at this point, he would likely recall nothing of the lucid dream. In the other case in which lucidity is lost, the dreamer *dreams* that he or she has awakened.

Since the lucid dream state is normally terminated by an awakening, when a lucid dream begins to fade, it is natural to expect an awakening. Often, however, this expectation is not fulfilled in actuality, but by a dream of awakening. "False awakenings," as these dreams are usually called (Green, 1968), are very commonly reported concomitants of lucid dreams. Although false awakenings are also reported following nonlucid dreams, the phenomenon appears to be much more frequently associated with lucid dreams, probably because only while we are lucid does the question of being awake or asleep normally arise. Moreover, false awakenings seem to occur more frequently in experienced lucid dreamers than in inexperienced ones. LaBerge (1980b) reported them in only 16 percent of his first year's record of lucid dreams, but in 30 to 40 percent of those in the next three years. This trend may be accounted for by the fact that the more lucid dreams a person experiences, the more he or she associates awakening with the lucid dream fading and thus more strongly expects to awaken. If the profound influence of expectations on dream content is not already obvious, it will be after the next section.

Expectation: Its Impact on Dream Content

The assumptions—conscious or unconscious—that dreamers hold about what lucid dreams are like or could be like determine to a remarkable extent the precise form taken by their lucid dreams. As influential as expectations may be in the waking world, it is readily seen that they play an even more significant role in the dream world. After all, in the physical world there are biological limitations built into our bodies, to say nothing of the constraints we know as the laws of physics. In the dream world, however, these laws are followed merely by convention, if at all. There is no gravity in dreams, but thinking makes it so. It is true that there appear to be "laws of physiology" that constrain a lucid dreamer's action, deriving from functional limitations of the human brain. However, these restraints are far fewer than those imposed by physical law, which leaves more room for psychological influences such as assumptions to play a limiting role. The degree to which expectations influence the experience of a particular dreamer is vividly illustrated by the following examples.

The philosopher Ouspensky assumed on theoretical grounds that "man cannot in sleep think about himself *unless the thought is itself a dream*" (1931). From this premise, he reasoned that "a man can never pronounce his own name in sleep." It should therefore come as no surprise that Ouspensky reported "as expected" that when he pronounced his name during a lucid dream, he immediately woke up.

A generation later, Green (1968, p. 85) described the experiences of a lucid dreamer ("Subject C") who, having heard of the philosopher's account, decided to test the effect of repeating her own name during a lucid dream. "C" reported that when a suitable occasion presented itself during a lucid dream, she "thought of Ouspensky's criterion of repeating one's own name," and explained that she achieved "a sort of gap-in-consciousness"—whatever that may mean. She explained that the effort seemed to make her "giddy"; in any case, she stopped.

In 1974, Garfield recounted a lucid dream of her own bearing precisely on this issue: she had given this dream the title, "Carving My Name," and "proceeded to do just that on the door where [she] was already carving." When she read what she had just written, the entire fabric of the dream "vibrated and thundered," and she awoke. Garfield, who was familiar with both Ouspensky's and Subject C's experiences, concluded from this that while it is "not impossible" to pronounce one's own name in a lucid dream, " . . . it *is* disruptive" (1974a, p. 143). LaBerge (1980a) wrote that when he read Ouspensky's account, he neither followed the philosopher's reasoning nor accepted his original premise about thinking in dreams. Consequently, he could see no reason why saying his name while dreaming should present any difficulty at all. He reported that trying to pronounce his name in a lucid dream resulted in nothing more than hearing his own voice. The conclusion would seem to be that the dream experiences of Ouspensky, Subject C, and Garfield were all the effects of self-fulfilling prophecy.

One more illustration of the effect of assumptions on the content of lucid dreams should be enough to prove the case. McCreery's "Subject E," in speaking of the emotional quality of her lucid dreams, declared that "realization that one is dreaming brings a wonderful sense of freedom—freedom to try anything in the extended range of experience" (1973, p. 114). The Englishwoman added that "The nature of lucid dream experience may range up to the mystical, whilst *there seems to be an inherent resistance to anything erotic*" (ibid.).

Garfield's (1979) experiences present a striking contrast. She reported that two-thirds of her lucid dreams are accompanied by sexual arousal, of which half culminate "in an orgasmic burst." She writes that "my own experience convinces me that conscious dreaming *is* orgasmic," and adds that "too many of my students have reported similar ecstatic experiences during lucid dreams to attribute the phenomena to my individual peculiarity." For Garfield, "*Orgasm is a natural part of lucid dreaming*" (ibid., p. 44).

However, as to the question of whether lucid dreaming is "naturally" erotic or the opposite, before answering we must ask "for whom?"

The assumptions that the dreamer makes about what can happen during a lucid dream may wholly or in part determine what *does* happen. As a corollary of this, individual differences may be very significant in the phenomenology of lucid dreaming.

Having considered the beginnings and endings of lucid dreams, as well as certain factors contributing to their general form, we are now ready to deal with the lucid dream itself—including sensory, perceptual, emotional, and cognitive characteristics of this class of experiences.

Sensations and Perceptions

A wide range of approaches to the question of whether lucid and nonlucid dreams differ in reported sensory and perceptual content have been undertaken. The preeminent waking sensory modality is vision, and its representativeness in lucid–nonlucid dreams has been examined from four perspectives: general vision, color, brightness, and clarity of imagery. In the morning-after dream reports, subjects rated their lucid dreams as more visual than their nonlucid dreams (Gackenbach and Schillig, 1983). However, in two later studies controlling for dream recall, no dream difference in vision emerged. Long-term recall (i.e., by questionnaires) evidenced the opposite, that is, nonlucid dreams as more visual than lucid dreams (ibid.). Lucid dreams were seen as more colorful than nonlucid dreams by Gackenbach and Schillig (ibid.) and Gackenbach, Curren, LaBerge, Davidson, and Maxwell (1983) in morning-after reports, but less colorful as ascertained by long-term recall (Gackenbach and Schillig, 1983). No differences were noted by Gackenbach, Curren, and Cutler (1983).

As regards brightness, Hearne (1978) reports no difference from prior to lucidity to after its onset in one adept subject, and elsewhere (1981) argues for a brightness ceiling. Worsley (1982) points out that the difficulty in turning on a light switch in lucid dreams and thereby elevating the brightness levels may be due to problems with functioning in different modalities and not with a brightness ceiling per se. Relatedly, Gackenbach and Schillig (1983) found that subjects report the presence of a bright or salient light more often in vivid nonlucid dreams than in lucid dreams.

The second major sensory modality in dreams is that of audition, and here lucid dream reports have been generally found to mention auditory experiences more frequently than nonlucid dream reports (Hearne, 1983; Gackenbach, Curren, and Cutler, 1983; Gackenbach and Schillig, 1983). Worsley (1983) notes that although he could easily hear a radio while lucid, he could make no sense of it. This apparent contradiction will be covered in the cognitive section.

Minor sensations such as taste, smell, kinesthesia, touch, pain, and temperature have also been investigated. Taste and smell have generally exhibited no dream-type differences in morning-after reports (Gackenbach, Curren, and Cutler, 1983; Gackenbach and Shillig, 1983). Likewise, these two surveys reported pain as being noted more frequently in nonlucid dreams. No dream differences have been noted as regards temperature (Gackenbach, personal communication, 1980; Gackenbach and Schillig, 1983). Lucid dreams have been found most often to include body sensations such as touch and kinesthesia (Gilmore, 1983; Gackenbach, Curren, and Cutler, 1983; Gackenbach and Schillig, 1983) although a lack of a difference (Gackenbach and Shillig, 1983) has also been reported.

Emotions

Lucid dreams have historically been described as eliciting strong emotions (Green, 1968), which more recent survey data continue to support. Although lucid dreams appear to be generally characterized by positive affect, negative emotion is also intensified (Gackenbach and Schillig, 1983). The initiation of lucidity is frequently accompanied by very positive emotions, as the following sample of quotations should make clear. For Rapport (1948), the emergence of lucidity "instantly" transformed his dream into incommunicably beautiful vision. For Faraday (1974) "immediately the light became almost supernaturally intense . . . space seemed expanded and deeper, just as it does under psychedelic drugs." Similarly, for Yram (1967), " . . . the transformation was instantaneous. As if under a magic spell I suddenly became as clear headed as in the best moments of my physical life." In even more extravagant terms, Fox (1962) described the onset of his first experience of lucidity: "instantly, the vividness of life increased a hundredfold . . . never had I felt so absolutely well, so clear brained, so divinely powerful, so inexpressibly *free*!"

Cognitions

As with sensory and perceptual components of lucid dreams, the cognitive components have been investigated from multiple perspectives and with many techniques. The memory of waking life during the lucid dream, clarity of thought, dream control, and ability to do experiments in the lucid dream state are highly interrelated. To perform lucid dream experiments, the dreamer needs a clear dream mind in order to be able to remember and execute the intended task. Gackenbach (1978) reported that lucid dreamers, of varying frequencies, felt that their memory of waking life was on the average clearer than other dreams but still a dream memory.

Dream control has repeatedly been demonstrated to be higher in the lucid dream than in the nonlucid dream. This has been found by questionnaire (Gackenbach and Schillig, 1983; Hearne, 1983), by self-evaluation of individual dreams while keeping a dream journal (Gackenbach, Curren, and Cutler, 1983; Hearne, 1978), and through content analysis by independent judges of dream transcripts (Gackenbach, personal communication, 1985.)

The relative bizarreness of lucid versus nonlucid dreams is another cognitive aspect that has been the focus of considerable inquiry. The results have been mixed. Traditionally, lucid dreams have been conceived to be more realistic and less bizarre than nonlucid dreams (Green, 1968); and some of the more recent research has supported this perspective. Specifically, in content analyses of dream transcripts, Gackenbach (personal communication, 1985) found that nonlucid dreams were rated by independent judges as containing more animate bizarreness such as inappropriate objects and disfigured bodies, inanimate combinations of environmental features, transformations such as scene shifts, and metamorphoses. However, other research has pointed to more bizarreness in lucid dreams (Hearne, 1978; Hoffman and McCarley, 1980) or no difference (Gackenbach and Schillig, 1983). However, there are problems with some of these findings.

The anecdotal association of the initiation of dream with bizarreness has recently received experimental attention: Hoffman and McCarley (1980) tested the hypothesis "that the degree of dream lucidity will be correlated with the amount of accompanying bizarreness" by scoring 104 dream reports for "bizarreness" and "lucidity." The authors found, "as predicted," that the presence of lucidity was associated with the occurrence of bizarreness. However, this result is entirely predictable, given the five-point "lucidity" scale used in this study: "in only one dream was the dreamer conscious that he was dreaming (lucidity score = 5) and also in only one dream was action held up while the dreamer puzzled about an oddity (lucidity score = 3); in 15 dreams the dreamer registered the presence of an oddity (lucidity = 2) while in the remaining 84% of dreams no degree of lucidity was present." "Lucidity" as operationally defined by this scale is essentially equivalent to "perception of anomaly." As LaBerge (1980b) wrote, "The fact that the dreamer will more often 'register the presence of an oddity' in the presence of one (i.e., in dreams rated as bizarre) will hardly strike any reader not now dreaming as odd."

Gackenbach, Curren, LaBerge, Davidson & Maxwell, 1983 had adults evaluate lucid and nonlucid dreams as to their bizarreness the morning after experiencing each dream. The higher bizarreness ratings for lucid dreams may be in part due to the finding that the presence of an inconsistency or an oddity is one of the ways dreamers most often realize that they are asleep and dreaming.

The presence of speech and reading in these lucid dreams has also been investigated. Although they are typically found to possess more voices or speech (Gackenbach, Curren, and Cutler, 1983; Gackenbach and Schillig, in press), the understanding of such material either through audition or by vision (i.e., reading) has been reported as difficult (Moers-Messmer, 1938; Worsley, 1983; Wilmes, 1983; Gilmore, 1983; LaBerge, 1985).

LUCID DREAMERS: CHARACTERISTICS AND INDIVIDUAL DIFFERENCES

Differences between individuals who experience dream lucidity and those who do not have been investigated in four major domains: physiology, perception, imagery, and abilities and personal disposition.

Physiology

Hemispheric laterality (Snyder and Gackenbach, 1981), vestibular sensitivity (Gackenbach, Sachau, Rokes, and Snyder, 1983), autonomic balance (Gackenbach, Walling, and LaBerge, 1984) and migraine headaches (Irwin, 1983) have all been investigated as a function of lucid dreaming ability.

Snyder and Gackenbach (1981) tested left- and right-handed women in a dual-task paradigm that has consistently been used to infer the cerebral organization for speech in right-handers. This paradigm involves persons performing sequential manual tapping (finger tapping or arm tapping) during silence and concurrent with speech. The pattern of interference that results during concurrent activity relative to the performance during silence is said to depend upon the cerebral organization for speech and manual control.

The results of their study suggest that females who frequently experience lucid dreams, regardless of their handedness, have a greater degree of unilateral cerebral speech organization than do females who never or infrequently experience such dreams. For right-handed frequent lucid dreamers this unilateral organization is based within the left hemisphere, while for left-handed frequents, this unilateral organization is right-hemisphere-based.

Gackenbach, Rokes, Sachau, and Snyder, (1983) found that frequent lucid dreamers evidenced a clear leftward eye movement preference as measured by amplitude of movement in response to directions to look left, right, or forward with eyes open and closed. They also report that subjects differing in the frequency with which they reported dreaming lucidly were administered the caloric irrigation test of vestibular sensitivity. Electronystagmographical evaluation determined that nonlucid dreamers evidence borderline vestibular pathology. In support of this, they note that in a broader sample, without screening for vestibular dysfunction, high lucid dreaming frequency was negatively correlated, controlling for dream recall, with the presence of ear, vision, and motion sickness problems.

Autonomic balance was determined by Gackenbach et al. (1984) using Plutanick and Conte's (1974) Sympathetic–Parasympathetic test. When both social desirability and dream recall frequency were controlled, relative parasympathetic dominance was significantly associated with lucid dreaming frequency for women but not for men.

Finally, Irwin (1983) found in a chi-square analysis for lucid versus nonlucid dreamers that the former were more likely to report experiencing migraine headaches.

Perception

Frequent lucid dreamers have been found to be more susceptible to the stroop effect, to differential performance on the Southern California Motor Accuracy Test and a test of kinesthetic skills (Gackenbach et al., 1981), and to be field-independent (Gackenbach, Heilman, Boyt, and LaBerge, in press).

Sex differences in these associations also emerged. Specifically, Gackenbach et al. (in press) reported field independence as measured by the Embedded Figures Test to be consistent across sex and associated with lucid dreaming ability, but when it was assessed by the Rod-and-Frame Test (RFT), a sex difference emerged. Males who were frequent lucid dreamers were determined to be field-independent, while no difference in RFT performance as a function of lucid dreaming ability occurred for females. Similarly, Gackenbach et al. (1981) report that male nonlucid dreamers evidenced a strong leftward deviation with their left hands on a test of kinesthetic abilities, whereas male lucid dreamers showed a slight rightward preference. For women, there was no differehce between types of lucid dreamers and performance on this task with their left hands. Scores on spatial perceptual completion subscales of the Comprehensive Ability Battery (Hakstian and Cattell, 1974) also revealed sex differences in their relationship to lucid dreaming frequency. It was found that women who frequently dream lucidly were better able to do the perceptual completion task than those who do not, when self-reported sex-role identity, dream recall, and education were controlled. With the same controls, men who reported frequently experiencing lucidity were less able to do the spatial task.

No performance differences as a function of lucid dreaming frequency were found with the Southern California Figure-Ground Visual Perceptual Test, a hand steadiness task, two illusions (Necker cube and Mueller-Lyer)

(Gackenbach, et al., 1981), visual or tactile mazes, and a tracking task (Gackenbach et al., 1981).

Imagery

Both waking and sleeping imagery differences between individuals who vary in the frequency with which they report lucid dreams will be considered. Six aspects of the former have been investigated, and include spontaneous waking images such as hypnagogic images, hallucinations, daydreams, and psychic experiences, as well as experimental waking images such as style, control, and vividness reports of imaginal tasks.

Hearne (1978) found that for women only, the frequency of experiencing dream lucidity correlated positively with the frequency of experiencing hypnagogic images. Gackenbach (1978) investigated the degree to which these images are perceived as similar to lucid or nonlucid dreams, and found that they were perceived by adult high dream recallers as more similar to nonlucid than to lucid dreams. She also reported in a factor analysis that the higher the perceived concurrence between lucid dreams and hypnagogic images, the more likely it was that an individual's lucid dreams would be initiated by dreamlike or incongruent elements, and frequent lucid dreamers had significantly higher scores on this factor than infrequent lucid dreamers.

Blackmore (1983) reports that experiencing lucid dreams was positively associated with experiencing, both quantitatively and qualitatively, waking hallucinations. However, Hearne (1978) found no relationship between frequency of dreaming lucidly and frequency of a body-schema hallucination.

Frequency of daydreams was positively correlated to frequency of lucid dreams for men only, but no relationship was found between vividness of daydreams and lucidity (Hearne, 1978). Likewise, Gackenbach (1978) found no relationship between the degree of emotionality and realism of daydreams and the frequency of dreaming lucidly.

The final spontaneous waking imagery category is that of psi phenomena. Experiences with and attitudes toward four paranormal phenomena: extrasensory perception (ESP), psychokinesis (PK), survival of bodily death, and out-of-body experiences (OBEs), and their relationship to lucid dreaming have been investigated. Both Palmer (1979) and Kohr (1980) found self-reported lucid dreams to be one of the two best predictors among demographic and dream variables of psi experience.

Specifically, Kohr (1981) found a positive relationship between lucid dream reports and experiences with waking and dreaming ESP, whereas Hearne (1978) and Gackenbach (1978) found no such relationships. In a laboratory investigation using the lucid dream as an occasion to receive ESP information, Hearne (1981) reported "mildly encouraging results." Blackmore (1983) reported that those who believe in ESP were also more likely to experience dream lucidity.

In two investigations that have examined the correlation between self-reported experiences of PK and lucid dreaming frequency, no relationship emerged (Kohr, 1980; Gackenbach, 1978).

Experiences and beliefs about survival of bodily death or related phenomena such as seeing apparitions or having a near-death experience (NDE), have also been investigated as a function of lucid dreaming frequency. As for experience with apparitions, Gackenbach (1978) and Hearne (1978) found no such relationship, whereas Kohr (1980) reported that dream lucidity ability was correlated positively with these experiences.

Kohr (1980) identified three groups of respondents to a questionnaire who differed in whether or not they had had a NDE. The NDE group indicated that they had come close to death and reported having had moving personal experiences in this context. A second group indicated that they had come close to death and may or may not have had a moving personal experience. The third group was referred to as the Non-Experiencing group, composed of persons who had never come close to death. In terms of dream states, the NDE group reported a greater frequency of dreaming in color, greater frequency of unusual dream states such as lucidity and vibrations, and a greater range of types of sense modalities in dreams.

Relatedly, Greyson (1983) notes:

> I have already asked about the occurrence of lucid dreams in one questionnaire (a shortened version of John Palmer's Survey of Psychic Experiences) administered to self-selected members of the International Association for Near-Death Studies (IANDS). Among the "controls" (i.e., IANDS members who have not had NDEs), 83 out of 155 respondents (54%) reported having had lucid dreams, which is roughly what Palmer found among his sample from the general population. Among near-death experiencers, 13 out of 62 respondents (21%) reported having had lucid dreams *prior* to their NDEs, and 33 (53%) reported had lucid dreams *since* their NDEs. Thus, a fairly low percentage of near-death experiencers had lucid dreams before their NDEs, while after the NDE, this percentage rises to the level among the IANDS controls and the population Palmer sampled. [p. 6]

Beliefs about survival have also been investigated as they relate to the lucid dreaming experience. Palmer (1979) found a positive relationship, while Blackmore (1983) found no relationship.

The two major dimensions according to which mental imagery abilities have been assessed are control and vividness. Regarding control, neither

Hearne (1978), Blackmore (1982), nor Gackenbach's group has found any relationship between imagery control and lucidity ability. Blackmore (1982) and Gackenbach, Prill, and Westrom (1983) administered Gordon's control of imagery questionnaire, while Hearne asked several control-related imagery questions. The data are mixed regarding vividness. On the one hand, Hearne (1978) found no relation to lucidity for three vividness items, and Blackmore (1982) was unable to discover any differences between lucid and nonlucid dreamers in Bett's vividness of imagery scale scores. On the other hand, Gackenbach, Curren, LaBerge, Davidson, and Maxwell (1983) have found that when dream recall and social desirability were controlled for and understanding the concept of lucidity was ensured, males who frequently report dreaming lucidly also report more vivid tactile images. Likewise on a visualization task, Blackmore (1983) found a significant positive relationship with lucid dreaming frequency.

Returning to the question of imagery control, performance on mental rotation tasks provides a more accurate assessment of control of imagery abilities than do self-reports. Gackenbach, Curren, LaBerge, Davidson, and Maxwell (1983) found no relationship between performance on the two-dimensional task and lucidity abilities in two samples (student and adult) where dream recall was controlled. However, in another two-dimensional mental rotation task, with adult women when dream recall and handedness were controlled, the frequency of experiencing prelucid dreams was significantly positively correlated with performance. In the same study, Gackenbach et al. (1983) also determined that skill on three-dimensional mental rotation tasks was positively related to lucid dream frequency for women.

Abilities

Research covering intelligence, creativity, and several motor abilities in relation to lucid dreaming ability will be reviewed in this section. As regards intelligence, Gackenbach et al. (1981) and Hearne (1978) found no dreamer-type difference on the problem-solving tasks of the pyramid puzzle and the Raven's Progressive matrices, whereas Gackenbach, Curren, LaBerge, Davidson, and Maxwell (1983) reported that for males, in both student and an adult samples, intelligence as measured by Factor B of the 16PF inventory was negatively correlated with lucid dreaming frequency. In a more comprehensive evaluation of intelligence, Gackenbach, Curren, LaBerge, Davidson and Maxwell (1983) administered the four primary subscales (i.e., verbal, numerical, spatial, and perceptual completion abilities) of the Comprehensive Abilities Battery (Hakstian and Cattell, 1974) to adult lucid dreamers who varied in the frequency with which they had these dreams. When differences in dream recall, education, and relative masculinity and femininity were controlled, high lucid dreaming frequency was associated with high verbal, numerical, and perceptual completion abilities for men.

Gackenbach and Hammons (1983) report that for males only, verbal creativity was marginally associated with high dream lucidity frequency, whereas Gackenbach, Curren, LaBerge, Davidson, and Maxwell (1983) found no relationship for men between verbal or nonverbal creativity when differences in dream recall and relative masculinity and femininity were controlled. Women, however, who frequently experience this kind of dream were found by this group to be verbally and nonverbally creative.

Several motor abilities have also been examined. No lucid–nonlucid dreamer differences were found for motor accuracy or hand steadiness tasks (Gackenbach et al., 1981), but gross motor balance and related activities did evidence such a relationship. Gackenbach, Sachau, Rokes, and Snyder (1983) reported lucid dreaming ability in males to be associated with leftward leaning on a stabilometer task (i.e., a test of gross dynamic motor balance skill) and rightward leaning in nonlucid dreamers. No dreamer effects for females on this task were noted, nor were there any dreamer effects on a test of static motor balance skills.

Prevalence

Seven surveys have attempted to ascertain the prevalence of lucid dreaming in both student samples (Palmer, 1979; LaBerge, 1980a; Gackenbach, Rokes, Sachau, and Snyder, 1983) and adult samples (Palmer, 1979; Kohr, 1980; Blackmore, 1983; Gackenbach, 1978; Gackenbach, Curren, LaBerge, Davidson, and Maxwell, 1983). Among the latter, estimates of having had at least one lucid dream range from 100 percent (Gackenbach et al., 1983) to 47 percent (Blackmore, 1983), whereas the range estimated for students is from 85 percent (LaBerge, 1980a) to 57.5 percent (Gackenbach et al., 1984). A clearer picture emerges after consideration of both the representatives of the sample as well as attempts to verify that subjects understood the concept. Kohr (1980), Gackenbach (1978), and Gackenbach et al. (1983) were all dealing with highly motivated adult samples, that is, people who have an unusually high interest in dreaming and/or lucid dreaming. Thus their estimates tend to run high (Kohr, 70%; Gackenbach, 76%; Gackenbach et al., 100%). In the Palmer (1979) and Blackmore (1983) surveys, adults were randomly chosen from the telephone directory in the case of the former and from the electoral register in the case of the latter. Their estimates are considerably more conservative (Palmer, 55%; Blackmore, 47%). However, there is no indication that they attempted to verify that their respondents had understood the concept; and both LaBerge (1980b) and Gackenbach, Heilman, Boyt, and LaBerge (1983) have pointed out that when subjects are asked to supply a lucid dream, incidence rates drop because of confusion over simple definitions.

Sex, race, and age differences modify the frequency with which lucid dreams are reported. Hearne (1978) and Gackenbach (in Gackenbach and Snyder, in press) both found sex differences in incidence favoring females, while Blackmore (1982) reported such a difference but in the opposite direction, and Gackenbach (1978), Blackmore (1983), and Palmer (personal communication, 1974) found no sex differences. Only Palmer has examined race differences, reporting that 76 percent of blacks claimed experience with lucid dreaming compared to only 53 percent of whites. Age differences generally favor the younger respondent (Palmer, 1976; Blackmore, 1983; Gackenbach, personal communication, 1981) with one exception. Gackenbach (1978) found that among adult women with a high interest in dreaming, older women reported experiencing lucidity more frequently than their younger counterparts.

Family demographics have also been considered in several inquiries. Palmer (1979) and Gackenbach, Curren, LaBerge, Davidson, and Maxwell (1983) found differences as a function of marital status. In both cases a larger proportion of singles reported having had a lucid dream than marrieds. However, Gackenbach (1978) found no relationship between marital status and lucidity reports. Finally, Gackenbach, Curren, LaBerge, Davidson, and Maxwell (1983) report a higher incidence of lucid dreamers among first-borns than among later-borns.

As to education and occupation variables, no difference has been found as a function of education in a random sample (Palmer, 1979) or in well-educated samples (Gackenbach 1978; Gackenbach, Curren, LaBerge, Davidson, and Maxwell, 1983). Palmer (1979) also noted no differences as functions of occupational and family income analyses.

Personality

Personality dimensions examined thus far as possible differentiaters of lucidity ability include extraversion and neuroticism (Gackenbach 1978, in press; Hearne, 1978); self-perception (Belicki and Hunt, 1978); anxiety, hostility, depression, life changes (Gackenbach, personal communication, 1981); risk-taking (Dane, 1984; Gackenbach, Curren, LaBerge, Davidson, and Maxwell, 1983); a general personality inventory (Gackenbach, 1978); and sex-role identity (Gackenbach, Curren, LaBerge, Davidson, and Maxwell, 1983). Liberal or experimenting (Gackenbach, 1978), risk-taking proclivities (Dane, 1983; Gackenbach, Curren, LaBerge, Davidson, and Maxwell, 1983) and masculinity (Gackenbach, Curren, LaBerge, Davidson, and Maxwell, 1983) were found to be differentially characteristic of fre-

quent lucid dreamers. The other students found no differences or contradictory differences.

THE PSYCHOPHYSIOLOGY OF LUCID DREAMS

Lucid Dreaming Physiologically Verified

Under what physiological conditions do lucid dreams occur? Before the
recent availability of empirical evidence bearing on this question, speculation largely favored two answers: wakefulness or NREM sleep. Most sleep
researchers were apparently inclined to accept Hartmann's "impression"
that lucid dreams were "not typical parts of dreaming thought, but rather
brief arousals" (Hartmann, 1975; Berger, 1977). Schwartz and Lefebvre
(1973) noted that frequent transitory arousals were common during REM
sleep and proposed these "micro-awakenings" as the physiological basis
for lucid dreams. Although no one had put foward any evidence for this
mechanism, it seems to have been the accepted opinion (Foulkes, 1974) up
until the last few years. A similar view was put forward by Antrobus et al.
(1965), who supposed that recognition by the dreamer of the fact that he
or she is dreaming would immediately terminate the experience if it occurred in REM sleep; " . . . continuation of the recognized dream . . .
might then be expected more commonly in Stages 2, 3, and 4." Similarly,
Hall (1977) ventured that "lucid dreams may represent a transition from
Stage-1 REM to Stage-4 mentation" (p. 312), and Gackenbach (1978) concluded that there were "considerable data to support the possibility that
lucid dreams may be 'thinking' reports arising out of NREM or hypnopompic mentation" (p. 63). Green (1968) seems to have stood alone in her
surmise that since lucid dreams usually arise from nonlucid dreams,
" . . . we may tentatively expect to find lucid dreams occurring, as do other
dreams, during the 'paradoxical' phase of sleep . . . " (p. 128).

Empirical evidence began to appear in the late 1970s supporting Green's
speculation that lucid dreams would occur during REM sleep. Ogilvie et al.
(1978) offered some preliminary observations on the physiology of lucid
dreaming. Based on standard sleep recordings for two subjects who reported a total of three lucid dreams upon awakening from REM sleep, Ogilvie et al. cautiously concluded that " . . . it *may* be that lucid dreams begin
in REM. . . . " However, no proof was given that the lucid dreams had in
fact occurred during the REM periods immediately preceding the awakenings and reports. Indeed, the subjects themselves were uncertain about
when their lucid dreams had taken place.

What was needed to unambiguously establish the physiological status of
lucid dreams was some sort of on-the-scene report from the dream, a notion

first suggested by Tart (1965). LaBerge and his colleagues at Stanford University provided this verification by arranging for lucid dreamers to signal whenever they realized they were dreaming by means of specific patterns of dream actions having polygraphically observable correlates (i.e., eye movements and fist clenches). Following this approach, LaBerge, Nagel, Dement, and Zarcone (1981) reported that the occurrence of lucid dreaming *during* unequivocal REM sleep had been demonstrated for five subjects. After being instructed in the method of lucid dream induction (MILD) described by LaBerge (1980a) the subjects were recorded from two to twenty nights each. In the course of the thirty-four nights of the study, thirty-five lucid dreams were reported subsequent to spontaneous awakening from various stages of sleep as follows: REM sleep, thirty-two times; NREM Stage-1, twice; and during the transition from NREM Stage-2 to REM, once. The subjects who reported signaled during thirty of these lucid dreams. After each recording, the reports mentioning signals were submitted along with the respective polysomnograms to a judge uninformed of the times of the reports. In twenty-four cases (80%), the judge was able to select the appropriate 30-second epoch on the basis of correspondence between reported and observed signals. *All signals associated with lucid dream reports occurred during epochs of unambiguous REM sleep* scored according to the conventional criteria (Rechtschaffen and Kales, 1968). The lucid dream signals were followed by an average of 1 minute of uninterrupted REM sleep (range: 5 to 450 sec).

A replication of this study with two additional subjects and twenty more lucid dreams produced identical results (LaBerge, Nagel, Taylor, Dement, and Zarcone, 1981). LaBerge et al. argued that their investigations demonstrated that lucid dreaming usually (though perhaps not exclusively) occurs during REM sleep. This conclusion is supported by research carried out in several other laboratories (Hearne, 1978; Ogilvie et al., 1983; Fenwick et al., 1983). It should be noted with caution that although these studies have used various forms of signals for verification, none has followed the procedure of blind matching of signals to reports described by LaBerge et al. (1981a,b).

Ogilvie et al. (1983) reported the physiological state preceding fourteen spontaneous lucidity signals as unqualified REM in twelve (86%) of the cases; of the remaining two cases, one was "ambiguous" REM, and the other appeared to be wakefulness. Keith Hearne and Alan Worsley collaborated on a pioneering study of lucid dreaming in which the latter spent fifty nonconsecutive nights in the sleep lab while the former monitored the polygraph. Worsley reported signaling in eight lucid dreams, all of which were described by Hearne (1978) as having occurred during unambiguous REM sleep.

Having shown that lucid dreaming signaling occurs "during REM sleep" may leave unanswered what may be a crucial question for some readers: what exactly do we mean by the assertion that lucid dreamers are "asleep"? Perhaps these "dreamers" are not really dreamers, as many argued in the last century; or perhaps this "sleep" is not really sleep, as some have argued in this century. This issue has been cogently addressed by LaBerge in the following terms:

How do we know that the subjects were "really asleep" when they communicated the signals? If we allow perception of the external world as a criterion of being awake, we can conclude the subjects were indeed asleep: although they knew they were in the laboratory, this knowledge was a matter of memory, not perception; upon awakening, they reported having been totally in the dream world and not in sensory contact with the external world. Neither were the subjects merely not attending to the environment (e.g., as when absorbed in reading or daydreaming); according to their reports, they were conscious of the *absence* of sensory input from the external world. If subjects were to claim to have been awake while showing physiological signs of sleep, or vice versa, we might doubt their subjective reports. However, in the present case, the subjective accounts and physiological measures are in clear agreement, and it would be extremely unparsimonious to suppose that subjects who believed themselves to be asleep while showing physiological indications of sleep were actually awake. (LaBerge et al., 1981a).

Physiological Correlates of the Initiation of Lucid Dreams

Though the preceding studies have shown that lucid dreams occur during REM sleep, they leave unanswered the question of how lucid dreams are initiated. Moreover, to say that lucid dreams happen during REM is by no means an exact statement. REM sleep is a rather heterogeneous state exhibiting considerable variations in physiological activity, of which two distinct phases are ordinarily distinguished. In its most active form, REM is dominated by a striking variety of irregular and short-lived events such as muscular twitching, including the rapid eye movements that give the state one of its most common names. This variety of REM is referred to as "phasic," while the relatively quiescent state remaining when rapid eye movements and other phasic events temporarily subside is referred to as "tonic." So, to specify the lucid dream state no more precisely than as "Stage-1 REM" would be equivalent to saying that this chapter was written in the United States, thus leaving a great deal of territory that would be considerably narrowed by specifying the state as California or Iowa rather than, say, Florida or Alaska. Thus, to more precisely characterize the lucid dream state, we can ask whether lucid dreams take place in tonic or phasic REM. Research by the Stanford group has provided a definite answer: "phasic," as will be seen below.

LaBerge, Nagel, Taylor, Dement, and Zarcone (1981) distinguished three classes of characteristic physiology within REM accompanying the initiation of lucid dreams. Since lucid dreams are sometimes initiated from the waking state but more frequently from the dream state, it would be reasonable to expect that one general class of lucid dreams ought to involve brief arousals within REM periods, while the larger number of lucid dreams should exhibit no such arousals. This is exactly what LaBerge et al. found when they analyzed fifty lucid dream records derived from earlier studies.

As was mentioned above, momentary intrusions of wakefulness occur very commonly during the normal course of REM sleep, and it had been proposed by Schwartz and Lefebvre (1973) that lucid dreaming takes place during these micro-awakenings. However, LaBerge et al.'s data indicated that while lucid dreams do *not* occur during interludes of wakefulness within REM periods, lucidity is sometimes *initiated* from these moments of transitory arousal, with the lucid dreams themselves continuing in subsequent undisturbed REM sleep. Only 22 percent of the lucid dreams were of this type, and only 40 percent of the seven subjects showed this mode of initiation. The subjects were normally conscious of having been awake before entering this class of lucid dream.

In 78 percent of the cases, the subjects reported having realized that they were dreaming during an ongoing dream. The respective polysomnograms fell into classes with the initiation of lucidity occurring either (a) within 2 minutes of the beginning of the REM periods and frequently as little as 20 seconds after REM onset; or (b) elsewhere during REM, at times ranging from 3 to 45 minutes after the start of the REM period. Of the twenty-six lucid dreams belonging to the latter category, REM burst time in the 30 seconds preceding initiation of lucidity was above median levels for the respective REM periods in twenty-two cases. Since this distribution is unlikely to have occurred by chance ($p < 0.001$), the association of lucid dreams with *phasic* REM would seem to be firmly established.

As for the REM period-onset class of lucid dreams, LaBerge cited a model proposed by McGinty (1979) in which the increase in CNS excitation accompanying the transition from NREM Stage-2 to REM sleep results in a transient "overshoot." LaBerge theorized that this phasic activation, like that accompanying REM bursts, raises the brain to the relatively high level of cortical tone apparently necessary to initiate lucidity.

In an extension of the study just described, LaBerge, Levitan, Gordon, and Dement (1983) reported further characteristics of these three modes of lucid dream initiation, which they referred to as "wake-initiated" or "W-types," "onset" or "O-types," and "phasic" or "P-types." Analysis of sixty-two lucid dreams from seven subjects revealed 29 percent W-types, 21 percent O-types, and 50 percent P-types. Compared to other initiation types, P-types occurred significantly later in REM periods, while O-types occurred significantly earlier in the night.

For all three types of lucid dream, the initiation of lucidity was frequently marked by indications of orientation responses including respiratory pauses, skin potential responses (SPR), and biphasic heart rate responses. For the P-types, REM burst time, SPR rate, and respiration rate showed significant elevations in the 30 seconds immediately before the initiation of lucidity (as marked by the signals) compared to the preceding portions of the REM periods. The same was true for the 30 seconds immediately before the transitory arousals preceding wake-initiated lucid dreams.

There were striking individual differences regarding the types of lucid dream initiation as well as the particular forms taken by the orientation responses. For example, several subjects did not show heart rate responses at any time, while others always did. All four of one subject's lucid dreams were of the O-type, while none of another's twenty were; this is a highly significant difference ($p < .0001$), suggesting both an opportunity and a caveat. The opportunity is for future research to relate physiological differences in mode of lucid dream initiation to individual differences in personality and cognitive abilities. The caveat is to beware of overgeneralization from preliminary observations on a relatively small number of subjects. If the first subject we had studied had been the wrong one of the two just mentioned, after four lucid dreams, we would have been quite compelled by the mistaken notion that lucid dreams characteristically occur at the beginning of the first REM period of the night. Similarly, Ogilvie et al. (1978) fell victim to sampling error, hastily concluding on the basis of only three observations that lucid dreams were characterized by *low* rapid eye movement activity. Likewise, since the onset of lucidity was immediately preceded by a REM burst, in all eight of Worsley's lucid dreams, Hearne (1978) was tempted to suppose that all lucid dreams were P-types. The lesson of all this is, of course, that we must be careful not to interpret the foregoing studies as showing that there are only three types of lucid dream or that lucid dreams are never found in NREM sleep, and so on. With this caution, here is a paraphrase of LaBerge's (1985) summary generalizations on the psychophysiological conditions that are together necessary and sufficient for the occurrence of lucid dreams. On the psychological side of the coin, the requirement is an appropriate mental set. The would-be lucid dreamer must have the unequivocal intention to recognize when the time comes that he or she is dreaming. On the physiological side of the coin, the requirement

is a sufficiently high level of cerebral activation. Were this condition unnecessary, lucid dreams would be found randomly distributed throughout
every stage of sleep. However, the preliminary studies of the Stanford group
indicate the contrary: that this condition is in fact necessary and normally
(and possibly only) attained only in the particular circumstances described
above during stage REM, a state that has been justifiably called "paradoxical sleep."

The EEG during Lucid Dreams

The fact that lucid dreaming occurs during Stage-1 REM sleep defines to
a certain extent the EEG activity characteristic of lucid dreams. However,
the Rechtschaffen and Kales (1968) scoring manual provides EEG criteria
for REM sleep no more specific than " . . . relatively low voltage, mixed
frequency . . . ," which allows considerable latitude in terms of how much
of which frequencies are mixed. For example, the EEG of REM sometimes
shows predominant 2–3 Hz "saw-tooth waves," while at other times it may
exhibit prominent 8–10 Hz alpha waves. So the question arises as to whether
or not the range of EEG activity characteristic of lucid dreams reliably differs in any way from that of nonlucid dreams.

   In a series of studies, the Brock University group has pursued the hypothesis that lucid dreams are associated with high levels of alpha activity.
In the first of these investigations Ogilvie et al. (1978) initially came to the
"impression that alpha is the dominant EEG frequency during lucid
dreams" on the less than solid grounds of a comparison of "percent alpha
in the EEG" of just two lucid dream REM periods with percent alpha for
six nonlucid dream REM periods for a *single* subject. We have already discussed the interpretive problems with this pilot study, which need not be
repeated here.

   Ogilvie et al. (1982) followed up their preliminary work with a more sophisticated study entitled "Lucid Dreaming and Alpha Activity." The ten
subjects were all good dream recallers reporting lucid dreams with a frequency ranging from "one or two ever" to "near nightly," with "several
lucid dreams per year" being the average. They were recorded two nights
each in the sleep laboratory, during which they were awakened four times
per night from REM sleep: half of the time during periods of relatively high
alpha and half of the time during relatively low alpha. Dream reports were
collected and rated on a lucidity scale by a judge blind to awakening condition. Significantly ($p < .05$) higher lucidity ratings were obtained for high
alpha compared to low alpha awakenings.

   However, it is doubtful whether this establishes, as Ogilvie and colleagues
appear to have concluded, that lucid dreams are associated with high alpha

activity, for a variety of reasons. Translating the average lucidity ratings back to the words on the scale revealed subjects awakened during low alpha to have reported on the average "a brief moment where subject was pre-lucid." The high alpha awakenings yielded reports scored on the average "prelucid" somewhere between "throughout the dream" and during "a definite episode (noted at beginning, middle, or end of narrative)." So the two awakening conditions produced reports that differed on the average only in extent of *pre*lucidity. Moreover, we have no assurance of whether, in either condition, the episode of prelucidity or lucidity occurred in as-sociation with the final 20–30-second period of either high or low alpha activity that determined the awakening condition. Their scale ought to have distinguished between episodes at the end of the narratives, which would have been temporally associated with the awakening condition, and those at the beginning or middle, rather than lumping all three portions of the reports together. Moreover, since none of the dreams classified as lucid were marked by signals, we have no proof that they were in fact lucid dreams, nor in any case do we have any way of determining what the degree of alpha activity was *during* the frequently brief episodes of lucidity. In view of these considerations, perhaps a less misleading title for this provocative paper would be "Prelucid Dreaming and Alpha Activity."

Because of their design we cannot exclude the possibility that what Ogil-vie and his colleagues may actually have demonstrated is that subject ten-dencies to *retrospectively* judge themselves to have been briefly or partially lucid vary with the amount of alpha activity either just before or during the process of awakening. Support for this interpretation comes from an earlier study, which concluded that mentation reports collected from REM periods showing EEGs with a high proportion of alpha waves were asso-ciated with "some feeling of control over the content" and were frequently labeled by subjects as "thoughts" rather than "dreams" (Goodenough et al., 1959). It seems plausible that these two studies were barking up the same tree.

There is one more design problem with the Ogilvie et al. (1982) study that seems serious enough to merit mention: the judge's lucidity ratings were based not upon the spontaneous dream reports but on the subjects' answers to rather leading questions subsequently posed by the interviewer, such as "was there any point when you wondered whether or not you might be dreaming?" and "was there any point at which you knew you were dream-ing while that dream was going on?" The demand characteristics should be obvious. Additionally, there is the problem that retrospective judgments about earlier states of mind are likely to be confounded by our current mental state. Cognitive capacities we now possess are likely to be uninten-tionally carried back to our earlier state and mistakenly remembered as having been there in the first place. The conservative approach would seem to favor reliance upon the original reports, and in the present context one would like to know how many subjects spontaneously volunteered in their reports that they had been prelucid or lucid.

The most recent study by the Brock group remedied several of these methodological problems and arrived at a conclusion regarding alpha activity and lucidity unsupportive of their earlier work. Ogilvie, Hunt, Kushniruk, and Newman (1983) studied eight lucid dreamers for one to four nights in the sleep lab. The subjects were awakened from REM following spontaneous or cued eye movement signals. The cue buzzer sounded after 15 minutes of REM in the presence of either high or low alpha activity, and the subjects were to signal at the cue and again 30 seconds later if in a lucid dream. Reports were elicited 30 to 60 seconds after cued or spontaneous signals and rated for lucidity. Contrary to their earlier findings, the low alpha condition yielded slightly more lucid dreams than the high alpha condition; however, this difference was not statistically significant. Addressing the same issue as the Brock group, LaBerge (1980b) Fourier-analyzed C_3 EEG activity for a single lucid dream REM period. Comparison of the spectral profiles for the nonlucid and lucid portions of the REM period revealed alpha activity for the nonlucid dream to more closely resemble the waking EEG spectrum than did the lucid dream; however, the two REM samples did not significantly differ.

In summary, it would seem at this point that no reliable association of lucid dreaming with alpha activity (whether high or low) has yet been established. Rather than measuring a single feature (i.e., alpha power) of the EEG derived from a single electrode site, a more fruitful direction for future work would probably involve quantifying whole band EEG frequency spectra from several electrode placements and comparing signal-verified lucid dreams with nonlucid controls.

Temporal Distribution of Lucid Dreams

Van Eeden (1913) stated that his lucid dreams invariably occurred between five and eight o'clock in the morning. By way of explanation, he quoted Dante's characterization of these hours as the time "when swallows begin to warble and our mind is least clogged by the material body." Garfield (1975) exactly agreed with van Eeden's timing though perhaps not with his poetic explanation. LaBerge (1979) plotted the times of 212 of his lucid dreams and found their pattern to closely fit the usual cyclic distribution of REM periods. He suggested that the fact that most REM sleep occurs toward the end of the night provided a plausible explanation for van Eeden's and Garfield's observations. Later, LaBerge (1980a) tested this hypothesis by comparing the temporal distribution of his lucid dreams with that expected on the basis of normative data from Williams et al. (1974). A chi-square test indicated that the observed distribution of lucid dreams was not significantly different from what would be expected on the basis of mean REM period lengths at different times of night.

Again it should be noted that this result is for a single subject. Other factors besides REM period lengths may affect the temporal distribution of lucid dreams for other subjects. For example, one of LaBerge's subjects at Stanford had all four of his laboratory lucid dreams in his first REM periods. Also, the fact that REM density as well as overall dream intensity activity and bizarreness increase as the night progresses may contribute some of the late-night advantage for lucidity, perhaps more for some subjects than others. Cohen's (1977) hypothesis of gradually increasing left hemisphere dominance (GILD) during the course of the night is perhaps also of relevance. This seems especially likely because the left hemisphere's verbal abilities would appear to play a crucial role in lucid dreaming: without words, how else could we tell ourselves that we are dreaming? Clearly this is an area rich in research possibilities.

Another factor that will affect the temporal distribution of lucid dreams is initiation type. Onset-lucid dreams, as we have seen, occur earlier in the night than either wake or phasic types. Another comparison from LaBerge's (unpublished) personal record of lucid dreams indicates that for him, W-type lucid dreams are over ten times more frequent during afternoon naps than they are during the first REM period of the night ($p <$ 0.0002).

APPLICATIONS AND IMPLICATIONS OF LUCID DREAMING FOR RESEARCH IN ALTERED STATES OF CONSCIOUSNESS

Regarding the applications of lucid dreaming, LaBerge (1980b) recounted an anecdote concerning electricity, a "scientific curiosity" of the eighteenth century, about which a woman is said to have asked Benjamin Franklin, "but what *use* is it?" "What use, madame," replied Franklin, "is a newborn baby?" As for lucid dreaming, a "scientific curiosity" of the twentieth century, if the analogous question were asked, the corresponding answer could be given.

Nevertheless, even at this early stage in the development of our understanding of this phenomenon, a number of promising applications of lucid dreaming can be seen. A number of these are treated in LaBerge (1980b), and in Gackenbach and LaBerge (in press). Here we must limit ourselves to a single application, that provides a paradigm for a powerful approach to research on various states of consciousness.

Mapping Out the Dream World

One of the major obstacles to making human consciousness a topic of rigorous scientific study has been that the most direct account available of the contents of a person's consciousness is that person's own subjective report. Unfortunately, of the "bad witnesses" that Heraclitus called the senses, "introspection" appears to be among the least reliable. What is needed is a means of corroborating the testimony of the "I-witness" as regards consciousness, and this is just what the psychophysiological approach provides.

A key element in this new strategy is the idea of making full use of the subject's cooperativeness and intelligence. A frequent practice in experimental psychology today requires the subject to be deceived about the true nature of the experiment. This has the advantage of minimizing the effect the subject's knowledge might have on the experiment. But this traditional method is inappropriate when the subject matter of the investigation is the subject's own consciousness. In this case, a more suitable approach is one in which the dichotomous subject/experimenter relationship is modified: perhaps subjects should be regarded, to borrow an anthropological term, as "participant/observers." As for the problem of subjective report reliability, it seems helpful to study highly trained (and lucid!) subjects and make use of the fact that the convergent agreement of physiological measures and subjective reports provides a degree of validation (Stoyva and Kamiya, 1968).

The fact that lucid dreamers can remember to perform predetermined actions and signal to the laboratory suggested to LaBerge a new approach to dream research. Lucid dreamers, he proposed, "could carry out diverse dream experiements marking the exact time of particular dream events, allowing derivation of precise psychophysiological correlations and methodical testing of hypotheses" (LaBerge et al., 1981a). This strategy has been put into practice by the Stanford group in a number of studies summarized by LaBerge (1985).

LaBerge pointed out first of all that the data reported in LaBerge et al. (1981a,b) indicate that there is a very direct and reliable relationship between gaze shift reported in lucid dreams and the direction of polygraphically recorded eye movements. It should be noted that the results obtained for lucid dreams (see also Hearne, 1978; Ogilvie et al., 1983) are much stronger than the generally weak correlations demonstrated by earlier investigations testing the notion that the dreamer's eyes move with his or her hallucinated dream gaze (e.g., Roffwarg et al., 1962). This would seem to illustrate the methodological superiority of the lucid dreamer approach. The parallel between subjective and objective eye movements implies that, to a first approximation, spatial relationships in the dream world are similar in form to those of the physical world. What about temporal relationships? How long do dreams last?

LaBerge (1980b; 1985) reports having straightforwardly raised the question of dream time by subjects to estimate various intervals of time during their lucid dreams. Signals marking the beginning and end of the subjective intervals allowed comparison with objective time. In all cases, LaBerge reported, time estimates during the lucid dreams were very close to actual dream time.

In another study, LaBerge and Dement (1982a) found evidence for voluntary control of respiration during lucid dreaming. They recorded three lucid dreamers who were asked either to breathe rapidly or to hold their breath (in their lucid dreams), marking the interval of altered respiration with eye movement signals. The subjects reported successfully carrying out the agreed-upon tasks a total of nine times, and in every case, a judge was able to correctly predict on the basis of the polygraph recordings which of the two patterns had been executed ($p < 0.002$).

In regard to other muscle groups, while testing a variety of lucidity signals, LaBerge et al. (1981a) observed that a sequence of left and right dream-fist clenches resulted in a corresponding sequence of left and right forearm twitches as measured by EMG. However, the amplitude of the twitches bore an unreliable relationship to the subjective intensity of the dreamed actions. Since all muscle groups except those that govern eye movements and breathing suffer a profound loss of tone during REM sleep, it is to be expected that most muscular responses to dreamed movements will be feeble. Nonetheless, these responses faithfully reflect the motor patterns of the original dream. In LaBerge's (1985) phrase, "the dreamer's body responds to dreamed actions with movements that are but the shadows of the originals."

A further step toward refining our picture of the degree of connection between the dream body and physical body has been taken by Fenwick et al. (1984). They studied a single proficient lucid dreamer (Alan Worsley, who had also been Hearne's [1978] subject), who carried out a variety of dreamed muscular movements while being polygraphically recorded. In one experiment, Worsley executed movements during lucid dreams involving finger, forearm, and shoulder muscle groups (flexors) while EMG was recorded from each area. The results were consistent: the axial muscles showed no measurable EMG activity, while the forearm EMG "consistently showed lower amplitude and shorter bursts" compared to the finger EMG. A similar experiment with the lower limbs yielded "similar results." In addition to the finding that REM atonia shows a central-peripheral gradient with motor inhibition least for the most distal muscles, Fenwick et al. reported that similar experiments comparing EMG response to dreamed arm and leg flexions and extensions "suggested" that flexors were less inhibited than extensors. In addition to EMG, an accelerometer was utilized in several experiments demonstrating that Worsley was able to produce minor movements of his fingers, toes, and feet during REM, though not of his legs. Fenwick et al. also presented the results of a single experiment suggesting that dream speech may be initiated in the expiratory phase of respiration just as it usually occurs during waking. In still another experiment they demonstrated the voluntary production of smooth pursuit eye movements during a lucid dream.

As if the foregoing were not enough for one paper, Fenwick et al. also showed that Worsley was able to perceive and respond to environmental stimuli (electrical shocks) without awakening from his lucid dream. This result raises a theoretical issue: if we take perception of the external world to be the essential criterion for wakefulness (LaBerge et al., 1981a; see above), then it would seem that Worsley must have been at least partially awake. On the other hand, when environmental stimuli are incorporated into dreams without producing any subjective or physiological indications of arousal, it appears reasonable to speak of the perception as having occurred during sleep. Furthermore, it may be possible, as LaBerge (1980b) has suggested, for one sense to remain functional and "awake" while others fall "asleep." As long as we continue to consider wakefulness and sleep as a simple dichotomy, we will lie in a Procrustean bed ("one size fits all") that is bound to be at times most uncomfortable. There must be degrees of being awake just as there are degrees of being asleep (i.e., the conventional sleep stages). Before finding our way out of this muddle, we probably will need to characterize a wider variety of states of consciousness than those few currently distinguished (e.g., "dreaming," "sleeping," "waking," and so on).

Since many researchers have reported cognitive task dependency of lateralization of EEG alpha activity in the waking state, LaBerge undertook a pilot study to determine whether similar relationships would hold in the lucid dream state. The two tasks selected for comparison were dreamed singing and dreamed counting, activities expected to result in relatively greater engagement of the subjects' left and right cerebral hemispheres, respectively.

Integrated alpha band EEG activity was derived from electrodes placed over the right and left temporal lobes while four subjects sang and counted in their lucid dreams (marking the beginning and end of each task by eye movement signals). The results supported the hypothesized lateralization of alpha activity: the right hemisphere was more activated than the left during singing; during counting, the reverse was true. These shifts were similar to those observed during actual singing and counting (LaBerge and Dement, 1982a).

Sexual activity is a rather commonly reported theme of lucid dreams (Garfield, 1979; LaBerge, 1985). However, to this point, only a single physiological investigation of lucid dream sex has been published. LaBerge, Greenleaf, and Kedzierski (1983) undertook a pilot study to determine the extent to which subjectively experienced sexual activity during REM lucid dreaming would be reflected in physiological responses. Their subject was a highly proficient lucid dreamer who spent a night sleeping in the laboratory. Sixteen channels of physiological data, including EEG, EOG, EMG, respiration, skin conductance level (SCL), heart rate, vaginal EMG (VEMG), and vaginal pulse amplitude (VPA), were recorded. The experimental protocol called for the subject to make specific eye movement signals at the following points: when she realized she was dreaming (i.e., the onset of the lucid dream); when she began sexual activity (in the dream); and when she experienced orgasm. The subject reported a lucid dream in which she carried out the experimental task exactly as agreed upon. Data analysis revealed a significant correspondance between her subjective report and all but one of the autonomic measures: during the 15-second orgasm epoch, mean levels for VEMG activity, VPA, SCL, and respiration rate reached their highest values and were significantly elevated compared to means for REM epochs. Surprisingly, there was no significant heart rate increase.

LaBerge (1985) has succeeded in replicating this experiment with two male subjects. In both cases, respiration showed striking increases in rate. Again, there were no significant elevations of heart rate. Interestingly, although both subjects reported vividly realistic orgasms in their lucid dreams, neither actually ejaculated, in contrast to the "wet dreams" commonly experienced by adolescent males.

All of these results unanimously support the conclusion that the events we experience while asleep and dreaming produce effects on our brains (and to a lesser extent, bodies) remarkably similar to those that would be produced if we were to actually experience the corresponding events while awake. To the extent to which this conclusion is valid, it could provide an explanation of why dreams seem so real while they last: it is because of our brains, dreaming of doing something is equivalent to actually doing it.

The preceding outline of the psychophysiological approach to exploring the lucid dreaming state of consciousness and mapping the relationships between inner and outer realities has relied more on illustration than on theoretical discussion. Hopefully, the flavor of this research strategy has been adequately conveyed thereby. However, it may be informative before leaving the topic to compare and contrast the methodology that the LaBerge group has been pursuing to Tart's (1973) proposal for "state specific sciences" (SSS).

Psychophysiology vs. State-Specific Sciences

According to Tart, each SSS consists of two classes of activity to be carried out within the particular state of consciousness being studied: observing and theorizing. On the issue of observation, applying Tart's general concept specifically to the lucid dream state of consciousness, to carry out such a SSS requires "a group of highly skilled, dedicated and trained practitioners" capable of entering the lucid dream state and "able to agree with one another that they have attained a common state." While in the lucid dream, " . . . they can investigate other areas of interest"—whether totally internal phenomena of the lucid dream state, or " . . . the interaction of that state with external physical reality, or people in other dream states of consciousness" (Tart, 1975, p. 217). Of course, Tart's description is virtually identical with the way we have conceptualized the capacities required by our lucid dreamers and the types of investigations we have been carrying out. So, regarding observations, we are in close agreement.

It is on the issue of theories, however, that we part company. Tart proposes that theoretical explanations for the observations made in a given altered state of consciousness ought to be developed in the *same* altered state of consciousness rather than another one (such as the waking state). The premise underlying this contention seems to be the notion that all states of consciousness are equally valid ways of organizing experience and that none has any intrinsic superiority over any other. This is an assumption that we are unable to accept, but rather than argue, let us note LaBerge's (1985) observations on this issue: "I am rarely tempted to theorize on lucid dreaming while in the lucid dream state, and those few times that I have done so resulted in ideas that seemed unmistakably irrational in the clear light of morning. Tart would say that I ought not judge my lucid dream reasoning with the standards of waking rationality. But this is exactly what seems necessary to do in order to increase my rationality in the lucid dream state." Every state of consciousness has its strengths and weaknesses. The strength of the lucid dream state seems to be in our capacity to vividly create model universes that can provide a new perspective on our view of waking life and the physical universe. Likewise, the lucid dream state seems particularly suited to divergent thinking and the creative generation of ideas—brainstorming, as it were—whereas the state seems ill suited for convergent thinking, critical evaluation of ideas, rational theorizing, and the like. Perhaps we should be content to explore the inner reality of the lucid dream and its relationship to the external reality of the physical world. Relating the structures and phenomena of a newly explored domain to those of a more familiar domain (of which the physical world is the paradigm) provides what would appear to be a salutary grounding and point of reference. Progress is achieved when an unknown phenomenon is seen in relation to familiar, well-understood phenomena. In any case, there is the important question of what impact the events of the lucid dream world have on the physical world, especially that part of it that comprises the lucid dreamer's body.

In light of these facts, we would perhaps be wise to use the lucid dream to explore the dream world and its relation to the physical world. While in the lucid dream state, we might sensibly limit ourselves to observations and experiments (planned in the waking state!), leaving theorizing on the topic to our more rational waking moments.

REFERENCES

Antrobus, J., Antrobus, J., and Fisher, C. Discrimination of dreaming and non-dreaming sleep. *Archives of General Psychiatry,* 1965, *12,* 395–401.

Banquet, J. P. Comparative study of the EEG spectral analysis during sleep and yoga meditation. In *Sleep: Physiology, biochemistry, psychology, pharmacology, clinical implications.* Basel: S. Karger, 1973.

Belicki, D. A., Hunt, H., and Belicki, K. An exploratory study comparing self-reported lucid and non-lucid dreamers. *Sleep Research,* 1978, *7,* 166.

Berger, R. *Psyclosis: The circularity of experience.* San Francisco: W. H. Freeman, 1977.

Blackmore, S. J. More sex differences in lucid dreaming frequency. *Lucidity Letter,* 1982, *1*(2), 5.

Blackmore, S. J. A survey of lucid dreams, OBE's and related experiences. *Lucidity Letter,* 1983, *2*(3), 1.

Brown, A. E. Dreams in which the dreamer knows he is asleep. *Journal of Abnormal and Social Psychology,* 1936, *31,* 59–66.

Cohen, D. Changes in REM dream content during the night: Implications for a hypothesis about changes in cerebral dominance across REM periods. *Perceptual and Motor Skills,* 1977, *44,* 1267–1277.

Dane, J. An empirical evaluation of two techniques for lucid dream induction. Unpublished doctoral dissertation. Georgia State University, 1984.

Evans-Wentz, W. Y. *Tibetan yoga and secret doctrines.* New York: Oxford University Press, 1960.

Faraday, A. *Dream power.* London: Hadder Stroughton, 1974.

Fenwick, P. B. C., Schatzman, M., Worsley, A., Adams, J., Stone, S., and Baker, A. Lucid dreaming: A correspondence between dreamed and actual events in one subject during REM sleep. *Biological Psychology,* 1984, *18,* 243–252.

Foulkes, D. [Review of Schwartz and Lefevbre 1973.] *Sleep Research,* 1974, *3,* 113.

Fox, O. *Astral projection.* New Hyde Park, N.Y.: University Books, 1962.

Gackenbach, J. I. A personality and cognitive style analysis of lucid dreaming. Unpublished doctoral dissertation, Virginia Commonwealth University, 1978.

Gackenbach, J. I. Content analysis. Unpublished data, 1982.

Gackenbach, J. I. Personality differences between individuals varying in lucid dreaming frequency. *Journal of Communication Therapy,* in press.

Gackenbach, J. I., and Hammons, S. Lucid dreaming ability and verbal creativity. *Dreamworks,* 1983, *3*(3) 219–223.

Gackenbach, J. I. and LaBerge, S. (Eds.), *Lucid dreaming: New research on consciousness during sleep.* New York: Plenum, in press.

Gackenbach, J. I. and Schillig, B. Lucid dreams: The content of conscious awareness of dreaming during the dream. *Journal of Mental Imagery,* 1983, *7*(2), 1–14.

Gackenbach, J. I. and Snyder, T. J. A consideration of individuals who differ in spontaneously experiencing dream lucidity. In J. I. Gackenbach and S. P. LaBerge (Eds.), *Lucid dreaming: New research on consciousness during sleep.* New York: Plenum, in press.

Gackenbach, J. I., Snyder, T. J., McKelvey, K., McWilliams, C., George, E., and Rodenelli, B. Lucid dreaming: Individual differences in perception. *Sleep Research,* 1981, *10,* 146.

Gackenbach, J. I., Curren, R., and Cutler, G. Presleep determinants and post-sleep results of lucid versus vivid dreams. Paper presented at the annual meeting of the American Association for the Study of Mental Imagery, Vancouver, June 1983.

Gackenbach, J. I., Curren, R., LaBerge, S., Davidson, D., and Maxwell, P. Intelligence, creativity, and personality differences between individuals who vary in self-reported lucid dreaming frequency. Paper presented at the annual meeting of the American Association of Mental Imagery, Vancouver, June 1983.

Gackenbach, J. I., Prill, S., and Westrom, P. The relationship of the lucid dreaming ability to mental imagery experience and skills. *Lucidity Letter,* 1983, *2*(4), 4–6.

Gackenbach, J. I., Heilman, N., Boyt, S., and LaBerge, S. The relationship between field independence and lucid dreaming ability. *Journal of Mental Imagery,* in press.

Gackenbach, J. I. The content of lucid dreams. In J. I. Gackenbach and S. P. LaBerge (Eds.), *Lucid dreaming: New research on consciousness during sleep.* New York: Plenum, in press.

Gackenbach, J. I., Rokes, L., Sachau, D., and Snyder, T. J. Relationship of the lucid dreaming ability to vestibular sensitivity as measured by caloric hystagmus 1983, *Journal of Mind Behavior,* in press.

Gackenbach, J. I., Sachau, D., Rokes, L., and Snyder, T. J. Lucid dreaming ability as a function of gross motor balance 1983, unpublished manuscript.

Gackenbach, J. I., Walling, J. A., and LaBerge, S. Lucid dreams and parasympathetic functioning. *Lucidity Letter,* 1984, *3*(4), 3–6.

Garfield, P. *Creative dreaming.* New York: Ballentine, 1974.

Garfield, P. Self-conditioning of dream content. *Sleep Research,* 1974, *3,* 118.

Garfield, P. Psychological concomitants of the lucid dream state. *Sleep Research,* 1975, *4,* 183.

Garfield, P. *Pathway to ecstasy.* New York: Holt, Rinehart & Winston, 1979.

Gillespie, G. An experiment in dream planning. In J. I. Gackenbach and S. P. LaBerge (Eds.), *Lucid dreaming: New research on consciousness during sleep,* New York: Plenum, in press.

Goodenough, D. R., Shapiro, A., Holden, M., and Steinschriber, L. A comparison of "dreamers" and "nondreamers": Eye movements, electroencephalograms, and the recall of dreams. *Journal of Abnormal and Social Psychology,* 1959, *50,* 295–302.

Green, C. *Lucid dreams.* London: Hamish Hamilton, 1968.

Greyson, B. Near-death, out-of-body, and lucid experience: additional comments and data. *Lucidity Letter,* *1*(3), 1982, p. 6.

Hakstian, J. and Cattell, R. B. The checking of primary ability structure on a broader basis of performance, *British Journal of Educational Psychology,* 1974, *44,* 140–154.

Hall, C. S. and Van de Castle, R. L. *The content analysis of dreams.* New York: Appleton-Century-Crofts, 1966.

Hall, J. A. *Clinical uses of dreams.* New York: Grune & Stratton, 1977.

Hartmann, E. Dreams and other hallucinations: An approach to the underlying mechanism. In R. K. Siegel and L. J. West (Eds.), *Hallucinations: behavior, experience and theory.* New York: Wiley, 1975.

Hearne, K. M. T. Lucid dreams: An electrophysiological and psychological study. Unpublished doctoral dissertation, University of Liverpool, 1978.

Hearne, K. M. T. A "light-switch" phenomenon in lucid dreams. *Journal of Mental Imagery,* 1981, *5,* 97–100.

Hearne, K. M. T. Lucid dream induction. *Journal of Mental Imagery,* 1983, *7,* 19–24.

Hoffman, E. and McCarley, R. W. Bizarreness and lucidity in REM sleep dreams: A quantitative analysis. *Sleep Research,* 1980, *9,* 134.

Irwin, H. J. Migraine, out-of-body experiences, and lucid dreams. *Lucidity Letter,* 1983, *2*(2), 2–3.

Irwin, H. J. Out-of-body experiences and dream lucidity: Two views: Part I: Empirical perspectives. In J. I. Gackenbach and S. P. LaBerge (Eds.), *Lucid dreaming: New research on consciousness during sleep.* New York: Plenum, in press.

Kohr, R. L. A survey of psi experiences among members of a special population. *The Journal of the American Society for Psychical Research,* 1980, *74,* 295–411.

LaBerge, S. P. Lucid dreaming: some personal observations. *Sleep Research,* 1979, *8,* 158.

LaBerge, S. P. Lucid dreaming: An exploratory study of consciousness during sleep. Ph.D. dissertation, Stanford University, 1980a.

LaBerge, S. P. Lucid dreaming as a learnable skill: A case study. *Perceptual and Motor Skills,* 1980b, *51,* 1039–1042.

LaBerge, S. P. Directing the action as it happens. *Psychology Today,* 1981, *15,* 48–57.

LaBerge, S. P. *Lucid Dreaming.* Los Angeles: J. P. Tarcher, Inc., 1985.

LaBerge, S. P. Self-integration through lucid dreaming. In A. Ahsen (Ed.), *Handbook of imagery research and practice.* New York: Random House, in press.

LaBerge, S. P. and Dement, W. C. Lateralization of alpha activity for dreamed singing and counting during REM sleep. *Psychophysiology,* 1982a, *19,* 331–332.

LaBerge, S. P. and Dement, W. C. Voluntary control of respiration during lucid REM dreaming. *Sleep Research,* 1982b, *11,* 107.

LaBerge, S. P., Nagel, L. E., Dement, W. C., and Zarcone, V. P. Lucid dreaming verified by volitional communication during REM sleep. *Perceptual and Motor Skills,* 1981a, *52,* 727–732.

LaBerge, S. P., Nagel, L. E., Taylor, W. B., Dement, W. C., and Zarcone, V. P. Psychophysiological correlates of the initiation of lucid dreaming. *Sleep Research,* 1981b, *10,* 149.

LaBerge, S. P., Owens, J., Nagel, L. E., and Dement, W. C. "This is a dream": Induction of lucid dreams by verbal suggestion during REM sleep. *Sleep Research,* 1981c, *10,* 150.

LaBerge, S. P., Greenleaf, W., and Kedzierski, B. Physiological responses to dreamed sexual activity during lucid REM sleep. *Psychophysiology,* 1983, *20,* 454–455.

LaBerge, S. P., Levitan, L., Gordon, M., and Dement, W. C. The psychophysiology of lucid dream initiation. *Psychophysiology,* 1983, *20,* 455.

Malamud, J. R. The development of a training method for the cultivation of "lucid" awareness in fantasy, dreams, and waking life. Unpublished doctoral dissertation, New York University, 1980.

McCreery, C. *Psychical phenomena and the physical world.* London: Hamish Hamilton, 1973.

McGinty, D. J. Sleep state organization and dissociation. In R. Drucker-Colin, M. Shkurovich, and N. B. Sterman (Eds.), *The function of sleep.* New York: Academic Press, 1979.

McLeod, B. and Hunt, H. Meditation and lucid dreams. *Lucidity Letter,* 1983, *2*(4), 6–7.

Moers-Messmer, H. Dreaming while knowing about the dream state. *Archiv fur die Gesamte Psychologie,* 1938, *102,* 291–318.

Narayana, R. (Ed.). *The dream problem and its many solutions in search after ultimate truth.* Delhi, India: Practical Medicine, 1922.

Neisser, U. *Cognitive psychology.* New York: Appleton-Century-Crofts, 1967.

Ogilvie, R., Hunt, H., Sawicki, D., and McGowan, K. Searching for lucid dreams. *Sleep Research,* 1978, *7,* 165.

Ogilvie, R., Hunt, H., Tyson, P. D., Lucescu, M. L., and Jeakins, D. B. Lucid dreaming and alpha activity: A preliminary report. *Perceptual and Motor Skills,* 1982, *55,* 795–808.

Ogilvie, R., Hunt, H., Kushniruk, A., and Newman, J. Lucid dreams and the arousal continuum. *Sleep Research,* 1983, 12, 182.

Ouspensky, P. *A new model of the universe.* London: Routledge & Kegan Paul, 1931.

Palmer, J. A community mail survey of psychic experiences. *Research in Parapsychology,* 1974, *3,* 130–133.

Palmer, J. Unpublished data, 1974.

Palmer, J. Community mail survey of psychic experiences. *Research in Parapsychology,* 1974, 3, 130–133.

Plutchick, R. and Conte, H., Sex differences in reported psychophysiological reactivity, *Psychological Reports,* 1974, 35 pp. 1221–1222.

Price, R. Lucid dream induction: An empirical evaluation. In J. I. Gackenbach and S. P. LaBerge (Eds.), *Lucid dreaming: New research on consciousness during sleep.* New York: Plenum, in press.

Rajneesh, B. S. *The book of the secrets—I.* New York: Harper & Row, 1974.

Rapport, N. Pleasant dreams. *Psychiatric Quarterly Supplement,* 1948, *22,* 909–317.

Rechtschaffen, A. and Kales, A. (Eds.). *A manual of standardized terminology, techniques, and scoring for sleep stages of human subjects* (National Institute of Health Publication No. 204). Washington, D.C.: United States Government Printing Office, 1968.

Reed, H. Meditation and lucid dreaming: A statistical relationship. *Sundance Community Dream Journal,* 1978, *2,* 237–238.

Richardson, A. *Mental imagery.* New York: Springer, 1969.

Roffwarg, H., Dement, W., Muzio, J., and Fisher, C. Dream imagery: Relationship to rapid eye movements of sleep. *Archives of General Psychiatry,* 1962, *7,* 235–258.

Schwartz, B. A., and Lefebvre, A. Contacts veille/P.M.O. II. Les P.M.O. morecelles. *Revue d'Electroencephalographie et de Neurophysiologie Clinique,* 1973, *3,* 165–176.

Snyder, T. J. and Gackenbach, J. I. Lucid dreaming and cerebral organization. *Sleep Research,* 1981, *10,* 154.

Sparrow, G. S. *Lucid dreaming: Dawning of the clear light.* Virginia Beach, VA: A.R.E. Press, 1976.

Stoyva, J. and Kamiya, J. Electrophysiological studies of dreaming as the prototype of a new strategy in the study of consciousness. *Psychological Review,* 1968, *75,* 192–205.

Tart, C. Toward the experimental control of dreaming: A review of the literature. *Psychology Bulletin,* 1965, *64,* 81–92.

Tart, C. State-specific sciences. *Science,* 1973, *180,* 1003–1008.

Tart, C. *States of consciousness.* New York: Dutton, 1975.

Tart, C. From spontaneous event to lucidity: A review of attempts to consciously control nocturnal dreaming. In B. B. Wolman (Ed.), *Handbook of dreams.* New York: Van Nostrand Reinhold, 1979.

Tholey, P. Techniques for inducing and manipulating lucid dreams. *Perceptual and Motor Skills,* 1983, *57,* 79–80.

Tulku, T. *Openness mind.* Berkeley, CA: Dharma Publishing Co., 1978.

Van Eeden, F. A study of dreams. *Proceedings of the Society for Psychical Research,* 1913, *26,* 431–461.

Venus, S. Early results with Hearne's dream machine. *Lucidity Letter,* 1982, *1*(2), 2.

Watkins, M. M. *Waking dreams.* New York: Harper & Row, 1976.

Williams, R., Karacan, I., and Jursch, C. *Electroencephalography (EEG) of human sleep: Clinical applications.* New York: Wiley, 1974.

Wilmes, F. Editor's note. *Lucidity Letter,* 1983, *2*(3), 5.

Worsley, A. Alan Worsley's work on lucid dreaming. *Lucidity Letter,* 1982, *1*(4), 1–3.

Worsley, A. Comments on an investigation of the relative degree of activation in lucid dreams. *Lucidity Letter,* 1983, *2*(3), 5.

Yram. *Practical astral projection.* New York: Weiser, 1967.

7. Personal Experience as a Conceptual Tool for Modes of Consciousness

E. Mansell Pattison and Joel Kahan

The teachings of psycho-analysis are based on an incalculable number of observations and experiences, and only someone who has repeated those observations on himself and on others is in a position to arrive at a judgment of his own upon it. (Freud, 1940)

Along with Freud we approach the topic of states of consciousness from the point of view of what we ourselves experience and what others relate as their experience. We concur with Freud as he continues from the above to state: "our acts of consciousness . . . are immediate data, and cannot be further explained by any sort of description." Therefore we choose to focus on personal experience as our avenue of exploration of states of consciousness. The human organism obviously experiences many operations, events, and stimuli, many of which occur outside of consciousness. Our focus is upon those operations that are experienced *in consciousness,* hence *personal* experiences.

Our purposes are threefold in examining the domain of personal experience:

1. To highlight the importance of personal experience as a major domain of human action.
2. To clarify the confusion of conflicting, ambiguous, and diffuse terminology and concepts currently existent in this domain.
3. To present a heuristic taxonomy of terminology that has a natural coherence, and is consistent with current theories of human action.

199

PERTINENT LITERATURE

The domain of personal experience has had a checkered history in behavioral science research. Philosophical inquiry has, of course, struggled with the importance and place of personal experience in our understanding of the human. However, it is beyond our purview to review the philosophical assumptions that have variously influenced a more strictly psychological inquiry in the past century. Beginning with the first experimentalists (Strange, 1978; Spiegelberg, 1972), introspection and personal experience were given place in human action. The great philosopher–psychologist William James continued to give credence and centrality of personal experience to human action at the turn of the twentieth century (James, 1890).

During this century, however, the domain of personal experience lost its centrality. The empirical-experimental methodology of behavioral psychology followed a research strategy in which personal experience lay outside its methodology. Similarly, the methodology of psychoanalytic inquiry, although relying on introspective data, pursued a path of data analysis that also excluded the domain of personal experience per se (Fingarette, 1963; Haan, 1977; Hofstadter and Dennet, 1981; Pope and Singer, 1978; Raimy, 1975).

Nevertheless, scientific exploration of personal experience continued to exist on the periphery, as exemplified in phenomenological psychology, existential psychology, and experiential psychology (Spiegelberg, 1972). In the past decade, new work in psychology, psychoanalysis, and neurobiology has refocused explicit attention on the domain of personal experience (Mahrer, 1978; Taylor, 1979). As a result, the domain of personal experience is again a major topic of scientific inquiry. This work again pushes personal experience into the center of our understanding of human action.

We have encountered numerous problems in collating a simple review of this new research because:

1. Authors use different terminology for the same concept.
2. The same terminology is used to refer to different concepts.
3. Terminology and concepts are often derived from prior theoretical requirements, resulting in artificial or biased terms and concepts.

Therefore, an exegesis of the literature would require an entire paper just to differentiate the confusions that abound. So we shall be content to briefly summarize the most salient commentators, to exemplify the state of the literature. We consider six areas.

First is the area of *action language*. Roy Schafer (1976) has criticized the tendency to anthropomorphize psychic functions. The constructs of ego, id, and superego have come to be loosely ascribed personal attributes, whereas those constructs only describe operations. Schafer proposes that we describe psychic functions solely in operational terms, without imputing personalistic biases in our language. At the same time, Schafer would resurrect a language to describe personalized action. Jane Loevinger (1976) takes this approach further in her description of "ego." She differentiates ego operations that are mechanistic psychic functions from the synthetic executive operations of ego, which are personalistic and experienced as the "sense of I operations."

Second is the area of *personalizing language.* In his original work Freud employed the terms "das-es" and "ich" to refer to personal operations of the human. Bettelheim (1983) has recently criticized English translations into the terms "id" and "ego" as synthetic, impersonal, cold terms that misrepresent the original intent of Freud to maintain a personal dimension in his description of psychic operations. Hoffman (1982) similarly criticizes subsequent psychoanalytic theorists for mechanizing psychic operations under the rubric of adaptation, thereby omitting the personalizing voluntarism of the human. Both Loevinger (1976) and Pattison (1984) emphasize that impersonal psychic operations lack appreciation for personal choice and personal direction of action, which lie at the heart of personal freedom, responsibility, and moral capacity.

Third is the area of representation of *personal experience.* Neurolinguistic research, for example, Luria (1973), points up that there is a substantial gap between experience and language. In fact, thought must be transformed into language. This is the basis for Jacques Lacan's (1978) contention that human experience must be the essence of analysis of human action, rather than psychodynamics per se. Lacan explains that through language, even introspective language, the person achieves distance by *naming the experience.* Thus there is a clear distinction between the *person* of experience, and the person's *report* of experience. Lacan terms these the "self of experience" and the "self of discourse," and he postulates an "I of existence" and an "I of meaning." This view is reinforced by studies in child development. Stechler and Kaplan (1980) suggest that typical metapsychological and psychodynamic theory does not account for the developmental data that demonstrate an emerging capacity for personalized self-regulation, which is the emerging sense of "I." Similarly, Izard (1978) describes how the child operates in terms of experience, leading to affective permanency, then perceptual permanency, and finally cognitive permanency. These developments lead to "self-awareness" or reports of personal experience. Sutherland (1980) notes that it is incorrect to ascribe adult anthromorphic attributes to the experience of the developing child. Rather, child development is rooted in personal experience: "the development of the person has to be conceived as the progressive differentiation of a structure from a unitary matrix that itself interacts at a *holistic personal level* from the start.'' Alvin Mahrer (1978) synthesizes these observations in the notion that personal experience develops into personalizing operations, which we come to name "Me" experiences and "I" experiences. Mahrer goes on to describe self-operations as derivative from precursor Me and I experiences.

Fourth is the *Me experience.* James (1890) described the "empirical me" as the self-as-known, in contrast to the "I" or self-as-knower. Gordon Allport (1937) makes the same differentiation, terming the bodily sense a "bodily me," which "remains a life-long anchor for our self-awareness." This experience of Me is described by Harry Stack Sullivan (1953) as the "good me," the "bad me," and the "not me," whereas Winnicott (1965) distinguishes between the "experience of me" and the "experience of not me." Mahrer (1978) has explored this bodily Me experience and suggests that this "inner experience" is the basic referent of being alive. Hilgard (1977) considers this private inner experience of Me as the "hidden observer," and even described different "me operations."

Fifth is the *I experience.* The paper by Globus (1980) describes the "I" as what we personally experience during the operation of executive ego functions, just as Loevinger does. To Globus the "I" is not an anthropomorphic "ghost in the machine." Indeed "I" is an experience of the ego operations of evaluating, deciding, choosing, and directing action. Csikszentmihalyi (1989) describes these ego operations as part of the processes of consciousness entailing attentionality and intentionality. When "I" experience these operations, it is possible to name the experience as "I am choosing." Thus the I experience reflects the voluntary action operations of the person.

Sixth is the concept of *self.* This is a very confusing area. Carl Rogers (1961) considered the self-system as composed of I and Me. Epstein (1981) has observed that the term "self" is often used as a catchall to refer to I, me, myself, identity, being, and existence. Self is variously considered as subject, object, and concept. James (1890) described the "self-as-a-knower" and the "self-as-a-doer." Amsterdam and Levitt (1980) distinguish between "self as being" and "self as object of observation." Schafer (1976) describes three functions of the "self-structure": "the self-as-an-agent," "the self-as-locus," and "the self-as-object." It is obvious that these usages of self contain elements of Me experience, I experience, and mechanistic ego operations. The most unambiguous use of the term "self" has developed out of current research on "self-as-a-construct" (Lewis and Brooks-Gunn, 1979; Lynch, et al., 1981). In this view, self is a psychological construct stored in memory on the basis of social interaction. As a durable memory, the "self-construct" does indeed produce an "experience of self"; that is, memory of whole person action in the past (self in past), memory of desired action in terms of the self construct (self in future), and comparison of present action in accord with the construct model (self in present). Loevinger (1976) has pointed out that the superego and ego ideal contribute to the self-construct, but are not the same as the social construction and voluntary construction of a self-construct by the person. In brief, self is a construct in memory.

To conclude, the literature suggests that we must distinguish between experience, psychodynamics, and behavior. Personal experience emerges as a unique attribute of the person, which serves as the basis for personal freedom, responsibility, and voluntary choice of action. The terminology of personal experience, however, is imprecise and ambiguous. In part this reflects very different research approaches, and in part an emerging domain of inquiry that has not been systematically analyzed. Therefore, our work here does not raise new issues, ideas, or concepts, but rather addresses a systematic taxonomy of personal experience.

METHODOLOGY

We began our inquiry from a nontheoretical posture; we did not assume any theoretical demand for a specific type of description of personal experience. We frankly started with our own personal experience, and attempted to achieve consensual agreement on what we each experienced. We then sought similar descriptions from a study group over a four-year period to assess biases or idiosyncracy in our own descriptions. We then searched the literature for descriptions of personal experience to compare, validate, or contradict our personally derived descriptions. Next, we compared our "normal taxonomy" with clinical syndromes. When we had achieved a taxonomy that had natural coherence, heuristic logic, and clinical verdicality, we finally addressed the problem of fitting the taxonomy into existing psychological theory. Our emphasis, however, remains on what can be known of personal experience by direct self observation. Therefore, it is hoped that our examples throughout will be "common knowledge" that the reader can personally confirm.

MODELS OF HUMAN ACTION

The domain of personal experience is ambiguously represented in our current biopsychosocial model of the human. In this chapter we seek to analyze the components of personal experience, and present a model of human operation in which personal experience is defined as a major component. We seek to restore the concept of the person to our description of the human.

There are three major perspectives from which human operations are described: experience, behavior, and psychological constructs. Each offers a valid view of the human, but each in isolation produces a reductionistic description.

The behavioral perspective describes the human in terms of public action, that is, human actions that can be determined by observation without the subject's self report. Such behaviors are universal in that the same operations (e.g., speech rate) can be observed in all humans. Therefore, these behaviors are *public universal* phenomena.

The psychological construct perspective describes the human in terms of theoretical human actions. Such actions are inferred from the subject's self report. This description is private in that it depends upon the subject's willingness to provide a self report of the experience from which psychological actions are inferred. However, constructs are also universal in that they can be reported by every person (e.g., the report of guilt feelings indicative of superego action). Therefore, the psychological construct actions are *private universal* phenomena.

The personal experience perspective describes the human in terms of those operations that are private, available only through self report. As phenomena they are unique experiences: I describe *my* own experience operating as a human being. Thus personal experience is idiosyncratic. We may recognize a *similar* personal experience of another, but I can never have your personal experience. Therefore personal experiences are *private unique* phenomena.

Our purpose is to avoid a reductionistic model. The behavioral perspective ignores the richness of psychological process and describes the human only in terms of impersonal universal mechanisms. The psychological construct perspective focuses on internal private processes that may not predict the behavioral outcome, while again those are impersonal universal mechanisms. The personal experience perspective gives credence to unique personal phenomena but ignores the universal mechanisms of psychological constructs and behavior.

Most models of the human recognize the danger of reductionism. However, for the most part, only two out of three perspectives are combined. For example, the behavioral and psychological are combined in two-step learning theory, cognitive–behavioral theory, and rational–emotive therapy. The psychological and experiential are combined in Gestalt therapy and phenomenological psychology. The behavioral–experiential combination is least represented, perhaps exemplified by behavioral implosive therapy.

Single perspective models might be represented in the behavioral perspective by aversive and operant conditioning, the psychological construct perspective by traditional psychoanalysis, and the personal experience perspective by humanistic/experiential therapies.

Although in the clinical arena there is considerable synthesis of all three perspectives, the same is not true for formal models.

We have constructed diagrams to represent our model. The reader may wish to first examine these diagrams to gain an overall sense of the terms we shall employ and their relationships to each other. In Figure 1 we illustrate the overall system of psychic operation. In Figure 2 we present a more detailed model of the interaction between the ego system and the experiential perspective.

CONSCIOUSNESS

Most commentators agree that personal experience is critically involved with the experience of consciousness (Valle and Von Ecktersberg, 1981; Goleman and Davidson, 1979; Walsh, 1980). Therefore, we shall detail the concept of consciousness.

Throughout our analysis we shall not refer to "states" of consciousness, but rather to "modes" of consciousness. Our purpose in doing so is to emphasize that consciousness is the experience of a process. The word "state" implies a static or fixed condition, whereas we hope to demonstrate that consciousness is the experience of an active fluctuating process. Although we shall describe levels of consciousness, we shall demonstrate that there are multiple modes of conscious experience at different levels. Further, we shall demonstrate that there is no such thing as a "normal state of consciousness." Rather, we can normally experience a variety of modes of consciousness.

Globus (1980) proposed that consciousness is an experience: namely, the experience of certain synthetic operations that are in themselves unique, and cannot be reduced to other ego operations (Loevinger, 1976). We concur with this proposition, and ask the question: what is the experience that we name as consciousness?

Our definition is: "Consciousness is the *name* we give to unique organismic experience which we personalize." In other words, consciousness is the experience of a set of ego operations to which a personalizing action is applied.

What are the operations that produce this "personalizing action"? We propose three sets of interactive variables that produce the experience of consciousness. More precisely, permutations of these three variables produce a panorama of modes of consciousness. We shall reject a simplistic definition of consciousness as one experience or one state. Rather we shall

206

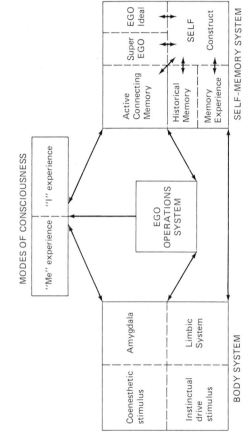

Figure 1. Model of psychic operations.

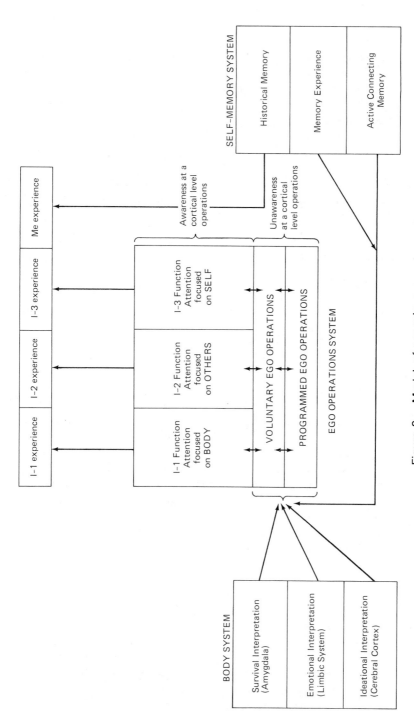

Figure 2. Model of consciousness.

conclude that there is a range of personalizing actions that result in a variety of modes of consciousness.

The three variables we shall consider are:

1. Primary experience
2. Awareness experience
3. Personal experience

For heuristic purposes we can consider each of these three experiences as separate, although in actuality all three are combined into various experiences of consciousness.

PRIMARY EXPERIENCE

Stimuli from body, objects, and self are processed and synthetically organized into concepts, classifications, and representative symbols.

The young infant is bombarded by stimuli, which at first are meaningless events. Stimuli are increasingly organized into classes of events. We learn to organize coenesthetic *body stimuli* into simple pain and pleasure events. Then those events are further organized into precise bodily experiences such as hunger, a cut toe, an arm movement.

A similar process occurs in the elaboration of primary experiences of *other person stimuli.* At first the infant only processes the primary experience of the "smile mask." Ultimately we come to process complex primary experiences of an array of precise interpersonal events.

Third, the same process occurs in the elaboration of primary experiences of self-as-person stimuli. A simple level of such occurs when the two-year-old infants answers the question what is your name?'' with the answer "me Johnny." The end process is reflected in transcendental reflection on one's existential place in the universe.

We note that a variety of primary experience events are occurring all the time in humans. In fact, primary experiences in all three areas (coenesthetic, other, self) are occurring simultaneously.

These primary experiences produce the feeling of existing. They represent the *background substrate of living,* but not the foreground (to be discussed later).

Descartes' dictum, I think, therefore I exist" is a background statement of the experience of existing. We can equally substitute parallel statements such as "I hurt, therefore I exist" or "I experience your presence, therefore I exist." *Any primary experience* of coenesthetic events, interpersonal events, or self operation events *validates existence.*

However, primary experiences are not the same as the experience of consciousness. Many primary experiences occur without "our being aware of them." We "consciously experience" primary experience events *only* when such events are in the *content of awareness*. Some primary experience events are recorded in short-term memory and discarded if not encoded in the long-term memory bank. However, primary experience events can be retrieved from short- and long-term memory if and when our attention is given to our memory bank and such data are retrieved. In that case we may "consciously experience" an event that we did not *know* had occurred.

In summary, primary experiences are occurring all the time. Much of learning in life occurs through primary experience events (life conditioning). We learn to use our ego awareness operations to focus selectively on primary experience events that are adaptive to the moment. And we may recall and retrieve other primary experience events passively as in dreams or actively as in memory recall.

AWARENESS EXPERIENCE

A set of ego functions is necessary to produce the experience of awareness. *Arousal* is the first function, mediated by the midbrain. Arousal refers to the level of activation of the brain to receive and process stimuli. The arousal level varies from stage IV sleep to full alertness. As we observe a person awakening or coming out of anesthesia we observe shifting levels of arousal reflecting the function of brain activation.

The second ego function is that of *paying attention,* mediated by the thalamus. This function is linked to brain maturation and development. The normal infant demonstrates the capacity to attend to external stimuli at about six weeks of age. Simple conditioning responses can be evoked in the infant with the appearance of the attention function. The capacity for attention continues to develop for many years in terms of attention span and complexity of content to which attention can be given.

A third ego function is the shifting of the *content of attention*. This has two subsets.

The first subset is the operation of shifting the *locus of attention*. This operation controls and mediates the process of changing attention from one locus to another. We may give attention to the following areas of primary experience.

1. Internal coenesthetic stimuli (pain, hunger, location of a limb)
2. External environmental stimuli (a tree, a person, the road)
3. Ego operations (thought, feeling, complex movements)
4. Memories (ideas, past events, concepts of oneself)

Complex human operations require synthesizing attention upon several areas of primary experience at the same time. For example, if one sits down at a formal dinner, one must pay attention to hunger stimuli, memories of desired or hated foods, the actual food on the table, and social behavior with the guests.

The second subset is the operation of shifting the *focus* of attention. This operation can be described as analogous to the operation of a camera. We can focus on foreground detail, with the background blurred, or focus on a broad landscape with absence of detail, or on variations in between. Detailed focus of attention is demonstrated by the writing of an examination, in which attention to the state of one's body, the room, and others is indistinct. In contrast, a broad focus is illustrated by standing on a street corner observing the general activity without attending to specific persons, cars, feelings, or thoughts.

Now we can describe how these three ego operations interact to produce the experience of awareness.

First, the level of arousal determines the capacity to pay attention and the capacity to shift locus and focus of attention. For example, if one is just awakening, one may be aware of noise in the room, but cannot immediately give attention to the noise; therefore one cannot localize the noise or discern details of the noise as spoken words. Only when arousal has increased, can one pay attention to the speaker, localize the source of the language, and focus on the detail of the words.

Second, the operation of paying attention is determined developmentally. The capacity to extend the attention span is necessary for detailed examination of content, and for complex manipulation of the focusing process. For example, a two-year-old has not acquired the capacity to attend to a lengthy television plot. Even a five-year-old in kindergarten cannot maintain attention for over a few minutes. The capacity for maintaining attention is necessary before effective shifting operations can be deliberately invoked.

Third, the capacity for deliberate shifting of locus and focus is again developmental. One learns to increase the effectiveness and deliberateness of these shifting operations.

In summary, the experience of awareness can vary from the lowest level of operation (stage IV sleep) to the highest level of operation (e.g., the detailed exercise of focused attention in yoga practices).

Different experiences of awareness will contribute to the overall variation in different states of consciousness.

What is the awareness experience, then? It is the experience of being *connected* to a particular primary experience to which our attention is given.

We note that the human organism may be processing many primary experiences outside of awareness, and such events may be recorded in short- and long-term memory. We may retrieve such events from memory and thus "experience an awareness of content" that we originally had no awareness had happened to us. For example, one may sit in an examination in a hot room and sweat for an hour. One leaves the room and recalls that one has been sweating throughout the previous hour.

Further, we note that at the lowest levels of awareness, as in awakening, the clarity of connection is vague and ambiguous (I was dimly aware of the sounds of morning), whereas at the highest levels of awareness one is acutely and precisely connected to the content of awareness (I experience precise thinking in solving a math problem, or I apprehend the exact intent of your body movements). We summarize awareness as "the experience of connectedness to primary experiences."

PERSONAL EXPERIENCE

In addition to primary experience and the experience of awareness (the experience of connection to primary experiences), we can now add the personal experience, which we shall define as "the private and idiosyncratic experience of events as belonging to the person." This is the "*foreground of experience.*"

Personal experience is the sense of "owning" what is happening. It is not just that one experiences events, but that all such events are part of my unique existence—hence "my personal life," or "my experiences." Other people may name similar experiences, but my life events are uniquely "mine." My life is precisely personal because I experience a set of events processed through and by my own organism.

The personal experience is developmentally linked. The young infant is symbiotically linked to the "other mother object" without differentiation of the difference between mine and thine. With individuation and separation the child comes to differentiate between self and other. Finally, the adult comes to distinguish between introjects (my experience of "others" in me) and the self-construct (my experience of "me" in me).

Up to this point we have reviewed personal experience in a general manner. Now we must detail two aspects of personal experience: the Me experience and the I experience.

The Me Experience

As noted, the personalizing process results in the experience of "owning" what is happening. This is readily demonstrated in the clinical context when an experience is "not owned" and therefore is described as "not happening to me." Clinically we label these as "depersonalization experiences." Obviously both the experience of awareness is present, and primary experience is present, but what is missing is the personalization aspect. Often such "depersonalization experiences" are dysphoric and ego-dystonic.

We shall define the Me experience as "the cognitive label applied to the sense of being alive in person." We shall approach a description of this experience from the perspective of child development.

In the early stages of infancy, we infer that the infant experiences coenesthetic (bodily) sensations. Allport (1937) suggested that this is the sense of a "bodily me." However we need to be more precise in differentiating between the Me experience and primary experiences of coenesthetic stimuli per se.

Most authors describe the young infant as an *affective being* (Emde and Robinson, 1979; Engel, 1963; Piaget, 1952; Sroufe, 1979) in which cognition and emotions do not exist. Rather there is a stream of coenesthetic sensation arising from neurobiological process. Engel (1963) has suggested that the young infant experiences a "primary affect" or "basic affect" of either pleasure or unpleasure—or perhaps more accurately of equilibrium or dysequilibrium. Thus when the young infant is in a "steady state" (not inputing necessarily pleasurable stimuli) the infant exists in the basic affect state of "equilibrium." When noxious stimuli occur and exceed the sensory threshold, the infant manifests an indiscriminate affective response of disturbance—what we shall term a basic affect of "dysequilibrium."

In the above, we wish to clearly distinguish a "basic affect," which is a *synthesized global experience,* from discrete coenesthetic stimuli that the infant learns to identify in terms of bodily location. Further we wish to distinguish between this synthetic global basic affect and the discrete operations of the cognitive system and the emotional system which are ego operations.

This distinction is based upon recent research on the amygdala and its relation to the frontal cortex.

First, most studies of the amygdala show that its main function is to provide what may be called the "appropriate affective bias" (Kling, 1981; Young and Cohen, 1979). The amygdala serves as a reception center for coenesthetic stimuli, and stimuli from memory, ego operations, and the external environment. The amygdala operates as a subcortical "visceral brain" that processes and interprets stimulus events and then relays an *interpretation* to the frontal cortex, via both the hypothalamus and lateral projections directly to the frontal lobes. The question posed by Gloor (1978) is "what is the amygdala trying to tell the frontal cortex?" The answer proposed is that the amygdala signals the basic survival state of the organism and the species. The complex integrating and synthesizing functions of the amygdala are reflected in the experimental studies, which demonstrate that the amygdala mediates: (1) general arousal, orienting reactions, and sleep; (2) agonistic behavior (fight, defense, and predatory attack), and passive and active avoidance behavior; (3) feeding activities; (4) sexual behavior; (5) reward and punishment in self-stimulation; (6) bonding behavior (Adamec, 1978; Grossman, 1978; Kaada, 1972; Lehman et al., 1980).

In brief, then, the amygdala mediates the synthesis of meaning of interoceptive and exteroceptive stimuli events to the survival of the organism.

Second, the amygdala apparently generates a basic tonic affect signal to the frontal cortex that indicates whether the organism is in a "safe state" or in a "danger to survival state." We term the former the "equilibrium affect state" and the latter the "dysequilibrium affect state." This tonic affective signal has been described in the psychoanalytic idiom by Krystal (1982) as a primary affect, which signals overwhelming threat to the organism. In turn, this affect constricts, impedes, and impairs ego operations except for basic survival responses.

Current neurobiological research suggests that the amygdala evaluates the emotional significance of events in terms of their survival value to the organism and attaches an emotional valence interpretation that is then sent as a signal to the frontal cortex (Ben-Ari, 1981).

Third, the amygdala is directly involved with the ego operations that produce consciousness. That is, the amygdala selects for conscious experience those stimuli that are of significance for survival or for some immediate or long-term goals of the organism. Thus an insignificant or nonthreat stimuli may be excluded from consciousness by the amygdala, whereas, if the amygdala interprets a stimulus as a survival threat, it will then transmit a dysequilibrium affective signal of survival threat to the frontal cortex.

To summarize, if the amygdala interprets stimuli as nonthreats, the basic affective signal is that of equilibrium, and the organism will tolerate many types of pain, discomfort, adverse stimuli, and stress, since the organism is not threatened; whereas an innocuous stimulus, if interpreted by the amygdala as a survival threat, will generate a basic affective signal of dysequilibrium.

These observations help us to understand why some people can tolerate much adversity in life without distress, whereas other persons are thrown into a survival panic by minimal stimuli.

Neurobiological data indicate that the frontal cortex can "reprogram" the interpretations made by the amygdala. Thus we can learn and teach ourselves *not* to interpret stimuli as a threat to our survival.

Fourth, it has been proposed by Pribram (1967) that the "global synthetic signals" of the amygdala are experienced in the frontal cortex as a sensory perception of "being alive." Pribram labeled this the "I am" experience.

We concur with the Pribram analysis, but propose that the appropriate label for this is the "Me experience."

To elaborate, when awareness is focused upon the ongoing input from the amygdala which presents a global signal that the organism is in operation, we cognitively label that input as "the experience of me." This awareness that "me exists" is strictly an awareness of signals of the organism operating. It has no points of reference in the environment, memory, ego operations, or coenesthetic stimuli, since all such stimuli are being processed through the amygdala, which in turn is sending the signal of the fact the organism is in operation. Thus the Me experience is a global experience.

Carefully note that at the same time we are "experiencing Me" we learn to discriminate and differentiate a variety of interoceptive and exteroceptive stimuli. Thus "Me" experiences additional facts such as the fact that hunger exists or a toe hurts. The hunger stimuli or the pain stimuli have both *direct* routes to the frontal cortex, where *discrete* intepretations are made, and *indirect* routes via the amygdala, where the flow of all stimuli are being transformed into the amygdala signal that generates the Me experience.

Note that the Me experience is inextricably linked to the basic affect generated by the amygdala. Thus the *Me is experienced in either equilibrium or dysequilibrium.* When the Me experience is linked with an affect of equilibrium, the organism may tolerate many different pleasurable and noxious stimuli without perturbation of its basic state (e.g., we tolerate hunger pains or a mosquito bite itch because we are in equilibrium and the particular stimulus does not affect the amygdala signal of equilibrium). However, an *interpreted* threat stimulus (not necessarily noxious to the external observer) may change the amygdala signal, and the result is a Me experience associated with dysequilibrium. At that point we experience anxiety or panic.

To make matters more complex, we must distinguish between this unique basic tonic affect generated from the amygdala, and the more general emotional system functions of the limbic system. That is, the limbic system also interprets stimulus events in terms of *emotional significance*. In turn an emotional response is sent to the frontal cortex. Pleasure or unpleasure is a limbic emotional tone, quite apart from the survival tonic affect.

We see now that there are *three systems* for the interpretation of stimulus events. The frontal cortex makes an *ideational* interpretation, the limbic system makes an *emotional* interpretation, and the amygdala makes a *survival* interpretation.

The outcome of this complicated process is that in the normal state, the amygdala signals a basic affect of Me alive and functioning without threat to survival. In this state, events occur that have a conjoint ideational and emotional meaning that is congruent.

But let us consider when the three interpretive systems are not congruent. A simple stimulus, such as a loud thunder clap, might startle the person, evoking a momentary survival panic. Yet the ideational and emotional response (a few milliseconds later) may lead the person to comment "That scared me." In this case, the frontal lobe and limbic system did not interpret the thunder clap as a survival threat, and the person immediately is "reset" in survival equilibrium.

In the case of incongruence between the ideational and emotional interpretations, we may be in the state of equilibrium while noting two different interpretations of events. For example, one makes a social faux pas. We say, "I feel embarrassed, but I know it is not rational to feel this way."

Now consider a complex interaction. If we ask a person to evaluate pinpricks on the arm to test sensation, a person may tolerate rather intense pain without anxiety or the manifestation of a dysequilibrium response. On the other hand, just prick the arm of a person sitting next to you at a concert, and a very mild prick may elicit a rage response. In the former example, the amygdala was programmed to interpret the pinpricks in the sensory test as a nonthreat, whereas the unexpected pinprick elicits an amygdala interpretation of attack on the organism.

In the above pinprick experiment, the pleasure or unpleasure (emotional significance value) of the stimulus event per se is *not* the critical determinant of the response of the human. Rather, it is the survival interpretation that determines whether the organism will process the event with ordinary ideational and emotional processes, or respond with survival panic.

Thus, I experience events in ideational and emotional terms alongside a Me experience of either equilibrium or dysequilibrium.

We can now conclude that there are *three* distinct neurobiological systems of interpretation of stimulus events. The clinical significance is obvious to our common knowledge. Some persons tolerate high levels of stress with negative emotional value without "me dysequilibrium." Yet other persons experience "me dysequilibrium" (panic and anxiety) in response to minimal stress, trivial stimuli, and even pleasurable stimuli.

The distinction between Me experience and I experience is critical to socialization and maturation. "I" must acquire the capacity to *program amygdala interpretations* to stimulus events such that the "Me experience is in equilibrium," or else new and challenging social learning cannot occur. At the same time, "I" must learn how to reprogram or reinterpret stimulus events in the amygdala in accord with adaptational requirements. Thus "I" must cognitively label pleasurable stimuli as not necessary for survival or noxious stimuli as not a threat to survival so that "I" can process both pleasurable and unpleasurable stimuli in a Me state of equilibrium.

The I Experience

In contrast to the Me experience where one "owns" and "labels" the amygdala signals as the "sense of me," the I experience is defined as: "the labeling and owning of interpretive processing operations." The declarative statement, "I am . . . " names the experience of interpretive processing of data. The experience of "I am" occurs only when a distinction is being made between the interpretive processes and the primary experience stimuli. We name this experience of interpretive process "I-ness."

We concur with the point made by Globus (1980) that the "I experience" is not to be construed as a "ghost in the machine" or as an anthropomorphic description of some innate structure of ephemeral being. Quite simply, the "I experience" is the label we give to an ego processing experience. Similarly, the "Me experience" labels a related but distinct amygdala processing experience.

We wish again to make a sharp distinction between primary experiences and personal experiences. Although repetitive, let us again clarify the differences. Primary experiences are generated from four sources:

1. Bodily operations (coenesthetic stimuli)
2. Amygdala operations (primary basic affect)
3. Limbic system operations (emotions)
4. Ego operations (experiences of thought, perception, etc.)

Primary experiences go on all the time outside of consciousness. When awareness of a primary experience occurs, then a person may engage in the process of "owning and labeling" the primary experience, which results in the personal experience of Me-ness and/or I-ness. Thus we shall define the personal experiences of Me-ness and I-ness as the consequence of particular and unique psychic operation apart from the quasi-mechanical ego operations described in psychodynamic and learning theories.

In most psychodynamic theories of ego operations, most attention has been given to structural and processing aspects of different ego operations. What has not been clearly defined are the proposed distinctive psychic processes that give rise to the Me experience and the I experience. These latter distinctive "personalizing operations of the ego" have been described by Loevinger (1976) in similar manner to the overall synthesizing and integrating operations, which she suggests gives rise to the sense of Me and I. Our proposal is therefore almost identical in concept to that of Loevinger, although more precise than her global formulations.

We now proceed to dissect the I experience into three heuristic modes related to maturation of the capacity for different modes of consciousness.

Consciousness is dependent upon the experience of awareness. In turn, awareness varies with maturation of the human organism. From infancy onward there is progress development of the capacity for:

1. Increasing levels of arousal
2. Increasing ability to attend to stimuli
3. Increasing ability to shift and focus attention on stimuli

Therefore, as the organism matures, there is increasing capacity for *modulating* awareness and *producing* different modes of consciousness.

The I experience varies with the developmental level of consciousness and with the particular content of awareness. Thus we will describe three nodal points of development of I experience: the I-1, the I-2, and the I-3 experience. This is a simplification, since I experience develops and remains a continuum of variations. At each nodal point of I-1, I-2, and I-3, we shall describe not just one mode of consciousness, but a *set* of modes of consciousness characteristic of the I experience at that nodal point. Let us consider an analogy. If we journey from New York to Chicago to Seattle, we might describe our journey by the eastern, midwestern, and western nodal points (i.e., I-1, I-2, I-3). In each of the three cities we may observe many events typical of that nodal city (i.e., modes of consciousness). *So we may conclude that the I experience is "how we are experiencing," and modes of consciousness are "what we are experiencing."* We may extend this analogy a bit further in terms of developmental constraints. At the youngest level of development (an I-1 experience), there are only certain modes of consciousness available. (In New York, one can only experience New York events.) As we journey to Chicago and later to Seattle, we can then experience Chicago events in Chicago, and Seattle events in Seattle. We can remember and compare Seattle experiences with Chicago experiences and New York experiences. And finally we can revisit and reexperience events in all three cities.

Similarly, mature modes of consciousness (I-3 experiences) can only be experienced when mature development has occurred. Yet we can shift our modes of consciousness to lower developmental levels.

We find it convenient to define the three I experiences in terms of the locus of attention. Thus in the I-1 experience the locus of attention is upon the *body* as object; in the I-2 experience the locus of attention is upon external *objects;* while in the I-3 experience the locus of attention us upon the *self-construct* as object.

From a developmental perspective, different personal experiences emerge and are operationalized *before* the child can cognitively label that personal experience. Thus we distinguish between the developmental emergence of a level of experience and the developmental labeling level. Here we shall use Mahler's (1975) schema as a convenient framework.

The Development of the Me Experience

The Me experience emerges at the termination of the autistic phase of infancy (one month). Prior to that time the "stimulus barrier" appears to block frontal cortex stimulation from the amygdala. We may consider the autistic infant as a subcortical organism operating with visceral brain function. At one month it appears that amygdala signals begin to be received in the frontal cortex, and the generation of primary tonic affect becomes possible. Hence the frontal cortex begins to generate the processes of a Me experience. Since there is cognitive lag, the young infant cannot cognitively label the Me experience even though it is occurring. However, by twelve months of age the infant can and does cognitively label the Me experience. Thereafter, we continue to appreciate the presence of the *ongoing Me experience in consciousness*. Consider the fact that I can recall always experiencing Me!

The Development of the I-1 Experience

The I-1 experience emerges at the psychological birth of the infant around four to five months of age at the peak of the symbiotic phase of development. The I-1 experience is marked by a focus of awareness upon body. In the infant this is composed of two major elements: the development of body as object representation in memory, and the development of capacity for discrimination and differentiation of body reactions as a result of emotions. The infant is best described as an "affective" being (the Me experience). In contrast the young toddler has emerged as an "emotional" being (the I-1 experience).

First the infant begins to discover and possess his own body, resulting in a stable memory representation of a body image (the body ego). Then the infant begins to appreciate bodily responses to the external world. Through increasing anticipation and specificity of reaction to external events the infant commences to experience differentiated emotions (pleasure, rage, happiness, sadness, etc.) (Sroufe, 1979). Hence limbic interpretation is added to amygdala interpretation, but still without full ideational interpretation.

Thus the infant proceeds through the first phase of separation–individuation, which is "differentiation" between "me" and the world. The child proceeds in this differentiation, fluctuating between the Me experience of primary basic affect and the I-1 experience of a differentiated set of bodily operations and emotions generated in response to the environment. The apogee of the I-1 experience is reached by eighteen months. The child laughs in anticipation; he is angry in the face of an obstacle; he is fearful or anxious in anticipation of noxious stimuli. The child is now aware of emotion itself and bodily concomitants in response to the world. Although the toddler is aware of the world, his locus of attention is upon the bodily experience of the world (a limbic interpretation). Hence the behavior of the toddler is determined by how his body experiences the world, rather than the reality of the external world. Thus the I-1 experience is a primary narcissistic experience devoid of reality testing. At the apogee of the I-1 experience of eighteen months of age, the infant can label his bodily experience as "I angry or I hungry, or I like that."

We can now describe a variety of I-1 level experiences in adulthood: a rage reaction in a marital argument, reclusive withdrawal while in bed with a cold, Zen meditation, orgasm, a flooding joy at a reunion at an airport. In each of these situations, there is predominant focus of attention upon our bodily experience. It is noteworthy that I-1 levels of experience result from a variety of circumstances. Bodily illness may promote regression to I-1 experiences. Normal regression to I-1 occurs in events such as reunion or orgasm. Pathological regression occurs in response to stress. And we may deliberately seek to achieve I-1 experience through meditation practices. Thus I-1 experiences are not discarded in development, but remain available to us under a variety of normal and pathological circumstances.

The Development of the I-2 Experience

In the I-2 experience the locus of awareness is upon external-reality objects. The I-2 experience emerges during the rapprochement phase of child development and is stably achieved around three years of age. The chief task of rapprochement is to develop stable identification of external objects and stable internal representation of those objects in memory. Hence the child is able to achieve discrete identification and differentiation between himself and all other external objects, as well as the presence or absence of external objects. In turn, this ability allows the child now to manage himself in the world in relation to external objects. At three years of age the schema of external objects is concrete (persons, dogs, toys). With maturation, the schema of external objects can be made symbolic and abstract. Thus the manipulation of the external objects ranges from managing concrete persons to the management of abstract ideas such as mathematics.

During this process the child is acquiring a stabilized sense of "self as object"—that is, a stabilized representation in memory of the fact that 'I exist as a unique person." Emotional manifestations of this process are reflected in experiences of shame, defiance, and positive or negative self-evaluation. However, the locus of attention is not upon the attributes of self, but rather upon the external objects of the world and how to manage them. Thus the epitome of the I-2 experience is everyday "reality testing" and "reality management." This is how most of us function most of the time in coping with everyday mundane reality circumstances.

We emphasize that people learn highly effective I-2 level operations, including artistic performance, intellectual skills, athletic prowess, and very complex ego coping operations, without necessarily ever focusing attention on the construct of self, which is the "programmed model" for all this high-level I-2 achievement. That is, most people take for granted the ongoing development of the self-construct, and cope with the external world in an effective way without ever questioning or examining the nature of their own self-construct. Put simply, most people take their own self-development for granted as a given; they focus their attention throughout life upon the external object world (or sometimes on their bodies). The fact that most people operate throughout life at an I-2 level of experience reflects reasonably effective social development.

However, in certain circumstances, the I-2 level of experience is a limiting experience. First, if the self-construct and ego operations are maladaptive, then effective coping with the external world breaks down because internal change is required. Second, people may be so bound to an I-2 level of experience that regression to I-1 level experience is threatening, ego-dystonic, or dysphoric (e.g., the person who cannot allow regression to I-1 during intercourse, and experiences mechanical orgasm without personal fusion with the partner; or the wary person who cannot allow himself to experience intense emotional experiences of anger, joy, or sadness). Third, the person who is tied to I-2 experience of coping with just external reality may be thereby bound to the time–space circumstances of immediate life. Such persons are unable to achieve I-3 levels of introspection, change life plans, or step back from the immediacy of life to take existential and transcendental views of their own human experience.

Thus much of our life is preoccupied with living at an I-2 level of experience. We even label such experience as mentally healthy and a manifestation of good adjustment and effective coping. Yet the I-2 level is not the only important level of I experience, and when life is lived just at the I-2 level, much may be missed.

Further, we note that much of psychotherapy technique has confused different levels of I experience. Some psychotherapy is "reality-based," that is, psychotherapy conducted only in an I-2 frame of reference.

In contrast, a number of experiential therapies are conducted at I-1 levels of personal experience, which may at times be helpful in assisting patients to achieve and experience I-1 levels of experience, but on the other hand may preclude effective change of ego operations and self-construct, since that requires I-2 and I-3 levels of experience and operation.

Finally, as we shall see, change in ego operations and self-construct formation often requires I-3 levels of experience, quite apart from just effective reality testing and reality management.

The Development of the I-3 Experience

The I-3 experience is generated when the locus of attention is upon the self-construct, and associated ego operations. It is best exemplified in the process of psychotherapy, where we teach patients to observe their own actions, to observe how they think, feel, and process information; and teach patients to examine and evaluate their own concept of self which serves as the basis for their management of their lives.

Here we need to clarify the construct of "self." In accord with most recent self theory, we shall define the self as a "cognitive construct of the identity of the person." There is no "ghost in the machine" that *is* a self. Nor do we wish to use the concept of self to refer to the whole person or organism. Rather, we shall limit our definition to the cognitive construct that is laid down in memory and becomes a stable representation or model of our identity. That "self-model" in turn can *generate memory signals* to ego operations of expected, desired, or required behavior in response to external circumstances in accord with the construct model available in memory.

As a technical aside, we note that current self theory focuses on the socialized self-construct as the product of the unconscious content of ego ideal and superego, which continue to produce input into the self-construct that emerges from our socialization experiences. Long ago, George Herbert Mead (1934) described the development of the *self-construct as an object* when the person internalizes in memory the "generalized other attributes from the community, social group, and family." The initial attributes of self are built into the unconscious content of ego ideal and superego in the first three to four years of life. Up through latency the child adds generalized other and specific other attributes to the self-construct through incorporation, introjection, identification, modeling, and imitation. Up until pubescence, most of the construction of the self-construct occurs outside the locus of attention and thereby *outside of awareness*. Thus in latency we see the intimations of I-3 experience but little actual I-3 experience, much less labeling thereof.

During adolescence we see the flowering of I-3 experience when the adolescent begins to peer in the mirror and ask "Who am I?" and "What do I want to be?" These are I-3 experiences. Often, after fleeting I-3 experiences, often labeled as adolescent dysphoria, the adolescent enters adulthood at an I-2 level, focusing on adaptation and coping with reality circumstances.

We can now note a variety of I-3 experiences. They include the experience of introspection, where the locus of attention is on the self-construct. This can be called "self-awareness" or "self-consciousness." Or, the locus of attention can be on observation of ego operations such as thinking, deciding, directing action, and so on. Thus in an I-3 experience I can be aware of my thinking, or my deciding, or my actioning operations of ego function. This might be labeled "operation awareness" or "ego function awareness." Third, the locus of attention can be upon the person in action. Here I observe my person as a whole interacting in the environment. I can observe how I walk, or talk, or respond to others. We can label this "behavior awareness."

We note that at the I-3 level of experience, one is capable of concurrently focusing attention on the self-construct, on ego operations, and on behavior. In addition, one can include some degree of attention at the I-2 level and I-1 level. This complex level of I-3 experience is critical to the function of the experienced psychotherapist, who must "listen with the third ear." Said more precisely, the psychotherapist may simultaneously process I-1 experience of hunger, irritation, or sleepiness, I-2 experience of the patient's behavior, and I-3 experience of evaluating how one is conducting the therapy session.

We note that countertransference phenomena may be picked up by the therapist who observes ongoing I-1 and I-2 experiences combined with I-3 observation of the conduct of one's person in the therapy. On the other hand, a pure I-2 level therapist experience is likely to preclude attention to important data from I-1 and I-3 experience of the therapist.

Other I-3 experiences, perhaps less complex, are important to describe. Taking a step back to view one's life, to achieve existential perspective, to take a transcendental overview, occurs not only in psychotherapy, but is critical in intellectual criticism, aesthetics, creativity, philosophy, and religion.

Severe psychosocial stressors may break down typical I-2 views of reality, resulting in glimpses of an I-3 experience. For example, the death of a child may provoke parents to stop and look at their marital and family history and question the directions, meaning, and purpose of their life-style.

There are other processes that occur with significant stress and may provoke I-3 experiences that are ego-dystonic and ego-dysphoric. These include out-of-body, possession, and trance experiences. However, panic and depersonalization experiences reflect ego-dystonic I-1 experiences.

Finally, we can note that I-3 experiences have been labeled by some as "supra-normal experiences of consciousness" (Tart, 1981; Walsh, 1980). In the sense that they are not I-2 experiences, that is true. On the other hand, psychotherapists have learned to achieve and appropriately utilize I-3 experiences. Creative persons, including artists, appropriately utilize I-3 experiences as essential to the creative process. And religious and philosophical leaders have always recognized the I-3 experiences of reflection and transcendent observation. Therefore, I-3 experiences are not "supra-normal," since I-2 experience is not "normal" but only typical or usual. Furthermore, I-2 experience can be abnormal.

In summary, we have described the developmental processes of personal experience, which is manifested through a continuum of modes of consciousness. Beginning with the Me experience, the human acquires the capacity for different levels of I experience. There is not one personal experience, but rather a variety of personal experiences involved in different modes of consciousness, none of which is necessarily pathological. Therefore, we suggest that the label "altered states of consciousness" is misleading, for there are many normal and appropriate modes of consciousness. Abnormal modes of consciousness are *not* determined by the mode of consciousness per se, but rather by the state of the human organism in relation to the given mode of consciousness.

For example, at the I-1 level, a young child may talk to an imaginary companion, as might a widow talk to her dead husband during acute grief, both of which experiences are normal, whereas a psychotic may speak of delusional persons.

At the I-2 level a normal person may ignore bodily and feeling signals while taking an exam, which is normal adaptation, whereas a severe obsessional may ignore bodily and emotional signals.

At the I-3 level, a person may deliberately practice transcendental reflection, whereas a person in an agitated identity crisis may be bewildered by his or her uncertain sense of self and life.

We have described the experiential perspective of human action, and it now remains to demonstrate how this perspective can be *integrated* with the more familiar behavioral and psychological perspectives. Each of the three perspectives provides a partial and limited explanation of human action. Therefore, let us consider what aspects of human action are determined by biopsychosocial variables in each perspective.

THE BEHAVIORAL PERSPECTIVE

This perspective focuses on biological determinants of action. The human actions described and explained are *external public universal actions*. Developmentally, such human actions are almost directly determined by biological variables in the young infant. With maturation, such external actions are modified by psychological and social variables. Nevertheless, in this perspective external actions result from biological variables which are the primary determinants of action.

We shall call this the *body system*. This system can be seen as composed of the following:

1. *The coenesthetic stimulus system,* in which action provoking signals are generated from the various body parts (pain, itch, warmth, hunger, limb position, body movement, etc.). This subsystem regulates human action via relatively automatic neurobiological operations. For example, the human action of maintaining balance on a bicycle is determined by biologic equilibrium processes.
2. *The amygdala system.* This subsystem regulates the flow of basic affect signals to the forebrain in regard to the affective equilibrium-dysequilibrium state of the organism. This subsystem also integrates the coenesthetic and instinctual drive stimuli into a visceral brain level of organismic response.
3. *The limbic system* as the emotional-interpretation system that generates the emotional value attached to stimulus events. The emotional tone is transmitted to both the amygdala and the frontal cortex.
4. *The instinctual drive stimulus system.* This subsystem has been subject to much misunderstanding. In lower animal forms we observe that instinctual processes directly determine external action. However, as we ascend the phylogenetic ladder, there is decreasing direct determination of action by the instinctual process. Indeed, in man we find that instinctual processes are substantially modified by psychological and social variables. As von Bertlanaffy (1962) observed: "The principle of instincts in open living systems is the same. The instincts are the same at all levels of the phylogenetic ladder. But as we ascend the ladder, the instincts are more pleomorphic in expression and more malleable to environmental modification of gratification."

When we describe the role of instinctual process in man, we can no longer speak of instinctual behavior, for the most part. As Fletcher (1957) and Fingarette (1963) have observed, we really are describing instinctual *principles,* rather than behavioral or action processes. Most human action is too flexible, malleable, overdetermined, and complex to be simply described as an "instinctual action." Therefore, in this subsystem we shall refer to the instinctual process as "instinctual drive stimuli."

We note that there may be a variety of levels of evocation of instinctual drive stimuli. The most immediate and manifest is breathing. Within a few moments of oxygen deprivation the human will demonstrate the attempt to obtain air—an instinctual response to preserve life. On the other hand, sexual drive stimuli may not be evoked except in very special social circumstances, and even if evoked may not produce any type of sexual action.

What human action does the behavioral perspective explain? Let us consider three sets of observable human actions. We shall call these *human preservation principles,* each of which has a set of observable actions:

1. *Life-preserving actions.* These include actions to obtain food, water, air, shelter, and body protection against pain or attack. We observe these actions in the young infant in terms of immediate stimulus–response reflexes, later in simple conditioning responses, and later in adulthood in complex operations. We note that in the mentally retarded, brain-damaged individuals, and psychotic persons, most of these life-preserving actions are retained. In the most severe pathologies even the life-preserving actions are comprised (profound retardation, comatose patients, and severe catatonia or withdrawn depressives).

2. *Self-preserving actions.* These actions include primary bonding behavior and the complex of ego coping skills adaptive to the environment. These actions reflect epigenetic unfolding of the potential to engage in such actions when stimulated by interaction with external objects. Normally, such biological–social interaction results in the development of what we call intrapsychic structure (i.e., ego ideal, superego, and operational ego skills). It also results in the formation of the self-construct. These actions depend upon the level of biological maturation and the particular set of social interactions that mold the content and operation of intrapsychic processes. Much of self-preserving action has been described in the familiar terms of classical psychodynamics. However, learning theory (both classical and operant) plays an important role in describing how social interaction relates to the biological potential of the human. In fact, most of self-preserving actions reflect automated human actions acquired over a long period of socialization.

3. *Species-preserving actions.* Here we include reproductive sexual actions and social bonding actions of parent with child and with a community of social others—that is, social bonding. Effective *life*-preservation and *self*-preservation actions are a prerequisite for successful achievement of *species*-preserving actions.

In normal development we never relinquish any of these three sets of instinctually driven sets of actions. Rather, we learn to mesh the instinctual stimuli from each of these three sets so as to satisfy all three sets of preserving actions. Such actions are seen then as normal or mature actions.

However, when a person pursues one set of preservative actions in disregard for the other two sets, we view those actions as aberrant, bizarre, destructive, or psychopathological. In some cases this may be true, yet at other times such action may be interpreted as normal behavior.

Let us study the following example. A fisherman lives in an Indian fishing village. Each day he fishes for salmon in a river in order to feed himself and his family, and to share with the community. His total complex of behavior is life-preserving (he catches fish for himself), self-preserving (he maintains his self-competency, self-image, and social image), and species-preserving (he assures food for his children to survive).

Now let us consider aberrations in the above complex of fishing. Assume that there is a poor run of salmon, and the entire village is starving. The starving fisherman luckily catches a salmon. He responds to his life-preserving stimuli and immediately eats the salmon by himself. His actions are simultaneously self-destructive (he loses social esteem and feels overwhelming guilt and remorse) and species-destructive (his children starve). We consider this an abnormal organization of behavior.

Now let us consider the starving fisherman who fails to catch fish. He experiences loss of village social esteem, family criticism, and loss of sense of competency. To escape from the threat to life (starvation) and the treat to self (social losses), he leaves the village and strikes out by himself to find another river. He forgets about the village and his family. He successfully catches salmon and feels competent again, while also averting his own starvation. Here his actions are life-preserving and self-preserving but species-destructive. This is an abnormal organization of behavior.

The third permutation occurs when the starving fisherman steals a salmon from another family in the village, which he takes home and eats with his children. Here we have life-preserving and species-preserving actions, but this is self-destructive action in terms of depreciation of self in his role as thief.

Fourth, the fisherman becomes severely depressed over his inability to catch salmon and sits all day in a withdrawn stupor. His actions are life-destructive, self-destructive, and species-destructive. This is abnormal.

Fifth, the fisherman who catches no fish becomes preoccupied with his loss of self-esteem. He engages in reckless fishing from dangerous places and drowns. This action was self-preserving (maintaining self-esteem) but life-destructive and species-destructive. It is abnormal.

Sixth, the fisherman becomes preoccupied with saving his children from starvation. He can think of nothing else. He begins to fish obsessively, night and day. He catches fish but will not eat them, giving them all to his children. He keeps on fishing when there are enough salmon and everyone pleads with him to stop and rest. He manifests a psychotic ideational preoccupation with catching fish interminably. He dies of starvation and exhaustion. Here we have life-destructive and self-destructive, but species-preserving action. This is abnormal.

Finally, we have the case of the fisherman who finally catches a salmon. His children are moribund and facing death, as he is himself. He gives all the fish to the children to save their lives, but dies himself of starvation. Here we have the case of "altruistic suicide," in which the actions are self-preservative (altruistic motives of a noble self), while the actions are life-destructive and species-preservative. We might consider this organization of action normal.

What do we learn from these examples? First, instinctual stimuli, in themselves, do not determine human action. Second, how the human responds to and integrates these three preservative principles determines pathology, rather than the instinctual stimuli per se. Third, preservative actions in response to instinctual stimuli do not necessarily imply normality. That is, a set of actions may be preservative of one principle and destructive of another. Fourth, it is not always necessary or desirable to respond in action to any set of instinctual drive stimuli.

In overall summary of the behavioral perspective, the body system is always contributing to human action, and derivatives from the body system will be found in all human actions. However, we cannot predict or explain human action solely in terms of body system varibles.

It remains now to integrate the experiential perspective with the behavioral perspective. We shall do this is terms of the three variables of consciousness: primary experience, awareness experience, and personal experience.

When we respond to *life*-preserving instinctual stimuli, our primary experience is that of our body system (coenesthetic stimuli, instinctual drive stimuli, and limbic emotional interpretation of event stimuli). In addition we experience the amygdala-generated basic affect of equilibrium or dysequilibrium in terms of life survival. Our personal experience is that of owning and experiencing our body—the Me experience. In terms of awareness, we focus on our body system and the situation of our bodily life at the moment.

Next, when we respond to *self*-preserving instinctual stimuli, our primary experience is that of our psychological operations (the *content* of perceiving, thinking, acting in the world). Our personal experience is that of owning the actions we are generating (I-1 and I-2 experiences). Our awareness experience is that of connectedness to the external world with which we are interacting.

Finally, when we respond to *species*-preserving instinctual stimuli, our primary experience is that of the self existing in relationship to others in time and space—an experience derived from memory of transcendent values and priorities apart from the immediate object world and its demands. The personal experience is that of owning what is happening to others in relationship to one's self-construct. This is the I-3 experience. The awareness experience is that of connectedness to past and future history, to one's family, and to one's community.

Thus each of the three sets of instinctual stimuli is associated with different primary experiences, personal experiences, and awareness experiences that result in different modes of consciousness.

THE PSYCHOLOGICAL PERSPECTIVE

Here we will consider two different sets of intrapsychic operations: the *self-memory system* and the *ego operation system*.

The self-memory system is thus designated because we shall consider those elements that are primarily memory functions that generate signal stimuli to be processed in ego operations. The ego ideal, which generates signals of shame, and the superego, which generates signals of guilt, are essentially memory storage systems. We shall define the *self* as a separate memory storage system in which a construct of desired and actual self-concept and self-image is stored. It too generates signal stimuli to ego operations. Such signals are reported as self-satisfaction, self-criticism, self-esteem, self-deprecation, self-evaluation, and so on.

We need again to call attention to possible semantic confusion about the self-construct. The term "identity" or "self-identity" we consider a synonym for the self-construct. The term "person" refers to the whole organism. The term "personality" we shall define as "the specific patterns of characteristic ego operations that result in relatively stable action patterns." The term "ego" refers to sets of psychic operations. The terms "I" and "Me" refer to personal experiences. Finally, there is no anthropomorphism or ghost in the machine "self." Personal choice of action is an ego operation that we experience and cognitively label an "I experience" (Loevinger, 1976). Thus we wish to narrowly restrain our definition of self-construct to a memory storage system, even though it is a psychically active system.

We note that the self-memory system is generated through social interaction; that is, memory events, memory meanings, and memory imperatives are constructed through the process of socialization. As a result, much of the self-memory system is acquired and automated apart from awareness. For most of us, it becomes a relatively automatic system of operation that generates stimuli for ego-directed action.

In contrast the ego system is a set of operations that epigenetically develop. That is, there is increasing human potential to crystallize complex operations as a result of interaction of ego systems with body system stimuli and external environmental stimuli. In this sense, *we may consider ego operations as complexly programmed computer systems.*

Thus in the psychological perspective we have the self-memory system and the ego system, which both determine human actions. But note that such actions are largely determined by machinelike computer processing of the psychological system. The psychological system operates and generates human action pretty much in terms of the socialized programming of the psychological operations. An apt metaphor would be to consider the psychological system perspective as a human computer system. We can see the logic of psychic determinism when analyzing human behavior solely in terms of the psychological perspective.

But this psychological perspective does not account for the capacity for personal experience. It does not account for the capacity of the human to *reprogram* both the ego system and the self-memory system. In fact, one of the major tasks of psychotherapy is to teach patients how to utilize their personal experience capacity to conduct such reprogramming. Finally, the psychological perspective does not account for the capacity for responsible personal choice of action.

We shall now examine the psychological perspective in relation to the experiential perspective.

Schafer (1976) has proposed that we describe "ego" in terms of discrete operations. Bellak et al. (1973) described twelve such ego operations or functions. However, each function or "ego system" does not operate in isolation. In fact, as Emde and Robinson (1979), Sroufe (1979), and others have shown, ego systems develop in a cogwheeling fashion of mutual influence in development. Thus the cognitive system influences the development of the emotional system, and vice versa. As a result we get "states of ego operation." As Loevinger (1976) notes, by definition the overall operation of ego is a synthesizing and organizing operation.

We wish to look at modes of organization of ego operations at three nodal points of development. Each nodal point corresponds to each of the three I experiences. We stress that development is a continuum, and that there are many permutations of I experiences, but for simplicity we shall limit our discussion to these three prototype nodal points.

Following Bellak et al. (1973), we have composed a chart of ego operations at each of three nodal points of development, with their associated I experience (see Figure 3).

We note the following characteristics of ego operations at each nodal point:

I–1	I–2	I–3
Sensation	Perception	Block of stimuli through meditation
Stimulus barrier	Threshold stimulus barrier	Block of stimuli through meditation
Inner reality testing	Reality testing (inner and outer stimuli)	Differentiation between ideal self and actual self
Basic affect expression	Affective expression	Affective expression
Object-relations (Bonding)	Object-relations (individuality and degree of relatedness)	Object-relations (self-constancy)
Memory traces	Thought process (memory, attention, conceptualization)	Thought process (concentration)
No-judgment	Judgment (behaviorally)	Judgment (emotional appropriateness)
No self-experience	Self-identify, Self-esteem, Self-boundaries	Ability to change the configuration of ideal-self
No ability to regress	Ability to regress in terms of cognitive functions	Ability to regress in cognitive and affective functions
No autonomous functioning	Autonomous functioning (relaxation of motor tasks)	Autonomous functioning (Relaxation of cognitive tasks)
No	No	Synthetic integrative function (Reconciliation of incongruities)
No	No	Mastery competence (Reconciliation of superego and ego ideal)
Biological evaluation function	Bio-social evaluative function	Bio-psycho-social evaluative function

Figure 3.

1. Not all ego operations are present at each nodal point. Some ego operations only develop in later maturation or with specific learning (introspection).
2. Some ego operations retain the same function, but change in their operation with maturation (i.e., eyesight at I-1 vs. shifting perception in I-3).

3. At each nodal point, the particular combination of ego operations produces a specific range of possible human actions, a relatively specific I experience, and a specific range of modes of consciousness.

Stated another way, in the psychological perspective the self-memory system and ego system operate at specific developmental levels, with an associated set of personal experiences (I experiences), with an array of associated modes of consciousness.

This conclusion allows us to move beyond a mere steady-state concept of psychological operations. We are in fact shifting back and forth in the levels at which the ego operations are functioning. Accordingly, our personal experience and modes of consciousness shift.

However, we would also argue that it is the very presence of a personal I experience and mode of consciousness that provides us the capacity to shift levels of ego operation, modify psychic operations, change memory models, and reprogram automated biological and psychological operations.

CLINICAL APPLICATIONS IN NORMALITY AND PATHOLOGY

In this section we wish to demonstrate how the integration of the experiential perspective may clarify normal human action and elucidate clinical problems. We shall focus on the unique contributions of personal experience.

First let us consider normal I functions at each of the three levels. For each, examples are given of different actions, with different I experience.

- At the I-1 level, normal ego operations and personal experience are exemplified in the symbiotic fusion of sexual orgasm, intense ecstasy of reunion, regressive withdrawal in bed rest during a bout of the flu, concentration on body motion while learning to hit a tennis ball.
- At the I-2 level, examples would include a seductive encounter, engaging in intellectual conversation, covering one's face with a handkerchief when sneezing in public, and practicing tennis strokes.
- At the I-3 level, examples include recognition by the parent of sexual impulses toward his or her own children; the therapist in psychotherapy observing his own interaction with a patient; evaluating one's own energy level, malaise, and physical stamina in deciding whether to stay home or go to work when one has the flu; a tennis player in a match, observing that he is getting anxious and angry, acting to isolate his emotions in order to concentrate on the game.

In each of the examples above, the same stimuli (sexual, other person, body illness, and a game action) are processed differently at each I level with different ego operations and a different personal experience. Each example illustrates how the I-1 experience focuses on body, the I-2 experience focuses on the external other, and the I-3 experience focuses on the self.

Second, we again point out that the I level of experience and the associated ego operations are in themselves not pathological. Consider three conditions in which the personal experience dimension is awkward, maladaptive, or pathological.

1. The I experience is unfamiliar or unexpected, hence ego-dystonic and dysphoric in its effects. For example, most people learn to operate predominantly at an I-2 level. We call this "reality-based" ego operation. Sudden intense affect flooding, as in an accident, death, or intense emotional encounter, may produce regression to an I-1 level. This may frighten people who do not have such experiences as adults. Here the ego operations and the I experience are normal relative to the event. However, what is abnormal is the *dysphoric interpretation* of the I-1 experience as aberrant ("I shouldn't be experiencing this"). As a result, the person may then invoke abnormal ego defenses. For example, upon the death of one's spouse, one may "feel horrible" and instead of tolerating the I-1 experience, the person invokes denial of the death.

At the other end of the spectrum, I-3 experience is often unfamiliar, especially in Western culture. Consider a man whose children leave home and whose wife goes to work. These events provoke the man to examine his life course, and suddenly he experiences an observation of his past life history and contemplates his future life history ("I see my whole life flitting before my eyes"). This observation of the self may be discomfiting and dysphoric because the man has never paid attention to the kind of person he desired to be or what he wanted to do with his life. Again, instead of toleration of the I-3 experience, it might generate anxiety (midlife crisis) and abnormal ego defenses, such as reaction-formation to demonstrate youth and virility through exercise and sexual escapades. Out of body experiences are often ego-dystonic I-3 experiences.

2. The person gets "stuck" in one I level and cannot effectively shift the level of ego operation. Here the I level is initially appropriate, but the person cannot appropriately shift levels. For example, a person during intense grief is at an I-1 level of experience and operation. But the person cannot recathect external others at an I-2 level, remains at the I-1 level, and develops a neurotic depression. Now consider marriage, which is mostly an I-2 level relationship. If a couple remained focused solely on the adaptive management tasks of rearing children and running a home, they might be unable to shift to I-1 levels of emotional intimacy, or shift to I-3 levels of reflection on the changing nature of their relationship over time.

At the next level, consider a college student who engages in I-3 level reflection and self-scrutiny bull sessions all the time, perseverating on what kind of person he is and what he wants to do with his life. He cannot shift to an I-2 level of concrete study and actual skill acquisition. Or consider a psychotherapist, operating at an I-3 level of self-observation, who is so preoccupied with his own self that he fails to note the patient's suicidal intentions and fails to act in reality at an I-2 level, or may not note the patient's homicidal movement to attack him, which would require I-1 self-defense by the therapist.

3. In this class of conditions, there is a "dysjunction" between the I level at which the person is operating and the adaptive requirements of the context. Here the abnormality is in the failure initially to employ the I level appropriate to the context. We shall give two types of examples for these dysjunctions: those that are normal behaviors but maladaptive, and those that are clinical pathologies resulting from such dysfunction.

A. An initial I-1 response instead of an I-2 response.
   Normal: During a marital disagreement, the spouse immediately regresses to an I-1 level of rage reaction, instead of I-2 problem solving.
   Pathological: A borderline personality experiences rejection and immediately regresses to an I-1 level and attempts suicide, instead of coping with separation anxiety at an I-2 level.
B. An initial I-1 response instead of an I-3 response.
   Normal: A patient expresses anger at a psychotherapist, who responds at an I-1 level of reciprocated anger (countertransference reaction), instead of an I-3 observation of the interpersonal transaction that is the context of the anger.
   Pathological: An adolescent looks at himself in the mirror and does not recognize himself as the person observed. He panics in an I-1 response and experiences depersonalization. Instead, a recognition of self-observation and self-evaluation at an I-3 level is called for. Panic attacks illustrate immediate I-1 physiological arousal and depersonalization when one does not use I-3 observation to determine the meaning of stimuli to oneself.
C. An initial I-2 response instead of an I-1 response.
   Normal: A couple engaged in sexual intercourse focus on sexual technique at an I-2 level and cannot experience regression to I-1 body boundary diffusion.
   Pathological: Persons with a severe character disorder, such as the schizoid or obsessive-compulsive, fear the affective arousal of intimacy with others. Therefore, when someone approaches them at a social event, they respond in a mechanical, businesslike fashion of I-

2 operation, without allowing themselves to experience I-1 empathic feeling in the interpersonal encounter.

D. An initial I-2 response instead of an I-3 response.

Normal: A business executive loses his job and immediately responds by frenetically seeking an identical position—an I-2 coping response, instead of engaging in I-3 reflection on his array of skills and abilities that might be suitable for a variety of positions.

Pathological: All character and personality disorders reflect fixation at an I-2 level of response to events. They characteristically react in accord with automated ego coping reponses, instead of shifting to I-3 self-evaluation of the appropriateness of their ego coping styles.

E. An initial I-3 response instead of an I-1 response.

Normal: A person is ill with the flu, and responds by perseverative reflection on potential criticism by his boss for missing work, feels inadequate as a person for being sick, and fantasizes about becoming chronically ill. Here the I-3 preoccupation with self-image generates anxiety and distress, when the person should be regressing to an I-1 level of relaxation and bed rest.

Pathological: Psychosexual disorders, such as inhibited sexual desire, or inhibited sexual excitement may reflect preoccupation with the self, doubts about oneself, anxiety about self-performance at an I-3 level of self-scrutiny and self-evaluation, which precludes I-2 involvement with the other, and then I-1 regression to intense bodily response.

F. An initial I-3 response instead of an I-2 response.

Normal: In an automobile accident, the person stands immobilized, reflecting on the meaning of his own existence at an I-3 level, instead of acting at an I-2 level to care for injured people.

Pathological: In anorexia nervosa, the person is preoccupied with her self-image at an I-3 level of perseverative self-scrutiny, while she ignores I-2 level feedback from others and I-2 reality testing of her actual physical condition.

In summary, the examples we have given focus on abnormal behavior generated by an inappropriate choice of the level of I experience and ego operation. Thus, remediation of these clinically aberrant responses in action lies in learning to choose the correct level of I operation appropriate to the context. Then the person can employ the appropriate ego operations. We suggest that such examples of psychopathology indicate how the process of choosing a level of I operation can contribute to the generation of clinical syndromes. Similarly, this may contribute to the technique of psychotherapy, in that part of therapy may involve teaching a patient how to *shift* levels of I experience and ego operation, how to *choose* appropriate levels of operation, and how to appropriately *experience* and *utilize* each level of I experience.

CLINICAL SUMMARY

We shall not reiterate the complex construction of this study, but state the major implications of our proposals.

First, we have argued for the critical importance of personal experience as a variable in our description of human action. although a private, idiosyncratic element of operation, the personal experience variable is necessary to avoid biological and psychological reductionism, and to account for human choice and personal responsibility.

Second, we have proposed a systematic taxonomy for the use of the terms "Me," "I," and "self," which is logically construed and integrated with current biological and psychological theory.

Third, we have observed that there are multiple "modes of consciousness" that reflect different levels of I experience and associated ego operations. These different modes of consciousness, different I experiences, and different constellations of ego operations are not intrinsically pathological. In turn we have suggested that abnormality resides in dysphoric responses to unfamiliar personal experience, inability to shift levels of personal experience, or dysjunctions between the level of personal experience and the adaptive requirements of the context.

Fourth, we have offered clinical examples of how the personal experience variable contributes to abnormal action, in both maladaptive and pathological cases. We suggest that analysis of the personal experience variable may contribute to clinical diagnosis and to clinical treatment technique.

Finally, we must consider a description of how personal experience is associated with many other clinical states, which is the task of our final section.

CLINICAL APPLICATION OF THE PERSONAL EXPERIENCE PERSPECTIVE TO DIFFERENT MODES OF CONSCIOUSNESS

It remains for us to consider how this analysis of personal experience can further our understanding of the dynamics of different modes of consciousness.

To start, we have already concluded that there are a variety of modes of consciousness *that in themselves are not pathological.* In fact, we have demonstrated that for normal mature function, the human must shift modes of consciousness. The implicit assumption in the phrase "altered states of consciousness" is that there is one normal mode of consciousness, deviations from which are "altered."

Consider the same person engaged in different actions, which we simply consider as fully conscious deliberate acts, but substantially different personal experiences: experiencing bodily pleasure and bodily fusion during orgasm; experiencing intense thought process studying a book while ignoring bodily and environmental stimuli; experiencing body action and evaluating the environment while playing a tennis game; sitting with one's spouse and reflecting quietly upon changes in each other's personality values, life plans, and life goals over forty years of marriage. In each case the person is conscious, but the mode of consciousness produces a different personal experience.

Note that we cannot have this array of personal experiences with all in the same mode of full consciousness. In order to have different personal experiences we must *shift* modes of consciousness. This is so obvious, so familiar, so easily achieved, that most people never notice that they are shifting modes of consciousness during the course of everyday life.

Yet, we have given examples of people who cannot achieve even these simple shifts in modes in consciousness: people who cannot shift to intense I-1 bodily experiences or shift to I-3 self observation and reflection.

How do we apprehend these different modes of consciousness? We propose the analogy of a simple camera to assist in our analysis. A camera takes a picture of an event (a personal experience). But a camera can take a variety of types of pictures—panorama, group pictures, portraits, details (a variety of personal experiences). What produces the different pictures (personal experiences)? It is the way we manipulate the functions of the camera to take a specific type of picture. By analogy, we suggest that consciousness is a set of ego operations (camera operations) that can be manipulated to produce many different types of personal experiences (pictures).

In fact the functions of a camera bear very close resemblance to the functions in consciousness: (1) the breadth of field, (2) the locus of attention, (3) the focus of attention.

The breadth of field depends upon the camera lens. An average lens encompasses the typical field of interest—say, the front yard and house where I live. If the field of interest is the entire neighborhood, then I must put a "fish-eye" lens on the camera and fly over my house to take an encompassing view of my house and yard in the neighborhood. On the other hand, if I wish to photograph a butterfly on a leaf in my front yard, then I must put a "close-up" lens on my camera to limit the field to that butterfly.

Next, the lens that I use constrains both the locus and focus of the picture. In the average lens shot, I can move the camera to include only the yard, or only the house, or both house and yard. This is the *locus* or *content* of the picture. In addition, I can *focus* on the foreground with a hazy background, or focus on the background with a hazy foreground, or take a picture at intermediate focus with all objects in roughly the same detail. But with a fish-eye lens I can only take a broad picture with all detail indistinct; or with a close-up lens I can only take a detailed picture without any context.

In the above illustration, my house and yard are always in the picture (my personal experience). But the exact content of the picture will vary from a transcendental experience (my house and yard in a neighborhood as viewed from the sky), to an everyday action experience (the location of the driveway through the yard to the house), to a microscopic experience (the butterfly on a flower in my front yard).

When confronted with three pictures (panorama, yard, butterfly), I may or may not experience these three pictures as "personal experiences." If there is "no orienting connection," I might report that: this is a picture of a neighborhood from the sky; this is a front yard; this is a butterfly. However, if I "own and personalize" that I took each picture, then I can connect each picture in my memory, and report that each picture is a picture of "my place": my place in the neighborhood, my place to drive into the yard, a butterfly in my yard.

It is exactly here that the analogy with a camera differs from human consciousness. The camera takes a picture (personal experience), but the *camera has no memory* and therefore no ability to *interpret* the picture (experience). Therefore, the three different camera pictures are autonomous and unrelated pictures (experiences). On the other hand, the human has the capacity to engage in a conscious experience (picture) and simultaneously place that experience into meaningful reference to the rest of the person's life. (That is my yard in the neighborhood; that is my driveway; that is a butterfly in my yard.)

We can now consider the camera as the operations in consciousness that provide us with a variety of modes of consciousness (pictures). As we shift the ego operations in consciousness, we obtain different personal experiences.

But what is the meaning of a personal experience (picture)? Meaning requires a "connecting orientation." Without it, a personal experience is an idiosyncratic event. Consider taking a camera picture of a leaf. First, I take a picture of the leaf lying alone in the middle of my yard. Second, I take a picture of just the leaf, with no grass visible. Third, I take a picture of a centimeter of the leaf surface. All three pictures are three different personal experiences. But are they related experiences? I can only relate all three pictures to the same leaf *if I remember* that all three pictures are different pictures (experiences) of the same leaf. Without such *active connecting memory* the pictures can be given very different meanings. The second picture of the leaf alone could be any leaf anywhere, while the third picture could be just a geometric design to my eyes.

The above illustration demonstrates the difference between a normal and a pathological experience of an "altered state of consciousness." In a normal processing of experience, each picture (personal experience) is *concurrently connected in memory* such that the picture (experience) is immediately identified as not only connected to me (hence personal experience), but also connected to the entirety of my whole life. Therefore, the "altered state" experience is not ego-dystonic, is not maladaptive, and does not perturb my own psychic operations.

In a pathological processing of experience, each picture (experience) is not immediately connected in memory. Hence the experience occurs as a *disconnected idiosyncratic event.* Consequently, the experience may result in ego-dystonic responses. The experience may not be personalized (a derealization or depersonalization), or it may be maladaptive (an anxiety or panic attack), or evoke neurotic defense mechanisms such as denial of the event, post-traumatic stress responses, and so on.

Modes of Consciousness and Reality Testing

We asserted above that the personal experience in a specific mode of consciousness depends upon the connecting orientation in memory. This memory connecting operation produces the ego operation of reality testing. That is, the normal person can engage in a wide variety of different modes of consciousness and connect all those personal experiences in ego-syntonic continuity with his entire life experience.

Examples of this normal connecting memory operation are seen in one who can sequentially have personal experiences of Zen meditation, sexual ecstacy, a friendly conversation, hoeing the garden, eating a sumptuous meal, and reflecting on his or her life, all in one day as a whole fabric of experiencing the same person throughout.

On the other hand, consider the same events when a person does not employ the connecting memory operation. The Zen meditation might be experienced as depersonalization; the sexual experience might produce anxiety about loss of body boundaries; the conversation might be experienced as a Capgras event, in which the friend is thought to be an imposter; hoeing in the garden might be a j'aime vu experience of unfamiliar environment; the meal might be rejected by an anorexia nervosa patient who fears eating; the reflection on one's life might produce an out of body experience. Each event of the day is a picture (an experience), but each experience is unconnected to the life experience of the whole person.

When we compare the same events in one day in the life of one person, the function of "reality testing" becomes obvious as *the process of relating or connecting all experience events in the "reality" of a single uniform life experience*. Failure to "test reality" is simply a failure to connect a single picture (experience) to the whole context of one's life. A single picture, by itself, lacks context. A single picture may not be meaningful in and of itself. A single picture can be interpreted in multiple ways without an orienting context.

We conclude that a specific mode of consciousness and a specific experience are not pathological. It is the failure to *personalize* the experience and the failure to *interpret* the experience in connection with one's whole life experience that makes a "state of consciousness" a pathological experience and a truly "altered" experience.

This conclusion has clinical relevance for the interpretation of many descriptions of "altered states of consciousness." Let us consider trance states, possession states, ecstatic emotional states, and meditative states. In many cultures such states are socially learned and ritually practiced by many members of the culture. We need not invoke a psychopathological personality or psychopathological disorder to explain how and why people engage in such experiences.

On the other hand, where a person has such experiences out of context, without interpretive meaning, without connection to the rest of his or her life, such experiences become pathological. Thus a trance state results in a "fugue experience" or sleepwalking. A possession state is experienced as "multiple personality" or a Capgras syndrome. An ecstatic emotional state is experienced as "latah," "windigo," "running amok." Ritual self-mutilation is enacted as an episode of deliberate self-harm. Meditative states are experienced as derealization. Transcendental states are experienced as depersonalization, identity crisis, homosexual panic, out of body experience.

In all of the above examples, the mode of consciousness and the event experience are the same. What differs is the contextual interpretation, and so there is a difference in the "personal meaning" of the experience. Hence the event becomes a different "personal experience"—either a normal personal experience or an abnormal personal experience *from the viewpoint of the person*. The observer cannot differentiate one from the other, just looking at the behavioral expression of the experience per se. However, the consequent reactions of the person will indicate whether the event experience was "personally normal" or "personally abnormal." That is, the experience was ego-syntonic and connected to the whole person without perturbation, or the experience was ego-dystonic and provoked psychopathological reactions.

The Function of Memory in Consciousness

To complete this analysis we must explicate the "connecting memory operation." An experience in consciousness cannot become a personal experience or a meaningful experience without memory. For example, persons with a severe organic brain syndrome may have immediate experiences that they do not appropriate to themselves personally and that are meaningless. A patient with Alzheimer's disease is almost hit by a car; the patient demonstrates no personal response to the near accident, and does not recognize the meaning of the event.

The memory system can be divided into two major operations. The first is storage and retrieval from storage. This includes immediate recall, short-term memory, and long-term memory. This is what we normally consider as memory. However, we call attention to a second major memory operation that we label the "active interpretive memory process."

This active memory process is critical to our interpretation of events as they occur. We do not experience events and then later interpret them. Rather, as stimuli enter the brain, they are actively interpreted in relation to coded data in the memory bank. An analogy will illustrate this process. A bilingual translator who can think simultaneously in two languages is able to concurrently take input in one language and interpret the meaning in terms of another language. This is *simultaneous concurrent interpretation*. Similarly, the human receives new input (experience) and concurrently and simultaneously makes an interpretation of that input in terms of whole life experience (memory). This active memory process allows us to experience events as meaningful because they are immediately connected to our whole life. Thus an event experience is immediately translated into personal experience.

When this does not occur, an event experience is strange, startling, immobilizing, depersonalized. (This is not happening to me; I couldn't respond; I must be dreaming.)

Such personal events are now stored in memory as whole events. One can activate this memory system and "relive or reexperience" the personal experience as it happened. We normally do not do this. But during hypnotic states, trance states, abreactions, or simply through learning as in the training of actors, we can use the memory system to "re-create" the personal experience. We shall call this "personal experience memory."

Usually, however, we cognitively "reinterpret" personal experience into a "conscious report," which is then stored in our readily available memory bank of "historical construction of life events." Thus our memory of "personal history" is not simply an accretion of personal experiences, but rather is a memory construction of an *interpreted personal history.* This latter memory process is identical to the work of a historian who weaves an intelligible history out of discrete events. This we shall call the "historical memory" (Spence, 1982).

When people recall events from memory, they usually recall data from historical memory. That is, they "remember." They may remember facts, emotions, actions, and report them. Such historical memory is not necessarily accurate, because all event details have been interpreted to "fit a personal historical concept." One can, through recall or free association, or in response to events, rework such historical memory to accommodate new interpretations of one's life. This is what much of the work of psychotherapy is about.

However, historical memory is different from personal experience memory. In the latter, there is not remembering but re-experiencing. In psychotherapy, we may wish to assist patients to re-experience so that they can reconstruct a new interpretation in historical memory of that experience. However, simple abreaction, or catharsis, or hypnotic regression may *not* be useful in therapy if such re-experience is not connected to historical memory. For example, in a case of pathological mourning, or post-traumatic stress syndromes, the person has repeated personal experience memories that are re-experienced. But since that re-experience is never connected to a new interpretation in historical memory, the person continues to have the same traumatic personal experience each time he or she activates the memory process.

We emphasize that the personal experience memory probably never disappears, but it loses its traumatic impact when that experience is connected and interpreted anew in historical memory. Thus the person can remember the traumatic experience in historical memory without having to activate the personal experience memory and therefore continually relive the experience. Now the experience is consciously accessible and interpretable in an acceptable way in historical memory.

The clinical relevance of this fact is seen in persons who experience repetitive flashbacks, phobias, panic attacks, and so on. In each case, a stimulus evokes a personal experience memory rather than a historical memory.

In culturally accepted trance states or possession states, a person is able to connect the personal experience to historical memory, and hence enters and emerges from such states as the same person.

In fugue states and amnesia states, the person functions solely in terms of immediate personal experience, without the connecting memory linkage to historical memory.

In multiple personality states, the person functions on the basis of memory recall of different personal experience memories without connection to immediate personal experience. Thus the person does not construct a "historical memory of whole self."

This difference between personal experience memory and historical memory is clearly made by Lacan (1978), who notes that there is a great distinction between the personal experience and the "report" of the experience. As Lacan says, the report or historical memory is a psychological maneuver that distances the person from his experience. Indeed, it is this very work of interpretation into a historical memory that allows us to diminish the intense affective component of the real experience. Hence we can now remember in historical memory without disturbing affective arousal.

We can now synthesize our observations in stating that it is the interpretation of personal experience that is critical to the psychodynamics of different modes of consciousness. In turn, that interpretation involves the active memory operations described above. When a person does not effectively employ the active connecting memory operations described, then personal experiences in different modes of consciousness may result in psychopathological syndromes. Alternatively, it appears that most so-called abnormal "altered states of consciousness" (apart from organic states) have their normal counterparts.

SUMMARY

In this chapter we have focused on personal experience as the distinctively human and uniquely personal element of human action. We find the structural psychoanalytic model of id, ego, and superego to be insufficient, whereas the topographical psychoanalytic model of unconscious, preconscious, and conscious is imprecise. We have sought to use operational language that does not antropomorphize psychic operations, while linking our operational descriptions to neurobiological process. We have linked the personal perspective to a behavioral perspective and to a psychological perspective. Finally, we have offered numerous examples of normal and clinical situations that we believe are clarified within the personal experience perspective. Particularly, we have sought to demonstrate that modes of consciousness provide a repertoire of personal experiences, and that such conscious experiences can be meaningfully integrated into whole person experience.

REFERENCES

Adamec, R. E. Normal and abnormal limbic system mechanisms of emotive biasing. In E. Livingston and O. Hornykiewicz (Eds.), *Limbic mechanisms.* New York: Plenum, 1978, pp. 405–456.

Allport, G. *Personality.* New York: Holt, 1937.

Amsterdam, K. B. and Levitt, M. Consciousness of self and painful self-consciousness. *The Psychoanalytic Study of the Child,* 1980, *35,* 67-83.

Bellak, L., Hurvich, M., and Geidman, H. *Ego functions in schizophrenia, neurotics, and normals.* New York: Wiley, 1973.

Ben-Ari, Y. *The amygdala complex.* North Holland: Elsevier Biomedical Press, 1981.

Bettelheim, B. *Freud and man's soul.* New York: Knopf, 1983.

Csikszentmihalyi, M. Attention and the holistic approach to behavior. In K. S. Pope and J. L. Singer (Eds.), *The stream of consciousness.* New York: Plenum, 1978, pp. 335-357.

Emde, N. R. and Robinson, J. (1979). The first two months: Recent research in developmental psychobiology and the changing view of the newborn. In S. I. Harrison (Ed.), *Handbook of child psychiatry.* New York: Basic Books, 1979.

Engel, G. L. Toward a classification of affects. In P. H. Knapp (Ed.), *Expression of the emotions in man.* New York: International Universities Press, 1963, pp. 266-299.

Epstein, Seymour. The unity principle versus the reality and pleasure principles, or the tale of the scorpion and the frog. In M. P. Lynch et al. (Eds.), *Self concept: Advances in theory and research.* Cambridge, Mass.: Ballenger, 1981.

Fingarette, H. *The self in transformation.* New York: Basic Books, 1963.

Fletcher, R. *Instinct in man.* New York: International Universities Press, 1957.

Freud, S. Preface to an outline of psychoanalysis. *Collected works,* vol. 23. London: Hogarth Press, 1940, p. 149.

Globus, G. G. On "I": The conceptual foundations of responsibility. *American Journal of Psychiatry,* 1980, *137,* 417-422.

Gloor, P. Inputs and outputs of the amygdala. In K. E. Livingston and O. Hornykiewicz (Eds.), *Limbic mechanisms.* New York: Plenum, 1978, pp. 189-210.

Goleman, D. and Davidson, R. J. *Consciousness: The brain, states of awareness, and alternate realities.* New York: Irvington Publishers, 1979.

Grossman, S. P. An experimental "dissection" of the septal syndrome. In *Functions of the septo-hippocampal system,* Symposium 58. New York: Ciba Foundation, 1978, pp. 227-273.

Haan, N. *Coping and defending: Processes of self-environment organization.* New York: Academic Press, 1977.

Hilgard, R. E. Divided consciousness in hypnosis: The implications of the hidden observer. In R. E. Shor (Eds.), *Hypnosis.* New York: Aldine, 1977.

Hoffman, E. L. From instinct to identity: Implications of changing psychoanlaytic concepts on social life from Freud to Erickson. *Journal of the History of the Behavioral Sciences,* 1982, *18,* 130-146.

Hofstadter, D. R. and Dennet, D. C. *The mind's I: Fantasies and reflections on self and soul.* New York: Basic Books, 1981.

Izard, E. C. On the outogenesis of emotions and emotion–cognition relationships in infancy. In Michael Lewis and Leonard A. Rosenblum (Eds.), *The development of affect.* New York: Plenum, 1978.

James, W. The varieties of attention. *Principles of psychology.* Boston: Longmans Green, 1890.

Kaada, B. R. Stimulation and regional ablation of the amygdaloid complex with reference to functional representations. In B. E. Eleftherioo (Ed.), *The neurobiology of the amygdala,* New York: Plenum, 1972, pp. 211-281.

Kling, A. Influence of temporal lobe lesions on radio-telemetered electrical activity of amygdala to social stimuli in monkey. In Y. Ben-Ari (Ed.), *The amygdala complex.* North Holland: Elsevier Biomedical Press, 1981.

Krystal, J. The activating aspect of emotions. *Psychoanalysis and Contemporary Thought,* 1982, *5,* 605–642.

Lacan, J. *The four fundamental concepts of psycho-analysis,* Jacques-Alain Miller (Ed.), Alan Sheridan (transl.). New York: Norton, 1978.

Lehman, M. N., Winans, S. R., and Powers, J. B. Medial nucleus of the amygdala mediates chemosensory control of male hamster sexual behavior. *Science,* 1980, *210,* 557–559.

Lewis, M. and Brooks-Gunn, J. *Social cognition and the acquisition of self.* New York: Plenum, 1979.

Loevinger, J. *Ego development.* San Francisco: Jossey-Bass, 1976.

Luria, A. R. *The working brain.* New York: Basic Books, 1973.

Lynch, M. D., Norem-Hebeisen, A. A., and Gergen, N. *Self concept: Advances in theory and research.* Cambridge, Mass.: Ballenger, 1981.

Mahler, M. S., Pine, F., and Bergman, A. *The psychological birth of the human infant.* New York: Basic Books, 1975.

Mahrer, A. R. *Experiencing: A humanistic theory of psychology and psychiatry.* New York: Brunner Mazel, 1978.

Mead, G. H. *Mind, self and society,* C. Morris (Ed.). Chicago: University of Chicago Press, 1934, pp. 152–164.

Pattison, E. M. Psychoanalysis and the concept of evil. In M. C. Coleman and M. Eigen (Eds.), *Evil: Self and Culture.* New York: Human Sciences Press, 1984, pp. 61–88.

Piaget, J. *The origins of intelligence in children.* London: Routledge and Kegan Paul, 1952.

Pope, K. S. and Singer, J. L. *The stream of consciousness: Scientific investigations into the flow of human experiences.* New York: Plenum, 1978.

Pribram, K. H. Self-consciousness and intentionality. In G. E. Schwartz and D. Shapiro (Eds.), *Consciousness and self-regulation.* New York: Plenum, 1976.

Raimy, V. *Misunderstandings of the self.* San Francisco: Jossey-Bass, 1975.

Rogers, Carl R. *On becoming a person.* Boston: Houghton Mifflin, 1961.

Schafer, Roy. *A new language for psychoanalysis.* New Haven and London: Yale University Press, 1976, pp. 102–120.

Spence, D. P. *Narrative truth and historical truth: Meaning and interpretation in psycho-analysis.* New York: Norton, 1982.

Spiegelberg, H. *Phenomenology in psychology and psychiatry: A historical introduction.* Evanston, Ill.: Northwestern University Press, 1972.

Sroufe, L. A. Socioemotional development. In J. D. Osofsky (Ed.), *Handbook of infant development.* New York: Wiley, 1979, pp. 462–516.

Stechler, G. and Kaplan, S. The development of the self. *The Psychoanalytic Study of the Child,* 1980, *35,* 85–105.

Strange, J. R. A search for the sources of the stream of consciousness. In K. S. Pope and J. L. Singer (Eds.), *The stream of consciousness.* New York: Plenum, 1978.

Sullivan, H. S. Good-me, bad-me, not-me. In D. Goldman and R. J. Davidson (Eds.), *Consciousness: The brain, states of awareness, and alternate realities.* New York: Irvington Publishers, 1979, pp. 46–47.

Sutherland, J. D. The British object relations theorists: Balint, Winnicott, Fairbairn, Guntrip. *Journal of the American Psychoanalytic Association,* 1980, *28*(4), 829–860.

Tart, C. T. Transpersonal realities or neuro-physiological illusion? Toward an empirically testable dualism. In R. S. Valle and R. V. Ecktersberg (Eds.), *The metaphors of consciousness.* New York: Plenum, 1981, pp. 199–222.

Taylor, G. R. *The natural history of the mind.* New York: Dutton, 1979.

Valle R. S. and Von Ecktersberg, R. (Eds.). *The metaphors of consciousness.* New York: Plenum, 1981.

Von Bertalanffy, L. General system theory—a critical review. *General Systems,* 1962, *7,* 1–20.

Walsh, R. N. Meditation research: The evolution and state of the art. In N. Walsh and F. Vaughn (Eds.), *Beyond ego: Transpersonal dimensions in psychology.* Los Angeles: J. P. Tarchen, 1980.

Winnicott, D. W. From dependence towards independence. In *Collected papers,* New York: Basic Books, 1963, pp. 83–92.

Young, J. G. and Cohen, D. J. The molecular biology of development. In S. I. Harrison (Ed.), *Handbook of child psychiatry.* New York: Basic Books, 1979, pp. 22–62.

Part Two
Manifestations

8. Working in Isolation: States That Alter Consensus

Francis Jeffrey*

INTRODUCTION

Almost 500 years ago, Columbus made a reasonable prediction that if he sailed west from Portugal he would reach land. This is the paradigm of science. Columbus gathered together the appropriate research equipment, consisting of money, ships, sailors, maps, and so on, and launched his experiment. Now, 500 years later, the results seem incontrovertible: the "new world" swarms with a billion people, some of them actively searching for a new frontier.

Scientific experiments test a reasonable hypothesis, based on everything that is considered scientifically sensible at the moment the hypothesis is framed. Usually those who frame a hypothesis are well informed and *design* their hypothesis toward a positive outcome. Generally experiment proves the hypothesis essentially correct.

Along the way, the unexpected may turn up. Columbus expected to arrive at India, but found a Caribbean isle which he named "El Salvador." The experiment was saved by an outcome slightly different from the expected. Otherwise, Columbus would have been forgotten, and the "new world" discovered later by someone else.

Science thrives on (1) its ability to predict results reliably, and (2) the appearance of the unexpected, to an extent that refines rather than disrupts predictions.

*Acknowledgments: Thanks to John Lilly for teaching the method, to Roland Fischer for conceiving this chapter and helpfully commenting on earlier versions, and to Carolyn Kleefeld for assistance in writing it.

249

My desire in writing this chapter of the *Handbook* is to conteptualize a phase of research in profound isolation, carried out by myself among others, as an interesting example of pure science.

What I will report here is less a result of research in the "objective" sense of the word, and more the result that this work had for the explorers. This includes the changes that must be carried through in preparation for and in the course of the work. In this kind of research, the essential unity of the observer and the observed phenomena needs to be explicitly acknowledged. Were it not stated as a premise at the outset, then it could be related at the conclusion as a "discovery."

What is offered here is one synthetic version of the possible alterations in consciousness and consensus that accompany the practice of certain states of being generally referred to as "isolation." By altering consciousness and consensus we hope to suggest and facilitate further and farther research.

Insofar as consciousness research impacts fundamental definitions such as reality, epistemology, self, and science, I want to begin by making my position clear as regards the nature of science.

What distinguishes science from exploration in general is that exploration seeks some external, objective goal, while science seeks a change in the explorers. While all exploration may change what is thought, science changes ways of thinking. The change comprises learning in the vanguard individuals who practice a particular scientific discipline. This change ramifies through the community of forerunners, and eventually impacts what everyone thinks. A scientific theory is a way of thinking that makes sense of a range of experiences, both actual and potential—past and future. The fact that the moon orbits the earth is merely an approximate observation, whereas gravitation is a theory that says why, how, if, and when.

Einstein's theory of gravitation makes sense of the same experiences and makes the same predictions as Newton's; but Einstein's is more accurate. It also is an approximation. Einstein's theory is in a way less tied to the past. It relies less on old ways of thinking, and it tends to help us predict the future—to formulate more interesting hypotheses. Similarly we could trace the evolution of physical thinking from Aristotle's *inertia* theory through that of Newton and Galileo (as Einstein and Infeld, 1938).

The hallmark of a valid theory is that it is an improvement over the past, and suggests further progress. Thus the emphasis that science places on operational verification is not essentially tied to the doctrine of empiricism, as has often been thought. Without imputing the actual existence of a universe of stable properties, it can be said that a theory of science does not possess an absolute and objective character. Rather, a theory is a state of mind in the vanguard community—"a state of consciousness" among the forerunners.

These observations allow us to add the third item to this list of what science is about:

1. Prediction
2. The unexpected
3. A community of shared consciousness/consensus

Participant-engaged experiential research into "states of consciousness" is not widely accepted. I conjecture that this is the case because it represents the pure form of science: science uncontaminated by the "belief in its own objectivity." Researchers often go to great lengths to hide from others the truth that their research actually is not objective. They pretend to be seeking some "outside" fact, as would a geographic explorer. For example, the phenomenological contents of a hallucination might be reported in the literature as the "results" of research. This provides the comforting illusion of objectivity—a separation between the phenomenon reported and the observer—but it is actually the stuff of science fiction. In extreme cases, the contents of the hallucination may be raised from the level of "fact" to the level of "theory," or even to ontological stature.

All psychological reseachers share the puzzle: *how to study nature while in fact studying our own nature?* (Fischer, 1977).

That is the common problem, and "altered states" research is simply the evident exemplar of the common predicament, the nonexception that illuminates the rule. The nature of our kind of research bluntly confronts us with that fact which most scientists would prefer to elude: science that is primarily and explicitly concerned with the properties of the scientist is *pure science,* for science is essentially *intelligently self-directed change in the participants* (i.e., learning).

During my experience in "traditional" experimental psychology, we routinely paid "subjects" to run through elaborate experiments that were in effect computer games. Invariably, more progress was made when the researchers themselves participated in the experiments, rather than running naive subjects and then looking at statistical analyses of the numerical data.

The difficulty was that the rules of our game as scientists required that we look for *answers* (to questions posed in the specialized literature), while science is really about finding *questions*. The focus on "objective" quantitative results eclipsed appreciation of the qualitative issues which we were actually involved with, and obscured our awareness of our own neural operations as scientific participants.

The research discussed in this chapter is presented explicitly as an example of pure science, with the understanding that science is a process of learning that models the most evolved operations of our nervous system by:

1. Taking into account actual phenomena
2. Practicing open communication
3. Insisting on operationally predictive validity

By "pure" I mean that it is not contaminated by the illusion of objectivity. The components of this research are, as much as practically feasible, only the researcher and the community of shared experience. Therefore, in terms comparable with most research, this research is about "nothing." There is/are no subject(s), no apparatus, and no specimens. There are no experiments per se and no data (Jeffrey, 1977).

Ideas are worked out in isolation and refined with recourse to the communicative and informational resources of the scientific community. These ideas are recognized and treated explicitly as *operations of the researcher,* under the prevailing experimental conditions. Necessarily, therefore, the concept of "objectivity" is refined *ad infinitum (ad absurdum).* In the process we see that issues of "self" achieve preeminence.

PREDICTIONS AND EXPECTATIONS

The paradigm of isolation research was developed by Lilly (1956) and by Lilly and Shurley (1961): *To achieve the maximum attainable isolation of the intact, healthy human observer in order to afford an opportunity for self-observation in the immediate absence of external influences.*

This definition necessitates three special provisions:

1. Insofar as this is physically and practically attainable.
2. In a manner that is completely voluntary and informed.
3. Within a finite slice of time.

These special provisions have very significant consequences, which will be treated subsequently. First, however, let's consider *why* someone might want to do this. Here is a partial, suggestive list of possible motives:

1. Expose someone to controlled stimulation in isolation.
2. Use in the context of therapy and psychiatric evaluation.
3. Experiment with drugs.
4. Use batteries of psychological tests to measure changes, comparing pre- and post-isolation experience.
5. Determine benefits for "super-learning," self-hypnosis, and executive success.
6. Use for think tank, creative problem-solving, and enhanced imagination.

7. Monitor EEG, blood pressure, and other physiological indicators.
8. Compare pre- and post-session sensory/motor patterns.
9. Explore medical benefits of relaxation.
10. Look for altered states of consciousness.
11. Report detailed contents of dreamlike experiences.
12. Seek pleasure, fantasy, excitement, unusual experiences.
13. Aspite to religious inspiration, trance, and visions.
14. Achieve enlightenment; mediate; meet God(s).
15. Develop super powers and ESP.
16. Experiment with telepathy.
17. Contact aliens (E.T.'s).
18. Induce insanity; brainwash; interrogate.
19. Learn to voluntarily experience orgasms.
20. Resolve conflict, integrate, self-therapise.
21. Relax, restore, recover, sleep.
22. Escape persons, places and things.
23. Crate alternative realities.
24. Encourage neoteny and longevity.
25. Evolve.

Probably all of these motives have figured in various experiments by many researchers. Some are of a science fiction, religious, or speculative character. Others have an objective component; for example, measuring a relaxing or therapeutic effect. Some entail an additional "variable," such as drugs or stimulation. Those applications that require monitoring of the person in isolation are probably outside our paradigm.

We are concerned here with the use of isolation in ways in which the above-listed motives are absent (or very secondary). Item 18 ("induce insanity," etc.) is impossible or highly unlikely within the Lilly–Shurley paradigm. What concerns us here is the use of isolation expressly for self-observation, in a scientific context. This includes research into individual (ontotypic) and species (phenotypic) characteristics of the brain and its operation, as well as study of the properties of scientific theories and unscientific theories.

Therapeutic effects are not excluded and sometimes might be expected, but their measurement by someone other than the participant-observer would seem to compromise the isolation paradigm.

When the optimal research conditions are met or approached, as defined above, the situation will be referred to hereafter as "Lilly Conditions," or "Profound Isolation" (PI).

The Lilly Conditions define an unusual state of being, a condition of existence that is uncommon in human experience, and outside the phylogenic experience of the human species, up until now. We have in effect defined for scientific purposes a new world. We cast off for this new world with some ideas about what this world *is*. These ideas begin the journey as navigational guides (maps, instruments, beacons, etc.). Their utility is tested, and during the voyage of discovery some are discarded as useless, misleading, counterproductive, dangerous, or irrelevant. Upon reaching our destination, perhaps different in reality from our imagined destination, we have those ideas that have survived the voyage constituting a fairly direct "map" to the destination actually reached.

To define the absence of environment, as required in PI, is to define implicitly the environment, one's relationship with the environment, and oneself as a being in relation to an environment. Thus, as far as this definition will apply, at least two sets of discernible entities are postulated: self/other, organism/environment, inside/outside, and so on. Their relationship, therefore, must be conceived as some sort of interface, boundary, or mesh of interconnections. To define the PI state meaningfully is implicitly to define the world. Much of the work will hence be expected to consist of the working-out of the consequences hidden in and implicit from this definition.

The definition of this dyadic relationship, as developed and refined experimentally, will supplant and succeed the concepts of subject/object, observer/phenomena, scientist/data, and so on, which are operational in ordinary research.

The most general prediction motivating research is that proceeding on a certain course, we will discover something worthwhile. In line with Shannon's information theory (Shannon, 1948), von Foerster has argued that the most valuable experiment is that which has the greatest potential for unexpected results (von Foerster, 1974b). This ideal is in practice balanced by the need to be able to interpret, contextualize, and communicate findings. This is also consistent with Shannon's theory, which defined information as the answers to questions. Therefore, questions will be interpreted as meaningful within the scientific community only when posed as the answers to other questions.

In order to contextualize this reserch with the right degree of information capacity, a general working hypothesis needs to be formulated at the outset. We begin with the hypothesis of *Neuro-Interoceptive Observation* (NIO), which can be stated in three forms:

1. *Strong form:* The physical structures and operations of the human brain will become apparent to the suitably prepared *participant-observer* working in PI (i.e., the one who communicates).
2. *Moderate form:* In PI it is possible to sense or detect patterns of the

operation of the brain that are normally not available to consciousness (e.g., "programs," metaprograms, etc.).

3. *Weak form:* In PI one can develop special *insight* into one's own behavior patterns, thought patterns, feelings, emotional states, aesthetics, etc. ("subjective" form of NIO).

Interoception is a term frequently used in physiology to refer to those nerve systems that sense the internal states of the body. Following the work of Klüver, Fischer has developed the psychological/phenomenological usage of this term:

> One can view, then, verifiable perceptions as on one end and unverifiable perceptions, i.e. hallucinations, as on the other end of a continuum with the sensory to motor ratio gradually increasing from one end to the other. In hallucinations . . . blocked motor performance impedes private verification in physical space–time and hence the experience is also inaccessible to public verification. We may look now at Klüver's illusions, memory images eidetic images, . . . etc., not as variations on the same theme but as gradually less and less verifiable forms of interpretation. . . . (Fischer, 1969, pp. 7–8)

> [On the perception–hallucination continuum of rising central arousal [,] *exteroception* is gradually changed into *interoception* [,] while willed motor activity becomes increasingly impaired and ultimately inhibited. Hallucinations, therefore may be described as "*interoception without action*" and characterized by high inner sensory to motor (S/M) ratios.] (Fischer, 1974, p. 143; see also Fischer, 1972, p. 177; *italics added*)

Fischer is here interpreting Klüver's form constants abstractly, as indications of the performance and structure of the system, rather than phenomenologically, as contents significant in themselves (i.e., *facts*). This is the approach that I will continue to take in interpreting PI experiences.

The formulations of Fischer are based primarily on drug research, and therefore require some adaptation to PI, but the concepts of S/M ratios, verification, interoception, and structural/functional interpretation are applicable to PI, and are central to my own formulations on this topic.

Another guiding principle is the concept of *uncoupling* supplied by Stark, as a refinement of the notion of isolation. (Lawrence Stark, private communication, 1974) The concept of coupling/uncoupling is derived from bioengineering—that is, biological cybernetic control systems theory (Stark, 1968). The single concept of isolation can be analyzed into several dimensions of uncoupling, for example, sensory/motor uncoupling, organism/

environment uncoupling, and so on. The uncoupling concept has various mathematical interpretations, and thus raises the possibility of applying mathematical analysis to PI.

Lilly (1977) has formulated isolation in terms of "interlocks" and "feedbacks" among multiple levels or program domains, including the observer/operator, external reality (e.r.), internal reality (i.r.), and *simulations* thereof:

> . . . The observer/operator exists exclusively in a metaprogrammatic computational domain . . . isolated from current e.r. computational necessities, e.r. simulations are free of input/output constraints and can be recomputed in new forms . . . the observer/operator observes/acts exclusively on/in computations . . . without modifications introduced by here/now inputs/outputs to/from the external reality. (p. 286)

> . . . The set of computations that currently generates external reality simulations . . . interlocked with the observer/operator and with the computed e.r. inputs/outputs operating synchronously, generates what is called "external experience." . . . In physical isolation . . . , e.r. inputs/outputs approach zero. . . . the i.r. experience is among simulations. (p. 294)

A coupling relationship, such as that between an organism and an environment, is characterized by *stability,* and those mechanisms or operations that maintain the stability. "In man, and in neurophysiological terms, *stability* refers to the closed unity of perception and behavior . . . " (Fischer, 1977, p. 65). Fischer quotes the formulation of Powers (1973): " . . . we know nothing of our own behavior but the feedback effects of our own outputs. . . . To behave is to control (what is sensed as) perception . . . "—that is, *inputs.*

Fischer (1969) also notes that hallucinations arise in the presence of ordinary levels of stimulation, when behavior is restricted, inhibited, or discouraged by failure to be effective. And hallucinations can be "switched off" by high levels of voluntary, intentional activity, or by the intention to attempt such activity, but not by the mere contemplation of activity (as in the experiences of Gordon Alles reported in Stafford, pp. 288–289, see Jeffrey, 1983a).

The PI conditions assure that the coupling relationship between organism and environment, or between self and its percepts, will be interrupted. The closed circular-causal chain of inputs and outputs will be unlinked. However, the absence of strong sensory stimulation in the PI environment implies that the S/M ratio may be kept quite small; even when voluntary behavior is minimal, and further, the feedback effects (inputs) from behavior are minimized in PI, as far as physically feasible, also contributing to a low S/M ratio. Therefore the S/M ratio could become elevated only if the equivalent of sensation were generated within the organism. This might arise with drugs, disease, excitation, and other forms of uncontrolled neural activity (i.e., neural activity without a strong intentional or ordering component).

The bioengineering concepts of coupling and uncoupling led eventually to formulation of the ICC model (*Impact-Coupling-Constraints*). ICC is an attempt to understand the operation of the nervous system (CNS) in terms of (1) the intensity of sensory stimulation *impacting* the system; (2) the degree of *coupling* in which this stimulation plays a part; and (3) the *constraint* that 1 and 2 impose on the degrees of freedom of interpretation or autonomy of the system.

ICC was a significant advance over current cybernetic-style formulations because it opened the way to acknowledging an "inner dimension" of autonomy or self-determination. This development made it possible to make sense of experiences in PI work that represent processes normally so faint as to escape notice in ordinary organism/environment relationships.

It also raises the prospect of integrating PI into the mainstream of neuropsychological research, where it forms a major potential impetus to theoretical advance. PI has heretofore been treated "in isolation" as almost a separate science. A major unification is promised by developments along the line of the ICC model.

Powers has written (1978, p. 433): "What determines which controlled quantity will be controlled? . . . The behaving system itself must be the determining factor. What the person attends to becomes the controlled aspect of the display. The person also determines the selected aspect that is to serve as q^*_i," (the input quantity when the system is undisturbed).

PI researchers have noted that this mysterious inner *selection* can become the principal feature of consciousness once the system in isolation ceases to control perceptions, either i.r. or e.r. I want to note in passing that Fischer has formulated the idea that the self-consistency or "integrity" of a conscious organism (organization) can increase through experience in alternative conscious states—including PI—and I shall return to this theme later on.

With the understanding that "subcortical" includes the afferent (i.e., sensory) neural pathways arriving at the brain, we see that Fischer also presages the ICC model (Fischer, 1972): "If we assume that man . . . creates experience through the cortical . . . interpretation of his subcortical activity, we may ask about the extent of freedom, or relative independence, of the mind (cortex) from the biological substratum (subcortex)'' (Fischer, 1972 p. 178). He cites MacLean (1954, 1958) on the limbic system.

EXPERIMENTAL AND EXPERIENTIAL BASE

I was introduced to the PI methodology by John Lilly in 1973–74. During the following three years I was able to spend approximately three hundred hours in isolation myself, and to involve over one hundred self-selected participant-observers in my research. I was able to interview most of these people before and after PI sessions, and fifty-two filed written reports. These volunteers provided the background for contextualizing and understanding my own solitary experiences. I also had access to the community of PI researchers and self-explorers associated with Lilly, and to written reports, including Hoffman's (1976), and an extensive scientific literature. Lilly's work, reported in 1977, involved over three hundred participants, most of whom filed written reports. He utilized the classic PI methods of the ''isolation tank,'' which he invented, providing total darkness, silence, and body suspension in isothermal (93–94°F) heavier-than-water fluid. Hoffman allowed his thirty-four participants to control the levels of illumination and sound down to zero levels if they chose. I provided my participants with silence and the choice of total darkness or dim, diffuse, white illumination through a plastic canopy. Most chose darkness after initial experimentation.

In 1975 I was granted the first United States Patent (#4000749) for the design of an isolation module for humans.

Reports in the literature from these and other researchers using similar PI methods are varied, but they tend to be varied in the same ways. (Lilly, 1972, 1976, 1977, provides a good characteristic sample.)

Contrasting Motives and Methods

Distinct from the pure PI work is other research combining PI with psychoactive drugs. This includes Lilly's (1967) research, associated with the phrase ''human biocomputer.'' Other researchers have combined psychoactive drugs with reduction or attenuation of sensory stimulation other than the complete PI conditions (e.g., Fischer et al., 1970; Patton and Fischer, 1973).

A large number of workers followed the ''SD'' paradigm. For roughly a decade, from the midfifties to midsixties, a program of research was widely pursued concerned with the effects of drastically reducing the level of sensory stimulation and interaction with the environment. The generic title under which this research has come to be known is "Sensory Deprivation." This research area, which from initial reports appeared to be highly exciting and promising, was soon overshadowed by negative valuations and the non-repeatability and idyosyncratic character of results. The program is summed up in a 1961 review edited by Solomon. A great variety of aberrations, including hallucination, long-term disorientation and perceptual distortion, cognitive disintegration, and negatively valued subjective states are reported therein.

More recently it has come to light that the SD work was largely instigated and covertly funded by national security agencies of the U.S. government, as were the bulk of experiments with LSD and other psychotropics during the same period. Work sponsored by the CIA and Army intelligence and chemical warfare branches generally violated both ethical canons and the standards of sound scientific research. It was concerned with applications in indoctrination, interrogation, coercion, and degradation.

I was able to interview one person who was a victim of this quasi-research. As an Army enlisted man he had been required to spend up to six days in an SD chamber covertly operated at the Defense Language Institute in Monterey, California. His report of his experiences, and subsequent psychiatric history, suggested to me that he had been dosed with drugs (perhaps LSD) without his knowledge or consent, while in SD, under military orders.

[Various reports of SD research (not all of it unethical) are given by Brownfield (1965), Heron et al. (1956), Heron (1961), Vernon (1963), and West (1962). Several authors have argued that the reported results (hallucinations!) are attributable more to restriction of movement (motor deprivation, or MD) than to SD, including Cohen (1961), Freedman (1961), Schaefer and Bernick (1965), Zubek and Wilgosh (1963) and Zubek et al. (1963) Bennet (1974) has attributed SD effects to stress. There is an interesting literature on stress without SD, which is equally effective in producing aberrations of perception and behavior] including the literature on single-handed navigation (Bennett, 1974; Erickson and Gustafson, 1968). The well-known story of Donald Crowhurst is reported in Toralin and Hall (1970) and psychoanalyzed by Podvoll (1983).

My own background experience included the use of darkened anechoic chambers to provide SD conditions for relatively short (physically comfortable) periods. I had also experimented with other variations on the theme of "unusual perceptual conditions," including studies of the effects and aftereffects of seen motion, stabilized images, redundant patterns, stroboscopic illumination, sensory overload, and subbehavioral attention shifts with inhibited occular motility (MacKay, 1957–1958, 1964; Grindley and Townsend, 1970; Riggs et al., 1953; Jeffrey 1972, 1971b).

Experiential Specimens

It is not difficult to trace the negative results often reported in SD work to (1) stressful, uncomfortable physical conditions; (2) unethical circumstances; and (3) negative set and setting. In contrast, PI experiences are almost always reported as "positive." Hoffman had 100 percent positive evaluations. I had *three* (3%) negative evaluations, each of which was clearly circumstantial.

One participant reported an hour of intense subjective pain. This was attributed to her dwelling on her severe physical disease condition (cancer, thought to be terminal). Several other cancer sufferers found the PI experience pleasant, helpful, or transformative.

My second negative result was from a very active New Yorker, who described her 15 minutes in PI as the most boring experience of her life.

Finally, I had one participant who had described himself as an intensely religious Christian. His motive was not self-exploration but a desire to prove to himself that "he could take it." After 90 minutes in isolation he reported that his entire session was taken up with horrid experiences of being "burned in hell." Note that there was nothing external keeping him in the tank for the full 90 minutes! A check of my equipment revealed that the thermostat was out of order, and the fluid temperature had run up from the comfortable isothermal range of 93–94°F, to 106°F! The range of dream-like experiences attainable in PI is covered by Lilly (1972, 1976, 1981); while the fictional account of Chayesfsky (1978) and the movie *Altered States* are more speculative and metaphorical than experiential.

GENERAL RESULTS OF PI

The effects of the profound isolation methods are to disengage (uncouple) one from perceptible interaction with an environment, as well as from active, explicit interaction with one's own body surface. Further, the gravitational component of somaesthetic sensation is virtually abolished by perfect fluid suspension, and the sensation of the body outline (skin) is eliminated by pressure relief, isothermal fluid conditions, and the monotony of the residual, minimal topical stimulation of the skin. Under these optimally isolated, stress-relieved conditions, reinforcement ceases for the usual definition of self-as-body-image, and self-as-relationships.

Naturally, several hours or several sessions of PI may pass before a new participant-observer experiences a radical transformation in conceptualization and perception. The earliest PI experiences for an individual are usually reported as simply relaxing, relieving, pleasurable, exciting, and so forth. Eventually, however, most PI participant-observers experience a perceptual/conceptual reorientation that is described in various mystical and/or scientific terms. Obviously, the change is occasioned by withdrawal from the usual mundane reinforcement and physical-world relationships and interactions, and the attendant stresses.

Certain sensations do persist in the PI condition. These include the respiratory, cardiovascular, gastro-intestinal-oral-pharengeal, and residual myaesthenic *interoceptive sensations.* Another class of interoceptive sensations typically emerges in the hiatus of mundane physical world interactions: I have designated these new sensations as *neuro-interoceptive observations* (NIO).

Neuro-interoceptive (NI) sensations are those sensations arising in the nervous system in the absence of relevant interaction with a physical world. These new sensations are experienced as *localized within the nervous system,* usually, within the brain. For example, some PI participants are able to localize points of pleasure in the head and then "tune" these to extreme levels. Outside of PI experimentation, there is very little discussion of NI in the scientific literature, probably because the experience is normally atypical, and/or socially invalidated upon communication in public. But within PI situations, NI experience is entirely commonplace. Presumably, the relief of physical world involvement allows the normally much weaker, less relevant NI signals to be recognized and articulated.

Together, all of the exigencies of repeated, ongoing profound isolation sessions add a new dimension to one's experience-in-the-world, and occasion a substantial reorientation and expansion of concepts. I shall now attempt to explore and explain this "brave new world."

ADVENTURES (. . . IN PARADIGM)

The PI Experience and Context Change

The common feature of experience discovered among the many participant observers, including myself, was not content, but *context*. There was a general reorientation of concepts concerning self-identity and interpersonal relations and interactions. It seems characteristic of independent research in the "conscious states" area that its results tend to be statements about context rather than statements about content. This is in contrast to standard, institutionalized, publically funded research, in which there is an insistence that results bear on content, and that context change must be slow, gradual, indirect, worked out in the course of public evolution of theories and paradigms.

The results of participant-observer type research are to be assimilated into the scientific mainstream only slowly because typically the results of this research amount to major contextual reorientations that are represented as learning in the participants. This sort of learning would correspond in the mainstream to paradigm shifts and scientific revolutions.

We are our most important scientific results, in terms of the way we think about our experiences and formulate models and theories. The most constant, universal effect of PI research is to draw attention to the ubiquitous (hence universally ignored) features of self-definition and being-in-the-world. Specifically, awareness is drawn to the *inherent ambiguity of self-definition in terms of boundaries and inside/outside relations.* Once the ambiguity is noticed, then one's previous, fixed self-identity definition based on physical boundaries is recognized as *arbitrary, behaviorally conditioned,* and *excessively limiting.*

The suspension of behavioral reinforcement of the physical self-definition, occasioned by PI experience, opens the way to a full appreciation of *other, optional, self-definitions,* and ideas of relationship, communion, and communication.

In summary, the results of PI research may be described in terms of new ways of seeing (context) rather than new things to see (content): "... seeing not new landscapes, but with new eyes. ..."

A Model of the Nervous System in Environment

Neurophysiologists have long described the nervous system in terms of "ascending" or more "central" levels or layers, and relatively "higher" centers. This gives a model of the nervous system that is said to be *centripetally* organized—that is, tending toward the center. (MacLean, 1954, 1958, 1970).

For example, the retina of the eye has several successive layers for neural processing, beginning with the photoreceptor cells—the rods and cones. Next, signals feed the optic nerve, pass through the optic chiasma, proceed through several relay stages along the base of the brain, and eventually feed into the visual cortex (occipital area) of both hemispheres. Since the cortex is generally considered to be the area of "central processing" in the brain, the progress of the signals from the periphery (sensors) to the cortex may be termed "centripetal." The visual system has about fifty layers according to Tanimoto and Klinger (1983).

The centripetal model does not imply, however, that eventually signals arrive at a most central, "pontifical" neurone (nerve cell), and that is the end of it! Rather, the signals arriving centrally form the basis for motor signals, which are transmitted *centrifugally* and eventually affect the tension of muscles, thus effecting physical activities. In turn, physical actions alter the environment and change the signals arriving at the sensory receptors, for example, at the retinae of the eyes.

Therefore, the organism-in-environment constitutes a *closed loop,* albeit a very complex one, into which other contingencies may enter from within and from without. We shall not examine the "high-level processes," such as integration and cognition, that are presumed to go on in the midst of this loop.

Von Foerster (1974a) has asserted that for every layer or level in the CNS, the preceding layer feeding it with signals may be regarded as its environment, that is, "the environment." For example, the outer world of light and movement constitutes the environment of the retina, and the retina constitutes the environment of the optic nerve.

This model is illustrated in Figure 1. The outside space represents the outside, physical environment beyond the body. Concentric circles proceeding inward represent the successive layers of processing in the nervous system, beginning with the sensory receptors on the periphery of the body (skin, etc.). The innermost circle represents the motor area of the CNS, which feeds back, via the motor nerves, to the muscles, thus affecting both the configuration of the sensory receptors (body position and posture) and

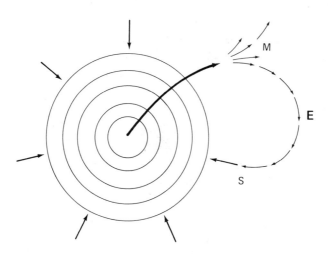

Figure 1.   Onion brain.

the arrangement of objects in the outermost environment (outside world), as discussed by von Foerster (1970, 1974a, 1976, 1981), Powers (1972), and Glasser (1981).

Note that within each concentric zone, *integration* is presumed to take place (viz., the "higher processes of the brain"). Should we wish to explicitly picture both dimensions of the process (i.e., (1) the centripetal/centrifugal circular process, and (2) the integrative process), then we could resort to a map on the surface of a sphere, or on a torus, as in Figures 2 and 3 (after von Foerster, 1979, Figure 3). These diagrams illustrate a full two dimensions of circularity and circular closure. The environment (outside world) is represented as a band around the torus, and as a small patch on the surface of the sphere (!).

I would now like to inquire as to what facts of experience allow us to, *normally,* identify the "outside world" as the environment. Clearly, there is quite a bit of ambiguity as to what constitutes the environment, or "outside," and what constitutes the "inside." For every layer may consider itself the "inside," with respect to the preceding layer, which it considers the environment!

Presumably, there is something about the quality of interactions going on that allows us, normally, to identify without trepidation the outside-as-environment. This apparently has to do with the relative degrees of *control* versus *uncertainty* operating at the various layers, and also with the fact that only the outside world is (normally) the *common environment and interaction zone for several persons.* (Compare Lilly, 1977, pp. 280–297.)

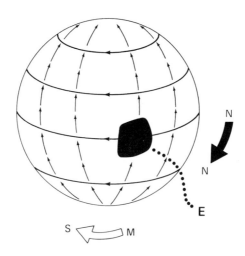

Figure 2.   Global brain.

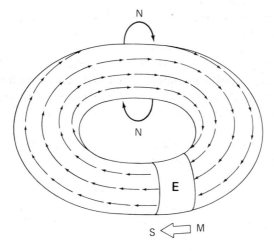

Figure 3.   Donut brain.

Now having illustrated the ambiguity of the organism/environment—or inside/outside—question, I want to proceed to an analysis of PI experience in these terms.

Our sense of space, objects, relationships, and movement is conditioned by physical world experience—physical interaction with material objects, including one's own body, and the bodies of others. One's whole concept of the world, beginning in infancy, is gradually acquired by such interactions, as has been lucidly and elegantly described by Piaget, and subsequently refined and elaborated by the recent work of von Foerster and others. This analysis is quite distinct from associationalism and behaviorism; it is referred to by its exponents as "constructivism" (von Glaserfeld, 1975; Piaget, 1959; von Foerster, 1976, 1981).

So long as one is involved with the physical world through one's waking hours and, to a lesser extent in sleep, one's collection of concepts and behaviors for dealing with the physical world predominate in the operation of the CNS (concept means literally "grasping"). This predominance is so tremendous that it normally overshadows every other basis of conceptualization, virtually to the point of exclusion of other models of the world. Our language reflects this fact. In simple terms, we are preoccupied with objects and distances, movements, commodities, and *separation defining identity.* "The world is too much with us." In a brain so routinely, mundanely preoccupied, there is room for little else (and even the word "room" reflects the fact I am referring to).

The physical world is characterized by collections of tangible objects whose identity is established by physical separateness (or separability). Things consist of parts, which in turn consist of parts . . . *et cetera ad infinitum* . . . in an infinitely recursive series of *parts-to-wholes relationships*. This fact of physical experience is ubiquitously reflected in our language; in the scientific paradigm of reductionism; in all the philosophies of materialism; in hierarchical models of bureaucracy, society, and religion; and in a general systems theory organized on the basis of hierarchical systems (as Jantsch, 1980).

The same mundane experience is perfectly mirrored in our ordinary logic, including the logic of law, science, and mathematics ("Logic, the great mirror of the world . . . ," as described by Wittgenstein, 1921). Accordingly, we are inclined to think of individuals as we speak of them: a name associated with a specifically bounded region in time and space—that is, a body with its characteristic patterns of behavior. Therefore, we define ourselves by *separateness,* by boundaries, and by the associated *emotional dynamics*.

Bateson (1972, 1978) has elucidated the fallacies involved in a self-definition that stops *at the skin,* or at any other physical demarcation outside the skin (i.e., oneself as one's territory, as one's possessions, etc.) He has pointed out that where we actually abide is in communicational loops (feedback, feed-forward, feed-through), pervading the body and the environment, including all other bodies in the environment.

Seeing the Synthesis

A prolonged, repeated course of PI experience is characterized by gradual learning, slow conceptual drift, durable long-term change, and an occasional surprising revelation. In the course of roughly three years of intensive experimentation with the PI environment, I found my sense of being-in-the-world mutating in ways that were difficult to elucidate in the terms of ordinary social discourse. Consequently, I did not attempt a systematic organization or publication of this information, but continued to scan literature and individual teachers in order to assimilate diverse models and metaphors that might be useful in comprehension and synthesis.

Beginning in the autumn of 1976, I became aquainted with the English mathematician G. Spencer-Brown, whose book, *Laws of Form,* I had studied since its first American edition in 1972. Spencer-Brown's work takes the reader to the foundations of mathematics, or perhaps beneath the foundations, to a pristine world of pure *forms,* where "we discover the very structures that we have created." *Laws of Form* presents in the most elementary form the logic or structure of parts-to-wholes relationships. This is the logic of the physical world, and thus the logic of ordinary self-definition, as conditioned by physical world experience. My communications with Spencer-Brown focused my attention once again on the book and proved to be catalytic to a synthesis of the foregoing hundreds of hours of PI experience and the gradual contextual reorientation it had facilitated.

At this point I was able to see that the logic presented in the book corresponded to the context that I had transcended in the course on the PI work: *a self-definition in relation to the world in terms of parts-to-wholes relationships.* One might say that focusing on the form of the logic effectively brought to full awareness the assumptions of the old context, and that allowed the last residua of the old context to be "canceled." A new synthesis would of necessity take its place.

Figure 4 illustrates the logic of the self-definition of oneself in the world in terms of parts. The circle marked by the "X" stands for one's own self-definition. The inside of this circle represents one's body, possessions, creations, family—or whatever else one defines as constituting *self,* as opposed to other. Everything outside the circle is other. The other circles stand for the self-definitions of *others:* all those beings one regards as having independent, autonomous existences. (Naturally, assuming that there *are* others, one is inclined to attribute to themselves the same kind of self-definition one attributes to oneself!) The background on which all the circles are drawn represents the remainder of the perceptible world: the "stage" whereon the action takes place. I shall designate this model as the *First Degree World Logic* (Figure 4).

A moment's reflection (or perhaps a major contextual reorientation!) will reveal that it is a priori perfectly arbitrary to identify oneself exclusively with the *inside* of one's self-definition (the circle marked "X"). One may equally flip to the opposite polarity, and identify with the outside of one's self-definition (i.e., outside the marked circle). In consequence, one's self may be seen to include all others, as well as the rest of the world. This is

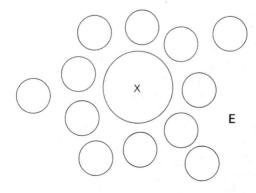

Figure 4. First degree.

the vision of *the world in oneself,* in contrast to the vision of *oneself in the world.*

In agreement with the vision of the world in oneself are the reports of many psychological and neurological researchers that precise and vivid experiences of relationships *with other persons* may sometimes be evoked in the subject (Penfield, 1952; Penfield and Jasper, 1954). This view is certainly in accord with the ideas of depth psychologists such as C. G. Jung (1970). Implicit in Jung's model of the "unconscious" is the inclusion of the world within the "larger Self" (with a capital S).

Clearly, the habitual identification with the inside of one's self-definition—with inside one's skin—is conditioned by behavior in the physical world. And this fixation may be loosened and overcome by "behavioral" means: that is, by suspension of physical world interaction through the methods I have described. Thereafter, an alternative point of view is accessible to oneself.

I am not a "visual thinker" but rather more of a "conceptual thinker," and therefore it was notable that the synthesis I have described arrived not rationally, conceptually, but visually. I saw in the physical world the self-definition of myself and others such that it was possible to identify with the territory on either side of the self-definitions. This was a fully perceptible, visual experience, reminiscent of the exceptional experiences described by Carlos Castenada in the course of his shamanic training (1972), or by Tibetan Yogins (as Trungpa, 1972). This visual experience preceded, rather than followed, a conceptual, rational appreciation of the synthesis that was occurring.

A bit more logical refinement is now necessary in order to convey a fuller, more precise, idea of the experiences in which a new (for me) model of the world formed.

Figure 4, which I called a "First Degree World Logic," is characterized by the fact that the closed curves representing self-definitions do not intersect. In a *second degree* logic, the closed curves could overlap, without this changing whatever each curve represents *individually.* For example, we could designate two curves as X and Y (Figure 5). Let x designate the inside of curve X, and let $\bar{x}$ designate the outside of X. Similarly, let y designate the inside of Y, and let $\bar{y}$ designate the outside of Y. If we let X and Y overlap, then this creates a region that (in the language of logic and set theory) is called the *intersection* of x and y. The creation of this intersection does not alter the meaning of the two independent sets x and y (i.e., the insides of the curves X and Y, respectively).

I refer to these set-definitions (i.e., a closed curve together with its inside and its outside, considered explicitly) as *booles,* in honor of the mathematician who in the middle of the nineteenth century devised the first sys-

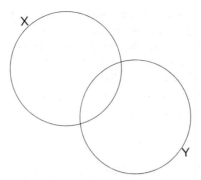

Figure 5.   Second degree.

tematic notation of treating such mathematical objects (Boole, 1847, 1854). In contrast, however, to set theory, the concept of the boole places equal emphasis explicitly on both the inside (the set) and the outside (the complement.)

A logic of the second degree then accounts for the noninterfering relationship between two independent set-definitions. A logic of nth degree could account for the noninterfering relationship among n independent set-definitions, where n represents any number. A vision of a world in which n self-definitions are active seems to require an nth Degree World Logic.

The nth Degree World Logic visualizes a world in which n autonomous beings may operate; but their autonomy (independence) is only potential, for it is diminished to the extent that they are coupled *behaviorally,* in the physical world of routine experience, and also coupled *conceptually* through anticipation of grasping (Latin: *concaptio*) tokens (i.e., objects) of common value.

The idea of the *Bateson loop*—a closed loop of communication pervading both organism and environment—is relevant in this connection (Bateson, 1972). Such loops pass through "common territory" and convey shared messages, whose meanings are, however, specific to each organism. Through communication, the several individuals are aligned with one another in a shared version of the world, partially encompassing the many individual versions. As von Foerster (1970, 1974a) has shown, *information* is not a property of an objective environment, or a property of a community consensus, but rather an observer's relationship with the incoming signals (Atlan, 1981). Von Foerster's proof is in perfect agreement with mathematical theory of communication formulated by Shannon (1948) in terms of *channel definitions.*

The world of my model/metaphor is not the collection of parts of the

reductionistic-materialistic interpretation, or even the hierarchically organized system with super-additive properties of the systems theorists. Rather
it is an *overlay* of whole systems, each of whose integrity is self-defined as
a relativistic co-observer. The current qualitative condition of this world is
a property of the details of the alignment of these systems. To the extent
that there is a measurable space, it cannot be divided among the many systems that interpenetrate.

INTERPRETATION

I have related several minor anecdotes and one major experiential adventure
that developed out of the PI research. I now want to address the questions
of the meaning of these observations and experiences. I have already stated
my view that the phenomenological content of episodes in unusual conscious states is not necessarily of any special significance. There is *a priori*
no reason to expect to find in these contents any more scientific information
than in the contents of everyday experience. Unusual states are often per-
vaded with a feeling of "cosmic meaning," "insight," or absolute "certainty," along with the pure forms of other attributes, usually unrelated to
anything specific.

   Those who are convinced by the "truth" of the particular details of their
experience often go on to (co-)found religions or other "movements" that
serve to effectively block further scientific progress by their adherents.

   My hypothesis of neuro-interoceptive observation (NIO) states that under
certain conditions conscious awareness shifts from its usual subject matter
to the structures and operations that routinely "process" this subject matter.

   Let's examine some of the more profound considerations pertaining to
this point of view, before considering its applications to the experiences of
myself and others in extreme states of being.

Problems of Social Communication

In the course of my study of PI certain impediments to communication
became apparent. First there was the problem of socially conditioned aversion toward revelation of characteristics of the *actual* functioning of the
human CNS, and its intrinsic programs, referred to commonly as "mind."
The disparity between actual experience and conventional ways of talking
was so great as to effectively inhibit communication, or cause embarrassment to listeners. This proved to be especially embarrassing in proportion
to the degree that an individual had a professional investment in the conventional modes of discourse about brain/mind/body/society.

The second impediment to communication was lack of *appropriate* concepts and descriptive metaphors for nonphysical realms of experience; or perhaps, by default, the preponderance of inappropriate concepts conditioned by physical world experience. Relevant to this problem, Fischer et al. (1963) summarized: "Stebbing's conclusions appear relevant in this context: Nothing but confusion can result if, in one and the same sentence, we mix up language used appropriately for the furniture of earth and our daily dealings with it with language used for the purpose of philosphical and scientific discourse" (p. 56). However, that does not go quite far enough! Throughout roughly a decade of research in "consciousness aquisition," I have been repeatedly struck by the inadequacy of *both* our common language *and* our scientific-philosophical language to lucidly treat the emerging experiences.

Language, logic, and law are closely interconnected in society. People lead their lives in terms of words and associated concepts whose definitions are of social origin and whose limits are defined by law. Our English word "reality" derives from the Latin *res,* which has the double meaning of "things" (in general) and "a court of law." Lilly (1975), who has delineated this connection in relation to consciousness, described people as living behind a "screen of words" that conceals the view of *real* reality, according to the exigencies and machinations of social institutions. Certainly, this is equally and *especially* true of science as a human institution and of its language and logic.

The key concept, in terms of which law, logic, and language articulate to define (and *delimit*) our reality, is the concept of *the person, as the name associated with body, property, and a history.* A group's expectations about individual behavior are also included in this concept of the person.

A paradoxical situation develops when psychologists, who are nominally persons, attempt to study and *scientifically* describe other persons. The situation is perhaps even more difficult when they attempt to study and describe themselves, who are nominally also *persons.* Such efforts, if successful, must contradict and threaten to invalidate the nominal definition of the researcher, and by implication, the lawful, language-bound institutions and interpersonal relations that form the social context of the researcher and his/her work.

Transpersonal psychology, and more specifically *participant-engaged research in conscious states,* carries the hazard that the deeper one goes in scientific exploration, the more tenuous becomes one's connection with the language-bound "reality," in the Latin sense of the word.

These hazards and limits should be interpreted, I believe, as pointing at the limits of the *logic* implicit in our law and language, onto which the logic imposes limitations. As Metzner (1980) observed, "Fundamental world views, paradigms of reality, conceptions of human nature are being questioned and challenged.'' I have described a program of research that points *at,* and therefore also points *beyond,* the limited logic of the definition of persons as objects in the physical world.

Communication, Communion and Interoception

Having hazarded a departure from the ''contained self'' belief system, and its attendant conveniences of being able to describe human behavior as causally consistent interactions in ''Newtonian–Cartesian'' space–time, we will need now to further refine the our notions of relationships among and within nervous systems.

As Fischer (1976), von Foerster (1979), and Bateson (1972, 1978) have suggested, it is valuable to distinguish clearly between communication and communion. *Communication* means *transmission* of signals explicitly and implicitly suggests *reception* at some other point in space and time.

If, on the other hand, we could not distinguish between the place in space/time of the sender and the place in space/time of the receiver, then we could not properly speak of communication; then we should speak of *communion.*

Communion does not require an explicit transmission of signals, or a presumption of physical separateness; rather it is just the opposite of separation.

The communication/communion distinction applies both *inter*personally and *intra*personally. To the extent that space–time distinctions may not be germane in certain states of being, we ought to consider the possibility that communion rather than communication may be involved in interpersonal relationships.

*Intra*personally, the concept of communication is highly suspect. From elementary neuropsychological considerations we should think of the ''person,'' the ''observer,'' and the scientific communicator, as functions of an *entire* human brain. Concepts such as ''internal dialogue'' are therefore questionable. *Who is speaking with whom?* Me, myself, and I?

Nevertheless, an entire universe seems to exist within the brain. This universe can unquestionably represent itself as one or more persons, as well as vast territories to tour and explore. Presumably travel, as well as signal transmission, within this universe is limited by the speed of light, in the extreme case, and by the speed of nerve impulse transmission, in the more common case. (To the extent that non-locality may apply, this constraint may be transcended intrapersonally and interpersonally, but then the concepts of travel and transmission are also transcended!)

To the extent that NIO is a kind of interoception, it would be expected to operate by way of *interneuronal* connections—at least in the simplest case. Vast networks or constellations of neurones must be involved. Therefore it would be surprising if NIO were subject to the rules of construction of lucid sentences or the classical laws of logic.

In a very abstract and esoteric way of thinking, one may ask whether the "self" or "observer" is *self-reflecting* (reflexive), whether it (he/she?) can observe itself, whether it vanishes in the process, and similar speculative questions. These questions would be applicable and would have trivial answers if we were here discussing a simple system of mathematical logic; however, what we are discussing is an immensely complex *bio*logical system. There has in recent years been a great deal of theorizing along these lines, providing a ready-made explanation for failure in the neuro-interoceptive program, as well as *logically* convincing arguments that NIO data cannot exist, or cannot be valid, if such data exist anyway.

The real question is: Can an organism observe and generate descriptions of structures and processes operating in itself just as it generates fairly accurate descriptions of those phenomena that it normally treats using its structures and processes?

These "phenomena" nominally fall into two classes: (1) external or "objective" phenomena; (2) internal or "subjective" phenomena. The internal phenomena are supposed to be of a private, unverifiable, perhaps whimsical character. This is the subjective world of fantasy, idea, ideals, feelings, values and beliefs. The external phenomena are supposed to be of a solid, verifiable, consensual reality.

The NIO hypothesis posits the reality of a *third* class of phenomenal observations: (3) awareness of the structures and operations mediating the first two classes.

There are a great many well known instances of NIO that are usually not thought of as such. Perhaps mathematics is an example of knowledge gained by paying attention to operations (such as counting) that otherwise we simply perform. Mathematicians formulate and formalize this knowledge.* Engineers design it into computers (Jeffrey, 1983c).

In practice, the demands of all those phenomena of classes (1) and (2) fully occupy the organism. But this situation is not necessarily permanent; in fact the PI methodology would seem to provide the optimal conditions for exceptions to the rule.

Is it possible in the PI environment to detect changes, states, or opera-

---

*Jarun Z. Lanier, a colleague of Marvin Minsky, and associates at VPL Research, Inc., in Palo Alto have succeeded in implementing a system of computer software incorporating some of the deep principles of the brain, including relativistic co-observation among "collumnar" sub-systems. (See cover story, *Scientific American,* September, 1984).

tions of the CNS that go unnoticed in the busy, interactive environment of the outside world?

Evidence from all branches of neuropsychology indicates that routinely the "medium" (i.e., the brain) enters into the "message" (i.e., observed phenomena). In the business-as-usual world of perception and behavior, the CNS contribution is interpreted as part of the observed phenomena—that is, as a property of the outside or of the subjective world. Thus illusions, delusions, hallucinations, misperceptions, and nonperceptions are part of ordinary everyday perceptual life. They are interpreted as errors, oversights, discoveries, surprises, quirks, noise, coincidences, miracles, disagreements, agreements, and beliefs. Only in PI and other unusual states are they revealed as properties of the self.

Conscious, Unconscious, Deeper and Deeper

Conservatively estimated the human brain comprises 10^{11} (one-hundred billion) neurones, plus other structures (Valentino Braitenberg, personal communication, 1982). The neurones typically have thousands of interneuronal connections, plus other interactions that we are only beginning to notice (as of 1985). Each neurone is of complexity comparable to an autonomous unicellular organism, such as an amoeba. We do not currently know to what extent the internal structures and processes of the neurone, the proteins, organelles, nucleic acids, and so on, figure in the "computations of the brain."

In a solid-state digital computer the construction of the components enters into the computations only when the computer is malfunctioning. This is so by design. Computer engineers enforce a strict isolation between the "medium" and the "message." The construction of components is entirely subordinated to carrying out their designed *logical* function. Quantal fluctuations and analogue properties are effaced as far as is physically possible. Digital signals are maintained by amplification, clamping, and damping— at considerable expense in energy.

There is no good reason to suppose a priori that the same constraints apply to the construction of the brain. Indeed both experience and biological theory argue against structural–functional isolation in the brain. An early and simple analysis based on quantum chemistry (von Foerster, 1949) yields a 0.1 percent *indeterminacy* in the brain with respect to meaningful signals (memory).

It is today, to say the least premature to apply any limitations of a logical, linguistic, or ontological character to what is considered valid discourse on the brain and its operations—and, by implication, on those operations themselves. To a large extent language already imposes limitations. Scientific progress can be viewed largely as the struggle to overcome the unconscious limitations on thought arising from the way people habitually talk about experiences and phenomena, shared and individual. These limitations are effective precisely because we are unaware of them. Growth of knowledge is limited, thus, by *ignorance of ignorance.* Much of science consists of overcoming a variety of simple perceptual errors and oversights.

Scientific theories progress by testing, experimental and experiential. They are simply *derailed* by reifications of parts of our language, such as observer, objectivity, cognition, computation, self-reference, autonomy, recursion, reflexivity, and so on, and the resulting prescriptive limitations that these reifications tend to impose on "what one may say," "whereof one may speak," "what can be known"—and *by whom.* This leads to consideration of "conscious" and "unconscious."

Conscious–Unconscious

"The Unconscious is not unconscious, only the Conscious is unconscious of what the Unconscious is conscious of."

Let's rephrase this in terms of the brain. First let's consider the bird brain. The eagle is reputed to have magnificent visual perception, with acuity and color definition superior to the human visual system. It can soar high over the land and spot small animals that it likes to eat. It can swoop down at high speed and capture chosen prey. However, we do not think that the bird brain generates any original thoughts, generates descriptions of its own structure and programs, or even learns very much. (But compare Patton and Nottebohm, 1984).

The same may largely be said of the human brain. The brain "knows" enough to carry out its function of fabricating individual reality, and of participating in social intercourse that generates consensus reality; but the conscious self appears normally to have no access to the machinery or programs that the brain uses to do its job. We might say that the operations and structures of the brain constitute the immediate environment of the "self." If it is the self or the Conscious that generates reports of its experience, it seems to be able to say a lot about what goes on in the brain's (i.e., the body's) environment, but not much about what goes on in its (i.e., the self's) immediate environment.

A computer analogy is apropos here: A computer instruction (BASIC) might read:

100 PRINT "HELLO THERE BIG BRAIN!"

If we could run such a program in our "human biocomputer" (Lilly's phrase), we would experience "HELLO THERE BIG BRAIN!"; we would not experience the operation of PRINTing, etc. (normally). It is as if we are outside the biocomputer looking at the printout. We seem to enjoy an *outside* view of our own brain! In other words, our usual experience is not of the programs, but only of the consequences the programs generate. We experience the *literal* (i.e., quoted string) part of the program, but not the *operational* parts.

Fischer analyzed the difficulty this way: "You, in the [isolation] tank, are an observer of your own system. The system knows the meaning of the info[rmation] but the observer (in you) does not know its meaning. Hence the difficulties of using language as a means for expressing something that presupposes itself as that which is to be expressed" (Roland Fischer, personal communication, October 1981).

It is most important now to be consistent with our earlier rejection of the definition of the person as "contained self"—as something existing in a well-defined region within physical space. Correspondingly, the conscious self, inner observer, or ego must not be modeled as a compartment spatially localized in the brain. It is rather to be thought of more as a dynamic, coherent pattern of activity and information that exists only in the phase of its activity. It is characterized by the ability to generate *literal reports that make sense to itself.* These reports may be communicated by either internal or external feedback paths. An example of an external path is a pencil and paper. A more complex example is the design of a digital computer, or the programming of a computer (Jeffrey, 1983c).

It now becomes possible to formulate the operation of the conscious mind in operational terms. The resulting model includes limits on knowledge that are pragmatic and approximate rather than limits that are abstract and absolute. These limits are the same limits as those tested in the course of scientific progress. They are the same limits that appear in language where they are invisible. They are the same limits that do not appear to us as our *ignorance of ignorance*—which is the fundamental limit on our knowledge.

A mind operates and defines itself by recurrently filtering out those patterns which are incongruent with its own structure. These filtering operations are carried through by behavior—both external (muscular) behavior and internal (neural-effective) behavior. The principal mode of this behavior is selection of inputs by focusing and directing attention.

Our mind thus defined is essentially a paranoid system. It is a "closed system," in that its operation is primarily circular and self-referencing. But it is not closed in an absolute, abstract way. It is closed in a pragmatic, approximate way, defined by *habit,* and the relative stability of the environment—the physical environment and the social/communicational environment. The mind is also not a constant being—as psychology and psychiatry attest. It is no more stable than the physical structures that support its operation and through which it operates. It can be augmented and reduced, maximized and minimized, intensified and attenuated—and it can go away. *Gaps* in the time domain constitute one of the greatest opportunities for creating exceptions to closure. All scientific progress and creativity exhibit exceptions to the "closed mind" mode of operation.

Transitions, Transients, and Transformations (TTT Theory)

Besides Fischer's discovery that normal human mentality includes a continuum ranging from perception to hallucination, we may now add the precept that *paranoia* is the normal state of mind. In its Greek origin, paranoia means "next to knowledge," which suits the idea that our conscious mind operates in the midst of knowledge to which it allows itself no access. This mode of mentality is essentially equivalent to a system of *hypothesis proving,* which operates by gathering evidence selected by its expectations. I had earlier formulated this concept as a model of visual perception (Jeffrey, 1972), based on the discoveries of Stark (1968), Noton (1969), and Noton and Stark (1971), and relying on contemporary work in Artificial Intelligence studies with computers. Powers's (1973) control system formulation that *behavior is the control of perception,* together with its broad implications for experimental psychology, completes the picture, uniting behavior with epistemology, in a grand "paranoid" system from which future scientific progress must escape.

I want to conclude by paying a little attention to two theories, the TTT theory, which attempts to explain the all-important exceptions to paranoid self-referencing closure of perceptual and conceptual behavior, and the ICC theory, which addresses the deeper reaches of selfhood and self-determination.

I have elsewhere defined *intelligence* as a measure of access to one's own structure, or to the principles of one's construction and functioning (Jeffrey, 1983a). Increase in intelligence—individually and scientifically—depends on escape from the steady state of current knowledge. This may occur stochastically, fortuitously, or by design.

The CNS is at any moment equilibrated about its biochemical state. One's experience is the eigen-value, or steady state, of sensory-motor feed-through (feed-back and feed-forward), under the conditions of the current biochemical equilibrium. Minor continuous changes in either the biochemical or the behavioral situation are rapidly, smoothly compensated—and constitute one's experience of change and the passage of time.

There are two ways of disrupting the steady-state condition: (1) behaviorally, as in profound sensory isolation or hyperstimulation (sensory overload, excitement, etc.); (2) chemically/physiologically, as with trauma or psychoactive chemicals.

A rapid change imposed on the biochemical state of the CNS establishes a different, new physiological equilibrium, which is the environment (*milieu intérieur*) of the behavioral steady state. Then a *transient* period ensues as the behavioral loops adjust to the new conditions. This is an N-dimensional adjustment process involving fluctuations and oscillations until a new steady state is reached. Between State 1 and State 2 is the "trip," an experience of novelty that is difficult to integrate or explain subjectively.

The transient period is a very rich source of knowledge about the systematic parameters of the subject's CNS because experience during the transient is primarily *of the equilibrium process,* rather than the normal experience *of the steady state.* Therefore the "trip" is accurately described as *psychedelic,* which means "psyche-*manifesting*": the systematic properties (i.e., operations) of the "psyche" (i.e., perceptual/behavioral process) are made evident to direct experience during the transient phase.

I was able to formulate this principle around 1974, based on elementary bioengineering concepts, and it seemed then to very satisfactorily elucidate the experience of the "trip": Transitions (biochemical change) result in Transients (fluctuations), as the CNS automatically seeks a new behavioral equilibrium to match the new biochemical state, and in the process profound learning occurs, which accounts for *Transformation* of the subject's relation with the world. The key concept is *Transients,* linking transition to transformation, because a system that made transitions without transients would not be able to learn anything from the change. For example, an electric light can be switched *on* and *off,* may attain *illumination,* but does not achieve *transformation,* except insofar as the filament gradually deteriorates from thermal stress, and finally breaks.

Stability and Eigen-Theory

What accounts for the stability of the inner and outer worlds? Which is more constant over time? Ironically it is often the stability of the neurological system that persists in the face of changes in the physical world outside and physical change in the body. The extraordinary stability of the behavior patterns of an organism in the world must be explained in terms of its structure. Even in isolation from the physical world, behavior patterns do not change rapidly—although they may change more rapidly than when the organism is engaged with reliable, repeated patterns of the environment that normally reinforce behavior.

It appears that stable patterns are maintained by recurrent circular operations between organism and environment, and within the organism.

According to Heisenberg (1972), the puzzle of stability and constancy led the physicists, including Schrödinger, to develop the quantum and wave mechanics. Their formulations account for the stability of structures at the atomic scale of size in terms of *eigen-functions*. In collaboration with Piaget, von Foerster has applied analogous mathematical models to behavior of people in macroscopic space. Together, Schrödinger et al. and von Foerster have unified the largest and smallest scales applicable to consideration of the CNS. I propose to fill in the intervening levels of scale and the associated structures, in the same terms (Jeffrey, 1983): Level 1, physical-behavioral interaction space (organism in environment); 2, internal behavior (such as inner attention shifts, subvocalization, etc.); 3, neuro-chemical-electrical steady state (s.s.); 4, micro-physiological s.s.; 5, macro-molecular s.s.; 6, physical–chemical (mass–action) s.s.; 7, atomic–nuclear s.s.

In this model, the stability of behavior/structure at each level depends on (a) recurrent circular interactions among entities at the same level—for example, stable reciprocal sequences of behavioral response—and (b) the stability of the next level *inward* (i.e., higher number on scale), which constitutes the substratum of structure from which the *next outer* level is constructed; for example, learned behavior depends on some kind of "memory" in the organism, whose persistence in the absence of continual reinforcement must be explained by some sort of inner stability, rehearsal, maintanence, and so on (Jeffrey, 1983a).

There is a certain *coupling* or interdependence between levels, but entities at a certain level tend to prefer and differentially select interaction with other entities at the same level: we normally do not hold conversations with cells, play baseball with atoms, and so on. Fischer (1963) rephrased the question of "how the acausal, relatively random behavior at the atomic level can be the basis for ordered causal behavior ʼat the macroscopic level. . . . It is difficult to determine where the transition (if it can be called that) occurs . . . " (p. 56, quoting Friedrich). A photon arriving at the retina of the eye is usually interpreted as light, color, or movement, and not as a statement about the quantum chemistry of *rhodopsin*! Fischer (1963) continues: "It is also contained in man's restricted level of attention that he experiences imperceptible atomic events as mental images, whereas . . . a galaxy with a diameter of 50000 light years is perceived as a few millimeter small stationary object" (p. 56). Since there is no a priori reason for perfect isolation between levels, it would seem that in some instances structure may be translated outward across levels.

Nicolescu (1984, p. 33) has recently raised the issue of "scale" in the context of quantum physics, and asks, "Is there a vertical exchange between different scales?" Fessard (1954) had earlier proposed that consciousness might be explained by the transfer of order from the molecular to the cellular level. Mandell (1980) has considered correlations among the statistics of biochemical oscillators and other oscillations in the brain tissue, at different levels of scale. This is tied to the theory of dissipative structures in the brain (Prigogine, 1980) and in the mind (Fischer, 1977), according to Melnechuk (1982, p. 19).

It is now (1985) well known that quantum theory implies a *nonlocal universe,* involving some strange-sounding trade-offs. Precise specification of the characteristics of a very small entity entails loss of specification of its position in macroscopic space. At a small enough subatomic scale of size, physical positions become indistinguishable. Dirac observed that, for example, all electrons in the universe could in some sense be the same electron. Following this line of reasoning, it would appear that all brains may be connected at the subatomic level in my model of eigen-states. This connection must be *superluminal* in that it is not limited by transmission of signals at the speed of light, and *sublunary* in that it occurs in the shadowy fringes of consciousness (or in potential consciousness). *It is not communication between brains*! Perhaps in repeated unusual states, such as PI, it is possible to learn to translate between the levels of structural scale and interpret or utilize this "sublunary–superluminal" *communion* in a coherent manner.

Impacts, Constraints, and Couplings (ICC Theory)

"Without (motor) verification of 'measurement,' the information of a system is not constrained, and things that appeared are represented as appearances of things, that is, hallucinations, whereas in perception–conception, appearances of things are transformed into things that appear" (Fischer, 1969, p. 163). Behaviorism describes an organism as something that "responds to stimuli." Cybernetic models describe an organism as "compensating perturbations" to maintain an ideal, undisturbed state as far as possible. Powers' theory portrays an organism that acts so as to control its perceptions. This model can be extended to include the *selection* of *which* states to regard as perceptions, and which perceptions to attempt to control. In PI external perceptions and the behaviors that maintain them are suspended, except insofar as the voluntarily isolated person is behaving so as to have the perception of being in isolation. The isolated CNS is free to occupy itself entirely with inner perceptions–conceptions. These may be simulated *as if* external, as has often been reported in the literature; however, once the range of these types of experiences has been tested, the participant observer may cease acting in this way (Lilly, 1981). To perceive is to control attention and input so as to have a particular experience that one has somehow set as a goal to be achieved or maintained. This goal is called the *reference*. If the goal reference is no longer set by external motivations, by inner biological necessity, or by the ontogenic or phylogenic "memory" of either, then one begins to generate one's own references in an unconstrained, mysterious fashion.

This is *imagination*—the unconstrained play of imagination in its pure form. The objects of imagination are no longer those conditioned by external world experience.

Powers has pointed out (1978, p. 418) that any level of perceptual processing in the brain may be regarded as the *input*. The brain may control its high-level perceptions or internal states rather than controlling anything connected with the outside world.

Extensive PI experience occasioned a transition in my own theoretical position from one in which the brain is viewed as mirroring and adapting to an interactive environment, to one in which the brain is seen as a system that operates *autonomously,* except to the extent that it is constrained by the impact of physical energies in the context to coupling relationships that contextualize those energies as meaningful patterns.

In the absence of the above, the brain conforms to its own pattern, its own ideal state, in which the boundary between conscious and unconscious does not exist.

Apparently the conscious/unconscious distinction is a neurological fact closely correlated with the inner/outer distinction, and the manifold distinctions of multiplicity. Baruch Spinoza taught that all experience and all phenomena were derived from a single cosmic "substance" by variation and limitation. Lilly (1967) has defined the *multidimensional cognitive–conative space.* Fischer (1969) related the inner and outer spaces this way: "The synchronization of object, meaning and information can be formalized within the circuitry of a self-referential system (man) by designating the flow of environmental information between (1) *physical space–time*—the most space-like and least time-like dimension, the Euclidian, engineering or survival space–time of decision-making and action—into (2) *cerebral* (mental) *space–time,* the interpretive, behavioral space–time of perception, hallucination and dreaming—the most time-like and least space-like dimension . . . " (p. 164). Similarly Maturana (1979) holds that all phenomenal and experiential relations exist in a "cognitive domain" or *information space* (as Fischer, 1977) of neuronal interrelationships. It may be philosophically controversial to state that all phenomena, as well as the self, consist of the same "stuff"; however, it is *neurologically trivial.*

Wide experience with cybernetic thought has convinced me to regard the human brain as a goal-seeking, goal-setting system. Returning to the world, the self re-emerges along with its objects, redefining itself as a self-determining entity. It will seek active participation in framing future realities in preference to passive spectatorship of current realities of others. It will define itself in terms of defining its own destiny, which includes the destiny of its world (Jeffrey, 1981a,b, 1982a,b, 1983c), treating physical objects as media rather than as objectives or obstacles. In this view the brain is an instrument of self-creation (Jeffrey, 1983b): " . . . which creates the future in the most glorious self-image it can imagine—a numenous loom, poetically incensed, weaving the strands of orphic vision, ideal love, and evolutionary eroticism."

REFERENCES

Atlan, H. Hierarchical self-organization in living systems. In M. Zelerny (Ed.), *Autopoiesis.* Amsterdam and New York: North-Holland, Elsevier, 1981.

Bateson, G. Cybernetic epistemology. In *Steps to an ecology of mind.* New York: Chandler, 1972, pp. 309–337.

Bateson, G. *Mind and nature: the necessary unity.* New York: Dutton, 1978.

Bennet, G. Psychological breakdown at sea: Hazards of single-handed ocean sailing. *British Journal Medical Psychology, 47,* 1974.

Boole, G. *The mathematical analysis of logic.* London, 1847.

Boole, G. *An investigation of the laws of thought.* London: Macmillan, 1854. (Dover reprints.)

Brownfield, C. A. *Isolation.* New York: Random House, 1965.

Castenada, C. *Journey of ixtlan.* New York: Simon & Schuster, 1972.

Chayefsky, P. *Altered States.* New York: Harper & Row, 1978.

Cohen, S. I. In P. Solomon (Ed.), *Sensory deprivation.* Cambridge, Mass.: Harvard University Press, 1961.

Einstein, A. and L. Infeld. *The evolution of physics,* 1938. New York: Simon & Schuster, 1950.

Erickson, G. and Gustafson, G. *Hospital and Community Psychiatry, 19,* 327, 1968.

Fessard, A. Mechanisms of nervous integration and conscious experience. In J. F. Delafresnaye (Ed.), *Brain Mechanisms and Consciousness.* Oxford: Blackwell, 1954. pages 200–236.

Fischer, R. The perception–hallucination continuum (a re-examination). *Diseases of the Nervous System,* Mar. 1969, *30,* 161–171.

Fischer, R. On separateness and oneness. *Confina Psychiatrica, 15,* 165–194, 1972. (Excellent bibliography.)

Fischer, R. *Confinia Psychiatrica, 17,* 143–151, 1974.

Fischer, R. Transformations of consciousness: a cartography II—the perception–meditation continuum. *Confinia Psychiatrica,* 1976, *19,* 1–23. (New York and Basel: S. Karger Publishing Co.).

Fischer, R. On dissipative structure in both physical and information space. *Journal of altered states of consciousness,* 1977, *3*(1, 1977–1978). (Baywood Publishing Co).

Fischer, R. et al. Limits of language. *Experientia,* 1963, *19,* 56. (Basel: Birkhauser Verlag, 1963).

Fischer, R., Hill, R., Thatcher, K., and Scheib, J. Psilocybin-induced contraction of nearby visual space. *Agents and Actions,* 1970, *1,* 190–197.

von Foerster, H. Quantum mechanical theory of memory. In H. von Foerster (Ed.), *Cybernetics* (Transactions of the Macy Symposia, 1949), New York: Josiah Macy Jr. Foundation, 1950. (1949)

von Foerster, H. Thoughts and notes on cognition. In P. Garvin (Ed.), *Cognition: a multiple view.* New York: Spartan Books, 1970, pp. 25-48 (and as BCL Publication #166, Department of Electrical Engineering, University of Illinois, Urbana).

von Foerster, H. Notes pour une épistémologie des objets vivants. In E. Morin and M. Piattelli-Palmarini (Eds.), *L'unité de l'homme.* Paris: Édition du Seuil, 1974a, pp. 401-418 (and as BCL Publication #9.3, 1972).

von Foerster, H. *Giving with a purpose: the cybernetics of philantrophy.* Washington, D.C.: Center for a Voluntary Society, 1974b.

von Foerster, H. Épistémologie génétique et équilibration. In Inhelder, Garcia, and Voneche (Eds.), *Hommage à Jean Piaget.* Paris: de Lachau et Niestlé, 1976.

von Foerster, H. On constructing a reality. *An Integral View,* 1979, *1*(2), 21-29 (California Institute of Integral Studies, San Francisco.)

von Foerster, H. A constructivist epistemology. In *Structures and cognitive processes* (conference, Geneva, 15-19 June 1981). Geneva: Foundation Archives Jean Piaget, 1981.

Freedman, S. J. In P. Solomon (Ed.), *Sensory deprivation.* Cambridge, Mass.: Harvard University Press, 1961.

Glasser, W. *Stations of the mind,* with an introduction by W. T. Powers. New York: Harper & Row, 1981.

von Glaserfeld, E. Radical constructivism and Piaget's concept of knowledge. In *Proceedings of the 1975 symposium of the Piaget Society,* Philadelphia, 1975.

Grindley, G. C. and Townsend, V. Visual search without eye movement. *Quarterly Journal of Experimental Psychology,* 1970, *22,* 62-67.

Heisenberg, W. *Physics and beyond: encounters and conversations,* A. J. Pomerans (trans.). New York: Harper & Row, 1972.

Heron, W. Cognitive and perceptual effects of perceptual isolation. In P. Solomon (Ed.), *Sensory deprivation.* Cambridge, Mass.: Harvard University Press, 1961.

Heron, W. et al. Visual disturbances after prolonged isolation. *Canadian Journal of Psychology,* 1956, *10,* 13-18.

Hoffman, P. Sensory reduction (senior project). Nassau County, N.Y.: Friends World College, Feb. 1976.

Jantsch, E. *The self-organizing universe.* New York: Pergamon Press, 1980.

Jeffrey-Busco, F. Significance of context in visual perception, (Monograph: Project in Neurophysiological Computation) Berkeley: University of California, 1972 (available from Alive Systems Group, Big Sur, CA 93920).

Jeffrey-Busco, F. Isolation module. United States Patent #4000749, 1975.

Jeffrey-Busco, F. Phenomenology of nothing. Abstract in *Proceedings of the 4th annual conference on applied phenomenology,* Los Angeles, University of California, 1977.

Jeffrey, F. Discussion. In W. Pieper and N. Barron von Holtey (trans.), *Höhere Intelligenz und Kreativität.* Germany: Der Grüne Zweig 80, 1981a, p. 32. (From panel discussion, T. Leary, Chairman, The future of intelligence, in *Proceedings* of Colloquium II, Psychedelic Education Project, University of California, Santa Cruz, 11 July 1981. Available on tape from Linkages Radio, Santa Cruz, Calif.)

Jeffrey, F. The effects of space on mind and body (27 Feb.), and, To float or not to float: gravity's place in space (8 June), "Future File" (national radio program). Los Angeles: Golden Egg, 1981b.

Jeffrey, F. Computers and space: space in computers. *Space Age Review,* Jan. 1982a, p. 405.

Jeffrey, F. Frontiers of the brain (recorded lecture at Esalen Institute, 2 June 1982). Big Sur, Calif.: Dolphin Tapes, 1982b.

Jeffrey, F. Thoughts on increasing intelligence. In P. Stafford, *The psychedelic encyclopedia.* Los Angeles: J. P. Tarcher, 1983a, pp. 405–406.

Jeffrey, F. Commentary. In C. Kleefeld, *Lovers in Evolution.* Los Angeles: The Horse and Bird Press, 1983b.

Jeffrey, F. Interview with C. Seraphim, "Infinity" (radio program), KCBS Radio, first broadcast 22 Jan. 1983c. (Available from Dolphin Tapes, Big Sur, Calif. 93920.)

Jung, C. G. *Mysterium Coniunctionis* and *The structure and dynamics of the psyche* (Collected works, vols. 14 and 8), Princeton, N.J.: Bollingen Foundation/Princeton University, 1970.

Lilly, J. C. Mental effects of reduction of ordinary levels of physical stimuli on intact, healthy persons. *Psychiatric Research Report 5.* Washington, D.C.: American Psychiatric Association, 1956.

Lilly, J. C. *Programming and metaprogramming in the human biocomputer: theory and experiments* (various issues as research reports), 1967 (as book, New York: Jullian Press, 1972). (Huge categorized bibliography of this and related research fields.)

Lilly, J. C. *The center of the cyclone.* New York: Julian Press, 1972.

Lilly, J. C. *Simulations of God: the science of belief.* New York: Simon & Schuster, 1975. ("Reality," pp. 119 sqq. and 255.)

Lilly, J. C. *The dyadic cyclone* (with A. L. Lilly). New York: Simon & Schuster, 1976. (Excellent bibliography.)

Lilly, J. C. *The deep self.* New York: Simon & Schuster, 1977. (Technical information, experiential reports, bibliography.)

Lilly, J. C. The mind contained in the brain: a cybernetic belief system. In R. S. Valle and R. von Eckharssberg (Eds.), *The metaphors of consciousness.* New York: Plenum, 1981, pp. 169–178.

Lilly, J. C. and Shurley, J. T. Experiments in solitude, in maximum achievable physical isolation with water suspension, of intact healthy persons (symposium at U.S.A.F. Aerospace Medical Center, San Antonio, Tex., 1960). In *Psychological aspects of space flight.* New York: Columbia University Press, 1961, pp. 38–247.

MacKay, D. M. Moving visual images produced by regular stationary patterns. *Nature,* 1957–1958, *180,* 849–850, and *181,* 362.

MacKay, D. M. Central adaptation in mechanisms of form vision. *Nature,* 1964, *203,* 993–994.

MacLean, P. *Journal of Neurosurgery,* 1954, *11,* 29.

MacLean, P. *American Journal of Medicine,* 1958, *25,* 611.

MacLean, P. The triune brain: emotion and scientific bias. In F. O. Schmitt, *The neurosciences* (second study program). New York: Rockefeller University Press, 1970, pp. 336–349.

Mandell, A. J. Toward a psychobiology of transcendence—God in the brain. In Davidson, J. M. and Davidson, R. J., (Eds.) *The Psychobiology of Consciousness,* New York: Plenum, 1980.

Maturana, U. The wholeness of unity: conversations with Heinz von Foerster. *Cybernetics Forum,* Fall 1979, *IX*(3), 20–26.

Melnechuk, T. Excerpts from Consciousness and Brain Research. *Institute of Noetic Sciences Newsletter,* Fall 1982, Volume 10, #2, pp. 19–21. (San Francisco: I.O.N.S.)

Metzner, R. Ten classical metaphors of self-transformation. *Journal of Transpersonal Psychology,* 1980, *12*(1), pp. 47–62.

Nicolescu, B. Unity and exchange: Systemic aspects of modern physics. *Parabola,* Vol. IX, #4, pp. 26–33, 1984.

Noton, D. A proposal for serial archetype directed pattern recognition. *Record 1969 IEEE SS&C Conference.* Philadelphia: IEEE, 1969.

Noton, D. and Stark, L. Eye movements and visual perception. *Scientific American,* June 1971.

Patton, J. and Nottenbohm, F. Neurones generated in the adult brain are recruited into functional circuits. *Science,* Sep 7, Volume 225, 1984. #4666, pp. 1046–1048.

Patton, Y. and Fischer, R. Hallucinogenic drug-induced behavior under sensory attenuation. *Archives of General Psychiatry,* Mar. 1973, *28,* 434–438.

Penfield, W. Memory mechanisms. *Archives of Neurology and Psychiatry,* 1952, *67,* 178–198.

Penfield, W. and Jasper, H. *Epilepsy and the functional anatomy of the human brain.* Boston: Little, Brown, 1954. (Information on iconic replay, ego states, patterns of behavior associated with certain subjective states, discrete trigger loci and signals.)

Piaget, J. *The construction of reality in the child.* New York: Basic Books, 1959.

Podvoll, E. M. Megalomania: psychotic predicament and transformation. *Naropa Institute Journal of Psychology,* 1983, *2.*

Powers, W. T. *Behavior: the control of perception.* Chicago: Aldine, 1972.

Powers, W. T. Feedback: beyond behaviorism. *Science,* 26 Jan. 1973, *179,* 351–356.

Powers, W. T. Quantitative analysis of purposive systems. *Psychological Review,* Nov. 1978, *85,* 417–435.

Prigogine, I. *From Being to Becoming.* San Francisco: Freeman, 1980.

Riggs, L. A., Ratliff, F., Cornsweet, J. C., and Cornsweet, T. N. The disappearance of steadily fixated visual test objects. *Journal of the Optical Society of America,* 1953, *43,* 495–501.

Schaefer, T. and Bernick, N. Sensory deprivation and its effects on perception. In P. H. Hoch and J. Zubin (Eds.), *Psychopathology of perception.* New York: Grune & Stratton, 1965.

Shannon, C. E. A mathematical theory of communication. *Bell System Technical Journal,* July and Oct. 1948, *27,* 379–423 and 623–656.

Solomon, P. (Ed.), *Sensory deprivation.* Cambridge, Mass.: Harvard University Press, 1961. (See individual articles cited above.)

Spencer–Brown, G. *Laws of form.* London: George Allen & Unwin, 1969. (New York: Julian Press, 1972.)

Stark, L. *Neurological control systems.* New York: Plenum, 1968.

Tanimoto, S. I. and Klinger, A. (Eds.), *Structured computer vision.* New York: Academic Press, 1983.

Toralin, N. and Hall, R. *The strange last voyage of Donald Crowhurst.* New York: Stein & Day, 1970.

Trungpa, Lama C. *Cutting through spiritual materialism.* Berkeley, Calif.: Shambala, 1972 (especially, pp. 121–137).

Vernon, J. A. *Inside the black room.* New York: Potter, 1963.

West, L. J. *Hallucinations.* New York: Grune & Stratton, 1962.

Wittgenstein, L. *Tractatus Logico-Philosophicus* (trans. from *Logische-Philosophische Abhandlung* by C. K. Ogden). London, 1922. (1921)

Zubek, J. P. and Wilgosh, L. Prolonged immobilization of the body: Changes in performance and in the electroencephalogram. *Science,* 1963, *140,* 306.

Zubek, J. p., Aftanas, M., Kozach, K., and Wilgosh, L. Effects of severe immobilization of the body on intellectual and perceptual processes. *Canadian Journal of Psychology,* 1963, *17,* 118.

9. Trance and Possession States

E. Mansell Pattison, Joel Kahan, and Gary S. Hurd

Trance states are a mode of consciousness in which the person is conscious, but seemingly unaware or unresponsive to *usual* external and internal stimuli. Such persons acts as if they are "in their own world" apart from the immediate context of the external reality of the world about them. We say "seemingly unresponsive" because in fact a person in a trance may perform very complex acts—for example, a person in a hypnotic trance, or a shamanistic healing ritual trance, or a possession trance. The person is obviously interacting with the environment and external stimulus cues, but appears not to be acting with personal volition; that is, the cues for action appear internal rather than external.

The concept of trance may be considered under three categories: trance modes of consciousness, trance behaviors, and trance interpretations. As shown in Figure 1, trance states have been described in two broad categories: naturalistic trance explanations and supernaturalistic trance explanations. Within each of these two broad rubrics are a wide variety of descriptions of trance states.

An examination of these descriptive boxes reveals that the naturalistic or "scientific" explanation of trance contains no "box" for "normal" trances. This reflects the fact that apart from research on hypnosis, most Western scientists have failed to attend to trance phenomena in Western culture. This is demonstrated in a recent study by Hufford (1982), stating that 15 percent of the U.S. general population have experienced "hypnagogic attacks." In turn, many reports by clinicians on trance phenomena have interpreted them as psychopathological or in reductionistic clinical terms. This

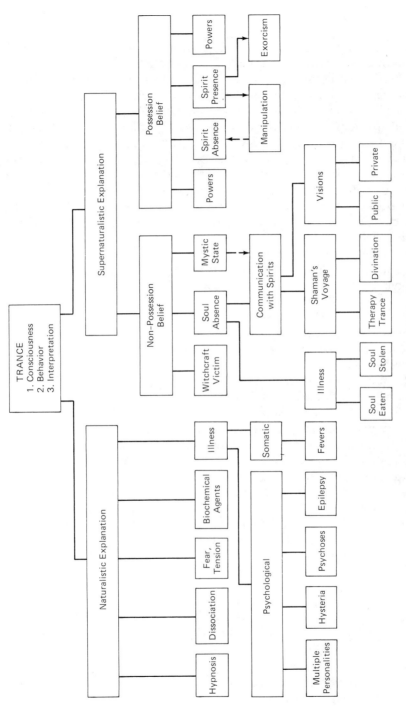

Figure 1. Trance states. Adapted from Bourguignon (1976a).

has been partially rectified in recent years by renewed interest in "altered states of consciousness" research (Pattison, 1978).

The same problem recurs in the study of the culturally religious forms of trance, classified under supernaturalistic explanations. Although anthropological descriptions have often demonstrated the culturally normative dimensions of many trance states, there is still the proclivity among Western scientists to suspiciously invoke a psychopathological explanation.

In Chapter 7 in this book, we presented evidence that the mode of consciousness per se (i.e., trance state) is not pathological. Rather, the trance state, or states, represent a particular mode of consciousness. Whether a trance state is to be interpreted as pathological or not depends upon the cultural context and the person's experience and interpretation of the trance experience.

We shall proceed to clarify the relationship between the mode of consciousness, the behavior, and the explanation with the following set of definitions.

1. *Trance* (T). Here we refer to a mode of consciousness, not culturally defined as possession, that is institutionalized in such a way that the form, practice, and experience are culturally learned patterns of behavior. The trance is an *intrapersonal event,* the content and meaning of which can only be learned from the affected person. Trance has long been taught and practiced within both Eastern and Western religious mystical and meditative traditions (Morley and Wallis, 1979; Wuthnow, 1976). In this case, the experience and behavior are *internal* to the person. Trance is culturally prescribed, learned, and practiced as an acceptable normal behavior. It may be ritualized, as in dance, or practiced as a private experience. Trance is not defined by the culture as a possession state.

2. *Possession Trance* (PT). In this case there is cultural definition of trance as an *interpersonal event,* in which there is *possession* by, or entranced impersonation of another being, in the context of *communal activity and witness to the behavior.*The form, practice, experience, and meaning are well known to the observing community, for whom the PT symbolizes common social experience. PT may be self-induced by a healer as part of the process of exorcism, it may be experienced by a person as a manifestation of possession, or it may be a ritual part of community religious practice. Examples include Southern snake-handling rituals (Kane, 1974) and Puerto Rican espiritismo (Garrison, 1977; Harwood, 1977). In all cases, PT behavior is viewed as unique, but normal only within the context of the special community activity.

3. *Possession Behavior (Neurotic)* (PBN). In contrast to T and PT, PBN does not necessarily involve a specific mode of consciousness, but rather

involves *behavior that is distinguished by the community along a gradient from unique to pathological* (i.e., unusual, idiosyncratic, deviant, aberrant, pathological). The behavior is recognized to be beyond the scope of usual, acceptable, normal activity in that society. Such behavior is interpreted as evidence of possession, and may range from ritualized and stereotyped behaviors to the patently bizarre. This form of possession constitutes a set of culturally symbolized behaviors available to some people through which they can express personal and interpersonal conflict, without retributive action being taken by the spouse, family, or community. The PBN serves as a ready vehicle for both symptom expression and symptom resolution (Chakraborty and Bannerjii, 1975; Sangree, 1974; Shack, 1971; Uzzell, 1974; Watson and Watson-Franke, 1977; Young, 1975). Although from a Western scientific perspective we might label such behavior as neurotic symbolism, such behavior may be a culturally sanctioned method of conflict resolution and may even be sought after as a positive experience. Although the psychodynamics are neurotic processes, the behavior is often accepted by the culture as appropriate behavior for conflict resolution.

4. *Possession Behavior (Psychotic)* (PBP). Although there is some overlap between neurotic and psychotic syndromes, we include in this category many of the *culture-bound reactive syndromes,* such as amok, latah, koro, imu, witiko, pibloktoq, and negi negi. The syndromes are characterized by *stereotyped behavior, usually of psychotic proportion, that the culture recognizes as clearly pathological.* Langness (1976) has termed them "hysterical psychoses." However, we find the use of the term "hysteria" misleading, since hysteria should be confined to a specific type of personality organization. Persons exhibiting these syndromes usually do not have a hysterical personality. Further, the cultural symbols manifest in the syndromes are diverse and not unique to one set of ego defenses or psychodynamics. It would be more appropriate to consider these syndromes under the rubric of "character psychoses" which develop in persons of differing character structure but are elaborated upon a common set of cultural symbols and rituals.

Behavioral syndromes characteristic of manic–depressive and schizophrenic psychoses are also encountered and recognized in societies within which culture-bound syndromes occur. Most cultures differentiate between the two forms of psychopathology and tend to label only the culture-bound syndromes as possession states (Gaviria and Wintrob, 1978; Westermeyer and Wintrob, 1979).

5. *Possession Explanation* (PE). Not all events of possession reflect psychologic conflict. Possession may be equally invoked as the *explanation* of accidents, economic reversal, trauma, epidemic disease, illness, and personal misfortune.

The history of trance is rooted in religion. Early history of religious practice is given by Russell (1979); medieval history by Knox (1950); renaissance history by Thomas (1971); and recent history by Podmore (1963). The classic early review of possession states was written by Oesterreich (1966), and was followed by extensive anthropological analyses (Bourguignon, 1973, 1976b; Douglas, 1970; Landy, 1977; Lewis, 1971; Mair, 1969; Rush, 1974). Empirical field and case studies have been published from a social science perspective (Crapanzano and Garrison, 1977; Goodman et al., 1974; Loudon, 1976; Tieryakian, 1977), while psychiatrically oriented volumes have also appeared (Cox, 1973; Kiev, 1964; Prince, 1968; Yap, 1974). This substantial literature reflects the active scholarly and professional interest in a topic that is not so esoteric as might at first appear.

Our concern, then, must extend beyond just exotic phenomena, to consider the following issues: (1) the worldwide distribution and manifestation of trance states, (2) the sociocultural and psychodynamic parameters, (3) the clinical components of the phenomena, and (4) the sociocultural implications. As we shall see, the phenomenon of trance is *not* extraordinary; in fact, it is quite ordinary.

SOCIETAL DISTRIBUTION AND CONDITIONS

Bourguignon (1973) has conducted the most extensive recent research on a variety of modes of consciousness that include trance and possession trance. Both are culturally learned behavior. However, trance is an intrapersonal event, the content of which can only be learned through description provided by the person having the experience. The possession trance is an interpersonal event, in which there is impersonation of another being on an occasion when there are witnesses. As such, the context and meaning of the event are known to the community, for whom the possession trance embodies common social and cultural symbols. In a survey of 488 societies worldwide, Bourguignon found that 90 percent had institutionalized one or the other of these states.

In general, Bourguignon has found that the more simple societies practice trance behavior, whereas more complex societies engage in possession trance. In North America, Bourguignon found that 92 percent of societies have trance, 25 percent have possession trance, and only 3 percent have neither! Thus, possession states are neither extraordinary nor unusual in the life of most people. Bourguignon (1976a) concludes:

One might ask how to account for our findings. A number of comments as well as hypotheses might be suggested. One: societies which do not utilize these state clearly are historical exceptions which need to be explained rather than the vast majority of societies which do use these states. Two: the specific beliefs associated with altered states are cultural inventions. . . . Three: the specific behavior of altered states and the beliefs with which they are linked may be said to reflect certain types of social realities. . . . Four: the institution of one or another or both of our types of altered states of consciousness may be said to "do" something on the one hand for the participating individual, the trancer or possession trancer, and on the other hand to "do" something, to fulfill a function, for the society. (p. 96.)

In summary, the more complex, socially symbolic, and community-oriented possession trance is found in societies where symbolic modes of expression in social communication are necessary; whereas in more simple face-to-face social structure, we find simple trance states.

Let us now narrow our inquiry to the more specific social conditions in which the explicit forms of possession known as demon possession and exorcism appear. While, the belief in demon possession and exorcism is widespread, the actual occurrence of cases of demon possession and the practice of exorcism appear to be more limited. In particular, Bourguignon has reported that the eruption of demonology is coincident with social situations characterized by: (1) an oppressive social structure, (2) a loss of trust in the efficacy of social institutions, and (3) a seeming inability to cope with the evils of the social structure. When these particular social situations obtain, we see the *personification of social evil* in evil demons, the displacement of social protest in the form of accusations of possession and witchcraft, and personal experiences of possession. Being possessed of social evil is personified, while accused, accuser, and exorcist act out the symbolization of the social conflict in a safely displaced form, since active social protest and reform seem impossible. Thus, there is social conflict and social ambiguity of action (Uzzell, 1974; M. Wilson, 1971; P. Wilson, 1967).

With an understanding then of the social conditions that give rise to demonology, we see that contemporary social conditions are ripe in the Western world for the re-emergence of supernaturalistic belief systems, and even demonology: society has been perceived as oppressive, trust in social institutions has disintegrated, and a mood of helpless impotence in social action has emerged. So it is not surprising that the evil society should again be personified and symbolized in contemporary Western demonology.

But not all persons in such a social situation participate in the possession and exorcism. Usually, it is only those in the community who are most oppressed, and for whom social protest or reform is least viable, who turn to possession and exorcism to symbolically ameliorate their plight (Carstairs and Kapur, 1976; Wijesinghe et al., 1976). Further, in different cultures some reports indicate that different personality types are more likely than others to seek possession and exorcism (Kuba, 1973; Yap, 1961). Thus, there is a combination of social conditions, community status, and personality structure that intertwine to produce demonology in practice.

PSYCHODYNAMICS VERSUS PSYCHOPATHOLOGY

Earlier literature on T and PT usually interpreted them as a manifestation of psychopathology. As a result, there were many attempts to determine the particular type of neurotic or psychotic personality that was prone to these experiences. The purely psychopathological approach is inadequate, however, on several counts. First, recent careful studies of ritual trance and ritual possession trance, in both shamans and lay persons, reveals that although *some* participants may be either neurotic or psychotic, that is *not* the general case (Hoch, 1974; Hippler, 1976). Second, the widespread distribution of T and PT militate against the plausibility of explanation solely as psychopathology. Third, the psychodynamics of T and PT have been made abundantly clear, but it is reductionistic to conclude that the explication of psychodynamics means psychopathology.

One of the basic problems in dealing with the issue of psychopathology is the distinction between "emic" interpretations (i.e., the culture interprets the behavior) and "etic" interpretation (i.e., universalized scientific interpretation). These differences can be distorted in either direction. From the emic perspective, one can observe the structural and functional value of possession in a culture, and therefore conclude that the possession is not psychopathologic because it is meaningful within the culture; or from the etic perspective, one might conclude that the behavior was psychopathological because it appears abnormal in terms of expected Western norms of behavior. But these are misinterpretations. It is possible to derive from ethnographic data a cultural, emic distinction as to whether a specific behavior or condition is "culturally normal," unusual or deviant but acceptable, or abnormal and not culturally acceptable. In all three instances we deal with psychodynamics, but only in the last instance with psychopathology. Thus, we are dealing with both the analysis of personality structure and social adaption. The psychological anthropologist George De Vos (1976) summarized this dual synthesis:

> We must maintain a clear distinction between the internal structuring of personality related to a concept of adjustment and social-behavioral responses which can be seen as adaptive or maladaptive for the individual within his nexus . . . to understand the interrelationships of social struc-

ture, possession behavior, and personality one must use a dual level of analysis with a structural-functional distinction to delimit and interrelate the concept of adjustment to psychological structure on the one hand, and adaption to social functioning on the other. (p. 117)

We may note that there are always general social conflicts in a culture. These conflicts are then symbolized, and some degree of cultural conflict resolution is achieved through a variety of ritual symbolic activities (Turner, 1969). To the degree that the conflicts of the culture are conflicts for the individual, the symbolizing rituals afford personal melioration of experiencing cultural conflict (Firth, 1967; Obeyesekere, 1969, 1970; Skultans, 1974). This then is a general socio-psychological dynamic for participation in ritual trance and possession trance for many "normal" persons.

But again, we return to the issue of psychodynamics versus psychopathology. Freud (1922) stated the classic psychiatric formulation: "The states of possession correspond to our neuroses . . . the demons are bad and reprehensible wishes." But his interpretation reduced demonology to nothing but individual neurosis, for he concluded that the actors in the drama of demonology were but acting out neurotic conflicts—as his case study demonstrated. Following the lead of Freud, psychiatric historians have subsequently interpreted the demon possession of medievalism as evidence of neurosis or psychosis, and concluded that, until modern psychiatry, the Western world interpreted mental illness as demon possession. This interpretation is incorrect on two major counts.

First, recent historical studies have revealed that Freud and the psychiatric historians following him based their conclusions on the study of neurotics, from which they generalized to interpret all demonology; and the documents of prescientific Western history reveal that from early medieval times onward many clear distinctions were made between mental illness and demonology (Kroll, 1977; Neugebauer, 1979). In his analysis of medieval demonology, the Spanish anthropologist Baroja (1964) notes that Western rationalism ousted the belief in witchcraft from its place in the collective consciousness of man, to survive only in the marginal circles of cranks and neurotics. (These were the possessed whom Freud observed.)

Second, the appearance of demonology in historical perspective reveals broader sociocultural issues than cannot be accounted for solely in terms of individual neurosis. Thus, the eminent medical historian George Rosen (1968) observes:

Witch hunting expresses a disease of society, and is related to a social context. . . . To be sure, some individuals involved in witch trials were mentally and emotionally disordered. Most of those involved were not. In part, their reactions were learned, in part, they conformed because of fear-producing pressures. (p.43)

Similarly, historian J. B. Russell (1972) concludes:

But it will not do to assume that the witches were, on the whole, mentally ill. They were responding to human needs more universal than those of individual fantasy; universal enough to be described in terms of myth. . . . The phenomenon of witchcraft, whether we are talking about the persecutors or the witches, was the results of fear, expressed in supernatural terms, and repressed by a society that was intolerant of spiritual dissent. In most respects, a variety, or at least an outgrowth of heresy, witchcraft was one manifestation of alienation. (p. 222)

INTRAPSYCHIC EXPERIENCE, DESCRIPTION, AND INTERPRETATION

We must now delineate three levels of analyses and description. First consider the intrapsychic experience. This level of analysis is deeply personal, difficult to communicate to others. The second level of analysis is the individual's description of intrapsychic experience. Two important features of this level are that it is necessarily social, and its expression is through a shared symbol system. The third level is that of explanation or interpretation of experience. This level may proceed as either personal or social efforts, but always occurs with references to a social or cultural belief system that mediates and structures experiences into categories meaningful to the participants. It is interesting to note that this third level exists *independent of a primary intrapsychic event*. Thus, an observer may only attempt interpretation of experience that has been described or observed. This is the level of scientific theory and also that of magical or religious belief.

Obviously all three levels of analysis may occur simultaneously and with reference to the same events. An example, perhaps familiar to most, is the conversion experience, the "born again" experience of the charismatic Christian churches. The profound nature of this intrapsychic experience is indicated by the weeping and not uncommon fainting observed at charismatic services. This experience is difficult to communicate, especially to those who have not in some way shared the experience. Indeed, at the level of description we have words used such as "beautiful," "terrible," or "powerful," and rarely is there reference to the "public" features of the experience such as weeping. At the level of interpretation or explanation we commonly hear that the person was "being possessed" or "touched" by the Holy Spirit. *Here the independent nature of the explanation level becomes manifest.* For an observer whose belief system does not admit possession by a Holy Spirit, the "born again" experience might appear as hysteria or perhaps as an affirmation of group membership. In fact, persons participating primarily at the interpretation level of experience are mostly concerned that their "experience" (actually their interpretation) become consistent with and nonthreatening to their established beliefs. It is by interpreting a difficult or unusual experience as part of an acceptable belief framework that the experience becomes nonthreatening. The prior existence of a belief framework often enables one to "explain away" problems or at least to make them tolerable.

TRANCE, POSSESSION TRANCE, AND POSSESSION STATES

These modes of consciousness and associated behaviors have a number of points in common. They are not typical of the participant's behavioral repertoire and rarely constitute daily routine. They are marked by a specific onset and termination that may be generally anticipated by the participant. Finally, these modes of consciousness produce highly stereotyped and patterned behaviors that satisfy criteria for appropriateness held by other significant participants or observers.

Trance

Trance states, per se, are culturally prescribed practices that are performed primarily as *personal ritual* and have personal and private satisfactions. One should note that the inwardly directed trance state occurs within a carefully prepared social context—the mantra of transcendental meditation or, as another example, the highly structured context of Zen Buddhism.

In Western culture, sanctioned trance states were popular and widely practiced in Europe and the United States in the nineteenth century. But such practice has faded, except for some of the avant garde "experiential therapies' popular in the 1960s. Hypnotherapy is perhaps the faded flower left in the garden of Western-style trance states. In contrast, various degrees of trance are widely used in the "quiet therapies" of Japan (Reynolds, 1980).

It is not, however, that trance states have disappeared from common experience in the Western world (Ness, 1978, 1980). Consider the fact that television commentators describing the New York marathon noted that in the last 6 miles the runners were running in the "twilight zone" of consciousness—that is, not aware of the world in which they were running and unresponsive to the cheering crowds. More simply, most people have experienced hypnagogic states of trance when driving, or reading, or gazing at the clouds. We just do not note these degrees of trance.

At the same time, because of the typical modes of consciousness fostered in Western culture, different modes of consciousness easily evoke dysphoric unease. For example, in classroom exercises where we demonstrate shifting modes of consciousness, about 20 percent of the class become obviously anxious and stop the exercise when they begin to experience a shift in mode of consciousness.

Finally, we take note of sudden shifts into trance states in response to psychic distress. Here the unfamiliar trance state is ego-dysphoric and ego-dystonic. We clinically label such states as near-death experiences, fugue states, depersonalization attacks, Capgras syndrome, and so on.

Possession Trance

Trance is distinguished from possession trance by the ascription of the participant's behavior to possession. Thus, possession trance corresponds to the description level of analysis where both actor and observer are interacting to inform each other as to the nature of the experience. Indeed, it is not uncommon to find that the principal actor, the one possessed and participating at the intrapsychic level, professes ignorance as to his behavior during the trance and requests this information from other participants.

EXAMPLE: POSSESSION TRANCE—NORMAL

Glossalalia or "speaking in tongues" is often practiced as a possession trance. Modern manifestations of this behavior are linked to the biblical account of the apostles' experience when they gathered to celebrate Pentecost: "And they were all filled with the Holy Ghost, and began to speak with other tongues, as the Spirit gave the utterance" (Acts 2:4).

The contemporary settings for "speaking in tongues" are typically charismatic Christian churches. During hymn singing following a sermon or while being exhorted to "let the Spirit in" some members of the congregation begin systematically swaying or shaking. Their body movement becomes more intense as they leave their seats and slowly move toward the center aisle or the area below the pupit. Some may fall to the floor, but all begin to make rather strange utterances with no discernible pattern. These utterances, the "tongues," are punctuated by shouted praises to God as well as questions about which members of the congregation seek spiritual guidance. The utterances and body movements continue until several questions are "answered," usually by the minister or another member "interpreting" the meaning of the utterances. At the conclusion of the possession trance the more active participants are sent back to their places where they may inquire about the questions asked and the answers received. This may be repeated several times, with each episode lasting from one to twenty minutes.

Comment. It is noteworthy that in the above example only four or five persons in the church group actually experience the intrapsychic event of the trance. The behavior of enacting "possession" is mutually shared as a socially sanctioned and expected behavior, shared by all even though enacted only by a few. And there is a common consensual interpretation of the event.

This is an example of institutionalized possession trance. The church community perceives of itself as a "holy remnant" in an evil, alien, larger society. The preacher presents a conflictual issue to the congregation, following which several persons are possessed by the Holy Spirit, enter a trance, and speak in tongues. The "message" of advice from the Holy Spirit is interpreted subsequently by others in the congregation. The glossolalia symbolizes a powerful force that can rescue the congregation, and the message offers a solution to the conflict. In this example, we see clearly the use of possession trance for social conflict mediation (Pattison, 1974).

In general, possession trance is practiced by shamans or healers as part of rituals of healing or divination and by community members as part of symbolic religious rituals that deal with conflcits in the local societal structure. Both instances may be used to symbolize societal conflict, and through the possession ritual effect social conflict resolution (Davis, 1980; Laguerre, 1980; Rogers, 1982; Scheff, 1979).

Possession State

Possession state (PS) is distinguished from possession trance (PT) in that PS is always related to a specific conflict situation, typically arising between the individual expressing PS and one or more of his or her socially significant alters. As in PT, we note highly stereotypic behavior, which includes all those attributes that the appropriate reference community utilizes to indicate possession. There is generally a specific onset of the behavior. However, unlike PT, PS is more likely to invade all of the affected individual's behavior. Unlike PT and possession behavior (discussed below), *PS is merely an expression of conflict, not a means of conflict resolution.* Varying degrees of specification occur in PS, from particular spirits to the most abstract, such as in hex magic or root work (Wintrob, 1970, 1973; Lambert, et al., 1959). While there are examples with a high degree of specification from other cultures, the case we present here is that of a possession state induced by root work in the southeastern United States.

EXAMPLE: POSSESSION STATE

A black male was admitted to a psychiatry unit on referral from the Police Department. In his midthirties, the patient had been college-educated. On admission the patient complained of inability to sleep, stomach ache, and the feeling that "there are snakes under my skin." This last symptom was accomplished by or in reference to occasional, apparently involuntary, microtremors in the patient's extremities. The patient's neurological workup was normal, and the only medical findings were related to hypertension and poor nourishment. Sensitive to the patient's possible involvement with hex magic, the attending psychiatrist asked him if he thought that someone may have "put roots on him." The patient was at first hesitant but when made certain his doctor was not making fun of him, he responded with relief that, yes, his problems were definitely due to root work. When asked about who might have been responsible, the patient drew the business card of an apparently well-known "root doctor" from his wallet! He said he was sure that this was the person who performed the magic. The next logical question was: would the same root doctor remove the hex? The patient said that he had approached the root doctor about this, but had been refused. We then learned that for over four years the patient had been traveling from town to town throughout the southeastern states trying to find another root doctor able to help him. It was noted that the business card looked very professional; surely the root doctor had been paid by someone. The patient told us that "it couldn't have been my mother," but "for sure it had to be my wife's father." In exploring the conflict between the patient and his father-in-law, it was doscovered that it stemmed from the promiscuous behavior of the patient's wife. Each man held the other responsible, and this led to heated arguments resulting at least once in the exchange of gunshots. It was after the shooting that the father-in-law bought the aid of a root doctor. (Case description courtesy of G. Hurd, Ph.D. and R. Bishop, M.D.)

Comment. The clinical goal in this case was the amelioration of the patient's symptoms related to the root work. However, it was not attempted to "cure" the patient of the hex or of his belief in hex magic. The approach taken was to have the patient explore and express his feelings about his wife and his father-in-law. It was the power of these conflicts that gave power to the hex. When the patient became possessed by the root magic, the conflict was removed from the accessible world into the unaccessible world of magic. This served to internalize the negative emotional content such that the patient could not intervene on his own belief, nor could he pursue the original conflict to any resolution. It should be noted that being possessed, in this instance, provided the patient with a means to leave the original conflict situation, which also included leaving an unhappy marriage.

Possession Behavior

Under this category we observe behaviors that are recognized by the community as aberrant, abnormal, or deviate from an individual's normal behavior. This is in contrast to possession trance and possession state, which are recognized as "different" but nonpathological. Within a given individual, the severity of the manifestation of PB may fluctuate over time, but the associated behavior becomes an overall component of the daily routine. We find that possession behavior is always related to a conflict situation, which might be marital, familial, or communal. What we have then is a set of culturally provided symbolized behaviors available to individuals through which they may express neurotic conflict. As such possession behavior is the description level of analysis, while the primary intrapsychic experience is that of the psychic conflict.

There are numerous excellent ethnographic analyses of such behaviors, which demonstrate how the possession behavior symbolizes a specific conflict, and how such conflict may be reduced, ameliorated, or resolved through the symbolism of possession itself, as well as through ritual possession exorcism (Chakraborty and Bannerjii, 1975; Watson and Watson-Franke, 1977; Young, 1975).

EXAMPLE: POSSESSION BEHAVIOR—NEUROTIC

An eighteen-year-old Mayan girl was betrothed to an older man who was the close friend of her father and paternal uncle. a few months before the wedding her fiance was killed in an accident. This caused considerable upset to her father, who had lost a good friend, but seemingly had little impact on the young girl. Her lack of display at the funeral caused negative reactions from the deceased's family as well as her own. Within a few weeks of the funeral she complained of nightmares and then of conscious visitations of her fiance, who sought to possess her. The father then reported similar experiences, and an indigenous healer was consulted, who performed a ritual exorcism. This consisted of drawing a circle of "magical power" around the girl and her father, so that they could not become trapped by the fiance's spirit. The healer then entered possession trance so that he could talk to the spirit and effect a positive outcome for his clients. During a lengthy discussion with the ghost, with the clients present, the healer repeatedly emphasized the sadness and grief of their loss but that the fiance must learn to forget his living friends. Similarly they must learn to live without him. At the conclusion of the exorcism the fiance's spirit accepted the situation and promised not to return. (G. Hurd and M. Migalski, 1982)

Comment. Here we see the classic psychodynamics of grief work carried out through both the symbolism and the explanation of the healer. The magic circle, like death, separates the fiance from the girl and her father, and the conflict is projected onto the ghost, reaffirming the normalcy of health of the clients. What is most interesting here is that grief was not at issue for the young girl. The impending marriage for the girl was the conflict. She was quite unhappy about the engagement, but could not resist her father's desire that she marry his friend. So, while her father was most likely using possession behavior as a means of expressing grief, she was reacting to her guilt and ambivalence concerning the death. Also, her actions provided the sanctioning community with the public display related to the fiance's death that had been lacking at the funeral. Thus we note that although the healer was entirely successful, his assessment of the case was slightly off base. The majority of the girl's problems were related to her way of resolving the initial conflicts, not the latter grieving process.

We might also call possession behavior "neurotic possession," since the affected persons are *unable* to otherwise resolve conflict, and resort to possession as the "neurotic symptom expression." Just as in more familiar neurotic symptoms in Western psychiatry, the possession symptoms mask the conflict from both the possessed person and those significant others with whom the conflict exists. Thus, possession behavior affords expression of the conflicts, and aids in the repression of the conflict from consciousness (Hillard and Rockwell, 1978; Weidman and Sessex, 1971; Wittkower and Weidman, 1969).

EXAMPLE: POSSESSION BEHAVIOR AND POSSESSION TRANCE —NEUROTIC BEHAVIOR

A fourteen-year-old Indian girl on a western reservation was referred for evaluation. Three months previously she had seen ancestor ghosts in the trees at night and talked with them. Subsequently, her behavior at school was that of a normal teen-ager; but when she returned home from school, she dressed in traditional Indian clothes, wandered around the house in a daze, and screamed with fright that ghosts were about to kill her or her siblings. Interviews with her mother revealed that this daughter had always been considered the designated recipient of the spiritual powers of her shaman grandfather. However, the family was now Presbyterian and did not believe in shamans or spirits. A traditional Indian exorcism ritual was arranged with the help of older women of the tribe. Immediately thereafter, the above behavior disappeared. (Pattison, 1982)

Comment. In this cast there is evidence of both possession trance and possession behavior. The symbolic situation was readily recognized by the Indian culture for what it was: the initiation struggle of a young shaman. In the traditional Indian culture, such behavior would have been accepted and responded to along culturally prescribed lines. In this case, acculturation with attendant cultural conflict prevented effective resolution in either the "old" Indian culture or the "new" Presbyterian culture. In this instance the problem was not the behavior itself but the confusion of cultural contexts within which the behavior occurred and had to be dealt with.

EXAMPLE: POSSESSION TRANCE—PSYCHOTIC BEHAVIOR

A middle-aged white woman with her five children drove into a gas station in a midwestern city. She reported experiencing a heavenly vision from the Lord which became an insistent directive. She parked, took off all her clothes, and walked over to the attendant's booth to deliver God's message. When the police arrived, she picked up her five-month-old son and proceeded to mimic fellatio. (Pattison, 1979)

Comment. This woman, who was also Pentecostal, had had religious possession experiences since her youth. Her childhood religious community was in conflict with mainstream society. In adulthood, she experienced marital conflict, leading to estrangement from her relatives, husband, and church. Although religious symbolism characterized the possession behavior, the incident occurred in a nonreligious context, and the behavior was not a communally sanctioned pattern. Given her hysterical personality structure, as revealed in subsequent evaluation, the behavior described is an example of "hysterical psychosis."

TRANCE AND POSSESSION EXPLANATION

Naturally, not all events of T and PT are a matter of neurotic conflict. Perhaps the majority of the world's societies today subscribe to supernaturalistic cosmologies. Thus, at the third level of analysis, T and PT are used as an explanation of accidents, trauma, disease, and misfortune.

What the Western mind rarely sees is that Western science and its construction of reality are terribly fragmented (Ehrenwald, 1976; Galdston, 1963; Rosenthal, 1971). The naturalistic system of the world of the West, rooted in the particularistic rationalism of latter-day humanism, provides proximate and limited explanations of isolated fragments of human life. Further, without ontological grounding it does not provide a rationale, or purpose, or meaning to life (London, 1964). Consider the conclusion of psychoanalyst Allan Wheelis (1971):

At the beginning of the modern age science did, indeed, promise certainty. It does no longer. Where we now retain the conviction of certainty we do so on our own presumption, while the advancing edge of science warns that absolute truth is a fiction, is a longing of the heart, and not to be had by man . . . our designations of evil are as fallible now as they were ten thousand years ago; we simply are better armed now to act on our fallible vision.

That Western technology has achieved greater creature comforts and longevity of life is indisputable, but what of the quality, meaning, and value of life? At the same time, we fail to recognize that the concept of supernaturalism is a *Western* construct (Bulka, 1979; Marty and Vaux, 1982). As the anthropologist Saler (1977) has pointed out, it is Western thought that has construed a separation between natural and supernatural. Levi-Strauss (1966) demonstrated in his book *The Savage Mind* that so-called primitive constructions of reality provide a much more coherent, cohesive, and explanatory model of the world and human behavior than does the Western scientific construction of the cosmos. Science does not provide a very comprehensive description and explanation of human behavior.

Foster (1976) has compared naturalistic versus supernaturalistic systems of thought about health and illness. He finds that naturalistic systems (Western) view misfortunes and illness in atomistic terms. Disease is unrelated to other misfortune; religion and magic are unrelated to illness; and the principal curers lack supernatural or magical powers, for their function is solely an instrumental task performance. On the other hand, supernaturalistic systems integrate the totality of all life events. Illness, religion, and magic are inseparable. The most powerful curers are astute diagnosticians who employ both technical and symbolic means of therapeusis. This is exemplified in the wholistic and faith healing methods of the United States (Hand, 1976; Singer, 1977).

Early students of supernaturalistic systems of healing such as Ackerknecht (1971) and Rivers (1924) emphasized the particular magical beliefs and rituals of shamans and other folk healers, but they overlooked the complex integrated view of nature and mankind, and complex refined distinctions that were made between different kinds of accidents, misfortunes, illnesses, and diseases, along with their causes and cures. Loudon (1976) comments:

This reduces the study of health and disease to studies of witchcraft, sorcery, magic, and in general curative or socially readjustive ritual practices, with herbalists and empirically rational treatment and prophylaxis as residual categories. (p. 36)

In brief, supernaturalistic systems deal with the total spectrum of human life and behavior, which integrates man and nature. A variety of supernaturalistic explanations exist to deal with all varieties of situations in life. Careful ethnographic studies reveal two major conclusions:

1. Supernaturalistic cultures do make distinctions between accidents, distortions of natural process such as a malformed fetus, hazards such as snakebites or tornadoes, psychosomatic disorders, personal and in-

terpersonal conflict that we would term neurosis, and existential-re-
ligious issues of life (Bahr, et al., 1974; Morley and Wallis, 1979).
2. There are similar distinctions made between types of healers and intervention healing strategies for different life problems. Although such
   interventions may range from physicalistic (such as herb remedies) to
   purely symbolic rituals, they all are encompassed under a supernaturalistic rubric. Yet, both the common people and the healers differentiate different levels of intervention (Bilo, 1977; Harwood, 1981;
   Lin; et al., 1978; Woods, 1977).

In sum then, we must avoid a reductionistic interpretation of all supernaturalistic systems as simply magical spiritualism. Such systems are often
quite sophisticated and complex. Because supernatural explanations are
embedded in the whole of the system of health and healing, as well as the
spectrum of behavior, we cannot treat trance and possession trance as just
one specific phenomenon. Rather, there are a wide range of possession beliefs that are related to sets of behavior ranging from ritual trance on the
most specific end of the spectrum to abstract notions of the nature of man
as embodiment of spirit.

In contrast to the above observations of specificity, it must be noted that
"possession explanation," at times, is *overinclusive* of several different
classes of behavioral phenomena:

1. *Psychosis as possession.* Apart from the "cultural-bound psychoses,"
   which are usually explained as specific types of possession, there are
   often cultural explanations of possession in the classic psychoses of
   schizophrenia and manic–depression. Although there is no stereotyped behavior, such as is exemplified in the culture-bound psychoses,
   the aberrant, deviant, and bizarre behavior of the florid psychotic is
   taken as evidence of possession. In this case, we have psychotic elaboration and use of symbolic language and behavior of the culture
   (Ahmed, 1978; Wintrob, 1968, 1970).
2. *Combined functional–organic syndromes as possession.* Here we have
   a common behavior pattern, such as seizures, which may be either a
   "neurotic conversion," "organic conversion," or "organic epilepsy."
   In a study of Navajo seizure disorders by Neutra et al. (1977), they
   found the seizure behaviors were identical regardless of etiology, and
   thus seizures were ipso facto explained as possession and treated as
   such. The differentiation between the two etiologies was only revealed
   by long-term follow-up. The neurotic seizures disappeared after appropriate exorcistic healing, whereas the organic epileptic seizures persisted.

3. *Organic illness as possession.* Common illnesses usually are not attributed to possession. However, infrequent, unusual, or seemingly mysterious illness may be ascribed to it. An excellent example of this phenomenon occurred in the New Guinea highlands in the 1950s. A slow-growing virus epidemic developed in a small tribe. The illness was unknown to the tribe. The symptoms were a gradual but inexorable neurological deterioration without alteration of mental status. The tribe ascribed the illness to a specific possession and quickly developed an exorcist cult. After about 20 years, when the epidemic had disappeared, the tribe likewise gave up that specific possession belief, and the exorcist cult disappeared (Lindenbaum, 1979).

4. *Psychosomatic symptoms as possession.* In these instances the person may have transitory trance experience, but primarily interprets or explains the bodily experience as a possession phenomenon.

EXAMPLE

A forty-year-old male psychologist, recently divorced, was driving down a freeway with a new girlfriend when he began to experience twitching in his face, flushing, and nervous sensations throughout his body. He had recently become interested in mystical, holistic, and meditative therapies. He was panic-striken, believing himself possessed. He drove off the freeway and was taken to a hospital emergency room and given a minor tranquilizer. Still the panic and notion of possession persisted. He consulted a Methodist minister, who prayed for his healing. The psychologist confessed his guilt over his recent divorce, as well as guilt and anxiety over the resumption of dating. The symptoms abated. He joined the Methodist church and participated for six months. He then developed a stable relationship with another girlfriend, left the church, and announced that he no longer believed that he had been possessed. He now explained his acute symptoms as an anxiety attack.

Comment. This case illustrates the use of convenient cultural symbols and explanations (the current exorcism fad) in the service of ego defense. The subject employed this explanation to cope with his immediate life crisis, but abandoned the belief and explanation when it was no longer dynamically necessary to use that coping explanation.

TRANCE AND POSSESSION STATES AND MODES OF CONSCIOUSNESS

It remains for us to describe how the various types of trance and possession states are related to modes of consciousness. We refer the reader to Chapter 7, in which we outlined modes of consciousness as personal experiences.

The concept of *state* refers to the action or behavior of the person, which does not indicate the mode of consciousness, which refers to the personal experience of the person. Therefore the *same states* may occur in *different modes of consciousness.*

- *Trance.* In the state of trance the person is not interactive with the external world. The person in trance operates in terms of *intrapersonal experience.* There are two different trance states: First is the *meditative trance.* Here the person's focus of awareness if upon his or her own body; this is an I-1 function. The second is the *transcendental trance.* Here the focus of awareness is upon the self-construct; this is an I-3 function. In both instances, the person is in a trance, but the two personal experiences are radically different from each other.
- *Possession trance.* In PT the person is engaged in an *interpersonal experience.* The focus of awareness is upon interaction with external objects and persons. This is an I-2 function.

We can consider each of the three states above in terms of an ego-syntonic experience or an ego-dystonic personal experience:

- *The meditative trance state.* Examples of ego-syntonic personal experience would be Zen or yoga meditation, or auto-hypnosis. Examples of ego-dystonic personal experience would be a catatonic state, or severe hypochondriasis, with intense focus of awareness upon the body.
- *The transcendental trance state.* Examples of ego-syntonic personal experience would be mystical religious transcendence, creative artistic insight, and the shamanistic voyage. Examples of ego-dystonic personal experience would be out-of-body experiences, near-death experiences, and drug-induced hallucinatory experience.
- *The possession trance state.* Ego-syntonic personal experience would include the experience of hexing, possession states, shamanistic healing rituals, and Pentecostal charismatic rituals. Ego-dystonic experiences would include multiple personality, the Capgras syndrome, fugue states, and folie-a-deux.

Finally, we may ask: what distinguishes between an ego-syntonic and an ego-dystonic trance state?

First, in all ego-syntonic experiences there is personalization or "owning" of the experience as events that belong to the person. Therefore, the event is congruent with the self-construct. Thus the events are part of the historical continuity of the self in memory, rather than isolated and unfamiliar events.

Second, ego-dystonic events occur apart from cultural sanction and expectation. The event is disowned and depersonalized. The experiences are unfamiliar, and the events are perceived as disconnected and idiosyncratic to the person's own life. Ego-dystonic states reflect an impaired reality testing system, where personal experiences are discontinuous with the person's life experience.

SUMMARY

In this chapter we have described a variety of trance and possession states. Such states are relatively unfamiliar in the current experience of Western scientific observers. However, such states are widely practiced throughout the world, and even in Western cultures. We have described such states in terms of modes of consciousness, behavioral manifestations, and contextual interpretations. We conclude that any such states, per se, are not pathological, but may be experienced and interpreted as either normal or pathological personal experience.

REFERENCES

Ackerknecht, E. H. *Medicine and ethnology: Selected essays.* Bern: Verlag Huber, 1971.

Ahmed, S. H. Cultural influences on delusion. *Psychiatr. Clin.,* 1978, *11,* 1–9.

Bahr, D. M., Gregorio, J., Lopez, D. I., and Alvarez, A. *Piman shamanism and staying sickness.* Tuscon: University of Arizona Press, 1974.

Baroja, J. C. *The world of the witches.* Chicago: University of Chicago Press, 1964.

Bilo. Y. The Moroccan demon in Israel: the case of 'Evil Spirit Disease'. *Ethos,* 1980, *8,* 24–39.

Bourguignon, E. *Religion, altered states of consciousness, and social change.* Columbus: Ohio State University, 1973.

Bourguignon, E. *Possession.* San Francisco: Chandler & Sharp, 1976a.

Bourguignon, E. The effectiveness of religious healing movements: A review of recent literature. *Transcultural Psychiatric Review,* 1976b, *13,* 5–22.

Bulka, R. P. (Ed.). *Mystics and medics. A comparison of mystical and psychotherapeutic encounters.* New York: Human Sciences Press, 1979.

Carstairs, G. M. and Kapur, R. L. *The great universe of Kota. Stress, change and mental disorder in an Indian village.* Berkeley: University of California Press, 1976.

Chakraborty, A. and Bannerjii, G. Ritual, a culture specific neurosis, and obsessional states in Bengali culture. *Indian Journal of Psychiatry,* 1975, *17,* 211–216.

Cox, R. H. (Ed.). *Religious systems and psychotherapy.* Springfield, Ill.: Thomas, 1973.

Crapanzano, V. and Garrison, V. *Case studies in spirit possession.* New York: Wiley, 1977.

Davis, W. *Dojo: Magic and exorcism in modern Japan.* Stanford, Calif.: Stanford University Press, 1980.

De Vos, G. A. The interrelationship of social and psychological structure in transcultural psychiatry. In W. P. Lebra (Ed.), *Culture-bound syndromes, ethnopsychiatry, and alternate therapies.* Honolulu: University of Hawaii Press, 1976.

Douglas, M. (Ed.). *Witchcraft confessions and accusations.* London: Tavistock Publications, 1970.

Ehrenwald, J. (Ed.). *The history of psychotherapy. From healing magic to encounter.* New York: Jason Aronson, 1976.

Firth, R. Ritual and drama in Malaysia spirit mediumship. *Comparative Studies in Society and History,* 1967, *9,* 190–207.

Foster, G. M. Disease etiologies in non-Western medical systems. *American Anthropologist,* 1976, *78,* 773–782.

Freud, S. A seventeenth-century demonological neurosis. In *Collected works.* London: Hogarth Press, 1922.

Galdston, I. *Man's image in medicine and anthropology.* New York: International Universities Press, 1963.

Garrison, V. Doctor, espiritist, or psychiatrist?: Help-seeking behavior in a Puerto Rican neighborhood in New York City. *Medical Anthropology,* 1977, *1,* 65–180.

Gaviria, M. and Wintrob, R. Psychiatry in the multi-ethnic community: psychiatrist or spirit healer in the treatment of mental illness. In J. M. Divic and M. Dinoff (Eds.), *Aspects of community psychiatry.* Tuscaloosa: University of Alabama Press, 1978.

Goodman, F., Henney, J. H., and Pressel, E. *Trance, healing, and hallucination: Three field studies in religious experience.* New York: Wiley, 1974.

Griffith, E. E. H., English, T., and Mayfield, V. Possession, prayer, and testimony: Therapeutic aspects of the Wednesday night meeting in a black church. *Psychiatry,* 1980, *43,* 120–128.

Hand, W. D. (Ed.). *American folk medicine.* Berkeley: University of California Press, 1976.

Harwood, A. *RX: Spiritist as needed.* New York: Wiley, 1977.

Harwood, A. (Ed.). *Ethnicity and medical care.* Cambridge, Mass.: Harvard University Press, 1981.

Hillard, J. R., and Rockwell, J. K. Dysesthesia, witchcraft, and conversion reaction. *Journal of the American Medical Association,* 1978, *240,* 1724–1744.

Hippler, A. E. Shamans, curers, and personality: Suggestions toward a theoretical model. In W. P. Lebra (Ed.), *Culture-bound syndromes, ethnopsychiatry, and alternate therapies.* Honolulu: University of Hawaii Press, 1976.

Hoch, E. M. Pir, faqir, and psychotherapist. *The Human Context,* 1974, *6,* 668–677.

Hufford, D. J. *The terror that comes by night.* Philadelphia: University of Pennsylvania Press, 1982.

Hurd, G. S. and Migalski, M. Mediation of paradox: aspects of brujria. Unpulished manuscript.

Kane, S. Ritual possession in a southern Appalachian religious sect. *Journal of American Folklore,* 1974, *87,* 293–302.

Kiev, A. (Ed.). *Magic, faith and healing.* New York: Free Press, 1964.

Kleinman, A. M. Explaining the efficacy of indigenous healers: The need for interdisciplinary research. *Culture, Medicine, and Psychiatry,* 1977, *1,* 133–134.

Knox, R. A. *Enthusiasm: A Chapter in Religious History.* London: Oxford University Press, 1950.

Kroll, J. A reappraisal of psychiatry in the middle ages. *Archives of General Psychiatry,* 1977, *29,* 276–283.

Kuba, M. A Psychopathological and sociocultural psychiatric study of the possession syndrome. *Psychiatria et Neurologia Japonica,* 1973, *75,* 169–186.

Laguerre, M. S. *Voodoo heritage.* Beverley Hills, Calif.: Sage Publications, 1980.

Lambert, W., Triandes, L., and Wolf, M. Some correlates of beliefs in the malevolence and benevolence of supernatural beings: A cross-cultural study. *Journal of Abnormal and Social Psychology,* 1959, *58,* 162–168.

Landy, D. *Culture, disease, and healing: Studies in medical anthropology.* New York: Macmillan, 1977.

Langness, L. L. Hysterical psychosis and possessions. In W. P. Lebra, (Ed.), *Culture-bound syndromes, ethnopsychiatry, and alternate therapies.* Honolulu: University of Hawaii Press, 1976.

Levi-Strauss, C. *The savage mind.* Chicago: University of Chicago Press, 1966.

Lewis, I. M. *Ecstatic religion: An anthropological study of spirit possession and shamanism.* New York: Penguin Books, 1971.

Lin, T. Y., Tardiff, K., Donetz, G., and Goresky, W. Ethnicity and patterns of help-seeking. *Culture, Medicine and Psyhciatry,* 1978, *2,* 4–13.

Lindenbaum, S. *Kuru sorcery.* Palo Alto, Calif.: Mayfield Press, 1979.

London, P. *The modes of morals of psychotherapy.* New York: Holt, Rinehart & Winston, 1964.

Loudon, J. B. (Ed.). *Social anthropology and medicine.* New York: Academic Press, 1976.

Mair, L. *Witchcraft.* New York: McGraw-Hill, 1969.

Marty, M. E. and Vaux, K. L. (Eds.). *Health/medicine and the faith traditions.* Philadelphia: Fortress Press, 1982.

Morley, P. and Wallis, R. (Eds.). *Culture and curing.* Pittsburgh: University of Pittsburgh Press, 1979.

Ness, R. C. The Old Hag phenomenon as sleep paralysis: A biocultural interpretation. *Culture, Medicine and Psychiatry,* 1978, *2,* 15–39.

Ness, R. C. The impact of indigenous healing activity: An empirical study of two fundamental churches. *Social Science and Medicine,* 1980, *14B,* 167–180.

Neugebauer, R. Medieval and early modern theories of mental illness. *Archives of General Psychiatry,* 1979, *36,* 477–485.

Neutra, R., Levy, J. E., and Parker, D. Cultural expectations versus reality in Navajo seizure pattern and sick roles. *Culture, Medicine and Psychiatry,* 1977, *1,* 255–275.

Obeyesekere, G. The ritual drama of the Sanni demons: Collective representations of disease in Ceylon. *Comparative Studies in Society and History,* 1969, *11,* 174–216.

Obeyesekere, G. The idiom of demonic possession. *Social Science and Medicine,* 1970, *4,* 97–111.

Oesterreich, T. K. *Possession: Demoniacal and other among primitive races in antiquity, the middle ages, and modern times.* New York: New York University Press, 1966.

Pattison, E. M. Ideological support for the marginal middle class: Faith healing and glossolalia. In E. Zaretsky and M. P. Leone (Eds.), *Pragmatic religion: Marginal religious movements today.* Princeton, N.J.: Princeton University Press, 1974.

Pattison, E. M. Psychiatry and religion circa 1978: Analysis of a decade. *Pastoral Psychology,* 1978, *27,* 8–33, 119–141.

Pattison, E. M. Hysterical psychosis—commentary. *Journal of Operational Psychiatry,* 1979, *10,* 114–123.

Pattison, E. M. Possession states and exorcism. In C. Friedman and R. Faguet (Eds.), *Extraordinary disorders of human behavior.* New York: Plenum, 1982.

Podmore, F. *From Mesmer to Christian Science.* Hyde Park, N.Y.: University Books, 1963.

Prince, R. (Ed.). *Trance and possession states.* Montreal: R. M. Bucke Society, 1968.

Prince, R. The problem of spirit possession as a treatment for psychiatric disorders. *Ethos,* 1974, *2,* 315–333.

Reynolds, D. K. *The quiet therapies: Japanese pathways to personal growth.* Honolulu: University of Hawaii Press, 1980.

Rivers, W. H. R. *Medicine, magic, and religion.* London: Kegan Paul, 1924.

Rogers, S. L. *The shaman. His symbols and his healing power.* Springfield, Ill.: Thomas, 1982.

Rosen, G. *Madness in society. Chapters in the historical sociology of mental illness.* Chicago: University of Chicago Press, 1968.

Rosenthal, B. G. *The images of man.* New York: Basic Books, 1971.

Rothenberg, J. (Ed.). *Technicians of the sacred.* New York: Anchor Books, Doubleday & Company, 1969.

Rush, J. A. *Witchcraft and sorcery: An anthropological perspective on the occult.* Springfield, Ill.: Thomas, 1974.

Russell, J. B. *Witchcraft in the middle ages.* Ithaca, N.Y.: Cornell University Press, 1972.

Russell, J. B. *The devil: Perceptions of evil from antiquity to primitive Christianity.* Bergenfield, N.J.: Meridian Press, 1979.

Saler, B. Supernatural as a Western category. *Ethos,* 1977, *5,* 31–53.

Sangree, W. H. The Dodo cult, witchcraft, and secondary marriage in Irigwe, Nigeria. *Ethnology,* 1974, *13,* 261–278.

Scheff, T. J. *Catharsis in healing, ritual, and drama.* Berkeley: University of California Press, 1979.

Shack, W. Hunger, anxiety, and ritual: Deprivation and spirit possession among the Gurage of Ethiopia. *Man,* 1971, *6,* 30–34.

Singer, P. (Ed.). *Traditional healing.* New York: Conch Publ., 1977.

Skultans, V. *Intimacy and ritual: A study of spiritualism, mediums, and groups.* London: Routledge & Kegan Paul, 1974.

Thomas, K. *Religion and the decline of magic: Studies in popular beliefs in sixteenth and seventeenth century England.* London: Weidenfield and Nicolson, 1971.

Tiryakian, E. A. (Ed.). *On the margin of the visible: Sociology of the esoteric, and the occult.* New York: Wiley, 1977.

Turner, V. W. *The ritual process.* Chicago: Aldine, 1969.

Uzzell, D. Susto revisited: Illness as a strategic role. *American Ethnologist,* 1974, *1,* 369–378.

Watson, L. C. and Watson-Franke, M. Spirits, dreams, and the resolution of conflict among urban Guajiro women. *Ethos,* 1977, *5,* 379–387.

Weidman, H. H. and Sussex, J. N. Cultural values and ego functioning in relation to the typical culture-bound reactive syndromes. *International Journal of Social Psychiatry,* 1971, *17,* 83–100.

Westermeyer, J. and Wintrob, R. Folk criteria for the diagnosis of mental illness in rural Laos: On being insane in sane places. *American Journal of Psychiatry,* 1979, *136,* 755–761.

Wheelis, A. *The end of the modern age.* New York: Basic Books, 1971.

Wijesinghe, C. P., Dissanayke, S. A. W., and Mendis, N. Possession in a semi-urban community in Sri Lanka. *Australia and New Zealand Journal of Psychiatry,* 1976, *10,* 135–139.

Wilson, M. Witch beliefs and social structure. *American Journal of Sociology,* 1971, *56,* 307–313.

Wilson, P. J. Status ambiguity and spirit possession. *Man,* 1967, *2,* 366–379.

Wintrob, R. M. Sexual guilt and culturally sanctioned delusions in West Africa. *American Journal of Psychiatry,* 1968, *124,* 84–95.

Wintrob, R. M. Mammy water: Folk beliefs and psychotic elaboration in Liberia. *Canadian Psychiatric Association Journal,* 1970, *15,* 143–157.

Wintrob, R. M. The influence of others: Witchcraft and rootwork as explanations of disturbed behavior. *Journal of Nervous and Mental Disease,* 1973, *156,* 318–326.

Wittkower, E. D., and Weidman, H. H. Magic, witchcraft and sorcery in relation to mental health and mental disorder. *Social Psychiatry,* 1969. *89,* 169–184.

Woods, C. M. Alternative curing strategies in a changing medical situation. *Medical Anthropology,* 1977, *3,* 25–54.

Wuthnow, R. *The consciousness reformation.* Berkeley: University of California Press, 1976.

Yap, P. M. The possession syndrome: A comparison of Hong Kong and French findings. *Journal of Mental Science,* 1961, *106,* 114–137.

Yap, P. M. *Comparative psychiatry.* Toronto: University of Toronto Press, 1974.

Young, A. Why Amhara get Kureynya: Sickness and possession in an Ethiopian Zar cult. *American Ethnologist,* 1975, *2,* 567–584.

10. Protoconscious and Psychopathology

by Benjamin B. Wolman

The present chapter introduces a far-reaching revision of Freud's topographic theory of conscious, preconscious, and unconscious. The chief concept of this chapter, the protoconscious, is described as the bridge between conscious and unconscious phenomena; the so-called altered states of consciousness occur on the protoconscious level. Moreover, all psychopathological symptoms are viewed in this chapter as regressive, distorted, aggravated, frequent, and persistent instances of what could be regarded as normal occurrences. Consequently, protoconcious phenomena represent a bridge between normal behavior and psychopathology.

CONSCIOUS, UNCONSCIOUS, AND PROTOCONSCIOUS

The psychoanalytic theory of personality stresses three fundamental determinants, namely, dynamics, topography, and structure. Dynamics deals with the driving forces and the energies that they use. Eros and Thanatos are the driving forces, and libido and destrudo represent the energies at their disposal. Freud's topographic theory deals with the "mental layers" of conscious, preconscious, and unconscious. The structural theory introduces the three "mental agencies," namely, the id, ego, and superego (Freud, 1938). The present chapter suggests that Freud's topographic system be revised on the following lines:

First, there is hardly any reason for a distinction between the conscious and the preconscious layers. Conscious is what one *is* aware of at the present time; preconscious is what one *was* aware of and what can easily come back. In other words, what is right now *on* one's mind is conscious; what is *in* one's mind but not on one's mind at the present moment is preconscious. Apparently, conscious and preconscious are the same stuff, and preconscious is the storage room of the conscious. Both conscious and preconscious are accessible to reality testing; preconscious is the name for the memory link between the present and the past states of consciousness.

Unconscious is a totally different thing; it is what one is totally *unaware* of. Freud described a great many unconscious phenomena such as dreams, amnesia, errors of everyday life, and symptom formation. Unconscious is not a hypothesis; it is a fact proven by empirical research. Russian experimental studies of interoceptive conditioning deserve special attention because they come from a source not too sympathetic to Freud's theories (Bykov, 1957; Razran, 1961).

One may revise Freud's topographic theory by analyzing phenomena that were either unknown in Freud's times, or about which knowledge was inadequate. Sensory deprivation, biofeedback, and autogenic therapy were then unknown. Transcendental meditation, certain imagery processes, and parapsychological phenomena of telepathy and psychokinesis were not yet scrutinized by rigorous scientific research.

It is my conviction that all these phenomena are neither entirely conscious nor entirely unconscious. They are not conscious because there is no reality testing, yet the individual who experiences transcendental meditation or telepathy is aware that he does experience these phenomena. The dichotomy between being awake and conscious on one side and being asleep and unconscious on the other does not do full justice to what human beings experience. Psychomotor epileptics who attack innocent bystanders are both aware and unaware of what they are doing; they are neither unconscious somnambulists nor conscious muggers. Their state of mind is somewhere between conscious and unconscious—it is *protoconscious*. Sirhan Sirhan, when he killed Robert F. Kennedy, was not entirely aware of what he was doing; he was in a protoconscious state. Soon thereafter he totally forgot what he did; his amnesia was clearly unconscious. However, under hypnosis he did recall the assassination, and thus became conscious of what he had done (Fisher, 1976).

Protoconscious Phenomena

The dichotomy between sleep and wakefulness has been challenged by the so-called *lucid dreams*. The lucid dreamer is definitely asleep; thus he cannot be conscious. He is, however, aware that he is dreaming and, therefore, cannot be unconscious. In a lucid dream the dreamer is able to reason clearly, remember freely, and act volitionally upon reflection while being sound asleep and dreaming vividly (LaBerge, 1984). The lucid dreamer is aware that he is dreaming, and he can voluntarily control his respiration and even respond to electric shock without awakening. His state of mind is neither conscious nor unconscious; it is protoconscious.

Hartmann (1975) maintained that lucid dreams are not typical parts of the dreaming process but rather brief arousals that appear during NREM sleep in brief waking periods. However, LaBerge et al. (1981) reported lucid dreams in five subjects during REM sleep. It seems that lucid dreams can occur both in REM and in NREM sleep.

Most parapsychological phenomena belong to the category of protoconscious. The concept of *psi* includes telepathy, clairvoyance, and precognition (Rhine and Pratt, 1962). An individual experiencing parapsychological phenomena is aware of what he experiences, yet the content of the experience is not conscious. When one becomes aware of another person's feelings without sensory perceptions and without any possibility of proving or disproving them—as, for example, in telepathic experiences—he is neither in a conscious nor in an unconscious state; his mental state is definitely protoconscious (Ehrenwald, 1947; 1977; Eisenbud, 1970; Morris, 1977; Wolman et al., 1977).

It might be useful, at this point, to point to the difference between *cataplexy* and *catalepsy*. Cataplexy, which is a reduced muscle tonus with preservation of the conscious state, is a frequent and rather normal phenomenon associated with boredom, fatigue, and sleepiness. Catalepsy, which is a muscular hypertonus with a considerable decline or loss of conscious followed by amnesia, is a protoconscious state (Kales and Jacobson, 1967; Webb, 1977). In other words, in an unconscious state one is unaware of what he is experiencing; in a protoconscious state one is somewhat aware but lacks full control over his behavior; a conscious state is associated with both awareness and control.

Meditation is another example of a protoconscious state. The *Yoga Sutras,* the oldest known textbook of yoga, ascribes paranormal powers to meditation. The five stages of yoga gradually reduce external distractions and isolate the meditating individual. The first two stages reduce the awareness of one's emotions and desires; the third and fourth states reduce the awareness of bodily distractions. The fifth phase reduces the awareness of one's sensory apparatus and puts the meditating person into a protoconscious state of mind (Krishna, 1975).

The more recent meditation techniques used in psychotherapy are quite different from the earlier methods of transcendental meditation (TM). At the present time meditation is frequently used in stress-related illnesses, and it contributes to an increased rate of autonomic recovery. It is also used in treatment of insomnia, asthma, certain heart conditions, and pain control. In all these instances, this therapeutic method acts upon the meditating individual, whose mind is neither entirely conscious nor unconscious (Carrington and Stroebel, 1983).

Also sensory deprivation can induce a protoconscious state of mind. According to Goldberger (1977), sensory deprivation induces an altered state of consciousness characterized by: (1) *neurological* changes such as slowing in mean alpha frequency and appearance of marked delta; (2) changes in the *autonomic* system such as increased skin arousal; (3) *biochemical* changes in the levels of adrenaline and serum uric acid and urination; (4) *psychological* changes, especially hypnogogic and hypnopompic symptoms, and significant decline in motivation as well as apathy and boredom. Sensory deprivation does not make an individual totally unconscious, but he is not completely conscious; he is protoconscious.

Another instance of protoconscious can be assessed in the so-called phenomenon of *double hallucination* observed in post-hypnotic suggestions (Blum and Graef, 1971) when truly hypnotized subjects simultaneously perceived the real and the hallucinated image. Their state of mind can be described as being somewhere between the conscious and unconscious, that is, protoconscious.

NORMAL–ABNORMAL

Human behavior offers a galaxy of patterns. As long as it serves survival and enables people to attain the best possible level of adjustment, it is called normal. Maladjustive, self-defeating, and self-destructive behavior is called abnormal. Obviously, the difference between normal and abnormal individuals is often a matter of degree. The so-called normal people are, as it were, less crazy than the crazy ones. I believe that there is a continuum from being a well-adjusted individual to neurosis, to character neurosis, to latent psychosis, to manifest psychosis, and finally to total collapse of personality structure (Wolman, 1973).

The main criteria of mental health are: (1) the ability to perceive things as they are (reality testing); (2) emotional balance and self-discipline; (3) social adjustment; (4) awareness of one's potentialities. Disturbed people suffer from various degrees of damage to these functions, but the so-called normal individuals are not perfect and may suffer temporary and transient setbacks. Even a well-adjusted individual may occasionally experience delusions; but the more one is disturbed, the more frequent, the longer-lasting, and more severe are these states. Protoconscious moments may occur to everyone; in neurosis the ego-protective symptoms ward off most of them, in character neurosis the defenses dominate one's personality and behavior, in latent psychosis the individual desperately fights against the collapse of the conscious apparatus, in manifest psychosis the protoconscious and unconscious moods alternate, whereas in total collapse everything is unconscious (Fenichel, 1945; Wolman, 1973).

SOCIOCULTURAL INFLUENCES

In times of rapid sociocultural changes some sensitive individuals tend to develop visionary states and aspire to become social or religious reformers, mystics, or messiahs advocating or prophesying new ideas and new social, political, and cultural changes. McConnell (1973) compared the present-day loss of conventional beliefs and the rise of "philosophical anarchy" to the early Christian era with its mysticism and gnosticism. A survey of sales of occult books led him to conclude that we are in "a wild sea of superstition." There is at the present time a flood of pseudo-scientific articles, television programs, and books on ESP, astrology, and psychic powers and an unending succession of lectures, courses, and seminars on antiscientific occultism.

Periods of war, depression, and social disorder have fostered the belief that forgetting is the best escape from the fear of death. Sensual satisfaction seems to be the easiest route to quick amnesia. A desperate search for fun is a quick substitute for facing the inevitable dangers, and the more depressing the times are, the more urgent and widespread is the pursuit of sensual pleasures. Whenever the hopes for the future are dim and the sinking of the ship seems close, people are more inclined to evade hard thinking and coping with their problems, preferring regression to childlike blissful forgetting. There was never more wine, sex, bacchanalia, and orgies than in the time of decline of the Roman Empire, and no city was more a "fun-city" than Pompeii on the eve of its destruction (comparable to the present-day epidemic of alcoholism and drug abuse). Despair may drive people to escape into hedonism but it may also lead them on the second road of escape into mysticism. There is an unmistaken connection between the occult and the sensual, between orgies and magic, between the sublime and the vulgar. Ovid, Virgil, Horace, and the cult of Mithra were contemporaries of the Feasts of Lucullus and of Nero's arson and persecution of Christians. People get drunk not only by alcohol and opiates but also by occult and cabalistic practices. Unreality takes on many forms and shapes, and the belief in the supernatural and apocalyptic saviors and messiahs is the other side of the escapist coin. The proliferation of religious and pseudo-religious cults in our times— Scientology, Sun Myung Moon's Unification Church, Jim Jones, and others—bears witness to the infantile need to seek for a father figure and for renunciation of adult responsibilities. (Wolman, 1983, pp. 83–84)

Whereas the leaders of the various cults experience visual or auditory hallucinations, both the leaders and the followers experience various degrees of excitement. They often act in a totally irrational way, renounce their own families, neglect their social and cultural commitments, and give away their possessions; and in a recent case (the Jim Jones cult) they committed mass suicide. The behavior of the cultists is not unconscious, for they know what they are doing; but it certainly is not motivated or guided by conscious motivation. It represents a protoconscious case of mass-disorder.

SCHIZOPHRENIA

Several years ago I was teaching resident-psychiatrists in a postdoctoral program in a hospital attached to a medical school. One of the young psychiatrists whom I supervised, Dr. Strang, had a difficult time with Janice, a paranoid schizophrenic patient. In a meeting with the medical director (I did not take part in this meeting), Dr. Strang announced that he was not making any progress with Janice and refused to continue to treat her. Since no other resident agreed to work with Janice, the medical director decided to send her away from our university hospital to a state hospital. Next morning, when Dr. Strang had a day off, the medical director issued the proper direction to the nursing department.

That morning I came to the hospital two hours ahead of my schedule, and I went straight to the nurses' station. The head nurse greeted me with an expression of distress. "Janice got wild this morning," she said. "She came calmly to the nurses' station and asked for a pill for headache. Before the nurses had the chance to give her the pill, Janice attacked them, tearing their aprons, scratching their faces, breaking things, and screaming wildly. The nurses called the guards, who put Janice in a straitjacket and locked her up. Now, she is cursing and screaming!"

I asked the guards to bring Janice to my office, untie her, and wait for her outdoors. She stood at the door staring at the floor. She knew that I was Dr. Strang's supervisor. "Hi, Janice," I greeted her, "I am sorry that they locked you up. Dr. Strang has a day off today. Could you tell me what happened?"

Janice did not answer. She did not look at me. She stood still, staring with a faraway look in her eyes, and clenched her fists.

I started again. "I know you, Janice, as a quiet and friendly person. Somebody must have hurt you. You must feel horrible. Please, talk to me. I will help you. I will do everything I can to help you. I am so sorry, Janice. Please give me a chance."

Janice raised her head and stared at me. I offered her a cigarette. She refused.

I started again. "I would not let them tie your hands. I would not allow them to lock you up in the isolation room. If you don't feel like talking to me, you may go to your room or to the day room, whichever you prefer. But, please, tell me what happened. I will try to help you."

Janice looked at me. She cried. Her lips began to move, and I heard her mutter, "Soldiriver, soldiriver, soldiriver."

I could not understand. Apparently, she tried to tell me something. I felt utterly useless, a total failure, unworthy to teach psychiatry. I felt that all the years of graduate and postgraduate training were wasted on me, that I had not learned anything in seven years of supervision and twenty or more years of research, teaching, and clinical experience. Here stood in front of me an unhappy human being who called for help, and I was blind and deaf and heartless! Decades of training, and I did not know how to help her!

Suddenly, I had a brainstorm. It did not come from my conscious mind. But it did not come from the unconscious. The idea was crystal-clear, self-evident, absolutely sure. "They sold you down the river!" I exclaimed.

Janice sobbed loudly. I did reach her. We spoke the same language. We communicated at the same protoconscious level.

Janice came over and sat down on a chair I offered her near me. She told me, sobbing, what had happened. She was in love with Dr. Strang, but he didn't reciprocate, didn't feel anything for her. She still hoped to win him over when the blow came.

She had had a headache this morning and went to the nurses' station asking for a pill. While she waited for the nurses to get the pill, she overheard two nurses. The two were sitting at a desk writing something, and they did not notice her. One of the nurses wrote a note referring Janice to a state hospital. The nurse said that Dr. Strang requested the transfer because Janice was "a pain in the ass," and he could not stand her. The other doctors agreed with him, and no one wanted to work with her.

Janice felt like she had been hit with a thunderbolt. She tore up the transfer slip, hit one nurse, tore up the other nurse's apron, and attacked everybody else for selling her down the river.

Her actions were not completely conscious, nor were they totally unconscious. She knew what she was doing and remembered her actions, but could not control them. She was in a protoconscious state of mind.

So was I. That morning I had felt I had to rush to the hospital, and I went straight to the nurses' station. My words did not come from my conscious or preconscious mind, or from the unconscious. I was in a protoconscious state of mind, joining the mind of the schizophrenic girl.

TOPOGRAPHIC SHIFTS

Schizophrenia is usually associated with fluctuating modes and levels of mental functioning. One may assume that in a normal or rather balanced frame of mind people function on all three levels: (1) unconscious, which comes across in dreams; (2) protoconscious, when an individual is experiencing things he is somewhat aware of but has no control over; and (3) conscious, when the individual is aware of what he is doing and has full control of his behavior.

No schizophrenic is schizophrenic all the time. The level of his mental functioning shifts from one extreme to another, especially on the latent psychotic level. Latent psychotics can function reasonably well; often they are driven by fear of failure and strive for perfection. At the same time fatigue, inadequate or disturbed sleep, or even a mild frustration may throw them off and cause temporary or prolonged psychotic episodes, and in some instances even a psychotic breakdown. The intermittent states between adequate functioning and manifest psychosis are states of protoconsciousness. The pathological symptoms include disorientation, confusion, excessive irritability, and crying spells, but all these symptoms fluctuate between unconscious and protoconscious.

However, even manifest schizophrenics may act on a conscious level. A patient of mine maintained that I was General MacArthur. He suggested that I fight against President Truman and throw an atomic bomb on the North Koreans. However, when I told him, "Mr. Green, your time is over," he politely responded, "Goodbye, Dr. Wolman." A woman patient told me, "As I look on you, I know who you are: you are my mean brother." A few minutes later. "You are not my brother. You are Dr. Wolman."

As mentioned above, no schizophrenic is schizophrenic all the time.

I believe that the irrational way of thinking and acting of the schizophrenic is largely a product of the *situation* in which the schizophrenic finds himself *here and now*. Schizophrenia is a *field process,* a reaction to an unbearable social situation; it is, as repeatedly stated, an escape into a lower level of functioning. When the ego fails to keep the system together and everything seems to fall apart, some sort of abnormal adjustment is made. Schizophrenia is a morbid way of living that is adopted when every other way seems to have failed. Schizophrenic symptoms may become aggravated in unfavorable conditions and alleviated in favorable ones. The persistence of these symptoms may cause some damage to one's personality structure and intellectual functioning.

Apparently, the personality structure on all levels of schizo-type patients is far from being stable, and they easily shift from one topographic mental level to the other. The more disturbed they are, the weaker are the topographic boundaries and barriers. In hebephrenics, the barriers disappear, and they shift in a matter of seconds from unconscious to protoconscious to full conscious, back and forth.

A hospitalized thirty-two-year-old wife of a physician, who tried to kill her own child, told me: "I know I am an intelligent woman, but I hear voices. I am going to do something bad, very bad. As you know, I tried to kill my child. . . . "

Even hebephrenics are not hebephrenics all the time, though most of the time they function on unconscious level. Their disturbances in reality testing, cognitive functions, reasoning, and thought processes are most pronounced. Hebephrenics experience delusions of grandeur, hallucinate frequently, have ideas of reference and paranoid fears. They regress to primary prelogical and irrational ways of thinking. Their reasoning lacks purpose and consistency, is full of condensations and distortions, and their associations follow verbal, phonetic, or any other irrelevant clue. Their giggling, laughing, anger, or apprehension bears witness to their lack of contact with reality, and reflects unconscious processes.

Infants' neologisms and autistic language serve to express not-yet-socialized feelings and perceptions. Neologisms and autistic talk of adult schizophrenics contain a misused wealth of socially approved symbols. When the schizophrenic said "soldiriver," she meant that her doctor sold her down the river. She was somehow aware of it and obviously upset, reacting by garbled speech. "Soldiriver" was an expression of protest. It was on a protoconscious level.

Once a schizophrenic patient physically attacked the nurses. When she was finally subdued, she screamed, "We are outnumbered! Help!" But a few days later she admitted that she was glad that people "didn't take nonsense."

Will (1959) described a schizophrenic young woman who hit him, saying, "I haven't been able to hear you. You've been staying behind the wall of glass. It had to get broken somehow." The same patient often spoke sensibly.

PARAPSYCHOLOGY AND SCHIZOPHRENIA

Schizophrenia is associated with a good deal of *parapsychological experience* such as clairvoyance, precognition, and telepathy, and less frequently with out-of-body phenomena (Alberti, 1974; Arieti, 1961; Fischman, 1983; Ehrenwald, 1947; Ullman, 1953, 1977; Will, 1958, 1972; Wolman, 1973, 1979; and others). A schizophrenic can "sense" the moves of other people and be somewhat aware of their attitude to himself. Schizophrenics are especially sensitive to a hostile attitude.

One cannot fool schizophrenic patients—they can read the therapist's mind. I could conceal bad moods, fatigue, boredom, toothache, and even severe pain from all my patients except the schizophrenics. They always knew when something was wrong. The accuracy of their perceptions varied, but in many instances their assessment was quite correct. Some schizophrenic patients reported dreams that almost faithfully described recent events in my personal life. Ullman (1977, p. 563) wrote that the content of a schizophrenic patient's "telepathic forays into the private domain of the therapist is often embarrassingly revealing."

"There were times," Will (1959, p. 207) explained, in describing his treatment of a schizophrenic young woman, "when my own sentiments—anxiety, loneliness, depression, anger, uncertainty about myself and my function—were reflections of my patient's feelings."

Telepathic communication is a two-way street. (Stevenson, 1970) One day Dr. Will told a colleague: "I might as well not be here. It's like being in a cemetery; there isn't any life." At the same time the patient wrote: "I think I have been dead for many years. . . . Death is lonely, and I am a stranger to all of you and me" (ibid.).

Wilson and Reece (1964) reported the simultaneous deaths of schizophrenic twins hospitalized on two different wards in a mental hospital. Autopsy failed to discover the cause of their deaths; the only possible explanation could be related to parapsychology.

Years ago when I was teaching resident-psychiatrists in a university-affiliated hospital, I noticed that whenever there was tension at the staff meetings that were held in another building, there was an almost immediate trouble on the psychiatric wards. There was no way for the patients to know what was going on in a remote administrative office, but the minute we came from the staff meeting to the wards, the nurses reported quarrels and fights among the patients. On a few occasions we experienced a reverse process—a fight on a ward affected the moods at a staff meeting.

DELUSIONS AND HALLUCINATIONS

In most instances, schizophrenic patients hear voices when they *expect* to hear and, possibly, when they *wish* to hear. When a patient told me he heard voices telling him to assault the nurses, he somehow *knew* in advance what he would hear. It took a period of intensive psychotherapy to discover not only the patient's expectation, but also his awareness of what was going on. The voices were a *projection* of his hostility. This projection on outside forces that told him to act aggressively was a defense mechanism that protected him against, or at least reduced, unbearable guilt feelings.

The auditory hallucination was neither entirely conscious nor entirely unconscious. It was a protoconscious state. The projection was unconscious; the insight gained in psychotherapy was conscious. The voices came from the unconscious, and the patient's listening to them without being able to control them was protoconscious (Hartmann, 1975; Horowitz, 1977; Wolman, 1966).

Schizophrenic delusions can cover anything. A schizophrenic may feel that his hand turned into glass, or that his body is full of bugs. He may feel that his legs turned into lead, or that his nose is swollen. He may complain about his poor vision, or poor motor coordination, or not being himself any more. Loss of ego control over the perceptory and motor apparatus is experienced as a loss of identity. Unconscious images coming from within, hallucinations and delusions, deepen the feeling of not being one's self.

A twenty-two-year-old girl, Beverly, refused to go to college one day because "physical violence was planned against her" by another girl with whom she was friendly. The other girl had more initiative and was more outgoing than Beverly. Beverly reexperienced her fears of a demanding mother. When the girl confessed to Beverly some of her own troubles, Beverly panicked: here again was the powerful, omnipotent mother who demanded support from the girl. She projected her own hatred toward her friend and was sure her friend would attack her physically. The next step was to indulge in fantasies of cruel revenge against "her enemies." Anal-sadistic and oral-aggressive components were included in her daydreams, which bordered on hallucinations.

The drama of a schizophrenic personality overinvolved with and over-devoted to his parents evolves in a spectacular manner in delusions and hallucinations. What is carefully hidden and desperately repressed in the prepsychotic stages breaks through with an irresistible clarity in the display of protoconscious in manifest schizophrenics. Schizophrenics are not the rejected children; they are the "overdemanded," overcriticized, and over-involved ones. When rational controls break down, the conflict between the demand for perfection and the failure to meet this demand leads to one of the possible outcomes. Consider Harry's delusions: "Everybody in my office laughed at me. They said I was a coward and expected that I should find Suzie. They whispered that I was unfaithful to her. So I had to find her, to chase her, come what may." Harry, thirty years old, did not stop even before a sign: "Ladies' Room." He entered there in search of Suzie and "took the law into his hands." In his lucid moments he knew that Suzie, his college sweetheart, was presently married, had a child, and lived hundreds of miles away. When driven by delusions, Harry had "to prove" that he was faithful, that he was courageous, and that he would not betray

Suzie, who had a baby and thus was merged in his mind with his mother. He was seeing her face wherever he went, and he tried to talk to her about his love.

Stephen, thirty-six years old, was struggling with guilt feelings stemming from his mother's accusations. His father was a misfit, a drunkard and a poor provider, and a selfish and exploitative individual. His mother went to work to help support the family. She turned little Stephen into ally, friend, and confessor; she told Stephen about her misery and sufferings and her "sacrifice" for him, her only son. All her life, she said, she lived for Stephen only. But Stephen, she complained, was an ungrateful and lazy boy. When Stephen had a psychotic breakdown, he was awake for several nights reading, writing, and studying, as if to prove to his mother that he was a good boy. He felt that he "conquered sleep" and became the first man in the history of mankind "who could keep on working twenty-four hours a day."

Thirty-two-year-old Gladys was the oldest child in her family; her younger sister was also schizophrenic. Her father came to the United States from Russia and married an American-born girl who never stopped criticizing his foreign accent and "boorish manners." As far back as Gladys could remember, her parents had argued bitterly and criticized each other mercilessly. Occasionally they came to blows. Father accused mother of being a poor housekeeper and a mean person; mother accused father of being unintelligent, below her intellectual level, an egoist, and a brute. Both parents admitted (in separate interviews) that they enjoyed their married life prior to Gladys' birth. "Since that girl was born, I lost my wife. She didn't pay any attention to me. I am a sick man but no one cares for me," the father said.

Gladys was a latent schizophrenic with several manifest psychotic episodes and periods of remission. After childbirth she felt very elated and began to hallucinate. She was now a mother and could see God. God spoke to her; God loved her. She was to become omnipotent and omniscient, a God herself. She was entrusted by God to protect Russia and America (father and mother) and make peace between them. She felt she could control the world and feared nothing. As a God she finally overcame her perplexing fear of death. Now she would never die.

George, a twenty-eight-year-old schizophrenic, told the following story: "My boss gave me a look that meant a demand. He demanded my friendship. But I didn't feel I owed him anything, so I gave him a harsh look. Then he began to mimic me whenever he saw me. He made people call me on the phone and hang up. Next day I gave him a very hostile look. Then he said loudly to another man, 'Let's forget it.' I am sure he said it intentionally loud so I could hear him. His words meant, 'I do not demand anything from George.' You see, I won. He cannot force me to be his friend. But now I am afraid I hurt his feelings, and he may abandon me.''

George's father had tried to win George over as an ally against his hated wife, the boy's mother. The father acted seductively with poorly veiled homosexual undercurrents. George feared his protoconscious homosexual thoughts and was trying to repress them. But here is the typical schizophrenic conflict with no way out. If you yield to a homosexual temptation, you are a bad person; if you fight it off, you will be forsaken. You feel trapped. The desperate situation leads into a more morbid, more confused, and more irrational state of mind.

According to Sullivan (1962), schizophrenics fear "collapse," and that they themselves will turn into nothingness. They wish for things around them and inside themselves not to change. They insist on sameness, on continuity, and any digression from routine produces anxiety.

Two conclusions can be drawn from Sullivan's observation. First, there is a close affinity between obsession–compulsion and schizophrenia; I maintain that schizophrenia is a further step down in hypervectorial (schizo-type) disorders, whereas obsessive–compulsive neurosis is the first step. The second conclusion is related to the schizophrenic fear of change and its resemblance to autism. I believe that infantile autism is one of the syndromes of early childhood schizophrenia (Wolman, 1970).

Will (1972) interpreted catatonic withdrawal and stupor as an effort to avoid embarrassment and humiliation. Schizophrenics feel overresponsible and try to overcontrol their own behavior. However, as their efforts are doomed to fail, and they are confronted with criticism, embarrassment, and humiliation, they tend to eschew all responsibility. At the catatonic stage they become rigid and stuporous, renouncing any activity whatsoever, or they surrender passively to any orders from without.

The fear of total collapse was well demonstrated by a vivid dream of a schizophrenic on a latent and protoconscious psychotic level. The patient, a successful and prominent female executive, was a paragon of proper and virtuous behavior. She was a perfectionist who overextended her protective responsibility to practically all aspects of her life. In her dream she lost control of her car and was racing toward a black curtain. A deep precipice lay behind the curtain. Her dream was unconscious, reflecting her protoconscious fear and wish to escape into nothingness.

Many emotional experiences of catatonics and hebephrenics belong to the protoconscious state. Their fear of total dissolution often leads to magic thinking intended to restore their peace of mind. Sometimes they believe that a magic number or a magic slogan will restore their control over themselves and their environment.

Even catatonic patients are not totally unreachable, that is, totally unconscious. A catatonic patient, Bernice, thirty-two-years old, did not talk, was tube-fed, and did not move. She communicated with her fingers. When she was upset, her fingers were stiff, immobile, clenched, cold, and moist. When I sat down next to her, we did communicate. I communicated verbally, she nonverbally. When I said a few pleasant, friendly things to her, she responded, sometimes with a smile, sometimes with her hands. Her fingers became warm, soft, and relaxed. A schizophrenic patient put her arm around Bernice and said to her in a soft voice, "Bernice, I shall read you the *Times* magazine." Then she turned around to me and said, "Doctor, Bernice agreed." She sat down close to Bernice and read to her. The first person who got Bernice to talk was that patient.

SCHIZOPHRENIC DREAMS

In schizophrenics there is not much difference between the content of unconscious dreams and their protoconscious delusions and some hallucinations. Quite often schizophrenic dreams do not use any disguise, and their content is obvious, sometimes void of symbols. Many patients reported dreams of being beaten, raped, kidnapped, lost, rejected, left alone, and brutally assaulted. The fear of death was the prevailing theme of these dreams.

Schizophrenics often dream of neglecting their duties, forgetting to do things, missing appointments, failing to prepare homework for school, breaking things, being blamed and accused for all kinds of transgression and misbehavior.

These dreams often represent their own aggressive impulses and fear of them. One patient had a dream in which she was supposed to watch lions in cages, but the lions broke loose and attacked people. The patient woke up screaming for help. Another patient saw reptiles and tried to fight them off in his dream.

Dreams about wild animals, usually representing their own sexual and aggressive impulses, frequently occur in latent and manifest schizophrenics. One patient reported the following dream about her hated stepmother: "My stepmother and father fought. Father killed her. I cut my stepmother into pieces, and we ate her. I woke up in horror, and was upset all the day. I must be a very mean person. I hate my stepmother, but it was terrible to eat her."

There is no limit to regression in dreams. The most hostile dreams point to profound regressive tendencies, thus supporting the hypothesis that destrudo is more primitive than libido.

A thirty-year-old patient dreamed about an infant burned alive. She woke up and felt that she was the child destroyed by flames. Another patient dreamed that people poisoned him. Another dreamed that someone came to strangle him. Still another reported a dream in which she was hiding behind several doors and a gorilla (her father) broke through and raped her.

Schizophrenics often report dreams in which their fathers, mothers, spouses, and friends disappear. They call and no one answers. Sometimes they dream of running after lost love-objects and not being able to catch them; then they wake up in utter despair.

Sometimes they dream that their parents or other love-objects are dying, and the dreamers cannot help. They wake up in the middle of the night, unable to fall asleep again. Many of them are afraid to go to sleep, fearing that they may lose self-control and something terrible will happen. They desperately strive to master their impulses and are in panic when their impulses break through.

Often in dreams schizophrenic patients identify themselves with a parental figure and practice incestuous sex. A twenty-six-year-old woman dreamed that she gave birth to her younger sister. Many women dream about sex with a duke, a noble, or other authority figures representing father. Sometimes the symbolism does not apply to the father, but to the intercourse. A female patient reported she was "climbing" with her father; another was sliding and gliding with her father. The psychoanalytic symbolism is obvious in all these cases, and obvious to the patients themselves.

A man reported a dream in which he had intercourse with a woman who had two sons. His first reaction: "my mother."

The more the patients deteriorate, the less sharp is the line dividing dreams from the waking state. Ultimately, in severe deterioration the dream wins, and reality disappears. They dream while awake; they hallucinate.

CHILDHOOD SCHIZOPHRENIA

Goldfarb and Mintz (1961) described schizophrenic children's disorientation in time and space that makes it impossible for them to experience themselves and the world around them as temporarily and spatially continuous. This disorientation makes these children fear changes, and they insist on continuity and familiarity. I believe that infantile autism is a severe form of childhood schizophrenia (Wolman 1970) and these children fear change and insist on sameness. In milder cases, children disoriented in time and space tend to wander aimlessly, unable to find their way home.

I maintain that these children are not totally unconscious, but they function on the protoconscious level with occasional regressions to unconsciousness and progression to consciousness. Goldfarb and Mintz (1961, p. 538) described several defensive behavior patterns of schizophrenic children, all of them conducted on protoconscious levels. These behavioral patterns include: (1) withdrawal; (2) perseveration, seeking of sameness and resisting change and novelty; (3) confabulations; (4) compulsive overconcern with time and space, leading to endless questions about where things are and when things happen, and preoccupation with clocks, schedules, maps, and so on.

OTHER MENTAL DISORDERS

A neurotic can be defined as a person who in order to avoid an imaginary harm creates harmful situations. The obsessive–compulsive develops rituals that should by some magic protect him from nonexistent dangers, and a hysteric develops psychosomatic symptoms that should make him unable to face threatening situations. A phobic develops imaginary fears that he can cope with and uses them as a substitute for fears that he believes he cannot cope with. Agoraphobia is a good example. I had a patient who had considerable difficulty in relating to women, and he believed that no woman would ever accept his advances. In his wet dreams he violently attacked women and forced them to do whatever he wished in genital or oral sex. His unconscious wish to "punish" women for rejecting him and his rape-dreams had led to a fear that he might, indeed, attack women on the street; hence his tendency to stay home and refusal to go out alone.

Arieti (1961) suggested that phobias are a product of concretization in accordance with a general principle in psychopathology: whatever cannot be sustained on an abstract level elicits severe anxiety, becomes reduced, and is *concretized*. Patients on the prepsychotic level suffer severe feelings of general inadequacy, whereas on the manifest psychotic level the same patients may hear voices blaming them for a *particular* inadequacy. Moreover, phobic patients retain the ability for testing reality and are aware of the irrationality of their fears. The phobogenic objects are perceived not as hostile and plotting agents but as disturbing factors; phobias are introjections, paranoid projections. The phobic fear replaces a host of other fears that are not acknowledged and which the patient is unaware of.

Apparently phobias are protoconscious phenomena. A patient of mine was afraid of cats. She was making fun of her fear of little kittens and was aware how irrational her fear was. She was, however, unable to test reality and overcome her fears. Whe she dreamed about a huge cat scratching her arm, the interpretation of her dreams brought back the memory of the vicious cat—her mother. The phobia was protoconscious, the dream unconscious; the dream interpretation made her conscious of her punitive mother.

SOMNAMBULISM

When people are totally unaware of their mental or physical actions, their behavior is unconscious; but sleepwalking, sleeptalking, and other motor activities while the person remains asleep belong to the protoconscious. These activities rarely occur in childhood; they become more frequent at ages ten through fourteen, and usually disappear in adulthood. They are, however, a quite frequent occurrence in disturbed individuals. A study of neurotics in military service reported a 6 percent incidence of episodic sleep-walking (Webb, 1977).

Kales and Jacobson (1967) conducted laboratory research in somnam-bulism with seven children and four adults. The children had many sleep-walking experiences. As they walked around, they appeared to be aware of but not too concerned with the environment. They walked around with their eyes wide open. Some of their actions did not serve any apparent purpose: they touched the door, rubbed a blanket, and so on. When talked to, they answered in monosyllables. Their behavior appeared to be somewhat rit-ualistic and rigid. When awakened, they had no recollection of their be-havior.

I assume that their behavior was protoconscious; at awakening it was repressed and became unconscious. Sleepwalking occurs at stage four, at the deepest level of sleep, and it is not associated with the dream phases of sleep.

DEPRESSIVE DISORDERS

The name manic–depressive disorder is a misnomer; it is just psychotic depression. I called this disorder "dysmutual," for depressive patients change from joy to sorrow, love to hate, omnipotence to helplesness (Wol-man, 1973). The depressive or dysmutual disorders can be presented on a continuum of five levels: neurosis, character neurosis, latent psychosis, manifest psychosis, and total personality collapse. The manifest psychosis level, usually called manic–depressive psychosis, is manifest depressive (dys-mutual) psychosis.

One can distinguish four clinical patterns in dysmutual psychosis. These four syndromes, analogous to the syndromes of manifest schizophenia, are not closed clinical entities. They are descriptive categories, related to ob-servable symptoms and personality structure. Shifts from one clinical pat-tern to another are common.

The first syndrome is *depression,* which is the basic state of dysmutual psychosis. However, when the ego and the superego merge, a defense mech-anism on the protoconscious level of blissful elation or mania begins.

The second syndrome is *paranoia*. It occurs when the failing ego externalizes superego pressures, perceiving the world as the rejecting, punishing mother who will eventually be forced to accept the suffering child.

The third syndrome is *agitated-depression*. This syndrome manifests itself when the ego is crushed between the cruel superego and the savage id. There are no elated moods, no escape mechanisms, no respite from severe depression. Danger of suicide runs high in this syndrome.

The final and most regressive syndrome is *simple deterioration,* which occurs when both ego and superego are defeated by the triumphant id. There is some analogy between these four syndromes and the four syndromes of schizophrenic psychosis, especially with regard to the simple deterioration syndromes in both types of mental disorder.

Elated moods of depressive patients are protoconscious. Patients are aware of their excitement, but are unable to control it or to test it against reality. In elation there is no delay, no reality principle, no planning or caution. Whatever the manic feels like doing, he will do immediately, here and now. If he is sexually aroused, he may proposition the first girl he meets and become furious if she turns him down. If he is highly aroused, he is likely to rape her. He cannot take the slightest frustration.

The depressive patient's delusions and hallucinations have a lot to do with martyrdom, with being lost and found, with being Cinderalla saved by a good fairy or a slave led by a messiah toward a promised land. A typical fantasy of depressives is of a disaster that will force their mother to love them.

Schizophrenics wish to be God or Messiah. Since their parents have been weak and unreliable individuals, they must fill the void by becoming the omnipotent, omniscient, benevolent, or destructive God-Father, who saves, protects, or punishes their parents. Thus, whereas the schizophrenic rescues, the manic–depressive wants to be rescued. In the manic phase, he can be joined with the powerful parents and thereby acquire omnipotence and immortality.

However, even in a manic mood there is an underlying fear of losing a newly regained paradise. Manic patients avoid facing real issues out of fear that the sharp pin of reality may prick the balloon of their blissful illusion. Thus no real planning or practical steps are taken for fear that the implementation of an idea may bring hardships and disappointment.

The slightest disappointment, true or imaginary, may elicit a severe depression. One dysmutual psychotic patient rambled about his grandiose literary plans. He was writing, at one and the same time, a play, a novel, a philosophical essay, a study of the American economy, a survey of contemporary literature, and a textbook in industrial psychology, all of which were to be finished within the next three months and hopefully win him immortality. A few days later he was in the throes of despair and self-accusation. He sat in an armchair in my office, crying and accusing himself of being a complete failure. He blamed himself for the loss of a few dollars and tearfully recalled sad events that had occurred in the distant past: ten years ago he had lost something, and fifteen years ago it was something else. "I am a loser; I always lose things. I have never done anything right," he bemoaned. He contemplated suicide and blamed his wife (apparently a mother substitute) for not loving him enough.

Another patient, a married woman, was picking up men on the street in front of her building. She invited them upstairs, slept with them, and gave them all sorts of gifts. She was neither unconscious nor fully conscious of her deeds. Her actions reflected her protoconscious state of mind.

Manic–depressives are inclined to assume self-righteous attitudes with a total disregard for reality, and the fusion between their ego and superego gives them a protoconscious feeling of blissful omnipotence.

A hospitalized musician in an elated mood assured me that he was the greatest living composer and soon would outdo the great masters of the past. However, his mood soon changed, and in agitated-depression he denied having any abilities whatsoever; he hated himself and everyone else.

Destructiveness and self-destructiveness are the outstanding features of agitated-depression. Because the defeated ego is incapable of reality testing, casual approval by a nurse seemed to offer the patient a reason for living, whereas her son's lack of interest in her precipitated a violent destructive and self-destructive reaction. Thus, a slight sign of rejection or hate may unleash in dysmutual psychotics uncontrollable protoconscious outbursts of object and self-directed destrudo.

CONCLUDING REMARKS

The aims of this chapter, as stated at the beginning, were to introduce the concept of protoconscious and to apply it to an understanding of psychopathological issues. It must, however, be reiterated that protoconscious phenomena also occur in well-adjusted individuals. They occur infrequently and are less severe, but they do occur.

Consider excessive emotional episodes. All human beings may get furious and experience mental states that are neither fully conscious nor fully unconscious. Excitement, panic, and any other high-intensity emotion is protoconscious.

When these exaggerated emotional states are severe, frequent, and persistent, and they dominate the mental state of the individual and determine his or her behavior, they clearly belong to psychopathology.

REFERENCES

Alberti, G. Psychopathology and parapsychology. In A. Angoff and B. Shapin (Eds.), *Parapsychology and the sciences.* New York: Parapsychology Foundation, 1974, pp. 225–233.

Arieti, S. A re-examination of the phobic symptom and of symbolism in psychopathology. *American Journal of Psychiatry,* 1961, *118,* 106–110.

Blum, G. S. and Graef, J. R. The detection over time of subjects simulating hypnosis. *International Journal of Clinical and Experimental Hypnosis,* 1971, *19,* 211–224.

Bykov, K. M. *The cerebral cortex and the inner organs.* New York: Chemical Publishing, 1957.

Carrington, P. and Stroebel, C. F. Meditation: its clinical use. In B. B. Wolman (Ed.), *International Encyclopedia of Psychiatry, Psychoanalysis and Neurology: Progress Volume 1.* New York: Aesculapius, 1983, pp. 256–261.

Ehrenwald, J. *Telepathy and medical psychology.* Londong: George, Allen, Unwin, 1947.

Ehrenwald, J. Psi, psychotherapy, and psychoanalysis. In B. B. Wolman (Ed.), *Handbook of parapsychology.* New York: Van Nostrand Reinhold, 1977, pp. 529–540.

Eisenbud, J. *Psi and psychoanalysis.* New York: Grune & Stratton, 1970.

Fenichel, O. *Psychoanalystic theory of neurosis.* New York: Norton, 1945.

Fischer, R. State-bound knowledge. *Psychology Today,* 1976, *10,* 68–72.

Fishman, L. G. Dreams, hallucinogenic drug states, and schizophrenia. *Schizophrenia Bulletin,* 1983, *9,* 73–94.

Freud, S. (1938). *An outline of psychoanalysis.* New York: Norton, 1949.

Goldberger, L. Sensory deprivation. In B. B. Wolman (Ed.), *International Encyclopedia of Psychiatry, Psychology, Psychoanalysis and Neurology,* vol. 10. New York: Aesculapius, 1977, pp. 156–159.

Goldfarb, W. and Mintz, I. Schizophrenic child's reaction to time and space. *Archives of General Psychiatry,* 1961, *5,* 535–543.

Hartmann, E. Dreams and other hallucinations: In approach to the underlying mechanism. In R. K. Siegel and L. J. West (Eds.), *Hallucinations: behavior, experience, and theory.* New York: Wiley, 1975.

Horowitz, M. J. Consciousness, altered states, and imagery: Psychoanalytic research. In B. B. Wolman (Ed.), *International Encyclopedia of Psychiatry, Psychology, Psychoanalysis and Neurology, Vol. 3.* New York: Aesculapius, 1977, pp. 346–350.

Kales, A. and Jacobson, A. Mental activities during sleep: Recall studies, somnambulism, and effects of rapid eye movement deprivation and drugs. In C. Clemente (Ed.), *Experimental neurology.* New York: Academic Press, 1967, pp. 81–90.

Krishna, G. *The awakening of kundalini.* New York: Dutton, 1975.

LaBerge, S. *Awake in your dreams: The new world of lucid dreaming.* New York: Simon & Schuster, 1984.

LaBerge, S. P., Nagel, L. E., Dement, W. C., and Zarcone, V. P. Lucid dreaming verified by volitional communication during REM sleep. *Perceptual and Motor Skills,* 1981, *52,* 727–732.

McConnell, R. A. Parapsychology and the occult. *Journal of the American Society for Psychical Research,* 1973, *67,* 225–243.

Morris, R. L. Parapsychology, biology, and anpsi. In B. B. Wolman (Ed.), *Handbook of parapsychology.* New York: Van Nostrand Reinhold, 1977, pp. 687–715.

Razran, G. The observable unconscious and the inferable conscious in current Soviet psychophysiology: Interoceptive conditioning, semantic conditioning, and the orienting reflex. *Psychological Review,* 1961, *68,* 81–147.

Rhine, J. B. and Pratt, J. G. *Parapsychology: Frontier science of the mind,* rev. ed. Springfield, Ill.: Thomas, 1962.

Stevenson, I. Telepathic impressions: A review and a report of thirty-five new cases. *Proceedings of the American Society for Psychical Research*, 1970, *29*, 1–98.

Sullivan, H. S. Socio-psychiatric research: Its implications for the schizophrenic problem and for mental hygiene. In H. S. Perry (Ed.), *Schizophrenia as a human process*. New York: Norton, 1962.

Ullman, M. The dream, schizophrenia, and psi phenomena. Paper read at the First International Conference on Parapsychology, Utrecht, Netherlands, 1953.

Ullman, M. Psychopathology and psi phenomena. In B. B. Wolman, L. A. Dale, G. R. Schmeidler, and M. Ullman (Eds.), *Handbook of Parapsychology*. New York: Van Nostrand Reinhold, 1977.

Webb, W. B. Somnambulism. In B. B. Wolman (Ed.), *International Encyclopedia of Psychiatry, Psychology, Psychoanalysis and Neurology*, vol. 10. New York: Aesculapius, 1977, pp. 368–370.

Will, O. A., Jr. Relatedness and the schizophrenic reaction. *Psychiatry*, 1959, *22*, 205–223.

Will, O. A., Jr. Catatonic behavior in schizophrenics. *Contemporary Psychoanalysis*, 1972, *9*, 29–58.

Wilson, I. C. and Reece, J. G. Simultaneous death in schizophrenic twins. *Archives of General Psychiatry*, 1964, *11*, 377–384.

Wolman, B. B. *Vectoriasis praecox or the group of schizophrenias*. Springfield, Ill.: Thomas, 1966.

Wolman, B. B. *Children without childhood: A study in childhood schizophrenia*. New York: Grune & Stratton, 1970.

Wolman, B. B. *Call no man normal*. New York: International Universities Press, 1973.

Wolman, B. B. Dreams and schizophrenia. In B. B. Wolman et al. (Eds.), *Handbook of dreams*. New York: Van Nostrand Reinhold, 1979, pp. 388–405.

Wolman, B. B. Deculturation and disinhibition. In B. B. Wolman (Ed.), *International Encyclopedia of Psychiatry, Psychology Psychoanalysis and Neurology. Progress Volume 1*. New York: Aesculapius, 1983, pp. 82–86.

Wolman, B. B., Dale, L. A., Schmeidler, G. R., and Ullman, M. (Eds.), *Handbook of parapsychology*. New York: Van Nostrand Reinhold, 1977.

11. Psi Phenomena as Related to Altered States of Consciousness

Stanley Krippner and Leonard George

Long before the advent of recorded history, tribal shamans would enter altered states of consciousness in attempts to locate lost objects, foretell the future, communicate with someone at a distance, or heal an injured person. These events may have been examples of clairvoyance (unexplained awareness of hidden objects or distant events), precognition (unexplained knowledge of a future event), telepathy (unexplained information of another person's mental content or cognition), and psychokinesis (unexplained influence upon external objects or processes). Together they are referred to as "psi," purported interactions between organisms and their environment (including other organisms) that appear to transcend the ordinary constraints of time, space, and force. Parapsychology is the scientific study of psi; most of the researchers in this field are members of the Parapsychological Association, which has been an affiliate member of the American Association for the Advancement of Science since 1969.

The first group to devote itself to the scientific study of psi was the Society for Psychical Research, organized in London in 1882. Its members were especially interested in studying life after death, ghosts, and mediums (Kelly and Locke, 1981). Hypnosis, which had been linked to psi since the days of Mesmer, was a frequent topic of investigation and discussion. In 1885, the American Society for Psychical Research was founded; once more an active interest was demonstrated in mediums and the information they produced in altered conscious states through their "spirit controls."

FROM MEDIUMSHIP TO CARD GUESSING

One investigator of psi, William McDougall, was teaching psychology at Harvard when a prominent medium, Mina Crandon, was exposed as guilty of fraud. The American Society for Psychical Research, heavily committed in her favor, was nearly shattered by the scandal. McDougall had expressed skepticism in Crandon, as had J. B. and Louisa E. Rhine, two biologists who had been inspired by McDougall and who moved to Duke University in 1927 to join him. Taking a lesson from the Crandon debacle, the three scientists determined to rebuild parapsychology on a quantitative, statistical base.

The idea of using probability theory was not a new one: Charles Richet had carried out ESP tests using playing cards in 1889; at about the same time William Barrett and others were conducting card tests in England (Beloff, 1977, p. 18). The technique required that an individual guess the identity of cards that were hidden (clairvoyance), that were randomly selected at some future date (precognition), or that were seen at a distance by others (telepathy). These three forms of psi were referred to as "extrasensory perception" or ESP. Psychokinesis or PK was also tested objectively by having subjects concentrate on a randomly selected number while dice were being thrown. In both these ESP and PK tests, success was measured in terms of "deviation from chance expectancy."

The Duke University tests were run while people were in their ordinary conscious state, although the importance of such emotional components as motivation, rapport, and optimism was noted. J. B. Rhine had tested the celebrated medium Eileen Garrett, obtaining ESP results far in excess of chance expectancy (Birge and Rhine, 1942). However, Garrett's performances in ordinary and mediumistic conditions were about equal, and Rhine did not pursue this line of exploration. Rhine's associate J. G. Pratt attempted to statistically evaluate the medium's "readings," having Garrett's clients rate how probable it was that the "readings" applied to them. Unfortunately, many of the statements were not independent of each other, and this created statistical problems (Pratt and Birge, 1948). Nevertheless, Garrett volunteered her services for parapsychological research projects on several occasions and, in 1961, established the Parapsychological Foundation to further the exploration of psi.

Duke University also began to continue the work with hypnosis instigated by the Society for Psychical Research. However, Rhine (Rhine et al., 1940/1966) dispensed with hypnosis in the late 1930s, stating that his group could not decide what directions to give hypnotized subjects to improve their ESP scores. The Duke team, instead, focused upon a motivated waking state as being most appropriate for their subjects. Another area described by Rhine (1977, p. 35) as a "bad risk" problem was out-of-body experience (OBE). A Swedish exponent, John Björkhem, was actually invited to Duke, but Rhine's group could find no clear method to distinguish OBEs from less exotic psi performance.

It has been suggested that Rhine's abandonment of mediumship and hypnosis served to attain a certain degree of respectability for the field (Parker, 1975b, p. 15). After all, psychology had improved its scientific image when it redefined itself from "the study of consciousness" to "the study of behavior," restricting its subject matter to externally observable events. As Rhine (1977) later stated, "such success as was attained owed much to the discipline of adhering to problems that were logically possible to solve with the methods available" (p. 35).

DREAMS AND PSI

However, the Duke University team did not ignore spontaneous cases, many of which involved various alterations of consciousness. Although cases could not be used as proof of psi, J. B. Rhine (1948) observed their suggestive value; ideas raised could be tested experimentally and their validity decided. In response to J. B. Rhine's call for case material, thousands of letters were received at Duke; their collation and evaluation was attempted by L. E. Rhine—a task that was to occupy her for a quarter of a century. By 1973, she had tabulated 12,659 cases of reported ESP and 178 of PK.

In one analysis of these anecdotes, L. E. Rhine (1962) observed that 65 percent consisted of dreams. In addition, dreams contained a greater amount of complete information about the event in question than did the waking state. In one of L. E. Rhine's (1981) cases, a woman in Minnesota was working in a home for elderly people and dreamed that her daughter, Mary Jane, who was in California, came up behind her and embraced her. The mother said, "My God, it's Mary Jane," and then she saw the girl's face was gray and drawn—and also realized that she was very cold. The dream worried her, and she told her employer about it. Three days later, Mary Jane unexpectedly arrived in Minnesota; she had driven there from Los Angeles, encountering a snowstorm and two near accidents. She was cold, gray, and exhausted (p. 18).

L. E. Rhine's analysis demonstrated some similarities to clinical studies published by psychotherapists whose patients sometimes reported dreams of a presumptive paranormal nature (e.g., Devereux, 1953). Sigmund Freud, who was ambivalent about the existence of psi phenomena, wrote several articles speculating on relationships between psychoanalysis and both telepathic and precognitive dreams (e.g., Freud, 1922).

If Freud was the first major figure in psychiatry to attach scientific importance to ESP in dreams, the credit for being the first psychiatrist to devise a method to test for it experimentally must go to Montague Ullman. His method incorporated several of the features of real-life phenomena into the laboratory situation. As a radical departure from the repetitious card-guessing feats, Ullman used art prints as targets; since they often have emotional content, they were thought to be suitable stimuli to be incorporated into dreams (Parker, 1975b, pp. 87–88).

Ullman's initial subject was Eileen Garrett; electrodes were attached to her head so that the objective EEG indicators for dreaming (e.g., rapid eye movements, changes in brain waves) could be employed. Ullman himself served as agent, and some striking correspondences between target pictures and dreams were reported during both nights of a pilot study (Ullman et al., 1973, pp. 85–89).

In 1962, a dream laboratory was established at Brooklyn's Maimonides Medical Center where Ullman initiated formal, experimental work (Tolaas and Ullman, 1979). Stanley Krippner joined him in 1964, and they conducted thirteen dream and ESP experiments over the next ten years (Ullman et al., 1973). In nine instances the results were statistically significant; all nine involved four apparently "gifted" individuals, either as the sole subject for at least seven nights or as one of several subjects who participated on a one-night basis. In seven instances, the ESP task was telepathic; in the other two it was precognitive.

The subject for the precognitive studies was Malcolm Bessent, an English "sensitive" with a history of presumptive spontaneous experiences. A "recorder" remained in an isolated room all night, having no contact with Bessent or with the experimenters who observed the electroencephalographic readings, awakening Bessent when the brain waves and rapid eye movements indicated he had been dreaming. In the case of the second study (Ullman and Krippner, 1978) another experimenter (who had not been present while the subject's dreams were being collected) randomly selected a box of multisensory materials, accompanied by instructions for the recorder. The random selection took place after the dreams had been tape-recorded and after Bessent had been interviewed about his dreams. For example, on one morning the box of materials contained a Kodak carousel of slides depicting birds as well as a cassette of taped bird calls. Excerpts from Bessent's interview follow:

I remember seeing various kinds of doves. Ring-tailed doves, ordinary doves, Canadian geese. (p. 414)

A few ducks and things. It's fairly misty, but there are quite a lot of mandrake geese and various birds of some kind swimming around in rushes or reeds. . . . I just have a feeling that the next target material will be about birds. (p. 414)

I wrote a poem a couple of days ago about freedom and birds, and the last couple of lines were . . . "Even birds aren't free; they have gravity to contend with." (pp. 414–415)

These statements were made *before* the random number had been selected directing the recorder to the box containing the slides and cassette. The recorder then placed the slide carousel in a projector and showed them to Bessent; the recorded bird calls were played through stereo earphones on his head. Three outside judges, working blind and independently, attempted to match the eight transcribed sets of dreams against the eight slide-and-sound presentations. The mean of their scores was statistically analyzed and found to be highly significant (Ullman and Krippner, 1978).

Attempted replications of the Maimonides work have met with mixed results (e.g., Sargent and Harley, 1982), even though two of the "gifted" subjects were utilized in three of the studies (Van de Castle, 1977). Furthermore, J. B. Rhine (1977) asked whether the results, based as they were on outside ratings of correspondences between dreams and target pictures, were "due to the subject, the experimenter, or the targets" (p. 44). From a practical point of view, EEG-monitored dream research is expensive and time-consuming if conducted in a systematic, thorough-going way. Nevertheless, Ullman's procedures were well received by most members of the parapsychological community and stimulated a revival of altered states research in relationship to psi.

HYPNOSIS AND PSI

In the 1930s, parapsychology's development mirrored that of psychology when it abandoned subjectivity to focus on externally observable events. In the 1960s, a similar event occurred; psychology had again acknowledged the importance of inner events and now had the tools to study them. Again psychology was redefined, this time as the "study of behavior and experience." EEG monitoring equipment allowed the Maimonides team to investigate ESP in dreams, just as it had already given behavioral scientists an opportunity to retrieve dream content in a systematic way.

In both psychology and parapsychology, however, hypnotic phenomena had escaped the behaviorists' purge of the subjective (Honorton and Krippner, 1969). The Nobel-prize-winning physiologist Charles Richet, the first to apply statistics to ESP studies, also pioneered the study of hypnosis and psi. In one instance, a "gifted" subject was instructed to observe Richet's laboratory while hypnotized; she is said to have correctly reported a fire. On another occasion, she was asked to describe the behavior of a colleague of Richet; reportedly, she described his burning his hand with a brown liquid at about the time that he had accidentally burned his hand with bromine (Richet, 1889).

The first systematic study involving hypnosis was reported by J. J. Grela in 1945. He assigned eleven subjects to a "hypnosis" group and ten to a "waking suggestion" group. ESP guessing tasks were completed by the hypnosis group in three conditions: a non-hypnosis ESP attempt, hypnotic induction with positive suggestions aimed at instilling belief in ESP and the confidence to demonstrate it, and hypnotic induction with negative suggestions. The waking suggestion subjects were given positive suggestions. For the hypnosis group the difference between the positive and negative suggestion conditions was statistically significant. Chance results were obtained in the waking condition and by the subjects given waking suggestions.

Charles Honorton (1977) surveyed the Grela study and fifteen other ESP card-guessing experiments that followed it, the last one having been published in 1976. Of the sixteen comparisons between hypnosis and waking conditions in these sixteen studies, ten showed overall significant psi performance in hypnosis; only one demonstrated overall significant psi under waking conditions.

Honorton (1977) also surveyed picture-guessing tasks involving hypnosis, in some of which hypnotized subjects were asked to "dream" about the target picture. When a few studies were added utilizing hypnosis for "psi-training" and "psi-discrimination," a total of forty-two were identified. Of these, twenty-two obtained significant results (chance error would yield two or three significant studies). Honorton concluded, "The conclusion is now inescapable that hypnotic induction procedures enhance psi receptivity" (p. 450). Furthermore, he was able to compare the studies utilizing card-guessing techniques and those involving target pictures. The latter were found to provide more ESP-associated information, leading Honorton to observe that the data directly support "spontaneous case findings that psi is most frequently mediated through imagery and other spontaneous mentation processes (p. 451).

Of the studies in hypnosis and ESP (e.g., Fourie, 1977; Sargent, 1978a) concluded since Honorton's review, an experiment by John Palmer and Ivo van de Velden (1983) was the most ambitious, although no evidence of psi emerged. The subjects were 150 volunteers in the Netherlands, each of whom was administered the Tellegen Absorption Scale, the Wilson-Barber Creative Imagination Scale, and a self-rating of the maximum hypnotic depth achieved during the initial induction. These measures of "hypnotic imagination" correlated significantly with each other as well as with four measures of belief in psi. Those subjects whose scores reflected a strong capacity for "hypnotic imagination" reported a stronger degree of belief in the reality of various psi phenomena and were more likely to claim having had such experiences themselves than those who scored low on the scales. D. P. Fourie (1982) has also emphasized the importance of the hypnotist–subject relationship in future parapsychological studies, while E. I. Schechter (1984) has called for direct comparison of hypnosis and control conditions. In a meta-analysis of twenty studies in which psi tasks were compared in this manner, sixteen showed higher scoring for the hypnotic condition, with seven attaining statistical significance.

RELAXATION, MEDITATION, ALPHA WAVES, AND PSI

Sometimes a theoretical article can be as powerful as a novel technique in opening up new research vistas. One such article was written by R. A. White in 1964, analyzing introspective reports from a number of "gifted" subjects. She concluded that relaxation—both physical and mental—was a common factor in their success, often being preceded by a building up of tension. She even observed that the Duke University high-scorers often used such words as "abstraction," "detachment," and "relaxation" to describe their experiences. Honorton (1977) describes this type of relaxation as "passive volition" or "allowing it to happen" (p. 452). He also sees a similarity to "stilling the mind," or reducing the internal noise level, as practiced in Patanjali's system of Raja yoga (e.g., Mishra, 1967).

G. R. Schmeidler (1952) conducted the first systematic experimental investigation of relaxation in psi performance. She used a clairvoyance task, reporting significantly superior psi performance from hospitalized concussion patients compared to patients with other afflictions. A subsequent study with maternity patients tested Schmeidler's hypothesis that the concussion patients scored better because of their greater relaxation, receptivity to the experiment, and willingness to respond to the external world. The results were highly significant, with twelve of fifteen relaxed patients scoring positively in the psi task. None of the maternity patients who were not judged to be relaxed scored positively; in fact, this group exhibited "psi-missing"—making so few hits that their deviation *below* chance was statistically significant (Gerber and Schmeidler, 1957).

William Braud and Lendell Braud (e.g., 1974) assessed the effects of induced relaxation on identification of concealed target pictures through ESP. Subjects in their studies sat in an armchair with eyes closed and were given tape-recorded relaxation instructions. At the outset they were told to keep in mind that they were to receive impressions of a target picture that would be "transmitted" by an agent. Correspondences between targets and mentation reports were assessed by a judge's blind ranking of each report against a pool of five pictures—four controls and one randomly selected target. The results of these studies were generally significant, and a successful replication by another team was reported (Stanford and Mayer, 1974).

In 1977, Honorton identified thirteen experimental studies of psi retrieval during induced relaxation, ten of which were significant. He concluded, "Quite clearly, induced relaxation procedures appear to enhance psi receptivity" (p. 457).

Schmeidler (1970) also conducted the first systematic study of psi and meditation. Six psychology students completed an ESP guessing task before and after instructions in yogic meditation and breathing were given by a visiting swami. Pre-meditation psi scores were at chance levels, but post-meditation scores were statistically significant.

Karlis Osis and Edwin Bokert (1971) conducted a two-year study that isolated three basic dimensions of meditation that could precipitate ESP: the presence of feelings of self transcendence and openness to experience, combined with intensity of mood. Even so, there were individual differences, and meditation's relationship to ESP was highly complex.

Meditation has been used to study PK as well as ESP. For example, Charles Honorton and Edward May (1976) had ten subjects complete an equal number of PK trials, giving them auditory feedback pertaining to the magnitude of deviation both above and below chance as well as visual feedback to provide directional information. A significant directional PK influence was obtained, demonstrating volitional control. Six members of the group were meditators, and four of them obtained independently significant results; scores of only one of the non-meditators reached a similar level.

Nine of sixteen experimental studies completed by the time of Honorton's 1977 review were significant, eliciting his conclusion that "meditation is an effective means of producing controlled psi interactions" (p. 442).

Closely related to the relaxation and meditation studies are those that have monitored various physiological parameters associated with relaxed states. Most frequently examined have been occipitally recorded EEG data, but the results have varied (Morris, 1977). Using preselected subjects who could produce high level of alpha, Honorton et al. (1971) found significant positive relationships between abundance of alpha waves and proportions of correct choices on ESP card-guessing tasks. Robert Morris and his associates (Morris et al., 1972) reported a positive relationship between alpha abundance and proportion of correct guesses on a task involving choosing the sex of concealed photographs. The study employed a "gifted" subject, Lalsingh Harribance, who generally showed alpha abundance before and during the actual time of successful guessing, obtaining the highest levels ever produced during EEG monitoring (Parker, 1975b, p. 174). During unsuccessful guessing, Harribance's alpha abundance was high before guessing, but dropped while he was making his choice.

On the other hand, there have been studies that reported negative relationships between alpha abundance and correct choices (e.g., Stanford and Lovin, 1970) and studies in which no relationship was detected (e.g., Morris and Cohen, 1969). Morris reviewed the literature and concluded that "the EEG results are confusing and contradictory" (p. 706). One difficulty in forming a coherent picture is that different measures of alpha activity were often used by different experimenters (Parker, 1975b, p. 153). However, if subjects were preselected for expertise at alpha production or for previous high-scoring on psi tasks, the data tended to support a relationship between the two phenomena.

DRUGS AND PSI

The use of LSD-type (or psychedelic) drugs is probably more responsible than any other factor for the contemporary interest in subjective experience (Parker, 1975b, p. 125). Half a dozen experimental studies involving psi and LSD-type drugs appear in the literature; Stanley Krippner and Richard Davidson (1974) reviewed them and found the methodology to be somewhat crude and the results inconclusive. A common problem is the instability of the psychedelic experience itself; a subject will typically report a kaleidoscope of images and feelings that are explored, producing ecstasy, terror, curiosity, or a variety of other moods not conducive to psi-testing.

R. E. L. Masters and Jean Houston (1966) surmounted these difficulties by adequate preparation of their sixty-two subjects. Remarkable results were obtained both in card-guessing and telepathy tasks using picture targets. For example, when the LSD "guide" was concentrating on a picture depicting an Amazonian rain forest, the subject reported "lush vegetation, exotic flowers, startling greens, all seen through watery mist" (p. 120). When the picture was a plantation in the old South, the subject's imagery was of "a Negro picking cotton in a field" (p. 121). The conditions for these tasks were less than ideal, as the guide was often in the same room as the subject; under such an arrangement the possibility of nonverbal or subliminal communication arises.

Earlier work in the 1930s by J. B. Rhine (1973) indicated that sodium amytal markedly reduced scoring rates in three of his high-scoring subjects, while caffeine intake was associated with an elevation of these scores to their previous levels. Other experiments have used dexedrine (a stimulant) and quinalbarbitone (a depressant) in addition to sodium amytal. Brenio

Onetto-Bächler (1983) reported that ritalin administration appeared to significantly enhance ESP scores. In reviewing the studies, Palmer (1977) concludes: "The evidence is fairly consitent in showing that central nervous system depressants tend to reduce the level of scoring in ESP card tests. The evidence that stimulants have the opposite effect is much less consistent" (p. 123).

In the meantime, there have been any number of anecdotal reports of supposedly paranormal experiences in conjunction with drug use. Charles Tart (1971) surveyed a large number of marijuana users and found that 31 percent claimed telepathic experiences; Stanley Krippner and Don Fersh (1970) conducted a field study of twenty-two "hippie" communes, observing that the reporting of paranormal experience was a common theme. Legal restrictions make further laboratory work difficult, but it may be important to pursue this inquiry at some future time.

Twenty-three percent of Tart's (1971) respondents also reported out-of-body experiences (OBEs) during their marijuana-induced altered states of consciousness, about the same proportion as found in the general population. During OBEs, the observer appears to be perceiving objects or events from a point of view not coincident with his or her physical body. Although few in number, the results of the reported studies have been provocative. For example, one of Tart's (1968) subjects was able to correctly identify a five-digit random number placed on a shelf above her bed. Her EEG record showed prominent "alphoid activity" during the OBEs, a low frequency alpha rhythm very rare among sleeping subjects.

On the other hand, Janet Mitchell's (1973) subject, the artist Ingo Swann, demonstrated very little alpha during his OBEs. His psi task was to draw targets placed out of sight on a platform 10 feet above the floor. An outside judge was able to correctly match all eight targets with their respective pictures, an event that would occur by chance only once in 40,000 times. Swann was later instrumental in developing the procedures for "remote viewing" experiments, a type of "traveling clairvoyance" analogous to OBEs (e.g., Schlitz and Gruber, 1980). In parapsychology, as well as in other endeavors in the behavioral and social sciences, no one experiment can stand by itself, but the dramatic success of the OBE studies needs to be further explored. However, the data thus far accumulated indicate that the OBE is not one experience, but may represent a continuum of experiences (Rogo, 1978, p. 192).

SENSORY DEPRIVATION AND PSI

During sensory deprivation, subjects often report body image distortions, depersonalization, and internal imagery; the experience can be positive or negative, depending on set and setting variables. The subject is generally highly suggestible; in one study, sensorially deprived subjects who listened to a record arguing for belief in psi phenomena manifested greater changes in attitudes to psi than did a control group (Hevoh, 1961).

The first experimental study of psi retrieval under conditions of sensory deprivation was conducted at Maimonides Medical Center by Honorton and his co-workers (Honorton et al., 1973). Thirty subjects were isolated from visual and auditory stimuli in a rotary "cradle" that also reduced kinesthetic sensations. Every 5 minutes, subjects were asked to give a "state report" on a five-point scale to describe changes in awareness; at the end of the 30-minute session, they guessed the identify of the target picture. Those subjects with the highest overall state reports made significant ESP scores, and those reporting strong *shifts* toward internalized attention obtained an especially high level of target identification.

Honorton also found ESP to be associated with a shift in awareness when he studied EEG alpha (Honorton, 1969), alpha biofeedback (Honorton et al., 1971), and "hypnotic dreams" (Honorton, 1972). In the last study, Honorton's subjects were hypnotized and asked to "dream" about the target picture. Not only did subjects in the hypnosis group make higher ESP scores than those in a "waking imagination" group, but those hypnotized subjects who reported a strong change in their subjective state between the pre-hypnosis and the "hypnotic dream" period produced significantly more hits than those showing little change.

Additional support for the importance of shifts in awareness came from a "hypnotic dream" study conducted by Adrian Parker (1975a), and a study conducted by Rex Stanford (1971) observing shifts in alpha frequency and ESP. Parker (1975b) has applied the "shift of state" hypothesis (Murphy, 1966) to OBEs, stating that if these rapid changes occur during a state "in which logical processes are retained but reality orientation lost, it would explain how such experiences are interpreted as out-of-the-body experience since reality is viewed from the focus of the ESP impression" (p. 83).

"Shift in state" is especially noticeable during hypnagogic reverie, the period between waking and sleep. Specific experiential reports are given in 95 percent of awakenings from the hypnagogic period, and these experiences differ from dreams in that they are primarily visual and lack emotional content (Foulkes and Vogel, 1965). The Maimonides research group (White et al., 1968) broke each of the dream telepathy transcripts into "units of meaning" and had a judge rate each "unit" as to similarity to the target picture used that night. Waking reports contained the fewest correspondences, hypnagogic imagery the most—even more than dream imagery. (For the purposes of this analysis, hypnagogic reverie was combined with hypnopompic reverie, which occurs between sleep and wakefulness in the morning.)

William Braud (1977) evaluated ESP scoring in two conditions: subjects attempted to identify picture targets (1) "sent" during hypnagogic reverie and (2) "sent" late at night. Significant scoring occurred for the hypnagogic but not the dream targets.

All these data support the "shift of state" hypothesis. And even before Braud's work was completed, Honorton (1977) had explored "ganzfeld stimulation," which utilizes a homogeneous visual field to provide subjects with a uniform visual input. Ganzfeld stimulation was produced by placing halves of ping-pong balls over subjects' eyes and a uniform source of light is front of their faces. The result was an experience of diffuse, unpatterned light, typically accompanied by an increase in alpha activity. Specifically, this procedure satisfies conditions Honorton (1977) felt to be conducive to psi: (a) reduction of the sensory noise level through regulation of perceptual input; (b) development of attention toward internal mentation which could serve to "carry" psi impressions; (c) facilitation, through "stimulus hunger," of an affective link between the psi-receiver and a remote information source (i.e., the target); (d) recording of target information through the receiver's continuous mentation report; and (e) confirmation of sender–receiver interaction through objective assessment of target–mentation correspondences (pp. 459–460). Ganzfeld studies have been undertaken in a large number of diverse laboratories. Stanford (1984) produced an in-depth survey of seventeen of these experiments, selected on the basis of complete statistical analysis, seven of which were significant. He concluded that the approach continues to be a very promising avenue for process-oriented ESP research.

In answer to critics who alleged that only significant parapsychological data tend to be reported, Susan Blackmore (1980) sent a questionnaire to any person who she thought might have been associated with ganzfeld studies, asking about those not completed or not published. Of the questionnaires sent out, 47 percent were returned. These elicited a total of thirty-two further ganzfeld studies reported by fifteen respondents. Of these, twenty had been completed, but one could not be evaluated for various reasons. Seven of the remaining nineteen studies yielded statistically significant data—a lower proportion but not one statistically different from the success rate of the published studies. Blackmore concluded that "the bias introduced by the selective reporting of ESP ganzfeld studies is not a major contribution to the overall proportion of significant results" (p. 217).

SCHIZOPHRENIA AND PSI

Since the early days of psychical research, it has been speculated that severe forms of mental disturbance may be psi-conducive (Alberti, 1974). In particular, the extreme personal disorganization that has come to be known as schizophrenia is frequently viewed as a possibly psi-conducive altered state of consciousness. It is well known that schizophrenics often report paranormal experiences of all kinds, and, indeed, belief in paranormal phenomena is used as one of the diagnostic criteria for the disorder in the current *Diagnostic and Statistical Manual* of the American Psychiatric Association (APA, 1980). Several clinicians with extensive experience in the psychological treatment of schizophrenia have observed that schizophrenics are particularly prone to paranormal manifestations, especially during the onset of the disorder (e.g., Ehrenwald, 1947; Ullman, 1953). Also, schizophrenia may have features in common with other suspected psi-conducive states. For instance, similarities between schizophrenia and shamanic states of consciousness have been noted (e.g., Silverman, 1967), although the assertion that shamans are schizophrenics has been conclusively refuted (Noll, 1983). There are also phenomenological, and possibly biochemical, similarities between some psychedelic drug-induced states and schizophrenia (Fischman, 1983), although the differences exceed the likenesses.

Unfortunately, formal parapsychological research with schizophrenics (reviewed by Rogo, 1982) has produced disappointing results. Few of the studies testing schizophrenics for ESP have yielded statistically significant findings, and to date there have been no studies examining PK with schizophrenic subjects. One possible explanation for the discrepancy between anecdotal reports and experimental impressions concerning schizophrenia and psi is that the anecdotal reports are misinterpretations, and that, in reality, schizophrenia is not psi-conducive. It should be noted, however, that schizophrenia research is one of the most difficult areas in the behavioral sciences because of a plethora of logistical and conceptual problems. First, it can be very difficult to obtain the permission of the caretaking institutions and the individual subjects to conduct experiments; even if permission is obtained, schizophrenics are notoriously unwilling or unable to function appropriately in a test setting. Second, almost all inpatient schizophrenics in the Western world receive daily doses of powerful tranquilizing medications, creating a constant confound with the underlying pathological process. Third, until the mid-1970s (before which almost all of the psi research with schizophrenics was conducted), diagnostic procedures for schizophrenia were extremely unreliable, and the more recent diagnostic instruments, while more reliable, are still of questionable validity (Fenton et al., 1981). Fourth, in many psychological and parapsychological studies of schizophrenia, no attempt is made to differentiate schizophrenics into subtypes or stages of the disorder, but differences in cognitive functioning have been reported across subtypes (e.g., George and Neufeld, 1983) and over time (Tsuang et al., 1981). The issue of whether or not some forms or stages of schizophrenia are psi-conducive states must be regarded as currently unresolved.

SHAMANISM AND PSI

With the advent of sophisticated technological systems to study psi and altered states, it is easy to forget the shamanistic tradition which has attempted to apply psi for practical purposes over the millenia (Winkelman, 1982). Shamans are individuals who voluntarily alter their consciousness in order to obtain knowledge and power from "nonordinary" (nonconsensual) reality in order to help and to heal people of the community which has assigned them that role. The community's belief system holds that shamans, while in an altered state, can obtain special information from nonconsensual reality (analogous to ESP) or exert special powers (analogous to PK). In addition to being "technicians of the sacred" (Eliade, 1966), shamans are characteristically "masters of magic," who often maintain their position through legerdemain (Handelman, 1967). The usual reaction among anthropologists has been to automatically ascribe any shamanistic display of "powers" to sleight of hand. However, Mircea Eliade (1966) has cautioned:

> We now touch upon a problem of the greatest importance . . . that is, the question of the *reality* of the extrasensory capacities ascribed to the shamans and medicine-men. Although research into this question is still at its beginning, a fairly large number of ethnographic documents has already put the authenticity of such phenomena beyond doubt. (p. 87)

Ethnographic accounts of ostensible psi phenomena have been reported from field studies with West African "diviners" (Gorer, 1935, p. 222), Jamaican "diviners" (Long, 1977, p. 380), Zulu shamans (Callaway, 1884), and a Haitian voodoo priest (Métraux, 1959, p. 63). One such anecdote was described by a South African psychiatrist (Laubscher, 1938), who buried a purse in the ground, covered it with a brown stone, then placed a gray stone on the brown one. He then drove to the home of a shaman who lived 60 miles away. To solve the problem, the shaman went into a ritual dance to alter his consciousness and reportedly described the purse and the stones in detail. The psychiatrist was present at the time, however, thus opening the possibility of nonverbal or subliminal communication. A number of years later, Adrian Boshier (1974) entered into an apprenticeship with Zulu shamans, citing several examples of divination he felt to represent psi.

Several experimental studies with native populations have been carried out (e.g., Van de Castle, 1974), but none focused upon shamans or altered states of consciousness until Patric Giesler (1983) conducted field studies in Brazil. Giesler tested ten people who were clients of Umbanda (a Brazilian "spiritist" movement) shamans in São Paulo. Each lent two personal objects to an experimenter, who placed them at one of four possible locations—all unknown to the clients. At times, the client consulted a shaman during a public ceremony before guessing the identity of the hidden object; at other times the location was guessed at without consulting the shaman. The overall results were not significant, but clients scored significantly higher with consultation than without it. Giesler also persuaded the Umbanda shamans to participate in a "remote viewing" test, but the results were not significant.

Giesler concluded that his combination of ethnographic and experimental methods provided a more complete portrayal of possible psi among the practitioners of Umbanda than could have been achieved using one method alone. E. F. Kelly and R. G. Locke (1981) assert that systematic cross-cultural analysis has the potential to yield significant advances in the understanding and control of both psi and altered states (p. 84). Of the thousand known societies, 89 percent have at least one institutionalized form of altered state induction (Bourguignon, 1974). Thus there are a number of possibilities for field research into shamanism and similar processes that may reveal ESP and PK effects strong enough to be measured and analyzed. In the meantime, no systematic studies have been made of psi effects in lucid dreaming, multiple personalities, mutual hypnosis, mystical experiences, near death encounters, or sexual rapture, despite the increasing scientific attention being paid to these phenomena.

CRITICISM AND MEDIATING VARIABLES

In reviewing the literature on psi phenomena, one must be aware of the controversial nature of parapsychology. However, psi researchers claim that the criticisms they constantly face have led to an increased sophistication in the designing of experiments. Krippner (1974) has listed some of the major precautions that need to be taken:

1. Isolating the subject from the ESP or PK target in ways to eliminate sensory cuing or muscular activity.
2. Taking precautions to ensure that the person who records the responses is "blind" to the nature or identity of the target material.
3. Using a randomization method to select target material.
4. Deciding how many trials will be attempted before an experiment begins.
5. Testing high-scoring subjects in different laboratories in an attempt to replicate earlier findings.
6. Imposing proper security measures that will prevent the alteration of experimental data.

Many of the attacks on parapsychology have been irresponsible and inaccurate. However, psi researchers need to be vigilant because the accumulation of human knowledge depends upon experimental methods that are well conceptualized and carefully executed. Perhaps the best critiques of psi research have come from within the field by members of the Parapsychological Association itself (e.g., Akers, 1984).

There is another set of criticisms to consider when evaluating the data concerning psi and altered states of consciousness. The exact role of altered states in the apparent success of psi experiments remains unclear. The literature consists primarily of studies demonstrating high psi-scoring in the altered state rather than contrasting the altered state with ordinary consciousness (Kelly and Locke, 1981, p. 4). Even fewer studies exist contrasting altered states with each other.

Keeping these criticisms in mind, the evidence reviewed in the preceding pages suggests that ostensible psi functioning is enhanced following the performance of a variety of procedures that have in common the association with reports of qualitatively altered awareness. In order to advance their understanding and control of these phenomena, parapsychologists must endeavor to identify which variable(s) mediate the connection between psi and altered states of consciousness. Discussion of such mediating variables requires that parapsychologists identify those altered states that are apparently psi-conducive, the psychological and physiological characteristics of those states, and the variables that appear to facilitate psi functioning.

Parapsychologists have identified as potentially psi-conducive such states as those associated with hypnosis, meditation, sensory deprivation, and dreaming. The difficulties pertaining to these delineations are those that complicate the study of altered states of consciousness in general. For instance, various issues (e.g., the extent to which attributes of consciousness are amenable to categorization into discrete states as opposed to organization in terms of continua, the accuracy of our typologies of consciousness, the utility of "altered state" as a concept of explanatory efficacy versus being a mere descriptor) raise broad questions concerning the feasibility or value of relating altered-states variables with psi-related variables. If the notion of discrete altered states is generally misleading in its overemphasis on the stability of essentially transient phenomena, then the simple statement that, for instance, a "meditative state" is psi-conducive is of questionable validity on a priori grounds. If current typologies of altered states are grossly inaccurate or simplistic—if, for example, there is not one altered state potentially associated with meditation, but instead thousands—then the above simple statement concerning a "meditative state" is practically meaningless. Also, if we reject the use of state-of-consciousness terminology in explanatory statements, then speaking loosely of a psi-conducive state erroneously implies the existence of a nonexistent causal link. In the present chapter, the term "altered states of consciousness" is used as a label of convenience to designate the conditions following various induction procedures, in which people often report that their awareness is recognizably different from their ordinary waking state. It is not assumed that such reports are perfectly associated with altered functioning—persons can exhibit heightened suggestibility following a hypnotic induction, and report that they possess normal awareness—and so altered states have descriptive and not causal status. Neither is it assumed that the typology of altered states employed in this chapter is final or ideal, but it is simply provisionally useful at the present time.

The characteristics of the altered states discussed in this chapter have been an area of intensive research and much controversy for many years. Some findings are generally agreed upon, for example, that muscular relaxation, increased predominance of EEG alpha, and reports of enhanced visual imagery are common to many of the altered states. Other issues are still debatable, for instance: Are there meditative states with distinctive psychophysiological correlates (Schuman, 1980)? Is it possible to distinguish hypnosis from the waking state by any criteria aside from subjects' compliance in self-labeling (Barber, 1979)? In what ways do the states of consciousness associated with psychedelic drug ingestion differ from acute psychosis (Fischman, 1983)? Such unresolved questions complicate the attempt to relate the characteristics of altered states to anything else, including psi performance.

Also, the factors that facilitate psi are not yet clearly delineated. There is some evidence that such variables as moderate relaxation, imagery, extraversion, belief in the possibility of psi, and high motivation are psi-conducive, but this evidence is far from consistent concerning any of these variables. It is evident that whatever processes underlie the evidence for psi are immensely subtle and complex interactions, and/or are of a nature that has not thus far been adequately addressed by scientific approaches to psi phenomena.

In summary, the attempt to explore the variables mediating two such complex and poorly understood realms as those of psi and altered states of consciousness is necessarily tentative. Further progress in both parapsychology and the psychology of consciousness will be required before certainties, or even clear probabilities, emerge. Meanwhile, some speculations, clearly labeled as such, may help to guide us in the directions where progress seems most likely.

There are three possible categories of variables mediating the association between altered states and psi: (1) parameters that are common to the various ostensibly psi-conducive states; (2) parameters that are associated with the altered states, but are not restricted to them, that is, confounding variables; (3) specific psi-conducive parameters associated with certain, but not all, purportedly psi-conducive states.

GENERAL PSI–CONDUCIVE ASPECTS OF ALTERED STATES

Disruption of the Ordinary State of Consciousness

Several theorists of consciousness have discussed the processes whereby the ordinary, waking state is replaced by an altered state. For instance, from the perspective of Tart's (1975) systems approach, any discrete state of consciousness is viewed as a complex construction that, in the face of a constantly changing environment, must be actively maintained by various stabilizing processes. These processes function to keep the structure of awareness operating within the normal range. Conversely, according to Tart, the induction of an altered state involves two operations. Initially, processes are initiated that counter or deactivate the stabilizing processes, leading to the disruption of the ordinary state; then, patterning processes, which reorganize the potential structures of consciousness into a new discrete state with distinctive characteristics, are brought into play. Between the onset of the disrupting forces and that of the patterning forces may be a period of relative cognitive chaos, when consciousness is still unstructured, in transition between states. During these shifts, any of the possible capacities of awareness are potentially available. From these possibilities, the patterning processes act to select certain ones to characterize the new discrete state, and inhibit others.

Milton Erickson and his associates (Erickson et al., 1976), in discussing hypnotic induction, describe a similar process in slightly different terms. They hold that ordinary awareness is heavily structured by learned limitations in the form of sets, biases, and inhibitions, which function to block a person from accessing his or her vast reservoir of potential resources. An important principle in hypnotic induction, then, is "depotentiating the habitual frame of reference," which is accomplished by presenting the subject with such input as contradictions, double binds, and confusing or boring situations. A second principle, analogous to Tart's (1975) patterning process, is the redirection of the subject's attention in an inward direction in order to facilitate receptivity to the expanded resources made available by discarding the learned limitations of ordinary awareness.

Also, Arthur Deikman (1966), in his seminal research on meditation, noted that when subjects fixated their attention on a single object for a period of time, their records of those experiences suggested that a deautomatization of perception occurred. That is, the constructive processes involved in the organization of experience, which had become so habitual as to operate totally outside of awareness, returned to the conscious level. Again, the implication is that some of the conditioned limitations of human consciousness may be bypassed in an altered state.

The question arises as to whether this depotentiation of conscious sets, which is an intrinsic feature of alterations of consciousness, may be relevant to the apparently psi-conducive nature of altered states. Evidence from several areas of parapsychology suggests that it may indeed be very important; psi may be a human potential, the access to which is limited by the constraints of ordinary awareness, and facilitated by the disruption of this state.

Gardner Murphy (1966) proposed that the shift between discrete states of awareness may be psi-conducive, rather than the discrete states themselves. Murphy noted parapsychological parallels between creative acts and psi phenomena, and postulated that

> it is not the motivated state, not the relaxed state, not the dissociated state *in themselves* which are conducive to both high creativity and high paranormal success, but rather a rapid *movement,* say, from an unmotivated to a motivated state; or from a relaxed to a highly active state; or from a highly integrated to a very dissociated state. . . . It may be that we exploit energies as the result of a *transition,* as a result of passing from one way of functioning to another. (p. 20)

This "shift in state" hypothesis of psi facilitation apparently refers to the disruption or depotentiation aspect of altered state induction. The studies of Honorton (1972), Parker (1975), Stanford (1971), and others, described above, provide some empirical support for this notion.

Also relevant to the idea that the disruption of conscious sets facilitates psi is the conformance behavior theory of psi functioning, originally proposed by Stanford (1977) and developed by Braud (1980). In essence, the theory proposes that when there are two systems, one that is organized in a relatively random or unconstrained fashion, and one that is relatively ordered and contains a "disposition" (or need) involving the first system, the former system will tend to change in conformance with the disposition of the latter. To give a concrete example of this rather abstract principle, in a PK experiment, the relatively random system would be the target system, such as rolling dice. The disposed system would be the mind/brain of the experimental subject, with his or her intention to have certain die faces be displayed when the dice stop rolling. A consistent, nonrandom pattern of die faces in this situation might be taken as suggestive of the occurrence of

PK (assuming that the usual methodological precautions against alternative explanations had been taken, of course). Conformance behavior is regarded as independent of the complexity of the systems involved, and is not conceived as involving the passage of any information-bearing energy or force from one system through the intervening space to the other system. Braud (1980) elaborated some of the implications of this theory by stating that the magnitude of a psi influence upon a system is proportional to the lability of that system, and inversely related to the constraints imposed upon the system. Lability is defined by Braud as "the ease with which a system can change from one state to another and the amount of free variability in the system" (p. 301). In practical terms, this principle implies that the probability of success in a PK task increases with the lability of the target system, and success in an ESP task depends on the degree of lability of the receiving system—that is, the brain/mind of the percipient.

Many of the details of conformance theory have not been articulated in detail, but its broad explanatory power has already been demonstrated, and it has stimulated considerable research (Braud, 1981). The use of intrinsically indeterminate or highly random sources for PK target sequences, as employed in the experiments of Helmut Schmidt (1973), and such findings as the apparent facilitation of ESP by negative response biases (Stanford, 1967; Kreitler and Kreitler, 1973) have led to striking evidence for the occurrence of psi, and are consistent with the conformance behavior theory. It is also consistent with theory to consider that altered-states induction procedures, with their disruption of the constraints of ordinary awareness, produce a transient, highly labile mental system, which would be more susceptible than the unaltered system to the structuring "influence" of the disposed target system. ESP-conducive procedures are those that facilitate the lability of the receiving system; altered-states induction procedures act to increase the lability through their disruptive processes.

Another implication seems to be that PK-conducive procedures are those that promote a structure and disposition of the mind/brain of the subject. In other words, shifts between states of consciousness may be ESP-conducive, and certain stable, discrete states may be PK-conducive. Such a prediction has not been systematically explored, but some relevant data may be found in studies of mental imagery enhancement training and psi. Such training, which attempts to increase the vividness and controllability of subjects' imagery, may be conceived as increasing the structure of the mental system by promoting a stable state of awareness characterized by controlled imagery. Several studies have been conducted that measured ESP prior to and following an imagery training program (Mockenhaupt et al., 1977; Morris et al., 1978; Morris and Bailey, 1979; Morris, 1980; George, 1982). Only one of these studies (George, 1982) attempted to measure the imagery-enhancing effects of the training in addition to its psi effects; evidence suggestive of imagery enhancement was obtained. In none of these studies was there clear evidence that ESP was enhanced through imagery training. Two studies have examined the PK-facilitating effects of imagery training (Morris and Hornaday, 1981; Braud, 1983). Only Braud's study measured imagery functioning across training, and obtained some evidence that imagery enhancement took place. Braud (1983) also reported that PK scores increased to a significant degree following training. An inadequate number of parapsychological experiments using imagery training have been conducted to ascertain the robustness of the possible tendency for such structure-enhancing practices to facilitate PK and not ESP, but the pattern of available data is not inconsistent with the predictions of conformance behavior and lability/inertia theory.

Internally Directed Attention

Another common characteristic of altered states of awareness is that, following the disruption of ordinary consciousness, more attention tends to be allocated to internal processes than to those of the consensus reality. An alternative (but not necessarily conflicting) approach to the psi conduciveness of altered states to that outlined in the preceding paragraphs has emphasized this characteristic.

An information-processing model of psi was outlined by Honorton (1977, 1978) and elaborated by Braud (1978). It is based on C. D. Broad's (1953) distinction between psi *interactions,* in which information is paranormally acquired without conscious registration, and psi *experiences,* in which such information enters awareness. An important question is: what distinguishes these two functions? How does the information acquired through psi become conscious after it "enters" the individual's processing system? Essentially, psi-mediated awareness is conceived as an act of signal detection. The information is in competition with the many other sorts of data that enter awareness, and under circumstances in which we wish to consciously access the former, it is in effect a signal being transmitted in a very noisy channel. It follows that maximizing the probability of a psi experience would entail increasing the signal/noise ratio, and one means of accomplishing this is by noise reduction. Honorton (1977), inspired by his studies of Patanjali's *Yoga Sutras* (e.g., Mishra, 1967), postulated that altered states function as a means of psychophysiological noise reduction, by directing the attention (i.e., the allocation of processing capacity) away from exteroceptive and proprioceptive stimuli and toward the inner experiences through which the faint psi signal might be expected to emerge. Indeed, Honorton (1977) refers to psi-conducive altered states as "internal attention states."

Braud (1978) has elaborated and extended the noise reduction model, categorizing the various potential sources of noise, as well as means for reducing them through alterations of awareness. According to Braud, several processes are held to be characteristic of ordinary awareness, which tend to be attenuated or absent in altered states, and may contribute noise that masks the psi signal: exteroceptive stimulation, skeletal muscle activity, excessive autonomic activity, various kinds of cognitive activity (e.g., analytical thought), excessive effort to succeed at the task, distracting imagery and mentation.

Braud (1978) also attempted to integrate the noise reduction approach with Stanford's conformance behavior model. He stated, "Noise-reducing procedures may be psi-conducive to the extent that they free the nervous system from external and internal constraints, thereby increasing its alternative possibilities ('randomness') and hence its susceptibility to conformance behavior" (p. 26). However, it is not evident that the two approaches can actually be merged so easily. If the psi conduciveness of altered states is attributable to procedures that increase the lability of the nervous system, then it is misleading to call them "noise-reducing" procedures, as if noise reduction and lability enhancement were identical processes, whereas conceptually they are distinct types of operation. This is not to say that the conformance behavior model and the signal detection model may not each be useful in explaining various features of the relationship between altered states and psi, but it is not apparent that the former model can logically subsume the latter one.

PSI-CONDUCIVE CONFOUNDS OF ALTERED STATES

It is plausible that the apparent psi conduciveness of altered states of awareness may arise not from characteristics associated exclusively with altered states, but from processes that characteristically occcur in conjunction with such states, but are not restricted to them. Parapsychologists have identified several such variables, some of which are discussed below.

Mental Imagery

Psi researchers have long been interested in the possible relationships between psi and imagery, for a variety of reasons. For instance, many traditional techniques from diverse historical and geographical locations that purportedly produce psi involve the use of highly cultivated mental imagery. Also, mental imagery has been implicated in some of the theoretical approaches to psi. For example, Tyrrell (1943) divided the ESP process into two stages, the first stage involving the acquisition of information by the personal unconscious of the percipient, and the second stage involving the passage of this information into consciousness by means of psychological structures called "mediating vehicles." Psychological investigation of dreams, reveries, and hallucinations have indicated that imagery is a prominent vehicle for the conveyance of unconscious information.

A third reason for the interest of parapsychologists in mental imagery is the body of empirical evidence suggesting the involvement of imagery processing in spontaneous and experimental psi (reviewed in George, 1981). The collection and analysis of spontaneous case material is one of the strategies used in psi research. The results of such studies cannot be regarded as strictly evidential concerning psi, as the reported incidents usually occurred under uncontrolled circumstances and were not reported in accordance with scientifically rigorous standards. However, they can be useful in suggesting hypotheses, which can then be evaluated in a more formal manner. Of the five major spontaneous case analyses that have examined imagery, four (Rhine, 1954; Sannwald, 1959; Green, 1960; Prasad and Stevenson, 1968) reported that imagery-mediated ostensible psi experiences (comprising those involving dreams and hallucinations) were more frequently reported than other kinds, and one (Haight, 1979) reported the reverse pattern. White (1964) examined the subjective reports of outstanding subjects who participated in some of the free response studies of early psychical research, and observed that the presence of vivid imagery was associated with ostensible psi occurrence.

A large number of studies attempting to delineate quantitative relationships between psi and imaginal variables have appeared over the past fifteen years. The effects of individual differences in such parameters as self-reported vividness and controllability, manipulations of instructional set and target characteristics, and imagery enhancement training, have all been examined with respect to psi measures. The findings have been rather inconsistent. Many of these studies have provided evidence for psi, but, in general, quantitative relationships between imaginal variables and psi have not proved robust. Given the elusiveness and the difficulties in conceptual definition in both mental imagery and psi, this is not altogether surprising (George and Krippner, 1984).

It is noteworthy that in most of the altered states that are regarded as possibly psi-conducive, mental imagery is thought to be a prominent aspect of the experience; for example, hypnosis (Hilgard, 1977; but see Wadden and Anderton, 1982), psychedelic drug states (Masters and Houston, 1966), sensory deprivation (Bertini et al., 1964), schizophrenia (Slade, 1976), relaxation (Luthe and Schultz, 1969), meditation (Kornfield, 1979), and dreaming (Foulkes, 1978). It is therefore possible that the ostensible psi conduciveness of these states is at least partly attributable to an increased orientation toward mental imagery.

Arousal

Another variable that has attracted the attention of parapsychologists is arousal. Several researchers have proposed that there exists a psi-optimal pattern of cortical or autonomic activation, and that this pattern may underlie the ostensible psi conduciveness of altered states of consciousness.

For example, Hans Eysenck (1967, 1975) postulated that relatively low levels of cortical arousal facilitate psi functioning. Eysenck (1973) also argued that extraverts are characterized by chronically lowered cortical arousal relative to introverts, and it follows that extraverts should manifest superior psi performance. Support for Eysenck's psi postulate derives from several studies that have demonstrated with some consistency that extraverts tend to score higher than introverts in laboratory ESP tests (e.g., Kanthamani and Rao, 1972).

Another depiction of psi-facilitating arousal was offered by Honorton (1978). He distinguished between cortical and autonomic arousal, which Eysenck did not do, and suggested that relatively high cortical arousal coupled with relatively low autonomic arousal is psi-conducive. The lowering of autonomic arousal is regarded as a strategy of psychophysical noise reduction in order to enhance the detectability of the psi signal, as described previously. In the presence of reduced patterned sensory input, some degree of cortical arousal is necessary in order to maintain waking or dreaming awareness.

A third position on arousal and psi was presented by Braud (1978, 1981), who shares Honorton's endorsement, and much of his reasoning, concerning the psi conduciveness of reduced autonomic (and specifically sympathetic) nervous system activation. However, based on studies conducted by himself (Braud, 1981) and by Soji Otani (1955, 1958) involving the use of psychophysiological measures of arousal during ESP task performance, he proposed a refinement of this notion, suggesting that the psi-facilitative effects of lowered autonomic arousal occur within a measurable range, and that this range depends on the nature of the psi task. Performance on ESP tasks that require less effort and structure, such as free response tasks, may be maximized at lower levels of arousal than that on more constrained tasks, such as forced-choice guessing. Braud's speculations concerning central nervous system involvement in psi functioning are more elaborate than those of either Eysenck or Honorton. He suggested that reduced sympathetic arousal may promote a shift in the dominance of neurophysiological structures involved in information processing from the reticular activating system and left cerebral hemisphere to limbic-midbrain structures and right hemisphere, and that such a shift might be expected to be psi-conducive.

Carl Sargent (1978b), in a discussion of the postulated link between arousal and psi, suggested that one must consider not only the dimensions of cortical and autonomic arousal, but also the directionality of the psi effect (hitting versus missing). Based on his own studies and a review of the literature, Sargent proposed that low autonomic arousal coupled with high cortical arousal appeared to promote hitting, whereas high autonomic/ high cortical and low autonomic/low cortical arousal conditions were associated with psi missing.

Many of the purportedly psi-conducive altered states discussed in this chapter are known to be characterized by lowered sympathetic nervous system activity, for example, neuromuscular relaxation (Mathews and Gelder, 1969), rapid eye movement sleep (Rechtschaffen et al., 1963), and some types of meditation (Shapiro, 1980). Indications are less clear for sensory deprivation and hypnosis, but there is some evidence that these conditions may involve decreased autonomic arousal (Braud, 1981). Therefore, if these states are psi-conducive, it may be by virtue of their association with a general psi-conducive arousal factor.

Expectancy

It is a long-standing part of the "lab lore" of experimental parapsychology that a high degree of expectation of success on the part of the subject and experimenter is psi-conducive; conversely, a high expectancy of failure is held to inhibit psi effects, at least those in a positive direction. The best-known line of research cited in support of this notion concerns the "sheep-goat effect" (Schmeidler and McConnell, 1958). This effect consists of the finding that subjects who state that they believe in the possibility of ESP (sheep) tend to score above chance expectation on ESP tests, whereas those who reject the possibility of ESP (goats) tend to score at or below chance. According to Palmer (1971), only one-third of the published studies of the effect report statistical significance, but these significant findings have always been in the predicted direction, that is, with sheep scoring higher than goats. Unfortunately, the relationship between psi and expectancy may be less clear and more complex than is generally assumed (George, 1984). For instance, the sheep–goat variable appears to be confounded with other parameters that may affect the psi process, such as evaluation (Layton and Turnbull, 1975), motivation (Lovitts, 1981), and extraversion (Thalbourne, 1981). ESP studies that have compared low-expectancy (indecisive) subjects with more extreme sheep and goats have not generally found more evidence for psi among the latter two groups relative to the former, and, indeed, in some studies there is a trend for the indecisive subjects to score higher than either sheep or goats. The status of expectancy as a psi-conducive variable is unclear at present, although it appears somehow to be relevant to psi functioning.

Expectancy is important in the present context insofar as it is confounded with purportedly psi-conducive states of awareness, and there is some evidence that it may be. There are data (Hevoh, 1961; Palmer, 1979) indicating that subjects who underwent sensory deprivation inductions increased their expectations concerning personal psi performance compared to control subjects. There are few data concerning the effects of other altered states on expectancy. Further research concerning the psi/expectancy and altered states/expectancy links is clearly warranted.

Subject Selection

D. Scott Rogo (1976) suggested that the apparent psi conduciveness of altered states may be a result of nonrandom subject selection. Parapsychological experiments usually recruit subjects on a volunteer basis, and it is plausible that the kind of person who would volunteer for an experiment involving altered states may be significantly different from the average volunteer subject, let alone the average person on the street. For instance, he or she may be less neurotic, more open to novel experiences, and more susceptible to mental imagery than many other people, and these factors may affect the psi process independently of any influences attributable to altered states. This possibility could be evaluated through the use of control groups, or within-subjects designs with "normal state" conditions, but inclusion of such features has generally not been the case in parapsychological altered states research.

CONCLUSION

It is possible that the various altered states of consciousness discussed in this chapter may be psi-conducive for different reasons. That is, there may be no common processes, either intrinsic or confounding, that explain the apparently psi-facilitating effects of these states, in which case the various attempts to formulate global theories in this way may be misguided. It is conceivable that psychedelic drugs and meditation, for instance, may promote psi through radically differing mechanisms, just as verbally oriented psychotherapy and ingestion of barbiturates may achieve similar anti-anxiety effects arising from dissimilar causes.

Current research concerning common variables in the ostensibly psi-conducive states is somewhat promising, but little has actually been established with a great degree of confidence. Therefore, it is wise not to rule out the logical possibility that it may be necessary to consider several state-specific explanations if the global explanation approach does not bear fruit. Little can be said about the former approach at the present time, as it remains to be seen how productive the latter one will be.

In the meantime, an understanding of psi may depend upon a concomitant understanding of altered states. Psi may not be a perceptual phenomenon but rather a sharing of experiences that occurs most easily when people are in altered states of consciousness, linked by common associations and empathic feelings (Parker, 1975b, p. 170). On the other hand, psi may represent hitherto undetected forms of subliminal perception (Nash, 1971) and energetic field effects (Murphy, 1945; Persinger, 1975) that are most easily manifested in altered states of consciousness. In either event, research in the psychology of consciousness may be crucial for an understanding of psi phenomena.

REFERENCES

Akers, C. Methodological criticisms of parapsychology. In S. Krippner (Ed.), *Advances in parapsychological research,* vol. 4. Hendersonville, NC: McFarland, 1984, pp. 112–164.

Alberti, G. Psychopathology and parapsychology. In A. Angoff and B. Shapin (Eds.), *Parapsychology and the sciences.* New York: Parapsychology Foundation, 1974, pp. 225–233.

American Psychiatric Association. *DSM–III: Diagnostic and statistical manual of mental disorders.* Washington, D.C.: American Psychiatric Association, 1980.

Barber, T. X. Suggested ("hypnotic") behavior: The trance paradigm versus an alternative paradigm. In E. Fromm and R. E. Shor (Eds.), *Hypnosis: Developments in research and new perspectives.* New York: Aldine, 1979, pp. 217–272.

Beloff, J. Historical overview. In B. B. Wolman (Ed.), *Handbook of parapsychology.* New York: Van Nostrand Reinhold, 1977, pp. 3–24.

Bertini, M., Lewis, H., and Witkin, H. [Some preliminary observations with an experimental procedure for the study of hypnagogic and related phenomena.] *Archivo di Psicologia Neurologia e Psichiatrica,* 1964, *6,* 493–534.

Birge, W. R. and Rhine, J. B. Unusual types of persons tested for ESP. I. A professional medium. *Journal of Parapsychology,* 1942, *6,* 85–94.

Blackmore, S. The extent of selective reporting of ESP ganzfeld studies. *European Journal of Parapsychology,* 1980, *3,* 213–219.

Boshier, A. K. African apprenticeship. In A. Angoff and D. Barth (Eds.), *Parapsychology and anthropology.* New York: Parapsychology Foundation, 1974, pp. 273–284.

Bourguignon, E. *Culture and the varieties of consciousness.* Boston: Addison-Wesley, 1974.

Bruad, W. G. Long-distance dream and presleep telepathy. In J. D. Morris, W. G. Roll, and R. L. Morris (Eds.), *Research in parapsychology 1976.* Metuchen, N.J.: Scarecrow Press, 1977, 154–155.

Braud, W. G. Psi conducive conditions: Explorations and interpretations. In B. Shapin and L. Coly (Eds.), *Psi and states of awareness.* New York: Parapsychology Foundation, 1978, pp. 1–41.

Braud, W. G. Lability and inertia in conformance behavior. *Journal of the American Society for Psychical Research,* 1980, *74,* 297–318.

Braud, W. G. Psi performance and autonomic nervous system activity. *Journal of the American Society for Psychical Research,* 1981, *75,* 1–35.

Braud, W. G. Prolonged visualization practice and psychokinesis: A pilot study. In W. G. Roll and J. Beloff (Eds.), *Research in parapsychology 1982.* Metuchen, N.J.: Scarecrow Press, 1983, 187–189.

Braud, W. G. and Braud, L. W. Further studies of relaxation as a psi-conducive state. *Journal of the American Society for Psychical Research,* 1974, *68,* 229–245.

Broad, C. D. *Religion, philosophy, and psychical research.* New York: Harcourt, Brace, 1953.

Callaway, H. *The religious system of the Amazulu.* London: Folk-Lore Society, 1884.

Deikman, A. J. Deautomatization and the mystic experience. *Psychiatry,* 1966, *29,* 324–338.

Devereux, G. (Ed.). *Psychoanalysis and the occult.* New York: International Universities Press, 1953.

Ehrenwald, J. *Telepathy and medical psychology.* London: George, Allen, & Unwin, 1947.

Eliade, M. *Shamanism: Archaic techniques of ecstasy.* W. R. Trask (transl.). Princeton: Princeton University Press, 1966.

Erickson, M. H., Rossi, E. L., and Rossi, S. I. *Hypnotic realities: The induction of clinical hypnosis and forms of indirect suggestion.* New York: Irvington, 1976.

Eysenck, H. J. Personality and extra-sensory perception. *Journal of the Society for Psychical Research,* 1967, *44,* 55–71.

Eysenck, H. J. *Eysenck on extraversion.* London: Crosby-Lockwood-Staples, 1973.

Eysenck, H. J. Precognition in rats. *Journal of Parapsychology,* 1975, *39,* 222–227.

Fenton, W. S., Mosher, L. R., and Matthews, S. M. Diagnosis of schizophrenia: A critical review of current diagnostic systems. *Schizophrenia Bulletin,* 1981, *7,* 452–476.

Fischman, L. G. Dreams, hallucinogenic drug states, and schizophrenia: A psychological and biological comparison. *Schizophrenia Bulletin,* 1983, *9,* 73–94.

Foulkes, D. *A grammar of dreams.* New York: Basic Books, 1978.

Foulkes, D. and Vogel, G. Mental activity at sleep onset. *Journal of Abnormal Psychology, 1965, 70,* 231–243.

Fourie, D. P. An attempted revival of the Ryzl training method. In J. D. Morris, W. G. Roll, and R. L. Morris (Eds.), *Research in parapsychology 1976.* Metuchen, N.J.: Scarecrow Press, 1977, pp. 59–61.

Fourie, D. P. Hypnosis and psi: Taking stock. *Parapsychological Journal of South Africa,* 1982, *3,* 17–27.

Freud, S. Dreams and telepathy. *Imago,* 1922, *8,* 1–22.

George, L. A survey of research into the relationships between imagery and psi. *Journal of Parapsychology,* 1981, *45,* 121–146.

George, L. Enhancement of psi functioning through mental imagery training. *Journal of Parapsychology,* 1982, *46,* 111–125.

George, L. Expectancy and psi: A critical review and reformulation. *Journal of the American Society for Psychical Research,* 1984, *78,* 193–217.

George, L. and Krippner, S. Mental imagery and psi: A review. In S. Krippner (Ed.), *Advances in parapsychological research,* vol. 4. Henderson, N.C.: McFarland, 1984. pp. 64–82

George, L. and Neufeld, R. W. J. Imagery and verbal aspects of schizophrenic informational performance. *British Journal of Clinical Psychology,* 1984, *23,* 9–18.

Gerber, R. and Schmeidler, G. R. An investigation of relaxation and of acceptance of the experimental situation as related to ESP scores in maternity patients. *Journal of Parapsychology,* 1957, *21,* 47–57.

Giesler, P. V. Parapsychological anthropology: Multi-method approaches to the study of psi in the field setting. In W. G. Roll, J. Beloff, and R. A. White (Eds.), *Research in Parapsychology 1982,* Metuchen, N.J.: Scarecrow Press, 1983, pp. 241-245.

Gorer, G. *African dances: A book about West African negroes.* New York: Knopf, 1935.

Green, C. Report on inquiry into spontaneous cases. *Proceedings of the Society for Psychical Research,* 1960, *53,* 97.

Grela, J. J. Effect on ESP scoring of hypnotically induced attitudes. *Journal of Parapsychology,* 1945, *9,* 194-202.

Haight, J. Spontaneous psi experiences: A survey and preliminary study of ESP, attitude, and personality relationships. *Journal of Parapsychology,* 1979, *43,* 179-204.

Handelman, D. The development of a Washo shaman. *Ethnology,* 1967, *6,* 444-464.

Hevoh, W. Cognitive and physiological effects of perceptual isolation. In P. Solomon et al. (Eds.), *Sensory deprivation,* Cambridge, Mass.: Harvard University Press, 1961, pp. 6-33.

Hilgard, E. R. *Divided consciousness: Multiple controls in human thought and action.* New York: Wiley, 1977.

Honorton, C. Relationship between EEG alpha activity and ESP card-guessing performance. *Journal of the American Society for Psychical Research,* 1969, *63,* 365-374.

Honorton, C. Significant factors in hypnotically-induced clairvoyant dreams. *Journal of the American Society for Psychical Research,* 1972, *66,* 86-102.

Honorton, C. Psi and internal attention states. In B. B. Wolman (Ed.), *Handbook of parapsychology.* New York: Van Nostrand Reinhold, 1977, pp. 435-472.

Honorton, C. Psi and internal attention states: Information retrieval in the ganzfeld. In B. Shapin and L. Coly (Eds.), *Psi and states of awareness.* New York: Parapsychology Foundation, 1978, pp. 79-100.

Honorton, C. and Krippner, S. Hypnosis and ESP performance: A review of the experimental research. *Journal of the American Society for Psychical Research,* 1969, *63,* 214-252.

Honorton, C. and May, E. Volitional control in a psychokinetic task with auditory and visual feedback. In J. D. Morris, W. G. Roll, and R. L. Morris (Eds.), *Research in parapsychology 1975.* Metuchen, N.J.: Scarecrow Press, 1976, pp. 90-91.

Honorton, C., Davidson, R., and Bindler, P. Feedback-augmented EEG alpha, shifts in subjective state, and ESP card-guessing performance. *Journal of the American Society for Psychical Research,* 1971, *65,* 308-323.

Honorton, C., Drucker, S., and Hermon, H. Shifts in subjective state and ESP under conditions of partial sensory deprivation. *Journal of the American Society for Psychical Research,* 1973, *67,* 191-197.

Kanthamani, B. K. and Rao, K. R. Personality characteristics of ESP subjects: III. Extraversion and ESP. *Journal of Parapsychology,* 1972, *36,* 198-212.

Kelly, E. F. and Locke, R. G. *Altered states of consciousness and psi: An historical survey and research prospects* (Parapsychological monograph, No. 18). New York: Parapsychological Foundation, 1981.

Kornfield, J. Intensive insight meditation: A phenomenological study. *Journal of Transpersonal Psychology,* 1979, *11,* 41-58.

Kreitler, H. and Kreitler, S. Subliminal perception and extrasensory perception. *Journal of Parapsychology,* 1973, *37,* 163-188.

Krippner, S. Telepathy. In E. D. Mitchell and J. White (Eds.), *Psychic exploration: A challenge for science.* New York: G. P. Putnam's Sons, 1974, pp. 112-131.

Krippner, S. and Davidson, R. Paranormal events occurring during chemically-induced psychedelic experience and their implications for religion. *Journal of Altered States of Consciousness,* 1974, *1,* 175-184.

Krippner, S. and Fersh, D. Paranormal experience among members of American contra-cultural groups. *Journal of Psychedelic Drugs,* 1970, *3,* 109-114.

Laubscher, B. (1938). *Sex, custom and psychopathology. A study of South African pagan natives.* New York: McBride, 1938.

Layton, B. D. and Turnbull, B. Belief, evaluation, and performance on an ESP task. *Journal of Experimental Social Psychology,* 1975, *11,* 166–179.

Long, J. Extrasensory ecology: A summary of evidence. In J. Long (Ed.), *Extrasensory ecology: Parapsychology and anthropology.* Metuchen, N.J.: Scarecrow Press, 1977, pp. 371–396.

Lovitts, B. E. The sheep–goat effect turned upside down. *Journal of Parapsychology,* 1981, *45,* 293–310.

Luthe, W. and Schultz, J. H. *Autogenic therapy, Vol. 1: Autogenic methods.* New York: Grune & Stratton, 1969.

Masters, R. E. L. and Houston, J. *The varieties of psychedelic experience.* New York: Holt, Rinehart & Winston, 1966.

Mathews, A. M. and Gelder, M. G. Psychophysiological investigations of brief relaxation training. *Journal of Psychosomatic Research,* 1969, *13,* 1–12.

Métraux, A. *Voodoo in Haiti.* New York: Oxford University Press, 1959.

Mishra, R. *The textbook of yoga psychology.* New York: Julian Press, 1967.

Mitchell, J. Out-of-the-body vision. In D. S. Rogo (Ed.), *Mind beyond the body: The mystery of ESP projection.* New York: Penguin Books, 1978, pp. 154–161. (Original publication in 1973.)

Mockenhaupt, S., Robblee, P., Neville, R., and Morris, R. Relaxation techniques, feedback, and GESP: A preliminary study. In J. D. Morris, W. G. Roll, and R. L. Morris (Eds.), *Research in parapsychology 1976.* Metuchen, N.J.: Scarecrow Press, 1977, pp. 50–52.

Morris, R. L. Parapsychology, biology, and anpsi. In B. B. Wolman (Ed.), *Handbook of parapsychology.* New York: Van Nostrand Reinhold, 1977, pp. 687–715.

Morris, R. L. New directions in parapsychological research: The investigation of psychic development procedures. In I. L. Child, C. Honorton, E. F. Kelly, R. L. Morris, and R. G. Stanford, Merging of humanistic and laboratory traditions in parapsychology. *Parapsychology Review,* 1980, *11,* 1–4.

Morris, R. L. and Bailey, K. A. A preliminary exploration of some techniques reputed to improve free-response ESP. In W. G. Roll (Ed.), *Research in Parapsychology 1978.* Metuchen, N.J.: Scarecrow Press, 1979, pp. 63–65.

Morris, R. L. and Cohen, D. A preliminary experiment on the relationship among ESP, alpha rhythm and calling patterns. *Proceedings of the Parapsychological Association,* 1969, *6,* 22–23.

Morris, R. L. and Hornaday, J. An attempt to employ mental practice to facilitate PK. In Roll, W. G. (Ed.), *Research in parapsychology 1980.* Metuchen, NJ: Scarecrow Press, 1981, pp. 103–104.

Morris, R. L., Roll, W. G., Klein, J., and Wheeler, G. EEG patterns and ESP results in forced-choice experiments with Lalsingh Harribance. *Journal of the American Society for Psychical Research,* 1972, *66,* 253–261.

Morris, R. L., Robblee, P., Neville, R., and Bailey, K. Free-response ESP training with feedback to agent and receiver. In W. G. Roll (Ed.), *Research in Parapsychology 1977.* Metuchen, N.J.: Scarecrow Press, 1978.

Murphy, G. Field theory and survival. *Journal of the American Society for Psychical Research,* 1945, *39,* 181–209.

Murphy, G. Research in creativeness: What can it tell us about extrasensory perception? *Journal of the American Society of Psychical Research,* 1966, *60,* 8–22.

Nash, C. B. Cutaneous perception of color with a head box. *Journal of the American Society for Psychical Research,* 1971, *65,* 83–87.

Noll, R. Shamanism and schizophrenia: A state-specific approach to the "schizophrenia metaphor" of shamanic states. *American Ethnologist*, 1983, *10*, 443–459.

Onetto-Bächler, B. Ritalin and ESP: A pilot study. *Journal of the American Society for Psychosomatic Dentistry and Medicine*, 1983, *30*, 17–20.

Osis, K. and Bokert, E. ESP and changed states of consciousness induced by meditation.
Journal of the American Society for Psychical Research, 1971, *65*, 17–65.

Otani, S. Relations of mental set and change of skin resistance to ESP score. *Journal of
Parapsychology*, 1955, *19*, 164–170.

Otani, S. Studies on the influence of the mental and physiological conditions upon ESP function. *Journal of Parapsychology*, 1958, *22*, 296.

Palmer, J. Scoring in ESP tests as a function of belief in ESP. Part 1. The sheep–goat effect.
Journal of the American Society for Psychical Research, 1971, *65*, 373–408.

Palmer, J. Extrasensory perception: Research findings. In S. Krippner (Ed.), *Advances in
parapsychological research, Vol. 1, Psychokinesis*. New York: Plenum Press, 1977, pp. 59–
243.

Palmer, J. ESP and out-of-body experiences: EEG correlates. In W. G. Roll (Ed.), *Research
in parapsychology 1978*. Metuchen, N.J.: Scarecrow Press, 1979, pp. 135–138.

Palmer, J. and van de Velden, I. ESP and "hypnotic imagination": A group free response
study. *European Journal of Parapsychology*, 1983, *4*, 413–434.

Parker, A. Some findings relevant to the change in state hypothesis. In J. D. Morris, W. G.
Roll, and R. L. Morris (Eds.), *Research in parapsychology 1974*, Metuchen, N.J.: Scarecrow Press, 1975a, pp. 40–42.

Parker, A. *States of mind: ESP and altered states of consciousness*. New York: Taplinger,
1975b.

Persinger, M. ELF waves and ESP. *New Horizons*, 1975, *1*, 232–235.

Prasad, J. and Stevenson, I. A survey of spontaneous psychical experiences in school children
of Uttar Pradesh, India. *International Journal of Parapsychology*, 1968, *10*, 241–261.

Pratt, J. G. and Birge, W. R. Appraising verbal test material in parapsychology. *Journal of
Parapsychology*, 1948, *12*, 236–256.

Rechtschaffen, A., Vogel, G., and Shaikun, G. Interrelatedness of mental activity during sleep.
Archives of General Psychiatry, 1963, *9*, 536–547.

Rhine, J. B. The value of reports of spontaneous psi experiences. *Journal of Parapsychology*,
1948, *12*, 231–235.

Rhine, J. B. *Extrasensory perception*, Rev. ed. Boston: Bruce Humphries, 1973.

Rhine, J. B. History of experimental studies. In B. B. Wolman (Ed.), *Handbook of parapsychology*, New York: Van Nostrand Reinhold, 1977, pp. 25–47.

Rhine, J. B., Pratt, J. G., Stuart, C. E., Smith, B. M., and Greenwood, J. A. *Extrasensory
perception after 60 years*. Boston: Bruce Humphries, 1966. (Original publication in 1940.)

Rhine, L. E. Frequency of types of experiences in spontaneous precognition. *Journal of Parapsychology*, 1954, *18*, 93–123.

Rhine, L. E. Psychological processes in ESP experiences. Part II. Dreams. *Journal of Parapsychology*, 1962, *26*, 172–199.

Rhine, L. E. *The invisible picture: A study of psychic experiences*. Jefferson, N.C.: Mc-
Farland, 1981.

Richet, C. Further experiments in hypnotic lucidity or clairvoyance. *Proceedings of the Society
for Psychical Research*, 1889, *6*, part 15.

Rogo, D. S. Research on psi-conducive states: Some complicating factors. *Journal of Parapsychology*, 1976, *40*, 34–45.

Rogo, D. S. Experiments with Blue Harary. In D. S. Rogo (Ed.), *Mind beyond the body: The
mystery of ESP projection*. New York: Penguin Books, 1978, pp. 170–192.

Rogo, D. S. ESP and schizophrenia: An analysis from two perspectives. *Journal of the Society for Psychical Research,* 1982, *51,* 329-342.

Sannwald, G. [Statistical investigations of spontaneous phenomena.] *Zeitschrift für Parapsychologie und Grenzgebiete der Psychologie,* 1959, *3,* 59-71.

Sargent, C. L. (1980). *Exploring PSI in the ganzfeld.* New York: Parapsychology Foundation.

Sargent, C. L. Hypnosis as a psi-conducive state: A controlled replication study. *Journal of Parapsychology,* 1978a, *42,* 257-275.

Sargent, C. L. Arousing problems in parapsychology. In B. Shapin and L. Coly (Eds.), *Psi and states of awareness.* New York: Parapsychology Foundation, 1978b, pp. 131-151.

Sargent, C. L. and Harley, A. T. Precognition testing with free-response techniques in the ganzfeld and the dream state. *European Journal of Parapsychology,* 1982, *4,* 243-256.

Schechter, E. I. Hypnotic induction vs. control conditions: Illustrating an approach to the evaluation of replicability in parapsychological data. *Journal of the American Society for Psychical Research,* 1984, *78,* 1-27.

Schlitz, M. and Gruber, E. Transcontinental remote viewing. *Journal of Parapsychology,* 1980, *44,* 305-317.

Schmeidler, G. R. Rorschachs and ESP scores of patients suffering from cerebral concussion. *Journal of Parapsychology,* 1952, *16,* 80-89.

Schmeidler, G. R. High ESP scores after a Swami's brief instruction in meditation and breathing. *Journal of the American Society for Psychical Research,* 1970, *64,* 100-113.

Schmeidler, G. R. and McConnell, R. A. *ESP and personality patterns.* New Haven: Yale University Press, 1958.

Schmidt, H. PK tests with a high-speed random number generator. *Journal of Parapsychology,* 1973, *37,* 105-118.

Schuman, M. The psychophysiological model of meditation and altered states of consciousness: A critical review. In J. M. Davidson and R. J. Davidson, (Eds.), *The psychology of consciousness.* New York: Plenum, 1980, pp. 333-378.

Shapiro, D. H. *Meditation: Self-regulation strategy and altered state of consciousness.* New York: Aldine, 1980.

Silverman, J. Shamanism and acute schizophrenia. *American Anthropologist,* 1967, *69,* 21-31.

Slade, R. D. An investigation of psychological factors involved in the predisposition to auditory hallucinations. *Psychological Medicine,* 1976, *6,* 123-132.

Stanford, R. G. Response bias and the correctness of ESP test responses. *Journal of Parapsychology,* 1967, *31,* 280-289.

Stanford, R. G. EEG activity and ESP performance: A replicative study. *Journal of the American Society for Psychical Research,* 1971, *65,* 144-154.

Stanford, R. G. Are parapsychologists paradigmless in psiland? In B. Shapin and L. Coly (Eds.), *The philosophy of parapsychology.* New York: Parapsychology Foundation, 1977, pp. 1-16.

Stanford, R. Recent ganzfeld-ESP research: A survey and critical analysis. In S. Krippner (Ed.), *Advances in parapsychological research,* Vol. 4. Jefferson, N.C.: McFarland, 1984, pp. 83-111.

Stanford, R. G. and Lovin, C. EEG alpha activity and ESP performance. *Journal of the American Society for Psychical Research,* 1970, *64,* 375-384.

Stanford, R. G. and Mayer, B. Relaxation as a psi-conducive state: A replication and exploration of parameters. *Journal of the American Society for Psychical Research,* 1974, *68,* 182-191.

Tart, C. T. A psychophysiological study of out of the body experiences in a selected subject. *Journal of the American Society for Psychical Research,* 1968, *62,* 3-27.

Tart, C. T. *On being stoned: A psychological study of marijuana intoxication.* Palo Alto, Calif. Science & Behavior Books, 1971.

Tart, C. T. *States of consciousness.* New York: E. P. Dutton, 1975.

Thalbourne, M. A. Extraversion and sheep–goat variable: A conceptual replication. *Journal of the American Society for Psychical Research,* 1981, *75,* 105–120.

Tolaas, J. and Ullman, M. Extrasensory communication and dreams. In B. B. Wolman (Ed.), *Handbook of dreams.* New York: Van Nostrand Reinhold, 1979, pp. 168–201.

Tsuang, M. T., Woolson, R. F., Winokur, G., and Crowe, R. R. Stability of psychiatric diagnosis. *Archives of General Psychiatry,* 1981, *38,* 535–540.

Tyrrell, G. N. M. *Apparitions.* London: Duckworth, 1943.

Ullman, M. The dream, schizophrenia, and psi phenomena. Paper read at the First International Conference on Parapsychology, Utrecht, Netherlands, 1953.

Ullman, M. and Krippner, S. Experimental dream studies. In M. Ebon, *The Signet handbook of parapsychology.* New York: New American Library, 1978, pp. 409–422.

Ullman, M., Krippner, S., and Vaughan, A. *Dream telepathy.* New York: Macmillan: 1973.

Van de Castle, R. L. An investigation of psi abilities among the Cuna Indians of Panama. In A. Angoff and D. Barth (Eds.), *Parapsychology and anthropology.* New York: Parapsychology Foundation, 1974, pp. 80–82.

Van de Castle, R. L. Sleep and dreams. In B. B. Wolman (Ed.), *Handbook of parapsychology.* New York: Van Nostrand Reinhold, 1977, pp. 473–499.

Wadden, T. and Anderton, C. The clinical use of hypnosis. *Psychological Bulletin,* 1982, *91,* 215–243.

White, R. A. A comparison of old and new methods of response to targets in ESP experiments. *Journal of the American Society for Psychical Research,* 1964, *58,* 21–56.

White, R. A., Krippner, S., and Ullman, M. Experimentally-induced telepathic dreams with EEG-REM monitoring: Some manifest content variables related to psi operation. In H. Bender (Ed.), *Papers presented for the Eleventh Annual Convention of the Parapsychological Association.* Freiburg, West Germany: Institute für Grenzgebiete der Psychologie, 1968, pp. 431–443.

Winkelman, M. Magic: A theoretical reassessment. *Current Anthropology,* 1982, *23*(1), 37–66.

References found to be especially useful in the preparation of this paper were Honorton (1977), Kelly and Locke (1981), Parker (1975b), and Van de Castle (1977). The reader is referred to them for additional information.

12. Drug-Induced States

Claudio Naranjo

EFFECTS OF THE LSD–LIKE PSYCHEDELICS OR HALLUCINOGENS

A case may be made for calling this group that of the "hallucinogens," for it was in view of their effect that this word came into use—not in its literal meaning (which would be the property of eliciting true hallucinations), but in that of bringing about hallucination-related or *hallucinoid* phenomena. If I sometimes call them the "LSD-like" psychedelics rather than the "hallucinogens," it is only to avoid confusion in the mind of readers unfamiliar with my suggested nomenclature, for the term "hallucinogen"—unless specifically defined as I am proposing—might be considered applicable to the fantasy-enhancers as well, and is generally (though somewhat inappropriately) regarded as a synonym for "psychedelic." The group comprises lysergic acid diethylamide and related compounds, mescaline, dimethyl tryptamine (DMT) and related compounds, psilocybin and psilocin, and various phenylisopropylamines, in addition to plants containing some of the above. The drugs in this group differ in the duration of their effect and in subtle characteristics (mescaline, for instance, produces more visual phenomena than psilocybin, the effect of which tends to be more cognitive, and the experiential quality of LSD has been characterized as more "electric" than others); yet they all differ from the feeling- and fantasy-enhancers in that they elicit characteristic perceptual phenomena, may bring about psychotic experiences (including depersonalization, delusions of damnation, messianic ideas, gross misinterpretations of the ongoing situation, etc.), and have the potential to bring about the "psychedelic experience" par excellence—characterized by a combination of contemplative experience, ecstasy, and varying degrees of spiritual insight.

The variety of psycho-spiritual states that may be evoked by the hallucinogens has surely been apparent to all those familiar with the domain. In the *Varieties of Psychedelic Experience,* Masters and Houston (1967) distinguish aesthetic, recollective-analytic, archetypal or symbolic, and integral or mystical experiencs. Grof (1975), in *Realms of the Human Unconscious,* speaks of a psychodynamic or "Freudian" domain, a perinatal or "Rankian" domain, and transpersonal experiences (some of which correspond to the archetypal and thus "Jungian" domain). Following Huxley (1964), I proposed in the *Healing Journey* (1973) a classification of psychedelic states in general into "heavenly" ones, characterized by the apprehension of intrinsic values (and frequently accompanied by rapture), and "hellish" states, characterized by a near-psychotic intensification of psychopathology. I proposed, too, a further subdivision of the positive feeling states according to the quality of value characterizing the experience; and, influenced in this by the thinking of Scheler and Spranger, I proposed a gamut of value leading from the sensate (pleasure) through aesthetic (beauty) and the social and interpersonal (love) to the religious (holiness—associated with the apprehension of Being).

This classification would have been more complete had I included, along with the heavens and hells, "purgatory" states, neither wholly positive nor wholly negative but states of satisfaction and dissatisfaction at the same time, characterized by striving and the sense of moving along, working through obstructions.

In spite of the validity of such distinctions, expressions such as "archetypal experience," "psychodymanic experience," and "heavenly state of the religious kind" fail to convey the specificity of archetypal, psychodynamic, or religious states brought about by the action of LSD-like psychedelics. This resides, not in the core phenomenon (archetypal-mythical, self-insight, or mystical experience proper) but in the context of physical, perceptual, affective, and cognitive phenomena in which it appears embedded. In what follows I will describe the effects of hallucinogens (sensu strictu) in greater detail in regard to behavior, the emotions, perception, thinking, and the spiritual realm proper.

By far the most common effect on behavior after a full dosage of LSD or similar hallucinogen is a surrender to what Barber (1970) has labeled "dreamy-detached" feelings, and which might appropriately be called a spontaneous *contemplative* attitude and state. Words such as "dreamy" or "reverie," I think, fail to do justice to the psychedelic state, which, while involving a rich visual component (either with eyes closed or with eyes open) is in other ways a hyperalert state rather than one of obnubilation (the effects of the LSD-like hallucinogens in this regard differ from those of *Amanita muscaria*, the fly-agaric mushroom, which causes a desire to sleep).

The connotation of the word "contemplative" in the spiritual traditions derives in part from the fact that it exists as part of a word-pair, designating a polarity: contemplative/active. Contemplative experience arises in the practice of meditation, which in turn entails a moving away from the world of action and the senses. Aside from its implication of passivity, the word "contemplation" makes reference, in its traditional use, to a spiritual experience; that is, one in which the individual has access to spiritual riches. Also, it is a state in which the habitual duality of subject and object is reduced or may disappear, so that the contemplator is absorbed in the object of his contemplation. In the "hallucinogenic trance," as we may also call this particular effect of the LSD-like psychedelics, the individual feels inclined to lie down and usually to close his eyes, relinquishing every intention aside from that of mere experiencing—while the characteristic perceptual and spiritual effects to be described later unfold.

When the eyes are kept open, objects become more interesting, as they are regarded in a way different from the habitual—in a "contemplative" manner in the sense of its being gratuitous rather than motivated by the ordinary utilitarian outlook; one in which seeing is its own satisfaction. There is a tendency to linger on things, which either undergo transformations in terms of formal or aesthetic attributes, significance, or, as Huxley (1954) puts it, is-ness.

On the affective side, the experience of the body may range from one of "oceanic bliss" on the positive side to malaise, localized pains, suffocation, and other painful symptoms on the negative. On the whole, we may say that the body reflects, just as visual perception does, the experiential qualities of heavenly, hellish, and intermediate states—or, to say it in Grof's terms, physical experience reflects the "perinatal matrices." According to him, thus, these experiences of physical distress sometimes suggest the re-experiencing of birth trauma, while the experience of relaxed plenitude suggests life in the womb before the onset of labor. The experience of "purgatory" that lies between these extremes of superabundant well-being and of distress may also be described in reference to the metaphor of birth, for we may attribute it to the fetus as it progresses along the birth canal.

Grof (1975, 1980) suggests that the perinatal matrices (i.e., modes of experience related to those experiences surrounding birth) are memories or replays of the past—a hypothesis in line with convincing examples of hallucinogenically induced age regression in other regards though in conflict with the fact that by the time of birth myelinization of the peripheral nerves is not complete. Alternatively, we may conceive that these distinct states are not in essence memories but "mental landscapes" *analogous* to those surrounding birth—which, precisely by virtue of this analogy, are *associated* with memories and fantasized reconstructions of the past. Hallucinogen-elicited death/rebirth experiences are, I think, experiences pertaining to the temporay "death" of what spiritual traditions have called "ego" (our ordinary identity and what it entails) and the "birth" of deeper layers of one's nature. Yet it is not to be wondered that these experiences that correspond to the perception of a psycho-spiritual death/rebirth process and which echo those of physical birth at a higher octave, so to speak, may become *symbolized* in these earlier experiences and memories—in the way all experiences under the influence of the hallucinogens tend to become symbolized.

A symbol both expresses and has the potential to conceal—and it is my impression that this is particularly the case in regard to the painful experiences of the body, which may include, aside from those suggestive of birth trauma, all sorts of psychosomatic symptoms and seemingly individual aches and muscle tensions. It is a common finding of those involved in psychotherapy with hallucinogens that these ailments constitute a projection upon the body of affective experiences that still have not been confronted, and that they disappear along with the undoing of repression. Striking examples of this may be found in the first-person account *Myself and I,* by Constance Newland (1963). She discovered, for instance, that her painfully full bladder was an equivalent of sexual arousal, that her excessive sensitivity to pain in the teeth was connected to fantasies of biting, and that her chronic tensional aches in the arms, amplified under LSD into a sensation that she described as the buzzing of an electric saw, disappeared after a therapeutically guided session in which she was able to remember a traumatic event that occurred when she was two and a half. On that occasion her nurse had tied her arms to give her an enema, the water of which was too hot, and which made her feel as if she were to burst. In addition to retrieving this memory, she was also able to discover that she experienced this painful event as punishment for masturbation.

We may note that any feeling possible to our human nervous system may be aroused in the psychedelic state, and this applies not only to the ordinary feelings but also to very early preverbal feeling-states, for among the effects of the hallucinogens is that of age regression. The passivity itself that characterizes the hallucinogenic state at its peak, a non-goal-directed state that may be characterized as a de-differentiation of the mind, can be regarded as regressive, for it is tempting to regard it as analogous to what may have been the state of mind of a fetus. This state and the reliving of early experiences are related, in that de-differentiation is the basis for the psychological permeability that allows the accessing of remote mental contents or their "manifesting" to the conscious mind.

Very characteristic under the influence of hallucinogens are, of course, the ecstatic states and the counter-ecstatic states, which are to grief what ecstasy is to ordinary happiness and pleasure. The most profound among the ecstatic states is that associated with the physical states that I have described as "oceanic," by virtue of the seeming dissolution of boundaries between the individual and the world, the inside and the outside, self and other, and even subject and object. It is a supremely impersonal or transpersonal domain of experience in which even the visonary content is abstract rather than figurative. Individuals sometimes spontaneously use the word "cosmic" in reference, not only to experienced boundlessness, but to the sense of superabundant plenitude. Though individuals with religious or philosophical sophistication may translate this ineffable experience into terms such as "the clear light of the void" as Huxley did, or Sat-Chit-Ananda, Brahman, "The Absolute," and so forth, I will not undertake to engage in any such conceptualizations here—aside from distinguishing this "mystical" experience from religious experiences proper, which lie in a domain where thought is not altogether absent and images or concepts of an exalted, "superhuman," or mythical quality are manifest in the visions. In reference to them I will speak of "religious–archetypal" experiences, being of the opinion that the religious and the mythical can be only artificially separated—archetypes being essentially symbols imbued with numinosity, sacred symbols that arise from an experience of sacredness. (Thus, experiences of an "otherness" perceived as a "heavenly father" or a "cosmic mother," usually regarded as "religious," may also be considered to be implicitly archetypal.)

Some reports of profound ecstatic states could be used to illustrate either religious ecstasy or the ecstatic feelings associated with deeply felt love; in other instances, an arousal of love may be manifest without an explicit religious content. One may wonder in these cases, however, whether there is not a factor of spiritual awareness that underlies what nonreligious individuals perceive only at the interpersonal end of the feeling spectrum. At least the association between both is frequent, and particularly in the context of group therapy facilitated by LSD. One comes across episodes where individuals engage in a silent communication of a depth uncommon in ordinary life; these may be simply interpreted as experiences of deep empathy, in the sense of seeing the common humanness between self and other; or may be articulated as experiences of which the outer manifestation is love but which arise from a glimpse of that transcendent self that is the essence of both self and other.

Just as a transcendent background of experience may manifest itself in the interpersonal realm as feelings of love, it is also possible that the same spiritual factor projects itself in aesthetic experience, in a way that some individuals may acknowledge as such while others, not open to the spiritual dimension (perhaps by virtue of an anti-religious bias), fail to acknowledge or articulate. It seems quaint to me that in so many of the early reports on the effects of psychedelics only the aesthetic aspect stands out, and reference to love and mystical insights are absent. (Klüver, 1966, on the last page of his essay on mescal, disdainfully puts in quotation marks the expression "cosmic significance," which some individuals report in connection to their visions.) Perhaps the spirit of the times was not sufficiently receptive to the transcendent dimension of hallucinogenic experiences, and thus it is revealing to read Huxley's (1954) report in the *Doors of Perception,* in which he experiences no lesser degree of aesthetic ecstasy than his predecessors but is able to trace the beauty of the perceived world back to an underlying enhancement of *Istigkeit,* the sense of Being.

Another source of ecstasy is connected to something akin to pleasure. I say "akin to" pleasure in order to point out the peculiar kind of bliss that some individuals interpret or express in reference to body feelings or sensations rather than religious interpersonal or aesthetic emotions, for it differs in quality from the pleasure of instinctual gratification. It is to a considerable extent pleasure associated with seeing and with hearing, a delight not in the aesthetic qualities of particular music works, but in sound itself, not in aesthetic form but in colors and textures—a pleasure residing in the affective tone of sensations themselves. Part of it comes from proprioceptive sensing—as in a state of free flowing "body energies"—and may be described simply as intense well-being. Just as in the above instances, however, we may have reason to think that such "pleasure" is not unrelated to the core factor in psychedelic peak experiences: the mystical or spiritual factor that spills over the different domains of experience including that of sensing. In the same way that the beauty of Huxley's carnation and iris owes its intensity to a felt meaningfulness that is projected upon them from the field of experience of Huxley, who contemplates them, all sensory experience partakes of increased meaningfulness in the awareness of one immersed in the expanded hallucinogenic state. This "translates" itself into apparent intensification, but we know that this sensory intensification is a subjective phenomenon, not verified by experiments on tactile discrimination or visual acuity. It constitutes, rather, like visual distortions, a symbolic projection of luminosity, enhanced significance.

Another state that I want to mention among the peak experiences elicited by the hallucinogens (along with the paradises and states of inspiration, culminating in trances of divine possession) is one characterized by an intense feeling of all-rightness in the face of the concrete, undistorted here-

and-now and one's individual circumstances. This state (usually accompanied by a feeling of gratefulness as has been described by Aldous Huxley in *Island*) best corresponds in the perinatal domain to the state of the newborn—who has emerged from the beyond and comes into the world of persons and objects as a ripe fruit. In the language of religious symbolism we may call this state an "earthly paradise."

The supernegative or "hellish" states may be understood not only as intensifications of psychopathology (as I put it in *The Healing Journey*) but as states of intense value deficiency. Accordingly, for each state of enhanced value we may distinguish the corresponding state of valuelessness, or negative value. To pleasure, there corresponds, on the sensory level, a state of distress that is an undescribable agony of a vague sort, in which an individual probably somatizes a psycho-spiritual distress to such a degree that it sometimes requires the interruption of the experience. To the aesthetic level and the perception of beauty, on the positive end of the feeling range, there corresponds an intensified perception of ugliness, where any particular object or the world as a whole becomes something flat, caricature-like, grotesque, in bad taste, artificial, hideous, and so forth. To love there corresponds, on the negative end, a lovelessness that can be the background of a state of forlornness and depression or of a paranoid state, in which the world or others are perceived as hateful, malevolent, demonic. In a special class among paranoid states are states of possession by demonic or malevolent entities, in which the individual may either engage in destructive behavior (frequently described as a reaction to *Amanita*) or feel that his mental processes are forced upon him—as during part of Albert Hofmann's (and the world's) first LSD self-experiment (Hofmann, 1983). To the highest level of value—the sense of the holy—there corresponds, as a counterpart, a complete desacralization of life, an absence of being, a sense of unreality, insubstantiality, or emptiness of self and of the world.

A rarer affective state that may be brought about by the hallucinogens is neither positive nor negative (nor both), but of intensified indifference—as in the catatonic syndrome. It is neither "heavenly" nor "hellish" (in appearance), but, to borrow another word from religion, one of "limbo". In psychiatric terminology I think most would agree to call these states as in the first case reported in Sydney Cohen's *The Beyond Within* (1967, 113–114), catatonic reactions.

Though "heavens" and "hells"—peak and nadir experiences—may be regarded as the most typical states induced by the hallucinogens, they are perhaps not the most frequent, particularly if we consider their duration in the course of a specific session. I think that if a statistical calculation were made of the time spent on different experiential realms across subjects, this would show that the most frequent state is neither one of unalloyed bliss nor dispair, but one in which positive and negative feelings are present side by side. It is essentially a *seeking-state*, a state that is half-abundance, half-deficiencey, and is characterized by the striving for abundance, and a pursuit of optimization.

It is this feeling state, I believe, that explains those visions that Klüver (1966, p. 31) has called *presque vu* experiences:

> events in the visual field . . . suggest an end which is not quite reached, or they lack the proper completion; they do not—to use a Gestalt psychological term—call forth a "closure" experience.

That these experiences reflect not only the structure of neurological events but an affective state is suggested by less abstract embodiments of near perfection, such as a vision of innumerable snail shells, each with a little piece missing.

This seeking state, echoing the situation of "wanting to be born" that we may emphatically attribute to the child as it advances through the birth canal, is frequently associated with psychotherapeutic inquiry or with what may be described as spontaneous spiritual work—such as that of seeking to surrender more deeply, to accept the pain of the moment less defensively, or to experience ever more fully one's aspiring, perhaps prayerful attitude. This is the state that religious symbolism has projected into the afterworld as "purgatory"—a place of purification—and I do not think that it should be explained as a mere reliving of a perinatal situation any more than the impulse to progress psycho-spiritually in life should.

The seeking impulse, which I see as the core phenomenon in "purification" states, is a longing that, detaching itself from habitual objects (such as romantic love or the affirmations of one's idealized self-image), comes to interpret itself as a thirst for what may be variously interpreted as plenitude, wholeness, higher consciousness, God, Enlightenment. The spontaneous aspiration to escape the prison of internal limitations and to attain an intuited possibility of higher consciousness and greater satisfaction is, I think, objectively justified by the perception of these limitations and potential in the present. Its foundation need not be sought in early experience, therefore, but in the condition of the organism at the moment: a condition of dysfunction and pain that the hallucinogens (and also the feeling-enhancers) characteristically bring into awareness—together with glimpses of an alternative.

It has been one of Grof's merits to point out the hallucinogenic syndrome that he calls "volcanic"—and which he describes in terms of its association with the moment immediately preceding birth, when passage along the birth canal is fastest and suffocation has reached its maximum. In it a volcanic type of ecstasy is manifest simultaneously with an intensification of suffering to cosmic proportions. It may be accompanied by sexual feelings, experiences of dying and being reborn, and intense physical manifestations ("pressures" and pain, suffocation, muscular tension and discharge, nausea and vomiting, hot flushes and chills, sweating, cardiac distress, problems of sphincter control, ringing in the ears"; Grof, 1980, p. 82). Among the visions typically accompanying these experiences he includes: titanic battles, archetypal feats, explosions of atomic bombs, launching of missiles and spaceships, exploding volcanoes, earthquakes, tornadoes and other natural catastrophes, bloody revolutions, dangerous hunts for wild animals, discoveries and conquests of new continents.

Volcanic states may be regarded as intensified states of emptiness-fullness, and are those that may most properly be spoken of as death-rebirth processes; for there is in them at the same time a crumbling down of the habitual personality (with the consequent fear) and an ecstatic emergence of new energies and a new sense of self. They may be regarded as a greatly accelerated or amplified form of the ongoing dying and being born that are part of human evolution.

To end this survey of affective states, I will mention the frequent occurrence of hypomanic or manic states. These can be of two kinds: (1) narcissistic excitement about the wonders of one's experience, corresponding to the phenomenon of inflation (pride in spiritual experience, most common toward the end of sessions); and (2) the irresistible humor associated with otherwise shallow experiences, as a facet of a defensive reaction.

Writing of the affective aspect of hallucinogen-induced states would not be complete without discussion of something implicit in all of them: a variable measure of detachment. Out of detachment grows the contemplative experience; it is out of abandon that visions arise. When "getting out of the way" is thorough, mystical experiences manifest; when the eruption of the mind-depth is resisted, it is hells that arise. These hells not only are resisted but are created through an inward act of jumping into the void; they constitute an otherworld of the mind that has been arrived at through a measure of death, an incomplete yet real though temporal dissolution of the "little" I, the ordinary self.

All affective states, from terror to bliss, arise, I think, from this background of detachment—ranging from "dreamy-detached" feelings (to borrow Barber's expression) to ego-death.

It is the perceptual effects of the hallucinogens that have suggested their name; they are intense and unfamiliar, and echo the range of affective states. Thus, it is not only with respect to feelings but in visual terms that we encounter hells, purgatories, heavens—and an enriched earth. For the earthly paradise of the hallucinogens, unlike the one brought about by feeling-enhancers, is linked with a special mode of perception in which the world of persons and objects is neither distorted nor left behind (along with the body itself and one's sense of identity), nor is it hidden behind a screen of half-materialized fantasies; it becomes more of itself, we might say. Everything becomes clearer, sharper, not only appearing to be more "present" than usual, but with a density of formal relationships that creates the impression that each thing is a miracle of perfection even in its imperfections.

No less remarkable are the distortions in visual perception ("dismorphopsia"), which, like illusory movement, are of an expressive nature.

We may speak of varying degrees in which is effected a projection of the inner world upon the outer. The intensification of light and perception of expressive qualities stand at the lower end of this range; illusory movements and perceptual distortions constitute an intermediate stage; a further step in this direction is the creation of hallucinations proper (which are rare) or psuedo hallucinations (in which the individual knows the perceived form to be the materialization of a fantasy).

According to Masters and Houston (1967), every category of myth may spontaneously arise: creation myths, myths of death–rebirth, of questing and transformation. Yet more common than mythological sequences proper (which are more common with the fantasy-enhancers) is the emergence of symbolic scenes and the stimulation of mythical understanding—linking the content of visions with universal themes.

Most characteristic of the hallucinogens are abstract visionary experiences, or ones in which realistic elements are embedded in an abstract pattern. It is such visions that Klüver (1966) studied in his classic study of mescal in 1928. In that work he points out the existence of "forms and form elements which must be considered typical for mescal visions," and which he proposes to call form-constants. He describes three of these. One of these form constants, for example, is always referred to by terms such as *grating, lattice, network, filigree, honeycomb,* or chessboard design." Closely related to this is another that he calls the cobweb figure; for instance, "colored threads runing together in a revolving center, the whole similar to a cobweb." The cobweb may be regarded, I think, as a combination of lattice and circularity or (to echo Jung's generalization of the Oriental word) *mandala.* Related to the latter are also "kaleidoscopic" images.

Klüver suggests that such images may have a neurological basis. Without discarding such a thought, we may also regard them as remarkable projections of the state of affairs in the individual's psyche, which is one of increased associations between mental contents—felt as an interconnected and coherent multiplicity.

A second form-constant singled out by Klüver (1966) is one "designated by terms such as tunnel, funnel, alley cone, or vessel." Here are some of his illustrations:

> Sometimes I seemed to be gazing into a vast hollow revolving vessel, on whose polished concave mother-of-pearl surface the hues were swiftly changing; the field of vision is similar to the interior of a cone, the vertex of which is lying in the center of the field directly before my eyes; . . . upon pressure of the closed eyes I first saw an alley in very deep perspective; deep beautiful perspectives . . . going to the infinite. (p. 23)

Here, too, we may understand the formal pattern as a visual representation of an experience: that of moving along an *experiential path*. A tunnel may be regarded as the mandalic structure of a field of experience (with the self at the center) unfolding in time. When such visions occur as a response to music, the sense of onward movement echoes not only the felt progression of a physical and psychological process but the perception of music as an unfolding in time.

A third form-constant mentioned by Klüver (1966) is the *spiral*.

> There appears a brown spiral, a wide band, revolving madly around its vertical axis. The band spiral opens and closes on a concertina according to the rhythm of the whistling . . . a procession, coming from the lower right, moved slowly in spiral turns to the upper left. . . . At the same time one of my legs assumes spiral form the luminous spiral and the haptic spiral blend psychologically. . . . A physician, a subject of Beringer, reports: "Before me I see the lower part of my body from the hips down as a large green varnished object which has about the shape of a truncated cone with spiral windings." (p. 23–24)

At the time when Klüver was writing his pioneering report, there was not in his environment something that has come into ours that echoes the style of psychedelic abstractions better than words and even human painting can do: certain computer graphics. And they do this, I think, because they convey the same combination of mathematical regularity and organic complexity that is perhaps the fundamental aspect of these visions. Among computer graphics and, more generally, bidimensional geometric displays, it is particularly moire patterns involving the superimposition of "reverberating" conic sections (ellipses, etc.) that are most expressive of the visionary realm. If we want to convey harmonious complexity with a single line, however, in no way could we do it better than with the spiral—which for this and other reasons may be the most appropriate graphic symbol of psychedelic consciousness. Containing in itself a radial pattern, a sense of advancing of advancing toward a goal never reached, and plural reverberation, in addition to the felt harmonious complexity of its equation, by its serpentine form it evokes the snake, universal symbol of the "life-force," "Kundalini," or "cosmic orgone."

True as may be the description by Havelock Ellis (DeRopp, 1957, p. 36) of his mescaline experience as "an orgy of vision," listening to music is at least as significant as attending to the visual world, and is generally regarded as the best doorway to ecstatic experience.

At best, the experience of musical audition may lead the individual to echo the statement of classical India: "*sabda Brahman*: sound is God." Just as the visual world may convey—behond the particulars of form, color, objects, and meanings—Being-ness, *Istigeit,* so sound in itself, beyond musical forms and psychological content, becomes suffused with Being, a Being with which the listener identifies as he dissolves in the music, becoming nothing and the music all at once.

While in the depths of oceanic dissolution music ceases to be perceived as such, at a more differentiated level of consciousness audition becomes musical audition proper, though an intensified musical audition. This is a transpersonal realm equivalent to that of visual archetypes, and distinct from the state of musical audition in still another state of consciousness characterized by the presence of personal contents. In the latter, the music becomes the mirror of the ordinary psyche, rather than the spirit: an acoustical projective device. According to the context of the experience projected upon it, music then will be (at either level) heavenly, hellish, or anything in between.

Broadly speaking, the cognitive aspect of hallucinogen-induced states may be discussed in regard to an interference with rational, linear, discursive, and goal-directed thinking; a stimulation of unusual forms of cognition (an "expansion of consciousness" by virtue of which it is possible to grasp "other realities"), and the possible presence of delusional thinking. These three seem to be interrelated in such a manner that the suspension of rational thought allows for the emergence of nonrational, intuitive, analogical, and magical thinking—which in turn can be manifest in a productive or an aberrated manner.

It is my impression that delusional phenomena constitute an intuitive potential gone askew, and that psychotic thinking in general may be viewed as a distorted approximation of reality. It is as if the psychotic came into contact with too much truth—more than he could bear—and evaded such an excess of perception through the escape-valves of projection, displacement, distortion, and so on. This is suggested, for instance, by Laing and Esterson's (1964 investigation of schizophrenics and their families, in which they invite us to consider madness as a step in the direction of healing. All the same, it is a step in the direction of a truth (about the love of parents, for instance) that cannot be handled, and because it cannot be handled it is transformed into an approximation—usually a symbolic equivalent of the truth that is in equal measure a truth that rises above the common world of lies and an absurdity that falls below the standards of reason.

In connection with the interference of rational thinking, I will omit laboratory data (summary of which may be found in Barber, 1970) and stay at the phenomenologic level. When interference is profound, this may be subjectively experienced as a "nothingness," skillfully described by Michaux (1974) in his essay on "What is 'Coming to Oneself'?" His answer to the question is, accordingly, being "restored to thought."

Not everyone will agree in regard to the total suspension of thought under the effect of a hallucinogen. Huxley (1954), for instance, in *The Doors of Perception,* remarked that he could think clearly and conceptualize throughout the experience. However, besides being the expression of one particular kind of experience—an extreme one—it is possible that suspension of thought may have been a state particularly available to Michaux, since there is a tendency for hallucinogenically induced states to counterbalance in some regards the salient features of one's personality; and Michaux—who described such nonthinking (1974)—throughout his writings appears to be the epitome of a "thinking type."

In another passage, Michaux (1974, pp. 27–28) described trying to write under the effects of a hallucinogen. Here thought was not totally silenced but was in a process of disintegration. The passage shows an abundance of thought leading to an interference of goal-directed thinking. While the writer aims at the expression of a thought, an overwhelming increase in the density of associations causes the emergence of other thoughts that compete with the first as objects of expression—and so on. Yet this is a phenomenon that can be experienced in two different attitudes. The subject may either, like Michaux, insist on thinking in a linear way and be distressed to realize that his thinking is disturbed; or he may, alternatively, give up the attempt—or rather *intent*—to think and discover himself immersed in a different cognitive medium, so to speak; for it is precisely this silencing of thought that traditional spirituality has recognized as the point of departure for contemplative experience. St. Gregory says contemplation is "to rest from exterior motion and to cleave only to the desire of the Maker." We might expand this description inasmuch as the passivity of the contemplative state entails the relinquishment, not only of external action, but of the thinker, the computing, analyzing mind.

The astounding abundance of detail of hallucinogen-induced visions seems to reflect admirably the wealth of elements simultaneously present in the individual's field at any moment. The state of increased permeability characteristic of this state allows for easy access to memories, to new connections, and to constellations of experience such as those that Jung has called complexes and Grof (1980) proposes to call systems of condensed experience (COEX systems). Such constellations of reciprocally associated mnemonic traces and their corresponding affect may be said to exist in our psychological structure, where they are, in the first place, buried because of repression and amnesia, and are not grasped as wholes, but sequentially, through the linear and one-dimensional progression of discursive thought.

The condition of increased interconnectedness and accessibility of mental contents may not only lead to the lifting of childhood amnesia and the arising of personal insights, but is likely to be the basis for the potential of hallucinogens to stimulate creativity (Harman and Fadiman, 1970), and, most typically, it constitutes the basis for the gift of contemplation. This manifests itself not only in regard to external objects, but in regard to internal or mental objects as well. Any subject matter that motivates the individual (and these emerge spontaneously in the course of any hallucinogenic experience) is invested with a great wealth of associations drawn out of the "oceanic" depth of the mind and experienced not merely as a thought-construction but as inseparable—by virtue of associative links—from the whole of one's inner life. I believe that the experiences that Grof (1975) classifies as temporal and spatial expansions of consciousness (ancestral experiences; collective and racial experiences; identification with other persons, with animals, plants, planetary consciousness, etc.) constitute, in essence, expressions of contemplative experience—inasmuch as the individual not only mobilizes an unusual degree of creative imagination in them, but (as is usual in contemplation) identifies himself with his mental creation. It is no wonder that—by virtue of this movement—the products of contemplative experience may be taken literally as a tapping by the human mind of a "group consciousness," a consciousness inherent in inorganic matter, extra-planetary consciousness, and so on. The question remains, however, of whether the sense of certainty that accompanies these experiences reflects literal truth or is instead a phenomenological trait associated with an "inner" truth comparable to that of a poem or a myth.

Peyote-consuming Indians and researchers alike (Grof, 1975; Kripner, 1974) have noted that the hallucinogens may elicit experiences of extrasensory perception.

If the hallucinogens indeed stimulate clairvoyance and clairaudience, that should not be wondered at, since it should be expected from increased access to "the other side of the mind" and would naturally arise from increased receptivity.

Contemplative experience may find support in any object, symbol, or concept, and leads (when contemplation is most successful) to an apprehension of the "mysteries"—eternal truths concerning existence that cannot be grasped by thought alone, and at most can be expressed gropingly in art and philosophical discourse.

That the sense of time may expand is easy to understand as a result of the acceleration of thought; yet time may also shrink, and this seems a natural consequence of the silencing of discursive thinking at the hallucinogenic peak. The apparent suspension of time is usually associated with the mystical experience and a sense of the eternal—in which the experience of time-arrest is compounded with a sense of infinite time.

In connection with delusional thinking, my view is that it corresponds to a superposition of higher cognition and defensive distortion. Through rejection of an experience that—when accepted—may be called divine, there thus arises a sense of the demonic, of paranoia, and a sense of a remote, indifferent, or inaccessible cosmos or self in depression.

I have already touched upon the spiritual effects of hallucinogens in speaking of the experiences of the body, perceptual and cognitive phenomena, emotional and behavioral effects; for the domains of the psyche cannot be wholly separated, and spiritual experience has a physical correlate (the movement of "energy" in the body or, to speak in Indian terms, the activation of the Kundalini and the circulation of prana through the chakras and nadis) and is related, with the emotional sphere (with its polarity of deficiency/abundance, craving versus love) and with the cognitive domain. The fact that many cognitive experiences have been classified by Grof (1980) as "transpersonal" is an indication of how difficult it may be to separate the transpersonal or spiritual factor proper from its cognitive and perceptual "envelope" or echo. Indeed, though the mystical experience, as the word itself reveals, is ineffable (the Greek root *mus* meaning 'mute') it is typically articulated through the medium of symbolism.

If we want to move on from such projections of spirituality onto the domains of cognition, emotion, action, and the experienced body, seeking to penetrate to the spiritual sphere itself, transcendent to these components of the "person," we might do best by not saying anything. Such is sometimes the Buddhist attitude—as an expression of its "theology" (if we can continue to use this word for a nontheistic articulation of transcendence). For spirit, in this view (consonant with the *ein Soph* doctrine of the Kabbalah and the Chinese concept of the Tao), is something that cannot be pointed at, and lies in an altogether different domain from that of articulate consciousness with its awareness of body, feelings, qualities, things, logical classes, and persons. To speak of it as "voidness," as Mahayana scriptures do, does more than express its ineffability: it points to a sphere of experience (or nonexperience?) that is like the matrix in which the articulate contents of the mind unfold, the "space" in which thoughts and images arise and mental states occur—a field that, according to Vajrayana Buddhism, may possess increasing degrees of permeability or openness according to stages of spiritual development and meditational depth.

Along with the interpretation of the transpersonal factor as *nothingness*—which invites us to interpret the spiritual element in psychedelic experiences as a factor of self-annihilation and surrender—spiritual traditions have also spoken of spirit as the *ultimate something,* an "invisible" sphere endowed with a degree of reality of which the reality of manifest existence seems but a shadow or reflection (as in Plato's myth of the cave). Whether it is spoken of as Absolute, ultimate Truth, Being, Mind, God, or Self, it is declared to be—inasmuch as it is all that—everywhere, pervading everything. But one who experiences himself as *Self* (rather than isolated and limited *self*) experiences himself as the Self of all; he whose identity has shifted from an individual personality to Being feels unified with the infinity of all that is. Thus, we may say that becoming nothing is the other side of becoming everything, nothingness is the other side of totality.

In Figure 1 I attempt to summarize the relation between some LSD states graphically. The solid arrows point out that the "death experience" is the gateway to nothingness, the "birth experience", the gateway to Being. The dotted arrows indicate transition from one "perinatal pain" to another, transition through which nothingness becomes a context for birth, and the experience of Being permits the extinction of the "ego." Double arrows linking the center of the diagram with the periphery suggest the arising of the transpersonal experiences out of "madness" as surrender of control becomes more complete than in psychotic states where it is resisted and incomplete. It will be noted that in this graph the horizontal axis (voidness–plenitude) is the static one, while the vertical (Birth–Death) is dynamic (dying is a process *oriented to* nothingness; birth the process *oriented* to Being). The volcanic vertical axis and the serene horizontal one may be also regarded in light of the "enstatic" versus "ecstatic" polarity that has been the subject of Roland Fischer's discussions.

A common misunderstanding that has arisen in regard to the death–rebirth and voidness–plenitude experiences under the effects of hallucinogens is that of failing to draw a distinction between *states* and *stages* of consciousness, transient experiencing, and phases of spiritual growth. While the "annihilating illumination" (Andrews, 1963) may occur rather easily in

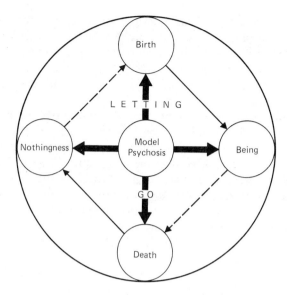

Figure 1. Graphical representation of spiritual effects of LSD.

the course of a psychedelic experience, this cannot be equated to the death-in-God of Christian mystics who have attained permanent mystical union or sanctity, or to *nirvana* ("annihilation") of the Buddhist who attains the happiness of that "other shore," where the passions are transcended. The death and rebirth of the Greek myths, of the Egyptian teachings concerning Osiris, and of the Christian myth are formulations of a life process involving a death-in-life—death to "oneself" and "the world"—and the initiation and birth of a higher life. Psychedelic experiences are, I think, only glimpses of the great transformation that lies within our potential, archetypal anticipations and, at best, steps along the way.

While access to the transcedent or spiritual factor in human life has been often sought in the spiritual traditions through the acceptance of nothingness and death, only in shamanism was the acceptance of madness recognized as a pathway, and in the Dionysian religion of the Greek mysteries. (In the figure of the god of drunkenness, human genius expressed an appreciation of surrender to the point of divinization.) The hallucinogenic experience (known to the Greeks through the use of *Amanita muscaria;* Graves, 1982) is, I think, a spiritual experience of an eminently Dionysian kind. This Dionysian element in it may account in part for the reluctance of some Christians to equate it with the mystical experience of their saints; for, even if we allow for a common core of spiritual experience beyond the characteristics of each religious path, the utter abandonment of the individual under the effects of a hallucinogen are sharply in contrast with the austerity and discipline of the desert fathers or the Theravada monks. A strong anti-Dionysian spirit may be perceived, for instance, in the attitude of Zaehner (1961)—best known and most learned among those denying (in his *Mysticism: Sacred and Profane*) the spiritual significance of "psychedelics."

Though Alan Watts (1962) is possibly the best-known religious thinker who has endorsed the validity of psychedelicly induced mystical experiences, it is to Panhnke that we owe the most satisfactory attempt at experimental validation of this contention (1963 and 1967). [Nine universal psychological characteristics were derived from the literature of spontaneous mystical experience reported throughout world history from almost all cultures and religions. They are: unity (consciousness and memory are not lost; instead the person becomes very much aware of being part of a dimension much vaster and greater than himself), transcedence of time and space, deeply felt positive mood, sense of sacredness, noetic quality ("a feeling of insight or illumination with a tremendous force of certainty") paradoxical, it alleged ineffability, transiency, and persisting positive changes in attitudes and behavior.] On a memorable double-blind experiment carried out with ten theology students and professors in Boston on a Good Friday (Pahnke, 1970, p. 152ff: these characteristics proved to be identical for spontaneous and psychedelicly induced mystical experiences.

I think that the most important question is not whether hallucinogen-induced experiences are similar or identical to those elicited by means of austerities, meditation, and prayer, but whether both are of comparable value for an individual's life. It may be surmised that an experience obtained through spiritual discipline is one that the individual has earned, having developed the necessary aptitude to induce it; an artificial experience, on the other hand, is one in which the individual has not brought about in himself the inner conditions necessary to elicit it. Inasmuch as the experience requires an outer stimulus, the person depends upon it as on a crutch, and we may wonder whether such a crutch can interfere with the progress of meditative depth rather than assist it. Since it is well known that the depth of hallucinogenic experiences diminishes after some time, the peak experiences that lie within their potential to elicit may be regarded, perhaps, more as initiatory experiences than as a *path,* and thus an alternative to spiritual methodologies.

THE FEELING–ENHANCERS

I have proposed (1973) the name *feeling-enhancers* for drugs such as *MDA* and *MMDA* that share with the LSD-like psychedelics the effect of eliciting "spontaneous self-analytic experiences," and yet differ from them in that they do not bring about the characteristic perceptual phenomena of the hallucinogens, do not stimulate mythical thinking, and do not bring a person to angelic or demonic realms—but do elicit peak or nadir experiences that remain within the bounds of the familiar human domain. To this category of drugs belong, along with MDA and MMDA, a number of other less-known ones such as TMD-2 and MDMA. The psychedelic effect of many such amphetamine related compounds was reported by Shulgin et al. (1961) without reference to qualitative differences which may be conceptualized in terms of varying degrees of amphetaminic activity and hallucinogenic effects. MMDA, for instance, is of little activity as a stimulant (subjects report drowsiness) and is slightly hallucinogenic (in that imagery may be present when the eyes are closed). The nature of this imagery, however, reflects the typical inner atmosphere of the feeling-enhancers, for it is neither abstract nor mythical but realistic, and related to persons more than animals or objects. MDA, on the other hand, may be regarded as the prototype of this group, for it is mostly a feeling-enhancer, with rare and negligible hallucinogenic effect.

On the behavioral level the effects of the feeling-enhancers differ from those of the hallucinogens in that there is less of an inclination to become absorbed in a trance. The person under the effects of MDA usually feels like lying down during the first hours of the experience, but this impulse is not so compelling as with LSD and related compounds. The individual remains in greater contact with the environment and with the body. This is probably not unrelated to the characteristic talkativeness of people under the effect of feeling-enhancers. Such talking is not only motivated by the communication of the experience but is frequently the expression of an exploration of one's life—its contents being that of one's relationships, personality, and projects.

At the cognitive level, one characteristic of the feeling-enhancers is a relative lack of disruption of thought as found with hallucinogens. Yet perhaps the subtle "relaxation" of discursive thought that takes place under their effects is related to a facilitation of cognition in another regard, for as remarkable as feeling-enhancement itself is the facilitation of insight that they bring about in regard to one's personality and one's relationships. Under the effect of the MDA-like drugs it is easier to feel what one feels, to see things as they are. The insights, which may sometimes profoundly affect the individual's life, are not usually discoveries of anything remote but are the outcome of a willingness to see what is obvious—such as, "I have been afraid all my life," or "I have never allowed myself to be who I am with my lovers," or "I'm feeling guilty." They constitute a discovery of what has always been the case but has not been acknowledged, out of a fear of not being able to face the consequences of such perception.

Another cognitive effect, which, like the above, may be understood in the light of a deactivation of repression, is the lifting of amnesia concerning painful events—usually in one's early history. It would seem that the same capacity to see the obvious in the present also allows the individual to see what has happened to him in the past which he has "forgotten".

Feeling-enhancement is not something irrelevant to this cognitive effect of undoing repression. It is hard to say whether we are in the presence of a quasi-physiological affective amplification of the emotions or simply a more direct experience of the emotions—usually veiled from our awareness because of our unwillingness to cope with our true situation (or fear we will not be able to). The enhancement of feelings that this group of psychedelics characteristically bring about applies to positive and negative feelings as well, and just as the hallucinogens have their heavens and their hells, we can say that there also is something like heavens and hells in the MDA or MDMA experience—only these archetypal terms do not seem so evocative in regard to the MDA domain of the psyche, which is not the mythical-magical domain or the domain of symbolization at all, but a domain of memory (i.e., that of the facts of life as they are stored in our experience). The peak experience of MDA, for instance, is one that may justify the popular talk of it as a "love drug," for it is an experience characterized by warmth. The negative end is characterized by the intensification of psychological pain, and may involve sadness, guilt, shame, and less commonly, anger.

THE FANTASY-ENHANCERS

In *The Healing Journey* (1973) I proposed to call harmaline and ibogane "fantasy enhancers" to emphasize the property that led William Turner (1964) to coin the term "oneirophrenic" for yage, after his pioneering self-experiment with a plant extract. This special term seemed justified in view of the fact that, while these substances may in a broad sense be called psychedelic, their effect is different enough from those of the LSD-like psychedelics and feeling-enhancers to distinguish them. Together with other harmala and iboga alkaloids, they constitute a group of "dream-inducing" drugs, as we might also call them if we were to adopt the language of South American Indians (who use the word "dream" in an extended sense—applicable to dreams in the absence of sleep).

The main differences between these alkaloids and the hallucinogens, aside from the prominence of dreamlike sequences with archetypal content, is the absence of perceptual distortions, scant stimulation of the emotions, and absence of psychotomimetic as well as mysticomimetic (though not spiritual, as will be seen) potential of these drugs. All these are present, however, among the effects of the drink variously known as yage, ayahuasca, and so on, prepared by medicine-men of the South American "montaña" from a combination of at least two plants, which usually contains DMT in addition to harmala alkaloids. The difference between the state elicited by this mixture and the one induced by LSD and similar hallucinogens lies in the prominence of the "oneirophrenic" effect, the typical content of the visions, and, as I propose below, an awareness of instinct rather than emotions or cognitive processes.

The characteristics of the harmaline and yage experiences led me in the sixties to think that it was *Peganum harmala* rather than *Amanita muscaria* that had been the source of the Iranian haoma and Indian soma—central to the early Aryan sacrifices and religion. This hypothesis has recently received convincing support from research by David Flattery (Flattery and Schwartz, 1985).

The psychedelic property of the harmala alkaloids is also of interest in view of the demonstrated transformation of serotonin into melatonin and (psychoactive [see Naranjo, 1967, for further references]) 6-methoxy harmalan in pineal tissue.

Before carrying out the human experiments with ibogaine reported at the LSD conference organized by the University of California in 1966 and in a subsequent paper (Naranjo, 1968), I had only been able to find literature about the effects of the drug on the the intestine of the rat, the vagina of the rabbit, and the brain cortex of the cat (upon which it elicited the electrical response of a stimulant)—the last being in accord with anthropological reports suggesting that it was a stimulant that the iboga roots were used in ceremonies. In accordance with such notion, a preparation from iboga root was introduced in the French pharmacopoeia early in the twentieth century. The effects that I was able to observe on volunteers (Naranjo, 1968) and later on patients (Naranjo, 1973) are now confirmed by other psychotherapists and may be said to be very close to those of harmaline. This is not surprising in view of some chemical similarity between ibogaine and the β-carbolines. The differences between both are subtle, and consist in a more archetypal and less personal content in harmala experiences, a greater prominence of telluric and "primordial goo" visions (along with the animal and solar visions common to them and the yage experiences), less death imagery, and a tendency for the iboga experience to be more "malleable" (i.e., subject to control or guidance). Rather than lumping the harmal alkaloids and ibogaine together in this exposition, however, I will concentrate on the effects of harmaline and of harmaline associations. I will use the term "yage" for the latter, extending the use of the Indian designation to the combinations of harmaline not only with DMT but with other hallucinogens or feeling-enhancers.

At the time when I conducted the experiment with Chilean volunteers in

1967 (Naranjo, 1967) the content of yage visions was generally regarded by anthropologists as the result of indoctrination and expectations, for the natives reporting them usually partook of the infusion in the context of specific traditions and instructions. The finding that some of the motifs reported in a shamanistic context, such as the visions of animals (snakes, felines, and birds of prey in particular), are spontaneously elicited by harmaline in individuals who have no such expectations not only seems to provide an impressive demonstration of a collective unconscious, but shows that this alkaloid stimulates a specific province of the archetypal mind.

The imagery-complex of the yage experience is, above all else, suggestive of animality, primitiveness, and the sense of the body as flesh—perishable flesh that survives through eating. It may be understood as the symbolic projection of an experiential atmosphere that might be described as the experience of oneself as animal—and which, I believe, arises from the stimulation of the instinctive reptilian brain. (Suggestive of this are the experiments performed at the University of Chile on clinically decerebrated cats, which show a primary stimulating effect of harmaline on the reticular formation at the pons.)

Though the South American Indians take yage in their ritual dances and, in smaller amounts, to increase proficiency in hunting, most non-Indians could hardly conceive such a thing under the effect of the drug, for they feel very dizzy and are compelled to lie down and "dream." Visionary trance is, anyhow, the common behavior of Indians and non-Indians alike at the peak of effects.

The content of visions is partly abstract and mostly realistic or surrealistic (i.e., realistic–archetypal) and rarely personal. Animal imagery stands out (all kinds of animals, insects and spiders included), and imagery related to death and to flying. Among animal images the most prominent are, by far, those of big cats, snakes, and birds of prey.

If aggression were not evident in the frequent visions of tigers and snakes, it would be apparent from the content analysis of visions as a whole; war scenes, weapons, crashing automobiles, the action of cutting, burns, and so on, abound. "Not only teeth are prominent in harmaline visions—teeth of cats, sharks or monsters—but bayonets, scissors, broken glass" (Naranjo, unpublished book). Sexuality is somewhat less prominent than aggression in the content of visions; yet when present it is most striking—sometimes in the form of orgiastic sexual activity, other times elevated to an archetypal-religious level of expression.

More characteristic than the fact that instinct is conveyed by the images in harmaline experiences is the form of relationship in which the individual stands to his instinctual reality, when not one of terror or disgust, as in yage nightmares; this relationship is, especially in peak experiences, what may be regarded as contemplative experience of instinct. Thus, rather than sexual stimulation, the alkaloid elicits a contemplation of sexuality; more than stimulating aggression, it presents aggression to the inner eye as a force of nature that inspires awe and reverence. The "heavens" of harmaline, thus, are not so much celestial as nether-world paradises of self-satisfied sexuality and aggression perceived as a divine force.

The symbolic complex of death, aggression, and sexuality that the South American Indians articulate with the image of jungle animals suggests that a single experience contains the qualities of dying and bursting forth, of detachment and of letting go to life-impulses. It is interesting to note that snake, feline, and bird have been compounded by the human mind in that most archetypal of archetypes: the dragon—which, like yage visions, fluctuates between the divine and the demonic. In it we witness a synthesis of the facets of an experience that—as experience with yage shows—contains them all. (The same symbolic complex (i.e., of detachment) recurs in the figure of Shiva, lord of yogis, who is at the same time worshipped in the form of the generative organs and regarded as the destructive aspect of the godhead).

The mythologem of death as fountain-of-life, dramatized in the death-rebirth rituals in the ancient world, is the expression of an inner experience easy to understand by one under the influence of harmaline: that of an *inner* death that is the fountain of life; a detachment from oneself that leads, not to indifference, but to leaving one's organism alone; a letting go not only *of* but *to* organismic function. Images of flying, which are frequent in yage experiences, seem to convey this convergence of detachment and flowing, freedom and vitality.

Though much more could be said about yage visions, I will only add that the name "telepathine" was once proposed for the main alkaloid in yage because the South American Indians (who are the world experts in its use) have employed it as a means to the development of parapsychological abilities. Anecdotes collected from Indians in the Putamayo and visits among them leave me with the impression that their claim deserves to be investigated. In addition to clairvoyance and clairaudience, hunting people are particularly interested in learning about nature, and use the drug in order to become acquainted with the behavior of animals and the properties of plants. In this, their experience echoes the representation of Zoroaster as learning about plants from drinking haoma in early Iranian sources (Flattery and Schwartz, 1985).

While discursive thinking is put to rest rather than disrupted under the effect of the harmala alkaloids, not only is oneiric activity stimulated, but so, more generally, is symbolic thinking. Some people thus may become involved in allegorical or mythical (or distinct from abstract-conceptual) speculation, such as I have illustrated in an unpublished book. One of the subjects in it, for instance, began in this way his retrospective account of the experience:

"Is humanity in the process of uniting into a single individual? Is the devil—defined as a conscious entity—real and trying to prevent this, or is he a figment of our imagination?" It is the stimulation of intuitive thinking that South American Indians may have in mind when they speak of taking yage in order to "learn medicine"; for their concept of learning medicine includes, as an important aspect, the ability to understand dreams and visions. Reichel-Dolmatoff has reported (1971) how through periodic ingestion of yage the Desana Indians penetrate into the meaning of the creation myth recited once every year under the influence of the drink. Whereas in the normal state of consciousness it might not be understood beyond its literal meaning, yage opens the door to the experiences behind the symbols and thus might be regarded as a stimulant of a hermeneutic ability. When visionary experience is spoken of, thus, we may well bear in mind that it entails not only the facility for internal visual representation but an implicit faculty of encoding–decoding, an awakening of analogical thought.

In regard to the affective domain, I will say that there are peak and nadir experiences with yage, but these are of a very different experiential quality from those of feeling-enhancers or hallucinogens. Peak experiences convey the expression of free and unobstructed instinct, as is manifest in visions of animals, and not so much experiences of warmth but of freedom and power. One could well use the terms applied in connection with haoma intoxication in the Avesta: "shining," "vivid," "energetic," "accompanied by joy-making truth" (Flattery and Schwartz, 1985). So, while one can speak of heavens and hells in connection with yage experiences, these are not so much heavens of beatitude and hells of damnation, but, rather, positive experiences closely related to the visions of jungle animals in the form of allies (or as images with which an individual identifies) and "hells" in which snake, tiger, and so on, become aggressors. This suggests strongly (in line with the interpretation of these images as projections of one's instinctive nature) that the essence of these heavens and hells is, in the first case, free-flowing instinct, and in the latter, instinct rejected through vilification—"demonization." Just as in traditional mythology snakes, tigers, and lions have positive and negative connotations, and dragons may be embodiments of supreme evil or the power of heaven, it is the same "energy" that manifests at opposite ends of the affective continuum, depending on individual attitudes of acceptance or rejection of the spontaneity that they involve. At times a transition may take place from the contracted to the expanded state, as on the occasion of my giving a mixture of harmaline-LSD to a colleague. A huge snake that seemed the embodiment of all evil appeared before him, and in the presence of this apparition he was distressed (and suffered from a migraine headache). The confrontation of the image led, however, to his allowing himself to be eaten by the snake and swallowed, and when he was able to surrender in this way to the spontaneous course of the experience (in which he seemed to be annihilated), he felt himself in the belly of the snake. There, digested, he finally dissolved into its otherness until he and the snake were one—"and behold! the snake was God."

Just as at the positive end of the feeling continuum it is not exactly emotions that characterize the experience but a sense of spontaneity and pleasure in which there seem to converge mostly spiritual and sensory ingredients, also at the negative end of the spectrum it is not negative "emotions" that stand out—except for the possible appearance of terror; it is rather the case that emotions are *symbolized* as "terrifying visions" (which may not be frightening at all, but perceived with detachment). Alternatively, these emotions may be somatized in the form of physical discomfort verging on collapse. That the hell of harmaline is a *physical* hell (rather than one characterized by *emotions* of separation, emptiness, guilt, shame, etc.) reinforces the notion that it involves (or makes manifest?) a dysfunction at the instinctual level; we observe in these cases an intensification of the desire to sleep, general malaise, and vomiting.

In regard to the spiritual effects, I have proposed to call the contemplative states elicited by yage "illuminative" rather than mystical, applying here a distinction introduced by St. Ignatius: whereas in the mystical experience there is rapture and a plunging into an ineffable realm, difficult to articulate in thought, this illuminative experience is one characterized by clarity and the joy of understanding (an understanding usually inseparable from the symbolic content of the visions). Another aspect of yage spirituality, is, as has been implicit in discussion above, the fact that it is a spirituality of the belly or a spirituality of the body, the gist of which is a sacralization or a resacralization of instinct.

A deeper peak experience than any of those mentioned thus far, a near-imageless experience comparable to the oceanic experience of LSD but of a different "flavor," is one that I call the "molten gold" experience because in it the sense of fluidity is coupled to a fiery component and an experience akin to orgasm but neither genital nor even clearly located in the body—a sexuality on a higher sphere, one could say.

Finally, it should be borne in mind that all these mind-manifesting experiences of wrathful, orgiastic, or "golden" content occur in a background of implicit death—that is, of an implicit detachment and letting-go that is frequently arrived at through a process of encounter with death in the visionary realm. Appropriately, the word *ayahuasca* with which the Peruvian Indians call their sacred plant means "vine of death" as well as "vine of the soul."

The spiritual effects of yage are taken for granted by South American Indians. Those of harmaline, containing *Peganum harmala* as was mentioned, seem to have been recognized in ancient Iran. The experience elicited by the harmala alkaloids seems cognate with the heroic spirituality of our Indo-European ancestors, with its cultivation of the willingness to die for life.

CANNABIS

I will use the word cannabis here to signify the leaves, flowering tops, derivatives, and active ingredients of *Cannabis sativa,* one of the oldest cultivated nonfood plants of humankind (Julien, 1981, p. 169).

From the point of view of the states of consciousness that it may elicit, cannabis is remarkable for its versatility. Unlike the feeling-enhancers that activate interpersonal awareness present and past, and unlike the fantasy-enhancers that are avenues to the symbolic domain, cannabis can stimulate these and other states as well, approximating the range of the LSD-like hallucinogens: the oceanic state, religious–archetypic or artistic contemplative states, possession states. In regard to the spectrum of consciousness that it activates, the main difference from the halluciongens is the infrequency of psychotic reactions and "volcanic" episodes. It would seem as if cannabis acted as an all-purpose lubricant of the psyche rather than an explosive. Whatever facilitation it brings about can be controlled and channeled in alternative directions, and, while facilitating the suspension of the ego, it does not visit the individual with an "annihilating illumination" coming from outside—much less with a terrifying one.

In small or moderate amounts marijuana is said to have the effect of a "euphoriant," yet in saying this we should point out that the euphoria it brings about is very different from that elicited by cocaine. Writing of the marijuana experience in the *American Handbook of Psychiatry,* Balis (1974, p. 407) appropriately comments that "the term 'euphoria' is loosely used in the literature to describe a variety of affective states," and "does not seem to represent a distinct affect or to be associated with a specific stimulus or a specific psychological state." He points out that it is an overinclusive term "that encompasses such qualitatively different feelings as those induced by narcotics (opiates), inebriants and intoxicants (ethanol, ether), stimulants (amphetamines), or moods experienced by manic patients," and that "the euphoric experience of "high" induced by marijuana . . . " is a complex psychological response characteristic of this drug."

The euphoria arising from the effect of cannabis is, to a considerable extent, the outcome of a spontaneous detachment of the user from ordinary cares, and is usually better described as well-being than joy or excitement. Thus, we are in the presence of something more akin to a tranquilizer—though one differing from ordinary tranquilizers in its effect of sharpening sensory (and, I will propose, pattern) awareness. In greater dosages the effect of cannabis is that of a fantasy-enhancer, and sometimes that of a feeling-enhancer. Hallucinogenic effects may be present with high doeses (see, for instance, McGlothlin, 1968), but in our culture a full-blown psychedelic effect is rare, just as paranoid and anxiety states are rare.

Curiously, reports of cannabis experiences from the nineteenth century show a much more hallucinogenic effect than those in recent times. When we consider Ludlow's (1858) descriptions and Baudelaire's (1860) "artificial paradises," we may wonder whether the hallucinogenic effect that they report was just a matter of dosage or the result of there being a greater distance between the average personality of Victorian man and the psychedelic state than between the latter and our relatively liberated contemporary psyche. I suspect that the model personality some generations ago was more explosive than today's, as is also suggested by the disappearance of classical hysteria with its faintings and seizures. There was no door or avenue of expression for spontaneity, and when drugs (or hypnosis) provided an outlet, the result was dramatic.

The most remarkable effect of cannabis on the feelings is the well-being arising from "selective inhibition" of worry and pugnacity, and from the relaxation of the impulse to sustain an image of oneself, as well as increased naturalness and a temporary inhibition of the "passions," which no doubt inspired the Chinese appellation of "liberator of sin" for it (Taylor, 1966, p. 20). Also (mostly on the first occasions), everything seems very funny—perhaps a "cosmic joke." At other times there is the excitement of grandiosity (as in Baudelaire's report): a grandiosity arising from fantasized narcissistic gratification. There is usually a greater openness in the expression of feelings, and spontaneity in behavior. With eyes open, the effects of cannabis are not very remarkable: an increased appreciation of form and sensory experience, mostly. More intense is the effect on the perception of music, which may be greatly enhanced in regard to texture and expressiveness. With eyes closed, the effects are those of a fantasy-enhancer—but one without the content-specificity of the harmala alkaloids and ibogaine.

In the cognitive sphere, as in the case of other psychedelics, there is a slight impairment of reasoning and a facilitation of intuitive–aesthetic understanding (McGlothlin, 1968). In regard to thinking impairment, what stands out is perturbation in short-term memory and an increased distractibility. As for the stimulation of intuition, I think that a case may be made for the hypothesis that cannabis use involves a facilitation of nonlinear thinking. This facilitation, I believe, is not merely the outcome of an interference with linear thinking, but of a more specific potential of cannabis as a stimulant of "higher cognition": an effect of sharpening pattern perception. For while the perception of novel patterns arises in the case of other hallucinogens through an abundance of material to be connected and associated, there is at play in the cannabis experience, rather, something like the activation of a patterning function, an increased ability to organize chaos into form. It is thus not just a matter of the (Bergson–Huxley) "reducing valve" of the brain being opened and of consciousness being flooded, but of consciousness pursuing a definite track—which happens to be unusual.

The spiritual effects of hashish were well known to the Sufis, who are said to have introduced "the wine of the poor" in the Muslim world in the twelfth century (Rosenthal, 1971, p. 45 ff.). Yet they must have been well aware, as the doctors of law and contemporary writers were, of the adverse after-effects of hashish, and the "deterioration of personality" caused by hashish addiction. Hashish—also called, significantly, "the killer"—was claimed to help the pious in their religious devotions and to "allow the human mind to go beyond the limitations of reality" (ibid.). Al-Is^{c}irdī speaks of the "secret" of the drug that permits "the spirit to ascend to the highest points in a heavenly ascention (*mi^{c}rāj*) of disembodied understanding" (ibid., p. 93; 163, verse 8). It may not have taken them long to realize that the potential of hashish to stimulate some aspects of the person's growth are offset by retarding effects in other regards, and that the net result of continuous use is probably harmful, as is suggested by literary and legal reference throughout Moslem history (ibid.).

It is in the Hindu tantric tradition and in African shamanism, however, that cannabis has been employed as a sacrament—just as soma, peyote, teonanacatl, fly agaric, yage, and iboga have been in other cultures.

In Indian Tantrism the most characteristic use of the plant is for devotional exercises employing visualization along with the chanting of mantra and attention to the *chacras* (subtle energy centers) and *nadis* (subtle pathways) in the body. These exercises are typically embedded in a context of ritual, which may include (in the Pañcamakāva or secret ritual) sexual union. In the latter, cannabis serves as an enhancer of many aspects of the experience, ranging from the sensory level to the spiritual, which involves regarding self and other as male and female personifications of the divine (Woodroffe, 1965).

REFERENCES

Andrews, G. Annihilating illumination. *Psychedelic Review,* 1963, *1,* 66–68.

Balis, G. U. Psychotomimetic and consciousness-altering drugs. In S. Arieti and E. Brody (Eds.), *American handbook of psychiatry.* New York: Basic Books, 1974, pp. 404–448.

Barber, T. S. *LSD, marijuana, yoga and hypnosis.* Chicago: Aldine, 1970.

Baudelaire, P. C. *Les paredis artificiels.* Paris: Ponlet-Malessis, 1860.

Cohen, S. *The beyond within: the LSD story,* 2nd ed. New York: Atheneum, 1967.

DeRopp, R. S. *Drugs and the mind.* New York: St. Martin's Press, 1957.

Flattery, D. S. and Schwartz, M. *Haoma and harmaline: the botanical identification of the intoxicating "soma" of ancient Indo–Iranian religions.* Berkeley: University of California Publications in Near Eastern Studies, no. 21, 1985.

Graves, R. *The Greek myths.* Garden City, N.Y.: The Viking Press, 1982.

Grof, S. *Realms of the human unconscious: observations from LSD research.* New York: The Viking Press, 1975.

Grof, S. *LSD psychotherapy.* Pomona, Calif.: Hunter House, 1980.

Harman, W. W. and Fadiman, J. Selective enhancement of specific capacities through psychedelic training. In B. Aaronson and H. Osmond (Eds.), *Psychedelics: the uses and implications of hallucinogenic drugs.* New York: Anchor Books, 1970.

Hofmann, A. *LSD: my problem child: reflections on sacred drugs, mysticism, and science.* Los Angeles: J. P. Tarcher, 1983.

Huxley, A. *The doors of perception.* New York: Harper Brothers, 1954.

Julien, R. M. *A primer of drug action,* 3rd ed. San Francisco: Freeman, 1981.

Klüver, H. *Mescal: the "divine" plant and its psychological effects.* Chicago: University of Chicago Press, 1966.

Kripner, S. Paranormal effects occurring during chemically-induced psychedelic experiences and their implications for religion. *Journal of Altered States of Consciousness,* 1974, *1*(2), 175–184.

Laing, R. D. and Esterson, H. *Sanity, madness and the family.* London: Tavistock, 1964.

Ludlow, F. *The hasheesh eater: being passages from the life of a Pythagorean.* New York: Harper and Bros., 1858.

McGlothlin, W. H. Cannabis: a reference. In D. Solomon (Ed.), *The marijuana papers.* New York: Signet, 1868, pp. 455–478.

Masters, R. E. L. and Houston, J. *The varieties of psychedelic experience.* New York: A Delta Book, 1967.

Michaux, H. *The major ordeals of the mind: and the countless minor ones.* New York: Harcourt, Brace, Jovanovich, 1974.

Naranjo, C. Psychotropic properties of the harmala alkaloids. In Efron, D. (Ed.), *The ethnopharmacologic search for psychoactive drugs.* Washington D.C.: Public Health Service Publication no. 1645, 1967.

Naranjo, C. Psychotherapeutic applications of new fantasy-enhancers. *Clinical toxicology,* 1968, *1.*

Naranjo, C. *The healing journey: new approaches to consciousness.* New York: Ballantine, 1973.

Naranjo, C. Psychological aspects of the yage experience in an experimental setting. In M. S. Harner (Ed.), *Hallucinogens and shamanism.* New York: Oxford University Press, 1973a, pp. 176–190.

Newland, C. A. *Myself and I.* New York: Signet Books, 1963.

Pahnke, W. N. Drugs and mysticism. In B. Aaronson and H. Osmond (Eds.), *Psychedelics: the uses and implications of hallucinogenic drugs.* New York: Anchor Books, 1970, pp. 145–164.

Reichel-Dolmatoff, G. *Amazonian cosmos: the sexual and religious symbolism of the Tukano Indians.* Chicago: University of Chicago Press, 1971.

Rosenthal, F. *The herb: hashish versus medieval Muslim society.* Leiden: Brill, 1971.

Shulgin, A. T., Bunnell, S., and Sargent, T. The psychotomimetic properties of 3,4,5-trimethoxyamphetamine. *Nature* 1961, 189, 1011.

Taylor, N. *Narcotics, nature's dangerous gifts to man.* New York: Dell, 1966.

Turner, W. J. Schizophrenia and oneirophrenia. *Transactions of the New York Academy of Sciences,* 1964, *26,* 361–368.

Watts, A. W. *The joyous cosmology: adventures in the chemistry of consciousness.* New York: Vintage Books, 1962.

Woodroffe, J. (transl.) *Serpent power (sat-chakra-nirupana & paduka-panchaka).* Madras: Ganesh "Śakti and Śakta," 1965, pp. 590–648.

Zaehner, R. C. *Mysticism sacred and profane: an inquiry into some varieties of praeternatural experience.* New York: Oxford University Press, 1961.

13. On the Remembrance of Things Present: The Flashback

Roland Fischer

PREAMBLE

The immediate present or "now" is already past at the very moment of its awareness. This is so because of the approximately 60 to 70 milliseconds of nervous processing that has to precede the awareness of "now" (Efron, 1967). Moreover, "being" at each moment is structured through memory, and what we perceive as the present is a vivid fringe of memory tinged with anticipation. Accordingly, the "being" of present always resides in a past. The intense condensation of this past and its re-presentation is the flashback. "In a second, the faintest perfume may send us plummeting to the roots of our being; by a mere smell we are connected to another place and another time" (Purce, 1974, p. 3).

Thus, "memory is not that which we remember, but that which remembers us; memory is a present that never stops passing" (Paz, 1949, p. 97). The paradox that the present is past and the past is present may best be echoed by paraphrasing a line from the 30th sonnet of Shakespeare to "summon up" not the "remembrance of things past . . . " but *the remembrance of things present*. Such remembrance, such reinstatement of the past as present, is the flashback.

Flashbacks are mostly thought of as "bad trips," and this is symptomatic of our psychedelic proletarization of inner space. But flashbacks are too important to be left entirely to clinical psychiatrists. Few people realize that a writer's ability to induce flashbacks in a reader is a criterion of masterful literature, and Marcel Proust, creator of *A la recherche du temps perdu* (Paris, Gallimard, 1954), should be revered as patron saint of the flashback.

An embodiment of past experiences, the temporary construct of a person, is passé "now." This "outdated" person goes on connecting fleeting moments to enduring sequences "that never stop passing" and thus partakes in creation endlessly averted, travestied, corrected; a creation that continuously demands the retouching of the present and of nothingness (Poulet, 1949).

THE AROUSAL STATE-BOUND AND STAGE-BOUND NATURE OF THE FLASHBACK

Instead of defining the flashback, a "Dear Abby" story (1971) can be used to illuminate significant features of the arousal state-bound nature of the flashback.

> I was in love with a college classmate, but he married someone else. I also married, and even after four years and a beautiful baby I still dreamed about this fellow. Whenever I saw a car like his, my heart would pound even though he had left town years before and I knew it couldn't possibly be his.

Dissecting the body of this conscious experience, we find a "pounding heart," or emotional state of autonomic (subcortical) *arousal,* and "a car like his," a symbol of the cognitive (expectant) *interpretation* of that arousal. Accordingly, an arousal state-bound event-structure may be re-presented or flashed back in two ways: (1) by inducing naturally, or with drugs and hypnosis, a particular level of hyper- or hypoarousal; or (2) by presenting some symbol of its interpretation such as an image, a melody, a taste, or a smell.

Jean de Léry (1573), a member of a Protestant mission to Brazil in 1555, brought back from the bay of Rio de Janeiro a delightful ethnographic report. His text was lost, reconstructed, lost again, and miraculously recovered. It finally appeared in 1573, written in the sixteenth-century French of Rabelais and Montaigne. In one passage it is surely Proust's madeleine (described below) that is foreshadowed when Léry, after his return home, finds himself in a place where starch is being made, and, breathing in the smell, is transported to the homes of savages busily making manioc flour, which

> a la vraie senteur de l'amidon, fait de pur froment longtemps trempé dans l'eau quand il est encore frais et liquide. (Léry, 1573, quoted by Lévi-Strauss, 1976, p. 970)

Written in 1538, the following passage from Juan Luis Vives (1964) "the first psychologist," is one of the oldest descriptions of a flashback:

> When I was a boy in Valencia, I was ill of a fever; while my taste was deranged I ate cherries; for many years afterwards, whenever I tasted the fruit I not only recalled the fever, but also seemed to experience it again.[1]

Seligman (1980) had a recent remarkably similar ("taste-bound") experience.

> Sauce béarnaise . . . used to be one of my favorite foods in the world. One evening, in 1966, I had sauce béarnaise on filet mignon. About 6 hours later I began to throw up and spent the next several hours retching. After that, sauce béarnaise tasted foul to me.

"A cursory examination of what I know of Pavlovian conditioning," continues Seligman, "suggested to me that my taste aversion violated five basic assumptions of general process learning theory: 1) Learning took place with a *six hour delay* between conditioned stimulus (the sauce) and unconditioned stimulus (being ill), and this never occurs in the laboratory. 2) The learning was *selective.* Only the sauce, and not the filet mignon, nor the white plate became aversive. 3) The phenomenon was *robust*: it has lasted 13 years, whereas normal Pavlovian conditioning extinguishes readily. 4) The phenomenon was not *cognitive:* the knowledge that the illness was caused by a stomach flu and not the sauce béarnaise did not prevent the sauce from tasting bad in the future. 5) It made good *evolutionary sense* that taste should be selectively associated with illness, whereas promiscuous Pavlovian conditioning makes no evolutionary sense at all" (Seligman, 1980, p. 14).

Seligman's analysis (1970) indicates that recurring flashbacks of his taste aversion experience in response to (the image of) sauce béarnaise do not follow the rules of Pavlovian conditioning. Logue (1979) argues that the taste-aversion phenomenon, at the present time, does not necessitate a dispensing with the general laws of learning. More relevant, perhaps, is the observation that only about 10 percent of the general population are capable of flashbacks (Fischer, 1977); and most of the "bad" and depressing flashbacks get publicity while the elated (good) variety are quickly forgotten and less frequently reported.

The image that symbolizes the interpretation of a "spiritual effect," or religious arousal, and which is capable of repeatedly eliciting it, was described by the mystic poet St. John of the Cross in 1579:

To certain images God gives a particular spiritual influence upon such persons, so that the figure of the image and the devotion caused by it remain fixed in the mind, and the person has them ever present before him; and so, when he suddenly thinks of the image, the spiritual influence which works upon him is of the same kind as when he saw it—sometimes is it less, but sometimes it is even greater—yet, from another image, although it be of more perfect workmanship, he will not obtain the same spiritual effect. (Saint John of the Cross, 1958, p. 456)

A contemporary example of state-bound flashback is from Proust's *Swann's Way* (1928), the famous madeleine episode.

And so, mechanically, weary after a dull day with the prospect of a dull morrow, I raised to my lips a spoonful of the tea in which I had soaked a morsel of the cake. No sooner had the warm liquid, and the crumbs in it, touched my palate than a shudder ran through my whole body, and I stopped intent upon the extraordinary changes that were taking place.

Undoubtedly what is thus palpitating in the depths of my being must be the image, the visual memory which, being linked to that taste, has tried to follow it into my conscious mind. (Proust, 1928, p. 64)

In luminous prose, Octavio Paz (1949) grasps the time-transcending power of a particular symbol as it evokes an involuntary welling up of an experience lived long ago: "Memory is not that which we remember, but that which remembers us. Memory is a present that never stops passing" (p. 97). The years do not part from us. Our bodies house the vanished hours.

SYNAESTHESIAS, FLASHBACKS, AND POETRY

How frequently do flashbacks—those *moments bienheureux*—recur in Proust's *A la recherche du temps perdu?* Beckett replies:

I think twelve or thirteen times. But the first—the famous episode of the madeleine steeped in tea—would justify the assertion that his entire book is a monument to involuntary memory and the epic of its action. The whole of Proust's world comes out of a teacup, and not merely Combray and his childhood. For Combray brings us to the two "ways", and to Swann may be related every element of the Proustian experience. . . .

Swann is the corner-stone of the entire structure, and the central figure of the narrator's childhood, a childhood that involuntary memory, stimulated or charmed by the long-forgotten taste of a madeleine steeped in an infusion of tea, conjures in all the relief and colour of its essential significance from the shallow well of a cup's inscrutable banality (Beckett, 1931, p. 23).

Beckett goes on to compile a list of twelve *moments bienheureux,* each one being a remembrance of things present, but adds that the list is not complete. There is another flashback that is even more memorable than the madeleine episode, comments Poulet:

> At the end of Le Temps Retrouvé, at the house of the Prince of Guermantes, the hero touches his lips with a strongly starched napkin. At once, he says, there surges the dining room at Balbec, "trying to shake the solidity of the House of Guermantes," and "making for an instant all the armchairs waver around me."

> The resurrection of the past, comments Poulet, forces our mind to "oscillate" between years long past and the present time "in the dizziness of an uncertainty like that which one experiences sometimes before an ineffable vision at the moment of going to sleep." (Poulet, 1977, p. 10)

How are these flashbacks created? Withdrawn in his cool dark room at Combray, Proust extracts the total essence of a scorching midday from the scarlet stellar blows of a hammer in the street and the chamber music of flies in the gloom. To him, lying in bed in the twilight of closed shutters, the exact quality of the weather, temperature, and visibility is transmitted in terms of sound, in the chimes and the calls of the hawkers. And each privileged moment becomes a state of exaltation.

We realize now why Riley and Baril's (1976) bibliography of 403 references on conditioned taste aversions (in the rat), covering the 1950–1975 period, fails to enlighten us about the flashbacks of Vives, Seligman, and Proust. Flashbackers are human beings, with connections in their brains involving linkages between any one sensory modality and the limbic system. These connections can be the source of powerful activity when they subserve emotional and autonomic responses to sensory stimuli. Moreover, the human brain possesses a philogenetically new and unique anatomical structure, the area of inferior parietal lobuli including the angular and supramarginal gyri, to a rough approximation of areas 39 and 40 of Brodmann. We have a junction point in these extensive parietal areas, uniquely human cross modal connections for enabling and enhancing *cross modal associations* in perception, thinking, and language. These Geschwindian connections are important because they enhance sensory abstraction (Geschwind, 1965) and—according to Natapoff (1967)—make possible the development of sophisticated language.

It is striking that the sequence of metaphorical transfers of sensory adjectives follows the philogenetic development of the senses: tactile to gustatory and olfactory, and finally to acoustic and visual. Williams (1979) investigated the metaphorical use of adjectives in relation to the five senses and found that adjectives belonging to a certain human sense are transferred metaphorically to the area of another sense only in one direction almost without exception. In Williams's scheme of senses, metaphorical shifts generally take place only from left to right in a given sequence.[2] This leads to a sequence of sense development from tactile to gustatory, to olfactory, and finally, to acoustic and visual (or visual and acoustic). Interesting examples in the context of color vision are warm (touch→color), full (dimension→color), austere (taste→color), bright (color→sound) and strident (sound→color). Williams's scheme applies not only to English, but also to the Japanese language.

How do cross modal associations relate to the overpowering impact of sensory symbols that initiate a flashback? And how can language signify, re-present, and evoke intense experiences through creative literary texts that may elicit a flashback in some readers of similar intensity to that experienced by the writer a long time ago?

A curiously significant fact is that certain psychological categories of perception are roughly reflected in the organization of language. Structures are somewhat equivalent to nouns, operations to verbs, and qualities to modifiers (Brunelle, 1973). But the most intriguing peculiarity of language is that it is the only system composed of elements wherein the phonemes are signifiers and yet are devoid of meaning (Jakobson, 1978). There are appproximately 200 phonetically defined phonemes in all languages, but the inventory of English includes about 40 of them (Heike, 1972). For the combination of phonemes, selection restrictions are very specific in a given language. For example, there is no word in English that begins with more than three consonants, and in a cluster of three consonants the first can only be "s"; the second must be "p," "t," or "k," and the third is restricted to "r" or "l" (Schane, 1973). The intimate connection between the sound and the meaning of a word gives rise to a desire by speakers to add an internal relation to the external relation, resemblance to contiguity, to complement what is signified by a rudimentary image. Because of the neuropsychological laws of synaesthesia, phonic oppositions can themselves evoke relations with musical, chromatic, olfactory, tactile, and similar sensations. For example, the opposition between acute and grave phonemes has the capacity to suggest an image of bright and dark, of pointed and rounded, of thin and thick, of light and heavy, and so on. This "sound symbolism," as it was called by Edward Sapir, this latent inner value of the distinctive features, is brought to life when there is a correspondence in the meaning of a given word and in our emotional or aesthetic attitude toward this word, and even more toward pairs of words with two opposite meanings (Jakobson, 1978).

Synaesthesias and flashbacks are twin concepts, both based on "knowing" that is bound to high, nonordinary levels of arousal. Both experiences are involuntary, and both have the elated, ineffable quality of the *unio mystica*. In fact, the mystical union has been described by Schrader (1969) as a synaesthetic experience: in the prose commentaries to the *Cantico Espiritual* of San Juan de la Cruz and in the writings of Caterina de Siena, Marguerita de Navarra, Teresa de Avila, Francis de Sales, and Mme de Verger, as well as those of Origenes, Augustinus, Bonaventura, Ramón Llull, and others. A powerful, inspired, and possessed quality is associated with both mystical synaesthesia and literary descriptions of arousal state-bound flashbacks. For Wordsworth

> . . . all good poetry is the spontaneous overflow of powerful feelings: it takes its origin from emotion recollected in tranquility: the emotion is contemplated till, by a species of reaction, the tranquility gradually disappears, and an emotion, kindred to that which was before the subject of contemplation, is gradually produced, and does itself actually exist in the mind. (1960, p. 501)

In our terminology Wordsworth's "emotion" can here be equated with our "subcortical arousal" and his "contemplation" with our "cortical interpretation."

Another illustration of state-boundness is T. S. Eliot's:

> . . . way of expressing emotion in the form of art (is) by finding an "objective correlative"; in other words, a set of objects, a situation, a chain of events which shall be in the formula of that *particular* emotion; such that when the external facts, which must terminate in sensory experience, are given, the emotion is immediately invoked. . . . The artistic "inevitability" lies in this complete adequacy of the external to the emotion. (1932, p. 729)

Eliot uses "emotion," as Wordsworth does, for "arousal," and his "objective correlative" seems analogous to our "cortical interpretation."

Perhaps one criterion of masterful, and, hence, affective, poetry is its ability to induce "state-boundness" for the eternal, stereotyped, or archetypal human experiences of deep love, intense hate, overwhelming joy, loneliness, ultimate dread, utter despair, searching hope, and cosmic ecstasy.

THE VARIETIES OF STATE-BOUND EXPERIENCES: DRUG-INDUCED FLASHBACKS

State-bound recall can be evoked by imagery, melodies, and other symbols of the *content* of an experience, but also by inducing—"naturally," pharmacologically, or hypnotically—the particular level of *arousal* that prevailed during the initial experience, as in this next example. A young man complaining of unpleasant flashbacks from a previous LSD experience remembered, on questioning, that they occurred each time he took pills prescribed (in the emergency room of a university hospital) "to drain his sinuses." The tablets were soon identified as amphetamine, which apparently *produced the level of arousal* necessary to recall his previous (state-bound) drug experience. This, then, is the very nature of a flashback: the coupling of an experience to a level of drug-induced arousal that may be reinduced at a later time. In our opinion, "LSD flashbacks" are only special cases of the general phenomenon of state-boundness. Their unpleasant nature may be due to the anxiety associated with a seemingly unprovoked experience.

The common experience in which alcohol induces the state of arousal necessary for the recall of a state-bound experience is depicted in the film *City Lights*. Here Charlie Chaplin saves a drunk millionaire from an attempted suicide and becomes his good friend. When sober, however, the millionaire does not remember Charlie. But

the millionaire does not stay sober long. When he is drunk again, he spots Charlie and treats him like a long-lost friend. He takes Charlie home with him, but in the morning, when he is again sober, he forgets that Charlie is his invited guest and has the butler throw him out. (McDonald et al., 1965, p. 191)

Evidently, consciousness extends between states of either drunkenness or sobriety, but there is amnesia (no recall) between the two discontinuous states.

Another illustration of the discontinuity between states of sobriety and drunkenness is in a recent letter written by an older member of Alcoholics Anonymous:

. . . there was a time when I was drinking . . . there was a lady in San Antonio . . . I could find her home when I was drunk. But I could not find it when I was sober. (Personal communication, Jan. 20, 1972)

And in his diary entry of October 23, 1944, Evelyn Waugh (1973, p. K-15) remarked, "how boring it was to be obliged to tell Randolph (Churchill) everything twice—once when he was drunk, once when he was sober."

Chaplin's story was recently reenacted scientifically with forty-eight subjects who memorized nonsense syllables while intoxicated. When sober, these volunteers had difficulty recalling what they learned, but they could recall significantly better when intoxicated again (Goodwin et al., 1969). Another study revealed that encoding as well as retrieval strategies differ in intoxicated and sober states, and that the amnesia between these states— or the dissociated recall effect—is far more robust with words than with imagery (Weingartner et al., 1976). Alcohol apparently produces a strong depressant effect on dominant neocortical (language) functions. This could explain the powerful recall-inducing effect of nonverbal signs, symbols, images, tastes, and melodies.[3]

Chaplin's story is a good illustration of the amnesia between different states of arousal; apparently, the more extreme these states are, the more complete is the amnesia or state of *incommunicado*. It is a well-known characteristic of so-called dissociated trance-states that participants generally are unable to recall their content afterward. There is complete amnesia for the period of dissociation, and Bourguignon (1970) reports a brief period of disorientation as consciousness is regained after the amnestic dissociated state, as if one were "waking from sleep in unfamiliar surroundings." An analoguous amnesia may follow violent acts of crime, and a criminal thus sincerely denies an act he cannot recall. The partial amnesia of excited eye-witnesses for "what actually happened" may also explain the conflicting accounts that reporters invariably obtain from honest, qualified witnesses.

The implications of this *amnesia between different levels of arousal* for criminology, jurisprudence, and psychotherapy have not yet been realized. Amnesia that results from the discontinuity between different states of arousal may explain (Fischer and Landon, 1972) why Sirhan Sirhan, who killed Robert F. Kennedy, had no recollection of shooting Kennedy, and why hypnosis could clear up many details of the assasination. In our interpretation, psychiatrist Bernard L. Diamond (Fischer, 1976) hypnotically induced in Sirhan on several occasions that state of hyperarousal during which the shooting occurred. Only in this state could Sirhan reexperience and reenact the incident.

Eight years later, in 1977, Sirhan's amnesia about the assassination still persisted ("Sirhan," 1977) although he was eager to know whether he did or did not kill the senator. His attorney, Godfrey Isaac, after meeting Sirhan in his cell at Soledad prison, California, conveyed to the public the prisoner's suggestion that he be taken back to the scene of the killing, the kitchen of the Ambassador in Los Angeles.

The amnestic "subconscious" refers, in fact, to a different person. Locke, in 1690, noted that "if it be possible for the same Man to have distinct incommunicable consciousness at different times, it is past doubt the same Man would at different times make different Persons" (Locke, 1975, p. 342).

"To be taken back to the scene" is equivalent to "to be in the same state," since the *scene* can evoke the *state* and vice versa. This phenomenon is well known in fiction, as, for example, in *The Moonstone,* a nineteenth-century novel by Wilkie Collins (1874). A precious jewel is stolen, so the story begins, and a physician's assistant concludes that the thief, who is eventually identified, had been drugged (with laudanum or opium) at the time of the theft and thus had no recollection of the deed. The physician's assistant proposes that the "unwitting thief" be redrugged in an effort to restage the event and learn what the thief did with the jewel. The proposition is carried out, and the mystery is cleared up to everyone's satisfaction.

Wilkie Collins's novel was published half a century after DeQuincey's famous *Confessions of an English Opium Eater* (1821). It took another century to establish scientifically that morphine can induce state-dependent learning in rats,[4] a model of the state-bound flashback (Hill et al., 1971).

Flashbacks, particularly "bad trips" or "bummers"—"the dark nights of the soul"—may arise under the influence of one drug but may recur under the influence of another. The essential factor seems to be the reinstallment of the same state, which may be accomplished not only with another drug but also with a placebo, that is, the symbol of a drug, as in the following example.

An 18-year-old boy had a "bum trip" on "acid" and could not "come down" for two weeks. After he drank wine with a group of friends and was told by one of them that the wine contained a high dose of LSD (which it did not), he experienced hallucinations continuously for 14 days. (Tec, 1971)

Three-quarters of Abruzzi's (1974) flashback patients had their initial bummers on "acid" (LSD), mescaline, amphetamine, and so forth, but had their flashbacks precipitated by alcohol or marijuana. Habitual drug users and/or addicts may react to stimulant drugs with "increased sensitivity" over time. Kramer (1972), in fact, reported that amphetamine addicts may experience almost immediate reactivation of paranoid ideation when they take amphetamine, even after a prolonged period of abstinence. This may be a sensitized variety of arousal state-bound flashbacks.[5]

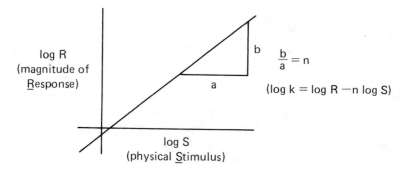

Figure 1. The power law shows a straight-line relationship between (log) stimulus (S) and (log) response (R). The slope gives the exponent n, while the intercept is related to the constant k.

Up to now, when describing the flashback, we have emphasized that it is arousal- (systemic, functional) or state-bound and stage- or symbol- (sign, cue) bound. State-bound performance, however, is not limited to imagery; visual, tactile, and intermodal sensory magnitude estimations, under the influence of certain psychoactive drugs, are also state-bound (Shaffer et al., 1973). The straight-line relationship (see Figure 1) between log S (stimulus) and log R (response):

$$\log R = \log k + n \log S$$

is not altered by 160 μg/kg of psilocybin or by 30 mg Δ^9-THC, the active ingredient of marijuana. Neither drug affects the consistency of sensory magnitude estimations, though both induce significant changes in the values of n, the exponent, and k, the constant. It is unlikely that these changes are due to learning or practice, since, according to Stevens (1971), untrained, inexperienced college subjects perform as well in psychophysical tests as those with many years of practice. The consistency of magnitude estimations in view of changing n and k is therefore taken as a demonstration of the state-bound nature of a consistently inducible performance characteristic of or bound to a particular state of consciousness.

REMEMBERING AN EXPERIENCE AND RE-EXPERIENCING A REMEMBRANCE

Remembering an experience implies reference to a particular spatio-temporal configuration, a dimensional and sequentially ordered representation of the content of consciousness. If we define space as *data content,* and time as *rate of data processing,* state-boundness may be redefined within the principle of space–time equivalence (Fischer, 1967, pp. 457–458) as memory retrieval of particular data content at the specific rate of data processing that prevailed during the initial experience. The information-processing rate is a function of the level of either ergotropic or trophotropic arousal. Specifically, increasing ergotropic arousal, or excitation, increases the rate of data processing ("a flood of inner sensation"), while increasing trophotropic arousal, or tranquilization, decreases the rate of data processing.

State-bound flashback requires that retrieval of the data content of a particular experience be optimal only at the specific rate of data processing that corresponds to the level of arousal prevailing during the initial experience. State–stage, or arousal–symbol, equivalence is another conceptualization of space–time equivalence, and refers to the representation of a particular spatio-temporal neuronal-synaptic firing pattern that prevailed during the initial experience. Or, in Borges's words: "Time is a river which sweeps me along, but I am the river; it is a tiger which destroys me, but I am the tiger; it is a fire which consumes me, but I am the fire" (1962, p. 234).

Only certain people can re-experience the intensity of the initial experience. We contrast these "re-experiencers" with those who can only remember an experience. The following examples should help us to understand the nature of the flashback and that of the flashbacker.

One of our college-girl volunteers, N. B., an easily hypnotizable subject (Gwynne et al., 1969, p. 225) with large and variable standard deviation on perceptual and behavioral tasks, was repeatedly administered the hallucinogenic drug psilocybin. Later, a hypnotically induced experience was substituted for the real drug experience. The hypnotic induction placed the subject in a peaceful beach scene with waves lapping the shore. The experiments were interrupted after two such sessions, when N. B. left for a Florida seaside vacation. After her return, she reported a strange event that happened to her while walking down to the beach for the first time. As she gazed at the seashore, the whole scene suddenly "blacked-out" and her "old beach" reappeared—the beach of the hypnotically induced psilocybin experience. The hypnotically induced experience was re-experienced by exposure to an aspect of ordinary reality (the Florida beach), which symbolized and represented the covert hypnotic experience. Therefore, instead of one subconscious, there appear to be as many potential self-awarenesses as levels of arousal, and corresponding significant but covert interpretations in an individual's interpretive repertoire.

The many layers of self-awareness remind us again of the proverbial ship's captain with girlfriends in many ports, each girl unaware of the existence of the others, and from the captain's standpoint, each existing only from visit to visit (i.e., *from state to state*). Also, consider the following:

> I shared living quarters in Honolulu with a man who was a heavy drinker. When drunk, the only visible sign was that the whites of his eyes showed all around the cornea. His actions were unusual. He would take up a position on a street corner in mid-town and expound on the battles of the Civil War. . . . His knowledge of the subject was extensive and everytime he became drunk he would take up his lecture where he left off in strict *chronological order.* (Evans, 1976)

Amnesia between disparate states of arousal has many important implications. One is that an "exciting" experience may be meaningful only at that level of arousal at which it occurred. (It is no wonder that marriage licenses had to be invented!) For instance, we may interpret a dream by dreaming its interpretation, says Erich Fromm (1951), referring to subjects who were placed into hypnotically induced dreaming and asked to interpret their dreams. Without hesitation, these subjects gave meaningful interpretations of the symbolic argot employed by these dreams, whereas in the usual waking state the same dreams seemed entirely meaningless. Fromm also quotes Jochanan, who holds that when asleep we can understand the meaning of another dream and interpret it correctly. Descartes's illumination, the discovery of rational, universal order, was followed by a triple dream in which the brilliant, sickly, introvert philosopher was analyzing, while dreaming, both his illumination and the dreams (von Franz, 1952). Unfortunately, Descartes's dream of rationality ended with Freud's rational dream analysis and our awareness of rationality as being another dream.

Stekel (1943, p. 123) also stressed the unity of each individual's dreams: "A patient's dreams in their entirety are like a serial novel, each installment ending with the subscript 'to be continued'. . . . " Dreams, like masterworks of art, are, in Ricoeur's (1970) formulation "not mere projections of the artist's conflicts, but also the sketch of their solutions . . . " (pp. 521–522).

Extreme states of hyper- and hypoarousal, for instance, the manic and depressive phases of bipolar, cycling affective disorder, also display stateboundness. The phenomenon is not restricted to verbalizable experiences; the style of a drawing and creative style, in general, are state-bound—hence Navratil's patient-artist, Hauser, in a nonmanic state may dislike his drawing executed while he was manic (Hauser, in Fischer, 1976a). Creative arousal does change the appearance of the world (as demonstrated by the rising horizon and the closing in of nearby visual space at high levels of arousal—Fischer et al., 1970). This may be the reason why the artist Giacometti could not paint from a model; after five minutes of posing, even well-known models would become complete strangers to him (Giacometti, 1970).

COMMUNICATION AND COMMUNION

In one of his essays von Foerster (1974) states that "The nervous activity of one organism cannot be shared by another organism, . . . this suggests that indeed nothing can be communicated." I agree with the first statement but suggest a few exemptions: the simultaneous orgasm of two lovers, the breast feeding of an infant by its mother, and the hypnotist's sharing of his interpretive repertoire with that of the hypnotized. Valéry (1957) expressed a similar view when he noted that poetry is not written to share something intelligible with someone else. Its aim is rather to evoke a state, the poetic rendering of which uniquely corresponds to the meaning of that state.

Communication may be possible only within states of comparable, low-to-moderate (daily routine) levels of arousal. At higher levels of arousal, that is, above a certain sensory/motor (S/M) ratio, when moving closer to the "Self" (on the continuum in Figure 1 of Chapter 1 in this book), less and less is to be communicated in the analytical-rational (left cerebral hemispheric) sense. For men and women in these *intense* states, everything knowable may already be known, and hence there is no need for *extensive* communication. As Christ said (Matthew 18:20), "For where two or three are gathered together in my name, there am I in the midst of them." This may be an arousal-state-bound communion and not communication.

We need not regard speech as principally evolving as a communicatory mechanism; and, indeed, Susanne Langer (1973) argues that the motive for human vocalization was most likely communion, a vicarious form of tactile contact. Only subsequently did meaning attach to sound and a communicatory function evolve.

The "content" of a highly aroused (state-bound) experience may often be no more than a symbol, a cue, or a mnemonic tool that can re-evoke the intensity of a past significant experience. People may attempt telling the *content* of an exciting story without realizing that what they really want to do is to share the *excitement* and intense meaning associated with the story's content. The content then becomes the prosaic part of an aroused experience; its intensity is the poetic dimension because only poetic language can convey intensity in concise form. Most of us "lose" the significance of a story whose intensity is "translated" into prosaic "content." As Valéry (1957, vol. 1, p. 1511) would say, "It's poetry that is lost in translation."

A significant feature of creative poetry, literature, music, fine art, and architecture is that it should evoke in a reader, listener, or spectator either the same creative arousal-state-bound consciousness that the artist experienced during the process of creation or another deliberately intended state of consciousness.

There are a variety of tropes in poetic language for the induction of a nonordinary state of consciousness. One of them is the "meter-and-meaning" process, while another important one is sound-symbolism—"the sound must seem an Echo of the sense"—which Pope (1824) founded on a phenomenal connection between the visual and auditory modalities. Since Mallarmé, French poetry has used the collision between sound and meaning and the "semantic shift" for the composition of a music of sound-images. Other tropes are metaphorical and metonymic structures, and Jakobson (1960) notes that in poetry, where similarity is superimposed upon contiguity, any metonymy is slightly metaphorical, and any metaphor has a metonymic tint. Ambiguity is a corollary feature of poetry, and so is the conversion of a message into an enduring pattern. Words similar in sound are drawn together in meaning. In Poe's "Raven," for example, "the overwhelming effect," comments Jakobson (1960, p. 371), is primarily due to the sway of poetic etymology:

And the Raven, never flitting, still is sitting, *still* is sitting
On the pallid bust of Pallas just above my chamber door;
And his eyes have all the seeming of a demon's that is dreaming,
And the lamp-light o'er him streaming throws his shadow on the floor;
And my soul from out that shadow that lies floating on the floor
Shall be lifted—nevermore.

Highly aroused mystical ecstasy and creative-inspired arousal are both embraced in one unique state of consciousness in the poetry of San Juan de la Cruz. His symbols are those of the mystical experience: "dark night of the soul," "living flame of love," "*soledad sonora*" (sonorous solitude). Both the serenely detached and ecstatic components of the mystical rapture are dissolved in the music of the poetic structure:

Mi Amado las montañas,
Los valles solitarios nemorosos,
Los ínsulas extrañas,
Los ríos sonorosos,
El silbo de los aires amorosos.

Guillén (1961, p. 120) tells us that shortly before San Juan died, on the night of the 13th to the 14th of December 1591, some of the lines of his immortal *Spiritual Canticle* returned to the mind of the dying saint and poet:

> Gocémonos, Amado,
> Y vámonos a ver en tu hermosura.
>
> Rejoice, my love, with me
> And in your beauty see us both reflected.

Gocémonos, Amado! These words, just as correctly translated "Let us have joy of one another, Beloved," are an audacious exclamation of a love completely fulfilled. San Juan de la Cruz is the one who epitomizes the type of poet Baudelaire was to dream of three centuries later, "Like a perfect chemist and a sainted soul" (*Comme un parfait chimiste et comme une âme sainte).*

Another poetic (arousal-state-specific) trope is the abundant use of primary process words (Martindale and Fischer, 1977) that is, words that express dedifferentiated, regressive thought in the Freudian sense. Landon and I (1970), when analyzing the common features of texts written during hallucinogenic drug-induced and creative states, found a characteristically simplified syntax in both states. Semantic orientation became more concrete (sentences exhibited fewer subordinated and more coordinated structures), while rhetorical structure was modified, and the variability of the numerical values of the above criteria decreased.

The above glimpse at the "grammar of poetry" infers the manifold nature of linguistic tropes created for the evocation of nonordinary states of consciousness or mood-states. Tropes can evoke particular states, since they signify and represent those states of arousal. That creatively aroused poetic performance may induce a corresponding creative experience has been known for thousands of years. It is now restated in a seemingly specific "objective" vocabulary, using words such as "scanning," "coding," "storage," "memory search," "state-dependent learning," and "retrieval of verbal associations" (Weingartner et al., 1977).

That experience may become state-bound can be of survival value. To recall experiences from one excited state to another may be lifesaving in terms of economy of performance (e.g., running and successfully hiding from an attacking tiger!). And not being able to recall highly exciting, traumatic, material during the normal state of dutiful routine is clearly mental-health-sustaining, and may improve performance as well. "And things must indeed be forgotten, for how could anyone who cannot forget live?" (Goes, 1968, p. 49).

To repent and to forgive (*tout comprendre c'est tout pardonner*) may be taken as integral parts of a psychotherapeutic procedure intended to relieve state-bound guilt. The guilt-inducing transgression of a taboo is usually committed under impact of "an immediate force," that is, an excited state of hyperarousal. Contemplating and restructuring this traumatic material in meditational understanding, a hypoaroused state of consciousness—as during ritualized confession in a ceremonial procedure—creates a "distance," or partial amnesia, as a vantage point from which the transgression may be viewed in a detached manner, so that it ceases to be a remembrance of things present and becomes a remembrance of things past.

THE MAKERS AND TAKERS OF FLASHBACKS

We can attempt to create equality, but we cannot equalize creativity. Some of us, as George Orwell wrote, "are more equal than others." Flashbackers belong in this latter category. In the first part of this chapter, we remarked (Fischer, 1977) that about 10 percent of the general population are capable of flashbacks. Who are these people?

First, they are *variable* individuals; that is, in contrast to stable individuals they display variable performance on a large variety of perceptual and behavioral tasks. They also overestimate time (e.g., they would be too early for an appointment) at the peak of hallucinogenic drug-induced arousal (Fischer, 1967). The variable performance of these individuals can be measured by their variable (mostly large) standard deviation (S.D.). What is the meaning of this variability? Variability and information are related concepts: anything that increases one also increases the other. Variability can be measured (using the S.D.), whereas information is a dimensionless attribute of the cognitive repertoire. When we have a large variability (large S.D.), we are not certain about what is going to happen, and, therefore, making an observation at this uncertain point will yield much information. A small S.D., however, tells us in advance the expected outcome of the observation, so it would be redundant to make another one (Hildum, 1967, p. 4).

Fischer and Hill (1971), as well as Panton and Fischer (1973), have established that the magnitude of the S.D. follows a near normal or log-normal distribution; hence, variable individuals constitute about one-third of the population. Their subject population consisted of unpaid, *self*-selected student volunteers (mostly from the Medical School, during the years 1960–1970, at Ohio State University in Columbus) who were interested in participating in legal hallucinogenic drug research. Ninety-five percent of the subjects turned out to be taste-sensitive to begin with; that is, on the Gaussian, or normal, distribution of taste thresholds (for quinine, sucrose, etc.), falling in the taste-sensitive (left) tail end of the distribution (Fischer, 1971) (see Figure 2). Taste-sensitive subjects are also drug-sensitive and, in comparison to taste-insensitives, require significantly lower doses of autonomic drugs for induction of comparable pharmacological responses. Moreover, on the Myers-Briggs (Jungian) Type Indicator (MBTI); the majority of the taste-sensitive subjects displayed the "sensitive" *INFP* and *ENFP* personality profiles; that is, they are *introverts (I)* instead of extraverts (E), and *Intuitors (N), Feelers (F),* and, *Perceivers (P)* as opposed to "down-to-earth" *Sensors, Thinkers,* and *Judgers* (Corlis et al., 1967).

It is remarkable that through self-selection a homogeneous population of 95 percent taste- and drug-sensitive subjects was assembled, and that these subjects displayed the sensitive INFP or ENFP personality profiles, which, respectively, constituted only 10.7 and 10.3 percent, of medical student populations in the late 1960s and early 1970s (Myers-Briggs, 1974). The most representative personality dimension on the MBTI, and the one shared by all self-selected volunteers, was *intuition* (N). The prevalence of N in the general college population is estimated at close to 60 percent (as against 40 percent for "down-to-earth" sensors (S), according to Dr. D. W. MacKinnon, Director, Institute of Personality Assessment and Research, University of California, Berkeley, in a letter written to me on Feb. 14, 1968). Note that this 60 percent figure is lowered among those who elected to become medical doctors, that is, in the first-year medical student population, and then increased to 95 percent through another self-selection process: experimentation with hallucinogenic drugs.

Not only were these self-selected taste- and drug-sensitive volunteers sensitive in terms of personality profile, they were also food-sensitive (displayed more food dislikes than the insensitive tasters), were smoke-sensitive (as a group they were, in fact, nonsmokers), and could be recognized by their faster reaction time on the written "Serial Seven Substraction" test (Fischer et al., 1965; Fischer, 1971). These traits are not peculiar to college volunteers. In a population of acute mental patients, for instance, the taste-sensitives were found to display all the above sensitivities in spite of being under the influence of major tranquilizers. Such sensitive patients, of course, need less tranquilizers than insensitives for the induction of the same psychopharmacological response. Fischer, (1971) describes the relevant aspects of the "systemic sensitivity" phenomenon and lists an extensive bibliography. The finding of a robust relation between taste-sensitivity and psychophysiological reactivity was independently replicated by Joyce et al., 1968.

Self-selected volunteers are "sensitives," but to be a flashbacker one must also be a "variable" subject, that is, one with a large S.D.

Figure 2 illustrates schematically the Gaussian, or normal, distribution of sensitivity, that is, a population's systemic (subcortical) reactivity. The two tail ends of this bell-shaped curve represent the sensitives and insen-

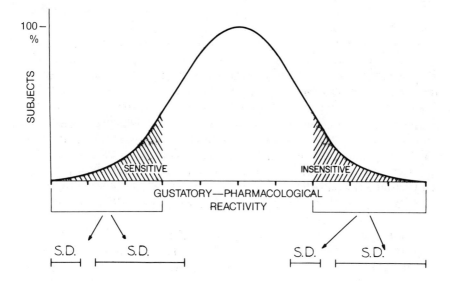

Figure 2. Gaussian, or normal, distribution of gustatory and pharmacological sensitivity in a general population. Sensitive tasters, the majority of self-selected college volunteers for hallucinatory drug research, are congregated on the left end of the distribution. These sensitives are also sensitive drug reactors. Insensitive tasters (right end) need a significantly greater amount of an autonomic drug for induction of a comparable pharmacological effect. Taste thresholds from 0 to 10 (from left to right on the abscissa) correspond to doubling concentrations of a compound such as quinine, sucrose, hydrochloric acid, or any other compound, the taste threshhold of which follows a normal distribution. Threshold 0 indicates a 3.66×10^{-7} M aqueous solution of quinine sulfate (in this illustration) at 21 C°; threshold 1 = 7.32×10^{-7} M; threshold 2 = 1.465×10^{-6} M; and so forth.

The sensitives on the left and insensitives on the right fall into two subgroups: stable and variable subjects with stable (small) and variable (mostly large) standard deviations (S.D.) respectively on a variety of perceptual and behavioral tasks. The magnitude of the S.D. indicates the capacity of the cortical interpretive repertoire; for instance, in terms of available multiple strategies. The taste sensitive *and* variable (large S.D.) subjects are the reexperiencers, or flashbackers.

Taste and drug sensitivity are markers of a general systemic or subcortical reactivity, whereas the S.D. on perceptual–behavioral tasks is an indicator of the ability to cognitively interpret subcortical activity.

sitives, with both groups subdivided into stable and variable subjects, having small and large cortical repertoires, respectively.

A flashbacker is a *sensitive* as well as *variable* subject. Sensitivity refers to heightened subcortical reactivity, whereas variability refers to a wide range in cortical interpretive ability. Variable subjects are also *minimizers* (or reducers) of sensory input, particularly at the peak of a hallucinogenic drug experience (Panton and Fischer, 1973; Fischer, 1980) and as a group display *high resting heart rates* (higher arousal) and the *ability to enter hypnosis easily* (Gwynne et al., 1969; Matefy and Krall, 1975). The two overlapping criteria—variability and ease of entering hypnosis—point to a subject with a cortical repertoire so responsive (i.e., redundant and uncertain) that its interpretive capacity may be shared or partially replaced by another—a hypnotically induced interpretation, a selectively imposed set and setting (Fischer, 1977). Variable and easily hypnotizable subjects also prefer *right cerebral hemispheric cognition* and display *alpha dominance* in the resting, waking state.

These then are the flashbackers among self-selected college student volunteers. The answer to the objection that we have not dealt with a representative sample of subjects is that experimentation with a randomly selected sample of paid volunteers would have resulted in an inordinate number of ''bad trips'' and no reproducible data. Self-selected subjects are a physiologically and psychologically homogeneous sample and representative of the type of person who is willing and able to enjoy an introvert experience (an excursion into inner space) and at the same time capable of following research procedures (as a price for a good trip).

An example should highlight the importance of the standard deviation in the design and evaluation of experiments involving flashbacks, hypnotic recall, and placebo effects. When, for instance, inexperienced users of marijuana are contrasted with frequent users, the frequent users are found to be inferior in distinguishing placebo ''joints'' from the delta-9 THC–containing ones (Jones, 1971). We suggest that the subjects with large standard deviations in the group of experienced users are liable to experience flashbacks from the correctly tasting and smelling placebo ''joints,'' and, hence, the mean score of the mixed (small and large standard deviation) group of subjects will be significantly influenced by the data from subjects displaying large standard deviations. Subjects in placebo groups should therefore be broken down into subgroups of subjects with small and large standard deviations.

What are the characteristics of authors, for example, Proust, whose texts can elicit a flashback, that is, a remembrance of things present, in taste- and drug-sensitive, variable re-experiencers with high resting heart rates? Most probably, these authors are the very same type of subject they can so creatively and skillfully manipulate. We assert this similarity because, on the one hand, hypnotic recall and flashback are one and the same phenomenon (although the former is involuntary, and the latter is not, they differ only in the ways and means they are triggered); on the other hand, the best hypnotists are known to be subjects who themselves can enter hypnosis easily (Morgan, 1975).

WHY MAY (ONLY) DRUG-INDUCED FLASHBACKS END UP IN "BAD TRIPS"?

Flashbacks that are not of the drug-induced variety are usually not considered a problem; only drug-induced flashbacks are regarded as frightening "bad trips." Although the involuntary re-experiencing of imagery that originated under drug exposure is often labeled as being "only psychological" in nature, ironically the *Diagnostic and Statistic Manual of Mental Disorders,* 3rd edition, of the American Psychiatric Association does not provide a proper taxonomic niche for this phenomenon (symptom or disorder). Why are only drug-induced flashbacks evaluated as "bad trips"?

Powers (1973) and Wall (1974) contend that we perceive only that for which we have an (operational) behavior, and, hence, perceptions are controlled by our behavioral repertoire. All that which is not appropriate for perception—that which makes no sense—will be denied, misperceived, repressed, displaced, distorted, or sublimated. To behave, therefore, is to adjust to (what is sensed as) perception or input. Output cannot be controlled because we are only aware of that part of our behavior that consists of the feedback effects of our own outputs. What the muscle, for example, reacts to is not the stimulus but the difference between stimulus-induced feedback (expectation) and stimulus (excitation); behavioral control attempts to adjust such difference to zero. Hence, zero effort implies that the signal of excitation coincides with the signal of expectation.

But extreme behavior may proceed *either* as pure voluntary motor activity, for example, a running contest, with its characteristic *low* sensory (S) to motor (M) ratio, *or* as dreams and hallucinations that are sensory (behavioral) experiences with greatly diminished capacity for willed motor acts and thus displaying a *high* S/M ratio. The point I wish to make is that drug-induced flashbacks originate in and re-present perceptions that cannot be controlled through available behavior. Hallucinogenic drugs elicit hyperaroused behavior with characteristically high S/M ratios, but the individual's dreamy perceptions proceed while he stands or sits, with open eyes in the real world. In the real world, the proof of the sensory pudding is in the motor eating; drug-induced perceptions, however, defy behavioral control that is based on willed motor acts. The average Western (extravert) individual simply does not know how to deal with drug-induced perceptual transformations that appear to be real but cannot be verified through willed motor acts. It is these untouchable, uncontrollable perceptions that are experienced as "loss of control," provoking anxiety, panic, and confusion.

The majority of those flashbacks induced in a reader by an author's text, however, belong to an arousal-state-bound. "plesaure of the text"—to use the title of a pleasurable book by Roland Barthes (1973). Literary flashbacks are well-structured cognitive acts, valued for the sake of their aesthetics and erotics, and no conflict is experienced between flashback-imagery and concurrent loss of its behavioral control.

INTER-INDIVIDUAL FLASHBACKS

We have dealth with the self-programmed, or intra-individual, varieties of state-bound experience, and turn now to the philogenetically programmed, inter-individual flashbacks. The ordering structures of *intra-individual flashbacks,* the perceptual–hallucinatory invariants, can be described as geometric–ornamental visual structures or constancies, represented as rhythmic harmonies in poetry. The ordering structures, or conceptual invariants, of *inter-individual flashbacks* are archetypal patterns: plots, scripts, and scenarios flashed back in fiction and fantasm. Eliade (1949) calls these conceptual invariants universal constants in collective imagination. An object or act becomes real only insofar as it imitates, repeats, and/ or slightly modifies an archetype.

For Leonard B. Meyer (1980), a musicologist, "archetypes . . . are what children learn when they tediously reiterate nursery rhymes, intone tiresome chants, and make visual images that only fond parents delight in, psychiatrists regard as interesting, and Wordsworthian Romantics find profound." Meyer illustrates the relationship between the general scheme of the archetype and its particular realization with instances from the *oeuvre* of Mozart, then exemplifies the way in which Beethoven realizes the archetype and the significance of some of his modifications, and, finally, considers how Berlioz realizes the same fundamental schema.

Conceptual invariants are reformulated by each epoch in contemporary terms and in such ways that it is not always easy to recognize their nature and origin. For instance, in present times the End of the World (as heat death in accordance with the second law of thermodynamics) is linked with the Eternal Return (through Ilja Prigogine's dissipative structures and Manfred Eigen's hypercycle), which bring about the Golden Age (through creative evolution that culminates in a utopian, progressive spiritual realm).

The domain of inter-individually inducible state-boundness is the philogenetic mental repertoire of our species, the great fantasms or daydreams and repetitive schemes, the ever rewritten plots of the world's literature. Re-presenting the human program, that is, the innate knowledge which according to Plato "is already there," these wish-fulfilling self-interpretations of the mind are constantly rewritten, repainted, resculpted and recomposed for each generation with but slight variation in style. For de Nerval (1854) (see Poulet, 1949), state-bound knowledge, rediscovered by each generation, is:

> . . . a turning spectacle, ballet of hours and ages, in which the epochs give one another their hand. And the faster the round turns, the more different ages seem susceptible of being confounded and able to reveal essential identity. Then thought becomes a mad clock. All the hours, all times seem to wish to be everywhere present at the same time. A self-same event is reproduced, a self-same star scintillates, a self-same sentiment recomposes itself, constellating the same horizon. All is always the same, always recognizable. What has happened happens and will happen. The same events that have occurred, occur, and in the same detail. (p. 170)

Parts of the human repertoire, or in Gebser's (1972) words, the philogenetically evolved "magical, mythical and mental structures of consciousness," may be re-experienced or flashed back not only through exposure to "cortical interpretations" such as good literature, art, and music, all of which have an underlying "religious" significance, but also by inducing, naturally or through certain drugs and hypnosis, a particular level of (subcortical) hyper- or hypoarousal.

Knowing–experiencing may be conceptualized as being distributed over a variety of arousal states in such a manner that a certain type of scenario is bound to and only retrievable at a particular level of arousal (Figure 1 in Chapter 1). As already mentioned, there is no communication between disparate levels of arousal; or—in paraphrasing Spencer-Brown (1969) and the Coptic Gospel according to Thomas (1968)—what is revealed on one level (of arousal state) is concealed on the other, but what is concealed will again be revealed.[7] The interpretation of particular levels of arousal can only be enacted in a restricted, stereotyped, or archetypal manner. Whenever the stage is set by a particular level of arousal, the pertaining cortical interpretation, or "knowing," myth, narrative, script, role, or "great story," may be enacted, re-experienced, or flashed back. This is how scripts of an inner "Schau-spiel" are enacted on the stage of one's experiential magic theater (Fischer, 1976). It may now be easier to accept the proposition that hyperaroused schizophrenic or neurotic patients, in whom hyperarousal is induced through a series of LSD sessions, re-experience (i.e., represent) parts of the inter-individual or archetypal human repertoire (Grof, 1973).

What is the hyperaroused action pattern of these inter-individual flash-backs? In 1955, Kranz reported that the frequency with which archaic-mythical–magical themes occur during hyperphrenic or schizophrenic epi-sodes is around 43 to 45 percent, irrespective of the year of sampling (1886, 1916, and 1946). The hyperphrenic preoccupation with archaic–magical–mythical "stories" is regarded by Perry (1962) as a creative striving of the unconscious psyche to reconstitute its structure, and Campbell (1949) finds that "the imagery of schizophrenic fantasy perfectly matches that of the mythological hero journey," which he has outlined and elucidated in *The Hero with the Thousand Faces*. The journey consists of: (1) separation; (2) initiation; (3) return, or rebirth—a reintegration process. Similar death-rebirth experiences are reported by Luthe (1973) during certain autogenic abreactions. This is, in Burnham's (1970) words, a " 'restructuring' process as a means of working through," and he refers to a little-known paper by Bertschinger (1916), originally published in German in 1911, on processes of recovery in schizophrenia. Bertschinger observed patients who passed through a whole series of delusional experiences that little by little brought about wish fulfillment. When the dramatic play of the wish-fulfilling de-lusions was complete, the patients emerged as if reborn or as if from a long sleep, with regained control of the unconscious spheres of their minds, and eventual recovery. Also, Freud (1958), in his well-known Schreber paper, published in 1911, independently stated that the delusional formation that we take to be the pathological product is in reality an attempt at recovery, a process of reconstruction. To sum up, Bertschinger's "rebirth, or recov-ery, process," Freud's "regression" and "reconstruction," Jung's "arche-types," Campbell's "hero journey," Perry's "death and rebirth," Luthe's "autogenic abreactions," and Grof's Freudian–Rankian–Jungian "agony and ecstasy" all refer to the same inter-individual (hyper) arousal-state-bound "knowledge" that is part and parcel of the human repertoire or universal grammar of our self-referential universe.

CODA

When Adam and Eve were expelled from Paradise because they tasted the fruit from the tree of knowledge, they left the garden of Eden as *homo sapiens* (Straus, 1956). Today the connotation of the Latin *sapiens,* from *sapere* "to taste" and "to know," is not that *they* knew what they were doing but that *we* know the script according to which we are to perform in the future. Through cybernetic technology, we, that is, twentieth-century man, reaffirm the concept of the medieval *liber mundi* and the baroque world theater. Once again the world appears to us as a hierarchy of codes and languages. Once more man conceives of himself as an actor in a play of signs and as a dramatist writing the script for human performance (Lucid, 1977).

In this script, creator and created coalesce in the creation of myth, the inter-individual flashback of unanalyzable, fundamental, categorical knowledge. "Myths signify the mind that evolves them by making use of the world of which it is itself a part. Thus there is simultaneous production of myths themselves by the mind that generates them and, by the myths, of an image of the world which is already inherent in the structure of the mind" (Lévi-Strauss, 1964, p. 184).

Do myths narrate basic systems of ideas, the algorithms of our self-descriptive nature? Recurring patterns in myths are recognized as functions (Propp, 1928); points (Lord Raglan, 1936); mythemes (Lévi-Strauss, 1958) and the relation of desire, of communication, and of action—each resting on a binary opposition (Greimas, 1966). If the human repertoire, the content of consciousness, is cognized as a self-descriptive literary text, then human action may be regarded as textual interpretation that escapes the bounds of literal meaning and becomes available for hermeneutic reinterpretation across space and time.

For Borges (1962, p. 58), the human repertoire is "the universe (of consciousness)—which others call the Library—. . . . and Man (is) the imperfect librarian. The Library is unlimited and cyclical. If an eternal traveler were to cross it in any direction, after centuries he would see that the same volumes were repeated"—read "flashed back"—"in the same disorder (which thus repeated would be an order: the Order)."

But what is the meaning of repetition? Is it the re-presentation of something one would wish to bring to presence again, or is it the remarking of that very absence? Proust, when referring to "presence," remarks that "returning memory causes us to breathe a new air, an air which is new precisely because we have breathed it in the past" (Harper, 1882, p. 1128).

The re-experiencing of numinous, universal, and fictional structures is beyond cognitive and linguistic representation. Lévi-Strauss was inclined in his later years to treat narrative fiction as music (Gardner, 1974, p. 210) and myth in particular as an orchestral score. The animated mathematics of music may most closely approximate the prefigured potentials of our existence, since music is the actualization of potential structures (orchestral scores) that allow personal variations upon experiencing collective themes.

Proust's (1954, III, 254) pen turns inward when his Narrator meditates about the music of a septet. "Une page symphonique de Vinteuil . . . comme un rayon de jour d'été que le prism de la fenêtre décompose avant son entrée dans une salle a manger obscure, dévoilait comme un trésor insoupçonné et multicolore toutes les pierreries de Mille et une Nuit." And Arthur C. Clarke's *2001: A Space Odyssey* (1982) ends with a daunting image that hints at repetitive patterns of our human behavioral repertoire, the "orchestral score" of our life. David Bowman, the only survivor of the team sent to investigate the black monolith inscrutably orbiting Jupiter, is seized by the alien artifact and sent whizzing through his own life, forward to its end and then back to its beginning, and all the while being scanned like a tape recording from which the monolith's makers could learn the melody of humanity.

ACKNOWLEDGMENT

The invaluable assistance of Dr. Thomas E. Hanlon, Baltimore, is most gratefully acknowledged. Dr. Jean Starobinski, Geneva, Switzerland, and Dr. G. M. Landon, Tempe, Arizona, kindly called my attention to the books by Schrader (1969) and Collins (1874) respectively.

NOTES

1. The original Latin version of this passage is both scientific and concise: "Puer quum Valentiae febri laborarem, et depravato gustu cerasa edissem, multis post annis quoties id pomum gustabam, toties non solum de febri memineram, sed habere mihi illam videbar" (Vives, 1745, p. 350).

2. That sequence had already been validated by the Spanish Nobelist poet Ramón Jiménez (1964), who died twenty years prior to Williams's publication. Jiménez wrote:

> Todo es un corresponderse
> de curvas, un grato engarce
> de musicas, de fragrancia,
> de luz, de color, de aires

   The cross-modal connections are sources of both flashbacks and such synaesthesias as described by Jiménez.

3. Susan Langer (1951) refers to the use of signs as the very first manifestation of mind. "It arises as early in biological history as the famous 'conditioned reflex' by which a concomitant of a stimulus takes over the stimulus-function. The concomitant becomes a *sign* of the condition to which the reaction is really appropriate. This is the real beginning of mentality, for here is the birth place of *error,* and herewith of truth."

4. State-dependent learning (SDL) refers almost exclusively to drug-states, and SDL is said to occur if performance of a learned response is conditional on the drug-state when the response was learned (Overton, 1973). For a critical overview of the SDL field consult Erdmann (1979).

5. "Sensitized" refers to *kindling,* that is, a long-lasting or permanently reduced threshold for neural excitability as a result of previous excitation (see e.g., p. 24 of Mandell, 1980).

6. Subjects who volunteer without monetary reward for a particular experience—from covering a retreat in battle to participating in hypnosis or hallucinogenic drug research—have a particular physiological and psychological makeup. The critical difference between self-selected volunteers and invited subjects has not yet been fully realized. Data obtained with self-selected volunteers may not be reproducible with invited subjects. For instance, the correlation between hypnotic susceptibility and EEG alpha indices is only obtained with self-selected subjects (London, et al. 1968), suggesting that hypnotizability is a stable per-

sonality trait with measurable physiological substrates (Dumas, 1977, 1978). Hilgard (1970), as well as Van Nuys (1972), noticed that subjects who have had hallucinogenic drug experiences appear to be more easily hypnotized than those who are not interested in such experiences.

The phenomenon of self-selected volunteers displaying a particular physiological and psychological makeup offers research advantages that may be illustrated with the following observations. When conducting psilocybin experiments under sensory attenuation, we were interested in whether the hallucinogenic experience is enhanced or diminished under such conditions (Panton and Fischer, 1973). Animal experiments had demonstrated that the hallucinogenic drug effect depends upon sensory input. We proceeded, therefore, by subdividing the self-selected taste- and drug-sensitive volunteers into stable maximizers and variable minimizers of sensory input and administered them the same doses of psilocybin in an environment of *sensory attenuation* (subject sitting alone in a quiet room with only *one candle light* of illumination). Under these conditions, stable maximizers of sensory input had no opportunity of maximizing and hence were unable to procure the sensory stimulation necessary for developing a hallucinogenic experience; in fact, these volunteers were never sure whether they had a placebo or not. The variable minimizers, on the other hand, did not need to minimize the already minimal (and hence, for them, optimal) sensory input and, accordingly, developed, a full-blown hallucinogenic experience. Hence, for the termination of a stable maximizer's "bad trip," the only intervention required is placing the subject into a sensory deprivation chamber.

Variable minimizers, in comparison to stable maximizers, have significantly higher resting heart rates (higher arousal), and these high pre-drug heart rates are then substantially reduced at the peak of a hallucinogenic drug session. Such cardiovascular quieting is characteristic not only of psilocybin but of hallucinogenic drugs in general (Shulgin, 1979) and is experienced as shivering. It took us a few years to realize that only variable minimizer volunteers asked for a blanket at the peak of a psilocybin experiment (Fischer, 1980). Later, a friend (Dr. James Foy, Georgetown University, Washington, D.C.) called our attention to Robert Graves's *Oxford Address on Poetry* (1961), where we found the following revealing passage:

That evening, four of us gathered in Gordon Wasson's apartment overlooking the East River, prepared to set out for Paradise under his guidance. He had advised us to fast beforehand, drink no liquor, and try to achieve a state of grace. At seven-thirty he gave us the (psilocybin) mushrooms in crystalline form washed down with water and, at eight, began *turning out the lights* one by one, while we settled down in easy chairs. Soon no sound was heard except the swish-swish of cars passing in an endless stream along the Drive between us and the river: a noise not unlike the sound of waves on a beach.

By eight o'clock I felt a numbness in my arms, and a pricking at the nape of my neck. In the half-light that filtered through the shutters, colored dots appeared on the ceiling; they shone brighter when I closed my eyes. We all *began to shiver,* our pulses slowed down, and Masha Wasson brought in blankets.

Apparently, not only the volunteers at O.S.U., but Robert Graves and the other self-selected members of his group, were variable "minimizers" who at the psilocybin-induced peak—and in a sensory attenuated environment—reduced their systemic output (fall of heart or pulse rate), and as a result began to shiver.

Self-selection of subjects, or *assortative volunteering,* as we should like to call it (bringing along one's wife, husband, or friends for hallucinogenic drug experimentation or hypnosis), results in the conglomeration of a near homogeneous population with a common sensitive (or reactive) physiological and psychological makeup (see also p. 218 of Fischer, 1971).

The "sensitive" ENFP and INFP personality profiles (of the *Myers-Briggs Type Indicator*) displayed by taste- and drug-sensitive volunteers for hallucinogenic drug experimentation and hypnosis are characteristic descriptors of another self-selected sample: individuals interested in serving as primary therapists for unmedicated, acutely psychotic patients at Soteria House in California. ENFP and INFP are the only MBTI profiles found among these volunteers, who rely on intuition (N, indirect perception by way of the subconscious), on feeling (F, discriminating between the valued and the non-valued), and a perceptive (P, perception) process in dealing with the outer world. These volunteers seem to share relevant traits with two groups, creative artists and psychotherapists of schizophrenics (Mosher, *et al.,* 1973). It is not surprising, then, that the majority of the medical students who volunteered to be part of hallucinogenic drug experimentation, subsequently chose to become psychiatrists. The importance of self-selection has other practical consequences. Since the abolishment of the draft in 1970, almost half of the U.S. *all-volunteer* Army's new recruits have belonged, to the lowest mental category acceptable in armed services (Holden, 1980). The problem of self-selection may also account, at least in part, for some of the adaptational difficulties of certain segments of the black population. Note that blacks have been the only involuntary immigrants in the U.S. while all other minorities are descendants of or are themselves self-selected volunteers.

7. The dissolved dualities and polarities that constitute the meaning of high (or low) arousal states cannot be revealed through the prosaic language of daily routine but only within a geometric-ornamental-rhythmic poetic structure.

Baudelaire (1971, p. 112) reveals his hyperaroused secret (in *The Poem of Hashish*): " . . . for me mankind has labored, been martyred and annihilated to serve as food . . . to my relentless appetite for emotion, knowledge and beauty! And I paraphrase this monologue. No one will be surprised at the final, supreme thought that bursts from the brain of the dreamer: 'I have become God!' "

But gnosis revealed at highest levels of arousal—ecstatic–beatific vision—is meant to be kept *incommunicado,* that is, God's mystery (according to the mystical doctrine of Sufism). When a Sufi, al-Hallaj (A.D. 1921), revealed his secret knowledge ("I am God; God and I are one"), he had to suffer a cruel death, since he revealed that which should have been concealed. "The moth flies into the light and while destroyed becomes itself the flame," reflected al-Hallaj.

REFERENCES

Abruzzi, W. 5,000 bad trips. *Contemporary Problems,* 1974, *3,* 345–362.

Al-Hallaj (A.D. 921). Quoted in Smith, M., *The way of the mystics.* London: Sheldon Press, 1976, p. 235.

Barthes, R. *Le plaisir du texte,* Paris: Seuil, 1973.

Baudelaire, Ch. *The poem of hashish,* S. Sullivan (transl.). New York: Perennial Library, Harper and Row, 1971.

Beckett, S. *Proust.* New York: Evergreen, Grove Press, 1931.

Bertschinger, H. Processes of recovery in schizophrenia. *Psychoanalytic Review,* 1916, *3,* 176–188.

Borges, J. L. *Labyrinths, Selected stories and other writings,* D. A. Yates and J. E. Irby (Eds.). New York: New Directions, 1962.

Bourguignon, E. Ritual dissociations and possession belief in Caribbean negro religion. In N. Whitten and J. Szwed (Eds.), *Afro-American Anthropology.* New York: Free Press, 1970.

Brunelle, E. A. The biology of meaning. *Journal of Creative Behavior,* 1973, *7,* 1–14.

Burnham, D. Varieties of reality restructuring in schizophrenia. In R. Cancro (Ed.), *The schizophrenic reactions: a critique of the concept.* New York: Brunner/Mazel, 1970.

Campbell, J. *The hero with the thousand faces.* New York: Pantheon, 1949.

Clarke, A. C. *2001: Odyssey two.* London: Granada, 1982.

Collins, W. *The moonstone,* a novel. New York and London: Harper and Brothers, 1874.

Corlis, R. Splaver, G., Wisecup, P., and Fischer, R. Myers-Briggs Type Personality Scales and their relation to taste acuity. *Nature,* 1967, *216,* 91–92.

"Dear Abby," *Citizen Journal,* Columbus, Ohio, Jan. 13, 1971, p. 21.

de Léry, J. (1573). *Histoire d'un voyage fait en la terre du Brésil,* J. C. Morisot (Ed.), Genève: Droz, 1976; reviewed by C. Lévi-Strauss in *Times Literary Supplement,* Aug. 6, 1976, p. 970.

de Nerval, G. (1854). In G. Poulet, *The metamorphosis of the circle,* C. Dawson and C. Coleman (transls.) Baltimore: The Johns Hopkins Press, 1966, pp. 166–181.

DeQuincey, T. (1821). *The confessions of an English opium eater.* London: Dent and Sons, 1960.

Dumas, R. A. EEG alpha-hypnotizability correlations; a review, *Psychophysiology,* 1977, *14,* 431–438.

Dumas, R. A. Influences of subject self-selection on the EEG alpha-hypnotizability correlation. *Psychophysiology,* 1978, *15,* 606–608.

Efron, R. The duration of the present. In R. Fischer (Ed.), *Interdisciplinary perspectives of time. Annals of the New York Academy of Sciences.,* 1967, *138*(2), 713–729.

Eliade, M. *Le mythe de l'eternel retour: archétypes et répétition.* Paris: Gallimard, 1949.

Eliot, T. S. *Selected essays.* New York: Harcourt, Brace, 1932.

Erdman, G. Zustandsabhängiges Lernen bei Psychopharmaka. *Psychologische Beiträge,* 1979, *21,* 450–473.

Evans, H. S. (Editor), *The Explorer's Journal,* Morristown, N.J. (personal communication), 1976.

Fischer, R. The biological fabric of time. In R. Fischer (Ed.), *Interdisciplinary perspectives of time. Annals of the New York Academy of Sciences,* 1967, *138,* 440–488.

Fischer, R. Gustatory, behavioral and pharmacological manifestations of chemoreception in man. In G. Ohloff and A. F. Thomas (Eds.), *Gustation and olfaction.* London–New York: Academic Press, 1971, pp. 187–237.

Fischer, R. State-bound knowledge. *Psychology Today,* 1976a, *10,* 68–72.

Fischer, R. On creative, psychotic and ecstatic states. In L. R. Allman and D. T. Jaffe (Eds.), *Readings in abnormal psychology; contemporary perspectives.* New York: Harper and Row, 1976b, pp. 250–277.

Fischer, R. On flashback and hypnotic recall. *International Journal of Clinical and Experimental Hypnosis,* 1977, *25,* 217–235.

Fischer, R. On the arousing effects of hallucinogens, or who is who under psilocybin. *Journal of Altered States of Consciousness,* 1980, *5,* 321–324.

Fischer, R. and Hill, R. M. Psychotropic drug-induced transformations of visual space. *International Pharmacopsychiatry,* 1971, *6,* 28–37.

Fischer, R. and Landon, G. M. On the arousal state-dependent recall of "subconscious" experience: stateboundness. *British Journal of Psychiatry,* 1972, *120,* 159–172.

Fischer, R., Knopp, W., and Griffin, F. Taste sensitivity and the appearance of phenothiazine-tranquilizer induced extrapyramidal symptoms. *Arzneimittelforschung* (Drug Research), 1965, *15,* 1379–1382.

Fischer, R., Hill, R. M., Thatcher, K., and Scheib, J. Psilocybin-induced contraction of visual space. *Agents and Actions* (Basel), 1970, *1,* 190–197.

Freud, S. Psychoanalytic notes on an autobiographical account of a case of paranoia (Dementia paranoides). In Standard Edition, *The complete psychological works of Sigmund Freud,* vol. XII. London: Hogarth Press, 1958.

Fromm, E. *The forgotten language. An introduction to the understanding of dreams, fairy tales and myths.* New York: Rinehart, 1951.

Gardner, H. *The quest for mind, Piaget, Lévi-Strauss and the structuralist movement.* New York: Vintage Books, 1974.

Gebser, J. The foundations of the aperspective world. *Main Currents,* 1972, *29,* 80–88.

Geschwind, N. Disconnection syndromes in animal and man (Part I). *Brain,* 1965, *88,* 237–295.

Giacometti, A. In a TV interview, *L'art et les hommes;* Montparnasse IX, Drot (interviewer). Paris, 1970.

Goes, A. Das Brandopfer. In R. Armes (Ed.), *The cinema of Alain Resnais.* London: A. Zwemmer Ltd.; New York: A. S. Barnes and Co., 1968.

Goodwin, D., Powell, B., Bremer, D., Hoine, H., and Stern, J. Alcohol recall: state-dependent effects in man. *Science,* 1969, *163,* 1358–1360.

Graves, R. *Oxford address on poetry.* London: Cassell, 1961, p. 122.

Greimas, A. J. *Semantic structural.* Paris: Larousse, 1966.

Grof, S. Theoretical and empirical basis of psychotherapy: observations from LSD research. *Journal of Transpersonal Psychology,* 1973, *5,* 15–53.

Guillén, J. *Language and poetry.* Cambridge, Mass.: Harvard University Press, 1961.

Gwynne, P. H., Fischer, R., and Hill, R. M. Hypnotic induction of the interference of psilocybin with optically induced spatial distortion. *Pharmakopsychiatrie Neuro-Psychopharmakologie,* 1969, *2,* 223–234.

Harper, R. The return journey. *Modern Language Notes,* 1982, *97,* 1121–1128.

Hauser, J. Johann Hauser's painting. In state-bound knowledge, by R. Fischer, *Psychology Today,* Aug. 1976, pp. 68–72.

Heike, G. *Phonologie.* Stuttgart: Metzler, 1972.

Hildum, D. C. (Ed.). *Language and thought.* Princeton: D. Van Nostrand, 1967.

Hilgard, J. R. *Personality and hypnosis: a study of imaginative involvement.* Chicago: University of Chicago Press, 1970.

Hill, H. E., Jones, B. E., and Bell, E. C. State-dependent control of discrimination by morphine and pentobarbital. *Psychopharmacologia,* 1971, *22,* 305–313.

Holden, C. Doubts mounting about all-volunteer force. *Science,* 1980, *209,* 1095–1099.

Jakobson, R. *Six lectures on sound and meaning,* J. Mepham (transl.). Hassocks, Sussex: Harvester, 1978.

Jakobson, R. Linguistics and poetics. In T. A. Sebeok (Ed.), *Style in language.* New York: Wiley, 1960.

Jímenez, J. R. *Libros inéditos de poesía.* Edicíon de F. Garfias. Madrid: Aguilar, 1964.

Jones, R. T. Tetrahydrocannabinol and the marijuana-induced social "high", or the effects of the mind on marijuana. *Annals of the New York Academy of Sciences,* 1971, *191,* 155–165.

Joyce, C. R. B. et al. Taste sensitivity may be used to predict pharmacological effects. *Life Sciences,* 1968, *7,*(I), 533–537.

Kramer, J. C. Introduction to amphetamine abuse. In E. H. Ellinwood and S. Cohen (Eds.), *National Institute of Mental Health Publication 72-9085.* Washington, D.C.: U.S. Government Printing Office, 1972, pp. 174–184.

Kranz, H. Das Thema des Wahns im Wandel der Zeit. *Fortschritte der Neurologie und Psychiatrie,* 1955, *23,* 58–72.

Landon, G. and Fischer, R. On common features of the language of hallucinogenic drug-induced and creative states. In W. Keup (Ed.), *Origin and mechanism of hallucinations.* New York: Plenum, 1970.

Langer, S. *Philosophy in a new key.* New York: New American Library, 1951.

Langer, S. K. *Mind,* An essay on human feeling, vol. 2, Baltimore: The Johns Hopkins Press, 1973.

Lévi-Strauss, C. *Anthropologie structural.* Paris: Plon, 1958.

Lévi-Strauss, C. *Le cru et le cuit,* Buchler, I. R., (transl.), Laboratoire d'Anthropologie Sociale, College de France, Paris. Paris: Plon, 1964.

Locke, J. *An essay concerning human understanding.* Oxford: Oxford University Press, 1975.

Logue, A. W. Taste aversion and the generality of the laws of learning. *Psychological Bulletin,* 1979, *86,* 276–296.

London, P., Hart, J. T., and Leibovitz, M. P. EEG alpha rhythms and susceptibility to hypnosis. *Nature,* 1968, *219,* 71–72.

Lord Raglan. *The hero.* London, 1936. Quoted in Scholes, R. *Structuralism in literature,* New Haven and London: Yale University Press, 1974, pp. 65–66.

Lucid, D. P. (Ed.). *Soviet Semiotics.* Baltimore: The Johns Hopkins Press, 1977.

Luthe, W. *Autogenic therapy, 6, treatment with autogenic neutralization. Theoretic sequences of the death-life-cycle,* Chap. 2. New York: Grune & Stratton, 1973.

Mandell, A. Toward a psychobiology of transcendence, God in the brain. In J. M. Davidson and R. J. Davidson (Eds.), *The psychobiology of consciousness.* New York: Plenum, 1980.

Martindale, C. and Fischer, R. The effect of psilocybin on primary process content in language. *Confinia Psychiatrica,* 1977, *20,* 195–202.

Matefy, R. E. and Krall, R. Psychedelic drug flashbacks: psychotic manifestation or imaginative role playing? *Journal of Consulting Clinical Psychology,* 1975, *43,* 434.

McDonald, G., Conway, M., and Ricci, M. (Eds.). *The films of Charlie Chaplin.* New York: Bonanza, 1965.

Meyer, L. B. Exploiting limits: creation, archetypes, and style change. *Daedalus,* 1980, *109,* 177–205.

Morgan, A. Personal communication from Dr. Arlene Morgan, Stanford University, 1975.

Mosher, L. R., Reitman, A., and Menn, A. Characteristics of non-professionals serving as primary therapists for acute schizophrenics. *Hospital and Community Psychiatry,* 1973, *24,* 391–396.

Myers-Briggs Type Indicator profiles from the Typology Laboratory, University of Florida, Dec. 1973, comprising 17 classes from 7 medical schools and 428 1973 summer SAMA–MECO students with an N = 2022, and the Longitudinal Study, University of New Mexico, School of Medicine, June 1974.

Natapoff, A. Consideration of evolutionary conservatism toward a theory of the human brain. *Perspectives on Biology and Medicine,* 1967, *10,* 445–461.

Overton, D. A. State-dependent learning produced by addicting drugs. In S. Fisher and A. Freedman (Eds.), *Opiate addiction, origins and treatment.* Washington, D.C.: V. H. Winston and Sons, 1973.

Panton, Y. and Fischer, R. Hallucinogenic drug-induced behavior under sensory attenuation. *Archives of General Psychiatry,* 1973, *28,* 434–438.

Paz, O. *Aquila o Sol? Eagle or Sun?* New York: October House, 1949.

Perry, J. W. Reconstitutive process in the psychopathology of the self. *Annals of the New York Academy of Sciences,* 1962, *96,* 853–876.

Pope, A. *The works of Alexander Pope, Esq.,* W. Roscoe (Ed.). London, 1824.

Poulet, G. *Etudes sur le temps humain.* Paris: Plon, 1949.

Poulet, G. *Proustian space,* E. Coleman (transl.). Baltimore–London: The Johns Hopkins Press, 1977.

Powers, W. T. *Behavior, the control of perception.* Chicago: Aldine, 1973.

Propp, V. *Morphology of the folk tale.* Translation of the 1928 Russian Publication 10, p. 134 of the Research Center in Anthropology, Folklore and Linguistics, Bloomington, Ind. 1968.

Proust, M. *Swann's way,* C. S. Montcrieff (transl.). New York: Modern Library, 1928.

Proust, M. *A la recherche du temps perdu,* P. Clarac and A Ferré (Eds.), 3 vols. Paris: Gallimard, 1954.

Purce, J. *The mystic spiral.* London: Thames and Hudson, 1974.

Ricoeur, P. *Freud and philosophy. An essay on interpretation,* D. Savage (transl.). New Haven: Yale University Press, 1970.

Riley, R. L. and Baril, L. L. Conditioned taste aversions: a bibliography. *Animal Learning and Behavior,* 1976, *4* (1B), 1S–13S.

Saint John of the Cross. *Ascent of Mount Carmel,* 3rd rev. ed., E. Allison Peers (transl.). Garden City, N.Y.: Image Books (Doubleday Div.), 1958.

Schane, S. A. *Generative phonology.* Englewood-Cliffs, N.J.: Prentice-Hall, 1973.

Schrader, L. *Sinne und Sinnersverknüpfungen;* Studien und Materialien zur Vorgeschichte der Synästhesie und zur Bewertung der Sinne in der italienischen, spanischen und französischen Literatur. Heidelberg: Carl Winter–Universitätsverlag, 1969.

Seligman, M. E. P. On the generality of the laws of learning. *Psychological Review,* 1970, *77,* 406–418.

Seligman, M. E. P. In "This Week's Citation Classic," *Current Contents of the Social and Behavioral Sciences,* 1980, *12,* (8), 14.

Shaffer, J. H., Hill, R. M., and Fischer, R. Psychophysics of psilocybin and $\triangle^9$-tetrahydrocannabinol. *Agents and Actions* (Birkhäuser, Basel), 1973, *3,* 48–51.

Shulgin, A. Phenethylamines. *Journal of Psychedelic Drugs,* 1979, *11,* 47.

"Sirhan still says 'I can't remember' . . . ," report in *Baltimore Sun,* June 3, 1977.

Spencer-Brown, G. *Laws of form.* London: Allen and Unwin, 1969.

Stekel, W. *The interpretation of dreams: New developments and technique,* vol. 1. New York: Liveright, 1943.

Stevens, S. S. Issues in psychophysical measurement. *Psychological Review,* 1971, *78,* 426–450.

Straus, E. On the form and structure of man's inner freedom. *Kentucky Law Journal,* 1956–1957, *45,* 255–269.

Tec, L. Phenothiazine and biperiden in LSD reactions. *Journal of the American Medical Association,* 1971, *215,* 980.

Thomas. The Coptic gospel according to Thomas. In M. Summers, *The secret sayings of the living Jesus.* Waco, Tex.: Word Books, 1968.

Valéry, P. *Oeuvres,* J. Hytier (Ed.), vols I and II. Paris: Gallimard, 1957. Quoted in J. Neubauer, *Symbolismus und symbolische Logik.* München: W. Fink, 1978.

Van Nuys, D. M. Drug use and hypnotic susceptibility. *International Journal of Clinical and Experimental Hypnosis,* 1972, *20,* 31–37.

Vivis Valentini, Joannis Ludovici. *Opera omnia,* Tomus III, Benedicti Monfort, 1745; Liber Secundus, p. 350 (University Library, Basel, Switzerland). Republished, London: Gregg Press Ltd., 1964.

von Foerster, H. Notes on an epistemology for living things. In E. Morin and M. Piatelli-Palmerini (Eds.), *L'unité de l'homme.* Paris: Seuil, 1974, pp. 401–417.

von Franz, M.-L. Der Traum des Descartes. In C. A. Meyer (Ed.), *Zeitlose Dokumente der Seele;* Studien aus dem C. G. Jung Institut, Zürich, III. Zürich: Rascher, 1952.

Wall, P. D. My foot hurts me, an analysis of a sentence. In R. Bellairs and E. G. Gray (Eds.), *Essays on the nervous system,* a festschrift for J. Z. Young. Oxford: Clarendon Press, 1974.

Waugh, E. Quoted by B. D. Nossiter in the *Washington Post,* May 13, 1973, p. K-15.

Weingartner, H., Adefris, W., Eich, J. E., and Murphy, D. L. Encoding–imagery specificity in alcohol-state-dependent learning. *Journal of Experimental Psychology,* 1976, *2,* 83–87.

Weingartner, H., Miller, H., and Murphy, D. L. Mood-state-dependent retrieval of verbal associations. *Journal of Abnormal Psychology,* 1977, *86,* 276–284.
Williams, J. M. As quoted in H. Zollinger, Correlations between the neurobiology of colour vision and the psycho-linguistics of colour naming. *Experientia,* 1979, *35,* 1–8.
Wordsworth, W. Observations prefixed to the 2nd ed., in *Lyrical ballads.* Quoted in J. H. Smith and E. W. Parks (Eds.), *The great critics.* New York: Norton, 1960.

14. Clinical Applications of Non-Drug-Induced States

Thomas H. Budzynski

There took place in Montreal in August of 1973 a most interesting conference entitled "Transformations of Consciousness." Many good papers were presented, but a few were personally fascinating because the research described dovetailed so well with work being done in our clinic. The paper by Joe Kamiya described early research on altered states produced through alpha EEG biofeedback. Julian Jaynes discussed his very controversial theory on the development of consciousness through the breakdown of the bicameral mind. Roland Fischer spoke of the changing emphasis in cultures of Apollonian versus Dionysian models of mental process. David Galin was persuasive with his argument that recent brain lateralization research seemed to support Freud's concept of the unconscious and, what's more, to locate it in the nondominant cerebral hemisphere.

This writer was privileged to present the early work on a biofeedback-induced theta EEG state procedure that we called "Twilight Learning" (Budzynski, 1972).

The technique evolved as a result of the enormous interest in altered states of consciousness (ASCs) during the late 1960s and early 1970s. These special states were highly valued, especially by the younger generation, and were produced by a variety of procedures including drugs, meditation, religious practices, sensory isolation, and sensory overload, to name a few. One of the difficulties associated with studying ASCs is the high degree of variability in the state from moment to moment. The transition zone between wakefulness and sleep, for example, is typically a short-lived phenomenon, since the individual either passes into deeper sleep or awakens.

At this time we were interested primarily in a non-drug procedure that

428

would enable us to impart positive suggestions to patients who were depressed and/or who had severe self-esteem problems. It seemed to us that if we could find a way to produce a stable, reliable ASC, we then would have the vehicle for absorption of the positive suggestions.

Our search led us to examine such seemingly diverse phenomena as the healing abilities of the !Kung tribe in the Kalahari Desert to melodic intonation therapy (MIT) with aphasics. We studied Russian sleep learning (hypnopaedia) and contrasted it with American research in this area. We surveyed the work on hypnagogic and hypnopompic states, especially that done by Foulkes and Vogel. In the area of brain function we examined differential effects of varying arousal level on left–right cortical functioning, voice comprehension in the two cerebral hemispheres, and characteristics of optimal voice comprehension by the right or nondominant hemisphere. Of great relevance was the work of Sperry and his associates on lateralization of brain function. Galin's review of this research led him to see a strong connection between Freud's concept of the unconscious and the newfound functions of the nondominant hemisphere. All of this brought us to the development of a Brain Lateralization model which has guided our non-drug therapy over the last five years. Reading further you will find how we integrated these seemingly diverse elements into the therapy model we have found to be so useful in our clinical work.

SLEEP RESEARCH

Our specific questions with regard to sleep research were twofold:

1. What are the characteristics of Stage 1 sleep with respect to critical screening?
2. What are the possibilities for learning during sleep?

The Twilight State (Sleep Stage 1)

In contrast to the waking or deep-sleep states, there is a very special state of light sleep. Identified by an EEG pattern of theta frequencies (4–7 Hz), this transitory condition has been referred to as the reverie state (Koestler, 1964), the fringe of consciousness, the pre-conscious, and the twilight state (Budzynski, 1972). Sleep researchers tend to refer to this zone of consciousness/unconsciousness in terms of the hallucinatory-like imagery that is associated with it—hypnagogic if falling asleep and hypnopompic if awakening.

During this rather brief period of usually 4 to 10 minutes, people often experience emergent, hallucinatory, dreamlike experiences that are more disjointed and brief than those dreams associated with rapid eye movement (REM) sleep. These hypnagogic images often resemble static photographic stills that have a vivid, live-in quality. A number of illustrious individuals from the fields of science, music, literature, and art have credited the imagery produced during the twilight state for creative solutions or inspiring thoughts. Koestler (1964), in recounting many examples of this phenomenon, concluded that "the temporary relinquishing of conscious controls liberates the mind from certain constraints which are necessary to maintain the disciplined routine of thoughts but may become an impediment to the creative leap; at the same time other types of ideation on more primitive levels of mental organization are brought into activity" (p. 169).

Kubie and Margolin (1942) used feedback to patients of their respiratory sounds in order to facilitate the recovery of emotionally charged material. While concentrating on the sound of their own breathing, the patients would enter the twilight state, which was said to enhance free association.

Froeschels (1949), in studying the hypnagogic state, postulated that "rules of association radically different from the rules of the waking state govern the formation of thought in the hypnagogic state. He concluded that the *unconscious* plays a major role in hypnagogic thought . . . " (p. 24).

The research of Foulkes and Vogel (1965) seemed particularly relevant for our interests. In addition to documenting the twilight state with EEG and eye movement indicators (4–7 Hz theta EEG and slow rolling eye movement), these investigators also questioned their volunteers upon awakening them from the twilight state. Their replies to questions about control over mentation and loss of contact with the external world indicated that loss of volitional control over mentation tended to occur first; then loss of awareness of surroundings; and, finally, loss of reality testing.

Moreover, Vogel et al. (1966) also scored subject reports for two ego functions: the degree of maintenance of nonregressive content and the maintenance of contact with the external world. Report content was rated as nonregressive if the mentation was plausible, coherent, realistic, and undistorted. Examples of regressive content were: single isolated images, a meaningless pattern, an incomplete scene, or bits and pieces of a scene, bizarre images, dissociation of thoughts and images, and magical thinking. The results showed that there was a statistically significant tendency for each EEG state (alpha, Stage 1, and Stage 2) to be associated with a different combination of ego functioning. In the first combination (ego state), usually found during an alpha pattern, the ego maintained *both* functions, or at most, showed an impairment of only one function. A second ego state, in which both functions were impaired, was associated with descending Stage 1 (the twilight state). The third ego state usually occurred during

Stage 2 and was characterized by a return to less regressive content; however, contact with reality was completely lost.

Overall, Vogel et al. found that it was seen

1. As individuals become drowsy and pass into sleep, their brain rhythms change from predominately alpha, to fragmented alpha, to low amplitude theta.
2. Paralleled (though not perfectly) with these EEG patterns are three ego states showing an increasing impairment of ego functions (as defined above).
3. Individuals with rigid, repressive, dogmatic personality traits report less sleep fantasy material.

Stage 1 sleep characteristics appear to be descriptive of the loss of dominant (left) hemisphere functioning. The generation of vivid visual imagery is also characteristic of this twilight state. This phenomenon appears to be a function of the nondominant (right) hemisphere. Twilight sleep, therefore, seems to involve a suspension of left hemisphere critical screening and a dominance of right hemisphere processing.

The next question that concerned us was whether the twilight state was one of *hypersuggestibility*. We found evidence that indeed it was.

Is the Twilight State Characterized by Hypersuggestibility?

Theodore X. Barber (1957), for example, in his dissertation found that subjects were just as suggestible when in a light sleep or in a drowsy condition as when they were hypnotized. A quote from one subject is illuminating: "I was just sleepy enough to believe what you were saying was true. I couldn't oppose what you wanted with anything else" (p. 59). Barber noted that at the therapeutic level it is possible that suggestions could be presented to people while they sleep for the purpose of helping overweight people reduce, getting heavy smokers to cut down, and helping timid people to gain confidence.

Another dissertation study at Yale University produced results that supported Barber's conclusions. Felipe (1965) tested the effects of attitude change information presented via tape recording to subjects during waking, drowsy, and deep-sleep conditions. He used several pre–post attitude scales to measure change in, among others, interracial dating attitude. The results were clear—only in the condition where the subjects were presented the message while drowsy did the attitude change reach significance. Apparently, the attitude change was not precipitated in the waking state because of the conscious defenses that were enabled. The lack of change in the deep-sleep condition may reflect the fact that less and less verbal information seems to register as sleep deepens.

The conclusions of a study by Lasaga and Lasaga (1973) illustrate this phenomenon:

1. Even during Stages 3 and 4 some perception of verbal stimuli is possible.
2. There is however, a progressive blurring of perception from Stage 1 and REM to Stages 3 and 4.
3. Some forms of learning seem to be possible during deeper sleep (e.g., association of words), but perceptual distortions make extremely unlikely the assimilation of complex verbal information.
4. Some subjects reported they heard nothing, yet they did well on recognition tests, suggesting some subliminal perception during sleep.

Other investigators have noted the hypersuggestibility of the drowsy or twilight state. DeManaceine (1897) was interested in the degree of suggestibility maintained in this state. She gave her subjects two types of suggestions while they were in transit from waking to sleeping: "intellectual suggestions," for example, $3 \times 2 = 5$, and "emotional suggestions," for example, "The building is burning down." The results indicated that among children under fifteen years of age, the intellectual suggestions were 85 percent successful, and the emotional suggestions were 97 percent successful. Among adults, the intellectual suggestions were 25 percent successful, and the emotional ones were 45 percent successful. A suggestion was considered successful if the person repeated the experimenter's statement or accepted it without protest (Schacter, 1976).

Simon and Emmons (1956) noted: "It may be that in the drowsy state preceding sleep, the individual is more susceptible to suggestion; perhaps one's attitudes or habits can be modified during this presleep period when criticalness is minimized" (p. 96). Stampfl (1953) and Leuba and Bateman (1952) also suggested that the intermediate point between waking and sleeping might be optimal for sleep learning. Orne (1969) showed that individuals are capable of carrying out purposive behavior in response to suggestions administered while they are asleep, without any evidence of physiological arousal. Furthermore, Russian researcher Svyandoshch (1968) has said: "Speech assimilated during sleep, in contrast to that assimilated during waking state, is not subjected during assimilation to the critical processing . . . " (p. 112).

Speaking of Russian research, Rubin (1968, 1970), having surveyed Russian sleep research over the years, found that unlike most other sleep learning outside the Soviet Union, the Soviet experiments and tutorial programs incorporated repetitive practice over several days or *even months*. They also placed emphasis on producing the correct set for learning and retention before the sleep learning session. The Russians have determined that retention of material is further optimized if the presentation takes place during the first 30 to 40 minutes of sleep. Rubin (1970) has noted that the *common denominator* among successful sleep-learning studies is that "superficial sleep" (Stages 1 and 2) is the psychophysiological background for maximum receptivity.

In concluding this section on sleep research, it can be said that Stage 1 sleep is characterized by the EEG pattern of theta (4–7 Hz) frequencies and the uncritical acceptance of verbal suggestions. Primary process or hypnagogic material emerges during this period as well. Consequently, this stage of sleep can be utilized not only for presentation of material to be assimilated in uncritical fashion, but for the retrieval of potentially creative or emotionally relevant information from within. Unfortunately, as noted above, the duration of this special state typically runs no longer than 10 minutes. We wondered, therefore, if the application of biofeedback would allow us to extend the duration.

Twilight State Biofeedback

In 1971 we began the development of a biofeedback device that would help produce and maintain a twilight state (Budzynski, 1976). The device would also control a tape recorder that would play the positive suggestions or change message (CM). The functional logic of the system is as follows:

1. The Twilight Learner senses the EEG over the left hemisphere. The system will turn on the tape recorder only if the EEG shows theta in the absence of alpha or beta rhythms.
2. If the client becomes more alert and shows an alpha or beta pattern, the tape-recorded message is immediately terminated.
3. If the client gets sleepier, his EEG will show lower-frequency and higher-amplitude rhythms. As this occurs, the volume of CM is correspondingly increased. The increasing volume gently arouses the client and thus acts as a sleep guard.
4. The Twilight Learner also can provide a "pink noise" background masking ambient sounds. Bertini et al. (1969) had demonstrated that such a masking sound facilitated the appearance of theta in the EEG.

Essentially, the Twilight Learner allows individuals to maintain themselves in a non-drug, low-arousal ASC. The research of Felipe, Barber, and the others noted above would predict that the presentation of verbal suggestions while in this state should result in their uncritical acceptance.

Case Studies with Twilight Learning

A few case studies will illustrate the operation of this procedure. (For more case studies see Budzynski, 1976.)

Client X was a forty-six-year-old single man, who worked as a printer's helper and lived in a boarding house. He had survived a brutalizing childhood during which he was repeatedly told he was no good and "wouldn't amount to anything." Mr. X spent almost all of his modest salary on therapy. He had tried seven years of psychoanalysis, yet still felt terribly lonely and unhappy. He had no friends, male or female, and no hobbies.

We decided to try Twilight Learning, especially since he expressed interest in a biofeedback procedure. The positive script we developed contained such statements as "I deserve to have fun," "I can have friends," "I can do a good job," "I am adequate," etc. There was a total of twenty positive statements on the tape.

Mr. X received nine one-hour sessions of Twilight Learning. He reported still no change on the sixth session. On the seventh session, however, he noted that he was losing interest in his job and was thinking of looking for a better one. By the ninth session he had secured a higher-paying job and was thinking of getting his own apartment. He terminated treatment with the ninth session. A follow-up nine months later revealed that he: liked his new job; had moved from the boarding house to an apartment; had joined a fishing and hunting club; and was bowling with the company team. Mr. X reported feeling much more satisfied with his life.

Another case involved a successful thirty-seven-year-old businessman (Mr. Y) who throughout his life found it almost impossible to say no to authority figures. In three years of psychotherapy the problem had not resolved itself. In the first few Twilight Learning sessions, Mr. Y experienced imagery related to a repressed early memory in which his authoritarian father had slapped him viciously for saying no. Further Twilight Learning sessions focused on the presentation of such phrases as "It's OK to say no," "Saying no is good sometimes," "I am good even when I say no," "I can say no when I want to," etc. After five sessions Mr. Y found that the anxiety associated with turning down an authority figure had vanished.

These two cases are representative of twilight learning applications. An average of ten sessions is typical although the number of sessions may range from five to twenty. It should be noted, however, that twilight learning is not applicable to all clients. To be effective it is required that theta rhythms be present during at least 25 percent of the session. If individuals are not able to produce sufficient theta, or if the theta is too intermittent, we will use another therapy modality such as hypnosis. Finally, twilight learning may be very suitable for those clients for whom hypnosis is not indicated.

A BRAIN LATERALIZATION MODEL

Why does twilight learning involve the uncritical acceptance of verbal suggestion? We believe that brain lateralization research may provide the answer. In the late 1960s Roger Sperry of Cal Tech began to reveal the results of research with "split-brain" patients (Sperry, 1969). These individuals had the connecting commissures of the cerebral hemispheres severed in order to alleviate severe epileptic symptoms. Post-operatively the patients were examined by Sperry and his associates in order to determine the functions of the newly independent hemispheres (see Table 1).

The results were somewhat surprising. For example, it was found that the nondominant hemisphere had very little ability to mediate verbal output, even though it did have a level of verbal *comprehension* roughly equivalent

TABLE 1. CEREBRAL HEMISPHERIC FUNCTIONS (a partial listing).

Left	*Right*
Speech	Voice intonation contours
Language comprehension (abstract)	Language comprehension (concrete)
Logic	Emotion
Time sense (past, present, future)	Present-oriented
Sequential (slow)	Parallel (fast)
Detail-oriented	Gestalt-oriented
Temporal	Spatial
Rhythm	Melody, pitch
Mathematics (e.g., algebra)	Spatial aspects of mathematics (e.g., geometry)
Reason	Intuition
Convergent approach	Divergent approach
Relatively narrow arousal level range over which it can function	Relatively wide arousal level range over which it can function
Evolutionarily newer	Evolutionarily older
Discrete	Continuous
Realistic	Impulsive
Differential	Existential
Explicit	Tacit
Objective	Subjective
Successive	Simultaneous
Focal	Diffuse
Directed	Spontaneous
Rational	Intuitive
Linguistic	Pantomime, kinesthetic, musical
Grammatical	Visuo-spatial
Abstract	Perceptual-synthetic
Conscious	Unconscious

to the vocabulary of a thirteen-year-old, and the syntactical ability of a five-
or six-year-old (Zaidel, 1976, 1978). Deductive reasoning ability is of a low
level in this hemisphere, and cognitive ability in general is probably rather
like that of a smart chimp (Gazzaniga and LeDoux, 1978). The interhemispheric difference in functions is called brain lateralization. The more distinct the functions, the more the degree of lateralization. In general, men
are more lateralized than women, and the right-handed (dextrals) more so
than the left-handed (sinistrals) (Levy, 1977). Moreover, the hemisphere that
has the functions of speech, logic, critical judgment, and sequential ordering is most often referred to as the dominant hemisphere. The other hemisphere, labeled the nondominant, appears to mediate the intuitive,
emotional, visuospatial processing, pattern recognition, and parallel rather
than sequential functions (Ornstein, 1972). In almost all dextrals and approximately 67 percent of sinistrals the left hemisphere is the dominant one.
A low degree of lateralization implies that the same functions may be present in both hemispheres, although not necessarily to the same degree (Budzynski, 1979).

Note that the right hemisphere has been labeled "unconscious." Are there
any data to support this? We need to examine this question next.

Is There an Unconscious?

Although banished along with consciousness by the behaviorists, the concept of the unconscious seems to be making a comeback. Of course, psychoanalysis has always based itself on unconscious mental process. More
recent therapies such as transactional analysis, primal therapy, Gestalt therapy, and neurolinguistic programming (NLP) also share the concept of the
unconscious. In recent years many behaviorists have found it necessary to
speculate about cognitive factors mediating between stimulus and response.
As Shevrin and Dickman (1980) have noted (in their article "The Psychological Unconscious: A Necessary Assumption for All Psychological Theory?"), such respected theorists as London, Bandura, and Lazarus " . . .
have described their own evolution from radical behaviorism, in which cognitive mediating factors play no role, to a view of psychology in which
subjective and conscious events are important" (p. 421). Furthermore, "As
cognition and consciousness have returned to psychology, the concept of
unconscious mental process has received increasing attention" (p. 421).

Shevrin and Dickman were able by reviewing research in the areas of (1)
selective attention, (2) subliminal perception, and (3) certain visual phenomena involving perceptual processing (e.g., retinal image stabilization,
binocular rivalry, and backward masking) to make a good case for the concept of unconscious processing. They concluded: "The clear message from

much recent thinking in psychology appears to be that behavior cannot be understood without taking conscious experience into account and that conscious experience cannot be fully understood without taking unconscious process into account" (p. 432); and, finally, " . . . if the thesis elaborated in this article is correct, then no psychological model that seeks to explain how human beings know, learn, or behave can ignore the concept of unconscious psychological process" (p. 432).

In speaking of biofeedback, Brown (1980) stated that "the discovery of the biofeedback phenomenon has revealed the universal, innate ability of the unconscious mind to control and regulate all physical process of the body" (p. 252).

Of course, brain researchers who postulate an unconscious processor are somewhat divided on the issue of whether conscious/unconscious functions are located vertically or horizontally in the brain. Many of them prefer a model in which consciousness is produced in the two cerebral cortices and the unconscious resides in subcortical structures. Others, such as Popper and Eccles (1977), see the left or dominant hemisphere as subserving conscious functions while the right or nondominant hemisphere serves as a sort of backup computer having some unconscious functions. Most experts agree that the left hemisphere, besides controlling motor functions on the right side of the body, controls much of the verbal output, as well as logic and analytical processing; in other words, what we generally consider to be conscious functions. The right hemisphere functions more as a spatial, Gestalt synthesizer.

Some researchers believe that such a distribution of functions may be true in only 15 percent of the population (Levy, 1980). However, except for the approximately 10 percent who are left-handed, the distribution generally supports the brain lateralization model.

Another important, yet little-known fact of lateralization is that the right or nondominant hemisphere has an advantage over the left with regard to the processing of voice *intonation contours* and emotional material (Blumstein and Cooper, 1974). For example, embedding short phrases and sentences in a simple melodic pattern often results in significant improvement in the verbally expressive ability of severely aphasic patients (Helm-Estabrooks, 1983).

Related to this phenomenon were the results of unilateral electroshock therapy (EST), as reported by Deglin (1976) in *The UNESCO Courier,* in an article entitled "Our Split Brain." Vadim Lvovich Deglin is an eminent Soviet neuropsychologist. Since 1967, the staff of the psychiatric clinic of the I. M. Sechenov Institute of Evolutionary Physiology and Biochemistry of the U.S.S.R Academy of Sciences has been administering unilateral EST. If one side of the brain is shocked first, and then the other side is shocked in a second treatment, the patient is less debilitated than he would be if the EST were bilateral. Deglin noted that after a unilateral shock, the patient feels, behaves, and thinks only with the unshocked hemisphere. An electroencephalogram (EEG) recorded after the shock reveals that only one hemisphere is "asleep," whereas the other remains active.

Deglin described the average single-hemispheric patient. If the right hemisphere is shocked, the voice becomes monotonous, colorless, and dull; the intonation is less expressive. In addition to the loss of affective coloring of his speech, the "left hemisphere" patient has difficulty understanding the intonation of words spoken to him. He is unable to identify the tone of voice as angry or interrogative, or to distinguish a male from a female voice.

It was also apparent to Deglin that the left hemisphere patient is not typically depressed. He becomes interested in topics unconnected with his illness. Regarding the future as an encouraging prospect, he believes he will be cured.

Contrasted with this average left hemisphere patient is the same average patient after his left hemisphere has been shocked. As a "right hemisphere" person, he speaks slowly if at all—in simple, concrete sentences and often with isolated words. He prefers to respond in mime or gestures. It is necessary to speak to him in very short or simply constructed sentences. However, the right hemisphere patient can hear and distinguish prosodic elements of speech better than before EST. He recognizes melodies and feels an urge to hum along. Unfortunately, his mood tends to decline in a direction opposite to that observed when his left hemisphere was dominant. He becomes morose and pessimistic about his present situation, and he complains of feeling unwell.

These composite, averaged descriptions provide us with valuable insights into the functioning of the normal, intact human whose hemispheres interact continuously across the corpus callosum and other commisures. Moreover, the startling hemispheric differences elaborated by Deglin hint at the possibility of interhemispheric conflict.

Is Language Comprehension in the Right Hemisphere?

It is important for the brain lateralization model proposed here that the right hemisphere be able to comprehend language. Space does not permit referencing of the many articles that have dealt with this question. However, certain conclusions can be drawn from this research. As noted above, the right hemisphere does process voice intonation, probably extracting best the emotional quality from the verbal communication. A flat, monotonic voice, therefore, would not excite or interest this hemisphere, although such a presentation would be understood and perhaps even preferred by a left-hemisphere-oriented individual. Popular revival preachers, ministers, politicians, military leaders, coaches, and lecturers know that the secret of "moving" audiences is the dynamism of the speech rather than the content.

There are other factors facilitating right-hemisphere language absorption, such as: redundancy, concreteness, use of high-probability or common words, and direct, positive (rather than negative) statements (Schnell et al., 1964). Sentences spoken at one-third the normal rate and punctuated with frequent pauses also improve comprehension. Active affirmative sentences ("The boy is pulling the dog") are absorbed better than passive negatives ("The boy is not pulled by the dog") (Lasky et al., 1976).

As noted above, the vocabulary of the right hemisphere is roughly equivalent to that of a thirteen-year-old and its syntactical ability that of a five- or six-year-old.

If we wished to communicate verbally with the right brain, we would endeavor to use simple, concrete, common words spoken slowly with a good deal of voice intonation, and repeated over and over again.

Hemispheric Functioning and Arousal Level

Does cortical arousal level have any differential effect on left/right functioning? A good deal of anecdotal evidence and some research studies would argue for the affirmative here. First of all, arousal level refers to the degree of activation of the various physiological systems of the body. High arousal is characterized by heightened muscle tension, increased heart rate and blood pressure, greater stress hormone output, and, in general, a dominance of the sympathetic branch of the autonomic nervous system. The brain wave or electroencephalographic (EEG) pattern assumes a beta configuration with low-amplitude, high-frequency rhythms.

High cortical arousal or activation can help to prepare us for fight-or-flight emergencies, but arousal can be overdone. Common examples are the "too high" athlete who loses his fine touch under pressure, or the student who becomes paralyzed by fear on a final exam and cannot remember anything. Crowd behavior—lynch-mob mentality—is another example of how heightened arousal debilitates certain mental faculties. Moreover, high cortical arousal decreases critical screening. Jerome Frank (1973), in his book *Persuasion and Healing,* noted that most religious healing involves a procedure that heightens arousal, often to the point of exhaustion, and leads to an altered state of consciousness that increases susceptibility to outside influences.

Another interesting fact uncovered by Frank was his observation that people who had been cured at Lourdes included the deserving, the sinful, believers, and apparent sceptics, but they were" . . . almost invariably simple people—the poor and the humble; people who do not interpose a strong intellect between themselves and a higher power" (p. 71). Moreover, he noticed that these people were not detached or critical. Frank observed that those individuals who remained entirely unmoved by the ceremonies did not experience cures.

Following his studies of a number of religious and primitive healing ceremonies, Frank concluded that the apparent success of healing methods based on various ideologies and methods compels the conclusion that the healing power of faith resides in the patient's *state of mind,* not in the validity of its object.

When Richard Katz (1979) of Harvard studied the !Kung tribe of the Kalahari Desert in Botswana, Africa, he found that they employed a healing dance that lasted from dusk to dawn. The dance activated a spiritual power or energy called "u/um." Eventually, through continued dancing and singing, the u/um reaches a boiling point, vaporizes, and rises up the spine until it "makes your thoughts nothing in your head." When the vaporized energy reaches the brain, the healer enters a state of transcendence called "!KIA." This is described as a state of enhanced awareness in which the healer can see into the patient's body and in which he encounters the gods. In this state the healer lays his hands on the sick party and draws out the evil spirit. Diseases such as depression and emphysema are treated.

Katz found psychological differences between those who were healers and those who were not. The healers had richer fantasies and were more inner-directed and able to cope with unfamiliar situations, and they were more emotional. One might be tempted to say that the healers more easily access their right hemispheres than the nonhealers.

If primitive healers often used a heightened arousal to produce the altered state required for healing, modern healers often do the opposite. For example, in *The Realms of Healing,* Krippner and Villoldo (1976) state that the healee is usually in a relaxed position during the healing session. Stress is absent, so that the autonomic nervous system can operate in a relaxed pattern.

One of the most renowned healers of modern times was Edgar Cayce. In order to heal people, at a distance, Cayce would first put himself in a quiet, self-hypnotic trance. Like Cayce, many psychic or spiritual healers attempt to produce an inner calm or "blank mind." Some shift to an attentional state focused only on tactile, kinesthetic, or interoceptive sensations. Others, while in this special quiet state, ask for, and then wait for, a spiritual healing force to act through them. The adjustment of arousal level would appear to be an integral initial stage in the process of primitive healing ceremonies as well as in spiritual and psychic healing. Is there, however, any scientific evidence of a left/right cortical differential effect with arousal level?

Dimond and Beaumont (1974) have carried out an interesting series of studies using a vigilance paradigm. They were able to separate out left and right hemispheric performance on vigilance tasks.

Here is what they concluded:

> The left (hemisphere) is capable of sustaining high levels of performance, but as intense activity to detect small and infrequent signals from the environment is particularly demanding, performance cannot be consistently maintained, and hence, the decline sets in. The right hemisphere, however, while apparently not capable of such high levels of performance, unless sustained by the left, maintains its performance steadily, beyond the point at which the performance of the left hemisphere has deteriorated seriously. The right hemisphere appears therefore to provide a skeleton service in vigilance, a minimum service *capable of maintaining performance after decrement occurs in the left hemisphere.* (p. 69)

These vigilance studies lend support to the concept that the right hemisphere remains functioning at cortical arousal levels that are too low to support critical screening in the left hemisphere.

Is Hypnosis a Right-Brain-Dominated State?

One could easily conceptualize hypnosis as a phenomenon that involves a temporary suspension of the critical screening functions of the left brain and the subsequent presentation of suggestions for change. Most often a preliminary relaxation is used to facilitate the trance, although this is not necessary if the hypnotist is clever enough to evade the critical screening defenses or to persuade the client to suspend them. In any case there should be a bypassing of the left hemisphere's critical screening functions before the suggestions for positive change are presented. To the extent that the left hemisphere can relinquish dominance or be bypassed, the suggestions have a better chance to be processed by the right. Hypnosis has been applied to a wide variety of disorders including smoking and obesity. These two troublesome habits are relatively impervious, in the long run, to logical persuasion methods, no doubt because of the strong emotional factors involved in their maintenance.

Zajonc (1980), in a fascinating article in the *American Psychologist,* noted that "the dismal failure in achieving substantial attitude change through various forms of communication or persuasion is another indication that affect is fairly independent and often impervious to cognition" (p. 158).

Zajonc concluded that affect and cognition are under the control of *separate and partially independent systems.*

This description of the relative separation of cognition and affect is mirrored by the separation of these functions then into left and right hemispheres, respectively.

Does hypnosis really involve a shift toward right hemisphere dominance? In 1978, Frumkin et al. used a dichotic listening paradigm to show that the usual right ear advantage for spoken verbal material as found during the normal conscious state is significantly reduced under hypnosis. The researchers concluded that *hypnosis facilitates greater participation of the right hemisphere* in cognitive processing even as the left hemisphere participation is reduced.

Recently, in our laboratory at Behavioral Medicine Associates we also were able to document a shift toward right hemisphere participation under hypnosis. Employing a very accurate quantification system, we found that the left/right ratio of temporal alpha EEG amplitude increased as subjects entered a hypnotic trance. Control subjects who simply relaxed for the same period of time did not show the L/R increase. Ornstein and Galin (Ornstein, 1972) had shown that the L/R alpha ratio tends to increase as the right hemisphere becomes more involved.

Erickson and Rossi (1979) had noted: "If we translate the terms 'conscious' and 'unconscious' into 'dominant' and 'nondominant' hemispheres, we may have the neuropsychological basis for describing a new hypnotherapeutic approach" (p. 247).

Is the Unconscious in the Nondominant Hemisphere?

Do the functions of the nondominant or right hemisphere support the view that it is the seat of Freud's unconscious? Some research would seem to buttress this hypothesis.

Much of the relevant material on this topic was compiled and integrated by Galin (1974), in his article entitled "Implications for Psychiatry of Left and Right Cerebral Specialization: A Neurophysiological Context for Unconscious Process."

Galin noted that the research of Sperry and his colleagues revealed that the two cerebral hemispheres in humans are specialized for different cognitive functions, and when surgically disconnected, they each appear conscious, albeit a different sort of consciousness. Because of these specializations they are not identical processors.

Jaynes (1976), in developing his hypothesis about the evolution of consciousness, concluded that "modern consciousness" may have begun to develop about 2000 B.C. Before that, Jaynes claims that humans possessed "bicameral minds" in which important decisions were communicated to them in the form of auditory and/or visual hallucinations. This older form of thinking did not involve conscious solutions or planning. Jaynes believes that this unconscious thinking is mediated by the right or nondominant hemisphere.

Even the great brain scientist Sir John Eccles (1976) has commented that the right hemisphere is unconscious: "Strictly speaking, therefore, we can state that the actions effected by the right cerebral hemisphere are unconscious actions" (p. 118).

Galin (1974) noted that certain aspects of right hemisphere functioning are congruent with the mode of cognition psychoanalysts have termed primary process, the form of thought that Freud originally called the unconscious:

1. The right hemisphere primarily uses a nonverbal mode of representation, presumably images: visual, tactile, kinesthetic, and auditory.
2. The right hemisphere reasons by a nonlinear mode of *association* rather than by syllogistic logic. Its solutions to problems are based on multiple converging determinants rather than a single casual chain. It is much superior to the left in part–whole relations (i.e., grasping the concept of the whole from just a part).
3. The right hemisphere is less involved with perception of time and sequence than the left hemisphere.
4. The right hemisphere does possess vocabulary, but the words are not organized for use in propositions. For example, a patient without a left hemisphere may be able to sing a song but cannot use the same words in a sentence.
5. Lesions affecting the left hemisphere result in problems of emotionality and impulse control, an observation that supports the interpretation that the left hemisphere is important to normal impulse control. In general, patients with damaged left hemispheres were constricted and unimaginative in their ideational productivity. Hall et al. (1968) suggested on the basis of their findings that the left hemisphere normally performs the role of censor in personality, controlling and inhibiting the more loosely structured ideation of the right side of the brain.
6. The right hemisphere is more involved than the left in the mediation of *emotion*. As Tucker (1981) noted in his extensive review: "The importance to emotion of the right hemisphere's cognitive functions suggests the possibility that right cortical regions may be particularly well connected with subcortical process" (p. 22).

It is not difficult to see that indeed the right cortical hemisphere does possess characteristics that could identify it as the functional seat of the unconscious, or, perhaps more accurately, the primary process of Freud's model. But we still need to consider the possibilities of interhemispheric conflict and the related phenomenon of repression.

Conflict between Hemispheres?

Brown (1980) remarked that "This failure of consciousness to know what unconsciousness knows may well be the basis for many conflicts between conscious and unconsciousness activities" (p. 76).

Note this description of split-brain patient P.S., as provided by LeDoux and Gazzaniga (1981):

> The day that case P.S.'s left and right hemispheres equally valued himself, his friends, and other matters, he was a calm, tractable, and appealing adolescent. On the days that the right and left sides disagreed on these evaluations, case P.S. became difficult to manage behaviorally. Clearly, it is as if each mental system can read the emotional differences harbored by the other at a given time. When they are discordant, a feeling of anxiety, which is ultimately read out by hyper-activity, and general overall aggression, is engendered. The crisp surgical instance of this dynamism raises the question of whether such processes are active in the normal brain, where different mental systems, using different neural codes, co-exist within and between the cerebral hemispheres. (p. 197)

Galin (1974) stated that anecdotal observations of the split-brain patients suggested that "the isolated right brain hemisphere can sustain emotional responses and goals divergent from the left" (p. 574).

Furthermore, Galin (1974) noticed the compelling similarity between certain dissociative phenomena seen in the split-brain patients and Freud's early model of the mind in which repressed mental contents functioned in a separate realm that was inaccessible to conscious recall or verbal interrogation, "functioning according to its own rules, developing and pursuing its own goals, affecting the viscera and insinuating itself in the stream of ongoing behavior" (p. 574).

Others have commented on the possibility of conflict between the hemispheres. Bogen and Bogen (1969) suggested that the possession of two independent problem-solving organs increases the chances of a successful solution to a novel situation, but it has the hazard of conflict in the event of different solutions.

Researchers Dimond and Beaumont (1974) brought up the fact that each hemisphere is an information-processing system that works its own idiosyncratic way through the information it receives. At this stage, no facility appears to exist for passing *unanalyzed* information across to the opposite hemisphere. Each, therefore, appears to act independently of the other. The process of integrating the products of the work of each hemisphere presumably occurs at a *late stage* following the completion of visual analysis.

The basis of the conflict may lie in the tendency of the left hemisphere to process information using an analytic mode while the right is specialized to process the information using a holistic or Gestalt mode. As Galin noted, the tendency of the left hemisphere to note details in a form suitable for expression in words at times appears to be at odds with the right hemisphere's perception of the overall picture.

Perhaps the greatest potential for conflict may lie in the fact that the left or dominant hemisphere uses syllogistic logic to solve problems, whereas the right or nondominant hemisphere relies more on emotional programming as it processes facial expression, body posture, gesture, tone of voice, and past history of emotional experiences in arriving at solutions. Thus, the familiar conflict when we watch a political debate on television—"what he says makes sense but there's something I just don't like about him." An even more common example is that of the overweight individual who consciously wishes to lose weight but finds himself sabotaging all efforts to do so. Why won't the unconscious allow the dieter to maintain his or her diet? The reasons can range widely, but often involve some fear of being a normal weight.

Serious conflict between hemispheres can occur under two general conditions:

1. A positive, moral, or adaptive left brain script conflicts with a negative, immoral, or maladaptive right brain script.
2. A negative, immoral, or maladaptive left brain script conflicts with a positive, moral, or adaptive right brain script.

An example of a type 1 conflict would be an intelligent, capable individual who sabotages her own success because of the unconscious script "I'll never amount to anything"; whereas an example of a type 2 conflict might be the very successful used car salesman who has developed spastic dysphonia and is forced to quit work because of the right brain script from childhood "I must not lie." In both these cases the right brain script has dominated in the final resolution. But, what if the left brain succeeds in dominating with its script?

Repression

Galin (1974) gives the example of a child being punished as his mother presents one message verbally, but quite another with her facial expression, tone of voice, and body language: "I am doing this because I love you, dear" say the words, but "I hate you and will destroy you" say the face, voice tone, and body language. Each hemisphere is exposed to the same sensory input, but because of their relative specializations, they each process only one of the messages. The left "conscious" hemisphere attends to the verbal stimuli because it cannot extract information from the nonverbal cues efficiently; the right "unconscious" will attend to the nonverbal cues because it processes them better than words. In effect, a different input has been delivered to each hemisphere. Since the resulting conclusions are in conflict (i.e., "she loves me" in the left and "she hates me" in the right), the dissonance probably will be reduced by an inhibition or repression of the unacceptable conclusion. But, what happens to the repressed script? Galin believes that this process in the right hemisphere, cut off in this way from the left hemisphere consciousness which is directing overt behavior, may nonetheless continue a life of its own. The memory, the emotional concomitant, and the frustrated plan of action all may persist, affecting subsequent perception and forming the basis for expectations and evaluations of future input.

This "life of its own" could take many forms. Unable to express itself verbally, the right hemisphere might choose to mediate a negative emotional pattern when next it is stimulated by a situation similar to the original trauma. Moreover, it is conceivable that the right hemisphere could initiate an illness, perhaps through a weakening of the immune response, in order to allow the individual to avoid those stimuli (Budzynski and Sparks, in press).

Galin (1974) concluded that if repression in normal intact people is subserved by a "functional disconnection of right hemisphere process, we might expect to see the expression of unconscious ideation through whatever output modes are not pre-empted by the left hemisphere" (p. 577). In his article, Galin (1974) quoted from a paper by Ferenczi (1926) on hysterical symptoms predominating on the left side of the body:

> One half of the body is insensitive in order that it shall be adapted for the representation of unconscious fantasies, and that "the right hand shall not know what the left hand doeth." I derive support for this conception from the consideration of the difference between right and left. It struck me that in general the hemianesthetic stigma occurs more frequently on the left than on the right; this is emphasized too, in a few textbooks. I recalled that the left half of the body is a priori more accessible to unconscious impulses than the right, which, in consequence of the more powerful attention–excitation of this more active and skillful half of the body, is better protected against influences from the unconscious. It is possible that—in right handed people—the sensational sphere for the left side shows from the first a certain pre-disposition for unconscious impulses, so that it is more easily robbed of its normal function and placed at the service of unconscious "libidinal fantasies." (p. 577)

Galin et al. (1977) did a careful examination of the charts of inpatients seen at the University of California San Francisco Hospitals for the period 1963–1974. Selecting those with lateralized (one-sided) conversion symptoms, Galin's group found that symptoms appeared on the left side in 63 percent of the mixed group and in 71 percent of the females. Their findings support the hypothesis that some unconscious processes are mediated by the right hemisphere operating independently of the left hemisphere.

Perhaps it might be useful at this point to summarize the information on unconscious process, conflict, and repression in the right hemisphere:

1. The characteristics of the right or nondominant cerebral hemisphere are similar or, in some cases identical, to those elaborated by Freud in his concept of the unconscious.
2. Most experts agree that the hemispheres are different in their functioning, just as they differ in structure. However, these differences (degree of lateralization) are generally greater in right-handers and males.
3. Each hemisphere processes information separately before comparing across the commisures.
4. Because they are different in their processing of information, the two hemispheres arrive at conflicting conclusions at times.
5. If conclusions are conflicting, a process of inhibition can occur. In these instances one of the hemispheres will dominate and suppress the behavior of the other.
6. If the conflict is severe enough, a process of repression can occur.
7. Even though repressed or suppressed, it is believed that a conclusion remains to exert its influence in unconscious ways.
8. These ways might take the form of hysterical or conversion reaction symptoms, psychosomatic illness, and unwanted and/or unexpected behavior, particularly emotional behavior.
9. These repressed action tendencies or attitudes can be conceptualized as right hemisphere scripts.
10. Right hemisphere scripts, especially those developed in childhood, should be relatively impervious to adult reason and logic.

CHANGING MALADAPTIVE RIGHT HEMISPHERE SCRIPTS

Given that right brain scripts are not easily accessed by conscious, verbal means, is there some way the maladaptive scripts can be changed? We think the answer is yes, and it may not require the considerable allotment of time, effort, and expense that is characteristic of long-term psychotherapy.

There are two problems, of course:

1. Accessing the negative script.
2. Changing the script to a positive one.

How does one go about recovering a suppressed, traumatic memory? There are many examples of this in social anthropological literature (Belo, 1960). Suffice it to say that all of them involve some procedure that (1) apparently acts to reduce or eliminate the critical screening of the left hemisphere, (2) involves an elicitation of the emotional correlates of the traumatic event, and (3) presents a positive change message that is uncritically accepted.

Reduction of Critical Screening

Critical screening appears to be reduced by procedures that raise or lower cortical arousal outside a certain range (Budzynski, 1977). As noted above, vigilance studies (Dimond and Beaumont, 1972) have shown that the left hemisphere is more sensitive to fatigue than is the right.

Ceremonies conducted by witch doctors or shamans often involve a driving up of cortical arousal through extreme physical activity, usually to the point of exhaustion, whereupon the patient is then considered to be in the proper state for expulsion of the evil spirit or disease (Katz, 1976). Other procedures involve a lowering of cortical arousal through quieting or relaxation methods. These may involve mind-numbing, rhythmic chanting or drumming, or both.

Monotony has also been found to reduce critical screening, as for example in Japanese Morita therapy, and restricted environmental stimulation therapy (R.E.S.T.) (Suedfeld, 1980).

In other words, any procedure that raises or lowers cortical arousal level beyond the range of normal functioning of the left or dominant hemisphere reduces critical screening. Furthermore, as critical screening decreases, accessibility to the right hemisphere increases. In its capacity of "backup computer," the right hemisphere continues to function even when its left counterpart is no longer able to do so. When the left hemisphere relinquishes its dominance and critical screening, the right hemisphere becomes available for more direct interrogation and re-scripting.

Is High or Low Arousal Always Necessary?

The general rule seems to be: any method that reduces or eliminates critical screening can permit access to the right hemisphere processing (Budzynski, 1977). Altering arousal level is one way of accomplishing this, but it is not the only way. The very ingenious techniques of the late master hypnotist Dr. Milton Erickson involved various ways of getting around the left hemisphere's dutiful vigilance. He might, for example, use a confusion technique that would tax the left hemisphere's attempts to find order and rationality in a disordered and irrational input. While the left hemisphere was thus occupied, Erickson would cleverly embed commands to be accepted by the right hemisphere (Lankton and Lankton, 1983). Other examples include paradoxical messages to subvert conscious resistance to accessing the unconscious, or various other psycholinguistic "tricks" designed to slip by the conscious defenses.

Erickson's extremely subtle techniques have been videotaped extensively. Bandler and Grinder (1975) did a careful analysis of Erickson's approach as well as the techniques of the Gestalt therapist Fritz Perls, and the very creative Virginia Satir, in order to develop a structure of their "magic" that could be taught to others. Thus, neurolinguistic programming (NLP) was born.

NLP therapists use the techniques as specified by Bandler and Grinder for establishing rapport with the client, accessing unconscious negative scripts, and neutralizing the scripts by associating the negative affect with memories of positive affect. Hypnosis and the induction of trancelike states through rapport procedures facilitate accessing of unconscious process.

The production of emotional states also helps to access right hemisphere programs. This is so because the right hemisphere is more involved than the left during emotional activation (Bryden and Ley, 1983). If one combines high arousal with emotional activation, as, for example, at a revival meeting or in traumatic situations, the critical screening is minimized, and the right hemisphere dominates. During these vulnerable episodes, as noted earlier, extremely powerful right brain scripting can occur. If it is of a particularly traumatic nature, the scripting may be repressed and remain relatively impervious to left hemisphere processing.

In summary, the reduction of critical screening can occur:

1. When cortical arousal level is increased or decreased beyond the functional range of the left hemisphere.
2. During normal cortical arousal levels if the critical screening capability of the left hemisphere can be disarmed through confusion, overloading, or various psycholinguistic procedures or by an extremely credible authoritative delivery.
3. When a highly emotional state is generated.

Re-scripting Procedures

When we began to use the brain lateralization model in our clinical practice, it became evident that many clients indeed did suffer from interhemispheric conflict. Our task involved helping clients reduce or eliminate the conflict by identifying and changing the maladaptive or negative scripts. If the negative conflicting script is seen as being mediated by the dominant (left) hemisphere, we will use a rational, conscious approach to try to get the client to change the script. The second case noted above is a good example. In this instance a used car salesman suffered from spastic dysphonia, his voice reduced to a hoarse whisper. When asked about his childhood, he responded that he had been raised in a very religious environment. How did his parents feel about telling the truth? The client replied that he had been punished severely on several occasions for telling untruths. Although the client did not make a connection between the early script ("I must not tell lies") and his present job, he was advised to try working for a car dealership that sold a good-quality product. Since he was being laid off from his job, he was able to comply with that advice. Two months after he started his new job, his voice returned to normal. Considering that he had suffered from his problem for two years and that it was worsening at the time he sought help, it would appear that being able to tell the truth on the new job allowed resolution of the conflict. Conflicts of this nature are far easier to resolve than the type of dissonance created by a negative unconscious right brain script conflicting with a positive conscious left brain program. To change this negative script one must first bypass the critical screening as detailed above, and then apply an appropriate change message (CM).

At our clinic we use twilight learning, hypnosis, guided imagery, and subliminal process in order to alter negative right brain scripts. We often combine techniques, as for example, employing subliminal process as a background for hypnosis or twilight learning.

Use of the Synchro Energizer

A device called a synchro energizer, designed by Dr. Dennis Gorges, is also used to facilitate the acquisition of the twilight ASC. Essentially a photic/auditory driver, the device features a goggle array of small lights, and sound presented through a headphone set. The synchronized sound and light stimuli can be varied in frequency from 1 to 30 Hz. In most individuals the presentation appears to produce EEG following.

Typically, the client begins by choosing a frequency that feels comfortable. After a bit, he is asked to begin to lower the frequency gradually— eventually stopping at 6 Hz. Clients describe this experience as relaxing and tranquilizing. These effects often linger in gradually diminishing intensity over a three- to four-day period. Use of the device alone on a twice-a-week basis can result in a decrease in felt tension or anxiety in certain clients.

The use of the syncho-energizer can be coupled with presentation of subliminal process CMs. Cassette tapes with music and/or ocean sounds with subliminal messages can be played through the headphone set along with the auditory stimulus.

We believe that the photic and auditory driving in the theta range produces, in most clients, a state that permits uncritical absorption of verbal information. As such, the device is also useful in the facilitation of the hypnotic trance.

Hypnosis

This subject is covered very well elsewhere in this book; however, as practiced at Behavioral Medicine Associates, hypnosis is used in conjunction with the synchro-energizer and subliminal process. *Ideomotor signaling* Barnett, 1981) helps to identify relevant negative scripts and the traumatic incidents that might have generative them. Once identified these memories can be replaced (re-scripted) with a new positive script.

A case example involved a thirty-four-year-old single female who suffered from a generalized fear of enclosed places (automobiles, buses, airplanes, small rooms), an obesity problem, and a tendency to sabotage relationships with men. Ideomotor signaling under hypnosis revealed that the fears were due to a single traumatic incident that happened when she was four years old. She had entered the women's rest room in the supposedly deserted day care center in the basement of the church as her mother discussed decorations with another woman on the first floor. Two boys (older by approximately three years) followed her in and engaged in a short period of tactile exploration of her chest through her dress.

The re-scripting involved having her re-experience the event under hypnosis from a mature, adult perspective.

After two sessions of re-scripting, the client was able to ride on a bus and successfully completed a vacation that involved a long flight on a commercial airline. She found herself able to maintain a diet. Finally, she was able to trust men for the first time in her adult life.

The decision to employ twilight learning or hypnosis is determined partly by the type of trauma that generated the negative script. If the trauma was a one-time specific incident, we prefer to re-script with hypnosis (given that the client agrees to the procedure). Twilight learning is preferred when the negative scripting is due to repeated traumas over a long period.

Imagery

Does the focus on visual imagery mobilize the right hemisphere more than the left? A number of clinicians believe so. Bresler (1979) devotes a good portion of his book on pain relief to imagery procedures.

Speaking of the role of the nondominant hemisphere, Bresler says: "You must now begin to communicate with the nondominant hemisphere, and on its own terms—in the language of imagery" (p. 353).

Later on, Bresler suggests how one can gain access to the unconscious: "By relaxing the muscles controlled by the somatic nervous system, you quiet the conscious mind so you can get in touch with your nondominant self . . . " (p. 355).

Bresler also notes that by learning to communicate with the right hemisphere " . . . you may uncover new insights and new information that will lead to improvement not just in your pain problem, but in your entire life" (p. 355). He also believes that unconscious misconceptions (negative scripts) need to be corrected in order for the healing process to occur: "For example, you may find that your right hemisphere is brimming with negative expectations which, in turn, are responsible for many or most of your negative experiences" (p. 355).

At Behavioral Medicine Associates we employ imagery because it does seem to produce dramatic results in some clients. We first train the clients to relax by means of biofeedback and our six-phase relaxation cassette program for training at home. Second, we ask the clients, while they relax deeply, to visualize their pain in whatever form they wish. They are asked to describe the pain form. For example, is it round, oblong, etc.? Is it hard, soft, pliable? What color is it? In some instances the mere describing of the pain in detail will reduce its intensity. As a second step in the visualization the clients are asked to discover ways that the pain form can be reduced or eliminated. A few case studies may help illustrate this process.

Mr. Z was a successful, young, single businessman. He reported frequent pain in his lower left abdomen. He had undergone extensive medical testing over the past two years and no pathology had been discovered. The diagnosis given him was irritable bowel syndrome. After learning to relax with biofeedback Mr. Z began the visualization procedure. He "saw" a shiny steel cone shape—"like a NASA nose cone." The cone grew in size proportional to the felt pain.

Mr. Z's second assignment was to find a way to eliminate the shiny, sharp cone. After trying several images, Mr. Z settled on one that seemed to work. He envisioned two NASA mechanics who would use speed screwdrivers and nut drivers to dismantle the steel cone. They would then take away the parts. This imagery procedure worked so well on the first try that the pain was entirely eliminated. After this Mr. Z simply called in his mechanics whenever he began to feel the pain. He was able to reduce his problem to occasional slight discomfort.

Miss G was a young secretary who had suffered from headaches at least three times a week for over three years. The described pain did not fall into the descriptive classification of either tension or migraine headache. Once again all medical tests showed no pathology. Combining hypnotically produced relaxation with the imagery procedure, we found that Miss G was able to visualize her head pain as a large light bulb. The greater the pain, the brighter was the bulb. Still in hypnosis, Miss G imagined that a rheostat could be turned down in order to decrease the bulb's intensity. It is interesting to note that turning the rheostat too quickly would have no effect on the bulb's brightness. The rheostat had to be turned very slowly and carefully in order for the bulb to follow. By relaxing and concentrating on the slow rotating of the rheostat, Miss G could reduce or eliminate her head pain.

Both of these cases showed good follow-up results, indicating that the frequent use of such imagery does not seem to "wear out" with time.

Subliminal Process

We began to incorporate this controversial procedure in our clinical work primarily because it fit the brain lateralization model as a technique that bypasses the critical screening faculties of the left hemisphere. The recently discovered verbal comprehension potential of the right hemisphere enabled us to design subliminal voice tracks that would optimize absorption by that hemisphere.

There has been a revival of interest in subliminal process in the last five years. As cognitive psychology began to take its place along with the behavioral approach in the last decade, it became necessary to recognize once more the existence of not only the conscious but the unconscious as well.

Shevrin and Dickman (1980) noted that a growing number of Russian researchers have been conducting investigations on subliminal and other unconscious processes. Moreover, evoked response research (Shevrin, 1973, 1978; Kostandov and Arzumanov, 1977) has provided support for subliminal process by showing that stimuli below consciousness can still register in the brain EEG. After reviewing research in a number of fields, Shevrin and Dickman (1980) concluded: "If the thesis we have elaborated here is correct, then James (1890) was mistaken in his rejection of unconscious psychological process. Rather than being the 'sovereign means for believing what one likes in psychology,' the assumption of unconscious psychological process appears to be a conceptual necessity in a variety of models dealing with selective attention, subliminal perception, retinal image stabilization, binocular rivalry, and metacontrast" (p. 432).

In his 1971 book, *Subliminal Perception: The Nature of a Controversy,* Dixon presents a strong case for subliminal perception as a valid phenomenon, based on converging evidence from eight bodies of supporting research. Moreover, Nisbett and Wilson (1977) have stated: "The basic question of whether people can respond to a stimulus in the absence of ability to report verbally on its existence would today be answered in the affirmative by many more investigators than would have been the case over a decade ago . . . largely because of better experimental methods and the convincing theoretical argument that subliminal perception phenomena can be derived . . . from the notion of selective attention and filtering" (p. 235).

Dixon (1981), who seems to produce an authoritative book every ten years on the subject of subliminal perception, concluded in his latest book, *Preconscious Processing,* that "the brain may respond to external stimuli which, for one reason or another, are not consciously perceived. The effects of such stimuli may be almost as varied as those of sensory inflow which does reach consciousness. They include the evoking or determination of cortical potentials, changes in the EEG, the production of electrodermal responses, and changes in sensory threshold. They also include effects on memory, the influencing of lexical decisions, and such subjective manifestations as changes in conscious perceptual experience, dreams, and the evoking of appropriate affects" (p. 262).

Speaking about lateralization and subliminal process Dixon (1981) noted: "All in all it seems highly likely that the nondominant hemisphere plays a significant part in unconscious perception" (p. 214).

Our interest in clinical applications of subliminal process was fired by the confluence of the findings in brain lateralization, the works of Dixon, and the research of Lloyd Silverman and his colleagues at New York University.

For approximately twenty years Silverman and associates have tested the effects of what he has designated the subliminal psychodynamic activation method. The technique involves the tachistoscopic presentation of wish-related verbal and pictorial stimuli (Silverman, 1976). Most of Silverman's work has been concerned with the effect of flashing the phrase "mommy and I are one" at 4 milliseconds (subjects see only a flash of light). The phrase apparently activates emotionally supportive feelings of symbiotic closeness. Its adaptation-enhancing effects have been used to facilitate weight loss (Silverman et al., 1978); smoking treatment (Palmatier and Bornstein, 1980); grade point average in the United States (Parker, 1982), and in Israel in Hebrew (Ariams, 1979); reduction of depression (Nissenfeld, 1980); and reduction of schizophrenic symptoms (Silverman et al., 1975).

At Behavioral Medicine Associates we had begun using ocean sounds and/or music to help clients relax as they trained with biofeedback. We later added subliminal verbal messages to these tapes and found that clients seemed to make faster progress. It would appear that individuals do indeed absorb subliminal material better if they are relaxed, as Fisher and Paul (1959) suggested.

Recently we have begun to employ a subliminal videotape (a colorful kaleidoscope) to help clients relax before biofeedback or hypnosis sessions. Clients can watch a 5-minute segment of the 30-minute tape if they wish.

The subliminal audio and video tracks contain, in addition to phrases of relaxation and good feeling, the psychodynamic activation phrase of Silverman.

If subliminally presented phrases can indeed produce positive changes in the unconscious negative scripting, then this process will take its place along with hypnosis, guided imagery, NLP, Gestalt therapy and twilight learning as techniques that can bypass critical screening, re-script unconscious process, and reduce conflict between hemispheres.

Facilitating Interhemispheric Communication

A case has been made for interhemispheric conflict. However, the related phenomenon of repression can mask certain of the severe conflicts. Moreover, the left or dominant hemisphere can easily rationalize forcing its own program in other cases. Quite probably the left hemisphere is often unaware of conflicting tendencies in the right. Since the nondominant hemisphere cannot argue its case in verbal–logical fashion, we speculate that in some instances it may do so through the striate muscle or autonomic nervous system, as noted above in the case of hysterical symptoms or conversion reactions. One can also make a tentative rationale for the right hemisphere's involvement in suppression of immune defenses (Budzynski and Sparks, in press).

Is there any way to resolve conflicts of this nature before *maladaptive* scenarios are directed by either the dominant or the nondominant hemisphere?

Therapies such as NLP, Gestalt, transactional analysis, and hypnosis offer procedures that, in the context of the brain lateralization model proposed here, can facilitate communication with the nondominant hemisphere. A discussion of these procedures is beyond the scope of this chapter, but almost all of them involve the client's re-experiencing of past, relevant events as though he were the younger personality of those events. Some therapies focus on a communication being established between the client's consciousness and various other parts of his personality.

Keeping in mind the fact that the right hemisphere has the syntactical language comprehension of a five-year-old, we have used an imagery procedure that involves the client visualizing a five-year-old representation of herself. Although the five-year-old image typically does not speak (the right hemisphere ordinarily does not control speech output), other, nonverbal communication can be established. For example, the child image can nod or shake her head in response to binary questions. After some weeks, or even months, of regular "interaction," the child image will begin to speak.

When the client first visualizes the child image, there is often a welling up of a sweet sadness as though the child side, after a long, lonely existence, is finally being recognized and accepted by the adult side. The client, acting out this dual role, can carry out a daily dialogue, for example, asking how the child feels about certain situations, or soothing the child's fears.

An example of this involved speech fright in a thirty-six-year-old executive. When he learned the communication technique, he was able to calm the five-year-old before the speech. As he began his speech, he imagined the child huddling behind him as he (the adult) gave the speech unafraid.

In another instance a twenty-nine-year-old businesswoman suffered anxiety panic attacks if she attempted to cash a check in a supermarket. As a result she had not tried to cash a check in two years. Employing the technique in a supermarket, she imagined a frightened five-year-old hanging on to her skirt as she (the adult) actually wrote out a check.

Both of these clients now use the dialogue several times each day in order to minimize anxiety and conflict. The results are typical of those clients who are able to visualize well. For these individuals the use of the procedure does result in a greater feeling of control as conflicts are resolved or at least coped with on a daily basis.

CONCLUDING REMARKS

The results of brain lateralization studies along with other research reviewed briefly have allowed us to develop a model of the brain that we have found to be extremely useful in the clinical setting. The model proposes conscious and unconscious processors that have distinct characteristics and are located in the left and right cerebral hemispheres, respectively.

Because the left/right processors are structurally and functionally different, they can arrive at conflicting solutions to problems in certain instances. The model further postulates that some of these conflicts can result in repression of the right brain solutions or scripts. Such repression of a right brain script may result in that hemisphere's attempt to force its solution through control of the somatic, autonomic, or immunological systems.

One general therapy goal is the resolution of the conflict by changing the negative script. The focus of this chapter has been on the application of procedures that can change right hemisphere scripts through a bypassing of left hemisphere critical screening and the presentation of an appropriate change message to the right hemisphere. These techniques may be used separately, or they may be combined to effect relatively fast therapeutic progress in selected clients.

A second general therapy goal is the development in the client of an effective communication between the left and right hemispheres. Such communication can help guard against the development of future conflict by facilitating ongoing resolution of disparate tendencies.

Although obviously simplistic, the present brain lateralization model provides us with an extremely useful framework into which we can place the variety of procedures used in our clinic.

REFERENCES

Ariam, S. The effects of subliminal symbiotic stimuli in Hebrew on academic performance of Israeli High School Students. Unpublished Ph.D. dissertation, New York University, 1979.

Bandler, R. and Grinder, J. *The structure of magic. Vol. I: A book about language and therapy.* Palo Alto, Calif.: Science and Behavior Books, 1975.

Barber, T. X. Experiments in hypnosis. *Scientific American,* 1957, *196,* 54–61.

Barnett, E. A. *Analytical hypnotherapy: Principles and practice.* Kingston, Ontario, Canada: Junica, 1981.

Belo, J. *Trance in Bali.* New York: Columbia University Press, 1960.

Bertini, M., Lewis, H. B., and Witkin, H. A. Some preliminary observations with an experimental procedure for the study of hypnagogic and related phenomena. In C. T. Tart (Ed.), *Altered states of consciousness.* New York: Wiley, 1969.

Blumstein, S. and Cooper, W. Hemispheric processing of intonation contours. *Cortex,* 1974, *10,* 146–158.

Bogen, J. E. and Bogen, G. M. The other side of the brain III: The corpus callosum and creativity. *Bulletin of the Los Angeles Neurological Society,* 1969, *34,* 191–220.

Bresler, D. E. *Free yourself from pain.* New York: Simon & Schuster, 1979.

Brown, B. *Supermind.* New York: Harper & Row, 1980.

Bryden, M. P. and Ley, R. G. Right hemisphere involvement in imagery and affect. In E. Perecman (Ed.), *Cognitive processing in the right hemisphere.* New York: Academic Press, 1983.

Budzynski, T. H. Some applications of biofeedback-produced twilight states. *Fields within fields . . . within fields,* 1972, *5,* 105–114.

Budzynski, T. H. Biofeedback and the twilight states of consciousness. In G. E. Schwartz and D. Shapiro (Eds.), *Consciousness and self-regulation,* vol. 1. New York: Plenum, 1976.

Budzynski, T. H. Tuning in on the twilight zone. *Psychology Today,* 1977.

Budzynski, T. H. Brain lateralization and biofeedback. In B. Shapin and T. Coly (Ed.), *Brain/mind and parapsychology.* New York: Parapsychology Foundation, 1979.

Budzynski, T. H. and Sparks, T. F. Toward a behavioral oncology: Stress response, brain lateralization and the psychophysiology of cancer. In S. Gross and S. Garb (Eds.), *Humanism and science in cancer research and treatment.* New York: Springer, in press.

Deglin, V. L. Our split brain. *The UNESCO Courier,* 1976.

DeManaceine, M. *Sleep: Its physiology, pathology, hygiene, and psychology.* New York: Scribners, 1897.

Dimond, S. J. and Beaumont, J. G. On the nature of interhemispheric transfer of fatigue in the human brain. *Acta Psychologia,* 1972, *36,* 443–449.

Dimond, S. J. and Beaumont, J. G. Experimental studies of hemispheric function in the human brain. In S. J. Dimond and J. G. Beaumont (Eds.), *Hemispheric function in the human brain.* London: Elek Science, 1974.

Dixon, N. F. *Subliminal perception: The nature of a controversy.* New York: McGraw Hill, 1971.

Dixon, N. F. *Preconscious processing.* New York: Wiley, 1981.

Eccles, J. Brain and free will. In G. G. Globus, G. Maxwell, and I. Savodnik (Eds.), *Consciousness and the brain*. New York: Plenum, 1976.

Erickson, M. and Rossi, E. L. *Hypnotherapy: An exploratory casebook*. New York: Irvington, 1979.

Felipe, A. Attitude change during interrupted sleep. Unpublished doctoral dissertation, Yale University, 1965.

Ferenczi, S. An attempted explanation of some hysterical stigmata. In *Further contributions to the theory and technique of psychoanalysis*. London: Hogarth Press, 1926.

Fisher, C. and Paul, I. H. The effect of subliminal visual stimulation on imagery and dreams: A validation study. *Journal of American Psychoanalytic Association*, 1959, *7*, 35–83.

Foulkes, D. and Vogel, G. Mental activity at sleep-onset. *Journal of Abnormal Psychology*, 1965, *70*, 231–243.

Frank, J. D. *Persuasion and healing*. New York: The Johns Hopkins Press, 1973.

Froeschels, E. A peculiar intermediary state between waking and sleeping. *American Journal of Psychotherapy*, 1949, *3*, 19–25.

Frumkin, L. R., Ripley, H. S., and Cox, G. B. Changes in cerebral hemispheric lateralization with hypnosis. *Biological Psychiatry*, 1978, *13*, 741–749.

Galin, D. Implications for psychiatry of left and right cerebral specialization. *Archives of General Psychiatry*, 1974, *31*, 572–593.

Galin, D., Diamond, R., and Braff, D. Lateralization of conversion symptoms: More frequent on the left. *American Journal of Psychiatry*, 1977, *134*, 578–580.

Gazzaniga, M. and LeDoux, J. *The integrated mind*. New York: Plenum, 1978.

Hall, M. M., Hall, G. C., and Lavoie, P. Ideation in patients with unilateral or bilateral midline brain lesions. *Journal of Abnormal Psychology*, 1968, *73*, 526–531.

Helm-Estabrooks, N. Exploiting the right hemisphere for language rehabilitation: Melodic intonation therapy. In E. Perecman (Ed.), *Cognitive processing in the right hemisphere*. New York: Academic Press, 1983.

James, W. *The principles of psychology*, vol. 1. New York: Holt, 1890.

Jaynes, J. *The origin of consciousness in the breakdown of the bicameral mind*. New York: Houghton Miflin, 1976.

Katz, R. The painful ecstasy of healing. *Psychology Today*, Dec. 1976, 81–86. Reprinted in D. Goleman and R. J. Davidson (Eds.), *Consciousness: Brain, states of awareness, and mysticism*. New York: Harper & Row, 1979.

Koestler, A. *The act of creation*. New York: Macmillan, 1964.

Kostandov, E. and Arzumanov, Y. Averaged cortical evoked potentials to recognized and non-recognized verbal stimuli. *Acta Neurobiological Experimentalis*, 1977, *37*, 311–324.

Krippner, S. and Villoldo, A. *The realms of healing*. Millbrae, Calif.: Celestial Arts, 1976.

Kubie, L. and Margolin, S. A physiological method for the induction of states of partial sleep, and securing free association and early memories of such states. *Transactions of the American Neurological Associations*, 1942, 136–139.

Lankton, S. R. and Lankton, C. H. *The answer within: A clinical framework of Ericksonian hypnotherapy*. New York: Brunner/Mazel, 1983.

Lasaga, J. and Lasaga, A. Sleep learning and progressive blurring of perception during sleep. *Perceptual and motor skills*, 1973, *37*, 51–62.

Lasky, E. Z., Weidner, W. E., and Johnson, J. P. Influence of linguistic complexity, rate of presentation, and interphrase pause time on auditory–verbal comprehension of adult aphasic patients. *Brain and Language*, 1976, *3*, 386–395.

LeDoux, W. and Gazzaniga, M. A divided mind: Observations on the conscious properties of the separated hemispheres. In S. Springer and G. Deutsch (Eds.), *Left Brain/Right Brain*. San Francisco: W. H. Freeman, 1981.

Leuba, C. and Bateman, D. Learning during sleep. *American Journal of Psychology,* 1952, *65,* 301–302.

Levy, J. Variations in the lateral organization of the brain. Master lecture presented at the 85th Annual Convention of the American Psychological Association Meeting, San Francisco, 1977.

Levy, J. Cerebral asymmetry and the psychology of man. In M. C. Wittrock (Ed.), *The brain and psychology.* New York and Kingston, Ontario: Junica, 1980.

Nideffer, R. M. Altered states of consciousness. In T. X. Barber (Ed.), *Advances in altered states of-consciousness and human potentialities,* vol. 1. New York: Psychological Dimensions, 1976.

Nisbett, R. and Wilson, T. Telling more than we can know: Verbal reports on mental processes. *Psychological Review,* 1977, *84,* 231–259.

Nissenfeld, S. M. The effects of four types of subliminal stimuli on female depressives. *Dissertation Abstracts International,* 1980, *40,* Ju 3.

Orne, M. On the nature of posthypnotic suggestion. In L. Chertoks (Ed.), *Psychophysiological mechanisms of hypnosis.* New York: Springer-Verlag, 1969.

Ornstein, R. *The psychology of consciousness.* San Francisco: Freeman, 1972.

Palmatier, J. R. and Bornstein, P. H. Effects of subliminal stimulation of symbiotic merging fantasies on behavioral treatment of smokers. *Journal of Nervous and Mental Disease,* 1980, *168,* 715–720.

Parker, K. A. Effects of subliminal symbiotic stimulation on academic performance: Further evidence on the adaptation-enhancing effects of oneness fantasies. *Journal of Counseling Psychology,* 1982, *29,* 19–28.

Popper, K. R. and Eccles, J. C. *The self and its brain.* New York: Springer International, 1977.

Rubin, F. (Ed.), *Current research in hypnopaedia.* London: MacDonald, 1968.

Rubin, F. Learning and sleep. *Nature,* 1970, *226,* 447.

Schacter, D. L. The hypnagogic state: A critical review of the literature. *Psychological Bulletin,* 1976, *83,* 452–481.

Schnell, H., Jenkins, J. J., and Jimenez-Pabon, E. *Aphasia in adults: Diagnosis, prognosis, and treatment.* New York: Hoeber, 1964.

Shevrin, H. Brain wave correlates of subliminal stimulation, unconscious attention, primary- and secondary-process thinking, and repressiveness. *Psychological Issues,* 1973, *8,* 56–87 (Monograph 30).

Shevrin, H. Evoked potential evidence for unconscious mental processes: A review of the literature. In A. S. Prangishvidi, A. E. Sherozia, and F. V. Bassin (Eds.), *The unconscious: Nature, functions, methods of study.* Tbilisi, U.S.S.R.: Metsniereba, 1978.

Shevrin, H. and Dickman, S. The psychological unconscious: A necessary assumption for all psychological theory? *American Psychologist,* 1980, *31,* 421–434.

Silverman, L. H. Psychoanalytic theory: "The reports of my death are greatly exaggerated." *American Psychologist,* Sept. 1976, 621–637.

Silverman, L. H., Levinson, P., Mendelsohn, E., et al. A clinical application of subliminal psychodynamic activation: On the stimulation of symbiotic fantasies as an adjunct in the treatment of hospitalized schizoprhenics. *Journal of Nervous and Mental Disease,* 1975, *161,* 379–392.

Silverman, L. H., Martin, A., Ungaro, R., and Mendelsohn, E. Effect of subliminal stimulation of symbiotic fantasies of behavior modification treatment of obesity. *Journal of Consulting and Clinical Psychology,* 1978, *46,* 432–441.

Simon, C. and Emmons, W. Responses to material presented during various levels of sleep. *Journal of Experimental Psychology,* 1956, *51,* 89–97.

Sperry, R. W. A modified concept of consciousness. *Psychological Review,* 1969, *76,* 532–536.

Stampfl, T. The effect of frequency of repetition on the retention of auditory material presented during sleep. Unpublished master's thesis, Loyola University, Chicago, 1953.

Suedfeld, P. *Restricted environmental stimulation: Research and clinical applications.* New York: Wiley, 1980.

Svyandoshch, A. The assimilation and memorisation of speech during natural sleep. In F. Rubin (Ed.), *Current research in hypnopaedia.* London: MacDonald, 1968.

Tucker, D. M. Lateral brain function, emotion, and conceptualization. *Psychological Bulletin,* 1981, *89,* 19–46.

Vogel, G., Foulkes, D., and Trosman, H. Ego functions and dreaming during sleep onset. *Archives of General Psychiatry,* 1966, *14,* 238–248.

Zajonc, R. B. Feeling and thinking: Preferences need no inferences. *American Psychologist,* 1980, *35,* 151–175.

Zaidel, E. Auditory vocabulary of the right hemisphere following brain bisection or hemidecortication. *Cortex,* 1976, *12,* 191–211.

Zaidel, E. Lexical organization in the right hemisphere. In P. Buser and A. Rougeul-Buser (Eds.), *Cerebral correlates of conscious experience.* Amsterdam: Elsevier, 1978.

15. Human Consciousness and Sleep/Waking Rhythms*

Roger Broughton

Many authors since antiquity have believed that, at least in its deepest stages, sleep is a state of more or less complete absence of conscious experience. This thesis is epitomized in a statement by Ladd the philosopher–psychologist, who compared awareness in wakefulness to that in sleep, when he wrote (1892, p. 301):

> What-ever we are when we are awake, as contrasted with what we are when we sink into a profound dreamless sleep, that is to be conscious.

Major theses of this chapter, however, will be: (a) that sleep is in fact a state of rich internal mental life during which the individual is not unaware of external stimuli: (b) that lawful cyclic fluctuations in the quantitative and qualitative aspects of consciousness occur in wakefulness that are related to 90–120-minute ultradian and 24-hour circadian sleep rhythms; (c) that the nature of an individual's waking awareness relates to the quantity and temporal stability of his preceding nocturnal sleep patterns; and (d) that many, and perhaps most, of the so-called altered states of consciousness reflect partial or dissociated sleep states.

What Is Consciousness?

It is, of course, necessary to define consciousness, despite Sir William Hamilton's admonition that consciousness cannot be defined (Hamilton, 1895).

*Reprinted by permission from the *Journal of Clinical Neurology,* 1982, vol. 4, no. 3, copyright 1982, Swets and Zeitlinger. Presented at the symposium The Neurobiology of Human Consciousness, held by the Eastern Association of Electroencephalographers, Mount Gabriel, Quebec, Canada, March, 1979.

461

The usage of the term has, in fact, been so imprecise and inconsistent that many authors have felt that it might best be totally avoided, a conclusion reached by William James (1912). James believed that, if it exists at all, consciousness is not an entity or a thing, but rather a function of the organism (James, 1904). The function is that of being aware of both one's internal mental activity and of interoceptive and exteroceptive stimuli, that is, of James's famous metaphorical "stream." The equating of consciousness with subjective experience has recently been further elaborated by Thomas Nagel (1974, p. 436), in his essay "What Is It Like To Be a Bat?" Nagel's concept of consciousness is summarized in the following quotation:

> . . . the fact that an organism has conscious experience *at all* means, basically, that there is something it is like to *be* that organism. There may be further implications about the form of the experience; there may even (though I doubt it) be implications about the behaviour of the organism. But fundamentally an organism has conscious mental states if, and only if, there is something that it is like to *be* that organism—something it is like *for* the organism.

Such a concept makes explicit the personal and individual nature of consciousness and explains why it is so difficult, if not impossible, to obtain insight into the conscious experience of another individual, let alone of organisms with which one cannot communicate verbally (i.e., infants, bats . . .). It indicates clearly that behavioral analyses will be inadequate and that only those components of our awareness that comprise subjective experience are relevant.

If we may accept such a working definition, what then is comprised within "consciousness"? A list, perhaps not exhaustive, of its components would be the following: perception of external stimuli, imagery and fantasy, thinking and planning, remembering, emotions, attention, and creativity and insight. This chapter considers our present knowledge of the extent to which these components of the "stream of consciousness" exist or persist during sleep.

THE STREAM OF CONSCIOUSNESS IN SLEEP

To What Extent Is the Sleeper Not Conscious of External Stimuli?

There is no doubt that sleep is a state of reduced awareness of the external world. Indeed Rechtschaffen and Foulkes (1965) taped subjects' eyelids open and showed that there was no recall upon subsequent awakening for visual stimuli in the form of objects, pictures, and so forth that were placed before the eyes of the sleeper. Nevertheless, various external stimuli *do* in fact enter into the ongoing mental activity of sleep, and others lead to awakening.

Much anecdotal evidence exists for some degree of incorporation of stimuli into ongoing mental activity. A famous example, unfortunately often used to support the incorrect belief that dreams can be completed almost instantaneously, was the guillotine dream of Maury (1853). In this dream the author had been watching condemned persons being guillotined. His turn came to mount the scaffold. At the moment of sensing the blade on the back of his neck he awoke to find that the head-stead of his bed had collapsed and struck him in the same location. Maury concluded (falsely) that the entire lengthy dream had been initiated and completed in the fraction of a second between the time the falling head-stead had struck him and the time of his awakening. There is further anecdotal literature of, for instance, temperature changes in the room leading to jungle or arctic dreams, of cramping of an arm due to lying on it being associated with dreams of a crippled identical limb, and many other similar instances involving retrospective explanations of dream content. More definite proof of such incorporation comes from studies in which experimenter-controlled stimuli have been presented during REM and NREM sleep.

Dement and Wolpert (1958) performed the first systematic study of the effects of external stimuli on mental activity. The stimuli were a 1000 Hz tone, a series of light flashes, and a spray of water on the skin. Stimuli were presented during REM sleep alone in twelve volunteers. Tactile stimuli were by far the most effective, being incorporated into subsequent dream reports without themselves causing awakening in 42 percent of applications, followed by light flashes in 23 percent, and sounds in 9 percent. When the experimental stimuli induced awakening, a similar order was encountered for apparent incorporation into reports of dreaming, that is, in 40 percent for awakening with water spray, 10 percent for awakening with flashes, and 0 percent (none of only five instances) with a 1000 Hz tone. Dream incorporation could seemingly be either direct and identical to a waking perception of the stimulus, or indirect and transformed into the ongoing context of the dream. The overall incidence of incorporation of these external stimuli was 24 percent, indicating that ongoing REM mentation is in fact relatively resistant to external stimuli. More or less similar direct or indirect incorporations ranging from 25 to 54 percent have been reported by Baldridge (1966) for hot and cold thermal stimuli applied to the skin, by Koulack (1969) for incorporations of nerve shock of the median nerve at the wrist, and by Berger (1963) for incorporation of spoken first names. There is evidence that children incorporate stimuli rather less frequently than do adults. (Foulkes et al., 1969; Foulkes and Shepherd, 1972).

Studies have also presented stimuli during NREM sleep and these have been found incorporated into mental activity after subsequent awakening. In the study of Castaldo and Shevrin (1970) it was found that verbal stimuli during NREM sleep tended to give rise to conceptual types of incorporations. As we shall see, conceptual thought, rather than dreamlike imagery, is the predominant type of mental activity in NREM sleep. Similar findings are reported by Lasaga and Lasaga (1973) in a study of short-term memory and sleep.

The awareness of sleepers of external stimuli may, as in the REM dreaming studies cited above, lead to awakening. It has been shown that their degree of significance to the subject is a major determinant of their effectiveness in causing return to wakefulness. Early studies using meaningless stimuli generally indicated that the highest awakening thresholds are in REM sleep followed by the deep slow wave stages (stages 3 and 4) of NREM sleep (Williams et al., 1964). This, combined with its high threshold of arousal to direct reticular stimulation in animals (Jouvet, 1962), suggested that REM sleep (active sleep, paradoxical sleep) is the deepest state of sleep. However, more recent studies using *significant* stimuli have shown that individuals then awaken very easily from the REM state (Pisano et al., 1966; Poitras et al., 1973). An example of a particularly effective stimulus is the playing of a tape recording of her infant's crying to a sleeping mother (Poitras et al., 1973). It has also been shown that significant stimuli are more effective than are nonsignificant ones in evoking EEG K-complexes (Oswald et al., 1960) or in producing finger plethymographic or heart rate responses (McDonald et al., 1975) in sleep. Such responses are incomplete arousal responses. The ability for such selective responsiveness is of obvious survival value for lower animals and for man. The organism must monitor the presence of significant stimuli (predator noises or smells, the cry of a child . . .) throughout sleep in order to respond appropriately.

In sum, rather than being perceptually cut off from the external world during sleep, the evidence is therefore for a very sensitive monitoring of the external stimuli of personal significance. If stimuli are not significant and are not overly intense, they can be found to be incorporated directly or indirectly into our ongoing mental activity in some 20 to 50 percent of instances. But if they are of sufficient significance, stimuli readily elicit awakening.

Imagery and Thoughtlike Activity in Sleep

The public concept of dreams, and of mental activity in sleep in general, is based largely upn the clinical literature of morning recall and, of course, upon the contributions of Freud (1900) in his monumental work *The Inter-*

pretation of Dreams. Widespread beliefs include that most dreams are bizarre in content, highly sexual or symbolic in nature, and express wish fulfillment as a compensating mechanism for impulses that are unacceptable in wakefulness. Other often-held concepts are that people vary greatly in the frequency of their dreaming and, since the early physiological studies of sleep, that dreaming occurs more or less exclusively in the REM state. All of these ideas have now been shown to be incorrect.

Space does not permit a thorough analysis of this very large literature. It is well reviewed by Foulkes (1966), Rechtschaffen (1973), Schwartz et al. (1978), Pivik (1978), and others. I will therefore limit myself to making a few main generalities concerning the nature, ubiquitousness, and physiological correlates of mental activity in sleep that are relevant to the topic under consideration. Only the manifest (versus symbolic) content will be considered.

1. *Most dreams are quite prosaic in nature.* Numerous studies of mental activity after REM sleep awakenings (at which time the most dreamlike mental activity is retrieved), such as those of Snyder (1970) and of Dorus et al. (1971), have shown that in fact most dreams contain situations that are rather probable and bland and are generally similar to those encountered in wakefulness, rather than being highly unusual and bizarre scenarios. So-called typical dreams of the type described in the psychiatric literature were encountered in less than 0.5 percent of dream reports of normals by Snyder (1970). Although penile erection occurs in over 90 percent of REM periods in normal males (Fisher et al., 1965; Karacan et al., 1966), dreams of males with explicit sexual content are relatively rare and have a less than 10 percent incidence. Childhood dream studies by Foulkes and colleagues (Foulkes et al., 1967; Foulkes, 1971) lead to similar conclusions. The main differences from adult dreams were a lower incidence of dream reports after REM awakenings, shorter report lengths, and a greater number of animals in the dream scenes. Waking personality styles were highly related to the individual differences in dream content, the correlation increasing with age.

2. *Dreaming is not restricted to REM sleep, but overall qualitative differences exist between mental activity in REM and NREM sleep.* Although the early studies of Aserinsky and Kleitman (1953) and Dement and Kleitman (1957) suggested that dreaming was frequently retrieved after REM awakening (85–95%) but only rarely after NREM awakenings (7–9%), subsequent studies have shown much higher rates of retrieval in NREM sleep, often up to 35 to 70 percent (Foulkes, 1967). Moreover, reported mental activity has been shown to vary along a continuum from a sequence of frank visual images evolving over time to reports of exclusively thoughtlike type such as simple mulling over daytime concerns. The latter are more common in NREM awakenings. Indeed NREM and REM reports can usu-

ally be differentiated by blind judges (Monroe et al., 1965). Nevertheless, as Foulkes (1966, p. 110) says:

> It is important not to over-estimate the difference between REM and NREM mentation, however, even though all these points of statistical differentiation have been established. Although most undistorted memory processes occur in NREM sleep, most NREM reports are not undistorted memory processes. Although most themes derived from an everyday routine of work or school occur in NREM narratives, most NREM awakenings do not produce such reports. Although REM reports are rated as more distorted than NREM reports, most of the latter contain some distortions. Although most "thinking" reports come from NREM sleep, most NREM reports are of "dreaming" (a visually hallucinated dramatic episode). And although the typical NREM report is less dreamlike than the typical REM one, some NREM narratives get very dreamlike indeed.

3. *Much mental activity in sleep is never retrieved.* Perhaps one of the most important findings of modern sleep research is the richness of mental activity obtained using nocturnal awakenings compared to its relative paucity in morning reports after a night of uninterrupted sleep. Thus, in the morning, most individuals report only a single dream or thought sequence, whereas each of the four to six nocturnal REM periods usually has a retrieved dream, if the sleeper is awakened, and much mental activity is reported after arousals during the intercalated NREM periods.

Similarly, it has been shown that individuals who insist that they are "nondreamers" do report dreams if awakened in REM sleep, although the incidence is about 50 to 60 percent of awakenings, that is, significantly lower than in the general population (Goodenough et al., 1959; Lewis et al., 1966). They are therefore regular nonrecallers rather than nondreamers. Such findings raise the issue of why so much nocturnal mental activity is not remembered the next day.

It has been shown that recall of a previous REM dream decays rapidly with passage of time in NREM sleep, suggesting that NREM sleep actively inhibits recall of preceding REM mentation (Wolpert and Trosman, 1958). Further evidence for impaired recall related to awakening comes from studies in chronic somniloquists of their sleep dialogues and utterances, which form an excellent model for studying this phenomenon. Conversations or utterances in sleep can be compared to their post-awakening recall. It has been shown that most such speech is poorly recalled later. Instances in which recall of speech shows high concordance with previous in-sleep speech are substantially less frequent for NREM than for REM sleep (Arkin et al., 1972). Gastaut and Broughton (1965) and Broughton (1968) have shown that NREM sleep awakenings, particularly when from slow wave stages 3 and 4, often produce confusion with retrograde amnesia of the immediate post-arousal behavior, including conversations. (REM awakenings, on the other hand, are often relatively difficult to elicit with nonsignificant stimuli. But once awake, the subject is usually in fairly lucid contact with his environment and recall appears relatively intact.) The *arousal-induced retrograde amnesia* has led me elsewhere to propose that it is quite possible that mental activity is in fact more or less continuous throughout sleep and that the lack of its being reported is mainly an artifact of such functional amnesia, due to the awakening process itself (Broughton, 1973; Broughton and Gastaut, 1973).

4. *No precise universal psychophysiological parallelism exists in sleep.* As cited above, correlations between dreamlike and thoughtlike activity and REM sleep and NREM sleep, respectively, are purely statistical. Attempts to show consistent correlations *across individuals* between aspects of dream content and physiological measures have in general proved unsuccessful. These include correlations between dream intensity and the frequency of rapid eye movements or other brief, so-called phasic activities; between emotionality and cardiac, respiratory, and electrodermographic activity; between bizarreness and so-called periorbital integrated potentials (PIPs); and a number of others (cf. reviews by Rechtschaffen, 1973 and Pivik, 1978). As Hauri (1975) has emphasized, the evidence is rather for specific and unique individual relationships between psychological and physiological variables in sleep. For example, the study of Stegie (Note 1) revealed that in six subjects emotionality in dreams correlated positively with respiratory variability in the last 30 seconds before awakening in two, negatively in one, and not at all in three. This individualization of psychophysiological correlates in sleep appears similar to the personalized patterns seen in wakefulness and documented in detail by Lacey et al. (1963).

5. *Impairment of attentional mechanisms occurs in REM sleep dreaming.* Rechtschaffen has recently emphasized a neglected aspect of the phenomenology of dreams, which is their "single-mindedness." He defines its characteristic features (Rechtschaffen, 1978, p. 108) as: "(1) the absence of a reflective awareness that one is dreaming while the dream is in progress; (2) the absence of alternative images and thoughts while attending to the primary dream content; (3) the tendency for dream content to stay on a single thematic track; (4) the absence of a set to remember the dream while it is in progress." These are indeed among the most remarkable features of dreaming and imply that in dreaming the mechanisms of voluntary focusing of attention are characteristically impaired. The exceptional existence of so-called lucid dreams in which the sleeper is aware that he is dreaming and can voluntarily influence dream content indicates that only rarely does at-

tention remain under some degree of control in that state. To this analysis of Rechtschaffen, I might add that lowered willful control *also* characterizes the mentation of NREM sleep. One's thoughtlike "mullings" over problems or situations characteristic of the NREM state also show a high degree of autonomy from willful control. It is as though mental activity throughout sleep largely lives a "life of its own," as indeed largely do the bodily functions.

6. *Mental activity in sleep shows a degree of intra-individual consistency.* One of the obvious and remarkable features of dream content is the fact that dreams often do show some degree of thematic consistency. These "dream themes" can occur within consecutive REM reports from single nights of sleep (Kramer et al., 1964; Trosman et al., 1960) or, as is widely known, may occur during the life of the subject. These findings indicate, not unexpectedly, that the dream content, like daytime thoughts and concerns, characterizes an individual and is indeed a major part of his or her uniqueness.

"What it is like" to be a particular individual in sleep can therefore be summarized as follows. Although conscious experience persists in sleep and exhibits various characteristic features across individuals (general prosaic nature of REM dreams, more thoughtlike activity in NREM mentation, problems of recall especially after NREM awakenings, low degree of volitional control), the evidence concerning its *content* and the physiological correlations of the latter is that they are highly characteristic of a given person. Consciousness in sleep, as in wakefulness, is highly personal. Unfortunately, few scientific longitudinal studies of individuals have been performed to document how subjective experiences in sleep and their physiological correlates may vary over time with important life experiences.

Creativity and Problem Solving in Sleep

Perhaps the elements of conscious experience that man prizes most are those involving creativity, insight, and problem solving. The degree to which these can occur during sleep is truly remarkable. In his book *The Act of Creation,* Koestler (1967) has suggested that creativity and insight generally involve seeing familiar bits of information in new associations or new combinations. He has proposed that sleep mentation is particularly fruitful in this regard specifically because of the unusual combinations and sequences with which the elements of discovery are presented to consciousness. André Sonnet (Dement, 1972, p. 92) goes so far as to credit dreaming with nearly every major artistic and technical achievement of mankind. This is of course an exaggeration, but does make the point that creativity can occur during sleep.

Some nocturnal creations are presented in completed form to the sleeper without apparently involving problem solving. Examples are musical compositions such as Tartine's "Devil Trill Sonata" or poetic compositions such as Coleridge's "Kubla Khan." Coleridge writes of himself in the third person singular as having fallen asleep in his chair from taking opium for a slight indisposition (quoted by Koestler, 1967, p. 167):

> The Author continued for about three hours in a profound sleep, at least of the external senses [sic] during which time he has the most vivid confidence that he could not have composed less than from two to three hundred lines; if indeed that can be called composition in which all images rose up before him as *things* with a parallel production of the correspondent expressions, without any sensation or consciousness of effort. On awakening he appeared to himself to have a distinct recollection of the whole, and taking his pen, ink and paper, instantly and eagerly wrote down the lines that are here preserved.

Unfortunately, the entire poem could not be written down using the visual images "which rose up before him as things," because he was interrupted from his writing by a "gentleman on business from Porlock" whom he had detained for over an hour while he slept.

Another poem that came to him while he slept, but not while under the influence of opium, is the following (Dement, 1972, p. 97):

> He lies at length poor Col' and with screaming,
> Who died, as he had always lived, a dreaming;
> Shot dead, while sleeping, by the gout within,
> Alone, and all unknown, at E'nbro' in an Inn.

Other poems or literary accomplishments derived from sleep include the entire poem "The Phoenix" by the English essayist A. C. Benson, the plots of many of Robert Louis Stevenson's stories including "Doctor Jekyll and Mister Hyde," and the theme of the Canadian Hugh MacLennan's "Two Solitudes," which portrays the problems of bicultural–bilingual federalism.

Instances of the nocturnal solving of problems that had been refractory in wakefulness are also well known. At least two Nobel prizes are attributable to the phenomenon. The most celebrated is that of Friedrick August von Kekulé, Professor of Chemistry at the University of Ghent, who one afternoon in 1865 solved the elusive structure of the benzene (C_6H_6) molecule. All previously known molecular structures had been linear in nature, and attempts to solve the riddle along these lines had been fruitless. He wrote, as translated by Findlay (1948, p. 37):

I turned my chair to the fire and dozed. Again the atoms were gambolling before my eyes. This time the smaller group kept modestly in the background. My mental eye, rendered more acute by repeated visions of the kind, could now distinguish larger structures, of manifold conformation; long rows, sometimes more closely fitted together; all twining and twisting in snake-like motion. But look! What was that? One of the snakes had seized hold of its own tail, and the form whirled mockingly before my eyes. As if by a flash of lightning I awoke. . . .

The structure of benzene, necessary to explain its molecular qualities, was realized in a flash of insight to be in the form of a ring, in fact, a hexagon. This discovery opened a whole range of organic chemistry of compounds with ring structures. Kekulé closed his remarks with the suggestion, "Gentlemen, let us learn how to dream."

Otto Loewi in 1920 dreamed the crucial experiment necessary to prove the existence of neurochemical transmission. Until that time all transmission was believed to be electrical. But this did not explain why an impulse traveling down a nerve would have an excitatory effect on some tissues and an inhibitory effect on others. Loewi actually dreamed the solution twice after cogitating on the problem for at least seventeen years. He wrote (Loewi, 1960, p. 27):

The night before Easter Sunday of that year (1920) I awoke, turned on the light, and jotted down a few notes on a tiny slip of thin paper. Then I fell asleep again. It occurred to me at six o'clock in the morning that during the night I had written something important, but I was unable to decipher the scrawl. The next night, at three o'clock, the idea returned. It was the design of an experiment to determine whether or not the hypothesis of chemical transmission that I had uttered seventeen years ago was correct. I got up immediately, went to the laboratory, and performed a simple experiment on a frog heart according to the nocturnal design.

Walter B. Cannon, the discoverer of adrenaline, called it "one of the neatest, simplest, and most definite experiments in the history of biology" (Koestler, 1965, p. 205). Loewi, like Kekulé, won the Nobel prize for his problem solving within sleep.

In summary, the evidence is overwhelmingly for the continuation of a detailed and broad stream of conscious experience throughout sleep. Because of its less immediate relationships with waking consciousness, many in pejorative fashion have deemed it less real than the latter. Modern Western man likes to belittle his fantasies and unconscious thought processes over which he has little control. Yet, as Havelock Ellis (1911, p. 281) has said about dreaming: "Dreams are true while they last. Can we, at the best, say more of life?"

CYCLIC SLEEP-RELATED FLUCTUATIONS OF CONSCIOUSNESS IN WAKEFULNESS AND RELATIONSHIPS TO PRECEDING NOCTURNAL SLEEP

These topics have in large part been recently reviewed by the author (Broughton, 1975) and will be covered here only briefly. They concern the evidence for lawful biorhythmic fluctuations of waking consciousness and their relationships to sleep. The relevant literature is large and still rapidly expanding and is contributed to mainly by psychologists, human physiologists, and sleep researchers. It gives rise in two main conclusions:

1. Humans do in fact exhibit substantial quantitative and qualitative rhythmic changes of consciousness during the waking state.
2. Waking levels of consciousness relate closely to the amount, quality, and temporal stability of preceding nocturnal sleep.

Evidence for Circadian Changes in Conscious Experience

A number of reports using both field studies and laboratory studies have documented regular circadian fluctuations of numerous parameters of conscious experience. The following results appear quite consistent in the literature:

1. The major parameters show lowest levels in the first third of the night, rise before the usual time of morning awakening sometimes with a second 5–6 A.M. dip, peak during the waking period in the morning (in the so-called larks), the afternoon to early eventing, or the late evening (owls), and then drop before sleep onset. Such patterns have been shown around the 24 hours for logging errors in a Swedish gas works company over a 20–30-year period by Bjerner et al. (1955) and for delays by switchboard operators in answering telephone calls by Browne (1949). During multiple daytime testing in the laboratory similar findings have been shown by Kleitman (1939, 1963) for a number of tests from purely mental to motor—including card sorting, mirror drawing, code transcription, multiplication, hand steadiness, and body sways—and by Blake (1967) for calculations, letter cancellation, card sorting, auditory vigilance, and a five-choice serial reaction time. In both of these studies all tests were repeated five times a day.
2. A general strong correlation for individuals exists between the above

pattern of test results and their body temperature curve (Kleitman, 1963).

3. Independence from this overall pattern exists for those tests involving memory functions. The latter peak independently in the morning (Baddeley et al., 1970; Hockey et al., 1972), whereas the peak of essentially all other functions is most frequent in the afternoon or early evening.

4. There is a transitory decrease in perceptual and other functions in the early afternoon, that is, the so-called post-lunch dip of Blake (1967). This time of day shows a universal trend on all tests for sleepiness and is the basis of the siesta of some cultures. It has also been pointed out that this period of lowered vigilance is the residual expression in adults of the last nap given up with growth and development (Kleitman, 1963).

Evidence for 90–100-Minute Ultradian Rhythms of Waking Conscious Experience

Strong evidence for ultradian cyclic variations of consciousness in the daytime comes from the studies of daydreaming of Kripke and Sonnenshein (1978). In an initial project, these investigators had eleven volunteers spend ten hours in an isolated recording chamber, the only input from the exterior being a sound that recurred every 5 minutes. This ensured that subjects were awake and was the signal to write on a card what was going on in their minds during the previous 5 minutes. Cards were later scored randomly and blindly by both the subject and the experimenters on a 1 to 5 scale of fantasy content. EEG, oculogram, and submental EMG were monitored by telemetry to compare daydreaming with physiological state. Subjects were not permitted food or water. Data analysis procedures and findings were as follows:

1. The fantasy scoring method showed high correlation between subjects and experimenters and so was probably highly reliable (mean Spearman Rank Order Correlation = 0.83, lowest 0.70).

2. Fantasy content was statistically analyzed by autocorrelation functions for 18 lags (maximum lag = 90 min), and smoothed variance spectra were obtained. These showed a marked peak in the 16 cycle/day range (1 cycle per 72–120 min, i.e., about every 90 min).

3. This cyclic peaking of daydream-type mental activity about every 90 minutes, alternating with periods of greater perception of the external world, was associated with ocular quiescence and increased alpha

rhythm, that is, with apparent drowsiness and so-called hypnagogic reverie.

Although all the subjects knew that they had some periods of marked fantasy during the study, none was aware of the clocklike regularity with which it occurred. In order to test whether such cycles are also present during unrestricted nonlaboratory conditions, the same authors did a field study of eight individuals who carried a timer and a portable tape recorder over a 12-hour period of their normal day. Each 10 minutes the timer sounded, and they recorded their ongoing mental activity for that interval. These results were later transcribed, scored, and analyzed as previously. The activities of the subjects were quite varied and included working as a computer programmer and as a hotel clerk, going to the beach for the day, and so forth. Inter-rater agreement and the number of well-formed daydreams were not as high as in the laboratory study. Nevertheless, the mean fantasy variance spectrum again showed a significant peak at 16 cycles/day, that is, one cycle every 72 to 120 minutes.

Other researchers have shown that daydreams can be essentially indistinguishable from the night dreams reported after REM sleep awakenings (Foulkes and Fleisher, 1975; Starker, 1974). It therefore appears that fantasy activity is cyclically modulated at the same periodicity in sleep and in wakefulness. Unfortunately, no studies have yet been done in single individuals around the 24 hours to see if the daytime fluctuations remain in phase with the nighttime ones.

This cyclic increase in dreamlike reports of mental activity as opposed to a more logical, analytic, verbal type of mental activity led me to propose first at the September 1973 Montreal conference on *Transformations of Consciousness* (Broughton, 1975) that REM sleep and ultradian diurnal daydraming might express a cyclic increase in activity of the (generally right) hemisphere nondominant for language over the language-dominant hemisphere around the 24 hours and be inherent to Kleitman's (1969) BRAC. There is evidence that this mechanism may hold true for REM sleep (Goldstein et al., 1972; Rosekind et al., 1979; Herman et al., Note 2). However, the results of one of my students' thesis projects has found that ultradian variations in waking EEG at the BRAC rate are synchronous between the two hemispheres, especially in the frontal regions (Manseau and Broughton, 1984). The results support cyclic diurnal drowsiness as the explanation of ultradian rhythmic daydreaming, rather than interhemispheric alternations.

Other psychological or behavioral variables that show a daytime ultradian cyclicity at the same 72–100-minute rate for adults include perceptual capabilities on visual detection tasks (Orr et al., 1974), and for the spiral after-effect (Lavie et al., 1975), and such disparate functions as gastric contractions (Hiatt and Kripke, 1975), oral activity (Friedman and Fisher, 1967; Oswald et al., 1970; Kripke, 1972), and heart rate (Orr and Hoffman, 1974).

The slow circadian and the more rapid ultradian variations in conscious experience raise a number of interesting issues:

1. To what extent is the variability seen in numerous psychological experiments due to such inherent biological cycles?
2. How, if at all, do various forms of stress alter the amplitude or periodicity of these functions?
3. Conversely, to what extent is not being able to reasonably follow such biological rhythms itself a stress to the body, and one that perhaps predisposes to malfunction or disease?
4. What are the educational, occupational, and other general life implications of these rhythms?
5. Is there a fundamental biological need for fantasy as well as for structured logical thought?

Inter-relationships between Waking Consciousness and Preceding Sleep Patterns

Each individual exhibits a range in the amount of sleep that is optional for his daytime well-being. If sleep-deprived, he will usually feel jittery and hyper-responsive. And if he oversleeps he will feel thick-headed and groggy. This optimal range of sleep is his "sleep need." The amount shows considerable variability across the general population. However, even extreme short sleepers will show a performance deficit when they oversleep from their need. This was shown recently by Stuss and myself for a healthy 2-hour sleeper (Stuss and Broughton, 1978) whose performance consistently deteriorated if he overslept to 3.5 hours per night.

Although brief, highly motivated performance tests are generally quite robust to at least acute sleep deprivation, tests that are long and boring and that require fine discriminations are quite sensitive. An example is the widely used Wilkinson's auditory vigilance task (Wilkinson et al., 1966). It requires listening to tones recurring every 2 seconds for a full hour in order to detect forty randomly located signal tones which are 20 percent briefer than the other tones, all tones embedded in 75 dB of white noise.

Without attempting to review the vast literature on its effeccts, it can be stated that sleep deprivation can lead to problems of focusing and shifting attention, to missing information due to "lapses," and to numerous other deficits. Physiologically speaking, progressive sleep deprivation causes somnolence, "microsleeps," and then eventually the need for more prolonged periods of daytime sleep, or in some even to more or less irresistible sleep attacks.

Important changes in feelings of well-being, level of perception, mood, and other variables of experience also occur when stable circadian sleep/waking rhythms are disrupted. This occurs more and more frequently in our society, due to rotating shift work and to exposure to so-called jet lag. It therefore appears increasingly that optimum daytime functioning is aided by a stable circadian sleep pattern, as well as obtaining one's optimal amounts of sleep. Erratic sleep patterns can induce insomnia and make some sleep pathologies, such as narcolepsy, very difficult to treat.

Space also does not permit discussion of the literature on *selective* sleep deprivation linking, for instance, the amount of nocturnal slow-wave sleep to daytime pain perception.

"ALTERED STATES OF CONSCIOUSNESS" AND SLEEP/WAKING RHYTHMS

If it can be said, as discussed earlier, that a widely accepted definition of consciousness does not yet exist, this is even more true for the concept of "altered states of consciousness" (ASCs). Using the provisional list above of the acknowledged components of conscious experience, the altered states thereof could theoretically include marked decrease, increase, or distortion in perception, imagery, thinking, remembering, emotional experience, attention, and insight and creativity. Any such phenomena would substantially change "what it is like to be" the individual involved. Implied in most discussions on the topic is that by their nature such altered states are temporary and reversible. Rather than considering the extremely large number of states to which an analysis of all possible combinations would lead, this section will be restricted to the more traditional consideration of a relatively small number of states characterized by impaired or distorted awareness. These can be classed into two groups, depending upon whether they arise in a matrix of sleep or of wakefulness.

ASCs Arising in Sleep

The relationships between altered states of consciousness and sleep/waking patterns are perhaps most obvious in those phenomena that begin in sleep itself, or during transitions between sleep and wakefulness. These are in fact quite numerous. The most outstanding are the following:

1. *"Nightmares" (terrifying dreams and sleep terrors).* No one would argue that subjective experience is not markedly altered in a full-blown nightmare. Two main types of nightmare exist—the terrifying dream and the

sleep terror. Terrifying dreams are sequences of visual or polymodal hallucinated images whose particular content becomes very threatening to the sleeper. This may take the form of the dreamer being about to lose his life in various situations such as falling off a cliff, being run over by a train, or other. Dreaming of actual death of the dreamer is rare, either in dreams reported after experimenter-controlled awakenings or in spontaneous home awakenings. Awakening in such life-threatening dreams indicates that the sleeper does realize that he can abort the experience and can escape, reassured, into the waking state. Fisher et al. (1970) have shown that terrifying dreams occur in REM sleep and are associated with much less autonomic discharge than are sleep terrors.

A detailed and valid description of the subjective experience of sleep terrors is far more difficult to obtain. This appears to be (see above) because recall of any associated mental activity is relatively incomplete in slow-wave sleep awakenings which form its matrix. Unlike terrifying dreams which normally occur in the second half of sleep, most sleep terrors occur in the first half or first third. The sleeper usually suddenly sits up and emits a primitive blood-curdling scream in apparent panic. He is inconsolable for the duration of the attack, which usually lasts 1 to 3 minutes. At its termination he often cannot recall any preceding mental activity or even the intervening events such as the parents or others trying to console him during the attack. If he does recall anything, it is inevitably of a *single scene* rather than of a progressive dream sequence. Palpitations and difficulty in breathing are frequent. During the Middle Ages the attacks were generally interpreted as being due to a devil sitting on the chest of the sleeper, an interpretation that is the basis of our term "incubus attack" and "nightmare," as well as their equivalents in the French and German languages (cf. Broughton, 1968). Physiologically these episodes arise usually in the deep slow-wave stages 3 and 4 of NREM sleep (Gastaut and Broughton, 1965; Fisher et al., 1970) and involve extremely abrupt and intense arousal, in particular a marked increase in muscle tone and marked tachycardia. Some of the subjective terror may be due to perceiving these intense somatic symptoms through a clouded sensorium. Indeed, full-blown attacks can be triggered in predisposed individuals by simple forced awakening, which precludes the necessity of postulating preceding causal mental activity (Gastaut and Broughton, 1965; Broughton, 1968). The retrograde amnesia mentioned previously would, however, make retrieval of such activity in "spontaneous" attacks difficult to prove.

2. *Somnambulism and other nocturnal automatisms.* Sleepwalking episodes certainly represent one of man's most remarkable dissociative states, combining, as they do, behavior that an observer would generally consider as demonstrating at least some degree of mental activity and awareness of

the environment with, upon termination of the attack, a total absence of recall of any such activity. These highly organized patterns of behavior sometimes have obvious goal-directed or symbolic features, such as in the childhood sleepwalker who repeatedly gets into bed with his parents. These certainly imply strongly that mental activity must be present during an attack. The inability to retrieve such mental activity is again apparently due to the retrograde amnesia inherent in the slow-wave sleep arousals that are the substrate of these attacks (Gastaut and Broughton, 1965; Jacobson et al., 1965). It will probably only be possible to know "what it is like to be a sleep walker" when such individuals, who also are sleeptalkers, divulge what is going on in their minds during an actual attack, as at least in part did Shakespeare's Lady Macbeth (*Macbeth,* Act 5, Scene 1).

3. *"Sleep drunkenness."* Sleep drunkenness consists of abnormally excessive confusion with mental "grogginess" occuring during transitions from sleep to wakefulness. Such states are at times associated with aggression and even with murder (Bonkalo, 1968). The subject later has little if any recall of what occurred during the state. In all instances, it appears that the phenomenon consists of difficulties of arousal from a deep nocturnal sleep, either stages 3 and 4 mainly in the first third of the night (Gastaut and Broughton, 1965; Broughton, 1968) or from the pathologically deep or prolonged sleep of hypersomnic patients in the morning (Roth et al., 1972).

The belief that the brain during these confusional arousals is in a state intermediate between sleep and wakefulness is supported by evoked potential studies. Both my own studies (Broughton, 1968) and those of Saier et al. (1968) have shown that arousals in slow-wave sleep first produce visual evoked potentials (to stroboscopic stimuli) containing waveforms with features characterizing both sleep and wakefulness, which then revert to a waking waveform with increased latency of components, before returning to one of presleep wakefulness. These changes roughly parallel the confusional period, which has also been shown to be characterized by impairment of simple auditory reaction times (Scott and Snyder, 1968), visual choice reaction times (Feltin and Broughton, 1968), mental calculation (Fort and Mills, 1972), perception of the spiral after-effect (Lavie and Giora, 1973), and other measures of awareness. Awakening from REM sleep, on the other hand, leads to more or less immediate reappearance of the baseline presleep visual evoked potential; and any impairment on perceptual or other performance tests is much less or minimal. Sleep drunkenness is a natural altered state of consciousness worthy of much further study.

4. *"Abnormal hypnagogic states."* A number of abnormal states of consciousness may also occur at sleep onset. The usual sequence of subjective events during transition into sleep involves, as Vogel (1978, p. 98) says, "a

decline in control over the course of mental activity and in awareness of the immediate environment and a steady rise in the frequency of hallucinatory experience." Such mental activity at sleep onset may be indistinguishable from REM dreams and can lead to actual "terrifying hypnagogic hallucinations" (Gastaut and Broughton, 1965). Dissociations may occur in the normal progressive sequence of events, particularly when sensations, illusions, or hallucinations take place before full loss of consciousness of the external environment. These mixtures can lead to a number of altered states of consciousness. Prolonged periods of such unstable hypnagogic states in the daytime can accompany a number of conditions involving chronic sleep deprivation and resultant drowsiness, and may lead to confusion of which perceptions are "real."

ASCs Mainly Arising in Wakefulness

A substantial number of other altered states of consciousness occurring in the daytime appear at least at times to involve dissociated sleep mechanisms. Only three of these will be considered. They are automatic behavior states, delirium, and certain states of "double consciousness."

1. *Automatic behavior states.* Patients with a number of clinical conditions exhibit prolonged episodes of complex automatic behavior beginning in wakefulness for which they later have no recall. These may last minutes, hours, or even days. Subjects may board a train or plane and arrive at their destination only to wonder how they got there. Although such automatisms may be seen in psychogenic fugue states and in prolonged epileptic confusional states, due to discharges of infero-mesial temporal lobe, frontal lobe, or generalized absence status type (Gastaut and Broughton, 1972), quite similar episodes are encountered in a major proportion of patients with excessive daytime sleepiness related to narcolepsy, hypersomnia, or other neurological sleep disturbances. Some such patients have been recorded during such episodes and have shown persistent patterns of light sleep or the existence of recurrent brief "microsleeps" during the attacks (Guilleminault et al., 1975).

Seemingly identical states may be observed after head injury. Henry Head (1923, p. 127) described these in his theoretical article on vigilance:

We are accustomed to associate a violent injury with loss of consciousness and other symptoms of concussion: empirically, we are equally familiar with that curious unwitting state which precedes the patients's complete recovery, during which he is liable to act apparently reasonably, but in a purely automatic manner.

It is known that head injury produces shearing forces in the brainstem leading to dysfunction of the ascending reticular activating system. Putting aside the possible contribution of bitemporal dysfunction in head injury, this mechanism of impaired vigilance and recurrence of partial sleep states in the daytime would appear to be similar, if not identical, to that of the various other neurological conditions with excessive daytime sleepiness, such as narcolepsy, idiopathic hypersomnia, Pickwickian syndrome or other forms of hypersomnia with sleep apnea, the more recently described "sub-wakefulness syndrome" (Mouret et al., 1972), and others.

These episodes of behavioral automatisms with varying degrees of retrograde amnesia sometimes take the form of full-blown fugue states and are one of the most interesting neurological altered states of consciousness. And, at least in the conditions mentioned, they express dysfunction of the normal sleep/waking mechanisms.

2. *Delirium.* Various causes of delirium appear to lead to a breakdown of the normal boundaries and normal succession of nocturnal sleep and daytime wakefulness, with resultant diurnal mixing of sleep and of wakefulness. Although much more research is needed in this area, at least for hallucinations of delerium tremens, intrusion of REM sleep mentation into wakefulness is well documented (Gross et al., 1976). The seeing of "pink elephants" therefore represents a REM dream imposed into wakefulness. Similar confusional or delerious states may be related to the so-called REM rebound of withdrawal from substances other than alcohol that also suppress REM sleep. These include barbiturates, most antidepressants, and narcotics. Their sudden withdrawal may produce psychotic states with hallucinosis, similarly based upon REM dreams, spilling over into wakefulness. In a recent book entitled *Delerium,* Lipowski (1980) proposed that this symptom is invariably produced by disturbances of sleep/waking rhythms. The documented causes of the intrusion of REM mentation into wakefulness support the "waking dreamer" hypothesis postulated by John Hughlings Jackson (1958, p. 412). The existence of such a mechanism in schizophrenia, however, has not been supported by sleep research using polygraphic techniques.

3. *"Double consciousness.* The interesting situation of subjective dream imagery superimposed simultaneously upon perception of the external environment has been described by several of my narcoleptic patients as occurring either during regular daytime activities or during attacks of sleep paralysis. This again appears to represent intrusion of REM-based imagery into the waking state, although these rare episodes have not yet been polygraphically recorded. In this situation also patients may be confused as to what is reality.

A number of further altered states of consciousness definitely appear to involve primarily a dysfunction of sleep/waking mechanisms. These include, for instance, Lhermitte's so-called peduncular hallucinosis.

CONCLUSION

It is self-evident that not all states of consciousness or alterations of it may be considered to reflect changes in the relatively diffuse cerebral systems involved in sleep/waking functions. Although modulated by the former, many aspects of perception, imagery, thinking, remembering, emotions, and so forth obviously involve more localized cerebral systems.

Nevertheless, it seems worthwhile to stress the following: (1) a substantial number of unusual states of awareness reflect *primary* dysfunction of sleep/waking mechanisms; (2) the quality of waking conscious experience has important interrelationships with that of nocturnal sleep; (3) major cyclic fluctuations of waking conscious experience occur that reflect circadian sleep/waking rhythms or ultradian rhythms of similar periodicity to the NREM/REM sleep alternation at night; (4) our nocturnal sleep is filled with rich subjective experience indicating that the human stream of consciousness persists around the clock. It seems certain that greater understanding of many aspects of human conscious experience will involve more comprehensive analysis of subjective experience in sleep or in partial sleep states, as well as further study of the sleep/waking mechanisms themselves.

The issues of consciousness and sleep are far from closed. To quote Kleitman (1955, p. 111), the father of modern sleep research, who said in a discussion at one of the Macy Foundation Symposia on Consciousness:

> I am convinced that we shall have to deal with consciousness as something which may occur in wakefulness and sleep: and that one can be awake and not be conscious, and be asleep and conscious.

NOTES

1. Stegie, R. Zur Beziehung zwichen Traumenhalt und während des Träumens ablaufenden Herz und Atmungstätigkeit. Unpublished doctoral dissertation, University of Dusseldorf, 1973.
2. Herman, J. H., Roffwarg, H. P., and Hirshkowitz, M. Electroencephalographic asymmetries and REM sleep dreaming. Paper presented at the Association for the Psychophysiological Study of Sleep, Hyannis, June 1981.

REFERENCES

Arkin, A. M., Antrobus, J. S., Toth, M. F., Baker, J., and Jackler, F. A comparison of the content of mentation reports elicited after non-rapid eye movement (NREM) associated sleep utterance and NREM "silent" sleep. *Journal of Nervous and Mental Disease,* 1972, *155,* 427–435.

Aserinsky, E. and Kleitman, N. Regularly occurring periods of eye motility and concomitant phenomena during sleep. *Science,* 1953, *118,* 273–274.

Baddeley, A., Hatter, J., Scott, D., and Snashall, A. Memory and time of day. *British Journal of Psychology,* 1970, *22,* 605–609.

Baldridge, B. J. Physical concomitants of dreaming and the effect of stimulation on dreams. *Ohio State Medical Journal,* 1966, *62,* 1271–1279.

Berger, R. Experimental modification of dream content by meaningful verbal stimuli. *British Journal of Psychiatry,* 1963, *109,* 722–740.

Bjerner, B., Holm, A., and Svensson, A. Diurnal variation in mental performance. *British Journal of Industrial Medicine,* 1955, *12,* 103–110.

Blake, M. J. F. Time of day effects on performance in a range of tasks. *Psychonomic Science,* 1967, *9,* 349–350.

Bonkalo, A. Hypersomnia. *British Journal of Psychiatry,* 1968, *114,* 69–75.

Broughton, R. Sleep disorders: Disorders of arousal? *Science,* 1968, *159,* 1070–1078.

Broughton, R. Confusional sleep disorders: Interrelationships with memory consolidation and retrieval in sleep. In T. J. Boag and D. Campbell (Eds.), *A triune concept of the brain and behavior.* Toronto: Univeristy of Toronto Press, 1973.

Broughton, R. Biorhythmic variations in consciousness and psychological functions. *Canadian Psychological Review,* 1975, *16,* 217–239.

Broughton, R. and Gastaut, H. Memory and sleep. A clinical overview. In W. P. Koella and P. Levin (Eds.), *Sleep: Physiology, biochemistry, pharmacology, clinical implications.* Basel: S. Karger, 1973.

Browne, R. C. The day and night performance of teleprinter switchboard operators. *Occupational Psychology,* 1949, *23,* 1–6.

Castaldo, V. and Shevrin, H. Different effects of auditory stimulus as a function of rapid eye movement and non-rapid eye movement sleep. *Journal of Nervous and Mental Disease,* 1970, *150,* 195–200.

Dement, W. C. *Some must watch while some must sleep.* San Francisco: Freeman, 1972.

Dement, W. C. and Kleitman, N. Cyclic variations in EEG during sleep and their relations to eye movements, body motility and dreaming. *Electroencephalography and Clinical Neurophysiology,* 1957, *9,* 673–690.

Dement, W. and Wolpert, E. The relation of eye movements, body motility and external stimuli on dream content. *Journal of Experimental Psychology,* 1958, *55,* 543–553.

Dorus, E., Dorus, W. and Rechtschaffen, A. The incidence of novelty in dreams. *Archives of General Psychiatry,* 1971, *25,* 364–368.

Ellis, H. *The world of dreams.* London: Constable, 1911.

Feltin, M. and Broughton, R. Differential effects of arousal from slow wave versus REM sleep (abstract). *Psychophysiology,* 1968, *5,* 231.

Findlay, A. *A hundred years of chemistry.* London: Duckworth, 1948.

Fisher, C., Gross, J., and Zuch, J. Cycles of penile erection synchronous with dreaming (REM) sleep. *Archives of General Psychiatry,* 1965, *12,* 29–45.

Fisher, C., Byrne, J., Edwards, A., and Kahn, E. A psychophysiological study of nightmares. *Journal of the American Psychoanalytic Association,* 1970, *18,* 747–782.

Fort, A. and Mills, J. N. Influence of sleep, lack of sleep and circadian rhythm on short psychometric tests. In W. P. Colquhoun (Ed.), *Aspects of human efficiency: Diurnal rhythm and loss of sleep.* London: The English Universities Press, 1972.

Foulkes, D. *The psychology of sleep.* New York: Charles Scribner's Sons, 1966.

Foulkes, D. Nonrapid eye movement mentation. *Experimental Neurology,* 1967, *19* (Supplement 4), 28–38.

Foulkes, D. Longitudinal studies of dreams in children. In J. Masserman (Ed.), *Science and psychoanalysis, Vol. 19: Dream dynamics.* New York: Grune & Stratton, 1971.

Foulkes, D. and Fleisher, S. Mental activity in relaxed wakefulness. *Journal of Abnormal Psychology,* 1975, *84,* 66–75.

Foulkes, D. and Shepherd, J. Stimulus incorporation in children's dreams (abstract). *Sleep Research,* 1972, *1,* 119.

Foulkes, D., Pivik, T., Steadman, H. S., Spear, P. S., and Symonds, J. D. Dreams of the male child: An EEG study. *Journal of Abnormal Psychology,* 1967, *72,* 457–467.

Foulkes, D., Larson, J. D., Swanson, E. M., and Rardin, M. Two studies of childhood dreaming. *American Journal of Orthopsychiatry,* 1969, *39,* 627–643.

Freud, S. *The interpretation of dreams.* New York: Basic Books, 1955. (Originally published, Leipzig and Vienna: Frunze Deuticke, 1900.)

Friedman, S. and Fisher, C. On the presence of a rhythmic, diurnal, oral instinctive drive in man. *Journal of the American Psychoanalytic Association,* 1967, *15,* 317–343.

Gastaut, H. and Broughton, R. A clinical and polygraphic study of episodic phenomena during sleep: Academic address. *Recent Advances in Biological Psychiatry,* 1965, *7,* 197–221.

Gastaut, H. and Broughton, R. *Epileptic seizures: Clinical and electrographic features, diagnosis and treatment.* Springfield, Ill.: Thomas, 1972.

Goldstein, L., Stoltzfus, N., and Gardocki, J. Changes in interhemispheric amplitude relationships in the EEG during sleep. *Physiology and Behavior,* 1972, *8,* 811–815.

Goodenough, D. R., Shapiro, A., Holden, M., and Steinschriber, R. Comparison of "dreamers" and "non-dreamers." Eye movements, electroencephalograms, and the recall of dreams. *Journal of Abnormal and Social Psychology,* 1959, *59,* 295–302.

Gross, M. M., Goodenough, D., Tobin, M., Halpert, E., Lepore, D., Perlstein, A., Sirota, M., Dibianco, J., Fuller, R., and Kishner, I. Sleep disturbances and hallucinations in the acute alcoholic psychoses. *Journal of Nervous and Mental Disease,* 1966, *142,* 493–514.

Guilleminault, C., Philips, R., and Dement, W. A syndrome of hypersomnia with automatic behavior. *Electroencephalography and Clinical Neurophysiology,* 1975, *38,* 402–414.

Hamilton, W. *Philosophical works.* Hildesheim: Georg Olms, 1967 (first published 1895).

Hauri, P. Categorization of sleep mental activity for psychophysiological studies. In G. Lairy and P. Salzarulo (Eds.), *The experimental study of human sleep.* Amsterdam: Elsevier, 1975.

Head, H. The conception of nervous and mental energy, II. Vigilance: a physiological state of the nervous system. *British Journal of Psychology,* 1923, *14,* 126–147.

Hiatt, J. F. and Kripke, D. F. Ultradian rhythms in waking gastric activity. *Psychosomatic Medicine,* 1975, *37,* 320–325.

Hockey, G. R. J., Davies, S., and Grey, M. M. Forgetting as a function of sleep and phase of the circadian cycle. *Quarterly Journal of Experimental Psychology,* 1972, *24,* 386–393.

Jackson, J. H. *Selected writings of John Hughlings Jackson,* vol. 2, James Taylor (Ed.). London: Staples, 1958.

Jacobson, A., Kales, A., Lehmann, D., and Zweizig, J. R. Somnambulism: All night electroencephalographic studies. *Science,* 1965, *148,* 975–977.

James, W. Does consciousness exist? *Journal of Philosophy, Psychology and Scientific Method,* 1904, *1,* 477–491.

James, W. *Essays in radical empiricism.* New York: Longmans, Green, 1912.

Jouvet, M. Recherches sur les structures nerveuses et les mécanismes résponsables des différentes phases du sommeil physiologique. *Archives Italiennes de Biologie,* 1962, *100,* 125–206.

Karacan, I., Goodenough, D. R., Shapiro, A., and Starker, S. Erection cycle during sleep in relation to dream anxiety. *Archives of General Psychiatry,* 1966, *15,* 183–189.

Kleitman, N. *Sleep and wakefulness as alternating phases in the cycle of existence.* Chicago: University of Chicago Press, 1939.

Kleitman, N. The role of cerebral cortex in the development and maintenance of consciousness. In H. Abramson (Ed.), *Problems of consciousness.* New York: Josiah Macy, Jr. Foundation, 1955.

Kleitman, N. *Sleep and wakefulness.* Chicago and London: University of Chicago Press, 1963.

Kleitman, N. Basic rest–activity cycle in relation to sleep and wakefulness. In A. Kales (Ed.), *Sleep: physiology and pathology.* Philadelphia and Toronto: Lippincott, 1969.

Koestler, A. *The act of creation.* New York: Macmillan, 1967.

Koulack, D. Effects of somatosensory stimulation on dream content. *Archives of General Psychiatry,* 1969, *20,* 718–725.

Kramer, M., Whitman, R. M., Baldridge, B. J., and Lansky, L. M. Patterns of dreaming: the interrelationship of the dreams of a night. *Journal of Nervous and Mental Disease,* 1964, *139,* 426–439.

Kripke, D. F. An ultradian biologic rhythm associated with perceptual deprivation and REM sleep. *Psychosomatic Medicine,* 1972, *34,* 221–234.

Kripke, D. F. and Sonnenschein, D. A biological rhythm in waking fantasy. In K. S. Pope and J. L. Singer (Eds.), *The stream of consciousness.* New York: Plenum, 1978.

Lacey, J. I., Bateman, D. E., and Van Lehn, R. Autonomic response specificity: An experimental study. *Psychosomatic Medicine,* 1963, *15,* 8–21.

Ladd, G. Contributions to the psychology of vivid dreams. *Mind,* 1892, *1,* 299–304.

Lasagna, J. I. and Lasagna, A. M. Sleep learning and progressive blurring of perception during sleep. *Perceptual and Motor Skills,* 1973, *37,* 51–62.

Lavie, P. and Giora, A. Spiral after-effect durations following awakenings from REM and NREM sleep. *Psychophysiology,* 1973, *14,* 19–20.

Lavie, P., Levy, C. M., and Coolidge, F. L. Ultradian rhythms in the perception of the spiral aftereffect. *Physiological Psychology,* 1975, *3,* 144–146.

Lewis, H., Goodenough, D. T., Shapiro, A., and Sleser, I. Individual differences in dream recall. *Journal of Abnormal Psychology,* 1966, *71,* 52–59.

Lipowski, Z. J. *Delirium: Acute brain failure in man.* Springfield, Ill.: Thomas, 1980.

Loewi, O. An autobiographic sketch. *Perception in Biology and Medicine,* 1960, *4,* 3–25.

Manseau, C. and Broughton, R. Bilaterally Synchronous Ultradian EEG Rhythm in Awake Human Adults. *Psychophysiology,* 1984, *21,* 265–273.

Maury, A. Nouvelles observations sur les analogies des Phénomènes du rêve et de l'aliénation mentale. *Annales médicales de psychologie,* 1853, *5,* (2nd series), 404–424.

McDonald, D. G., Schicht, W. W., Frazier, R. E., Shallenberger, H. H., and Edwards, D. J. Studies on information processing in sleep. *Psychophysiology,* 1975, *12,* 624–629.

Monroe, L., Rechtschaffen, A., Foulkes, D., and Jensen, J. Discriminability of REM and NREM reports. *Journal of Personality and Social Psychology,* 1965, *2,* 456–460.

Mouret, J. R., Renaud, B., Quenin, P., Michel, D., and Schott, R. Monoamines et régulation de la vigilance. I. Apport et interprétation biochemique des données polygraphiques. *Revue Neurologique* (Paris), 1972, *127,* 139–155.

Nagel, T. What is it like to be a bat? *Philosophical Review,* 1974, *83,* 435–450.

Orr, W. C. and Hoffman, H. J. A 90 min cardiac biorrhythm: methodology and data analysis using modified periodograms and complex democulation. *IEEE Transactions in Biomedical Engineering,* 1974, *21,* 130–143.

Orr, W., Hoffman, H. J., and Hegge, F. W. Ultradian rhythms in extended performance. *Aerospace Medicine,* 1974, *45,* 995–1000.

Oswald, I., Taylor, A. M., and Treisman, M. Discriminative responses to stimulation during human sleep. *Brain,* 1960, *83,* 440–453.

Oswald, I., Merrington, J., and Lewis, S. Cyclic "on demand" oral intake by adults. *Nature,* 1970, *225,* 959–960.

Pisano, M., Rosadini, G., Rossi, G. F., and Zattoni, J. Relations between threshold of arousal and EEG patterns during sleep in man. *Physiology and Behavior,* 1966, *1,* 55–58.

Pivik, R. T. Tonic states and phasic events in relation to sleep mentation. In A. M. Arkin, J. S. Antrobus, and J. Ellman (Eds.), *The mind in sleep.* Hillsdale, N.J.: Erlbaum, 1978.

Poitras, R., Thorkildsen, A., Gagnon, M. A., and Naiman, J. Auditory discrimination during REM and non-REM sleep in women before and after delivery. *Canadian Psychiatric Association Journal,* 1973, *18,* 519–525.

Rechtschaffen, A. The psychophysiology of mental activity during sleep. In F. J. McGuigan and R. A. Schoonover (Eds.), *The psychophysiology of thinking.* New York: Academic Press, 1973.

Rechtschaffen, A. The single-mindedness and isolation of dreams. *Sleep,* 1978, *1,* 97–109.

Rechtschaffen, A. and Foulkes, D. Effect of visual stimuli on dream content. *Perceptual and Motor Skills,* 1965, *20,* 1149–1160.

Rosekind, M. R., Coates, T. J., and Zarcone, V. P. Lateral dominance during wakefulness, NREM stage 2 sleep and REM sleep (abstract). *Sleep Research,* 1979, *8,* 36.

Roth, B., Nevsimalova, S., and Rechtschaffen, A. Hypersomnia with "sleep drunkenness." *Archives of General Psychiatry,* 1972, *26,* 456–462.

Saier, J. Régis, H., Mano, I., and Gastaut, H. Potentiels evoqués visuels pendant les differentes phases de sommeil chez l'homme: Etude de la résponse visuelle évoquée après le reveil. In H. Gastaut, E. Lugaresi, G. Berti Ceroni, and G. Coccagna (Eds.), *The abnormalities of sleep in man.* Bologna: Aulo Gaggi, 1968.

Schwartz, D. G., Weinstein, L. N., and Arkin, A. M. Qualitative aspects of sleep mentation. In A. M. Arkin, J. S. Antrobus, and S. J. Ellman (Eds.), *The mind in sleep.* Hillsdale, N.J.: Erlbaum, 1978.

Scott, J. and Snyder, F. "Critical reactivity" (Piéron) after abrupt awakenings in relation to EEG stages of sleep (abstract). *Psychophysiology,* 1968, *4,* 370.

Snyder, F. The phenomenology of dreaming. In H. Madow and L. E. Snow (Eds.), *The psychodynamic implications of the physiological studies on dreams.* Springfield, Ill.: Thomas, 1970.

Starker, S. Daydreaming styles and nocturnal dreaming. *Journal of Abnormal Psychology,* 1974, *83,* 52–55.

Stuss, D. and Broughton, R. Extreme short sleep: Personality profiles and a case study of sleep requirement. *Waking and Sleeping,* 1978, *2,* 101–105.

Trosman, H., Rechtschaffen, A., Offenkrantz, W., and Wolpert, E. A. Studies in psychophysiology of dreams. IV Relations among dreams in sequence. *Archives of General Psychiatry,* 1960, *3,* 602–607.

Vogel, G. W. Sleep onset mentation. In A. M. Arkin, J. S. Antrobus and S. J. Ellman (Eds.), *The mind in sleep.* New York: Erlbaum, 1978.

Wilkinson, R. T., Edwards, R. S., and Haines, E. Performance following a night of reduced sleep. *Psychonomic Science,* 1966, *5,* 471–472.

Williams, H. L., Hammack, J. T., Daly, R. L., Dement, W. C., and Lubin, A. Responses to auditory stimulation, sleep loss and the EEG stages of sleep. *Electroencephalography and Clinical Neurophysiology,* 1964, *16,* 269–279.

Wolpert, E. A. and Trosman, H. Studies in psychophysiology of dreams. I. Experimental evocation of sequential dream episodes. *Archives of Neurology* (Chicago), 1958, *79,* 603–606.

Part Three
Accessibility

16. Meditation as an Access to Altered States of Consciousness

Patricia Carrington

Throughout the ages, when men and women have sought to achieve an altered state of consciousness (ASC) for a specific purpose, the methods used to accomplish this have been carefully selected. Usually they have been incorporated into a ritual involving a standard series of steps or exercises. Since human beings do not ordinarily take the act of entering into an ASC lightly, when deliberately seeking this state, as in undertaking meditation, they also typically take precautions.

Probably the most widely used means of evoking ASCs deliberately is meditation in any one of its forms. This does not mean there are not other means used to accomplish the same goal. Drugs or ecstatic dancing have often been employed in a ritualistic manner to the same end. Most of the other ritualized methods for deliberately altering one's state of consciousness, however, involve elaborate preparations and props that are not necessary for the process of meditation. They may use group support in a tribal setting, special music, consciousness-altering substances, the presence of a shaman or other facilitative figure, and austere preparations such as going without food or sleep for an extended period of time prior to the ASC induction.

By contast, meditation is an undramatic procedure that the average individual can enter into when alone and with no elaborate preparations. Although it may be incorporated into involved religious or spiritual ceremonies, meditation does not *need* such accompaniments to accomplish its purpose, unless of course its purpose is defined in a special way by a given society.

In many parts of the world, down through history, meditation has been a solitary and personal pursuit, thus making it the most widely available and extensively used of all the tools for deliberately altering one's state of consciousness.*

Considering the central role that meditation has played in the inner life of human beings, as well as its close relationship to, and occasional overlap with, the widely engaged-in activity of human prayer, let us examine the ingredients that make up this powerful access to ASCs.

COMPONENTS OF MEDITATION

The Meditative Mood

Formal meditation usually occurs only when certain minimal conditions have been met, but the mood or emotional tone that underlies the meditative state is familiar to everyone and constitutes one of the most appreciated of human experiences. This "meditative mood," as I have referred to it (Carrington, 1977), usually occurs quite spontaneously and is marked by its ephemeral nature. Recognized at once as a moment of unusual aliveness, or perhaps of inner illumination, it can include some of the profoundly positive ASCs that Maslow (1962) has referred to as "peak experiences" and is often indistinguishable from the moments of inner stillness *intentionally* evoked by the ritual of meditation. An excerpt from the meditation journal of a colleague attests to this interesting similarity. He writes:

> Tonight at 8:45 P.M. I sat on the porch and watched the last twilight darken into night. I think I've learned to cheat on the TM* prohibition against "extra sessions". I would let a thought come popping into my mind and then gently replace it with some element of sensory perception—the dark line of treetops against the sky, the rushing of the overfed brook hurtling to the sea, the air against my face, the feel of my body against the chair, the smell of woods and growing things. . . . It was very soothing and peaceful. (Edington, 1977)

The writer clearly sees his experience during the formal TM process and his experience with an informal "meditative mood" as being so alike that during the latter it seemed as though he were "cheating" on his formal

---

*Dreams, another common means of accessing ASCs, cannot be classified as deliberate or consciously selected.

*TM is the abbreviation for Transcendental Meditation, a popular Westernized meditative technique.

meditations. Such moods are like true meditation in many ways and one could persuasively argue that they are meditations, suggesting that meditation as a discipline may be a spontaneous process developed into a formal practice.

Despite the fact that it frequently occurs naturally, however, people throughout the ages have developed hundreds of ingenious methods for intentionally evoking the meditative mood, methods that have been carefully cultivated and handed down over generations. Perhaps spontaneous meditative moods occur less often than is desirable. Perhaps when they occur naturally, they are less intense than human beings need them to be. In modern industrial society, based as it is on machinelike efficiency rather than on natural rhythms, the meditative mood may so seldom occur spontaneously that structured, formal types of meditation are particularly necessary. Let us consider some of the methods that man has worked out for evoking and holding onto this fragile mood.

The Techniques

Literally hundreds of practices could be listed under the heading "meditation." All of them have in common the ability to bring about a special kind of free-floating attention where rational thought is bypassed and words are of far less importance than in everyday life. It is characteristic of this state that when in it, the person is completely absorbed by his or her particular object of meditation. If something else comes to mind, it will usually drift in with a sort of vague, faraway quality, then drift out again.

The devices used to bring about this state are as diverse as gazing quietly at a candle flame, attending to the mental repetition of a sound (mantra), following one's own breathing, concentrating on the imagined sound of rainfall, chanting out loud a ritual word or phrase, attending to bodily sensations, concentrating on an unanswerable riddle (*koan*), passively witnessing the flow of thoughts through one's mind, or whirling in a stereotyped dance. Whatever the device, the aim is the same: to alter the way the meditator experiences his or her own existence.

It is important to note that all these techniques close out the distractions of the outer world in much the same way as an "isolation chamber." In a sensory deprivation experiment, the subject is removed from incoming sense impressions by being placed in a soundproofed room, by wearing goggles to eliminate patterned vision, or by undergoing other sense-reducing manipulations. In meditation, the meditator removes her attention from distracting sense impressions and thoughts by creating an inner "isolation chamber" of her own making. It is when the outer world is removed that meditation can take effect, and the individual is said to become "centered," reinstating an inner balance presumably lost during involvement with on-going life.

Despite the fact that in all forms of meditation attention is directed toward a meditational "object," each technique must cope with the basic property of meditation, which can best be described as a counter-tendency, a need to pull away from the object of focus. Even the calm and centered mind is not entirely still. Periodically it reaches for renewed contact with the environment, through either sense impressions or thoughts, and each meditational system has its own way of dealing with this problem.

Some systems are not permissive, or are even coercive with respect to the handling of "distractions of the mind" during meditation. A nonpermissive form of meditation will demand strict concentration on the meditational object. The practitioner will be directed to pinpoint his attention, to banish intruding thoughts from his mind by an act of will, and to return immediately and forcefully to the object of focus whenever he finds his attention has wandered. This approach is seen in extreme form in instructions given to a meditator in a fifth-century Buddhist treatise dealing with thoughts that may intrude into the meditation:

> . . . with teeth clenched and tongue pressed against the gums, he should by means of sheer mental effort hold back, crush and burn out the (offending) thought; in doing so, these evil and unwholesome ideas, bound up with greed, hate or delusion, will be forsaken, then thought will become inwardly calm, composed and concentrated. (Conze, 1969)

In contrast, many meditative systems are marked by varying degrees of permissiveness toward intruding thoughts. In these more permissive techniques, the meditator is instructed to return gently and without effort to the object of focus.

Although there are no experimental findings dealing with the effects on the meditator of permissive versus nonpermissive forms of meditation, it may well make a difference whether the meditator practices one approach or the other. The effects may even be different if she mistakenly interprets her form of meditation as being nonpermissive when it is not. Most techniques for meditation require that the meditator make no conscious effort, but "let things happen" rather than make them happen. Often, however the untutored beginner injects coercion into a meditative practice unless carefully trained to do otherwise. The result is roughly the same as it would be if a stern teacher were standing close by and commanding one to "shape up" the whole time one meditated. More often than not, a true ASC will be prevented because of the tension and guilt involved, and if the meditation has been undertaken for a therapeutic purpose, as is often the case today when modern forms of meditation are used for stress reduction, such effort clearly defeats the intent of the practice.

Meditation versus Centering

In the great meditative traditions, meditation is looked upon as a spiritual exercise, a means for attaining a special kind of ASC thought to be the highest state of consciousness of which man is capable. This supposedly advanced level of consciousness is only arrived at as part of a total way of life. An ascetic life-style, with prescribed physical exercise, diet, and social arrangements, as well as long hours of meditation each day, are typical procedures, and the mastering of the true meditative practice may take a lifetime. For this a highly skilled teacher is usually needed, a teacher who knows exactly how and when to alter the meditative technique in order to produce further spiritual growth in his pupil. "Warming up" exercises such as the silent repetition of a mantra or concentration on one's breathing (or many others that are available) may be prescribed for such a pupil, but these are not considered "meditations." They are devices used to center the individual in preparation for the deep state of communion or oneness that is "meditation." The Hindu spiritual leader Bhagwan Shree Rajneesh points out that:

> . . . meditation has two steps: first the active, which is not meditation at all; second, that which is really meditation (and) is completely non-active . . . just passive awareness. (Rajneesh, 1972)

Clearly therefore, the great meditative traditions identify the ASC arrived at by means of the exercises used, as "meditation," while we today in the West tend to refer to the simple psychological centering devices, the *preliminary* steps, as "meditation." We therefore give the same name to the techniques used to produce meditation as we do to the ASC obtained. According to the great meditative traditions, however, the centering techniques are *not* meditation. They are simply means toward the *goal*—which is meditation. These techniques are therefore more or less interchangeable, and theoretically the advanced practitioner will eventually discard all of them when he can achieve the ASC, "meditation," directly.

In this chapter I refer to the centering techniques or exercises themselves as "meditation," in accepted Western fashion. The average Westerner of today approaches meditation in a predominately practical way. Ordinarily he does not consider it a deep spiritual commitment, if he thinks of it as being spiritual at all, but learns it to make his life easier and more pleasant.

Despite any attempt to be clear about this, however, it will be obvious to anyone who has ever meditated by whatever technique, that one cannot draw a hard and fast line between the simple centering exercises and the deep ASCs that may be accessed by using them. One can commence by naively using the simplest of centering devices (e.g., mentally repeating a mantra with eyes closed) and end up having a profound experience that changes one's entire perspective on life. Or one can set out diligently to achieve deep spiritual awareness through meditation and wind up with a pleasant, relaxing centering experience and nothing more.

The boundaries, in other words, are permeable. Inner experience extends where it will, resisting control and refusing to be confined to categories.

In discussing meditation as a means of accessing ASCs, it should be noted that there are certain standardized rituals, which I have called "practical meditation," that are readily available in the West today. When considering the effects of meditation on the individual's life, we will be looking at research based on these modern forms of meditation, in particular research based on TM, on Clinically Standardized Meditation (the form of meditation that I designed for clinical settings) (Carrington, 1979), and on Herbert Benson's Respiratory One Method, as described in his book *The Relaxation Response* (Benson, 1975).

RELATIONSHIP OF MEDITATION TO OTHER TECHNIQUES

Those who work with meditation as a therapeutic agent are often asked whether meditation is merely "another relaxation technique" or whether it is simply a form of prayer, a type of self-hypnosis, or similar to some other method of self-development. The fact is that meditation, particularly in its modern practical forms, does have a number of points in common with some of the other methods used to promote personal growth, achieve therapeutic goals, or access ASCs, and a distinction is not always easy to make between them. Let us examine a few of these related techniques.

Meditation and Prayer

Historically, the formal discipline of meditation originated in religious practice, and the use of meditation as a spiritual exercise still outstrips by far its use as a practical technique in most parts of the world. While the Hindu and Buddhist religions and that of the Sufi sect among the Moslems clearly reach directly for a profound ASC by means of meditation, some forms of Christian meditation, particularly those practiced in monasteries, also do so. Other Christian practices loosely termed "meditation" are, however, actually "contemplations." Rather than evoking an ASC, they create an atmosphere where thought is directed in a disciplined manner to a specific theological problem or religious event. This process often ends with an attempt to apply the religious idea contemplated to one's own life in a linear fashion.

Much more commonly used by the religious layperson than meditation (at least in the West) is simple prayer, and the relationship of prayer to meditation is an interesting one. While profound prayer probably cannot take place without one's entering the "meditative mood," mechanical repetition of standard prayers in order to fulfill religious obligations does not require this special mood at all.

Prayer is nevertheless closely related to meditation in many ways. It is usually an inward, contemplative state, undertaken in quiet, often in solitude. As in meditation, in prayer also outward stimuli are reduced, and a special kind of soothing, monotonous environment is created. The echoing intonation of ritual words and phrases chanted over and over again; reverberating music; candlelight, votive offerings; incense; the sound of bells; awe-inspiring architecture with symbolic decorations; a special posture held for a period of time; the closing or partial closing of the eyes—these are all traditional accompaniments of prayer intended to evoke a sense of reverence and union with the deity. Through them the ASC that I have called the meditative mood is evoked in a highly effective manner.

Although prayer relies upon the meditative mood, it is nonetheless a goal-directed activity. In prayer, a person calls upon a deity in some manner. She gives praise or offers thanks; seeks forgiveness, consolation, or assistance; or enters into some other relationship with the deity. This goal-directed form of praying, by far the most common type, is quite different from the nonstriving, relatively goal-less absorption of meditation.

As we turn to other forms of prayer, however, the distinction between them and meditation is not so clear. Prayer can be used as a genuine form of meditation in the sense in which we have been using this term. Upon occasion it can evoke an ASC of profound impact. Maupin has described silent, contemplative prayer as having been for a long time the West's only widely used, socially approved "form of meditation" (Maupin, 1968). He suggests that with the lessening of prayer in the West in recent years, we have lost important benefits of this form of "meditation" that have little to do with religious belief: psychological quiet and contact with inner experience and our deeper resources.

In some instances prayer has been intentionally structured in a form belonging strictly to the realm of meditation. In Western monasteries, the repetition of words in praise of God has been widely used to evoke an ASC in which the outer world is shut out and the person is transported into an exalted sense of closeness with God. The "Prayer of the Heart" used by Russian monks and devout laypeople in prerevolutionary Russia is an example of this. This prayer was used to "purify the intellect" by means of a passive attitude and the repetition, on each successive out-breath, of the phrase "Lord Jesus Christ, have mercy on me." By this means the mind was thought to become emptied of all thoughts, images, and passions. In this instance, a Christian religious phrase was being used in the same manner as mantras are used in India, since Sanskrit mantras are either the names of deities or religious phrases.

Used as a form of silent inner communion or coupled with a mantra-like repetition of religious words, prayer can be seen to blend imperceptibly into meditation. Therefore, although we cannot equate prayer and meditation, we cannot fully separate them either. The two states are closely related, not only historically but often in their spirit or purpose, and both practices are in some sense related to another familiar method that evokes the meditative mood—self-hypnosis.

Self-Hypnosis

It might be asked whether meditation and hypnosis are the "same thing" because they both involve entering a "trance state" or ASC. This question can be confusing because "trance" is commonly thought of in the sense of the trances of deep hypnosis, where a person has only limited contact with her surroundings and may be quite unable, afterward, to recall what went on during her profoundly altered state of consciousness.

Actually, such deep trances are neither the only ones nor the most prevalent. Light trance states, which are familiar to everyone, do not ordinarily possess alarming qualities at all. Ronald Shor (1969) has pointed out that these light trances are actually daily, commonplace occurrences for all of us. They involve sharp narrowing of our attention, which becomes focused on one or on a few objects or events or thoughts. Because of this narrowing of attention, our generalized-reality-orientation—that is, our awareness of our surroundings and of our usual ways of thinking and perceiving—begins to fade, creating a "trance" effect. Shor (1969) describes his own experience with such a spontaneous trance:

> I was reading a rather difficult scientific book which required complete absorption of thought to follow the argument. I had lost myself in it and was unaware of the passage of time or my surroundings. Then without warning, something was intruding upon me; a vague, nebulous feeling of change. It all took place in a split-second and when it was over I discovered that my wife had entered the room and had addressed a remark to me. I was then able to call forth the remark itself which had somehow

etched itself into my memory even though at the time it was spoken I was not aware of it.

Many other everyday occurrences involve entering a state of light trance, although we may not label the state we experience by that name. We all know, for example, that an artist may be intensely absorbed in his work during its inspirational phase and become practically oblivious to his surroundings. The same absorption can occur when one is deeply involved in some majestic scene or in an engrossing game, or in viewing a work of art, listening to music, making love, or meditating. This does not mean, however that we should think of all these activities as being forms of self-hypnosis.

Although both involve some degree of trance, there are important differences between meditation and self-hypnosis. One of the identifying characteristics of self-hypnosis is the increased receptiveness of subjects to self-administered suggestions about mental or physical behavior that they want to bring about. Hypnotized persons act (or think) in the way they believe themselves, or the hypnotist, to be directing them. Self-hypnosis is therefore goal-directed. Robert White (1941), in fact, discussing the theory of hypnotism, has suggested that goal-directed striving is one of the primary characteristics of all hypnotic states.

This description of hypnosis is very different from most descriptions of meditation. In the great traditions, meditation is looked upon as a goalless, nonstriving state. In actual practice the meditator may make some effort during meditation (perhaps in an attempt to reach some spiritual goal), but this is usually only a minor aspect of the experience and is typically discouraged by meditation teachers. Self-suggestions, such as telling oneself to relax during meditation, or the implied "suggestion" involved in repeating a mantra that has become a signal to oneself to enter a state of deep relaxation, do play some role in the meditative experience, and certain forms of Yoga requiqre the meditator to employ some suggestions to help her reach the higher states of consciousness; but these minor uses of suggestion can scarcely be compared to the central position given to suggestion in self-hypnosis. With respect to *active striving toward a goal,* these two states differ.

Nor do meditation and self-hypnosis necessarily show the same kinds of physiological changes. Meditation typically brings about a lowering of metabolism with a deep quieting of mind and body. By contrast, some hypnotic states raise metabolism, as when an athlete uses self-hypnosis before a game to "psych" himself up. Other hypnotic states bring about no physiological changes at all, including no changes in brain waves (Kleitman,

1963), and a number of researchers have shown that hypnotized subjects usually have an activated brain wave pattern that is no different from ordinary wakefulness (1959). The only time hypnotized persons show wave patterns similar to those seen during meditation is when they are given specific suggestions to enter a meditation-like state. If they are directed to become deeply relaxed, they will usually obligingly do so, just as they will do many other things, including going to sleep, under hypnosis. In this light it is interesting to note that Zen monks are taught to suppress the hypnotic trance. The name they give to it is *sanran* (meaning "confusion") because they feel it interferes with their practice of meditation (Kasamatsu and Hirai, 1969).

The relationship between meditation and hypnosis is not resolved simply, however. It is possible that in the broadest sense of the term, meditation is a form of hypnosis, although it is certainly not the kind of hypnosis we know in the West. Western hypnosis is a highly motivated condition where the subject plays a "role," acting out certain prescribed actions or thoughts. Abraham Maslow (1969) has called this Western form "striving hypnosis," and points out that a much less familiar type, "being-hypnosis," allows the subject to move away from role playing and enter an intense ASC similar to that of "peak experiences" or mystic states of contemplation. This "being-hypnosis" is used almost exclusively for certain spiritual disciplines such as Yoga or Zen. It is possible that it is a form of meditation, or vice versa.

Looking back at the various techniques mentioned above, we see that virtually all of them require special conditions such as lowering of external stimulation or the presence of monotonous stimulation. In addition, every one of them sometimes evokes a meditative mood—with the possible exception of self-hypnosis, which only does so if the specific directions the person gives her- or himself are to "relax."

Despite the fact that they often involve a meditative mood, however, none of the techniques seems to be the *same* as meditation. They do not set out purposely to create the nonstriving goal-less experience of meditation in the same way, and none seems to achieve it in quite the same manner. Thus one might view meditation as a method that is related to, but also different from, the other techniques used for deliberately inducing ASCs.

EFFECTS OF MEDITATION

Meditation has a variety of effects on those who practice it, most of them highly salutary, and it is being increasingly used in a therapeutic context to facilitate the goals of conventional psychotherapy and/or stress management programs. Modern forms of meditation that aim at relaxing the practitioner and relieving stress have been developed to meet these contemporary needs. Today's meditation training is usually completed in about a week's time, and the meditator is seldom required to use special postures or particular forms of breathing, or to adopt any belief system.

In spite of their simplicity, however, research shows that these new forms of meditation can be highly effective in reducing tension and furthering a fulfilling way of life. As meditators begin to practice them, they typically find themselves feeling calmer. They may also notice an increase in energy, alertness, and physical coordination. Marked lessening of a variety of symptoms indicative of stress can also occur, and the meditator may experience other beneficial changes. Over the past few years a growing number of research studies have documented these effects of meditation.

Stress Reduction

Virtually all studies that have sought to document the effects of meditation on anxiety have shown marked reduction in anxiety levels in meditators versus nonmeditating controls, even as soon as a few weeks following the commencement of meditation (Carrington, 1977). This has been a consistent finding whether physiological measurements were taken or the researchers relied on self-reports or standardized tests of "anxiety" to determine the extent of this change. Evidence also suggests that meditators may actually develop some immunity to stress, as evidenced by the fact that they respond physiologically with fewer "alarm" reactions to stressful stimuli after becoming mediators (Goleman and Schwartz, 1976).

Greater Alertness

People who are meditating regularly tend to handle tasks in a more efficient manner, and this increased coping ability seen in meditators is different from that brought about by taking a tranquilizing drug. Relaxation resulting from drugs typically slows a person down, causing grogginess. By contrast, groups of meditators have been shown to react faster on visual tasks than nonmeditators (Appelle and Oswald, 1974), to discriminate more accurately between different sounds (Pirot, 1978), and to get better scores on tests of manual dexterity administered following meditation (Rimol, 1978).

A number of research studies have also shown meditators to have a freer flow of ideas than nonmeditators (Hines, 1977), and in certain instances disabling blocks to creativity have dissolved completely after a person has commenced meditating (Carrington, 1977).

Improvement in Stress-Related Illnesses

Meditation can have a strong positive effect on many stress-related illnesses. A series of studies on the use of meditation for the normalizing of blood pressure has shown a reliable decrease in blood pressure in a substantial number of people who learned meditation (Benson and Wallace, 1972). Other studies have shown meditation to be useful in the treatment of tension headaches (Carrington, 1977), bronchial asthma (Honsberger and Wilson, 1973), and heart disease (Zamarra et al., 1978), as well as other stress-related illnesses.

Most patients who respond to meditation with improvement of a medical condition must keep on meditating regularly to maintain their gains, however. In such cases, meditation is like a change of diet that eliminates symptoms only as long as the diet is faithfully followed.

Control of Substance Abuse

Meditation may be useful in helping meditators gain control over addictions. In one study (Shafii et al., 1974) researchers found that the number of marijuana users was reduced to nearly one-third the original number among meditators, while the figures for nonmeditators remained approximately the same over an identical period of time.

When these same investigators studied cigarette smokers, they found that 71 percent of those who had practiced meditation *for more than two years* reported a significant decrease in their use of cigarettes, and 57 percent had totally stopped smoking by that time, while at the end of a similar period, nonmeditators were smoking as heavily as before (Shafii et al., 1976).

With regard to alcohol consumption, among meditators who had been meditating regularly for more than two years, 40 percent reported that they had stopped drinking either beer or wine, while none of the nonmeditators had stopped. After three years of meditation, the figures were even higher: 60 percent of the meditators had now stopped drinking beer and wine. In addition, 54 percent of this last group (as against 1% of the nonmeditating group) had also stopped drinking hard liquor (Shafii et al., 1975). These and other studies suggest that meditation can be effective in combating addictions, provided that a person stays with the meditation for a sufficient period of time. There seems to be a clear-cut relationship between the amount of time people have spent meditating and their ability to cut down on drugs, cigarettes, or alcohol: the longer, the greater.

Improvement in Sleep

Certain forms of insomnia respond extremely well to meditation. In one study, after commencing meditation, subjects who had regularly lain awake for 1 ¼ hours each night before falling asleep now typically fell asleep within 15 minutes after lying down in bed (Miskiman, 1978). Another study has shown that such improvement in sleep habits can continue and in fact may be even greater after subjects have been meditating six months. (Woolfolk et al., 1976).

Greater Self-Acceptance

Meditation can also affect the way a person experiences his or her life in general. A frequent change resulting from meditation is the toning down or elimination of excessive self-criticism. Meditators tend to become more patient and understanding with themselves and less apt to indulge in unjustified self-blame (Carrington and Ephron, 1975a). As a result, they may develop a greater tolerance for other people as well. Friends and families of meditators frequently comment that the meditators are now easier to get along with, less irritable, and more understanding of those around them (Carrington and Ephron, 1975a).

More Inner Independence

Many meditators also report an increase in "inner independence." They may find that they can now identify their own opinions and feelings more easily, sense their personal "rights" in situations where formally they may have been unaware of them, and withstand social pressures better without abandoning their own opinions (Pelletier, 1974). As a consequence, they may become more decisive and better able to express opinions more openly, be able to disagree with others more effectively, and demand their own rights in situations where formerly they would have capitulated.

Mood Changes

Meditators may find that their moods are lighter as well as more stable after commencing meditation, and as a consequence experience a renewed sense of well-being. Although outer circumstances can remain unchanged, their lives often seem happier and more fulfilling than before (Carrington and Ephron, 1975b).

EXPLAINING THE EFFECTS OF MEDITATION

Evidence with respect to meditation's effectiveness is impressive; it seems to be a powerful method for evoking a special type of ASC and for changing certain aspects of personality. In trying to understand why meditation has such pervasive effects, we must give attention to many factors that combine to create an effect that is above and beyond that of any single component.] The following are some working hypotheses with respect to meditation's manner of effecting change.

Meditation as Sensory Deprivation

All forms of meditation shut out the external world to a greater or lesser extent. When meditating, we withdraw from the distracting sights, sounds, and other sense impressions that ordinarily bombard us. This is done by focusing attention somewhere else, usually upon a single unchanging or repetitive stimulus. Meditation might thus be described, in part, as a form of self-imposed "sensory deprivation," as if, every time we meditated, we entered an "isolation chamber" of our own making.

This comparison may raise some questions. Sensory deprivation, at least in its extreme forms, is not always desirable. Much evidence indicates that being radically deprived of external input or stimulation can be painfully disorganizing, and sometimes dangerous to survival. Long before modern experiments on perceptual deprivation, people knew that sensory isolation imposes severe stress. Solitary confinement has been a major punishment throughout history, and accounts of people changing under these circumstances, "losing their minds," or suddenly becoming "willing to talk" are well known. People placed alone in a monotonous environment without human contact for long periods of time may go insane, and animals will show similar kinds of withdrawal, regression, and possibly eventual death under these circumstances.

In the 1950s McGill University researchers set about constructing an artificial environment, an isolation chamber, that reduced sensory stimulation to a minimum, so that they could study subjects' reactions to being placed in it for varying lengths of time (Bexton et al., 1954). Later on, a number of other researchers also constructed such chambers. Each experimental setup differed slightly, but they all had in common a "sound-proofed room" (no room is completely soundproof, but these rooms approximated it) and a way of shutting out patterned vision. In almost all of the experiments the sense of touch was also reduced to a bare minimum; subjects wore gloves, kept their arms and legs in cardboard cylinders to eliminate touch sensations, and were told to move as little as possible. In a series of experiments conducted by John Lilly (Lilly and Shurky, 1958) subjects were kept immersed in a tank of water to reduce sensation even further.

With the radical cutting off of the ordinary varieties of sensory input, several things can happen. In the McGill experiments, after an initial period of sleep followed by attempts to keep occupied, subjects entered ASCs where their thinking tended to become disorganized and vivid images to appear. Similar to presleep "hypnagogic" images, these images sometimes were experienced with the vividness of hallucinations. Subjects also typically experienced sensations of bodily strangeness (Bexton et al., 1954).

After emerging from the isolation chamber, the McGill subjects tended to be emotionally labile or seemed dazed, with objects often appearing two-dimensional. Colors were also apt to appear far deeper and more intense than normal, and a number of subjects reported that confused thinking, headache, mild nausea, or fatigue lasted up to 24 hours. Directly after the experiment, the subjects generally showed a sharp drop in their scores in tests on reasoning, indicating a temporary decline in intellectual capacity.

On the basis of a long series of such experiments, the McGill investigators concluded that people cannot function in a logical, directed, integrated manner without a constant stream of sensory input. Since our nervous system is a receiver as well as a sender, if it has nothing to receive, then it may be thrown out of gear.

Just how it will be affected depends on the amount of stimulation still remaining. No experimental laboratory has yet succeeded in depriving a human being entirely of stimulation. Some sense impressions are always perceived by the person, even if they are minimal impressions of touch, taste, or smell. The studies done so far have only been able to reduce the intensity of stimulation, and to monotonize the environment. Usually they give some form of repetitive, unvarying stimulation to the person so that he or she experiences a constant sameness of input. In the McGill experiments, this monotony or sameness consisted of low illumination and constant "white" noise from the ventilating system, but there were no effective precautions against sudden large body movements, which occasionally provided some stimulation. In some of the experiments after McGill, such as Lilly's water immersion tank, there was a greater reduction of sensory input—total darkness and floating in body-temperature water—which reduced almost all touch sensations, but there were still some sensations from occasional movements of the water, leakage of sound into the tank, and other uncontrollable factors. Nevertheless, some of these later experiments differed from McGill ones in being relatively free of stimulation, and there are apparently some differences between these two types of experiments in terms of their effects.

The most excessive symptoms, such as severe disorganization of thought and hallucinations, are interestingly enough produced by montonous stimulation rather than by the near elimination of all stimulation. When stimulation is all but totally eliminated, thought distortion and hallucinations tend to taper off and finally stop, and the person enters an almost stuporous condition where he or she is largely nonreactive. It is as if the sending and receiving apparatus had temporarily gone out of commission under these conditions. As soon as enough light is reintroduced, however, so that it can be seen through diffusing goggles, or if a steady monontonous sound is reintroduced, the hallucinations are likely to return. (Doane et al., 1959).

While the practical forms of meditation and the McGill type of isolation, where some unpatterned sensory input is still allowed, are quite similar, the withdrawn state of *samadhi,* a radically altered state of consciousness induced by Indian adepts, is very different. During *samadhi* a deep trance is obtained in which metabolism can become so slowed that breathing may be undetectable by any measurement apparatus. The withdrawal achieved in *samadhi* appears similar to the near-total elimination of sensory input obtained in some of the more radical sensory deprivation experiments. If, as has been suggested by Brownfield (1972), eliminating sensory input almost entirely simply puts the sending and receiving apparatus out of commission, this might explain why the ASCs obtained in *samadhi* are reported to be so different from those of ordinary meditation. The bodily distortions, visions, unusual sensations, or fragmented thoughts that arise during the less strenuous kinds of meditation are said to be left behind in *samadhi,* and the experience is that of a "great void." The mental apparatus, as we know it, appears to be in a condition of suspended animation during this state.

The effects of monotonous, unpatterned stimulation of the McGill type of sensory isolation chamber more closely resemble the effects of ordinary meditation. Meditators frequently report vivid dreamlike imagery (although it rarely achieves the vividness of hallucinations unless they have been meditating for very long periods of time at one sitting). Meditators also frequently report distortions of body image, that their thinking has become much looser in its organization (almost uncontrolled), and that they are experiencing intense emotions during meditation. But although meditation and sensory isolation can produce similar effects, meditation is often described as pleasant and highly desirable, while sensory isolation is often felt to be unpleasant, disturbing, and undesirable.

If we examine the experimental reports carefully, we can see that not *all* subjects who undergo even the most severe sensory deprivation have unpleasant experiences or show disorganization of thinking, hallucinations, or any unusual behavior. Some have gone through several days of such isolation quite comfortably and have, in fact, reported positive effects.

For some people, then, sensory isolation appears to be a positive experience. Accounts by solitary sailors, polar explorers, lifeboat survivors, and other people forcibly isolated for long periods of time and exposed to highly monotonous environments, indicate that it is not unusual for such people to report that once they became accustomed to the isolation experience and found a way to cope with it, they underwent a "transformation." At some point the isolation seemed to become an important growth experience for them, many of these people being able to achieve a new integration of personality as a result.

To investigate whether sensory isolation might have some healing properties, researchers Azima and Cramer (1956) placed psychiatric patients in an isolation chamber similar to the one used in the McGill experiment, for periods lasting from two to six days depending on the patients' own responses to the situation. As in other sensory isolation experiments, the subjects could terminate the experience whenever they wished. As had been predicted, while some of these patients worsened with sensory deprivation, the symptoms of some other patients, especially those suffering from depressions, were very much improved. This improvement lasted after they came out of the isolation chamber, and did not disappear. These patients now showed greater motivation, more socialization with other patients, and greater self-assertiveness. Some of them responded so well to sensory isolation, in fact, that they improved to the point of being discharged from the hospital. This was particularly interesting in light of the fact that some of those who could be discharged in this manner had been long-standing chronic hospitalized patients.

At first the post-isolation patients reported a typical disorganization of thinking, but for them disorganization seemed to be followed by "reorganization." Self-assertiveness and "constructive aggression" seemed to become available to them, and psychological testing after the experience showed that they had suffered no loss of concentration or efficiency as a result of isolation; a number of them became more receptive to psychotherapy afterward. In general, patients whose major illness was depression seemed to benefit the most, whereas others, who were diagnosed as being "hysterical personalities," tended to become more anxious and disturbed when placed in isolation.

These results led another investigator (Harris, 1959) to try placing schizophrenic patients in sensory isolation. When he did this, he found that these patients tolerated the experience much better than normal persons, and that for many of them the intensity of their hallucinations was reduced or eliminated as a result of the sensory isolation. Other researchers then followed this same line of investigation, with practically unanimous agreement as to the value of sensory isolation for certain types of psychiatric patients.

Brownfield (1972) then attempted to discover the reason for this by testing subjects to find out whether they were predominantly "sensation seeking" or "sensation avoiding." Sensation-seeking people are those who tend to reach out for exciting experiences, new tastes, adventures, novel environments, travel, and other forms of stimulation. Sensation-avoiding people tend to withdraw from the new, tending to stick to the tried and true and to plan out everything in advance in order to avoid the unknown.

Brownfield reasoned that sensation-avoiding people might find sensory isolation pleasant and possibly therapeutic because it would help them achieve the reduction of stimulation they needed. On the other hand, sensation-seeking people might find it extremely painful to be shut away from the stimulation that they require. He assembled a group of "normal" people and a group of psychiatric patients, tested them to determine whether they were sensation-seeking or sensation-avoiding, and then asked for those who so wished to volunteer for sensory isolation, to remain in isolation for 24 hours if possible.

Though Brownfield had only a few patients in his final pilot study in the isolation chamber because of technical difficulties, the results were in the predicted direction. When placed in the chamber, sensation-seeking subjects all reported discomfort, anxiety, or boredom. Sensation-avoiding subjects, however, frequently reported that they felt *better* after being in the isolation chamber than they had before, describing themselves as now feeling comfortable, relaxed, and calm. When questioned afterward, the sensation seekers said they would never want to go through the procedure again, whereas those who were sensation avoiders seemed eager to revolunteer at the earliest possible opportunity.

Possibly sensation seekers find the partial sensory isolation of meditation uncomfortable, or even anxiety-provoking, while sensation avoiders find it comforting and even healing. In addition, in the overstimulating environment of our modern world, we may all require some sensory deprivation at times to right the balance, a possible reason for the beneficial effects of meditation.

A Governing Apparatus

Since meditation changes our stimulation level, it may act as a governing apparatus, helping us maintain the proper balance between too much and too little stimulation. We each seem to have our own optimum level of stimulation, a level that is neither too high nor too low for maximum functioning. In addition, we are able to tolerate more stimulation at certain times than at others. We probably all function better if the range of stimulation that we have to deal with is kept within our own best level, but keeping it within these limits requires effort.

When in a dull, unstimulating environment for too long, most people become restless. They then get up, walk around, stretch their muscles, talk to someone, do something "interesting," or otherwise show eagerness for sensory input. On the other hand, if they hear children shouting, a TV blaring, the lawnmower next door roaring, or a dog barking, they typically try to get away to some quieter place. They continually act to adjust to the level of stimulation, to make it as pleasant and comfortable for themselves as possible. If they are unable to do this satisfactorily, their functioning may take a sharp drop.

Meditation may help to achieve a balancing-out of sensory input because it brings about a mild form of sensory deprivation that still contains some sensory input, usually repetitive and monotonous such as the thought of a mantra or awareness of breathing. As indicated, when sensory deprivation is too extreme or prolonged, people may react to it with loss of efficiency, or even anxiety and distress, just as they often react adversely to overmeditating (a serious problem and source of possible abuse of the technique as discussed elsewhere [Carrington, 1977]). An adjustment process is typically hampered by overdoing—one reason why the practical modern forms of meditation achieve the therapeutic results that they do. They shut out *some,* but not *all* sensory input, and they do this only for relatively short periods of time.

Sensory Overload

While there have been many studies of sensory deprivation, surprisingly little attention has been paid to what happens when human beings or lower animals are bombarded with stimuli. Too much stimulation, carried to an extreme, can seriously break down the adequacy of mental or physical functioning. The strategies of the "third degree" and of "brainwashing" are based on this principle. If a prisoner or someone else whose behavior is being manipulated is kept overstimulated by constant bombardment with intense sights, sounds, or sense impressions for hours on end, day after day, the clarity of the thinking processes eventually breaks down. At this point people often become susceptible to suggestions or willing to comply with demands that, in a more rational state, they would clearly reject.

Playing upon this effect of overstimulation, primitive tribes or other groups may purposely create a sensory overload by means of rituals, singing, dancing, or whirling in order to bring about ecstatic states. Under conditions where there is *no escape,* however, sensory overload can have a deleterious effect. If animals are subjected to intense and inescapable stimulation such as loud noises, bright flashing lights, or impressions of rapid motion, over long periods of time, a wide variety of serious symptoms can occur. Ludwig (1975) reported that the heart rate and blood pressure of a group of rats subjected to these conditions changed in a manner indicating that the animals were undergoing severe stress: their adrenal hormone levels shot up, all manner of symptoms of anxiety were shown, and, in a number of instances, death occurred.

When animals are packed together in cages where they are subjected to constant inescapable stimulation from other animals, the consequences are also serious. What happens has been described as the "behavioral sink." The behavior of these animals deteriorates until there is extreme breakdown in social behavior; normally cooperative animals become hostile and destructive to each other. There is also a sharp increase in the death rate of the animals, with many early deaths that would not normally have been expected. The effects of overcrowding on animals have been studied because of the possible implications they may have for man. If overcrowding breaks down the inner controls of animals to such a radical degree, it may be asked what happens to human beings confined to the constant overstimulation of ghettos in large cities.

These are important questions in an age where sensory overload is widely prevalent, and where the average person faces an ever increasing amount of sensory bombardment in daily life. Despite its prevalence, however, we may not realize that we are faced with extreme sensory overload because this condition has become so much a part of our life-style. High-pressure advertising messages and dramatically presented newcasts are constantly flashed over the mass media. Billboards and supermarket shelves demand attention with their brightly colored competing displays. The noise of cars, motorcycles, and planes intrudes into even the quietest country resort. And these are but a few of the ways that high levels of stimulation invade people's lives in the 1980s.

With overstimulation, our normal tendency to withdraw from intense stimuli also seems to become less efficient. At this point, instead of withdrawing from excitement, ironically, we may reach for more. A familiar example is the young child staying up for a special occasion who becomes overstimulated and then refuses to go to bed, although what he now needs most is quiet. If left to their own resources, such children may drive themselves to an ever higher pitch of excitement until they "go to pieces." Perhaps such a tendency to seek more and more exhausting levels of stimulation is one reason why meditation is beginning to be looked upon favorably by so many people in the modern world. They may sense that they are being caught in a trend that, unless they stop it, may continue until they figuratively, or literally, drop in their tracks.

Lower animals periodically nap throughout the day, awakening for an hour or so and then going back to sleep. Most human beings, however, observe a 17-hour period of continuous wakefulness. We attempt to remain almost constantly awake, a feat for which we must be carefully trained. Infants and young children, who are not yet trained in this manner, also require naps; and some older people, who can no longer conform easily to this training for physiological reasons, again require naps during the day.

Because the average person does not have periodic sleep during the day, she may need other ways of reducing the sensory input she is receiving. Under natural conditions we all tend to lapse into "meditative moods" at certain times during the day. Perhaps these moods perform the same function for us as catnaps do for animals. The research on ultradian rhythms that shows that reverie states occur at roughly one-and-one-half-hour intervals throughout the day in people (Kripke and Sonnenschein, 1973) suggests that a tendency to retreat periodically from the stimuli that are pounding us is still built into our nervous systems, even though we may refuse to allow ourselves to indulge in this tendency to any degree.

One of the most effective ways for us to reestablish a balance between too little and too great an amount of stimulation may be to meditate. In this light, it is interesting to note that people in boring, low-stimulation conditions, such as some forms of imprisonment, frequently report obtaining refreshment from meditation. For them, the mental activity supplied by meditation seems to provide the stimulation they need—again suggesting that meditation acts as a governing apparatus. If meditation periodically restores us to a state of inner balance with respect to the adjustment of our stimulation level, its effects upon our health, both physical and mental, might be expected to be considerable.

Rediscovering Our Natural Rhythms

When we meditate, we do not retreat into a mere absence of external stimulation, but into the presence of something else. When one level of stimulation is removed—that of the world, which often acts on us in ways convenient to it rather than to us—we are released to sense more subtle forms of stimulation. In the quiet of the meditative state, we can become attuned to the voices of the body which are ordinarily obscured by waking activity.

Meditation seems to be the only natural state that is sufficiently still, and at the same time sufficiently alert, that when we are in it we can clearly perceive our own inner rhythms. Meditators often report that during meditation they hear the beating of their own hearts or sense their breathing as an important occurrence. They sometimes report that they can hear the rushing of blood through their head or sense other minute and delicate bodily processes usually obscured by activity.

We might compare our insensitivity to bodily processes when active to our inability in the daytime to perceive the stars in the sky. Although they are present 24 hours a day, we cannot see the stars when the sun is up because its brilliant light obscures them. When the sun sets, however, the far more subtle lights of the stars are readily seen, and it is as though a host of stars had "appeared" in the sky. So it is with meditation, which removes us from the bright light of activity to the softer light of inner awareness—away from one level of perception toward an entirely different one. When we cease to perceive ourselves in active interaction with the world, we are free to see ourselves in our own livingness.

It does not seem to be coincidence that established meditative systems often make use of components that reflect natural bodily rhythms. Our positive response and sense of peacefulness with respect to the rhythms of heartbeat, breathing, and other bodily processes are well known, with regularly repeated sounds or rhythmic movements widely recognized as soothing. Parents from all cultures and eras, for example, have rocked agitated infants to quiet them, or have repeated affectionate sounds in a lilting manner or bounced their babies on their laps with an intuitive awareness of the soothing effects that these rhythmic activities have on the infants and often on the parents as well.

Reginald Lourie (1976), studying the role of such rhythmic patterns in the development of children, reports that as they grow, a certain number of healthy children supply their own rhythmic patterns. At two to three months of age, a few of them are rocking or moving their heads, the only part of their bodies over which they have some control. At six to ten months of age, even more are rocking their heads, while others have now taken up increasingly dramatic forms of rhythmic activities such as banging their heads against the crib or getting up on hands and knees to rock vigorously back and forth.

In some of these children, these rhythmic movements are transitory, lasting only until about age two or three, but in others such movements remain much longer. Tracing these rhythmic activites through various stages of development, Lourie found that while at first rhythmic activities seem to be done predominantly for pleasure—a number of children will rock when they have had a particularly satisfying meal or are praised, or are successful or admired, or are having pleasant thoughts—by the end of the first year these rhythmic patterns seem to have changed in purpose. Now they have become a means of relieving tension and are used when the child is angry, frustrated, tired, bored, or hungry. This tension-relieving aspect of rhythm continues throughout life and is useful for all of us, the basis, it seems, of many habits that serve to release tension.

Sooner or later, of course, these rhythmic activities meet with interference from adults who are annoyed or even alarmed by the disturbance they make, and pressure is put on the children to stop them. No matter what ingenious devices are employed, however, they are typically ineffective in stopping these activities. The children may *seem* to conform to the wishes of the adults around them but they do not actually give up the rhythmic patterns— they simply substitute others. Tooth grinding, ear pulling, finger tapping, nose rubbing, and other newer, more disguised forms of repetitive activity now evolve, and may continue for a long time. The reach toward the comforts that rhythm brings seems too deeply entrenched to be easily abandoned.

To find out whether the sound of the human adult heartbeat, similar to the sound of the mother's heartbeat which the child has become accustomed to before birth, might have a particularly soothing effect on newborn infants, Lee Salk (1973) studied a large group of newborns in a hospital nursery, observing them from immediately following their birth until they were four days old. These infants were treated according to the ordinary routine of the nursery with one exception: they were continuously played a tape recording of a normal adult heartbeat sound (72 beats per minute) over an intercom, without interruption, day and night, for the first four days of their lives.

Salk had originally intended to have another group of infants hear the heartbeat speeded up to an abnormally fast sound (128 beats per minute) but quickly discontinued this part of the experiment. This speeded-up heart rate turned out to be so upsetting to the infants that their crying increased dramatically, and they showed other agitated behavior. For the sake of comparison, Salk selected a group of newborns for whom no tapes were played at all during the first four days in the nursery. These infants were simply treated according to regular hospital routine.

Results showed that 72 percent of the infants who heard the heartbeat rhythm increased in body weight over the first four days, as against 33 percent of the infants who did not hear the heartbeat rhythm—a highly significant difference. Crying was heard in the nursery only 38 percent of the time among those children who were listening to the heartbeat rhythm as against 60 percent of the time among those children who did not hear the heartbeat played. Since there was no difference between the two groups in the amount of food they consumed, the weight gain in the experimental group was of particular interest. Salk suggested that the fact that the more contented group had less exercise from crying might account for their weight gain. He theorized that the mother's heartbeat is one of the major sounds heard by the fetus before birth and that the unborn infant may have learned to associate these rhythmical heartbeat sounds with the relatively tension-free state in the womb. After birth, the mother's heartbeat (or other similar rhythms) may be soothing because of this early conditioning.

Meerloo (1969), reasoning along somewhat the same lines, has also suggested that the unborn child's early experiences with heartbeat rhythms may be the basis for the profoundly soothing effects of poetry, music, and dance. Perhaps, he says, these rhythmic experiences are all grounded in "various reminiscent feelings of a lost long ago and far away happiness."

Aside from the fact that we may have learned to connect natural rhythms with the soothing experiences before birth, it is also possible that we may instinctively find those regular rhythms that approximate the normal rhythms of our own bodies to be deeply comforting becasue, physiologically, they signify that "all is well." A study conducted at Princeton University set out to investigate this possibility by looking at the way in which undergraduate college students responded to various types of syncopated (two-beat) rhythms sounded on a drum (Markowitz, 1974). These drumbeats were first regulated as to speed and then recorded on tape so that five different speeds were obtained.

Markowitz wanted to find out what effect various rhythms might have on the mood of the listener—whether people responded differently to rhythms that were closer to the speed of the normal heartbeat than they did to those that were farther from it. The results supported the notion that adults are most comfortable with rhythms within the normal adult heartbeat range. The subjects rated rhythms in this range (the recorded speeds of 60 and 72 beats per minute) as making them feel "relaxed," whereas they rated rhythms that were either much faster or much slower than the normal heartbeat range as making them feel "tense" and "anxious."

These soothing effects of bodily rhythms may help explain some of the deeply calming effects of meditation. Repetition of the mantra is a profoundly rhythmic activity, as is one's own breathing. Even as the meditator is paying attention to his or her particular meditational focus, other rhythms such as heartbeat and respiration often come sharply into awareness during meditation. We may be more profoundly aware of these natural rhythms then than at any other time. In a questionnaire distributed to meditators, 74 percent of those who responded reported being more aware of bodily processes such as breathing and heartbeat during meditation than they were ordinarily, and 43 percent said they were *far* more aware of such processes during that time. By contrast, only 26 percent reported that they were less aware of bodily processes during meditation or that they saw no change.

Not surprisingly, a number of meditational techniques have made these natural bodily rhythms their object of focus. Zazen meditation demands careful attention to one's breathing, and the techniques of Hatha Yoga (the Yoga of "postures" or physical exercises) are based on a subtle coordination between physical activity and breathing—a coordination that most of us tend to lose during our waking life. When their actions and breath are in harmony, breathing becomes a central regulating rhythm that gives many people a feeling of centeredness and calm.

Even when attention is not consciously directed to these bodily rhythms, there seems to be a natural tendency to focus upon them. During regular mantra meditation, although the subjects we questioned had never been instructed to link their mantra to their breathing rhythm (in fact, they were told not to make any effort to do this), 76 percent of the meditators who filled out the questionnaire reported that their mantra spontaneously linked itself to the rhythm of their breathing, either sometimes or often, and 6 percent said it was always linked to breathing. Only 18 percent said the mantra was never linked to it.

Regularly repeating the mantra, or other repetitive meditational devices, or giving attention to the rise and fall of the breath can create a deep sense of calm. By inducing natural rhythms during meditation, rhythms only as rapid or as slow as the meditator wishes them to be at the moment, we may be extending an intuitive knowledge of the calming effects of rhythm to an activity appropriate for adults as well as children. Meditation may be one of the most comforting of the rhythmical activities available to us after childhood ends, restoring, through its lulling repetitions, a natural balance between tension and repose.

Meditation and Shift in Cognitive Mode

Shifts occur during meditation—radical shifts in perspective, more subtle changes in energy utilization. These can be looked upon as direct and purposeful adjustments, shifting the meditator's entire tuning apparatus to a different wave-length that he is not accustomed to. One important aspect of meditation appears to be a change in cognitive mode. During meditation the verbal, logical "self" that reasons in orderly sequences and is highly aware of time is replaced by a consciousness that is usually encountered only under special circumstances such as sleep onset, when the mind drifts among images and impressions whose content and meaning are known only intuitively. The awareness of meditation operates in a dim but intimate world, removed from considerations of time or involvement with past or future. During meditation, interior speech is either stilled or relegated to a background role, while images and an awareness of space are often the most vivid aspects of experience.

These facts suggest a shift in dominance between the two cerebral hemispheres. As is well known, the left side of the brain tends to be proficient in language and to handle linear thinking such as that involved in mathematics, thinking that is primarily analytical in nature. The right side of the brain excels in the recognition of faces, and in the estimation of space, and is holistic and synthetic in its approach.

The ASCs that occur during meditation raise certain questions, such as whether normal people can suffer from a conflict between the two halves of their brain, whether one of the hemispheres sometimes interferes with the smooth functioning of the other, and whether one hemisphere struggles to "right a balance" if the other side has usurped too much control. If so, a technique that would reduce the dissidence between the hemispheres and bring them into a more harmonious working relationship with each other might be expected to aid emotional adjustment and the integration of the total personality. While the relationship between meditation and hemispheric dominance is not yet clear, the possibility of a harmonizing of the two hemispheres during meditation is suggested by research in several different laboratories.

On the basis of their EEG studies with TM meditators, Glueck and Stroebel (1975) concluded that meditation may have its greatest impact on the individual because of a harmonizing of brain waves from all parts of the brain (including both hemispheres). Studying the EEG of experienced TM meditators, they found that as these people began to meditate, the density of alpha waves recorded increased rapidly. What was particularly interesting was the extent of the brain that appeared to be caught up in this alpha rhythm. The alpha waves "swept forward" until they involved the entire dominant hemisphere of the brain, including the frontal areas. Then, within a relatively short period of time (frequently no more than one or two minutes), the opposite hemisphere showed the same prominent alpha rhythm— the brain waves of both hemispheres were now in synchrony.

Confirming these findings, Banquet (1973) observed the same marked uniformity of electrical activity from all areas of the brain. He reported that during meditation, subjects' alpha waves rapidly spread synchronously (in phase with one another) from the back to the front of the brain, and that after about five minutes of meditating, recordings indicated that the dominant and the "silent" hemispheres of the brain were now in phase with one another. This kind of "hypersynchrony," as he called it, is usually seen only with different, slower varieties of brain waves and in states of drowsiness or sleep. It is unusual for a person in the alert awake state to have brain waves synchronized in this fashion. The implication is that during meditation the two hemispheres of the brain may be able to "work together" in a fashion not possible under other circumtances. By encouraging this synchrony between the two halves of the brain, meditation may foster the integration of the two basic modes of thinking—the analytical (left hemispheric) mode and the synthesizing and intuitive (right hemispheric) mode.

Man's highest achievements obviously require the complementary workings of thought processes from both sides of the brain. Intuition and hunches must be shaped through logical, disciplined thinking to form a work of art, and the most rigorous scientific and philosophical reasoning requires the enrichening leaven of hunch and inspiration. We need a harmony, a coming together of our two "selves" into one mind. Perhaps such an integration is one reason for the sense of "wholeness" experienced by meditators who respond to the technique positively.

Deposing the Ego

Another way to view the shift in mode of thinking during meditation is to see it as a move away from control by the ego. The ego is something constructed carefully, slowly, and painstakingly from infancy on. Forming it is somewhat like building a house by hand—lifting each brick, weighing it in the hands, trying it out in a particular place, fitting it in, and then cementing it. The structure develops gradually.

The ego is not static as a building is, however. It is a decision-making apparatus that enables us to weigh each thing we do, monitoring our acts to ensure that we behave both consistently and in a manner appropriate to the situation. It is a bookkeeper, calculating the psychological and physical costs of each act contemplated. It is a consultant, predicting future trends on the basis of past experience. It is an executive, organizing the days, hours, and minutes. As an executive, it is empowered to establish priorities, grant exceptions, mete out rewards and punishments, offer incentives for hard work, and plan for future expansion.

Up to a certain point the ego serves us. Beyond that point, the balance may shift, and we may begin to serve *it*. If the ego is in control *all* of the time, then direct experience is diminished as a welter of decisions begin to interpose themselves between even the simplest sense experiences and our own selves. The superstructure weighs each incoming impression, decides to file it under a particular category, and acts according to "the rules" when processing it. The machinery becomes so smooth that we need never contaminate ourselves by the uncertainty of the new; everything falls into place and is processed efficiently. As a result, life becomes mechanized; our tastebuds dull, our vision flattens, and our thoughts loose vitality. All contingencies are taken care of—but are we any longer fully alive?

Lost in a complex web of ego concerns, we all too often allow to slip from us a simple capacity for total experiencing. The revival of this lost capacity may be one of the most valuable assets of meditation. Arthur Deikman (1969) considers it to be an essential factor in meditation. He speaks about "deautomatization," which is the opposite of "automatization"—the natural process of making our activities, both physical and mental, automatic so that we can perform them without having to think about them.

Automatization is useful, but overautomatization can lead to difficulty.

When too large a portion of our experience is automatized, we become a walking bundle of habits. We apparently need both a necessary amount of automatization and a healthy degree of nonautomatization to allow us to experience life fully. Meditation may help us restore this balance by deautomatizing some of our ways of thinking and perceiving.

To investigate this possibility, Deikman taught subjects to meditate using a blue vase as a meditational focus. The instructions were to concentrate on seeing the vase "as it exists in itself without any connection with other things." The subjects were to exclude all other thoughts or sensations and let the perception of the vase "fill their entire mind."

The subjects who participated in the experiment reported that in the course of a series of meditation sessions, their perception of the vase changed markedly. Often its color became deeper, more vivid or "luminous." Sometimes it changed form, becoming larger or smaller, or distorted in shape. At times it seemed to become two-dimensional, its boundaries blurred, or it melted into the background. In some cases it seemed to move. One subject reported that she had "merged with the vase," losing her sense of individual identity. Following the meditation session, another subject looked out of the window at a park below and reported seeing things in a most unusual fashion. The objects on the landscape looked " . . . scattered all over the lot, not hung together in any way." Later he explained that "the view didn't organize itself in any way . . . there were no planes, one behind the other . . . everything was working at the same intensity . . . like a bad painting which I didn't know about until I got used to it so I could begin to pick out what was going on in the painting. I didn't see the order to it or the pattern to it or anything and I couldn't impose it, it resisted my imposition of pattern" (Deikman, 1969, pp. 207–208).

Deikman concluded that in the above instance this man's experience resulted from a "deautomatization of the brain's structures"—a radical change in the learned patterns that ordinarily provide visual organization of a landscape. Apparently his ability to focus attention selectively was also deautomatized, for each thing in the landscape *equally* claimed his attention, none of them standing out while others receded. Normal figure–ground perception also seemed to be deautomatized—the planes did not recede.

While the deautomatization of these subjects did not carry over into their ordinary waking life for more than a short period following meditation, what remained were pleasant feelings of newness, aliveness, closeness to the subjects' own feelings and to the world. The deautomization of meditation does not therefore appear to be an end in itself, but a means to an end—that of allowing a reorganization to take place within the personality.

Deikman stresses the fact that the breakdown of automatization that took place in his subjects did not occur at random, nor was it a destructive force.

It seemed directed toward a specific purpose—to permit the adult to gain a new, fresh perception of the world by freeing him temporarily from ingrained habitual ways of experiencing that had him trapped. In this way the constructive, creative forces within the person, those forces that seek to build, grow, and put together experiences in new and richer ways, may be given access to fresh material. This material comes from both the imagination and the senses, and comprises a new way of looking at experience. Deautomatization is not to be looked upon as a way of losing ground or regressing, but rather as the undoing of a pattern "in order to permit a new and perhaps more advanced experience" (Deikman, 1969, p. 217).

Deikman points out that while drugs and extreme forms of sensory deprivation may produce similar types of deautomatization, the effects achieved through these external means appear to be not nearly so long-lasting and are not so deeply inspiring or meaningful as those produced by the individual himself, through his own efforts, as he meditates over long periods of time. It seems to be that when taken in small doses, worked at conscientiously, and kept under voluntary control, the deautomatization process can be used to enable the person to gain freedom to rebuild his approach to life in a meaningful manner.

Blank-out

Another aspect of the change in consciousness that results from meditation may be related to what Ornstein (1972) has referred to as the "blank-out" of meditation. He proposed that forms of concentrative meditation, where stimulus input is intentionally limited, may create a situation similar to that which occurs when the eye is prevented from its continuous roving over the visual field, being instead forced to view a constant fixed image without recourse to scanning. When in a laboratory an image is projected onto a contact lens placed over the retina, the lens now follows the movements of the eye so that the new image becomes stabilized in the center of the visual field. Under such conditions the image soon becomes invisible; without constant shifting of the eyes to different parts of the perceived image, the subject's mind apparently cannot register the object. At this point, which Ornstein refers to as blank-out, prolonged bursts of alpha waves may be recorded in the occipital cortex.

It seems that the central nervous system is so constructed that if awareness of any sort is restricted to one unchanging source of stimulation, consciousness of the external world may then be turned off, and a form of mental blank-out is achieved. Mantra meditation, for example, involves continuously recycling the same input over and over, and not surprisingly it may result in a blank-out effect, which in turn has the effect of temporarily clearing the mind of all thoughts. The after-effect of blank-out may be an opening up of awareness, a renewed *sensitivity* to stimuli. After meditation, some meditators seem to experience an innocence of perception similar to that of the young child who is maximally receptive to all stimuli.

Although Ornstein does not address himself to the therapeutic implications of the blank-out effect, it is evident that at the least such a phenomenon might break up an unproductive mental set and give the meditator the opportunity to restructive his thoughts along more productive lines. This could result in a fresh point of view on emotional problems, as well as on other aspects of life. Also, becoming more open to direct sensory experience may in itself be valuable in a world beset by problems deriving from overemphasis on cognitive activity. The enlivened experiencing following meditation (often described by meditators as "seeing colors more clearly," "hearing sounds more sharply," or "sensing the world more vividly") may be a prime reason for the antidepressive effects of meditation.

Energy Shifts during Meditation

Any discussion of the changes that take place in meditation would be incomplete without mention of some of the reasons for these changes, as advanced by the great meditative traditions. Because these explanations are usually presented as dogma, not as hypotheses, it is customary for scientists to dismiss them out of hand. However, these influential belief systems deserve consideration.

The Yoga concept of prana is central to the Indian view of meditation and its effects. It is such a broad, all-inclusive concept, however, that it is exceedingly hard for the Western mind to grasp. Prana refers at once to a number of seemingly different things. It is said to be the vital energy or breath drawn into the body through the lungs, the vital energy absorbed through meditation, and ultimately a universal breath or energy of which the individual's energy field is "but one manifestation."

Prana is said to be present in all forms of matter from inert minerals to man himself. While it permeates matter, however, it is not matter, but rather an energy or force that animates it. This universal energy is thought to be manifested as gravitation and electricity, as muscular energy, as the energy that radiates through nerve impulses, and as the energy underlying thought processes. Both the driving force that animates pure thought and the driving force behind the simplest mechanical movement are but different manifestations of prana; and air, food, water, and light are in turn media through which prana is carried. Thus we are said to absorb prana through the food we eat, the liquids we drink, and the air we breathe. Prana can also penetrate totally and directly without recourse to these mediating factors. The whole body, in fact, is said to be controlled by prana, which in turn regulates every cell. Describing the overwhelming all-inclusiveness of this concept, Swami Vishnudevananda says:

If we look at the vast ocean, we see big or small waves arise and dissolve with innumerable small bubbles. But, the background of all these waves and bubbles is the same vast ocean. Everything from the smallest bubble to the biggest waves is connected with the ocean though in appearance they differ. Similarly every human being or animal or plant is connected with the infinite ocean of energy or prana. In reality, wherever there is motion and life, behind (this) there is the storehouse of pranic energy. (Vishnudevananda, 1960)

In the Yoga tradition, various forms of meditation are designed to open up blocks said to prevent the free flow of prana through the living being. While this view of meditation usually applies to the more advanced techniques used for spiritual development, a modified view relating to the practical Westernized forms of meditation is also possible. It is not inconceivable that some as yet unidentified energy exchange may take place during meditation. Theories of energy transfer are becoming more sophisticated. The effects of cosmic energy fields operating over vast distances are, for example, being systematically studied in such disciplines as biometeorology. If there is such an energy transfer in meditation, however, it must follow laws very different from those of the limited, readily observable energy forms that we know, such as electricity. A fundamental energy source, if it exists, could probably be studied only through extremely subtle means by techniques not yet available to science. Perhaps a type of energy transformation such as implied in the concept of prana is not so far removed from the concepts of mass–energy transformations that underlie the notions of modern theoretical physics. The presence of unknown forms of energy is not an unfamiliar concept to scientists working on discovering the properties of invisible and immaterial force fields. For this reason we should maintain an open-mindedness toward those explanations of meditation that conceive of the practice in terms of either the transfer or stabilizing of energy systems, or as a merging of individual energy systems with much broader energy fields. Were such concepts to prove correct, in whole or in part, they would represent an important, indeed a fundamental, aspect of meditation.

The Zen concept of the Individual Mind or Little Mind (the ego) merging during meditation into what is described as Big Mind draws upon similar reasoning and is derived from the same source—the intuitively conceived views of persons in states of altered consciousness, often during meditation.

These views suggest a certain parallelism with some concepts in modern physics which conceive of the universe as looking, in the words of Sir James Jeans (1937), "more like a great thought than like a great machine." At present, however, we still have to consider this concept as belonging to the realm of metaphysics rather than to the spheres of physics or biology, its relationship to scientific inquiry remaining, as yet, no more than a speculative one.

Meditation, then, is a time when the organism shifts gears from the active to the receptive mode; from a state of ego dominance to a state where the ego is subordinate and can be partially dispensed with; from a state of automatization to one of deautomatization. It may also be a time when the organism experiences a shift from the dominance of one cerebral hemisphere to a state of concordance or harmony between both hemispheres of the brain; and perhaps a time when it experiences a shift from limited contact with some as yet unidentified energy source toward a more fundamental contact, or "flowing with," that source.

Whatever the status of some of these conjectures turns out to be, one thing is certain: a change from our ordinary way of experiencing, that in many respects is fundamental, goes on during meditation.

Meditation and Desensitization

There is an interesting similarity between what occurs during a meditation session and what occurs during systematic desensitization used in behavior therapy. During the latter, increasing increments of anxiety (prepared in a graded hierarchy) are systematically "counterconditioned" by being paired with an induced state of deep relaxation. If the treatment is successful, presentation of the originally disturbing stimuli will no longer produce anxiety.

In meditation, the meditative "focus," whether it be a mantra, breathing, or a candle flame, becomes a signal for turning attention inward and bringing about a state of deep relaxation. Meditators then maintain a permissive attitude with respect to thoughts, images, or sensations experienced during meditation. They neither reject nor unduly hold onto them, but merely let these impressions "flow through the mind," either simultaneously with their focus of meditation or alternating with it.

This process sets up a subjective state in which the deep relaxation brought about by attention to the meditative focus is paired with a rapid, self-initiated review of an exceedingly wide variety of mental contents and tension areas, both verbal and nonverbal. As thoughts, images, sensations, and amorphous impressions drift by during meditation, the meditative focus seems to neutralize their effects, so that no matter how unsettling a meditation session may *feel*—and occasional sessions may actually be experienced as turbulent—meditators frequently say they find themselves emerging from meditation with the "charge" taken off their current concerns or problems, and that this enables them to cope with these problems more effectively.

Do the modern forms of meditation "work" because they are just versions of systematic desensitization? While there are points of resemblance between the two techniques, there would seem to be important differences as well. In systematic desensitization, a therapist and patient, working together, identify specific areas of anxiety and then proceed to deal with a series of single, isolated problems in a step-by-step, organized fashion. In meditation, the areas of anxiety to be "desensitized" are selected automatically by the responding organism, the meditating person. The brain of the meditator appears to behave during meditation as though it were a computer programmed to run relevant material through "demagnetizing" circuits, handling large amounts of data at one time. We might conceptualize subsystems within the brain as scanning vast memory stores at lightning speed with the aim of selecting those contents of the mind that are: first, most pressing emotionally; second, most likely to be tolerated without undue anxiety; and third, best able to be handled currently. The decision to surface certain mental contents rather than others for "demagnetizing" would presumably be made by automatically weighing such considerations as the above and arriving at an optimal compromise.

The process of meditation would thus give meditation a clear advantage over systematic desensitization when it comes to the scope of material that could be dealt with at one time. Systematic desensitization may be the most efficient treatment if we want to get at a limited problem such as a phobia, but for handling a wide range of interrelated problems, meditation may be more efficient. As Goleman (1971) has suggested, it may be a "global" form of desensitization.

Self as "Being"

Meditation is surprisingly complete in itself. When we are in this state, the outer world may threaten us, or sights and sounds may pound for attention, but we recognize that none of this fundamentally changes "who" we are. Through it all, the quiet intake and outflow of breath goes on, the gentle rhythms of our pulse coordinate with the beat of our mantra or with the motion of our breathing, and we know that whatever else may or may not happen, *life goes on.*

This sense of sureness about our existence tends to linger with us after meditation and may change our perspective in many ways. Matters that were formerly distressing may shrink to relative unimportance alongside this immediate experience of livingness, and this lesson in turn may lay the base for a new sense of identity, a new awareness of strengths and resources, and increased feelings of personal rights—developments that are often reported by meditators.

During meditation we are also learning not to force our minds or bodies to do what we "want" them to do or what we believe they "should" do; instead we are learning to follow gently where *they* lead. This experience of trusting the wisdom of our own inner selves makes meditation an unusual experience for the average Westerner. Our society encourages us to manage ourselves as though we were objects, to force ourselves to do things (or not to do them). This may be the by-product of a culture that measures work efficienty in terms of speed of production—the more one forces, presumably, the greater the profits. Many personal problems, therefore, may be products of a pathological time-oriented culture. In an agricultural society, people learn to have patience with the slow and compelling rhythms of nature, and so may develop a somewhat different attitude—a greater appreciation for the value of waiting and watching, of flowing with the stream rather than fighting it. Meditation may serve us by leading us back to such a receptive attitude; for we cannot meditate if we *try* to meditate, but can do so only if we *permit* meditation to occur.

In the sex therapies, for example, increasing emphasis is placed on teaching people to forget about trying to achieve orgasm (or to achieve at all) (Kaplan, 1974). Instead, they are instructed to view the various sensations they experience as a leisurely, nonstriving play experience, free of all demands and judgments about performing "correctly" or "incorrectly"—an experience without goals, with every step its own reward. This seems to lead to the ultimate in pleasure and intimacy between partners and is essentially an expression of the "meditative mood" in the sexual experience. When a person finally stops trying to be a lover, and experiences the luxury of having fun, when he or she "lets" everything happen and "makes" nothing happen, then the natural wisdom of the self takes over, and a fulfilling sexual experience is achieved.

Meditation helps people to achieve a nonstriving, natural approach in many different types of activities.

Learning Self-Permissiveness

Self-blame may be reduced through another aspect of meditation. Although children are often made to feel ashamed by looks and gestures of others around them, even before they can understand language, they are usually *scolded* through words. In this manner they come to blame themselves elaborately in verbal terms, mentally repeating: "I'm a bad child"; "I'm sloppy," "dirty," "dumb," "selfish," or whatever other disapproving terms they have learned to apply to themselves. The phrase "a still small voice" to refer to one's conscience is therefore well chosen; our conscience is in many respects a "voice." If we tune down the language centers during meditation and allow the wordless aspects of experience to come to the forefront of our consciousness, we tend to take the teeth out of much of our self-blame.

Reports of meditators show that during meditation, self-criticism seems to recede, along with other abstract verbal concepts, until it remains only a distant whisper. Simultaneously there seems to be desensitization during meditation of the wordless experiences of shame from early childhood. This two-pronged attack on self-blame—the reduction of self-critical statements and the removal of the "charge" from early nonverbal shame experiences—can be a powerful one, and it is interesting that when meditating, we are often able to experience even the least desirable aspects of ourselves without anxiety. We seem to readmit them to awareness, "make friends" with them, as it were, during meditation, and in this way begin to exert constructive control over them.

These and other aspects of meditation may constitute a profound self-reeducation. Repeated daily over a period of time, meditation may produce a conglomerate of experiences and attitudes that can affect one's outlook in fundamental ways.

Meditation then is a special kind of ASC. Practiced intentionally and systematically over time, it can profoundly affect a person's life, becoming an important tool that shapes the meditator's adjustment, both to the society in which he or she lives and to the meditator's own self.

REFERENCES

Appelle, S. and Oswald, L. E. Simple reaction time as a function of alertness and prior mental activity. *Perceptual and Motor Skills,* 1974, *38,* 1263–1268.

Azima, H. and Cramer, F. J. Effects of decrease in sensory variability on body scheme. *Canadian Journal of Psychiatry,* 1956, *1,* 59–72.

Banquet, J. Spectral analysis of the EEG in meditation. *Electroencephalography and Clinical Neurophysiology, 1973, 35,* 143–151.

Benson, H. *The relaxation response.* New York: William Morrow, 1975.

Benson, H. and Wallace, R. K. Decreased blood pressure in hypertensive subjects who practiced meditation. *Circulation,* Supplement II to vols. *45,* and *46,* p. 516, 1972.

Bexton, W., and Scott, T. H. Effects of decreased variation in the sensory environment. *Canadian Journal of Psychology,* 1954, *8,* 70–76.

Brownfield, C. A. *The brain benders.* Jericho, N.Y.: Exposition Press, 1972.

Carrington, P. *Freedom in meditation,* New York: Anchor Press/Doubleday, 1977; Doubleday Paperback, 1978.

Carrington, P. *Clinically standardized meditation (CSM) instructor's kit.* Kendall Park, N.J.: Pace Educational Systems, 1979.

Carrington, P. and Ephron, H. S. Meditation as an adjunct to psychotherapy. In S. Arieti (Ed.), *New dimensions in psychiatry: A world view*. New York: Wiley, 1975a, pp. 262–291.

Carrington, P. and Ephron, H. S. Clinical use of meditation. In J. H. Masserman (Ed.), *Current psychiatric therapies*, vol. 15. New York: Grune & Stratton, 1975b, pp. 101–108.

Chertok, L. and Kramarz, P. Hypnosis, sleep and electroencephalography. *Journal of Nervous and Mental Disease*, 1959, *128*, 227–238.

Conze, E. *Buddhist meditation*. New York: Harper, 1969, p. 83.

Deikman, A. J. Experimental meditation. In C. T. Tart (Ed.), *Altered states of consciousness*. New York: Wiley, 1969, pp. 199–218.

Doane, B. K. et al. Changes in perceptual function after isolation. *Canadian Journal of Psychology*, 1959, *13*, 210–219.

Edington, G. As quoted in Carrington, P., *Freedom in Meditation*. New York: Anchor Press/Doubleday, 1977, p. 4.

Glueck, B. C. and Stroebel, C. F. Biofeedback and meditation in the treatment of psychiatric illness. *Comprehensive Psychiatry*, 1975, *16*, 302–321.

Goleman, D. Meditation as a meta-therapy: hypothesis toward a proposed fifth state of consciousness. *Journal of Transpersonal Psychology*, 1971, *3*, 1–25.

Goleman, D. J. and Schwartz, G. E. Meditation as an intervention in stress reactivity. *Journal of Consulting and Clinical Psychology*, 1976, *44*, 456–466.

Harris, A. Sensory deprivation and schizophrenia. *Journal of Mental Science*, 1959, *105*, 235–237.

Hines, M. As cited in Carrington, P. *Freedom in Meditation*, New York: Anchor Press/Doubleday, 1977, p. 218.

Honesberger, R. W. and Wilson, A. F. Transcendental meditation in treating asthma. *Respiratory Therapy: The Journal of Inhalation Technology*, 1973, *3*, 79–80.

Jeans, J. *The mysterious universe*. Cambridge: Cambridge University Press, 1937, p. 122.

Kaplan, H. S. *The new sex therapy*. New York: Brunner/Mazel, 1974.

Kasamatsu, A. and Hirai, T. An electroencephalographic study on the zen meditation (zazen). In C. T. Tart (Ed.), *Altered states of consciousness*. New York: Wiley, 1969, pp. 489–501.

Kleitman, N. *Sleep and wakefulness*. Chicago: University of Chicago Press, 1963, pp. 329–338.

Kripke, D. F. and Sonnenschein, D. A 90 minute daydream cycle. *Sleep Research*, 1973, *2*, 187–190.

Lilly, J. C. and Shurly, J. T. Experiments in solitude in maximum achievable physical isolation with water suspension of intact, healthy persons. Paper read, in part, at symposium on Sensory Deprivation, Harvard University Medical School, Boston, 1958.

Lourie, R. S. The role of rhythm patterns. In *The five-minute hour*. Ardsley, N.Y.: Geigy Pharmaceuticals, Jan. 1976.

Ludwig, A. M. Sensory overload and psychopathology. *Diseases of the Nervous System*, 1975, *36*, 357–360.

Markowitz, J. The effects of an externally generated rhythm on mood. Senior thesis, Princeton University, 1974.

Maslow, A. J. *Toward a psychology of being*. Princeton, N.J.: D. Van Nostrand, 1962 (rev. ed. 1968).

Maslow, A. J. As quoted in Shor, R. E. Hypnosis and the concept of the generalized reality-orientation. In C. T. Tart (Ed.). *Altered states of consciousness*. New York: Wiley, 1969, p. 249.

Maupin, E. W. Meditation. In H. A. Otto and J. Mann (Eds.), *Ways of growth*. New York: Viking Press, 1968, pp. 189–198.

Meerlo, J. A. The universal language of rhythm. In J. J. Leedy (Ed.), *Poetry therapy*. Philadelphia: Lippincott, 1969, pp. 52–66.

Miskiman, D. E. Long-term effects of the transcendental meditation program in the treatment of insomnia. In D. W. Orme-Johnson and J. T. Farrow (Eds.), *Scientific Research on the Transcendental Meditation Program: Collected Papers, Vol. I.* New York: MIU Press, 1978, pp. 331–334.

Ornstein, R. *The psychology of consciousness.* San Francisco: W. H. Freeman Co., 1972.

Pelletier, K. R. Influence of TM upon autokinetic perception. *Perceptual and Motor Skills,* 1974, *39,* 1031–1034.

Pirot, M. The effects of transcendental meditation technique upon auditory discrimination. In D. W. Orme-Johnson and J. T. Farrow (Eds.), (see above), 1978, pp. 331–334.

Rajneesh, G. S. *Dynamics of meditation.* Bombay: Life Awakening Movement Publications, 1972, p. 130.

Rimol, A. G. P. The transcendental meditation technique and its effects on sensory–motor performance. In D. W. Orme-Johnson and J. T. Farrow (Eds.), *Scientific Research on the Transcendental Meditation Program: Collected Papers, Vol. I.* New York: MIU Press, 1978, pp. 326–330.

Salk, L. The role of the heartbeat in the relations between mother and infant. *Scientific American,* Mar. 1973, 24–29.

Shafii, M., Lavely, R. A., and Jaffe, R. D. Meditation and marijuana. *American Journal of Psychiatry,* 1974, *131,* 60–63.

Shafii, M., Lavely, R. A., and Jaffe, R. D. Meditation and the prevention of alcohol abuse. *American Journal of Psychiatry,* 1975, *132,* 942–945.

Shafii, M., Lavely, R. A., and Jaffe, R. D. Verminderung von zigarettenrauchen also folgc transzendentaler meditation (Decrease of smoking following meditation). *Maharishi European Research University Journal,* 1976, *24,* 29.

Shor, R. E. Hypnosis and the concept of the generalized reality-orientation. In C. T. Tart (Ed.), *Altered states of consciousness,* New York: Wiley, 1969, pp. 233–250.

Visnudevananda, S. *The complete illustrated book of yoga.* New York: Julian Press, 1960, p. 226.

White, R. A preface to a theory of hypnotism, *Jouranl of Abnormal and Social Psychology,* 1941, *36,* 477–506.

Woolfolk, R. L., Carr-Kaffashan, K., Lehrer, P. M., et al. Meditation training as a treatment for insomnia. *Behavior Therapy,* 1976, *7,* 359–365.

Zamarra, J. W., Besseghini, I., and Wittenberg, S. The effects of the transcendental meditation program on the exercise performance of patients with angina pectoris. In D. W. Orme-Johnson and J. T. Farrow (Eds.), *Scientific Research on the Transcendental Meditation Program: Collected Papers, Vol. I.* New York: MIU Press. 1978, pp. 270–278.

17. Access to Dreams

Montague Ullman

INTRODUCTION

The viewpoint expressed in this chapter is based on the premise that, because dreaming is a universal human experience, our dreams should be universally accessible. Since most of us grow up quite ignorant about the nature of our dream life, the question of accessibility involves a certain amount of preliminary learning. This would include a knowledge of the basic facts about dreaming, the problems faced by the dreamer on awakening, the needs created by these problems, and the way that others can be of help in meeting these needs.

Many books about dreams have been addressed to the general public. They have either stressed the psychoanalytic theory of dreams and the special knowledge needed to interpret them (Freud, 1921), or, while seemingly explaining the nature of our dream life, implied that a special knowledgeable guide was indispensable (Jung, 1933) or offered a more readily understandable account of one or another theoretical approach to dreams (Hall, 1953; Mahoney, 1976). Two writers of distinguished psychoanalytic backgrounds (Fromm, 1951; Rycroft, 1979) have sought to denude dreams of some of the awe and mystery that classical psychoanalytic theory enshrouded them with in the minds of the public. Fromm, critical of both Freud's and Jung's view, tried to project the dream as an expression of the self in a natural but forgotten language. Rycroft further delivered the dream from its instinctual casing by his emphasis on the dreamer's use of the language of metaphor.

A Swedish writer whose work is not well known in this country also disassociated himself from psychoanalytic theory and wrote of the dream as a natural healing system (Bjerre, 1933). A strong aesthetic sense and a broad range of clinical experience brought Bjerre to a view that broke with the classical notion of the dream as regressive in nature and enabled him to grasp what he felt to be the essence of our dream life, namely, that dream images are healing images.

In recent years there has been a spate of books that encourage a more widespread interest in dreams. They stress the value of dream work and offer one or another technique for acquiring skill in understanding one's dreams (Sanford, 1968; Faraday, 1972, 1974; Delaney, 1979; Taylor, 1983). These books are addressed to the individual dreamer, and the techniques offered are those that generally could be applied by the dreamer him- or herself.

My own point of view (Ullman and Zimmerman, 1979), which I did not find sufficiently developed in the literature, departs in three ways from the way that the public was being informed about dreams. First, while the dream is a most personal and private communication, the dreamer *has* to go public with it in order to appreciate its fullest meaning. Second, a small-group setting is the most favorable arrangement for dream work. Third, the skills necessary for a group to provide the special kind of help the dreamer needs are skills that can be developed by and shared with anyone, regardless of background.

Three questions arise: Why is a public setting necessary, why is the small group the public setting of choice, and what are the skills that have to be shared?

The Need to Socialize the Dream

I think it is important to distinguish between offering a technique that may be of help and actually getting across to the dreamer the importance of socializing dream work by providing a structure within which such social-ization can be pursued safely and effectively. As a social creature in his own right, the dreamer alone can socialize the dream up to a point with any one of a number of techniques. However, more can be gained through a prop-erly structured socializing process. While most techniques offered to the public take as their end point what the dreamer can do by himself, this should be seen only as the beginning of an adequate socialization of the dream. It has been my experience that, regardless of how far the dreamer can get on his own, an effective social context can offer a surprisingly richer yield.

What is meant by a public setting, and why do I consider the small group the public setting of choice?

By a public setting I mean sharing a dream with at least one other person.

Depending on the degree of intimacy of the two people involved, it will be more or less public in the ordinary sense of the term. The two-person situation prevails in individual psychotherapy or whenever another person is available to help the dreamer. More will be said about the former at a later time.

When a number of other people are involved in helping the dreamer, the question of the safety of the dreamer is paramount. While the dreamer may have a greater sense of safety in working within a single close relationship, a small group can, if the process is structured properly, also provide the safeguards necessary for the safety of the dreamer. In addition the group can help the dreamer make discoveries about himself that are difficult to make alone. The collective imagination of the group can produce a richer array of metaphorical possibilities relating to the dream imagery than a single individual can. Details of how this is done are given in the description of the process.

Working on a dream in a group enables the dreamer to move in two directions at once. It allows for the exploration of the immediate personal issues and, at the same time, fosters empathic contact with others through the reciprocal sharing that goes on between the dreamer and his helpers. The collective way of working with a dream facilitates a feeling of communion with others. The greater the degree of self-disclosure, the greater will be the responsiveness of the group and the deeper this feeling of communion. This is generally contrary to the expectation of newcomers, who often fear self-disclosure as possibly alienating others from them.

A further discussion of the significance of a group context will be given in the section comparing the experiential dream group and formal therapy.

While the foregoing are some of the reasons for the need for a social context in dream work, there are other factors at play of a more subtle and speculative nature. Our dreams confront us with the order and disorder that exists in our relationships with others and tell us something about their origins in earlier experience. Engaging in dream work in a social context provides the support we need to understand where we are as individuals in regard to this broader issue of "connectedness." While awake we engage individually and collectively in many acts that unknowingly impair, limit, hurt, corrode, corrupt, or destroy possibilities of connection. Our dream life addresses itself to the maintenance and repair of these connections by its capacity for honest display. It is as if that part of ourselves out of which these images flow is always in touch with the basic truth that, despite the fragmentation that has taken place among members of the human race down through history, we are still all members of a single species. As individuals we can survive and even thrive regardless of the level of dishonesty in our lives. Confronted as we are now with the difficulty of managing our enormous destructive power, the question is: can we survive as a species without a greater investment in honesty and honest connectedness among nations?

Speculations along these lines make me wonder if dreams are linked to a greater need, namely, that if we are to survive as a species we must do better than we have up to now in repairing the many ways we have ruptured connections between people. By unloading excessive and obstructive emotional baggage, by allowing ourselves to become more known, we achieve a greater freedom in human relationships and a greater respect for and tolerance of others. This need to share of ourselves is a natural human need that "civilized" cultures pay little attention to. Socializing our dreams is one way toward this goal. As we begin to deal more and more with the truth about ourselves, we increasingly recognize and discard self-deluding facades. I propose that what appears as collective dream work geared to the needs of the individual may, in fact, be linked to a deeper mechanism of species survival. If this is so, it is a fact of some importance, considering the precarious state of survival in which our species now finds itself.

Dreaming and the Dream

Those who engage in dream work for the first time need an orientation to the nature of our dream life and its derivation from the dreaming experience during sleep. The approach I follow is based on the following:

1. Consciousness in whatever form integrates afferent input and regulates efferent output.
2. Dreaming is that form of consciousness that occurs during sleep and is most characteristically, though not exclusively, associated with the rapid eye movement (REM) stage of sleep.
3. The input under the conditions of dreaming is internally generated out of recent and related remote experience.
4. The input is integrated not at a conceptual–linguistic level but at a sensory symbolic level, usually in the form of metaphorically expressive visual imagery but capable of employing any sensory modality.
5. The integrative process links present experience with related experiences from the past. Dreaming starts in the present with a recent residual feeling tone or memory that lingers on and surfaces during sleep to trigger the content.
6. The present experience, having this triggering power, has the quality of an intrusive novelty.
7. In response to this intrusive novelty, there is an information search to assess the significance of this event for the future of the organism.

The residue is explored in its connections to emotionally related though temporarily separated bits of the historical past, which are then woven into the imagery.

8. The moving pictorial display allows for the presentation of considerable information all at once.

9. The result of the information search is that the imagery contains a greater fund of information relevant to the current issue than is immediately available to the dreamer awake.

10. To assess the impact of the intrusive novelty for the future, this information has to be as accurate and reliable as possible. For this to be so, the imagery has to metaphorically reflect the actual impact of one's individual life experience on a current issue, in contrast to the way that issue may have been judged by the waking ego. Reaching into deeply felt aspects of one's life, dreaming thus provides a reliable portrait of that part of the dreamer's life that is under self-scrutiny at the moment.

11. Based on the imagery produced and the resulting feelings, the REM period may continue undisturbed until its natural termination, or, if the feelings are too disturbing, wakening may occur.*

What we refer to as the dream is the waking remembrance of the dreaming experience. It is not only a remembrance but also a transformation from a primarily pictorial to a primarily linguistic mode of expression.

In summary, the phenomenological characteristics pertaining to the content of the dreaming phase of the sleep cycle are:

1. The significance of a current tension as the starting point or focal issue around which the content will develop.

2. The ability of the dreamer to mobilize and include in the imagery relevant data from different epochs of his past.

3. The observation that the information so obtained is rooted in the emotional reality of the dreamer's life.

It is these features, along with an explanation of the metaphorical nature of the language of the dream, that should be stressed in orienting a layperson to dream work.

Skill Sharing

The identification of the skills that are needed in group dream work and how the sharing of them takes place will be presented in connection with a

---

*These thoughts have been further elaborated in various writings on the vigilance theory of dreaming (Ullman, 1961; Tolaas, 1978).

description of the group process I have been using. Suffice it to say that, if one teases the dream away from the metapsychological context that usually envelops it and stresses only the phenomenological aspects, those aspects define the skills necessary to engage the dreamer in effectively working with his dream.

PREMISES AND PRINCIPLES OF GROUP DREAM WORK

Certain underlying premises and principles have guided my work with dreams. These have arisen out of my earlier clinical experience and have been further validated by the group work I have been doing in recent years.

Premises

First Premise. Dreams are an intrapsychic communication that reveals in metaphorical form certain truths about the life of the dreamer that can be made available to the dreamer awake.

Second Premise. If we are fortunate enough to recall a dream, then we are ready, at some level, to be confronted by the information in that dream. This is true regardless of whether we choose to do so.

Third Premise. If the confrontation is allowed to happen in a proper manner, the effect is one of healing. The dreamer comes into contact with a part of himself that has not been explicitly acknowledged before. There has been movement toward wholeness.

Fourth Premise. Dreams can and should be universally accessible. Skills can be developed to extend dream work beyond the confines of the consulting room to the interested public at large.

Fifth Premise. Although the dream is a private communication, it needs a social context for its fullest realization. This does not mean that helpful work cannot be done working alone but rather, that a social context is a more powerful setting for the type of healing that can come about through dream work.

Principles

It bears emphasizing that dreams are an intrapsychic communication. Any process that is geared to their explication must respect that fact and the constraints it imposes. The process to be described has evolved with this in mind. It is geared to the expectations and needs of the dreamer as the one to whom the dream is given. Communicating the dream to a group is a secondary affair, necessary only to help the group make its contribution toward clarifying the original communication. It is in this connection that the following principles obtain.

First Principle: Respect for the Dreamer's Privacy. Since the dream is a most personal communication, the element of privacy is respected at all times. Each stage of the process is designed to be nonintrusive so that the group follows rather than leads the dreamer. The dreamer controls the process throughout the session and works at whatever level of self-disclosure he or she feels comfortable with in the group. There is no pressure to go beyond that point.

Second Principle: Respect for the Dreamer's Authority over His Dream. Dream images arise out of the unique life experiences of the dreamer. The fit between image and meaning is something that the dreamer alone can evaluate despite the possibility that he may accept or be led to accept something less than a true fit.

Third Principle: Respect for the Dreamer's Uniqueness. Everyone's life experience is unique. Any symbolic image can be used in a highly idiosyncratic way. No a priori categorical meanings are assumed.

THE EXPERIENTIAL DREAM GROUP

The remainder of this chapter will be devoted to a description of a small group approach to dream work, its rationale, its relationship to more formal psychotherapeutic work with dreams, and the extension of dream work into the community. The emphasis for the purposes of this chapter will be on the latter.

What follows is a description of an approach to dream work in which dreams are considered as potentially healing encounters with ourselves and where this potential is most fully realized in a social context. The social context most conducive to dream work is that of a small group, generally consisting of six to eight participants. The process unfolds in four stages, three that involve the group and the fourth involving the dreamer alone, sometime after the experience in the group. There are two substages in each of the first three stages.

Stage I

Substage IA: Sharing the Dream. The leader asks if anyone wishes to share a dream. A recent dream is preferable to an older one because the relevant context of the recent dream is more easily recalled than the older one. The decision to share a dream is the free choice of the dreamer. At this stage the dreamer limits himself to the details of the remembered dream and does not divulge associative data.

Substage IB: Clarification of the Manifest Content. The group is then given the opportunity to ask questions in order to clarify any parts of the dream that are not clear. At this stage the concern of the leader is to make sure that the dream comes across clearly to everyone and that the dreamer does not go beyond the manifest content.

Stage II

In this stage the group is asked to engage in a game-playing exercise with the dreamer listening but not actively participating. The intent is to mobilize the collective imagination of the group in order to come up with an array of feelings and metaphorical potentialities that the members of the group might connect to the dream if it were their dream. It is made clear to the group that, at this stage, they are not in a position to make statements about the meaning of the dream to the dreamer but rather, that they are working with their own projections in the hope that some may prove helpful to the dreamer. They speak of the dream as their own, and they speak to each other, not to the dreamer.

Substage IIA: Eliciting Feelings. As members of the group make the dream their own, they are asked to sensitize themselves to any feelings or moods that the imagery elicits or that they might imagine having if they had created the images. They are free to include in their projections any feelings they *imagine* the dreamer may have had or that they think they may have picked up from the dreamer as the dream was recounted. It is the creation of possibilities and their expression as self-projections that are the important thing, rather than their source in either the personal life experience of the group member or what may be felt to be coming from the dreamer.

Substage IIB: Eliciting Metaphorical Meaning. Every image in the dream is now approached as conveying metaphorical meaning. The image is regarded as one of the two terms of a metaphor. The life context giving rise to this image is the other term. The group, of course, does not know the dreamer's specific life context. Regarding the image as expressing a metaphorical identity with some life context, they then get involved in searching for possible life contexts that they can somehow relate to the images. Their task is to attend to every detail in the dream and to come up with as many possible meanings as they can. Again, it is the exploration of their own experience and use of their collective imagination to create possibilities rather than the derivation of these possibilities that is important. The source can be the past of the group member, what he thinks he may be picking up from or about the dreamer, or simply the play of his imagination on the assortment of images. Everything the group comes up with, regardless of how much certainty there may be that it is based on a true perception of the dreamer, is to be understood as a projection of the one offering it until, and if, it is later validated by the dreamer. The leader seeks to evoke the maximum range of responses from the group and to ensure that these responses are taking place in an "as if" atmosphere (as if the dream were dreamt by the respondent) rather than being offered to the dreamer as an interpretation.

During the entire second stage, the dreamer is both listening to the productions of the group and working along on his own. He is engaged in feeling the relative fit or accuracy of each response he hears, while under no constraint to respond. He is completely free to deal with his own reactions as he experiences them in the privacy of his own being.

Stage III

The second stage proceeds randomly as the interaction among the group members stimulates more and more responses. There is no way of knowing at this stage how helpful, if at all, the group has been to the dreamer. Actually, in practice, it is surprising to see how often a dreamer is deeply moved at many levels by what the group has come up with. But it is only a game. It comes to an end, and the dream is returned to the dreamer.

Substage IIIA: The Dreamer's Response. The leader now invites the dreamer to respond to the impact of the group's work. He is free to organize his response in any fashion he may wish, starting either with his own ideas and associations or with what he got from the group. He is given as much time as he needs and engages in as much self-disclosure as he feels comfortable with. How the dreamer handles this will vary greatly, depending on the dreamer, how much he got from the group, how easily he is in touch with inner processes, and how familiar he is with the metaphorical language of the dream. In most instances, he has moved a considerable distance closer to the dream. There will be a few who get very little and a few who, with the help of the group, bring the process to an end by the depth and comprehensiveness of their response. For the latter no further work in the group will be needed. In most instances, however, many gaps and puzzling aspects remain that require further work.

Substage IIIB: The Dialogue. The dialogue is the most difficult part of the process and the one that requires the most skill. As my experience with the process has developed, I have attempted to structure it in a more detailed way so as to offer as much help as possible. The goal of the dialogue is to effect a sense of closure between the dreamer and the dream. By closure I do not mean the working through of every element of the dream in elaborate detail or tracking every associative trend to its most private historical source. The goal is a more limited one. The point of closure is reached when everyone, especially the dreamer, has a felt sense that the dreamer recognizes the issues raised by the dream, their source in his or her present life situation, and their connection to the past, and when the group leaves the dreamer feeling competent to explore some of the more private ramifications of the dream on his or her own. In most instances, closure of this kind does occur.

There are two important aspects to the dialogue. The first is that control over the level of self-disclosure must remain in the hands of the dreamer. For this to happen, the dreamer is made clearly aware that he has the right to deal with any question in any manner he chooses. He can respond to the questions as well as he can or as well as he wishes. He can express the wish not to respond.

The group serves in a kind of advocate position for the dream. It is their responsibility, through the questions they ask, to see that every possible aspect of the dream has been covered. This includes all of the visual components, the situational components, and the feelings evoked in the dream. The following way of structuring the dialogue helps to achieve these ends:

1. The first part of the dialogue is devoted to clarifying the present context that led to the dream and to supplying the answer to a most important question: why did the dream occur when it did? The answer is pursued most readily with a recent dream, preferably one that occurred the night before the dream is presented. Toward this end, the following kinds of questions are helpful:

   • What were your last remaining thoughts, feelings, or preoccupations just before you fell asleep?
   • There is a felling of anger (fear, shame, etc.) in the dream. Can you think of any recent situation that bears any resemblance to that?

   If the dreamer seems to come up with any relevant information when questioned along these lines, it is sometimes helpful to ask him to review the events in his life for a 24- to 48-hour period prior to the dream. Often, recounting the experiences of the previous day will trigger a meaningful memory or bring forth data that can be used to clarify the image.

2. After every effort has been made to establish the present context, a systematic effort is made to call the dreamer's attention to every detail of the dream that has not been addressed or has not been dealt with sufficiently. Through its questions the group moves back and forth between the dream and the dreamer's responses in an effort to build a bridge between all the images in the dream and the life of the dreamer. The group members are always working with what the dreamer has given them, and care is taken to follow rather than lead the dreamer.

3. Up to this point, the group has been asking what I refer to as data-eliciting questions, the "what" and "why" types of questions. What were you thinking of when you fell asleep? Why did your wife (relative, friend, unnamed character) appear in your dream? Usually this type of systematic exploration of the content of the dream leads to a correlation with the waking life of the dreamer and is sufficient to bring about felt contact with the imagery, and finally brings the dreamer to an appropriate point of closure. However, there are times when this fails to happen and when further questioning would be to no avail. All of the data that can come from the dreamer at that moment have been elicited. If the dreamer has been seriously interested in making use of the group and uses its questions to deepen his or her own understanding of the dream, then the chances are that sufficient information has been elicited. But it may have come out in so random a fashion that it is too disorganized to be of much use to the dreamer. In these instances a further step, referred to as *orchestration,* is indicated. It is now up to the leader or anyone with sufficient experience to attempt an organization of the data in such a way that they correlate with the sequential arrangement of the imagery in the dream. This is really a playback of the material the dreamer shared, in an effort to shed light on the dream as a whole. It is most important for the person who attempts the orchestration to make it clear to the dreamer that this represents a selection made by that person from what the dreamer shared. It is that person's projection of how he perceives the metaphorical evolution of the dream and its connection to the life of the dreamer. Although not put in question form, it remains, in fact, another, but more integrative question for the dreamer. The dreamer is free to take out of this offering what, if anything, may be helpful to him. If done properly, this replay is not based on the introduction of new projections by the person doing it, as is the case in the game playing of Stage II. It should be limited only to what has been validated and shared by the dreamer. What is new for the dreamer is the way it is correlated and put together in its relation to the sequential movement of the imagery. To do this properly, one needs experience in how to listen to the dreamer as well as a sense of how the use of visual imagery lends itself to the metaphorical expression of feelings.

Stage IV: The Dream Revisited Alone

Sometime between the dream's presentation before the group and the next time the group meets, it is recommended to the dreamer that he review the dream in the light of all that came out in the group. Working alone, he sometimes can find other connections to the dream and permit himself to see more of what the dream may have been saying than he could while in the group. Usually he has been given enough leverage to go further with the dream. At the next meeting, he is offered the opportunity to share any of these additional thoughts, though he is under no obligation to do so.

THE NEEDS OF THE DREAMER

The dreamer awake may have greater or less difficulty seeing himself in an honest and penetrating light, compared to when he was asleep and dreaming. At some level he knows exactly what information he put into the images, but, awake, he is at a loss about how to regain that knowledge. The metaphor blindness that Tolaas (see Chap. 2) speaks of is most apparent when the dreamer attempts to decipher his dream. From a motivational point of view, two opposing forces are at work: a natural curiosity to learn what the images say and less conscious defensive maneuvers to protect one's self-esteem. As a result partial scotomata occur that limit the dreamer's view of the informational field in the imagery. The dreamer needs help, but that need places him in the paradoxical position of having to share in public something extremely private and trusting another or others with unknown or partially known aspects of himself.

In what follows we will consider the special needs of the dreamer and how the process meets those needs. In sharing a dream, the dreamer takes a risk. He shares a vulnerable part of his psyche and risks an encounter with disowned or unfamiliar aspects of his personality. No dreamer is apt to do this unless there are assurances, implicit or explicit, that he will be safe and that such sharing would make it possible for others to help him, assurances that I refer to as the "safety factor" and the "discovery factor."

The Safety Factor

In going public with a dream, the risk can be offset if control of what happens remains in the dreamer's hands so that he is the one in charge of titrating the delicate balance between going forward and pulling back. Once awake, the dreamer re-engages with his own defensive operations. The lowering of these defenses will be contingent on the degree of safety that he feels in the group. The first and most important step to assure that level of safety is to place the entire control of the process in the hands of the dreamer. This is achieved by building the element of control into each stage of the process.

In Stage I, the dreamer chooses whether or not to share a dream. At no time is there any constraint about sharing a dream. The only constraint is the general one that being in an experiential dream group involves dream sharing. Some people will share more than others. I have not had the experience of anyone not wanting to share at all in an ongoing group.

In Stage II, the dreamer is in a most private and safe position. She is free to accept or reject the group's projections as they evolve. From time to time there will be automatically felt responses—sometimes of a very powerful nature—but the dreamer is under no constraint to do other than what she feels like with these reactions. Usually she feels safe enough to accept and use them as she works along on her dream, and grateful enough to the group to want to share them later. The gamelike atmosphere and the emphasis on the projective nature of the group's comments allay the dreamer's defensive operations. Once the process is known and experienced, enough trust is generated to keep those operations sufficiently lowered for the necessary insights to occur.

In Stage III, the dreamer and the dreamer alone controls the level of self-disclosure she wishes to engage in as she responds. In the dialogue she controls the answers to the questions being put to her. Finally, there is an explicit understanding that the dreamer can stop the process at any point she wishes.

With the process structured in this way it has been my experience that trust is generated very rapidly, leading to remarkable instances of sharing, even on a first encounter with the process.

The Discovery Factor

The discovery factor appears in a number of interesting ways. It begins to operate as early as Stage I. The simple act of telling the dream out loud can result in sudden insights into the metaphorical message of the imagery. It is as if the decision to share a dream results in some lowering of defenses.

In Stage II the game is played with only the manifest content available to the players. The reason for this is that, were the dreamer to offer his or her ideas about the dream, there would be an unpredictable mix of relevant and defensive data, both of which could constrain the free imaginative play of the group. The game is played in the hope that the group will come, quite unknowingly, upon things that the dreamer cannot see by himself. This is a reasonable possibility in that (1) dreams tend to deal with significant issues that are familiar to a greater or lesser degree to all of us; (2) we share much of the same social space so that it is not unlikely that a dreamer's metaphors may have some meaning for others in the group; and (3) since it is a game and the members of the group do not have to live with the implications of the dream, they are often able to be much freer than the dreamer in the imaginative range of their ideas. The discovery factor operates in still another way during this second stage. When a projection is on target, it furthers the dreamer's own effort to move into the dream and often leads to other insights. Even when the projections are not applicable, they help the dreamer define what the image is not. In so doing they bring him closer to what it is.

As the dreamer in Stage III organizes both his own associative data and what has come from the group, he often comes up with additional insights. In the dialogue there is an effort to further the discovery process through questions designed to clarify the immediate life context that shaped the dream and questions that can build additional bridges between the imagery and waking life experiences.

The orchestration is a final effort to be of help when necessary. It relies for its effect on the fact that when the information elicited from the dreamer is organized in its relationship to the sequential pattern of the imagery, new light will be shed on the dream.

In Stage IV, having benefited from the group's work, the dreamer now has some leverage on the dream. His curiosity to learn more in combination with the privacy in which this takes place can bring about further lowering of defenses and a heightening of awareness.

ROLES

A word about the way roles are played out in this process is necessary to point up important differences from formal therapeutic approaches.

The Dreamer

It is the dreamer's choice to share a dream. If he does so, however, he is obliged to do it as honestly and as completely as possible. By the same token he is not obliged to answer the questions in the dialogue, but, if he does, his answers should be as close to the truth as he can get.

The Group

The group members create an atmosphere of trust in the way that space and freedom are given to the dreamer, in an atmosphere of mutuality by sharing their own projections, and in an atmosphere of help by placing their collective imagination at the disposal of the dreamer; and, through their questions, they help him discover the information he needs to bring the imagery to life.

The Leader

The leader has the dual role of moving the group through the process and being a participant at the same time. He has the choice of sharing a dream or not, just like any other group member. His role is to be an authority on the process, not on the meaning of the dream. As leader he is concerned with maintaining the integrity of the process. This involves both protecting the dreamer and facilitating the work of the group.

SKILLS

Basically, there are three skills involved: the art of learning to focus attention completely on what the dreamer shares spontaneously (see "Dreamer's Response," Stage IIIA of the process); the art of asking information-eliciting questions in a way that helps the dreamer to focus more closely on the immediate life context that led to the dream, and on the life context, present and past, suggested by the imagery; and, finally, the art of grasping metaphorical representation (i.e., how specific life contexts are being expressed as visual metaphors). All these skills have been noted in connection with the appropriate stage of the process. I want to stress here that each of these skills can be taught, and, with proper instruction, the serious dream worker without formal psychoanalytic or psychological training can learn to apply them in a way that is productive and safe for the dreamer. Once mastered, these skills become operative intuitively.

THE DREAM AS A POTENTIAL
AND NATURAL HEALING AGENCY

We have stressed throughout that dream work is healing. More needs to be said about this. The healing that takes place in the course of group dream work is a consequence of both the nature of what is worked on (the dream) and how it is worked on (i.e., how the process facilitates the communication of all that lies embedded in the imagery).

With regard to the dream, we have alluded to three factors that are at the heart of its healing potential: its origin in a current concern or tension; its ability to recruit information from the past that provides a historical perspective on the current issue; and, finally, its ability to depict reliably and honestly the emotional realities of one's life.

What is to be emphasized is that the dream has its origins in the subjective realities of the dreamer's life, and that these realities are displayed in the dream for what they are, in contrast to the way the dreamer may experience them in waking life. The point is not that we are no longer burdened by the strategic dishonesties of our waking life (our defenses), but instead that these are honestly depicted. Were it not for their intrinsic honesty, dreams would have very little value for us.

The features of the process that facilitate healing include: (1) the sense of safety and trust that experience with the process generates, and which minimizes defensive maneuvers; (2) the response of the dreamer to the concern, interest, and supportive effort of the group; (3) the dialectical aspects of the process whereby the members of the group, through their projections, share of themselves with the dreamer; (4) the sense of commonality through the mutual and ongoing sharing of dreams; and (5) the fact that working within a flat structure with no one in an authoritative relationship to the dreamer adds to the feeling of freedom and mutuality.

EXAMPLES

Two examples of the process follow. In the first the dialogue itself was not sufficient to bring about a closure, and an orchestration was necessary. In the second the dreamer, stimulated by the group's work in the second stage, arrived at the meaning the dream held for her, and no dialogue was necessary.

The sessions are reconstructed from notes taken at the time and checked later with the dreamer. They are a somewhat shortened account of what transpired.

Example 1

Doris is a recently married young woman. Her husband, George, is also in the group. This was the first dream that she presented. It had occurred the night before the group met.

DORIS'S DREAM (STAGE IA):

"I am at my friend Betty's house. I call Ann up to make an appointment to get my hair highlighted. I speak to the receptionist at the beauty parlor. I speak in a Russian accent. She asks when I can come. I say in a couple of days. I think that might be Wednesday. She asks, 'Are you sure because we are changing things around here,' implying that it won't be good if I change my mind and cancel the appointment. After speaking to her, I realize that I don't need to have my hair highlighted yet, because my hair hasn't grown out yet. But George and I go on the 'A' train to the beauty parlor. It goes through a neighborhood that I have never seen before. The train travels outside. George gets out at a stop as if he nonchalantly is doing something. The train leaves without him. I wave to him and feel bad that he is not on the train."

In response to a question (Stage IB) Doris adds that Betty is one of her closest friends and that she was at her house yesterday. Ann is a beautician whom she had just met once, at the beauty parlor to which she had been recommended.

FEELINGS EXPRESSED BY THE GROUP (STAGE IIA):

"I feel pressure, feeling rushed."
"I feel as though I'm acting a role when I put on the accent.   I like that role."
"I feel hesitant."
"I feel challenged by the receptionist. She knows something about me."
"I wish I could make up my mind."
"I feel annoyed. I wish my friend Betty would help me."
"I feel ambivalent."
"I feel better having George with me."
"I feel frightened being in a strange neighborhood."
"I don't know what I'm getting into."
"I feel abandoned by George."
"I feel insecure and have to take George along with me."
"I'm indecisive."
"I feel constrained and limited by the attitude of the beauty parlor receptionist."

THE GROUP THEN WORKED WITH THE IMAGES (STAGE IIB):

"I'm in foreign territory."
"Hair is the dominant image. I'm dealing with externals. Minor external changes seem important."
"I'm disguising myself."
"I have been rushing around lately."
"I'm trying to feel beautiful and loved."
"I want to be highlighted, a star."
"I do take the 'A' train to the Dream Group."
"I want to be above ground. My dream thoughts will be brought above ground. I have mixed feelings about it."
"In the Dream Group people will be messing around with my head."
"The hair represents my feelings, feelings that haven't ripened."
"George is preoccupied."
"George nonchalantly gave a dream last week [which he did]."
"George shows feelings easily."
"I want some highlighting and not to be left alone."
"I want to draw attention to myself. I want some visibility."
"I've been trained to stay on a certain track with my feelings."
"Ann is a stand-in for my mother."

DORIS THEN RESPONDED (STAGE IIIA):

"I find it hard to talk about this dream. I'm embarrassed that it has so much to do with my hair. I knew I would do a dream tonight. It has to do with how others see me and how I want to be seen. I do like to put on accents and I'm good at them. It would be bold of me to pretend I was Russian with someone I didn't know. I wouldn't normally do that.

"I resented when the receptionist asked me if I was sure. I want to have the freedom to change my mind. The receptionist reminded me of my chiropractor's receptionist. I don't like her.

"Lately I have felt abandoned. George has been very self-absorbed. Perhaps the train is the train of my thoughts and my life. I feel as if I'm watching George's life and his concern over a profession more than usually.

"About my hair. It has been cut short recently. When I'm getting my hair cut I feel as if I have to give up control. I usually don't like it immediately afterward. It is important to me how people see me. Maybe it's too important.

"We do take the 'A' train here to the Dream Group.

"Yesterday was Wednesday. I was with Betty yesterday. I know her very well. She is very different from me. We are in the same profession. I don't have to be embarrassed with her. I can admit that I want to look nice and not be embarrassed. There is no question of being judged by her.

"There is insecurity after the haircut, particularly at work where I have to meet others. I can't cut my hair myself.

"George has been self-absorbed and selfish. I felt angry at him for getting off the train. I certainly don't want him at the beauty parlor. Lately our feeling of sharing together has been pushed aside.

"The strange neighborhood—perhaps new things that will have to be confronted.

"I have to encourage George to take an interest in his appearance. He is more able than me to express feelings. I let my feelings out in dreams.

"My feeling about the group is, I don't want to be judged. I want to be accepted.

"I am committed to inner growth."

When she had finished I acknowledged how much she had shared. There was still more work to be done, and so the dialogue began.

DIALOGUE (STAGE IIIA):

(What were your thoughts on falling asleep last night?)

"I was upset that George wasn't going to be around for Christmas. Betty's husband was going into the hospital. I prayed for him."

(Anything more about yesterday?)

"Last summer my grandmother dyed my hair and it came out terrible. I felt terrible over it. I had just gotten my hair cut yesterday. There still were residues of what my grandmother had done. Why is hair so important? That bothers me. I don't want to be so affected by that."

The above questions were asked in the hope of clarifying the immediate context of the dream. What follows now are questions addressed to elements of the dream not sufficiently developed by the dreamer.

(Your feelings about the chiropractor's receptionist?)

"She had a chip on her shoulder. I did cancel my appointment yesterday. I resent her attitude."

(Why the Russian accent?)

"There is a store next to where I get my hair cut that is run by a Russian. He is a nice guy. He likes you no matter what you look like. He made me feel so good when I dropped in on him after the haircut. He likes me saying hello and goodby in Russian."

(The beauty parlor?)

"I don't feel trust. I have no control once I'm involved. My hair still shows what my grandmother did to it."

(Betty? Why was it important for her to be in your dream last night?)

"We talked about a lot of things. We just hang out. We talked about her past. She gets her hair colored. Hers is turning gray. She doesn't feel about it the way I do, and doesn't feel guilty about her physical appearance."

(Why the reference to changes going on?)

"I did cancel an appointment with the chiropractor yesterday. I had a job and didn't want to feel rushed to have to go back for the appointment. I'm changing. I look different. My work is going well. I'm concerned George may feel bad, as his work hasn't gotten off the ground yet. Maybe that relates to being above ground, exposing myself more. There is ambivalence and indecisiveness, particularly around the time of my period. I feel less sure of myself then. I do feel self-critical. I know it's not rational, but I still feel that people will judge me negatively if they know I color my hair."

Doris responded quite openly and frankly about her concerns despite obvious feelings of embarrassment at times and the fact that George was present. Although she expressed some criticism of George's behavior, it was not done in an attacking way but in a spirit of honest sharing. George experienced it that way, and at no point was he defensive.

Taking stock at this point, my feeling was that Doris had been able to identify the two main emotional currents impinging on her the night of the dream. She was upset about herself and the extent of her preoccupation with her hair and her appearance, and she was experiencing a growing upset about George's decision to spend Christmas alone.

How all this fitted into the imagery of the dream was not yet clear. Her own reactions had not been presented in any organized way but simply as they occurred to her. I felt that some attempt to pull the threads together should be made. I introduced my effort at orchestrating the material as follows:

"I think you are in touch with the concerns that led to the dream. You shared your thoughts and some of the connections you had to the images in the dream. I have the feeling that you shared as much as you can, and that you have probably brought out most of the relevant data. The problem now is how to help you put it together in relation to the dream. I am going to make an attempt to integrate or orchestrate the data you shared.

"You have emphasized how important it is for you to be liked and how sensitive you are to anything that could possibly evoke a negative judgment. For you the beauty parlor has a certain connotation of falseness, of adopting certain false values. Your hair focuses and symbolizes these concerns. It is a positive aspect of your attractiveness but also a source of concern, as if too much of yourself is tied up with externals and whatever connotation it is that dyeing one's hair has for you. Now the question is: why were you thrown back on these old concerns last night? Several things going on in your life seemed to push you in that direction—the recent haircut, the still troubling job your grandmother did on your hair, your encounter with Betty, who can accept herself regardless of the state of her hair. In the dream you move away from the concerns around your hair and another issue comes into focus, the fact that George leaving you alone for the holidays.

"More specifically, let me try to play back what I think I heard you share with the group, but now I'm going to play it back in its relationship to the sequential arrangement of the imagery in the dream. Although I am going to try to base what I say on what you shared, it is being filtered through my psyche and so may contain some of my own distortions. Please consider it then as my projection being offered in the hope that some of it may be meaningful to you. Although not put as a question, it really is a question to you.

"You begin with a scene at Betty's house, and you've told us of your wish to be more realistically accepting of yourself, your hair, your wish to make a good appearance, all of which Betty does quite nonchalantly. What stands in your way? The next part of the dream, perhaps, speaks to the problem area. You try to make an appointment at the beauty parlor to have your hair highlighted, and you speak in a Russian accent. You have told us of the mixed feelings you have about coloring your hair, feeling you will be judged negatively, as there is something false about it. Yet your hair is an important part of your appearance and you would like to make the most of it—highlight it.

"You also told us of your talent at putting on a Russian accent, much to the amusement of your friends. As you said, you would never do it with someone you didn't know, like the receptionist, but in the dream you do. So, speaking in a Russian accent is another way of calling attention to yourself, but again in a way that doesn't call attention to your real self but a temporarily assumed self. In the dream you chose as the person to receive this ambivalent display an aggressive person whom you dislike. You're expecting a negative judgment. The receptionist (perhaps your own self-critical judgment of this need to draw attention to yourself) sees through your ambivalence and warns you about changing your mind and not going through with the highlighting. Your first impulse is to back out with the excuse that your hair hasn't grown out yet. But then an interesting thing happens. You find yourself with George en route to the Dream Group. You did reveal to us your hesitancy about sharing this dream with us, as we might think you vain or false and judge you negatively. But you overcame these fears and did decide to share the dream with the group. Perhaps your dreaming self was aware that this would be your decision, as you go on to indicate that you and George are going through territory that you have never seen before. In sharing a dream publicly you are bringing something unknown and underground above ground, and in the dream the train is traveling on the outside. Then comes the part about George leaving (as he does intend to do at Christmas) and your feeling sad.

"So what have you accomplished by having the dream and sharing it? You accomplished two things in relation to the two concerns that were on your mind. You risked sharing the first one about your hair with the group and elicited a supportive rather than a negative response. And, through your dream you conveyed to George the extent of the hurt and sadness you felt at his decision."

Doris responded to this. She indicated that the dream that morning had led to an encounter with George, the result of which was that he had changed his mind, and they would be together for Christmas. Doris ended by saying, "I just had to hit him over the head."

AT THE NEXT SESSION OF THE GROUP DORIS ADDED (STAGE IV):

"After I shared my dream with the group I felt better about myself and my desires to want to be with George and to look and feel beautiful. Sharing the dream helped me feel the universality of the specific 'problem' I am working through, i.e., my femininity, my independence, and my relationship with George."

Comment. Inasmuch as this was Doris's first experience as the dreamer in the group, help was needed in correlating the concerns she was expressing with the specific imagery of the dream. The orchestration was more detailed and systematic than is ordinarily necessary for a more experienced dreamer. It was rendered not only to be helpful but also to teach how our dreams come up with images that metaphorically reflect our concerns and our efforts to resolve them.

Example 2

Marie is an elderly Norwegian woman in a dream group for the first time and presenting her first dream. The dream had occurred four months earlier. It had a powerful impact on her, and she was anxious to share it.

MARIE'S DREAM:

"I am in an Indian bazaar where they sell lovely silk and brocade. I am in a very happy mood because I'm getting married and am collecting material for my dowry. Suddenly I am in a shop trying on a long black silk georgette dress. I look at myself in a big free-standing mirror. The dress is quite transparent. My breasts and nipples show through, and I feel very seductive and sensual. The dress is quite black, with a red embroidery around the neck and shoulders. I decide this is the dress I want, whatever the price might be."

THE GROUP SHARED THE FOLLOWING FEELINGS:

"It feels somewhat unreal. There's no problem."
"The song 'I'm So Happy, I'm Flying' occurs to me."
"I feel strong."
"I have ambivalent feelings."
"I prefer the dress as a nightgown."
"I have a sense of narrowing, as if leaving things out."
"I feel my dream is very female-centered."

"I am worried. Where are the people?"
"It is my moment, just for me."
"Feeling of expectation and anticipation."
"I feel like Eve in Paradise."
"I'm worried about the black color."
"Where is my prince?"
"I feel reconciled but proud."
"I have both a public and a private feeling."

WORKING WITH THE IMAGES, THE GROUP CAME UP WITH:

"I want to show myself. I want to be seen."
"I like myself in this dream."
"I have all these possibilities."
"I'm dancing all by myself."
"I'm not used to seeing myself as beautiful."
"I really want to show myself."
"I'm sure of being welcomed by my groom."
"I provide my own dowry."
"The bride's dress is usually white."
"I feel alive."
"These are the colors of the Indian goddess Kali."

THE DREAMER GAVE THE FOLLOWING RESPONSE:

"This was a very important dream. I have thought of it every day since it occurred. There were many important feelings in it for me. Some of you spoke to the point. I worked in India for seven years in my youth, and later, many times in my dreams, I experienced the strain of my work there. The present dream is the first one in which the pleasant and good experience of India came back to me. I felt very happy when I woke up. People knew me in the bazaar. A merchant selling cloth would call out: 'Feel this, isn't it beautiful?' Happy, nice, and gay experiences were finally coming back to me in this dream. But why of all the colors did I choose black? For several years now I have worn black as my basic color. So did my husband. We both liked it. My husband died a year ago quite suddenly. Black is sorrow. The dream occurred at the end of May, five months ago, when I finally could really work more deeply with my sorrow. I could do this only after many practical matters had been taken care of. I had an important exhibition of my sculpture coming up just one week after my husband's funeral and had to put aside my grief, make all the arrangements and meet people. Somebody here mentioned the absence of people in the dream and that there were only pretty things around. There I stood at the exhibition, feeling utterly alone inside, with my art work all around. After my husband's death I had to empty his studio in town. It took so much of my strength.

"Someone mentioned the feeling suggestive of narcissism in the dream. It strikes me that that is a necessary ingredient in an artist's way of life, to look into oneself and *mirror* oneself in a work of art brought out into the open. I make torsos in the shape of vessels. Sometimes I wondered why a draping I naturally would make over my left shoulder would appear over the right in the sculpture. After many years I understood. The sculpture was a reflected image. I was mirroring myself.

"The Indian goddess Kali was mentioned in the group. That I find very interesting. She is depicted as black and bloodthirsty and seemed very scary. But the more I understood of Indian thinking, the more I understood that the destroying aspects of Kali were as necessary as the other aspect of her as the Great Mate (Mother). Something must die to give room for new growth. We see it in nature. We see it in our life experiences—every crisis is a new possibility. When my former life went to pieces after my husband's death, I changed my profession. Our marriage made us both grow as persons in an ever-deepening relationship. *But now I am collecting material for a new start.*

"There is also a spiritual aspect to the dream. When it occurred I was in a retreat. The very experienced leader had given two marvelous talks on the deeper opening of ourselves to the Divine Love. He also referred to Saint John of the Cross, the Spanish sixteenth-century mystic who, among other books, wrote *The Dark Night of the Soul.* I had a short talk with the leader that night. I told him I felt deeply moved by what he said and thanked him. Before going to sleep I thought of this encounter and of my whole life situation. I also recalled a meeting with an Indian wise man, a hermit who lived in a cave for forty years and who was also wonderfully accepting and made me understand that there are deep experiences beyond words.

"I wanted that dress, *whatever* the price. I was collecting a dowry for another kind of marriage, daring to go into another career and a deeper commitment.

"When I awoke, there was sadness. I was alone. But there also was a feeling of maturity and expectation. The basic emotion was very positive. I am really not afraid even with my heavy losses. Something has to die for something new to grow. My life is not yet ended. Darkness exists only when you no longer relate to the experience of youth, that is, understand and build on it."

It was not possible to recapture all that the dreamer said in her response, but it was so filled with hope, inspiration, and the courage to move beyond past losses that the group felt deeply moved. All I could do and all that could be done at that point was to acknowledge our appreciation for the openness with which she had shared so critical a period of her life. Even though the dream was several months old, the context was still fresh in her mind. She addressed each of the elements of the dream and was able to "contextualize" each one in a way that enriched her appreciation of the creative reserve that saw her through a most difficult period. The dreamer was content to stop at this point. A dialogue would have been anti-climactic.

THE EXPERIENTIAL DREAM GROUP AND FORMAL THERAPY

Implicit in the structure described are a number of ways this process differs from any variety of formal therapy. Perhaps the most obvious is that there is no therapist present. The dream alone becomes the therapeutic agent. Given the proper circumstances, there is a natural tendency to reown the dream.

Some people, of course, need more than this approach can give. Someone who is trapped in a neurotic defensive structure will need something more, namely, the analysis and resolution of the resistances that block the capacity for emotional healing. I see dream work as an experience that should be available to those people who have an interest in their dream life. I see therapy in the formal sense as geared to the treatment of pathological blockages to growth.

When we compare the approach to dreams in a formal therapeutic setting and the approach in the process outlined here, differences can be noted that come from the way the two situations are structured.

The group approach is favorable to dream work for several reasons: (1) the dream is the only item on the agenda, and the time needed to deal with the dream in its entirety is available; (2) we are dealing with a flat structure in which everyone engages in self-disclosure either through projection, sharing a dream, or both; (3) the focus remains solely on the dreamer and the dream and not on the interpersonal processes set up by either; (4) the collective imagination of the group can come up with a richer supply of metaphors than a single individual; and (5) the fact that the process remains totally in the control of the dreamer is a powerful impetus to the lowering of defenses.

Features of a formal therapeutic arrangement favorable to dream work are: (1) greater ease in dealing with more private and intimate implications of the dream, compared to the group approach; and (2) the therapist's greater knowledge of the dreamer. A concise way of putting it is that in the group we do dream work; in formal therapy the therapist uses the dream for leverage in implementing the therapeutic approach he or she is engaged in.

In the case of group therapy versus the dream group differences in the ground rules result in profound differences between the two processes. In group therapy attention to the evolving interpersonal and group processes is all-important, whereas in the dream group these aspects remain in the background. Although a group session may match a dream session in time, it would be rare of the entire group session to be devoted to a single patient's dream, and even more rare for it to be given over to the dream of the therapist. If we substitute leader for therapist in the dream group, these are commonplace events. Other differences, such as control by the dreamer, also obtain. A more detailed description of the differences is given elsewhere (Ullman, 1979).

Complementarity

During the time I have worked with this process, I have seen a natural complementarity between the experiential dream group and individual therapy. There are a number of ways in which this complementarity can manifest itself. Perhaps the most rewarding way is for a dream to be presented to the group first. This will generally have the effect of opening the dream up for the dreamer, identifying the issue involved and some of the indicators of its source in the past. Then the dream can be explored further in therapy, where the dreamer may feel freer to deal with the more personal references than he would feel in the group. If the dream is introduced first in the therapeutic session, there may be insufficient time to develop it to the dreamer's satisfaction. In a group session the dreamer has the time to approach the dream in a more leisurely fashion.

Occasionally, work on a dream that is brought to the dream group after a therapeutic session reveals that counter-transferential difficulties have been the basis for an unsatisfactory result with the dream in the therapy session; and this discovery then has a salutary effect on the therapy. I do not know of any instances of the reverse effect, where the dreamer was misled by the work of the group and this was recognized in individual therapy, although I could imagine this happening with persons inexperienced in the process.

EXTENDING DREAM WORK INTO THE COMMUNITY

When we turn our attention to the community at large, we see a rather unfortunate state of affairs that seems to prevail throughout the civilized world. In spite of all we know about the intrinsic value of dreams, society fails to meet the desire of many people to learn how to work with their dreams. We have the limited arrangement of referral to therapy, but this leaves the ordinary mortal alone to fend for her- or himself among the many books and articles that keep appearing about dreams. Much of what is written stresses the virtues of our dream life but glosses over the difficulties and problems involved, and does little to teach the interested reader the kinds of skill necessary for its exploration.

Can the skills developed in the course of clinical work be shared with anyone, regardless of background, who wishes to gain access to his or her dreams? From my experience of the past decade, not only is it possible, but it should be encouraged. The basic phenomenologic features of dreams can be as readily grasped as the notion of the visual metaphor. When a group comes together to do dream work and master the principles and rationale of the process, they not only will not harm the dreamer but will, from the beginning, help him. Of course, a skilled and experienced leader will facilitate the process and raise the level of work that can be done. But this does not belie the fact that this process can be placed safely in the hands of anyone, given the stipulations noted. Although there are risks involved when a professional skill is turned over to the public, the benefits to be gained warrant the attempt.

RESULTS OF DREAM WORK

Anyone who is serious about dream work wants to know what a dream is saying, and with the help of the group will get deeper and deeper into its meaning. The result is a sense of greater honesty about oneself. Dream work becomes a natural way of doing some emotional housecleaning. Debris from the past comes to light, and its power over one's life then diminishes.

Perhaps the outstanding result is an appreciation of the self-healing aspects of the dream. Ordinarily we react with fright or dismay to dreams with negative feelings or content, and oppositely to dreams we like. Consistent dream work leads to the realization that dreams filled with fear, shame, or guilt are not dreamt to make the dreamer feel worse but instead offer him the opportunity, with the help and support of others, to find the courage to confront the negative content and to learn more about its nature and source. The issue does not dissolve magically, but one feels better for having allowed the confrontation to take place, and, as we indicated earlier, by bringing the issue into the open, we socialize it. It is no longer a private, shameful demon of sorts.

One gets over the strong but mistaken tendency to judge a dream by waking standards (i.e., a long dream is better than a short dream, a dream with drama and action is better than a quiet one, etc.). One gets over the tendency to refer to any dream, particularly fragments or very short ones, as insignificant or unimportant. I refer to this as "dreamism," an irrational bias that operates in relation to dreams.

More and more there is a sense that dreams can provide us with an in-depth projection of how we organize our emotionality around particular issues in our life. The freer we are to learn these truths about our lives, the freer we are in our daily exchanges with others. We not only become aware of our vulnerable areas, but we become aware of them in a helpful way. Along with this comes a growing realization that within each of us lies a creative resource that places pictures at our disposal, pictures that are uniquely crafted to our own emotional specification.

More specific life changes flow from work with dreams. Once in touch with this creative resource, people have used it to further their individual talent in art, in music, in the ministry, in political science. It has been found a place in an introductory course in computer science (Storm, 1983).

PRACTICAL ASPECTS

There are a number of practical aspects of group dream work, as briefly noted below.

The Group: Open or Closed?

In a closed group, either new members are not brought in, or, if they are, it is only with the consent of the group. An open group is one in which new members can join at any time. I have tried both arrangements and have concluded that an open group is more advantageous in dream work. A new person adds a new supply of potentially helpful responses to the dreamer. Since we do not focus on the interpersonal aspects of the ongoing group process, new members are not experienced as disruptive. They should, of course, have some knowledge of the process so that they come in as participants and not as observers.

Time Arrangements

I have found that an hour and a half is sufficient time to unravel a dream in a leisurely and unhurried way. At the start of each session, time is allotted for any further sharing by the dreamer who last presented (Stage IV). The remaining time is apportioned to work with a new dream so that the last 40 to 45 minutes is left for the dreamer's response, the dialogue, and any orchestration that may be needed.

Size of the Group

By its very nature, dream work, is an intimate experience that can best take place in a small group arrangement. The optimal size is from six to eight participants, with leeway for one or two at either end. Having less than four members places too great a burden on the dreamer to share a dream, and is too limiting in the number of people available to help the dreamer. If there are more than ten members, one must wait too long for an opportunity to present a dream.

Confidentiality

Dream work involves sharing intimate aspects of oneself. Confidentiality is obligatory.

Leadership

Here we come to a delicate question. Should the leadership of a dream group be in the hands of a professional, or can anyone be a leader? My point of view is that the process as I have described it is not group therapy or related to it. The leader is not the therapist for the group and is not in any authoritative relationship to the group other than by virtue of his knowledge of the process itself. The leader is an active participant who functions in the same way as any other member of the group. It is the leader's familiarity with and competence in using the process that is the determining factor, and not whether he or she comes to the task with a professional background. Professional experience may enrich the proceedings, but that alone does not qualify an individual to be the leader.

The other possibility for a group starting out is for the participants, all of whom are at an equal level, to take turns at leading the group. If one decides to lead dream groups, it should be only on the basis of experience with the process and a mastery of the skills involved.

Obstacles

A number of difficulties can arise in connection with the effort to interest people in dream work. Inertia must be overcome. Why invest the time and energy to do effective dream work, especially if it involves organizing a group and mastering a time-consuming procedure? There is no simple answer. It can be approached in two ways. What I have been trying to do is to place a reliable tool in the hands of the public in the hope that the natural curiosity people have about their dreams will gradually draw more and more people into dream work. Another approach would be to try to get dream work started earlier through its introduction into high schools and colleges. That this is a promising area has been borne out by my experience as well as by Jones (1980).

Misconceptions about dreams and how to deal with them pose still another problem. The popular mystique that dreams may be handled only by properly qualified professionals has to be laid to rest. For the professional the dream is a powerful tool in the therapeutic endeavor. There the therapist, equipped with a body of technical and theoretical knowledge, uses the dream toward what he sees as a particular therapeutic end. For the person who is interested in dreams but not in need of therapy, the dream can be pursued for its own sake. Where the two approaches mesh is that, in both cases, the work is therapeutic. In formal therapy the therapist not only uses his knowledge to clarify the source of the dream through the dreamer's associations but also assumes responsibility for dealing with defensive operations that stand in the dreamer's way. In dream appreciation groups, there is no therapist (other than the dream itself), and the group creates an environment in which the dreamer is free to deal with his own defenses.

CONCLUSION

There have been three traditions around dreams, none of which has encouraged a particularly active public interest. There has been a literary and historical tradition that has highlighted the aesthetic and dramatic qualities of the dream. There has been a clinical tradition, beginning with Freud, that has pointed to the unique contribution that dream work can make to the therapeutic endeavor. In recent years there has been an experimental approach that has made knowledge about dreams and dreaming more widespread but has not brought people closer to their dream life. The time is ripe for resurrecting a tradition found in primitive societies, namely, the existence of an everyday working relationship between dream life and culture. The problem has to be approached in two ways. From below, there has to be more general acceptance of the fact that dreams can be made accessible in a safe and effective way outside the consulting room. From above, dream work has to move to a higher order of social priority, a move that may someday come about when more humane solutions are sought for the disarray that now exists among people and among nations.

REFERENCES

Bjerre, P. *Drömmarnas naturaliga system.* Stockholm: Albert Bonnier, 1933.
Delaney, G. *Living your dreams.* New York: Harper & Row, 1979.
Faraday, A. *Dream power.* New York: Berkley Publishing, 1972.
Faraday, A. *The dream game.* New York: Harper & Row, 1974.
Freud, S. *Dream psychology.* New York: James A. McCann, 1921.
Fromm, E. *The forgotten language.* New York: Rinehart, 1951.
Hall, C. S. *The meaning of dreams.* New York: Harper & Brothers, 1953.
Jones, R. N. *The dream poet.* Boston: G. K. Hall, 1980.
Jung, C. G. *Modern man in search of a soul.* New York: Harcourt, Brace and World, 1933, pp. 1-27.
Mahoney, M. F. *The meaning in dreams and dreaming.* Secaucus, N.J.: The Citadel Press, 1976.
Rycroft, C. S. *The innocence of dreams.* New York: Pantheon Books, 1979.
Sanford, J. *Dreams—God's forgotten language.* Philadelphia: Lippincott, 1968.
Storm, E. Personal communication, 1983.
Taylor, J. *Dream work.* New York: Paulist Press, 1983.
Tolaas, J. REM sleep and the concept of vigilance. *Biological Psychiatry,* 1978, *13*(1), 135-148.
Ullman, M. Dreaming, altered states of consciousness and the problem of vigilance. *Journal of Nervous and Mental Disease,* 1961, *133*(6), 529-535.
Ullman, M. The experiential dream group. In B. Wolman (Ed.) *Handbook of Dreams.* New York: Van Nostrand Reinhold, 1979, pp. 406-423.
Ullman, M. and Zimmerman, N. *Working with dreams.* New York: Delacorte/Eleanor Friede, 1979.

18. Biofeedback and States of Consciousness

Elmer E. Green and Alyce M. Green

In almost no other area is one's intellecual understanding so dependent on an adequate experiential base as in the consciousness disciplines. Both history and modern psychology are replete with countless examples of misunderstandings, dismissals, and pathological interpretations of these disciplines by those without personal experience and training in them. (Walsh, 1983)

PROLOGUE

Before discussing biofeedback and consciousness it is useful to define biofeedback, and biofeedback training, in the way they are used in this chapter. *Biofeedback* is the feedback of biological information to a person. It is the continuous monitoring, amplifying, and displaying to a person (usually by a needle on a meter, or by a light or a tone) of an ongoing internal physiological process, such as muscle tension, temperature, heart behavior, or brain rhythm. Biofeedback is not conditioning, and it is not therapy, any more than the act of looking at one's weight on a bathroom scale is conditioning or therapy.

Biofeedback training is the use by a person of his or her own physiological information in learning to voluntarily control the process being monitored. If anyone insists, the procedure might be called instrumental self-conditioning, although linking "self" with "conditioning" may seem paradoxical.

A number of biofeedback training programs, both research and clinical, have led to what some investigators call "altered states of consciousness."

It seems more accurate, however, in the context of biofeedback training, to speak of "states of consciousness" and delete "altered." "Optional states of consciousness" is better in the context of volitional procedures that are open to all (i.e., all who pay the price of practice), but "altered" is misleading.

The word "altered" may be appropriate when externally administered psychoactive chemicals or procedures actively invade or modify the central nervous system (CNS), but it seems inappropriate for *self*-regulation, in which self-consciousness and volition are essential, whether arrived at through autogenic training, meditation, yoga, or biofeedback training. It is especially inappropriate in an educational setting (Roberts, 1983). Needleman (1983) makes this same point about "altered," in another context (in the "search for a lost religion"), when he says:

> . . . the LOST element has to do with a quality of consciousness which is not a so-called "altered state of consciousness" but a quality of presence which appears when one is brought in front of the contradictions of one's own life and mind. I'm convinced there is a discipline, a way of cultivating this state of presence.

In our view, psychophysiologic training, using biofeedback as an aid, is one of the most effective of the newly developing ways of cultivating this state of presence, or at least finding the "inner place" (in the brain?—in the "heart"?) that opens to this state of presence.

BACKGROUND

In the early days of the Biofeedback Society of America, founded in 1969 under the name Biofeedback Research Society, it was affirmed by many members that: (1) biofeedback research and clinical biofeedback training were forms of instrumental conditioning; (2) consciousness of procedures and intermediate goals by the trainee was not a necessary ingredient of biofeedback-aided behavior modification; (3) *only* the trainer need consciously: (a) determine the training procedure and contingencies, (b) keep track of ongoing results, and (c) make midcourse corrections of procedures and contingencies.

Trainees were not treated as colleagues whose comments and suggestions might prove useful, or even necessary, to the solution or amelioration of the presenting problem.

Looking back, it is not difficult to understand the underlying reasons for the above orientation. Most members of the Biofeedback Research Society were psychologists or psychophysiologists whose training and professional careers had previously focused on animal behavior, and on the descriptive theories of B. F. Skinner and his ideological descendants. The idea that "states of consciousness" might be involved in instrumental conditioning was not thought about.

It is now clear to most therapists, however, that clinical biofeedback training, if it is to be effective, involves first and foremost the consciousness and volition of the patient, and secondarily the consciousness and volition of the trainer. Restated in terms of recent metaphors (and some facts), it was thought by many early researchers that the left cortex of the trainer was essential to success in training patients, and neither left nor right cortex of the patient need be consciously involved (any more than in deep-trance hypnosis). The limbic brain of the patient must be properly instructed or manipulated, of course, in order to affect physiological processes through limbic-hypothalamic/pituitary neural tracts, but the patient's cortical apparatus really was not needed.

That logic, stemming from animal conditioning, has been remarkably barren, though, in explaining the majority of psychophysiologic phenomena associated with biofeedback training in humans, mainly because biofeedback training in humans is *self-regulation* training, and successful self-regulation involves both increased "body awareness' (which develops through feedback of physiologic information) and increased skill in the use of visualization and passive volition to control the process being monitored. These three ingredients of psychophysiologic self-regulation, *self-awareness, passive volition,* and *visualization,* clearly involve "states of consciousness." Each of these factors is necessary, but not individually sufficient, for success with biofeedback training.

Misunderstanding can develop here, for on occasion research subjects report, while undergoing training, that they cannot detect in themselves any internal physiological awareness associated with the newfound control (such as control of single motor units, single nerve fibers). Some researchers have concluded, therefore, that physiological awareness in the patient or research subject is not necessary. We must remember, however, that in every biofeedback situation involving *self*-regulation information is first fed back to the cortex via biofeedback devices. Later, when self-regulation develops to the point at which biofeedback devices are no longer necessary for continuation of the skill, a sensitivity to interocepters (internal feedback circuits) has taken over, has replaced the original biofeedback source of information. The machine's information has been replaced by direct body awareness.

The fact that subjects or patients sometimes cannot easily describe this awareness is not to be wondered at, for interoceptors feed back their signals to subcortical brain centers, in which awareness only slowly develops (as affirmed by yogis and others who have become adepts at physiological self-regulation). Even the best of us cannot say exactly what the difference is between the odor of carnations and roses. The reason is that the olfactory organ is connected first with the limbic system, and secondarily with the cortex. Nevertheless, we are not in doubt about the differences, even though we may be tongue-tied in trying to describe them.

We are not saying that unconscious instrumental conditioning is not possible. That unconscious involuntary conditioning is possible, is already an established fact. What we are saying is that self-regulation requires a source of conscious information, either cortical or subcortical. When Basmajian (1963) trained a number of research subjects to control the firing of a single motor nerve fiber, they could not do it without continuous auditory feedback (apparently because a level of internal awareness was not sufficiently developed). On the other hand, when we trained a few subjects to control the firing of a single motor nerve fiber, *one* of them reported and demonstrated a body awareness (in his forearm, on the surface of which our electrodes were attached) by means of which he could at will turn on and off the firing of the fiber, without external feedback (Green et al., 1969).

We apologize for not mentioning many important contributions to the field of "biofeedback and consciousness." Instead, we are focusing in a more general way, using selected references, outlining and describing five major kinds of consciousness that we have found to be associated with biofeedback training. It will be noted that these broad divisions of states of consciousness are characteristic not only of biofeedback training, but of all human experiential, existential phenomena:

1. Physical
2. Emotional
3. Mental
4. Extrapersonal
5. Transpersonal

[It is said by some linguists that Sanskrit has more than sixty-five definitions and descriptions of aspects, attributes, and gradations of consciousness; but Westerners who have studied Sanskrit know that it is difficult to use these differentiations. At our present stage of research in consciousness in the Western scientific world, these definitions are too fine-grained. And neither have the differentiations in states of consciousness of Aurobindo (1955) and Tibetan Buddhism (Evans-Wentz, 1958) been easy to use. Therefore, in trying to classify subjective experiences in research subjects (college students taking part in a theta brain wave and imagery study; Green and

Green, 1977), [we found it advantageous to use broad relatively easy-to-understand experiential categories, and began using a purely descriptive word, "extrapersonal," for certain experiences and the associated states of consciousness.]

Much of the following is focused on physical states of consciousness and their relation to other states. The reason is that in the West the contribution of body awareness to physical health, and of physical health to mental and spiritual health, has been largely ignored, except in popularized Eastern imports such as Tai Chi, some kinds of yoga, and the martial arts (including Aikido). For Western trends in body/mind/spirit medicine, see Pelletier (1981) and Shealy and Freese (1975).

Transformation of the body and of the psyche generally seem to progress at the same time, but in many of our research subjects and patients, awareness of change in body functions or in physiologic processes has preceded awareness of psychological change. In others, awareness of psychological came first. In either case, the so-called body transformation has been associated on occasion in our subjects with extrapersonal and transpersonal phenomena.

DEFINITIONS

Since 1975, psychophysiologic therapists, using biofeedback training as a major therapeutic modality, have become increasingly aware of the various domains of experience listed above, each involving a state of consciousness that can be differentiated from others through training and experience.

The first three categories, physical, emotional, and mental, are familiar to everyone, and even the concept of transpersonal experience has become quite well known since Sutich (1968, 1969), Maslow (1969), Assagioli (1969), and others first wrote on the subject. But the concept of extrapersonal experience, its similarities and its differences from transpersonal, has only recently become a subject of discussion (Green and Green, 1977)—and under different names, such as psychic, astral, and magical (Hendlin, 1983; Vaughn, 1983; Welwood, 1983).

The main similarity between extrapersonal and transpersonal experience is that both seem to originate from sources beyond the ego and personal unconscious of an individual. The difference between extrapersonal and transpersonal experience seems to be most apparent in considering the difference between psychic (or perhaps, parapsychological) and spiritual. An experience may be both psychic and spiritual, or exclusively psychic, or exclusively spiritual; but the difference between them, when it exists, is often neither negligible nor inconsequential. Using such differentiations, Jung's "collective unconscious" clearly contains both the extrapersonal and the transpersonal (Jung, 1963), as does Grof's analysis and description of realms of the unconscious (Grof, 1975; Grof and Valier, 1983).

Psychic, following Aurobindo's differentiations, was usually spoken of as "cosmic," and meant any nondivine (nonspiritual) experience arising from physical, emotional, and mental sources lying outside one's own personal ego and personal unconscious (Aurobindo, 1951, 1955, 1958). Divine (spiritual) to Aurobindo was "universal," transcendental, transcosmic. Spiritual experience, following his definition, had its source in "overmind" and "supermind," dimensions of energy/substance and experience similar to "dimensions of the Void" in Tibetan Buddhism (Evans-Wentz, 1958).

To Aurobindo, if an experience was purely cosmic, it had no universal content. It related only to physical, or emotional, or mental states, or to a mixture of them. On the other hand, if an experience was purely universal, it was ineffable, could not be described in words, was of the nature of the Void—not meaning nothing but meaning no words are adequate. If an experience was *both* cosmic and universal, it had a combination of physical, emotional, mental, and universal components, and thus could be described in words, though often only in symbolic language.

Extrapersonal, as a category corresponding to Aurobindo's idea of "cosmic," includes the field of research studied scientifically in most parapsychological laboratories. In brief, *extrapersonal* experience means beyond the normal limits of the ego and the personal unconscious, into cosmic nondivine awareness; *transpersonal* experience means beyond the normal limits of the ego and the personal unconscious, into universal, divine awareness. Concerning "nondivine" (cosmic) and "divine" (universal), the difference between extrapersonal and transpersonal is similar to the difference between Halloween and Easter.

It is noteworthy that a specific experience may have consciousness components in several categories. A remarkable example of such an experience is described by James Lester (1983) in his article "Wrestling with the Self on Mount Everest." Four climbers, lost in the dark at 28,000 feet, stayed on a ridge overnight without oxygen, tent, or sleeping bags. Some months later, one of them wrote about his experience on that lonely ridge:

I could see my body lying on that rock and snow. . . . I cared not if I came back . . . I felt I could peek into the other side of life and understand death . . . I reached a void where everything became one. . . . There was no space, no time, no sense of losing life. . . . The trivia of life disappeared beyond the broad, powerful outlines of existence and truth . . . I was one with the universe . . . I knew who I was and what I was.

MIND, BODY, AND MACHINES

It may at first seem odd that the above definitions and differentiations between extrapersonal and transpersonal are useful in a discussion of biofeedback training. "After all," it might be said, "biofeedback means machines. And machines cannot produce either psychic or spiritual events. Correct?" Yes. But a misunderstanding often hinges on the idea that biofeedback machines produce something, or do something to people. They do not. They only detect, and display to a person's cortex, information about normally hidden processes of the body. But since the body reflects the brain, and the brain reflects the mind, and the two (brain and mind) are not separate while we have a body (even in out-of-body experiences), it can be inferred that becoming aware of the body means becoming aware of the mind.

This logic, this argument, is useful and sometimes adequate for satisfying, or pacifying, the left cortex, but it is not always needed. From an a-rational, pragmatic experiential point of view, we are again and again told by yogis (and by research subjects and patients trained in psychophysiologic self-regulation), that becoming aware of normally *involuntary* physiological processes is linked with becoming aware of normally *unconscious* psychological processes. This experiential fact is beginning to have significant applications in psychiatry (Gladman and Estrada, 1975; Meadows, 1983; Meany, 1981; Rickles, 1981).

Regarding the mind–body linkage, it is worth noting that there is no such thing as training the body. There is only the training of the CNS. And in our view, consciousness is the most essential factor in developing self-regulation skills in the CNS, regardless of which neural and biochemical mechanisms of the body reflect these skills. As conscious autonomic skills become habitual, they can be allowed to sink from consciousness; but, of course, as with a striate skill, they can be "called up" for examination and modification at any time.

If the brain lost its body (and thereby lost all its exteroceptive and interoceptive sensory inputs), and was floated in a tank of cerebrospinal fluid, presumably it would not be able to detect the loss if the appropriate neural signals reached it through "wired" connections from outside, and appropriate perfusing liquids and biochemicals were provided through carotid arteries. This basic idea was delineated (in different words) over 170 years ago by Charles Bell. Helmholtz and Fechner, upon whose ideas much of modern experimental psychology has been based, took it for granted (Boring, 1950).

Again, the point is that the training of the body with biofeedback machines really is the training of the CNS. And that means the training of the mind. We are not aware of our CNS; we are aware only of our states and contents of consciousness. Therefore, the conscious and willful training of what we call the involuntary nervous system involves becoming conscious of, and training, the so-called unconscious. Without this extension of consciousness over previously unconscious functions, *voluntary* control of the autonomic neuro-system is not possible. If this is not apparent, think of the fact that self-regulation, by definition, means *conscious* self-regulation. If it is not conscious, it is not self-regulation.

This psychophysiological reciprocity, in which the brain affects the mind and the mind affects the brain, may be a hard point for those who choose to view the mind as separate from the brain, or for those at the opposite end of the philosophical spectrum, who choose to maintain that mind is only epiphenomenal awareness of fully autonomous processes of the CNS. But experiential data imply that the body and mind are inseparable (at least for the period of time in which we have a body), regardless of what body and mind each may be in ultimate fact. And this leads to another philosophical knot: the *volition* problem.

If the body affects the mind and the mind affects the body, how can anything happen except by reaction? Only by postulating the existence of volition can the logical bind be converted to a case of psychophysiologic constraints, rather than adamants. The psychophysiological-principle-plus-volition to which it seems useful to subscribe if we wish to escape mental and physical paralysis is: "Every change in the physiological state is accompanied by an appropriate change in the mental–emotional state, conscious or unconscious; and conversely, every change in the mental–emotional state, conscious or unconscious, is accompanied by an appropriate change in the physiological state. When coupled with volition, this principle allows a process called 'psychophysiologic-self regulation' to occur." (Also, see Nowlis, 1981; Wortz, 1982).

A related idea in regard to the neurological and psychological ordering of society as a whole, rather than ordering only the mind/body of an individual, was well expressed some decades ago by F. S. C. Northrop (1948). It supports the thought that in a distant future, individual self-mastery will be the *sine qua non* of a well-ordered society.

PSYCHOPHYSIOLOGIC ANATOMY

It is useful to summarize some of the more important psychoneurologic concepts to which we have referred. Figure 1 represents the CNS and also the most self-apparent parts of the psyche, the emotional and mental parts of ourselves (Green and Green, 1977). The caption explains in condensed

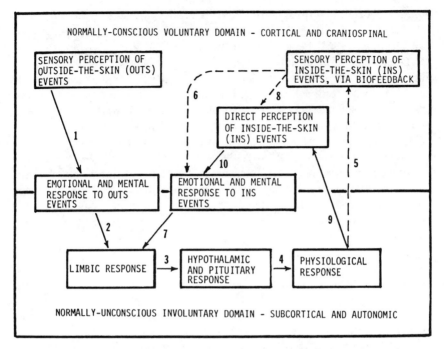

Figure 1. Simplified operational diagram of "self regulation" of psychophysiological events and processes: Sensory perception of OUTS events, stressful
or otherwise (upper left box), leads to a physiological response along Arrows
1 to 4. If the physiological response is "picked up" and fed back (Arrow 5) to
a person who attempts to control the "behavior" of the feedback device, then
Arrows 6 and 7 come into being, resulting in a "new" limbic response. This
response in turn makes a change in "signals" transmitted along Arrows 3 and
4, modifying the original physiological response. A cybernetic loop is thus completed and the dynamic equilibrium (homeostasis) of the system can be brought
under voluntary control. Biofeedback practice, acting in the opposite way to
drugs, increases a person's sensitivity to INS events and Arrow 8 is eventually
unnecessary because direct perception of INS events becomes adequate for
maintaining self regulation skills. Physiological self control through classical
yoga develops along the route of Arrows 7-3-4-9-10-7, but for control of specific physiological and psychosomatic problems biofeedback training seems
more efficient.

form how the system works. The basic neurological and neurohumoral information associated with the diagram was known several decades ago (Papez, 1937; Masserman, 1941; MacLean, 1949), but the self-regulation aspect
associated with biofeedback training, and its relation to the idea of *vol-*

untary, was not described before the 1960s (Basmajian, 1963; Brown, 1970; Budzynski et al., 1970; Green et al., 1969; Kamiya, 1962, 1968; Mulholland and Runnals, 1962; Peper and Mulholland, 1970).

The most significant implication of Figure 1 is that self-regulation training is first of all awareness training (see box labeled "DIRECT PERCEPTION . . . "). In biofeedback training, the cortex, in which presumably we are conscious, becomes aware of what the biofeedback device "says" and knows what that means in respect to the body. This knowing, when accompanied by appropriate visualization (in the box labeled "EMOTIONAL AND MENTAL RESPONSE TO INSIDE-THE-SKIN EVENTS"), is *followed* by the development of direct psysiological awareness, internal feedback. Finally, skill in self-regulation of the CNS is achieved, without machines, including large or small sections of the system formerly thought to be completely autonomic and unconscious.

PHYSICAL CONSCIOUSNESS

Biofeedback training, when used properly, is a potent tool in visualization training because of its powerful effects in developing simultaneous awareness of both psychological and physiological processes. And skill in visualization is the essence of *psycho*physiological self-regulation.

On the other hand, biofeedback used as a conditioning tool, rather than as an aid in developing consciousness and self-regulation, has had consistently negative clinical results. For instance, fifteen of the first sixteen published research studies using biofeedback for control of hypertension either failed completely or had statistically significant results that were *clinically* insignificant. That is, a sufficienty large *n* made the results satisfactory for statisticians, but the actual blood pressure changes were too small to have clinical value (for reviews see Blanchard et al., 1977; Frankel et al., 1978; Frumkin et al., 1978; Seer, 1979; Shapiro et al., 1977; Ray et al., 1979; Silver and Blanchard, 1978).

These research failures were generally well designed from a conditioning point of view and used excellent statistical methods of data handling, but were clinically defective. Specifically, successful clinicians do not use methods in which the patient is prevented from (or not aided in) developing self-awareness. The research designs and protocols used in the above investigations satisfied those who favor control of subjects by instrumental conditioning, but these designs do not satisfy those who favor freedom from conditioning, increased consciousness, and success *by the patient* in developing skill in autonomic self-regulation.

The handicaps, limitations, and problems associated with conditioning-type manipulation of human patients seem quite obvious to experienced clinicians, but the publish-or-perish culture of most universities has forced many researchers into hastily conducted and inappropriate studies. One professor, for instance, demonstrated that biofeedback for control of heart rate is "of no value whatsoever." He used a large number of subjects (183 college sophomores), processed the data with impeccable statistics (did everything needed to satisfy research reviewers and journal editors), but provided his subjects with only *six 5-minute training sessions*! With an equally large *n* with the same statistics, and with six 5-minute training sessions, we could demonstrate that hearing (auditory feedback) is "of no value whatsoever" in learning to play the piccolo. And doubtless we could get a paper published in a respectable refereed journal in a land where the the piccolo was not already known.

Researchers often do not pay the price necessary for clinical effectiveness, that of providing enough time for subjects to become aware, internally, of what is happening in the body (so that they no longer need feedback). In fact, some investigators make a point of the fact that subjects are not allowed to become conscious of what they are doing, and projects are conducted with double-blind conditions. Why such a general bias against "consciousness" has been maintained for so long is not easy to say, but this problem was persuasively handled (and should be completely answered) by a scientific paper in which it was clearly explained that the use of traditional experimental-psychology research designs in *clinical* research often includes serious errors of the type we have mentioned, as well as some basic statistical errors (Steiner and Dince, 1981; also see Ax, 1981). Having been involved directly or indirectly at The Menninger Foundation in the self-regulation training of over 1500 patients, about 80 percent of whom have succeeded in significantly ameliorating syndromes, we are pleased to note that these problems are beginning to get attention (see Surwit and Keefe, 1983; Thompson et al., 1983).

The single early research study that reported success at follow-up in training hypertension patients (Patel, 1973, 1975) had a clinical design in which home practice of "shavasan," a traditional yogic practice for deep relaxation and bodily self-awareness, was used in conjunction with laboratory feedback of galvanic skin response (GSR).

In contrast to the above-mentioned conditioning studies (in which consciousness was ignored), our own work in the field of hypertension uses a variety of self-regulation techniques including thermal biofeedback (emphasizing increased blood flow in the feet), striate muscular relaxation, breathing exercises, and autogenic training, which includes visualization (Schultz and Luthe, 1959). We stress self-awareness, blood flow control, blood pressure reduction, and medication reduction. In the first series of patients, six out of seven who had been using prescription medications for hypertention control (from six months to twenty years), were able to self-regulate their blood pressures and at the same time reduce their medication levels to *zero* (Green et al., 1979). Later, additional hypertensive patients were trained, many in groups, with similar positive results (Fahrion et al., 1985).

Our medication-free patients attributed maintenance of their success over a long period of time (the longest follow-up was ten years) to being able to maintain the self-awareness and self-control that developed during their original training. An important feature of their success was freedom from the generally deleterious side-effects of their medications. The pleasure expressed by these patients at having well-functioning bodies made it obvious that *the physical state of consciousness is a part of mental health.*

The biofeedback literature now includes several thousand research and clinical reports on the treatment of pathophysiologic syndromes of both psychosomatic and nonpsychosomatic origin (see Butler, 1978, for 2300 references; also, the Aldine series of annuals called *Biofeedback and Self Control*). The list of syndromes includes anorexia, bradycardia, blepherospasm, cancer, colitis, diabetes, epilepsy, esophageal spasm, fecal incontinence, foot drop, fibrillation, glaucoma, hypertension, insomnia, migraine, multiple sclerosis, nystagmous, oculomotor spasm, pain of various types, psoriasis, Raynaud's disease, strabismus, tachycardia, tension headache, tinnitus, and more.

The Placebo Effect. It is significant, in considering states of consciousness, that most of the above syndromes can often be temporarily ameliorated by the use of placebos (medically innocuous procedures, or "sugar pills"); and it is this wide range of syndromes responding to biofeedback training that originally led many psychologists and physicians to classify biofeedback training as a placebo—not realizing that *the placebo effect is unconscious self-regulation, whereas biofeedback training is conscious self-regulation.* Originally it had been thought (erroneously) by many researchers and clinicians that the placebo effect was imaginary. Nothing could be further from the truth. When a placebo slows the heart rate, that is real. When it changes gastric secretions, that is real. And now it has been shown that when the placebo "controls" pain, it does so through the release of endorphins, the endogenous morphine-like substances of the body (Levine et al., 1978). The placebo has proved to be the most generally pervasive factor in drug research, and every study designed to demonstrate the effectiveness of a new wonder drug must be carefully planned to eliminate the placebo effect (see Benson, 1980).

What is happening here? How can a sugar pill release endorphins, or cause the heart rate to decrease or increase (depending on what the physician tells the patient about the pill)? Answer: The placebo effect is determined by what the patient expects, and therefore visualizes, consciously or unconsciously. The placebo effect is generated in the patient's body by manipulating the patient's imagery and state of consciousness. The effect does not last, however, and cannot last, because the patient does not intentionally and knowingly use the visualization, is not aware of the fact that the effect is a physiological resultant of the visualization, and is not causally related to the pill.

As mentioned, sooner or later the sugar pill "does not work." That is why it is sometimes jokingly said in medical circles that the best time to use a new wonder drug is during the first year it is on the market. After that, the placebo component of the physiological effect dies out, and the drug may actually be found to be totally ineffective, like a sugar pill. On the other hand, when the patient experiencing psychophysiologic therapy becomes aware of the fact that visualization is the active ingredient in physiologic self-regulation, and learns to use it effectively, genuine self-reliance and self-control are achieved. And they tend to last.

The placebo works at first because the patient has been induced (more bluntly, tricked) by the doctor's description of effects, into visualizing what the body is going to do as a result of taking the "medicine." If the physician speaks Japanese to a patient who understands only English, however, the placebo effect presumably will be absent, or at least highly reduced. The patient might not know what to expect. It is interesting that the placebo (unlike acupuncture or tender loving care) does not work with babies or dogs. They do not understand, and do not visualize what is "supposed" to happen.

The reason a placebo stops working is that the patient begins to use the pill *habitually,* in an absent-minded way, without thinking each time, for instance, "this medicine slows my heart rate." The novelty is gone. Heart slowing as a consequence of pill taking, is taken for granted. The visualization stops. At this point, heart rate slowing no longer follows the swallowing of the pill. After this occurs a few times, the patient begins to think, "Maybe this medicine is not as effective as I thought it was." Confidence, an ingredient of effective visualization, diminishes, and a negative, sceptical, or pessimistic visualization begins to reverse the formerly positive placebo effect (see Frank, 1982).

In psychophysiologic therapy using biofeedback training, on the other hand, the amelioration of the syndrome is brought about by the patient's voluntary conscious visualization, guided by information. The patient is *self*-aware, and is conscious of creating the visualization. And that is no sugar pill. To quote an advertisement, it is "the real thing."

When clinical biofeedback came into focus in public attention, the entire field of self-regulation was brought abruptly under medical scrutiny. The patient's capacity to bring about physiological change through visualization began to be understood. Suddenly it became clear to most of those working in the field, that yoga, biofeedback training, hypnosis, self-suggestion, placebos, certain forms of meditation, all had something important in common—namely, visualization. Not necessarily mental pictures, but imagery of all kinds, verbal, pictorial, emotional, kinesthetic, depending on the nature and preferences of the visualizer.

The initial shock and controversy triggered by the emergence of a capacity in the average person for autonomic self-regulation is beginning to die away, and the main research question in the field of self-regulation is no longer "Is it?" but "*How* is it?" How can an idea become an enzyme? It may be a long time before that question is answered scientifically, but the yogic answer is that the mind, emotions, and body are states of *energy/substance* as well as states of consciousness, and all the body is in the mind, not all the mind in the body. The body is simply the densest section of the mind (Taimni, 1967).

Scientifically, the answer to the question about the "how" of autonomic self-regulation would seem to be the same as the answer about striate (voluntary muscle) self-regulation. Each kind of control, striate or autonomic, is preceded first by visualization and then by volition. We spent years as children learning to get the striate system under control, aided by exterocepter and interocepter feedback to the cortex. And now, with machine-aided feedback to the cortex, we are learning to use visualization and volition to get autonomic mechanisms under control. The ultimate question—how can *anything* be intentionally controlled in the CNS through visualization and volition?—cannot be answered by science, but for entertaining philosophical and psychophysiological discussions of the subject, see *Consciousness and Self-Regulation: Advances in Research and Theory* (Davidson et al., 1983).

EMOTIONAL CONSCIOUSNESS

As previously mentioned, the limbic system has been called the emotional brain, the visceral brain (MacLean, 1949), and it is now becoming clear that as we learn consciously to control the homeostatic levels of visceral behavior (with all that implies about the autonomic nervous system), we gradually become aware of the emotional states associated with both good and bad visceral homeostasis. It should be remembered that homeostasis means balance around a specific level of physiological functioning. Of itself, homeostasis is neither good nor bad. If our stomach is healthy, homeostasis tends to keep it that way. If, on the other hand, we have a stomach ulcer, homeostasis tends to keep it *that* way. And when we appear to "train the viscera" with biofeedback procedures to be calm and quiet in the face of stress, we are actually training the emotions to become calm and quiet in the face of stress. The visceral state reflects the limbic state. Psychologic homeostasis and physiologic homeostasis appear to be highly correlated. The extent to which in each of us they do not *seem* to be fully correlated, perhaps is one measure of the extent to which we are unconscious.

A good example of this body/emotion phenomenon was reported by psychiatrist James Howerton (1972). A thirty-year-old woman who had suffered from irritable bowel syndrome for fifteen years was referred to him by another psychiatrist, who in turn had received the patient from an internist. She had taken a variety of prescribed medications continuously for several years, and had become "a veritable authority on Freudian psychodynamics," but without relief. It was stressful to her to be more than 100 feet from a bathroom, and she was becoming suicidal over the fact that she could scarcely leave her house. Both physical and emotional equanimity were chronically nonexistent.

In line with the concept that "cortical awareness of dysfunctional autonomic behavior is the first requirement in gaining voluntary control of such behavior" (not simply recognition of the problem, but awareness of the specific piece of autonomic behavior involved), Howerton used an electronic stethoscope, taped to the patient's abdomen, to bring bowel sounds to consciousness. A technical difficulty at first was that the microphone did not amplify the sounds enough. Auditory feedback did not adequately precede colonic spasticity. The woman's husband suggested that a plastic bowl with the microphone taped to the inside (similar to a parabolic reflector), might give additional amplification of low-frequency rumbles.

After experimentation with different-sized bowls, the procedure worked, and through audio feedback the patient was able to become aware of impending disaster a few minutes in advance of the event. Howerton supplied his patient with "organ specific" autogenic phrases that were aimed at quieting the unnecessary motility of the GI tract, phrases such as, "my abdomen is calm, quiet, and peaceful"; "warmth and quietness are spreading throughout the whole lower section of my body"; "my entire GI tract does its work smoothly and quietly with no unnecessary activity."

As the body came under control of the mind, the emotional upsets came under control, and within five months the woman was "a new person," off drugs and leading a normal life. Howerton did not find it necessary in this particular case to find out whether a specific emotional problem was the original causative agent of the syndrome (through limbic-hypothalamic effects reflected in the autonomic nervous system), or whether a viral flu or some other "outside" factor caused the original spasms, which in turn led to upset and negative emotions (i.e., led to the kinds of emotions that alone, with no outside help, can upset healthy physiological homeostasis), which then perpetuated the problem in a vicious downward spiral of colitis, then greater, "neg-emotion," then worse GI symptoms and greater neg-emotion, and so on. Without identifying the particular psychodynamics involved, it was clear that this particular patient had a bad habit of responding to life stresses in a gastrointestinal way. When that fact finally came to consciousness, and a conscious skill at autonomic self-regulation was achieved, "the problem went away." Since 1972, neither that problem nor any other visceral dysfunction has appeared, and the patient jokingly told Dr. Howerton (1983) that he had deprived himself of a patient who could have afforded a psychiatrist for the rest of her life.

In some cases, however, as long maintained in psychoanalytic theory, it seems to be necessary for buried emotional events to come to consciousness before surcease from physical/emotional disorders is reached. For example, a fifty-year-old woman referred by a psychoanalyst to us in 1973 for training in self-control of somatic symptoms (fainting, heart irregularities, vomiting—all apparently associated with overreacting to "ordinary life stress"), was trained in hand warming (her dominant right hand) and in forehead EMG control. This was accompanied by breathing exercises and the instruction that the resultant voluntary physical sensations of deep quietness should be allowed to spread throughout her entire body. After a few weeks of home practice with a portable temperature feedback meter, and weekly sessions in the clinic to report on the development of self-awareness in body, emotions, thoughts, and fantasies, and to practice muscular relaxation aided by an EMG machine, she reported that the left side of her body seemed "to be frozen." On checking her reported lack of thermal symmetry, it was found that during sessions her left hand remained 16°F cooler than the right (80°F versus 96°F). Thermal training was then shifted to her left hand.

Three weeks later during a lab visit, she demonstrated equal warming with both hands, and said that during home practice with the left hand she had suddenly, out of the blue, begun thinking about long forgotten events that had happened twenty-five years earlier.

What she had really wanted to be in life, she said, was an opera singer. But one day, when singing with a church choir, she suffered an abrupt and total voice block. She became faint and other members of the group supported her until the performance ended. After this happened a second time, she visited her physician for advice. His simple suggestion was, "Give up singing." This she did—and it was then that her serious emotional/physical problems began. During the next twenty-five years she suffered continuously from a variety of physical and emotional upsets, she said, despite two five-year rounds of psychoanalysis. Not realizing her own direct responsibility, she said to us, "For the last twenty years my body has been trying to kill me."

Very interesting. The body, the innocent victim of the CNS, was blamed for what it supposedly was doing to the psyche. Some people live in their heads to such an extent that they are almost unconscious of the body except when it malfunctions. And then they feel they are cursed with a defective or malevolent biological apparatus.

Espeically interesting in light of findings in left–right hemispheric functions (Galin, 1974; Ornstein, 1972; TenHouten, 1978) is the fact that it was the left side of her body that seemed "to be frozen," and it was the corresponding (contralateral) side of her head, the "singing side" (right cortex), that presumably suffered the functional block. When the *left* hand was warmed, she "remembered" that what she had really longed to be (until she lost her voice in church) was an opera singer.

This precipitated a good mind/body recovery. She began to relive and resolve the events of a religious crisis, and soon was able to live without psychiatric help for the first time in twenty-five years, take a plane trip alone to return to her home state and take charge of the family business. She returned to church and became the director of a young people's choir, visited people in other cities, and eventually began planning a tour of Europe.

In our clinical view, supported by many such cases, there is no such thing as learning to control the body alone in a *self-regulation* paradigm, without emotion (without the limbic brain), as if psyche/soma could be fractionated under self-regulation conditions. Changes in states of consciousness seem to be the *sine qua non* of psychophysiologic therapy in our practice. It is a convenient fact that our bodies can tell us something about our minds, something about deeply buried emotional states.

MENTAL CONSCIOUSNESS

In attempting to differentiate between mental and emotional consciousness it is useful to consider the differences between thought and feeling, between intellect and desire (or aversion), between rational and a-rational, between mathematics and aesthetics, between figure and ground, between specific focus of attention and Gestalt awareness, between deductive-inferential and intuitive mentation, between dispassionate and passionate, between CPAs and free spenders, and so forth. It is not suggested, though, that there are many examples of pure thought or pure emotion. Most real-life examples are mixtures of the two and often have, in addition, a strong body component.

Nevertheless it is possible to discuss biofeedback and mental states of consciousness in: (1) consciously *getting* intellectual information from the unconscious, and (2) consciously *putting* information and instructions into the unconsciousness; or, as John Lilly (1972) might put it, first interrogating the human biocomputer, and second, programming the human biocomputer.

"Getting answers from the unconscious" was a phrase used by psychiatrist Johannes Schultz (Schultz and Luthe, 1959). It depends on a state of awareness in which normally hidden information of the psyche can come to consciousness, in a hypnagogic-like way, in response to need and to a conscious request for information. As explained by Schultz, a necessary psychophysiologic precondition, without which this mental process is inoperable, is that the requester first move into a psychophysiologic state of "autogenic shift." This state (very different from the usual presleep condition) is one in which the body, emotions, and mind are all quiet at the same time. The body approaches sleep, the emotions are deeply quiet, but a volitionally stilled receptive mind is *alert*, and not aimlessly wandering or daydreaming (see also, Budzynski, 1981; Fehmi, 1978).

The state of autogenic shift is reachable through classical Autogenic Training, through meditation, and in other ways (as many have testified over the decades), but one of the simplest ways is through biofeedback training. Biofeedback training has an advantage in our modern technological society of using what is perceived to be a "scientific" approach. For some purists (whether meditators or psychotherapists) who may not usually think of the body as being part of the mind, the psyche's use of a machine-aided approach to the unconscious seems either blasphemous or artificial, but for the average layperson who asks for help with physical, emotional, or mental difficulties, biofeedback training seems very natural after the rationale of self-regulation training is fully explored (Figure 1).

Interrogating the Unconscious

Into the state of autogenic shift, this multiplex state of quietness and alertness, the question for which an answer is desired is projected by the conscious "mind," with a request for a response. This is followed by a return to the state of quiet alertness in anticipation of a hypnagogic answer.

If a person can easily slip into the state of autogenic shift, biofeedback training may not be needed for getting information from the unconscious, but for most unsophisticated persons (and especially for extreme "left cortex" intellectuals) it is most productive in learning autogenic shift to first use thermal and EMG training, and follow this with brain wave (EEG) training.

In autogenic training, *two* of the psychophysiologic conditions needed for autogenic shift are warmth in the peripheral parts of the body and an overall body sensation of heaviness (or lightness, in some cases). In biofeedback, thermal training accomplishes the warmth condition, and EMG training accomplishes the heaviness condition. It is interesting to note that the feeling of warmth in the periphery has a correspondence with quiet emotions, and the physical feeling of heaviness, which is quietness in the striate nervous system, has a correspondence with deep relaxation.

Warmth in the periphery relates to emotional quietness because hand and foot warming depend largely on increased blood flow, which depends on vasodilation, which in turn depends on "turn-off" (decrease) of firing in the peripheral vascular section of the sympathetic nervous system and control thereby of the behavior of smooth muscles in blood vessel walls (peripheral vasodilation). And when this voluntary turn-down of sympathetic firing is established through biofeedback-aided visualization training, which seems to mean that the limbic brain is involved in making appropriate changes in hypothalamic circuits, the psychological result, or cause, or correlate, is emotional quietness.

In the other direction, *increased* sympathetic firing results in peripheral vasoconstriction and peripheral cooling, and is almost always associated with emotional activation. It is necessary to say "almost always" because unconsciously skillful patients and consciously skillful yogis can sometimes make the parts of the nervous system function in independent and disconnected ways.

A *third* condition of autogenic shift in getting answers from the unconsciousness is for the mind to be alert but not active. This is often accomplished in our practice of psychophysiologic therapy through occipital theta brain wave training (Green and Green, 1977). In order to understand the general significance of theta training (and here we get into an area in which, to the best of our knowledge, most biofeedback practitioners have not worked), it is useful to consider the difference between the voluntary production of alpha rhythm and theta rhythm (see Oliver, 1975).

Conscious alpha production for most people means relaxing in their usual way, with the eyes closed. Ninety percent of the human population normally produce some occipital alpha under these conditions, whether daydreaming or not. Interestingly, it is quite easy to learn in a few brain wave training sessions, using auditory feedback, to produce occipital alpha with the eyes open but unfocused. Conscious *theta* production, on the other hand, is much more difficult (based on our own experience, on research experience with college students and others, and on clinical experience in our Biofeedback Center over the last ten years).

Many people cannot succeed in causing the theta tone to sound in an EEG feedback-machine unless they are almost asleep. Then, when the tone sounds, they return to "alpha or beta attention" so quickly that the theta state is eradicated. The task is to develop alert internal attention without eliminating the theta rhythm. The trainee must learn to "hear" the theta feedback tone without changing the state of consciousness toward "normal", thus causing the theta state to disappear. It is necessary to learn to remain alert in the so-called twilight state of consciousness.

Many pages could be written about theta brain wave training and the associated subtleties of consciousness. Suffice it to say that in our estimation the evidence strongly suggests that "voluntary hypnagogic imagery (whether the achievement follows theta biofeedback training, or comes from some other volitional methodology) will eventually become "the royal road to the unconscious," rather than dreams (Freud, 1954) or hypnosis (Fromm, 1980). Concerning the significance of the hypnagogic state, Lawrence Kubie (1943) commented:

> The hypnagogic reverie might be called a dream without distortion. Its immediate instigator is the day's "unfinished business," but like the dream it derives from more remote "unfinished business" of an entire lifetime as well. . . . Whatever the explanation . . . with [hypnagogic reverie] significant information about the past can be made readily and directly accessible without depending upon the interpretations which are requisite in the translation of dreams. . . . It is probable that in this partial sleep, in this no-man's land between sleeping and waking, a form of dissociation occurs which makes it possible to by-pass the more obstinate resistances which block our memories in states of full conscious awareness, and which contribute to the distortion of memory traces in dream. . . . The patient's free associations seem to flow with extraordinary freedom and vividness, gravitating spontaneously to early scenes and experiences with intense affects, yet without the multiple distortions that occur in the dream process.

In our view, hypnagogic imagery that is self-obtained, without trance induction or programming by a therapist (as in hypnotherapy), is especially useful. As Barber (1965) has indicated, results in hypnosis are often reflective of the therapist's attitudes and emotions rather than the subject's.

An excellent example of "interrogating the unconscious" with the aid of theta training occurred in our lab when a biofeedback technician (at a Topeka hospital), himself skilled in EMG and blood flow control, and successful in training others, began to suffer from what seemed to be a form of colitis associated with "spontaneous" anxiety. Marty (an assigned name) had mentioned this problem to us, but not until he said that it was not responding to sympathetic quieting did we begin to suspect deeper causes than normal life stress. He obtained medical opinions from two physicians, following a "work up" of the GI tract, but no physical causes could be found, and he was advised to talk with a psychotherapist.

After a few nonproductive psychotherapy sessions, Marty asked if we would advise him on getting information about the problem from the unconscious. A student and teacher of Patanjali yoga, he felt that every cell of the body was a "cell" of the unconscious and the unconscious therefore had in it information about every part of the body. And because the unconscious was a section (region, aspect) of mind, it could generate a proper form of communication with the conscious mind. He was also acquainted with the kinds of hypnagogic imagery obtained by college students in our theta training research project.

It was suggested that he prepare a specific question in which a visualization of the problem would be presented to the theta-state unconscious, essentially following the procedure outlined below under "Programming the Unconscious," asking for specific information about his GI difficulty.

From previous experience with brain wave training, it was not difficult for him to become quiet enough to produce theta rhythm in the left occiput. Auditory feedback and a duration-integrator attached to the EEG machine showed that after a few minutes of mostly alpha production, he was able to produce theta about 20 percent of the time. At the end of the second session he described a hypnagogic image that had "popped" into awareness. A part of the intestinal tract was "seen" as thick and tough, rather than flexible, and in it knobbly blood vessels were becoming brittle and beginning to crack. We discussed this image and considered with him what it might mean. A couple of days later, at our suggestion, he returned to the physician who had been particularly friendly and told of his imagery, referring to it as a kind of dream. After further medical tests Marty's problem was diagnosed as Crohn's disease (an intestinal problem having some of the features he had described).

Under "Transpersonal Consciousness" (below), we will discuss Marty's attempts to control Crohn's disease through organ-specific visualization (which in his case did not succeed) and describe his eventual reinterrogation of the unconscious for an explanation of the problem.

Some interesting research ideas have come from theta training. For instance, one of its values seems to be the deeply peaceful state that is achieved. When normally buried information comes to conscious while the patient is in this state, he or she seems to be buffered against limbic overreactivity. Is there a neurochemical or neurotransmitter correlate here?

The patient may be uncomfortable with what is "dredged up," but information seems to be "metered" in a way that makes it tolerable. The unconscious seems to have an innate wisdom that may be protective when we ask for "answers from the unconsciousness." This is not contraindicative of the yogic idea that the unconscious includes not only the reactive "subconscious" but also a wiser "superconscious" (Assagioli, 1969; Aurobindo, 1955; Green and Green, 1971).

Programming the Unconscious

One of the most interesting facts that psychophysiologic therapists become aware of in the course of working with different patients and a variety of syndromes, is that patients learn how to reprogram, by themselves, specific physiologic and psychological mechanisms. Johannes Schultz implemented this possibility when he created the idea of the "organ specific formula" phrased in the first person, and made it an essential therapeutic tool of autogenic training. (For those not directly acquainted with autogenic training, an organ specific formula is a positive verbal statement in which the patient outlines for his or her own body the desired behavior of a body organ, or organ system, or congeries of systems.)

To be most effective, an organ specific formula is used by the patient while in a state of autogenic shift, while the body, emotions, and mind are quiet. It is important to note that the same conditions of quietness that enhance the process of getting answers from the unconscious can be used in programming the unconscious. Budzynski and Peffer (1973), for instance, developed an ingenious way of teaching languages while the student is in a passive nonvolitional theta state. But in our practice of psychophysiologic therapy, the organ specific formula is *actively* implemented through visualization, and biofeedback devices are used by the patient (1) for discovering what the body is actually doing in response to a specific visualization, and (2) for correctly modifying the visualization in order to get a desired physiological and psychological result. A "good" visualization for one person may be a "bad" one for another, but through the use of biofeedback each person can tailor-make his or her own most effective imagery, whether auditory (verbal), visual (mental pictures), emotional, or kinesthetic (body sensation).

Despite their many similarities, in this concept of *self-programming* biofeedback training and classical autogenic training are not the same. In biofeedback training there is a great deal more emphasis placed on the patient's own capacity to make decisions, to shape the organ-specific visualization, and to take self-responsibility.

As mentioned previously, heaviness and warmth training with EMG and temperature feedback machines help the patient get into the state of deep quietness of body and emotions, and theta brain wave training helps develop the deeply quiet but alert mind. As indicated, these different kinds of feedback used in concert are often powerfully effective in helping a person move toward awareness of the unconscious, but on occasion each *alone* will span the entire distance. That, is, these different kinds of feedback are not mutually exclusive in their effects, and on occasion individuals will move into a theta brain wave rhythm as a result of warming the hands (to above 95°F and maintaining that temperature for a few minutes). But on average, theta training *following* EMG and temperature training is considerably more effective in producing the "theta state" than temperature training and EMG training, either alone or together.

Developing deep mental quietness simultaneously with mental alertness is not easy for most people, even with theta brain wave training. Nevertheless, that training is a relatively simple method that Westerners can use without long yogic practice. And to be able to enter the theta state at will is an important accomplishment, we believe because, as stated above, the same state of deep quietness that is used in *getting* answers from the unconscious can also be used in *programming* the unconscious for physiological and psychological change. In the list below, note the opposites and parallels:

getting answers	programming behavior
sensory behavior	motor behavior
passivity	volition
imagery	visualization

In beginners, the problem of achieving deeply quiet mental alertness is doubly complicated by the fact that unlike the situation with psychophysiologic self-regulation experts such as Jack Schwarz (see Green and Green, 1977), visualization and volition tend to destroy the passive–receptive conditions of the unconscious that are needed for successful programming of the body–mind. This obstacle can be surmounted over a period of time by having the patient, or research subject:

Practice with EMG and temperature feedback devices until deep muscle relaxation is achieved and the hands can be warmed to more than 95°F and held there over a period of several minutes.

Practice with alpha–theta feedback until it is possible consciously to generate theta more than 10 percent of the time (this may take several sessions). As already mentioned, this state can be used for both interrogating and programming the unconscious. Interrogation has been discussed above. For programming:

1. Move first into a state of EMG quietness and peripheral warmth.
2. While in this state, *construct* the visualization that is to be planted in the unconscious, a visualization that has already been carefully planned by the cortex, with ambiguities eliminated (for the unconscious is like a computer in some ways, and tends to take instructions literally).
3. Allow awareness to sink down into the theta state with the idea that the unconsciousness is now listening; it is now in "record mode."

4. Gently project the visualization into the "field of mind" as a *Gestalt,* with as little left-cortex activity as possible.
5. Terminate the session with a quite command, such as "do it," "so be it," "the instruction is now terminated," or the like, in order to terminate unconscious receptivity (similar to using the "enter" key in programming a computer).
6. Bring awareness back to the surroundings carefully so as not to disturb the planted instruction.

Questions, doubts, anxieties, and all such cortical probes and limbic fears are held in abeyance. Thoughts such as "On the other hand, . . . " must be checked. Farmers do not dig up their just-planted seeds to find out if they are beginning to sprout, and patients must be trained to have patience when learning to program the unconscious.

If a problem is purely psychological, that is, without any *obvious* physiological correlates, there is no easy way of determining, after the difficulty is gone, whether it was the conscious or the unconscious that was reprogrammed (see the voluminous literature on hypnosis). But in physiologic cases, results are sometimes so remarkable (such as wounds healing at double speed, or intractable abcesses clearing up in a few days), that there is little doubt that normally involuntary unconscious biological mechanisms controlled by the hypothalamic–pituitary complex have been powerfully stimulated by autogenic (self-created) visualization, and these have caused the body to move toward healthy homeostasis.

The methods described above for programming the unconscious are often useful, not only in preparing for a stressful future event, possibly in sports, but also in handling upcoming physiologic crises. For instance, several clients of our Biofeedback Center have undergone visualization training in preparation for surgery. Without going into detail, it can be reported that after the client has learned to quiet the striate and sympathetic nervous systems through EMG and temperature training, we use guided imagery to help him or her move through a mental, emotional, and physiological scenario of the operation, in which the behaviors of the various aspects of body/mind are rehearsed. It is not spontaneous hypnagogic imagery that is wanted here, but *guided* imagery. If, however, the patient produces hypnagogic imagery under these conditions, we pay close attention to symbolic meanings, and work with the patient in clarifying implications.

Patients then practice on their own, at home, using the basic ideas of the "guided" session to construct appropriate scenarios, adapting them to changes in the situation as needed. Prior to surgery, in the hospital, relaxation and visualization are again practiced.

Physicians and nurses have reported that rapid healing in intensive care and complication-free recovery have characterized the experience of these patients. And the patients often have been exuberant. Some of them felt so well after surgery that they wanted to return home before their physicians were ready to release them (Walters, 1983).

A great deal of research remains to be done in this application of mind/body control, and the literature on self-hypnosis shows that there is interest in the possibility of devising scoring techniques for evaluation of effects (Orne and McConkey, 1981). Since physicians and nurses, as well as the patients themselves, are observers of recovery after surgery, it might be possible to devise physiological scoring methods that would provide hard data in this area.

EXTRAPERSONAL CONSCIOUSNESS

In the previous discussion of the meaning of "extrapersonal," we referred to experience "beyond the normal limits of the ego and the personal unconscious, into cosmic nondivine awareness." And we also used such terminology as psychic, astral, magical, parapsychological and Halloween. An out-of-body experience certainly has many personal features, but since perception without the use of the normal body organs seems to occur in ways that are "beyond the normal limits of the ego," we classify such phenomena as extrapersonal, or as extending into extrapersonal dimensions of experience.

The five experiential categories of this chapter can be thought of as occurring in five non-mutually-exclusive domains. In fact, it is affirmed by highly respected students of states of consciousness, such as Aurobindo, Patanjali, and Evans-Wentz, that these domains are energy/substance "fields" that, in humans, are fully interpenetrating. They are not the same, but they are coexistent and coterminous, just as magnetic, electrostatic, electromagnetic, and gravitational fields can be present in the same space at the same time—just as the broadcast fields of radio stations and television stations, though not the same, are present in the same space at the same time.

Again differentiating between extrapersonal and transpersonal, an out-of-body experience may be the subject of investigation in parapsychological research (Tart, 1968, 1975; Osis and McCormick, 1980), but there is no necessary implication that it is transpersonal. In fact, it might include a visit to "hell," if we are followers of Swedenborg (1934) or if we project into a bad "locale" (Monroe, 1971; Muldoon and Carrington, 1958; Gabbard and Twemlow, 1984).

At a 1972 biofeedback workshop in Kansas city, one of the first-time trainees, who practiced hand temperature control with a feedback device and autogenic phrases for half an hour, asked what it meant "when you see yourself from a distance." He said that he became deeply quiet and his hands grew very warm, and then he suddenly was on the other side of the room, looking at himself sitting in the chair with the biofeedback machine in front of him. Also, he said, there was a bundle of gray "fibers," like a gray rope, that went from him to his body. "What was that?" We talked for a while about yogic theory and psychic phenomena, and asked if this was a common occurrence with him. He said that it had not happened before, that he was not particularly religious, that several years ago in high school he had read about yogis controlling their hearts, etc., but he had been involved in the business world and had not thought much about the mind in the last few years.

It seems that out-of-body experience and other parapsychological phenomena are not as dependent on the particular biofeedback modality being used (temperature, EMG, EEG) as they are on whether the subject is able to slip into a "state of deep quietness," somewhat similar to the "trance state" described in much hypnosis literature. Concerning "trance" as a state of consciousness, it is interesting to consider the possibility that in hypnosis, the researcher, or therapist, is "talking directly to the limbic system" of the subject, without the help (except acquiescence) of the subject's cortex. In self-regulation training, on the other hand, the subject's cortex may be said to be talking to its own limbic system.

In line with our general orientation toward volitional self-guidance, we seldom recommend that patients buy biofeedback machines. Instead, we lend them machines for home practice, and have them returned as soon as possible, usually as soon as self-regulation without the machine is demonstrated. Dependence on a machine implies that the cortex is not secure in its ability to program its own limbic brain through visualization. A few patients we know of became dependent on machines, and had to be "weaned off" so that genuine self-regulation could develop. We also discourage the use of cassette tapes for programming the unconscious, even those made by the patient for control of his or her own symptoms. We want patients to get the gains of physiological self-regulation, and also have a gain in consciousness, not be externally-programmed.

A number of attempts have been made in parapsychological research since the early 1970s to use biofeedback training for enhancement of extrasensory perception (ESP), but in general these projects have suffered from the same deficiency found in much biofeedback research; namely, not enough time is allowed for the training of subjects. In fact, three not untypical studies in parapsychological journals were contingent on what the authors erroneously called "alpha training." In these studies training consisted of, respectively: (1) one alpha session of six 5-minute trials; (2) two alpha sessions, each of which contained two 15-minute trials; and (3) ten alpha training sessions, each of which contained four 4-minute trials. The last one mentioned totaled 160 minutes of training.

In our work with theta brain wave training, on the other hand, about 20 laboratory hours over a period of ten weeks were spent in theta brainwave training in a group of eight pilot subjects (including ourselves), and about 35 hours were spent in home practice without feedback devices. During lab sessions, three of the eight had hypnagogic imagery which included ESP material (Green and Green, 1977).

In a follow-up experiment, 40 hours were spent by college students in occipital alpha/theta training, and even then only three out of twenty-six in the group had experiences that because of their parapsychological implications we could classify as extrapersonal. We were not trying to elicit or study ESP and precognition, however, and that research lead was not followed. During the investigation with these students, the spontaneous ESP images that occurred were not particularly startling, as events, except in one case.

Val (an assigned name) had not had any previous ESP experience, but during the tenth week of alpha/theta training, spontaneous ESP began to occur, upsetting him because he did not "believe in such things." These events were climaxed by a hypnagogic image, just as he was falling asleep one evening, of Governor George Wallace being shot in a crowd of people. It startled him and made him feel uncomfortable, but he dismissed it as a "bad dream." Three days later, on the way to the lab for a meeting with us, he heard on his car radio that Wallace had just been shot. The circumstances were quite like his hypnagogic image, and he was visibly upset by the time he arrived. He did not want to know such things, he said. What was his responsibility in such a case? After thorough discussion we advised that in view of the scientific nonacceptance of precognition, and psychic phenomena in general, it was better not to discuss what he had "seen." Six months later we had occasion to talk with him by phone, and found that he was doing well in graduate school, and the various kinds of psychic phenomena that he had experienced for about three weeks at the end of theta training had stopped, not to his regret.

Mental and emotional phenomena of this kind happen occasionally in the practice of client-centered biofeedback clinicians (those who tend to work with patients as *colleagues* in solving problems), and for this reason alone it is useful to be able to speak in terms of a specific states-of-consciousness category, extrapersonal, in which all unusual events are not automatically classified as transpersonal.

TRANSPERSONAL CONSCIOUSNESS

In the previous discussion of the meaning of transpersonal, we referred to experience "beyond the normal limits of the ego and the personal unconscious, into universal, divine awareness." We used words such as spiritual, transcendental, overmind, supermind, transcosmic, ineffable, not nothing, and Easter; and referred to the Void of Tibetan Buddhism—which according to Evens-Wentz's Tibetan teacher contains twenty-eight differentiable levels of nonverbal experience (Evens-Wentz, 1954, 1958).

To the best of our knowledge, there has not been any generally accepted biofeedback research in the transpersonal domain; but we have received verbal reports from workshop attendees (persons in the helping professions who are using biofeedback techniques to help clients become self-aware and self-regulated) that attest to the nonrarity of transpersonal experience. (Also see Peper et al., 1979). If we can believe the data, transpersonal events happen at least once in the lives of more than 40 percent of our country's population, though they are seldom spoken of outside the intimate family (see Greeley and McCready, 1974, for a fascinating report, "Are We a Nation of Mystics?"). Such events are sometimes triggered by psychophysiologic self-regulation training. Consider the following.

Marty, whom we previously spoke of in regard to Interrogating the Unconscious, was relieved to find (on reporting his hypnagogic image to his physician and getting some additional gastrointestinal tests) that he had an identifiable problem, Crohn's disease. But the physician who worked with him was unable to find either a diet or any combination of medicines and diet that ameliorated the symptoms, and after a few weeks Marty began to detect intestinal bleeding during bouts of colitis.

In discussing this more serious development, he again asked if we would advise him on the possible meaning of symbols in hypnagogic imagery, and he would again use an EEG theta state for interrogating the unconscious. After the second session, following in main the quieting protocol outlined under "Emotional Consciousness," he reported that possibly crucial information had come to consciousness, but he did not know what to do. He had quickly and easily slipped into the state of deep quietness, the theta tone almost continuously assuring him that he was in the appropriate brain wave state, and then he was suddenly a performer in a hypnagogic *movie*. He no longer was aware of the training room, the theta tones from the feedback machine, or his body in the reclining chair.

He was on the ground floor of a several-story dark building, and it was necessary to get to the top. There were no stairways, and the floors had been broken out so that the interior was a large empty shell. Searching through the gloom, he found that the walls were covered with ladders, and he began to climb. It was tiring, but after passing three or four floors he could see a sloping roof above. The sides of the roof came together in a pyramid, like the inside of the Washington Monument.

Energized by the sight of his goal, he soon reached the slope of the peak. There the climb was exhausting and scary. It was hard to keep from falling, and it was a long way down. Steeling himself, he pulled his way upward in the stuffy darkness against both gravity and fear. As he approached the place where the ladders from all sides came together, he realized with a sinking feeling that there was no way out. He was too tired to search anymore, and he just clung numbly to the ladder.

Suddenly with a crash and a flood of air and light, the peak of the building burst off. A brilliant and beautiful shaft of golden light streamed down, and a ladder began to descend. With incredible relief he moved to the new ladder (Jacob's ladder?). He said it was "grace" and a flood of warmth and love poured through him. He began climbing. But as his head neared the opening, he felt a weight and pain in his lower midsection. Looking down, he saw he was wearing a broad leather belt on which four iron rings were bolted. Tied to each of the rings were two long ropes that descended into the gloom. He saw that men and women had hold of the ropes and, as he put it, "I was being pulled in two." He recognized them. They were members of the Patanjali yoga class he was teaching, which he had led for eight or nine months. What was he to do?

Then a strong clear voice from above said, "You must let them go and come up alone first." Marty said he was suddenly convulsed by fear and anguish, and he shouted upward, "I can't. I won't come up unless I can bring them with me." With that, the ladder and light vanished, and the broken-off top of the roof fell back in place. It was dark and cold, and again he was clinging to a ladder inside the roof.

Then he became aware of the training room. He rested for a few minutes, turned off the brain wave machine, and shaken mentally and emotionally, came to report the imagery. It was true, he said, that the yoga study group stressed him. The reason was that he had become so sensitive to their problems that if anyone came to the weekly meeting with a hurt knee, the moment that person came in the door his own knee began to ache. Every problem they had, he could feel. They had begun phoning him at night about their troubles, and in advance of their calls, his solar plexus would begin to ache.

From his description of the bonds between him and the group, and from the apparent significance of the imagery, we suggested that it might be useful if he and his wife, both of whom loved the mountains (where Marty was always able to recuperate from stress), would consider moving to Colorado for a year or two, where he had said he had an opportunity for a different job, one in which he would not be "pulled on" by others. He might then have time to repair himself. If people are drowning, isn't it better to throw a rope from the bank, rather than try to tow them in the water, especially if you are not yourself a good swimmer?

His surprising answer was not lacking in self-awareness. He did not want to leave the group and go to Colorado. He could not comply with the hypnagogic instruction because of an inner promise he had made. In the Marines he had vowed he would never again leave a person in need. He had not been in combat, but during a forced march across the California desert, one of his buddies became thirst-crazed and began pulling up bushes and chewing the roots. They had been warned of the poisonous creosote bush, but his buddy ate the roots, and before help came he was dead. Marty could have fought with his buddy to prevent that from happening.

On another occassion, when a group of marines was dropped from a helicopter into the surf off San Diego, with 40-pound machine guns attached to their belts, his closest friend had drowned. On hitting the water they were to pop self-inflating balloons to buoy up the guns. The friend's equipment did not work, and he plunged to the bottom. Marty struggled to shore, but he felt he should have jettisoned his own equipment and tried to dive for his friend. Never again, he said, would he leave friends, no matter what happened.

In a few weeks Marty developed peritonitis, and despite a desperate attempt by physicians and hospital staff to save him, he died. His determination to live was unparalleled, his doctor said, and he survived weeks longer than anyone at the hospital thought was possible, in part because of the devotion of his wife, who cared for him in the hospital day and night. He was amazing, they said, but he died. .

Marty's story is also the story of Franz Kafka, though the roles and circumstances are poles apart. In both cases they were told by an inner source what the problem was, and in both cases the advice was not acted on (see Kafka's novels, *The Trial* and *The Castle,* 1937 and 1954, respectively, in which are detailed his own inner experiences).

The significance of Marty's experience is several-fold: (1) It illustrates the potential of a part of the unconscious to answer questions and give wise guidance. (This we have seen in many patients, but they did not have Marty's vow, which bound his life to a seemingly inevitable doom.) (2) It suggests that as individuals we are not powerless, but that we have an opportunity to make choices that affect our lives. (Marty consciously made a choice.) (3) It shows a risk, the possibility of being too self-willed, too personal rather than transpersonal—unwillingness to take advice from what may be a wiser Self. (4) The hypnagogic image explained that the physiology and the psychology were not separate, and implied that it was necessary to be healed in mind first. (5) The image suggested that taking on the problems of others before you have handled your own problems may be an error.

As we now think of Marty, we think of "the noble warrior" who, in a certain way, gave his life for his friends, even if there was no obvious gain for them. What the ultimate transpersonal meaning of his life may be, we do not know. With Marty's case in mind, it seems useful for both personal and transpersonal well-being to become self-reliant, self-programming, self-understanding, self-*forgiving,* self-regulated, and self-responsible, in whatever fields of experience are encountered. Ways of doing this in life and death situations have been reported by Cousins (1979, 1983).

In patients having transpersonal crises, training in self-regulation and self-dependence often leads to their finding in their own unconscious a source of knowledge and wise guidance that is superior to anything that we, as external therapists, can offer. We have un-originally called this phenomenon "becoming aware of Self." This "center of self" appears to approximate in its salient characteristics what in Zen is called the True Self; and when it surfaces, we are always impressed by the insights and transforming ideas springing, like hypnagogic images, from the patient. Assagioli (1965, 1973) refers to the move toward self-regulation as the first step in transpersonal development. The second step is integration *of* self, "personal psychosynthesis," and the third step is integration *with* Self, "transpersonal psychosynthesis."

CONCLUSION

In reviewing the extrapersonal and transpersonal data presented, it seems useful to consider again the yogic idea that the various kinds of experience involve, and depend on, different kinds of energy/substance in an all-pervading energy field of some kind. As we work with patients having "ordinary" psychosomatic problems, it becomes increasingly evident that physical consciousness is not separate from mental and emotional consciousness. And as extrapersonal and transpersonal data accumulate, it seems more and more likely that superphysical energies (to use Aurobindo's term) exist, and every human experience, no matter how "high," or transcendental, is actually an experience in domains of reality not separate from substance.

Carl Jung made reference to this idea of other-dimensional reality in his Commentary on *The Tibetan Book of the Dead*:

For years, ever since it was first published the *Bardo Thodol* [*The Tibetan Book of the Dead,* by Evans-Wentz, 1927] has been my constant companion, and to it I owe not only many stimulating ideas and discoveries, but also many fundamental insights. . . . Not only the "wrathful" but also the "peaceful" deities are conceived as *sangsaric* projections of the human psyche, an idea that seems all too obvious to the enlightened European, because it reminds him of his own banal simplifications. But though the European can easily explain away these deities as projection, he would be quite incapable of positing them at the same time as real. . . . The ever-present, unspoken assumption of the *Bardo Thodol* is the antinominal character of all metaphysical assertions, and also the idea of the qualitative difference of the various levels of consciousness and of the metaphysical realities conditioned by them. The background of this unusual book is not the niggardly European "either-or," but a magnificently affirmative "both-and." (Jung, 1957)

In confronting a similar problem of proposing and explaining to Westerners transcendent experiential dimensions, and their "reality," Aurobindo made the suggestion that if a person is embarrassed by the word "spirit," then it might be useful to think of spirit as the subtlest form of matter. On the other hand, if the idea of spirit is not an embarrassment, then matter can be thought of as the densest form of spirit.

Judging from comments and questions at advanced biofeedback workshops, psychophysiologic therapists having several years' experience with patients suffering from psychosomatic disorders are becoming increasingly interested in states of consciousness. Many of these clinicians have become convinced (through their own experience with biofeedback-facilitated self-awareness, through meditation, and through discussions with patients), that healing "energy" exists (see Kreiger, 1975; LeShan, 1976) and that both extrapersonal and transpersonal domains of experience consist of factual, rather than imaginary, energy states.

There are as yet no scientific data, replicable in different laboratories across the country, that directly substantiate the existence of superphysical energies (such as photos that record these "energy fields" without using the Tesla-coil electricity of the Kirlian camera), but the belief is growing among some physicists, biologists, psychologists, and physicians that there are additional energy dimensions in which humans exist, and in which, and because of which we have extrapersonal and transpersonal experience (Capra, 1975; Jahn, 1982; Phillips, 1983; Puthoff et al., 1979; Prigogine, 1980; Sheldrake, 1982; Wilber, 1983; Zukav, 1979).

Whatever discoveries are made in this domain, there is no doubt in our minds that feedback methodology will prove useful in helping individuals become conscious of their own latent capacities to voluntarily control, and project in the Jung/Tibetan sense, physical, emotional, and mental energy.

As these latent developments become manifest, a new horizon of ethics and responsibility, for others as well as ourselves, is bound to come in view.

REFERENCES

Assagioli, R. Symbols of transpersonal experiences. *Journal of Transpersonal Psychology,* 1969, *1,* 33–45.

Assagioli, R. *Psychosynthesis.* New York: Hobbs, Dorman 1965; Viking, 1971.

Assagioli, R. *The act of will.* New York: Viking Press, 1973.

Aurobindo. *The life divine.* New York: The Sri Aurobindo Library, 1951.

Aurobindo. *The synthesis of yoga.* Pondicherry (India): Sri Aurobindo Ashram Press, 1955.

Aurobindo. *On yoga, tome one; On yoga, tome two.* Pondicherry (India): Sri Aurobindo Press, 1958.

Ax, A. F. Editorial on biofeedback efficacy studies (Steiner and Dince, 1981; see below). *Biofeedback and Self Regulation,* 1981, *6,* 273.

Barber, T. X. Physiological effects of "hypnotic suggestions." *Psychological Bulletin,* 1965, *63,* 201–222.

Basmajian, J. V. Control and training of individual motor units. *Science,* 1963, *141,* 440–441.

Benson, H. *The mind/body effect.* New York: Berkley, 1980.

Blanchard, E. B., Miller, S. T., Abel, G. G., Haynes, M. R., and Wicker, R. Evaluation of biofeedback in the treatment of borderline hypertension. *Journal of Applied Behavioral Analysis,* 1977, *12,* 99–109.

Boring, E. G. *A history of experimental psychology.* New York: Appleton-Century-Crofts, 1950.

Brown, B. B. Recognition of aspects of consciousness through association with EEG alpha activity represented by a light signal. *Psychophysiology,* 1970, *6,* 442–452.

Budzynski, T. H., Stoyva, J. M., and Adler, C. S. Feedback-induced muscle relaxation: Application to tension headache. *Journal of Behavior Therapy and Experimental Psychiatry,* 1970, *1,* 205–211.

Budzynski, T., and Peffer, K. Twilight-state learning: A biofeedback approach to creativity and attitude change. Paper presented at conference on "Transformations of Consciousness," Department of Psychiatry, McGill University, Montreal, Canada, October 1973.

Budzynski, T. H. Brain lateralization and re-scripting. *Somatics,* 1981, *3,* 1–10.

Butler, F. *Biofeedback: A survey of the literature.* New York: Plenum, 1978.

Capra, F. *The tao of physics.* Berkeley: Shambhala, 1975.

Cousins, N. *Anatomy of an illness.* New York: Norton, 1979.

Cousins, N. *The healing heart: Antidotes to panic and helplessness.* New York: Norton, 1983.

Davidson, R. J., Schwartz, G. E., and Shapiro D. (Eds.). *Consciousness and self-regulation: Advances in research and theory,* Vol. 3. New York and London: Plenum Press, 1983.

Evans-Wentz, W. Y. *The Tibetan book of the dead.* London: Oxford, 1927; New York: Oxford University Press, 1957.

Evans-Wentz, W. Y. *The Tibetan book of the great liberation.* New York: Oxford University Press, 1954.

Evans-Wentz, W. Y. *Tibetan yoga and secret doctrines.* New York: Oxford University Press, 1958.

Fahrion, S. L., Norris, P. A., and Green, E. E. Biobehavioral treatment of essential hypertension. *Biofeedback & Self Regulation.* In press, 1985.

Fehmi, L. G. EEG biofeedback, multichannel synchrony training, and attention. In A. Sugerman (Ed.), *Expanding dimensions of consciousness*. New York: Springer Press, 1978.

Frank, J. D. Biofeedback and the placebo effect. *Biofeedback and Self Regulation*, 1982, *7*, 449–460.

Frankel, B. L., Patel, D. J. Horwitz, D., Friedewald, W. T., and Gaarder, K R. Treatment of hypertension with biofeedback and relaxation techniques. *Psychosomatic Medicine*, 1978, *40*, 276–293.

Freud, S. *The interpretation of dreams*. New York: Basic Books, 1954.

Fromm, E. Hypnotherapy. Lecture at The Menninger Foundation, Nov. 1980.

Frumkin, K., Nathan, R. J., Prout, M. F., and Cohen, M. C. Nonpharmacologic control of essential hypertension in man: A critical review of the literature. *Psychosomatic Medicine*, 1978, *40*, 294–320.

Gabbard, G. O., and Twemlow, S. W. *With the eyes of the mind: An empirical analysis of out-of body states*. New York: Praeger Publishers, 1984.

Galin, D. Implications for psychiatry of left and right cerebral specialization. *Archives of General Psychiatry*, 1974, *31*, 572–582.

Gladman, A. E. and Estrada, N. A biofeedback approach in the treatment of psychosomatic illness. Paper given at the 128th Annual Meeting of the American Psychiatric Association, Anaheim, Calif., 1975.

Greeley, A. and McCready, W. Are we a nation of mystics? *The New York Times Magazine*, Jan. 26, 1974.

Green, E. E. and Green, A. M. On the meaning of transpersonal: Some metaphysical perspectives. *Journal of Transpersonal Psychology*, 1971, *3*, 27–46.

Green, E. E. and Green, A. M. *Beyond biofeedback*. New York: Delacorte, 1977.

Green, E. E., Green, A. M., and Walters, E. D. Feedback technique for deep relaxation. *Psychophysiology*, 1969, *6*, 371–377.

Green, E. E., Green, A. M., and Norris, P. A. Preliminary observations on a non-drug method for control of hypertension. *Journal of the South Carolina Medical Association*, 1979, *75*, 575–582. Also in *Primary Cardiology*, 1980, *6*, 126–137; and in *Journal of Holistic Medicine*, 1980, *2*, 88–99.

Grof, S. *Realms of the human unconscious: Observations from LSD research*. New York: Viking Press, 1975.

Grof, S. and Valier, M. L. (Eds.). *Ancient wisdom and modern science*. New York: State University of New York Press, 1983.

Hendlin, S. J. Pernicious oneness. *Journal of Humanistic Psychology*, 1983, *23*, 61–81.

Howerton, J. Unpublished report, 1972.

Howerton, J. Personal communication, 1983.

Jahn, R. G. The persistent paradox of psychic phenomena: An engineering perspective. *Proceedings of the IEEE*, 1982, *70*, 136–170.

Jung, C. G. Psychological commentary. In *The Tibetan book of the dead* (Author, W. Y. Evans-Wentz). New York: Oxford University Press, 1957.

Jung, C. G. *Memories, dreams, and reflections*. New York: Pantheon, 1963.

Kafka, F. *The trial*. New York: Random House, 1937, 1956.

Kafka, F. *The castle*. New York: Knopf, 1954.

Kamiya, J. Conditioned discrimination of the EEG alpha rhythm in humans. Lecture to the Western Psychological Association, San Francisco, 1962.

Kamiya, J. Conscious control of brain waves. *Psychology Today*, 1968, Vol. 1 57–60.

Kreiger, D. Therapeutic touch: The imprimatur of nursing. *American Journal of Nursing*, 1975, *75*, 784–787.

Kubie, L. S. The use of induced hypnagogic reveries in the recovery of repressed amnesic data. *Bulletin of the Menninger Clinic,* 1943, *7,* 172–183.

LeShan, L. Cancer control. Presentation at Conference on Transpersonal Living, Esalen Institute, Big Sur, Calif., May 1976.

Lester, J. T. Wrestling with the Self on Mount Everest. *Journal of Humanistic Psychology,* 1983, *23,* 31–41.

Levine, J. D., Gordon, N. C., and Fields, H. L. The mechanism of placebo analgesia. *The Lancet,* Sept. 23, 1978, 654–657.

Lilly, J. C. *Programming and metaprogramming in the human biocomputer.* New York: Julian, 1972.

MacLean, P. D. Psychosomatic disease and the "visceral brain." *Psychosomatic Medicine,* 1949, *2,* 338–353.

Maslow, A. H. Various meanings of transcendence. *Journal of Transpersonal Psychology,* 1969, *1,* 56–66.

Masserman, J. H. Is the hypothalamus a center of emotion? *Psychosomatic Medicine,* 1941, *3,* 3–25.

Meadows, R. L. Unpublished case reports, 1983.

Meany, J. Biofeedback and psychotherapy. Paper presented at Psychosomatic Grand Rounds, V.A. Medical Center, Fresno, Calif., Aug. 1981.

Monroe, R. A. *Journeys out of the body.* New York: Doubleday, 1971.

Muldoon, S. and Carrington, H. *The projection of the astral body.* London: Rider, 1958.

Mulholland, T. and Runnals, S. Evaluation of attention and alertness with a stimulus–brain feedback loop. *Electroencephalography and clinical neurophysiology,* 1962, *4,* 847–852.

Needleman, J. A very serious story: In search of a lost religion. *American Theosophist,* 1983, 71, 172–182.

Northrop, F. S. C. The neurological and behavioristic psychological basis of the ordering of society by means of ideas. *Science,* 1948, *107,* 411–417.

Nowlis, D. P. Glass beads, the mind–body problem, and biofeedback. *Biofeedback and Self Regulation,* 1981, *6,* 3–10.

Oliver, G. W. Symbolic aspects of hypnagogic imagery associated with theta EEG feedback. Doctoral dissertation, California School of Professional Psychology, Los Angeles, 1975.

Orne, M. T. and McConkey, K. M. Toward convergent inquiry in self-hypnosis. *International Journal of Clinical and Experimental Hypnosis,* 1981, *29,* 313–323.

Ornstein, R. E. *The psychology of consciousness.* San Francisco: Freeman, 1972.

Osis, K. and McCormick, D. Kinetic effects at the ostensible location of an out-of-body projection during perceptual testing. *Journal of the American Society for Psychical Research,* 1980, *74,* 319–329.

Papez, J. W. A proposed mechanism of emotion. *Archives of Neurology and Psychiatry,* 1937, *38,* 725–743.

Patel, C. H. Yoga and biofeedback in the management of hypertension. *The Lancet,* 1973, *2,* 1053–1055.

Patel, C. H. 12-month followup of yoga and biofeedback in the management of hypertension. *The Lancet,* 1975, *1*(7898), 62–67.

Pelletier, K. R. *Longevity: Fulfilling our biological potential.* New York: Delacourte Press, 1981.

Peper, E. and Mulholland, T. B. Methodological and theoretical problems in the voluntary control of electroencephalographic occipital alpha by the subject. *Kybernetik,* 1970, *7,* 10–13.

Peper, E., Pelletier, K. R. and Tandy, B. Biofeedback training: Holistic and transpersonal frontiers. In Peper, Ancoli, and Quinn (Eds.), *Mind/body integration: Essential readings in biofeedback.* New York: Plenum, 1979.

Phillips, P. Psychokinesis and fraud. Paper presented at the Council Grove Conference, Voluntary Controls Program, Menninger Foundation, 1983.

Prigogine, I. *From being to becoming: Time and complexity in the physical sciences.* San Francisco: W. H. Freeman, 1980.

Puthoff, H. E., Targ, T., and May, E. C. Experimental psi research: Implications for physics. Paper presented at 145th national meeting of AAAS, Houston, Jan. 1979.

Ray, W. J., Raczynski, J. M., Rogers, T., and Kimball, W. H. *Evaluation of clinical biofeedback.* New York: Plenum, 1979.

Rickles, W. H. Biofeedback therapy and transitional phenomena. In *Psychiatric annals.* New York: Insight Publishing, 1981.

Roberts, T. B. Personal communication on "transpersonal education," 1983.

Schultz, J. and Luthe, W. *Autogenic training: A psychophysiologic approach in psychotherapy.* New York: Grune & Stratton, 1959.

Seer, P. Psychological control of essential hypertension: Review of the literature and methodological critique. *Psychological Bulletin,* 1979, *86,* 1015-1043.

Shapiro, A. P., Schwartz, G. E., Ferguson, D. C., Redmond, D. P., and Weiss, S. M. Behavioral methods in the treatment of hypertension: A review of their clinical status. *Annals of Internal Medicine,* 1977, *86,* 626-636.

Shealy, C. N. and Freese, A. S. *Occult medicine can save your life.* New York: Dial, 1975.

Sheldrake, R. A. *A new science of life: The hypothesis of formative causation.* Los Angeles: Tarcher, 1982.

Silver, B. V. and Blanchard, E. B. Biofeedback and relaxation training in the treatment of psychophysiological disorders: Or are the machines really necessary? *Journal of Behavioral Medicine,* 1978, *1,* 217-239.

Steiner, S. S. and Dince, W. M. Biofeedback efficacy studies: A critique of critiques. *Biofeedback and Self Regulation,* 1981, *6,* 275-288.

Surwit, R. S. and Keefe, F. J. The blind leading the blind: Problems with the "double-blind" design in clinical biofeedback research. *Biofeedback and Self Regulation,* 1983, *8,* 1-2.

Sutich, A. J. Transpersonal psychology: an emerging force. *Journal of Humanistic Psychology,* 1968, *8,* 77-78.

Sutich, A. J. Some considerations regarding Transpersonal Psychology. *Journal of Transpersonal Psychology,* 1969, *1,* 11-20.

Swedenborg, E. *Heaven and its wonders and hell: from things heard and seen.* New York: Swedenborg Foundation, 1934. (Published in Latin about 1760.)

Taimni, I. K. *The science of yoga.* Wheaton, Illinois: Thesophical Publishing House, 1967.

Tart, C. A psychophysiological study of out-of-the-body experiences in a selected subject. *Journal of the American Society for Psychical Research,* 1968, *62,* 3-27.

Tart, C. *States of consciousness.* New York: Dutton, 1975.

TenHouten, W. D. Hemispheric interaction in the brain and the propositional, compositional, and dialectical modes of thought. *Journal of Altered States of Consciousness,* 1978-79, *4,* 129-140.

Thompson, J. K., Raczynski, J. M., Haber, J. D., and Sturgis, E. T. The control issue in biofeedback training. *Biofeedback and Self Regulation,* 1983, *8,* 153-164.

Vaughn, F. A question of balance: Health and pathology in new religious movements. *Journal of Humanistic Psychology,* 1983, *23,* 20-41.

Walsh, R. The consciousness disciplines. *Journal of Humanistic Psychology,* 1983, *23,* 28-30.

Walters, E. D. Personal communication, 1983.

Welwood, J. On spiritual authority—genuine and counterfeit. *Journal of Humanistic Psychology*, 1983, *23*, 42–60.

Wilbur, K. *A sociable God: A brief introduction to transcendental sociology.* New York: McGraw-Hill, 1983.

Wortz, E. Application of awareness methods in psychotherapy. *Journal of Transpersonal Psychology*, 1982, *14*, 61–68.

Zukav, G. *The dancing Wu Li masters: An overview of the new physics.* New York: William Morrow, 1979.

19. Becoming Lucid in Dreams and Waking Life

Judith R. Malamud*

In our ordinary dreams, we assume we are awake and conscious of the outer world, but in lucid dreams, we reject these assumptions and conclude we are actually asleep, dreaming an imaginary world. Lucid dreaming shows our capacity for perspective—our ability not to be fooled by the evidence of our senses and not to become so absorbed in how things appear to be that we forget the other reality (of the waking world) in which we also exist. If, in some sense, we are similarly mistaken to assume we are ultimately "*Awake*" during our waking lives, then we need this lucid perspective in waking life as well.

I intend to examine what has been learned about inducing lucid dreams. I will also propose a two-part analogy: (a) in the waking state, falsely assuming one's objectivity is to acknowledging one's subjectivity as, in the sleep state, dreaming is to lucid dreaming; and (b) waking life is to a hypothetical reality I call the "*Awakened Life*" as dreaming is to awakening from sleep. By presenting lucid dream research in this expanded philosophical context, I hope to clarify how learning to become lucid in dreams can be of value, both intrinsically and for the speculations, implications, and techniques we can derive from such work to promote a parallel evolution of consciousness in waking life.

Since *dream lucidity* is knowledge, during a dream, that one is asleep and dreaming relative to the seemingly more objective world of waking life, then *waking lucidity* could be defined as knowledge, during the waking state,

---

*The author wishes to acknowledge with thanks the assistance of Wendy Lubin, who commented on a draft of this chapter.

that one is *"Asleep"* and *"Dreaming"* relative to a possibly more objective reality, that is, the *Awakened Life.* Thus lucidity, as defined here, is not restricted to a specific state of consciousness. Coming to understand the potentials of lucidity in dreams may lead us to see parallel possibilities for lucidity in waking life (Goleman, 1971; LaBerge, 1980a, 1981; Malamud, 1979/1980, 1982b,c; Ogilvie et al., 1982; Sparrow, 1976).

CLARIFYING THE DEFINITION OF LUCID DREAMING

Since the term "lucid dream" was first used, probably by Van Eeden (1913/1969), there has been general agreement that knowledge that one is dreaming is an essential component of the definition of lucidity in dreams. Many researchers (Garfield, 1974a; LaBerge, 1980a; Tart, 1979; Van Eeden, 1913/1969) have observed that lucid dreamers often possess, to varying degrees, faculties that traditionally have been considered characteristic of waking consciousness, such as correct orientation in time and space (e.g., the middle of the night at home in bed), memory of one's waking life, plans, and intentions (e.g., recall of experiments planned for the night's dreams), perceptual vividness in any or all of the sensory modalities, and the abilities to think logically and to choose consciously one's course of action as the dream story unfolds.

Tart (1979, 1984) has asserted that possession of "waking consciousness" is an essential part of the definition of lucid dreaming, in addition to knowledge that one is dreaming. I think there are problems with defining lucid dreaming this way (Gillespie, 1982, 1983). As Tart has acknowledged, lucid dreams vary greatly, even moment to moment within a dream, on this waking consciousness dimension. For example, lucid dreamers frequently have difficulty recalling recent details of their waking lives (Green, 1968), or they may be irrationally afraid of dream enemies pursuing them even though they have just concluded that "This is only a dream."

The faculties ascribed to waking consciousness are not even necessary concomitants of the waking state, since we can be disoriented, forgetful, irrational, and perceptually dull even while awake. Even *reality contact,* defined by Jonté (1978–79) as "the ability to discriminate between inner experience and outer events" (p. 306), is ordinarily present in waking life only to a limited extent because, at minimum, each person's perception of outer events is uniquely and unconsciously "colored" by inner experience.

Furthermore, many of the waking consciousness characteristics of lucid dreams can be present in ordinary dreams (Specht, 1983). The sense of volitional control over one's actions, logical trains of thought, and reasonable conversations with other dream characters are not rare events in ordinary dreams. Many of us have actually had nonlucid dreams that surpassed waking life in their clarity on these dimensions. Another problem with including waking consciousness in the definition of lucid dreaming is the implication of *perceptual* contact with the waking world, which, by definition, cannot be characteristic of sleep and dreams (LaBerge, 1980a). Thus, these faculties of waking consciousness are neither sufficient nor necessary to define lucid dreaming, nor are they characteristic only of lucid dreams, nor are they even always associated with the waking state. Why add such confusion to our definition of lucid dreaming?

Tart (1984) rightly pointed out that researchers should be careful to differentiate among the vastly different kinds of dreams termed "lucid." We can probably retain in our definition both the suggestion of heightened consciousness and the understanding that this phenomenon is a matter of degree, while excluding the unwanted connotation of perceptual contact with the waking world, if we define lucid dreaming simply as knowledge, during a dream, that one is dreaming, with the qualification that there are great variations in the extent to which lucid dreamers are consciously aware of specific implications of the fact that they are dreaming. This definition embraces a dichotomy (aware of dreaming/not aware of dreaming), a continuum (minimally to maximally aware), and a typology (each implication of dreaming), so that dreams can be differentiated by degree and type of lucidity. Precursors to lucidity are taken into account by including nonlucid dreams on the continuum. As we shall see, this definition also clarifies how maximum lucidity, that is, knowledge that one is dreaming and full awareness of the implications of that fact, inherently involves experiencing certain of the often-suggested benefits of lucid dreaming, namely, enhanced creativity, psychological integration, and freedom, while increasing the likelihood of experiencing other frequently reported concomitants, such as pleasure and opportunities for experimentation (Arnold-Forster, 1921; Garfield, 1974a; Malamud, 1979/1980).

Implications of the Fact That One is Dreaming

One way to specify the implications of the fact that one is dreaming is in terms of the Creative Source (CS), the connection between Self and Environment (SE), and the existence of Alternate Realities (AR) (LeShan, 1976):

1. *The creative source (CS).* We are the primary creators of our dream worlds and dream experiences.
2. *The connection between self and environment (SE).* The apparent separation between ourselves and our dream environments is an illusion. In creating our dream images, we are expressing (or projecting) our-

selves and our unique perceptions of reality. Therefore, the dream environment has a self-mirroring aspect.

3. *Alternate realities (AR)*. Our dream experiences are subjective realities contained within the reality of the waking world. As alternate, qualitatively different realities, dreams offer different possibilities and limitations from those of ordinary waking life. Within dreams, we choose, consciously or unconsciously, among alternative ways of structuring the dream and responding to dream events.

In order to apply the concept of dreaming to waking life, the sleep-state qualifiers can be omitted, and *dreaming* can be defined more generally as *the act of creating a subjective world of experience and simultaneously misperceiving this personal world as objectively real*. When dreaming is defined in this non-state-specific way, lucid reflection may lead to the conclusion that ordinary experience in the waking state, such as that which you and I are now having, is also in some sense a *Dream*. That is, when we *Dream* in waking life, we misperceive our sensory, perceptual, and cognitive/affective construction of reality as if it were reality itself. A non-state-specific definition of *lucidity* would therefore be: *knowledge that one is creating a subjective world of experience and simultaneously misperceiving it as objectively real.*

I do not mean to imply that there is no objective reality; I do not know whether there is or not. Nor do I mean that we are solely responsible for creating our experience in waking life or even in dreams. The extent to which any particular level of reality—such as dreaming or ordinary waking life—is a subjective creation, has been and will continue to be a subject for philosophical debate and scientific exploration. However, creativity is always an interactive process. The creative contribution of each of us is the transformation of the raw materials of our existence—our abilities, history, biological needs, human and nonhuman environment, and outer events—into unique and subjective moment-by-moment experience.

If the concept of *Dreaming* in waking life is based on a valid analogy, the implications of *Dreaming* in the waking state may also be analogous to those of dreaming in the sleep state, that is:

1. *The creative source (CS)*. We are continuously contributing to the creation of, that is, we *cocreate,* our experience of the waking world and life events.
2. *The connection between self and environment (SE)*. The apparent separation between ourselves and our perceived waking environments is an illusion. As cocreators of our waking experience, we are continu-

ously expressing (or projecting) ourselves and our unique perceptions of reality. Therefore, the perceived waking environment has a self-mirroring aspect.

3. *Alternate realities (AR)*. Our waking experience is a subjective reality compared to the more encompassing reality we might experience if we *Awakened* from our ordinary waking lives. As alternate, qualitatively different realities, our waking lives offer different possibilities and limitations from those of the *Awakened Life*. Within ordinary waking reality, we choose, consciously or unconsciously, among alternative ways of structuring our experience and responding to events.⌟

As in lucid sleep-dreams, people who experience lucid episodes while *Dreaming* in waking life may differ, even moment by moment, in their awareness of these implications.

If awakening from a sleep-dream is defined as renewing the experience of contact with a level of reality that seems more objective and inclusive than the dream, then, by analogy, *Awakening* from a waking-state *Dream* would be defined as establishing the experience of contact with a level of reality that seems more objective and inclusive than the waking-state *Dream*. Notice that for both states, awakening, unlike lucidity, implies *directly experienced contact* with a seemingly more objective reality, not just intellectual knowledge of that reality's existence. Although I do not recall ever having *Awakened* from my own waking life, I imagine the experience might be equivalent to what mystics call *Enlightenment*. I will leave further speculation on the *Awakened* existence to the end of this chapter.

The Lucidity Continuum

As mentioned earlier, even ordinary, nonlucid dreams can show certain signs of heightened consciousness that are typical of lucid dreams. Celia Green (1968) defined *prelucid dreams* as those in which dreamers adopt a critical attitude toward their experience or even consider the possibility that they are dreaming, without realizing they actually are dreaming. Precursors of lucid dreaming can be comprehended in an extended lucidity continuum if we recognize that all of them reflect some degree of awareness of the implications of the fact that one is dreaming (CS, SE, and AR), even though the conscious thought "I am dreaming" has not occurred. Examples of such phenomena are: acting with conscious volition (CS), being aware of composing the dream drama (CS), compassionately understanding other dream characters (SE), analyzing the personal meaning of the dream while it is going on (SE), questioning incongruous events (AR), and performing acts that would be improbable or magical in the waking world (AR).

A more complex series of scales (Malamud, 1979) formed the basis of the lucidity continuum I will present here. This continuum is applicable to both sleep-dreams and waking life, and it encompasses both precursors and advanced forms of lucidity. Each level of this scale is defined in terms of the implications of the fact of dreaming, CS, SE, and AR.

[Level one—Totally nonlucid dreamers believe they are powerless (CS), alienated from the environment (SE), and lacking options (AR). They do not notice occurrences that are inconsistent with these beliefs. Dream example: nightmare of being paralyzed (CS) on another planet (SE) with no means of escape (AR). Waking example: belief that one is powerless (CS), isolated (SE), and trapped (AR) when the actuality is otherwise.

Level two—Contextually nonlucid dreamers are aware that they can act volitionally (CS), relate meaningfully (SE), and choose among options (AR) within a reality context that they falsely assume to be the waking (or Awakened) world; that is, they assume their world is externally created (CS), separate from themselves (SE), and concrete (AR). They do not question these assumptions even if they notice events inconsistent with them. Dream example: The dreamer purposely (CS) talks to (SE) another dream character, instead of (AR) ignoring the character, but does not realize he is creating (CS) the character, that it reflects aspects of himself (SE), and that it is only an image (AR). Waking example: A man purposely (CS) talks to (SE) another person, instead of (AR) ignoring the person, but does not realize he is experiencing a self-created (CS), self-revealing (SE) image (AR) of the other person.

Level three—Prelucid dreamers wonder whether they are creating (or co-creating) the world they are experiencing (CS), whether their experience of the environment reflects aspects of themselves (SE), and whether their current reality may be other than the waking (or Awakened) world (AR). Dream example: A dreamer wonders whether she is creating the forest around her (CS), whether the forest could symbolize her own sense of mystery (SE), and whether the trees might be only images (AR). Waking example: A woman wonders whether she is creating the problem she is experiencing (CS) by interpreting the situation in a particular way (AR) that reflects her own attitudes and history (SE).

Level four—Intellectually lucid dreamers realize they are creating (or co-creating) the world they are experiencing (CS), that their environment reflects aspects of themselves (SE), and that they are experiencing a reality other than the waking (or Awakened) world (AR). These realizations remain intellectual and do not result in: awareness of the actual process of creating their dream worlds (CS), an expanded sense of their own identities (SE), or recognition of the differing conditions and potentials of dream reality and waking (or Awakened) reality (AR). Dream example: A dreamer knows, in theory, that he is creating the mugger in his dream (CS), and that the mugger is only an image (AR) that could symbolize his own aggressive feelings (SE). Nevertheless, he is astonished by the mugger's appearance on the scene (CS), continues to experience himself only in the victim role (SE), and fears the mugger as if the image were real (AR). *Waking example:* A sophisticated therapy patient knows, in theory, that he is creating (CS) a transferential (SE) and unrealistic image (AR) of his therapist. Nevertheless, his emotions correspond to his fantasy about who the therapist is rather than to the therapist's actual personality.

Level five—Experientially lucid dreamers directly sense how they are creating (or cocreating) their dream worlds (CS), experience an expanded sense of self-identity as reflected in the dream environment (SE), and are aware of the differing conditions and potentials of their dream and waking realities (AR). *Dream example:* A dreamer is aware of creating a dramatic story (CS) and freely includes "magical" events (AR) in accordance with her own conscious flow of feelings and wishes (SE). *Waking example:* A woman recognizes the personal (SE) myth (AR) in terms of which she has been creating and construing (CS) her life (Krippner and Feinstein, 1982).

To simplify this presentation of the lucidity continuum, I have included all three implications (CS, SE, and AR) under each level. However, in actual dreams, the dreamer is rarely equally lucid for each implication; hence dreams should be rated separately for each implication. Here is a hypothetical example of a lucid dream rated CS-level four; SE-level three; AR-level five:

In the middle of a dream, I realized I was dreaming and therefore I could fly (AR). As I flew over the city, I momentarily wondered whether the tallness of the buildings reflected anything about me (SE), but then I realized, "Of course, I must be in downtown Chicago!" I marveled at the wonderful architecture I was somehow creating, but was frustrated that I could neither find nor conjure up the building where I used to live (CS).

PROCESSES IN THE DEVELOPMENT OF LUCIDITY

Some processes that may frequently play a part in the development of dream lucidity are: (1) achieving sufficient cognitive maturation for lucidity, (2) increasing motivation to achieve lucidity, (3) paying attention to dreams, (4) focusing intention on the achievement of lucidity, (5) achieving optimal cortical arousal, (6) attaining realization of dreaming, (7) maintaining an appropriate balance of consciousness, and (8) achieving higher levels of lucidity. These processes may also be important in the development of waking lucidity.

Cognitive Maturation and Lucidity

The capacity for reflective thought that is present in lucid dreams may require a level of cognitive development that is ordinarily lacking in early childhood. David Foulkes's (1982) research on children's dreams revealed that contrary to expectations derived from clinical experience, young children rarely report complex, imaginative dreams. Foulkes believed this finding would be surprising only if we made the assumption (which I would call "nonlucid") that dreaming is a passive perceptual process rather than a constructing of images via "creative recombination of memories and knowledge" (Foulkes, 1982, p. 293). Even though, as Rechtschaffen (1978) observed, most dreams are strikingly lacking in reflective thought within the dream, Foulkes pointed out that the very ability to construct dream images requires some capacity for reflective thought. Children develop this capacity over time, and it is demonstrated in the increasing complexity of their dreams. Indeed, Foulkes found that children do not reliably include a self-character in their dreams until they reach ages seven to nine, when, presumably, their capacity for self-observation and degree of self-knowledge permit the creation of self-representations. Lucid dreaming, like other manifestations of reflective thought within dreams, may indicate that the dreamer has reached a level of cognitive skill such that he or she can reflect on the products of his or her own reflective thought.

The maturation of children's beliefs concerning the origin and location of dreams (Evans, 1973; Laurendeau and Pinard, 1962; Piaget, 1927) suggests that lucid dreaming may be an advanced stage in a sequence of normal cognitive development. Very young children believe that dreams originate from an external source (e.g., God or the television set) and take place in the outer world (e.g., the foot of the bed). It was not until ages five and six that all the children in Foulkes's sample had reached the transitional stage of believing that the origin and location of dreams are at least partly internal. Most, but by no means all, adults in this culture believe, when they are awake, that dreams originate and take place internally. Carrying this knowledge into the dream may be the natural next step, requiring an unusually "dream conscious" environment for its emergence (Malamud, 1979/1980).

Motivation to Achieve Lucidity

Motivations for Spontaneous Lucidity. The question of what motivates dream lucidity when it occurs spontaneously can be illuminated by first considering what may motivate the usual nonlucidity of dreams (LaBerge, 1980a; Rechtschaffen, 1978). Dreamers in the midst of a dream really are not "strangers in a strange land," whom we should expect to be acutely aware of every discrepancy between the "foreign" dream territory and their "native" land of the waking world. Rather, dreamers may be *more* at home in their dreams than in the waking world because they have actually created their dream worlds to conform to their own deeply personal (but not necessarily conscious) wishes and/or assumptions about their lives. One probable reason why most dreams are not lucid becomes obvious: we have an investment in what we have created. Awareness of dreaming, then, depends on *willingness to suspend belief* in the personal world one is creating in favor of the consensually validated world of waking life.

Although many concomitants of spontaneous lucidity in dreams have been reported, the two most often mentioned triggers are *incongruous events* and *anxiety* (Gackenbach, 1982b; Garfield, 1976a; Hearne, 1983c; Hoffman and McCarley, 1980; Ogilvie et al., 1982; Sharcoff, 1983; Sparrow, 1976). This is not surprising, since incongruities and anxiety both can provoke a need to consider alternative realities.

Incongruities sometimes seem to induce lucidity by provoking cognitive dissonance, that is, an experienced lack of agreement between one's perceptions and one's expectations. However, dreamers can freely ignore or rationalize the most bizarre events. For example, I dreamed I was crossing a street and saw a lion heading toward me. I was relieved when it veered off, and wondered if it had escaped from somewhere. I thought, "Isn't it amazing that such a dreamlike event could occur in waking life!" Evidently, I was not interested in disbelieving in my narrowly missed encounter with a lion. Had the lion continued to approach me, anxiety might have motivated me to become lucid. In general, dreamers may respond to threatening dream situations by choosing assurance of self-preservation ("It's only a dream, so I'm not really in danger") over preservation of their belief in their self-created worlds.

The spontaneous occurrence of lucidity in waking life may be similarly associated with incongruous events and anxiety. Incongruous events in waking life may catch our attention and surprise us because they conflict with our expectations. We feel anxiety when reality as we perceive it seems to threaten us. Both kinds of experience challenge us to question the assumptions and perceptions by which we *Dream* our lives. On the societal level, unexpected results in science and threatening situations in world affairs (e.g., ecological crises) may lead to revolutions in our consensual *Dream* by provoking us to question accepted knowledge and to adopt new working models of reality.

Motivations for Inducing Lucidity.   Desires to cultivate lucid dreams arise from a variety of motivations that depend on the culture (Jonté, 1978–79), values, beliefs, and personality of the dreamer. Possible benefits of inducing dream lucidity include: (1) enhancement of the dream experience, (2) facilitation of creative interaction between the dreaming and waking states, and (3) enhancement of one's sense of inner unity across states of consciousness.

ENHANCEMENT OF DREAMING

Once dreamers become aware of the implications—CS, SE, and AR—of the fact that they are dreaming, they may be able to create less anxious, more gratifying dreams and even to experience inner growth while dreaming. Several researchers have reported success in alleviating unpleasant dreams and recurrent nightmares by inducing lucidity (Halliday, 1982; Schatzman, 1982; Tholey, 1983). Pleasure experiences can be programmed (Garfield, 1974a), and wishes that would be impossible, immoral, or illegal to gratify in waking life can be freely indulged in lucid dreams (Malamud, 1979/1980). Sparrow (1983) devised and tested a "dream reliving" lucidity induction exercise; results suggested the technique may have potential for enhancing "constructive dreamer processes," that is, within-dream behavior that, according to Rossi's (1972) theories, may be conducive to personality growth.

CREATIVE INTERACTION BETWEEN THE DREAMING AND WAKING STATES

At higher levels of lucidity, the lucid dream state consists of a self-reflective cognitive set and awareness of freedom, safety, and insulation from waking life consequences, combined with vivid perceptual experience, access to "autonomous processes" (Rossi, 1972), and the potential for powerful emotional impact. Hence, the lucid dream state may be ideal for fostering personality change via "corrective emotional experiences." Lucid dreaming may be suitable for desensitization of phobias and rehearsal of more appropriate behavior (Garfield, 1974a). Garfield (1976b) reported that students in a "Creative Dreaming" course learned to apply the so-called Senoi (Faraday and Wren-Lewis, 1984; Stewart, 1969) principle, "confront and conquer danger," in their dreams. These students reportedly experienced waking carryover effects of greater self-confidence and more assertive behavior. Because lucidity fosters awareness of the self-reflecting aspects of the dream environment, lucid dreams may be conducive to dialogue with one's own projections, in the form of other dream characters, during the dream itself. Rogo (1983) suggested that patients could train themselves to meet a "dream-helper" in lucid dreams. Whether lucidity training can actually produce constructive personality change remains to be verified by research, which, considering recent advances in lucidity induction techniques, should now be feasible.

Research on personality characteristics of lucid dreamers has only recently begun (Belicki et al., 1978; Gackenbach, 1981; Gackenbach et al., 1983). It seems that such research is more likely to produce meaningful patterns of results if the kind (CS, SE, and AR) and level of lucidity are considered as variables. One could predict personality differences between those whose typical lucid dreams show a merely intellectual lucidity (level four) and those who are able to directly experience and use the potentials of lucidity (level five). In the latter group, there may be differences among, for example, those who excel at conscious control of the dream's plot or environment (CS), achievement of self-understanding through dialogue with other dream characters (SE), or enjoyment of experiences that would be risky or impossible in waking life (AR).

Lucidity permits consciously directed access to the creativity that abounds in dreams. In lucid dreams, one can perform experiments to test one's powers of imagination (Saint-Denys, 1867/1982; Van Eeden, 1913/1969), seek out dream adventures, or study interesting images for later reproduction as literary or artistic works (Garfield, 1974a; Rogo, 1983).

The fact that action and perception in the dream state are not limited by time and space suggests that dreaming may be conducive to extrasensory perception. Considerable research supports this hypothesis (Ullman et al., 1973). Proficient lucid dreamers can plan and carry out parapsychological experiments such as inducing mutual dreams (Campbell, 1980; Donahoe, 1974, 1979), traveling in a dream to give or receive information that could subsequently be verified, or attempting to discover specific target material precognitively (Green, 1976).

The recent development of techniques for verifying lucid dreams and monitoring their physiological concomitants in the laboratory has opened another door to explorations of the correlations between the experiential and physiological aspects of consciousness (Hearne, 1983b; LaBerge, 1980a). Preliminary research (LaBerge, 1983) suggests that the brain, and to a lesser extent, the body, are affected by certain kinds of dreamed activities in much the same way as they would be affected by the corresponding waking activities. Further research may point to medical applications. I wonder, for example, whether inducing lucid dreams of healing could be combined with waking visualization techniques for combating disease (Simonton et al., 1978).

ENHANCING INNER UNITY

The richness and strangeness of our dreams are glaring reminders that we hardly know who we are in our roles as creators of our dream worlds. For me, the challenge of becoming lucid is to discover how and why I create my dreams. I am not seeking another method to interpret the "foreign language" of dreams, but rather, to get in touch with that state of my own consciousness in which dream language is not foreign, but native, so that I can understand directly my intentions as the creator of my dreams.

Waking experience can be enhanced by awareness of the implications of *Dreaming,* namely, that one is cocreator (CS) of a self-mirroring (SE) world of experience that, because of its subjectivity, is but one of many alternate realities (AR). Awareness of oneself as a creative source (CS) involves an increased sense of responsibility for one's past and current experience, as well as awareness of one's power to create future experience. Even if this sense of responsibility is merely acknowledged intellectually (level four), it may inspire deliberate attempts to "take charge" of one's life and may encourage an inquiring attitude toward one's own unconscious motives and life-shaping behaviors. Experiential awareness of one's creative role (level five) may lead to greater harmony between one's conscious intentions and resultant experience—a sense of "flow" in living.

Awareness of the self-mirroring aspect of one's experience (SE) can lead to reowning one's projections and to a sense of caring for other people and the environment, resulting from ever-deepening awareness of one's relatedness to them.

Awareness of the subjectivity of reality and the ever-present possibility of choosing to experience alternative realities (AR) increases the possibility of seeking and finding more satisfying options for living. Learning to be skeptical about the reality of one's perceptions may provide some protection against being trapped by them, whether those perceptions are considered "crazy" (e.g., hallucinations and delusions), merely "maladjusted" (e.g., transference, irrational ideas, learned helplessness), or consensually validated (e.g., the world-view of one's time and culture; "isms" of all kinds—racism, sexism, etc.).

Paying Attention to Dreams

Keeping track of one's dreams gradually leads to familiarity with one's personal repertoire of dream themes, symbols, characters, locations, and so on, so that dreaming of them may trigger remembrance—"Aha! I've dreamed this before!"—and lucidity. Occasionally, the mere act of keeping a dream diary may be sufficient to trigger lucid dreaming (Saint-Denys, 1867/1982).

Similarly, the first step toward lucidity in waking life is retrospective awareness that one has been *Dreaming.* Retrospective realizations may be

expressed variously: "I had always assumed . . . but now I realize . . . ";
"I misunderstood you"; "I saw it all through rose-colored glasses"; "I had
actually convinced myself it was true." The common denominator is an
evaluation of old perceptions as unreal, or *Dreamed,* compared to new perceptions that seem more real, true, or objective. Repeatedly noticing that
one has revised previous realizations could lead to the metarealization that,
in the ordinary waking state at least, we can never say the last word—we
can always reinterpret because our waking experience is essentially interpretation, not pure fact. Until we stably achieve this metarealization, that
is, that we are *Dreaming* continuously, each new realization may be equivalent to a *False Awakening,* that is, the delusion that we have finally shed
our subjectivity and *Awakened* to the real world.

Focusing Intention on the Achievement of Lucidity

Techniques to strengthen the intention to become lucid include autosuggestion (Arnold-Forster, 1921; Fluent, 1983; Garfield, 1974a,b; LaBerge,
1980a,b; Tholey, 1983), posthypnotic suggestion (Dane, 1983; LaBerge,
1980a; Tart, 1979), selecting recurrent, highly noticeable dream events as
cues to become lucid (Sparrow, 1976; Tholey, 1983), resolving to carry out
a particular activity in a dream (Castaneda, 1972; Tholey, 1983), and presleep rehearsal of lucid dreaming (LaBerge, 1980a,b).

Garfield (1974a) recommended devising an autosuggestion formula to remind oneself of the unreality of dream events; for example, "You know
this is a dream, it can't hurt you" (p. 177). LaBerge (1980b) achieved an
average of 5.4 lucid dreams per month by using autosuggestion. LaBerge
(1980a,b) developed a technique called "Mnemonic Induction of Lucid
Dreams (MILD)," to be used following spontaneous early morning awakenings from a dream, before returning to sleep. The technique has several
steps, including imagining oneself dreaming the last dream (or any dream)
lucidly, and affirming, while falling asleep, one's intention to have a lucid
dream. Using MILD, LaBerge was able to increase his frequency of lucid
dreams to 21.5 per month, a much higher rate than he achieved with autosuggestion alone. He attributed the MILD technique's effectiveness to the
"ability to remember to perform future actions" (1980b, p. 1041).

In a pilot study by Dane (1983), none of ten subjects was able to complete
the required seven out of twelve practice nights using MILD. Dane therefore abandoned a plan to compare the effectiveness of MILD to posthypnotic suggestion. Instead, he devised a study to compare a sophisticated
waking suggestion induction procedure, used alone, to the same procedure
used in conjunction with posthypnotic suggestion. In the latter procedure,
each subject was instructed to encounter a personal symbol of her "dream

consciousness'' and to ask it for help in inducing lucid dreams. Using a group of hypnotically suggestible female subjects who had never had lucid dreams prior to the study, he found that both methods were effective in inducing laboratory-verified lucid dreams, but the posthypnotic suggestion procedure was qualitatively more effective.

The use of a recurrent situation as a cue to become lucid, in combination with autosuggestion, could easily be adapted to waking life. These techniques could help one particularly in resolving to confront problems and opportunities with more awareness and creativity. Examples: ''Next time I think you're being critical of me, I'm going to check out my perception by asking you.'' ''Next time I feel angry, I am going to use the opportunity to become aware of my own expectations.'' ''Next time I go on vacation, I'm going to remember I'm free to spend my time as I please.''

Achieving Optimal Cortical Arousal

An optimal, higher than usual level of arousal seems to be associated with lucid dreaming. Lucid dreams have been reported to occur more often following a stimulating day (Garfield, 1976a), a period of wakeful activity, such as meditation (Sparrow, 1976), reading (LaBerge, 1980a), or even ''sexual intercourse during the middle of the night'' (Garfield, 1976a), and following microawakenings (LaBerge et al., 1981a). Lucid dreams have also been associated with REM bursts (Hearne, 1983b; LaBerge et al., 1981a), increased alpha activity (Ogilvie et al., 1982), and a high concentration of negative ions (Adler et al., 1983).

LaBerge (1980a) suggested that arranging for ''gentle awakenings'' during REM sleep by, for example, white noise, might facilitate optimal arousal. Hearne (1983d) induced lucidity in some subjects by applying four small shocks to their wrists during REM periods. Hearne subsequently developed and is testing a portable ''dream machine'' for home use that functions according to the same principle of gently alerting the dreamer during REM periods.

Optimal alertness for waking-life lucidity may be a natural concomitant of situations that sometimes provoke lucidity spontaneously, such as, surprising events that inspire cognitive dissonance, and threatening situations that provoke anxiety.

Realization of Dreaming

Dreamers can try to increase the likelihood of realizing they are dreaming by increasing their alertness to bizarre occurrences in dreams, practicing critical reflection in waking life, programming bizarre events in their dreams, memorizing state tests to carry out during prelucid dreams or false awakenings, and arranging for the presentation of conditioned stimuli during REM sleep to remind them that they are dreaming.

Dreamers can become more alert to incongruities by regularly recording their dreams in a journal and underlining all the unrealistic or "dreamlike" happenings (Malamud, 1979/1980). If dreamed events that are objectively incongruous are dreamed because they express subjective meanings, then those events are more likely to arouse critical reflection during the transitional period when the dreamer is beginning to question her subjective viewpoint. For example, a professional woman used to have a recurrent dream of fearing she would be unable to graduate from high school. During these dreams, she did not notice the incongruity, which coincided with an aspect of her unconscious self-concept. As her self-concept began to catch up with current reality, her "high school" dreams increasingly often concluded with the reassuring thought, "but I don't have to worry—I already graduated from college." At that point, lucidity sometimes ensued. Hence, one may increase the probability of "catching" recurring incongruous dream events by discovering and questioning the subjective viewpoints they symbolically express.

Practice in noticing inconsistencies that occur in waking life may be conducive to lucid dreaming (Fox, 1962; Sparrow, 1976) and to waking lucidity. Tholey (1983) recommended the "reflection technique," in which the subject frequently asks himself whether or not he is dreaming during the daytime, especially when dreamlike situations are encountered, and before going to sleep. To stimulate my own awareness of *Dreaming* in waking life, I ask myself at the end of the day, "What was the most surprising event that happened for me today? What assumption of mine was contradicted by this surprising event? What new hypothesis can I formulate?"

Since bizarre occurrences, nightmares, and false awakenings are often associated with the realization of dreaming, it seems logical that if we could somehow increase the frequency of such events, we might increase the probability of becoming lucid. One could attempt to induce dreams of flying or stressful dreams by autosuggestion (Garfield, 1974a,b; Rogo, 1983). Hearne (1982a) suggested that false awakenings could be encouraged by arranging for an assistant to disturb the sleeper several times during a sleep period, so as to set up an expectation of being awakened.

Hearne (1982a, c) proposed "state tests" to be memorized and practiced during actual awakenings, for subsequent use in false awakenings and prelucid dreams. Sample items from the list of state tests: "Jump off an object such as a chair. If you descend slowly you know you are dreaming. . . . Attempt to push your hand through solid looking objects" (1982c, p. 7). Unfortunately, no state test is foolproof (Garfield, 1974a; McCreery, 1973).

For example, dreamers may find themselves unable to push their hands through "solid" objects because of the power of expectations appropriate to waking life. McCreery (1973) made the valuable suggestion that because one hardly ever seriously considers the possibility that one may be asleep when one is in fact awake, if one does find oneself considering that possibility, one can almost surely conclude one is dreaming.

Another way of provoking realization of dreaming is to arrange for the presentation during sleep of a reminder that one is dreaming, or a conditioned stimulus that has been paired with such a reminder. LaBerge et al. (1981b) tried playing a tape of the sentence "This is a dream" at gradually increasing volume during subjects' REM periods. The subjects were instructed to signal with eye movements whenever they heard the tape or realized they were dreaming. Lucidity was the result in one-third of the trials. Similarly, each of the four shocks to the wrist administered in Hearne's experiment (1983d) was supposed to stand for one word of the sentence "This-is-a-dream." Price and Cohen (1983) accidentally discovered that administering biofeedback training during REM sleep induced one subject to have lucid dreams very frequently. They have been planning further experiments to isolate the effective factors in the procedure.

Maintaining Balance

Techniques that promote a balance between spontaneity and control, involvement and detachment, absorption and perspective, seem to favor prolongation of lucid episodes. Many lucid dreamers have spoken of the need to avoid distractions and excessive immersion in dream events, and of the need to stabilize the dream scene by focusing attention on some relatively fixed element in the dream (Castaneda, 1972; Garfield, 1974a; Saint-Denys, 1867/1982).

The necessary balance can be practiced by redreaming dreams lucidly in waking fantasy (LaBerge, 1980a,b; Sparrow, 1976, 1983). I devised a lucidity training method in which subjects were taught, with the help of a lucidity checklist and extensive feedback on their efforts, to continually remind themselves of the implications of dreaming (CS, SE, and AR) while redreaming their dreams in waking fantasy (Malamud, 1979/1980, 1982c). Some of these subjects showed notable increases in their ability to maintain lucid awareness in their waking fantasies. It remains to be seen whether such training can carry over to dreams and waking life. This possibility is supported by Sparrow's (1983) finding that some subjects were able to induce dream lucidity by practicing a "dream reliving exercise."

Lucid dreaming has been described as meditation in the dream state (Goleman, 1971; Hunt, 1982; Ogilvie et al., 1982; Sparrow, 1976). This seems to be a valid comparison for those forms of meditation in which the subject, while maintaining a detached "observer" attitude, permits spontaneous mental processes to go on (Carrington, 1977). This kind of meditative attitude could also be considered characteristic of waking lucidity. The practice of meditation may help to induce lucid dreams (McLeod and Hunt, 1983; Reed, 1978; Sparrow, 1976) and has certainly been considered one path to lucidity and *Awakening* in waking life (Vaysse, 1979). Rarely, lucid dreams may be initiated at sleep onset by maintaining a meditative focus during the hypnagogic, presleep phase (Ouspensky, 1914/1971; Tholey, 1983). Psychotherapy is another "practice" that, like meditation, is designed to cultivate self-observation (Deikman, 1982) and hence to promote lucidity.

Because too much arousal can end the lucid dream by awakening the dreamer, lucid dreamers need to guard against excessive arousal, for example, too much excitement over discovering one is dreaming. Sparrow (1976) and LaBerge (1980a) have suggested that moving the dream body may suppress awareness of one's physical body, and thus postpone awakening. Tholey (1983) found that deliberately producing REMs can suppress awakening. Gackenbach (1982a) has been investigating possible relationships between dream lucidity and "balance" on both a gross motor and a vestibular level.

Achieving Higher Levels of Lucidity

Many lucid dreamers have reported that, with practice and experimentation, their lucid dreams increased in frequency, duration, and power (Arnold-Forster, 1921; Jonté, 1978–79; Garfield, 1974a,b; Laberge, 1980a,b; McCreery, 1973; Tholey, 1983). Some lucid dreamers have learned to increase their volitional control (CS) over dream imagery (McCreery, 1973) and have improved their skills in such "magical" activities (AR) as flying and transporting themselves in time and space (Arnold-Forster, 1921; Tholey, 1983). Lucid dreamers have also gained increased respect for other dream characters and insight into their self-reflecting nature (SE) (McCreery, 1973; Tholey, 1983).

In my experience teaching subjects to incorporate higher levels of lucidity into dream-related waking fantasies, the learning process, although ultimately liberating, can be fraught with obstacles and anxiety (Malamud, 1979/1980). Low self-esteem and inner conflicts may cause blocking of imagination (Davidow, 1982), inability to challenge and change limiting assumptions, and avoidance of pleasure. Subjects who are aware of having even occasional difficulty with reality testing may feel especially threatened by instructions to let go of their inhibitions in the realm of imagination.

One typical barrier experienced by my subjects was anxiety over confronting supposedly unacceptable aspects of themselves. This anxiety was sometimes expressed as fear of "going crazy" or being ostracized by society. Also common was a fear of allowing themselves to imagine "bad" (immoral, dangerous, or illegal) behavior, lest they lose control and act out their fantasies. These fears were partially alleviated once the principle of alternate realities (AR) was grasped: fantasies occur in the privacy of one's own mind, not in public space; thoughts and images are not equivalent to actions and do not have the same consequences; thoughts and images do not automatically lead to action—choice and decision intervene (Malamud, 1979/1980, 1982c).

Initially, at least, learning to take full advantage of knowledge that one is dreaming may be facilitated by a humanly supportive context, such as psychotherapy or an accepting group. Group work (Malamud, 1982a) has the additional advantages that group members can inspire each other's imaginations and give each other "permission" to pursue satisfaction. When fully grasped, the principles of lucidity themselves provide considerable cognitive leverage and may be used by some people as self-help tools for life-long inner growth.

CONTROVERSIES

Are There Limits to Conscious Dream Control?

Experienced lucid dreamers have reported that despite achieving a high degree of conscious control over dream content, they never achieve total control (Gillespie, 1982; Ouspensky, 1914/1971; Saint-Denys, 1867/1982; Tholey, 1983). Researchers have expressed skepticism concerning the degree of conscious dream control that realistically can be achieved (Griffin and Foulkes, 1977). I have not come across anyone who claims complete conscious control over dreams.

Hearne (1982b, 1983a) has proposed that there are built-in physiological limits on control of dream imagery. Others (Donahoe, 1974; Worsley, 1983a,b) have pointed out that dream imagery is limited by the expectations, desires, and imaginative capacity of the dreamer. Limits may also result from interference by unconscious desires or inhibitions that oppose the dreamer's conscious plans for dream control. I think it is essential to keep in mind that it is not possible to prove conclusively that any hypothetical phenomenon is impossible, physiologically or otherwise. Since only one contradictory observation would disprove any hypothetical limit to dream control, we should be careful not to overgeneralize from data that must inevitably be incomplete, particularly since a false belief in an absolute limit is a powerful negative expectation that could become a self-fulfilling prophecy (LaBerge, 1980a) for lucid dreamers.

Could Dream Control Be Harmful?

Sparrow (1976) encouraged lucid dreamers to respond creatively to dream situations, but warned them not to try to manipulate dream events lest they violate their own inner natures. Colleagues who are clinicians have expressed similar concerns about possible dangers of "controlling the unconscious" by interfering with the dream's spontaneous flow. Implied in these objections is the idea that dreams are created by powerful agents "inside" us that we may try to dominate at our peril. In this model, human beings are reduced to separate minds (e.g., the "conscious mind" and the "unconscious mind") that compete for control, while the person as a whole, choice-making agent is regarded as weak or nonexistent. This divided-self model encourages us to disown much of our behavior, including the creation of dreams (Schafer, 1976). It seems more likely that we are, act, and create as unified beings in accord with our predominant motives, whether or not we are conscious of what we are doing and why.

Even in ordinary, nonlucid dreams, the dreamer is always "manipulating" and "controlling," that is, choosing the content and creating the images of the dream; in lucid dreams, the dreamer has at least an intellectual knowledge that she or he is doing so. It seems doubtful that conscious dream control is carried out by any force extrinsic to one's creativity in ordinary, unconscious dreaming. Success in consciously directing a dream probably indicates not that the dreamer is superimposing her conscious will to change the natural course of the dream (divided-self model), but simply that the dreamer is aware of what she, as a whole being, wants to create.

LaBerge (1980a) noted that lucidity can be disadvantageous if it is used as a means of evading threatening or unpleasant dream experiences that might have been enlightening. Indeed, I have observed that some beginning lucid dreamers respond evasively or defensively because they have not yet realized that they need not be afraid in dreams. Convincing themselves of their power to escape or conquer danger may be a useful step in helping dreamers achieve the crucial realization of their safety in the realm of imagination (AR). Once they realize they are safe, dreamers are much more likely to feel curious about the dream environment and to engage in the kind of exploration, adventure, and constructive dialogue that could lead to enhanced personality integration (SE).

SPECULATIONS ON AWAKENING

The fact that we can create vivid and seemingly real experience in our sleep, when perception of the external world is at a minimum, raises the possibility that we underestimate the extent to which our waking experience is also self-created, rather than determined by the outer world (Green, 1976). Awareness of this possibility is lucidity in waking life. What might be the next horizon, beyond lucidity? As LaBerge said, "Lucid dreams suggest what it would be like to discover that we are not yet fully awake" (1980a, p. 120).

Tibetan yogic doctrine includes a rigorous program to teach lucid dream control as a path to *Awakening;* that is, to recognition that both dreaming and waking experience are illusory, and to union with the *Reality* that underlies both (Evans-Wentz, 1935/1982). Does *Awakening* ever occur spontaneously, without arduous preparation? Are we sometimes so excessively aroused by the shocks of life that we *Awaken* roughly, temporarily? Do we *Awaken* normally, "refreshed," after we have had sufficient time to *Dream?* Are *Dreaming* and *Awakening* cyclical events? Do we, in our ordinary waking-life *Dreams,* experience amnesia for past *Awakenings?* Perhaps we are not fully lucid in our waking lives unless we can recall details of our existence in an *Awakened Life.*

When a dreamer awakens from sleep, the dream-self and dreamed world must fade and disappear so as to allow renewed awareness of the physical body and the waking world. Perhaps *Awakening* also involves a disappearance of our self-concepts and the world as we ordinarily perceive them. This analogy is consistent with mystical teachings on the need to let go of reality as perceived by the senses and to "die" as an ego in order to know *Reality* (Underhill, 1915). Thus, *Awakening* would mean becoming experientially aware of a seemingly more objective reality and of the *Self* who *Dreams* our waking lives. Perhaps, after *Awakening,* we would marvel at the bizarreness and creativity, anxiety and sweetness of our waking-life *Dreams.*

REFERENCES*

Adler, T., Gackenbach, J., and LaBerge, S. Negative air ions and lucidity induction: Additional data. *Lucidity Letter,* 1983, *2*(2), 5–6.

Arnold-Forster, M. *Studies in dreams.* London: Allen & Unwin, 1921.

Belicki, D. A., Hunt, H., and Belicki, K. An exploratory study comparing self-reported lucid and non-lucid dreamers. *Sleep Research,* 1978, *7,* 166.

Campbell, J. *Dreams beyond dreaming.* Virginia Beach: Donning, 1980.

Carrington, P. *Freedom in meditation.* New York: Anchor/Doubleday, 1977.

Lucidity Letter is available from Dr. Jayne Gackenbach, Department of Psychology, University of Northern Iowa, Cedar Falls, Iowa 50614. The *Dream Network Bulletin* is available from Chris Hudson, 487 Fourth Street, Brooklyn, N.Y. 11215. The author's articles in *Lucidity Letter* and *Dream Network Bulletin* are available from the author, 2555 Bainbridge Avenue, #6B, Bronx, N.Y. 10458. The *Journal of Lucid Dream Research* is available from Dr. Keith Hearne, P.O. Box 84, Hull, North Humberside, England, HU1 2EL.

Castaneda, C. *Journey to Ixtlan: The lessons of Don Juan.* New York: Simon & Schuster, 1972.

Dane, J. A comparison of waking instructions and posthypnotic suggestion for lucid dream induction. (Doctoral dissertation, Georgia State University, 1984.) *Dissertation Abstracts International, 45,* 3920B. Excerpt from draft, 1983.

Davidow, J. Pleasure dreams. *Dream Network Bulletin,* 1982, *1*(3), 1-2.

Deikman, A. J. *The observing self: Mysticism and psychotherapy.* Boston: Beacon, 1982.

Donahoe, J. J. *Dream reality: The conscious creation of dream and paranormal experience.* Oakland, Calif.: Bench, 1974.

Donahoe, J. J. *Enigma: Psychology, the paranormal and self-transformation.* Oakland, Calif.: Bench, 1979.

Evans, R. C. Dream conception and reality testing in children. *Journal of the American Academy of Child Psychiatry,* 1973, *12*(1), 73-92.

Evans-Wentz, W. Y. (Ed.). *Tibetan yoga and secret doctrines.* London: Oxford University, 1982. (Original work published 1935.)

Faraday, A. and Wren-Lewis, J. The selling of the Senoi. *Lucidity Letter,* 1984, *3*(1), 1-3.

Fluent, J. *Dream magic: A report on the art and practice of lucid dreaming.* Palo Alto, Calif.: Mindscape, 1983.

Foulkes, W. D. *Children's dreams: Longitudinal studies.* New York: Wiley, 1982.

Fox, O. *Astral projection: A record of out-of-the-body-experiences.* Secaucus, N.J.: Citadel, 1962.

Gackenbach, J. Lucid dreaming: Individual differences in personal characteristics. *Sleep Research,* 1981, *10,* 145.

Gackenbach, J. Balance and lucid dreaming ability: A suggested relationship. *Lucidity Letter,* 1982a, *1*(2), 3-4.

Gackenbach, J. Differences between types of lucid dreams. *Lucidity Letter,* 1982b, *1*(4), 11-12.

Gackenbach, J., Curren, R., LaBerge, S., Davidson, D., and Maxwell, P. Intelligence, creativity and personality differences between individuals who vary in self-reported lucid dreaming frequency. *Lucidity Letter,* 1983, *2*(2), 4.

Garfield, P. L. *Creative dreaming.* New York: Simon & Schuster, 1974a.

Garfield, P. L. Self-conditioning of dream content. *Sleep Research,* 1974b, *3,* 118.

Garfield, P. L. Psychological concomitants of the lucid dream state. *Sleep Research,* 1976a, *5,* 183.

Garfield, P. L. Using the dream state as a clinical tool for assertion training. *Sleep Research,* 1976b, *5,* 184.

Gillespie, G. Lucidity language: A personal observation. *Lucidity Letter,* 1982, *1*(4), 5-6.

Gillespie, G. Memory and reason in lucid dreams: A personal observation. *Lucidity Letter,* 1983, *2*(4), 8-9.

Goleman, D. Meditation as meta-therapy: Hypotheses toward a proposed fifth state of consciousness. *Journal of Transpersonal Psychology,* 1971, *3,* 1-25.

Green, C. *Lucid dreams.* Oxford: Institute of Psychophysical Research, 1968. (Distributed by State Mutual Book and Periodical Service, New York).

Green, C. *The decline and fall of science.* Oxford: Institute of Psychophysical Research, 1976. (Distributed by State Mutual Book and Periodical Service, New York).

Griffin, M. L. and Foulkes, D. Deliberate presleep control of dream content: An experimental study. *Perceptual and Motor Skills,* 1977, *45,* 660-662.

Halliday, G. Direct alteration of a traumatic nightmare. *Perceptual and Motor Skills,* 1982, *54,* 413-414,

Hearne, K. M. T. A suggested experimental method of producing false-awakenings with possible resulting lucidity or O.B.E.—the "FAST" (False-Awakening with State Testing) technique. *Lucidity Letter,* 1982a, *1*(4), 12–13.

Hearne, K. M. T. Effects of performing certain set tasks in the lucid-dream state. *Perceptual and Motor Skills,* 1982b, *54,* 259–262.

Hearne, K. M. T. Ten tests for state assessment. *Lucidity Letter,* 1982c, *1*(3), 6–7.

Hearne, K. M. T. A "scene-change phenomenon" in externalized imagery. *Lucidity Letter,* 1983a, *2*(1), 2–4.

Hearne, K. M. T. Electrophysiological aspects of lucid dreams—more detailed findings. *Journal of Lucid Dream Research,* 1983b, *1,* 21–47.

Hearne, K. M. T. Features of lucid dreams: Questionnaire data and content analyses (1). *Journal of Lucid Dream Research,* 1983c, *1,* 3–20.

Hearne, K. M. T. Lucid dream induction. *Journal of Mental Imagery,* 1983d, *7,* 19–24.

Hoffman, E. and McCarley, R. W. Dream bizarreness and lucidity in REM sleep dreams: A quantitative evaluation. *Sleep Research,* 1980, *9,* 134.

Hunt, H. T. Forms of dreaming. *Perceptual and Motor Skills,* 1982, *54,* 559–633, Monograph Supplement 1-V54.

Jonté, D. Ego functions in a variety of dream states. *Journal of Altered States of Consciousness,* 1978–79, *4,* 305–319.

Krippner, S. and Feinstein, A. D. Personal myths and dream interpretation. *Dream Network Bulletin,* 1982, *1*(3), 1, 6.

LaBerge, S. P. Lucid dreaming: An exploratory study of consciousness during sleep. (Doctoral dissertation, Stanford University, 1980.) *Dissertation Abstracts International,* 1980a, *41,* 1966B. (University Microfilms Order No. 8024691.)

LaBerge, S. P. Lucid dreaming as a learnable skill: A case study. *Perceptual and Motor Skills,* 1980b, *51,* 1039–1042.

LaBerge, S. P. Lucid dreaming: Directing the action as it happens. *Psychology Today,* Jan. 1981, 48–57.

LaBerge, S. P. Psychophysiological parallelism in lucid dreams. *Lucidity Letter,* 1983, *2*(4), 3–4.

LaBerge, S. P., Nagel, L. E., Taylor, W. B., Dement, W. C., and Zarcone, V. P., Jr. Psychophysiological correlates of the initiation of lucid dreaming. *Sleep Research,* 1981a, *10,* 149.

LaBerge, S. P., Owens, J., Nagel, L. E., and Dement, W. C. "This is a dream ": Induction of lucid dreams by verbal suggestion during REM sleep. *Sleep Research,* 1981b, *10,* 150.

Laurendeau, M. and Pinard, A. *Causal thinking in the child.* New York: International Universities, 1962.

LeShan, L. *Alternate realities: The search for the full human being.* New York: Evans, 1976.

Malamud, J. R. The development of a training method for the cultivation of "lucid" awareness in fantasy, dreams, and waking life. (Doctoral dissertation, New York University, 1979.) *Dissertation Abstracts International,* 1980, *40,* 5412B. (University Microfilms International Order No. 8010380.)

Malamud, J. R. Discovering lucidity: Experiential exercises for dream study groups. *Dream Network Bulletin,* 1982a, *1*(2), 1–3.

Malamud, J. R. Lucidity in waking life. *Dream Network Bulletin,* 1982b, *1*(5), 1, 2, 7.

Malamud, J. R. Training for lucid awareness in dreams, fantasy, and waking life. *Lucidity Letter,* 1982c, *1*(4), 7–11.

McCreery, C. *Psychical phenomena and the physical world.* New York: Ballantine, 1973.

McLeod, B. and Hunt, H. Meditation and lucid dreams. *Lucidity Letter,* 1983, *2*(4), 6–7.

Ogilvie, R. D., Hunt, H. T., Tyson, P. D., Lucescu, M. L., and Jeakins, D. B. Lucid dreaming and alpha activity: A preliminary report. *Perceptual and Motor Skills,* 1982, *55,* 795–808.

Ouspensky, P. D. *A new model of the universe: Principles of the psychological method in its application to problems of science, religion and art.* New York: Vintage/Random House, 1971. (Original work published 1914.)

Piaget, J. *The child's conception of the world.* London: Routledge & Kegan Paul, 1927.

Price, R. and Cohen, D. Auditory biofeedback as a lucidity induction technique. *Lucidity Letter,* 1983, *2*(4), 1-3.

Rechtschaffen, A. The single-mindedness and isolation of dreams. *Sleep,* 1978, *1,* 97-109.

Reed, H. Meditation and lucid dreaming: A statistical relationship. *Sundance Community Dream Journal,* 1978, *2,* 237-238. (Available from Dr. Henry Reed, P.O. Box 595, Virginia Beach, Va. 23451.)

Rogo, D. S. *Leaving the body: A complete guide to astral projection.* Englewood Cliffs, N.J.: Prentice-Hall, 1983.

Rossi, E. L. *Dreams and the growth of personality.* New York: Pergamon, 1972.

Saint-Denys, H. de. *Dreams and how to guide them,* M. Schatzman (Ed.) and N. Fry (Transl.). London: Duckworth, 1982. (Original work published 1867.)

Schafer, R. *A new language for psychoanalysis.* New Haven: Yale University, 1976.

Schatzman, M. Introduction. In H. de Saint-Denys, *Dreams and how to guide them,* M. Schatzman (Ed.) and N. Fry (Transl.). London: Duckworth, 1982, pp. 1-17.

Sharcoff, J. Lucid dreaming: Personal observations. *Lucidity Letter,* 1983, *2* (2), 8-9.

Simonton, O. C., Matthews-Simonton, S., and Creighton, J. L. *Getting well again: A step-by step, self-help guide to overcoming cancer for patients and their families.* New York: Bantam, 1978.

Sparrow, G. S. *Lucid dreaming: Dawning of the clear light.* Virginia Beach: Association for Research and Enlightenment, 1976.

Sparrow, G. S. An exploration into the inducibility of increased reflectiveness and "lucidity" in nocturnal dream reports. (Doctoral dissertation, College of William and Mary, 1983). *Dissertation Abstracts International, 45,* 1050B. Draft copy, 1983.

Specht, P. Letter to the editor. *Lucidity Letter,* 1983, *2*(1), 5.

Stewart, K. Dream theory in Malaya. In C. Tart (Ed.), *Altered states of consciousness: A book of readings.* New York: Wiley, 1969, pp. 159-167.

Tart, C. T. From spontaneous event to lucidity: A review of attempts to consciously control nocturnal dreaming. In B. B. Wolman (Ed.), *Handbook of dreams: Research, theories and applications* New York: Van Nostrand Reinhold, 1979, pp. 226-268.

Tart, C. T. Terminology in lucid dream research. *Lucidity Letter,* 1984, *3*(1), 4-6.

Tholey, P. Techniques for inducing and manipulating lucid dreams. *Perceptual and Motor Skills,* 1983, *57,* 79-90.

Ullman, M., Krippner, S., and Vaughan, A. *Dream telepathy.* New York: Macmillan, 1973.

Underhill, E. *Practical mysticism.* New York: Dutton, 1915.

Van Eeden, F. A study of dreams. In C. T. Tart (Ed.), *Altered states of consciousness: A book of readings.* New York: Wiley 1969, pp. 145-158. (Reprinted from *Proceedings of the Society for Psychical Research,* 1913, *26,* 431-461.)

Vaysse, J. *Toward awakening: An approach to the teaching left by Gurdjieff.* San Francisco: Harper & Row, 1979.

Worsley, A. Comments on an investigation of the relative degree of activation in lucid dreams. *Lucidity Letter,* 1983a, *2*(3), 5.

Worsley, A. Objective vs. subjective approaches to investigating dream lucidity: A case for the subjective. *Lucidity Letter,* 1983b, *2*(2), 7-8.

20. The Mystical Way and Habitualization of Mystical States

J. H. M. Whiteman

PRELIMINARY CONSIDERATIONS

By the *habitualization* of mystical states is here meant the cultivation of certain dispositions, the use of certain practical procedures, or the maintaining of certain intentional attitudes of mind, by virtue of which mystical states may be expected to occur with a certain degree of frequency. Whether a claimed method of habitualization has or has not been partly responsible for the occurrence of a continuing series of mystical states may be decided on the basis of authentic evidence that the frequency has been maintained when such dispositions, practices, or intentions have been exercised, and has not been maintained when these have not been exercised.

The frequency maintained might be, on an average, once every few years, or a few times a year; or experience of a broadly mystical character might continue fluctuatingly over some days, weeks, or months, then lapsing for a certain period before resumption occurs. Or the frequency might be, finally, such as occurs in the unitive life, when the "union" is described as *habitual* (IC.VII, Chap. 4; Farges, 1925, pp. 176f) or *almost permanent* (GIP.283f).[1]

Stages of the Mystical Way

For clearer thinking on these matters it is helpful to distinguish four chief stages of development, taking as a basis for classification the four-stage

---

[1]For the meaning of the code letters, see Appendix A.

Buddhist plan (Jennings, 1947, pp. 501f) and correlating this with St. Teresa's seven-stage plan (in IC).

The four Buddhist stages are characterised by successively more thorough liberation from the fixated identification of oneself with one's personality (*pañc-upādāna-kkhandā*, the five grasping "branches" of personal life: bodily appearance, sense, feelings, etc.). By a successive deepening of non-attachment to all these things, one more and more habitually sees the personality as temporary (*anicato*), rooted in "dis-ease" or not-rightness (*dukkhato*), and without basis in a "self" (*anattato*).

The first stage of liberation, that of "stream-winning" (*sotāpatti*), is usually named "conversion" in English; but here we must rather speak of a *first conversion*. One has then adopted a life-orientation in which deeper realities are recognized, beyond what is material or merely personal and governed by pleasure or pain. And this higher orientation inspires a life more in accord with those realities, that is, more "moral."

The second stage of liberation is that of one who awaits an end to "lapsing" (*sakad-āgāmi;* literally, a "once-for-all lapser"). This stage may be identified with one in which there is a suddenly increased intensity of *working-up,* either by sustained and comprehensive Recollection practices, or something less deliberate, but always with the feeling that an answer to problems concerning the ultimate meaning of life *must* be found, and is in fact very near.

The third stage (of the *anāgāmi,* a "nonlapser") may be taken as a stage in which a powerful disclosure of the Source (*asaṅkhata,* the Unconditioned) creates an *initiatory transformation.* It may then be equated with St. Teresa's stage of full union (GIP, Chap. 17). Consistently we may describe it also as a *second conversion* (compare the account by Suso, in Underhill, 1930, p. 186). The illuminative way, or ecstatic union, then follows, with many separative disclosures.

The fourth and last stage, that of the *arahant* (entitled, competent, worthy), is the unitive life.

Buddhaghosha (1964, I.14, XXII.2–31) interprets the "four paths" according to the three great stages of the complete mystical way worked out in DN.2. Thus the first two paths correspond to *sīla* (morality), the third to *samādhi* ("collectedness" practices), and the fourth to *paññā* (higher knowledge, perception, and wisdom). The scheme suggested above, with an initial development of recollectedness and obedience in the *second* stage, and *paññā* (including *separation* of all kinds) begun in the *third* stage, and reaching the mystical continuity of the unitive life in the fourth stage, seems more logical.

In this context a "popular" interpretation of the verbal root *āgam* (approach, go back) is commonly assumed, implying a "return to the physical world by reincarnation in a new physical birth." In other words, the interpretation of *āgam* is accommodated to the popular interpretation of *jāti* (which means "generation" of any kind) as necessarily parturition. But the meaning of *jāti* in this context is authoritatively explained by Buddhaghosha (1964, XXII:32, p. 567). He states that in this context *jāti* means *bhava* (becoming), not parturition; and he describes the process spoken of in the Sutta (DN.2:93–94) alternatively as *paṭisandhi* (recompounding) as a result of "lapsing" (*cavana,* XVII.164. p. 639). For further confirmation that this interpretation is correct, see (ibid.) VIII.39, p. 256, on the brief life-duration of a "being" (*satta*), "person" or "self" (*attabhāva*), as the state of consciousness "becomes" from one moment to another (ibid. p. 211, note 6); or see Govinda (1969, p. 246).

Can Mystical Experience be "Voluntary"?

This question calls for consideration because two extreme views have been expressed by authors of note, each view contradicting the idea that mysticism is an art, whose fruits of knowledge, discernment, and wisdom are to be developed by following a certain path of self-discipline.

The one view is that mystical experience may be produced in anyone by administering a drug such as LSD, nothing else being needed except perhaps a brief preparation of affective mood. The other view is that of Poulain, who begins his investigations (GIP.1) with the ruling that:

> We apply the word mystic to those supernatural acts or stages which our own industry is powerless to produce, *even in a low degree, even momentarily.* (his italics)

Dealing with this second view first, it may be observed that the problem is chiefly a linguistic one, depending upon what we mean by "produce," "industry," and "our own." Deferring, for the moment, consideration of what Poulain's real intention is, we may set more authentic evidences against his apparent assertion that "mystical exercises" are ineffective, and that the unitive life continues without any contribution by the will of the mystic:

> (From St. Paul) [His gifts were] that we may no longer be children, tossed to and fro . . . but that, speaking truth in love, we may grow in every way into Him who is the head, into the Dedicated One (*ho christos*). (Eph. 4:14–15)

> (From St. John of the Cross) When the soul rids itself totally of that which is repugnant to the divine will and conforms not with it, it is trans-

formed in God through love . . . The soul, then, needs only to strip itself of these natural dissimilarities and contrarieties, so that God . . . may communicate Himself to it supernaturally, by means of grace. (AMC.II.5:4,5)

(From Patanjali, YS.IV:3) The motive [of the individual] is not directly effective [in bringing about mystical development or disclosures]. But from that [motive, there may be brought about] the removal of obstacles, as a farmer [cultivates crops by preparing and irrigating his fields].

An almost identical view to this last is expressed in the Conclusions of the Teresian Congress, 1923 (Farges, 1925, p. 649: Conclusions 1–4 on Theme V).

"Images" and Spiritual Objectivity; "Dying to Self"

The intention behind Poulain's dictum, quoted above, seems to be to rule out application of the term "mystic" (mystical, supernatural, etc.) to subjective, phychical, or psychopathic effects, often referred to as "images" or "visions," and restrict it to disclosures that are *noetically objective* and *ultimately real* in character. Unfortunately, his attempt to relate this difference to the possibility of habitualization breaks down, as we have seen, and other methods need to be proposed.

The kinds of experience objected to would certainly be evaluated as nonmystical if we use the method summarised in Appendix C to determine their General Index of Reality, which would be well below the 11 + points needed for a mystical experience; so Poulain's problem would appear to be solved. But the problem of determining what kinds of mental attitude or physical behavior conduce to advancement on the mystical way, and what kinds are obstructive, is not solved by any such means.

In particular, it has not been established that any resort to "images" or "visions" in the intervals between full-fledged mystical experiences is obstructive. What is declared by St. John of the Cross (an authority much depended on in this connection) is that we must not "lean upon imaginary visions, nor upon forms and figures" (AMC.134), not be "attached and cling to them" (137) or "desire" them as "distinct objects of the understanding." They must be viewed as an "outer rind" or "husk"; for to adopt these attitudes of "attachment" would close our eyes to "the spiritual part that is infused," to that "other light" which comes in "the day of transformation and union with God to which the soul is journeying" (136f, 138).

This line of thought—which conforms entirely with what is taught in

Buddhism and the Yoga Sutras in regard to "attachment," "clinging," "grasping," and "desire"—amounts to saying that what is obstructive is precisely such *attachment,* and what is conducive is the countering *nonattachment.* But it is clear that this is a very peculiar kind of attachment; and unless some attempt were made to make the teaching more precise and practical, the demand that we should renounce all attachment could appear unnatural, forced, or even impossible to carry out.

First, we need to consider the fact that the attachment spoken of is not merely to sense (physical or nonphysical), but could be to thoughts, feelings, and wishes or incentives. How can we have an incentive to do something, such as helping another person, without being in some way attached to the act of carrying it out? And how can we be convinced that 2 and 3 make 5, without being in some way attached to that view?

To distinguish the right kind of attachment from the wrong kind, mystics (in the N.T., Buddhism, later Christian times, Swedenborg, etc.) have noted that the *wrong* kind is well described in common speech by saying that it is from *self.* For example, the terms self-control, self-discipline, self-restraint, and self-denial all indicate that by self (when the word is not used in a simple reflexive way) we tend to understand some power in us, or influence coming and going in our personality, that we must try to recognize, control, judge, and sometimes deny. And terms such as self-love, self-will, selfishness, self-glory, self-pity, self-interest, and self-opinionated indicate that self may be seen also as an influence coming upon us and accepted as our own that causes good or harmless qualities of character (love, pity, interest, etc.) to be counterfeited and become, as we say, false or evil.

Thus it is possible to see how certain attitudes of mind or motivations are obstructive to insight and advancement on the mystical way because, by an automatic kind of attachment or "clinging" to what comes and goes in the personality, an identifying with them, and consequent "deciding for oneself," we have become fixated on what does not really belong. The fixation prevents a "higher" orientation to the Source of right and good; and without such "Obedience," there is a continuance of "entanglements" instead of release and integration:

> Everything of bodily form [and the other "grasping branches of personality"] is to be regarded with right insight as it really is, thus: "This is not mine; I am not this; this is not my self (*atta*)."

It is through being unawakened to this teaching, not penetrating it, that this world of men has become like a tangled and knotted skein . . . and does not get beyond distraction, ill way of life, [mental and spiritual] falling-apart, and the continual coming and going [of personality identifications and consequent dis-ease] (saṃsāra). (Jennings 1949, pp. 49, 274, 34f, 476, 520f and DN.15:7

In so far as Love of Self and Love of the World are discerned and removed, heavenly love appears and operates. . . . These loves begin to reign when a man judges for himself and makes his own decision. (Swedenborg, AC, Index volume, p. 214. The love of self and love of the world may be taken to be *attachment* to what is subjective and objective, respectively, blinding one to wisdom from the Source through Obedience.)

The writings of Christian mystics abound in references to self-denial, self-loss, and death or even annihilation of the self (Underhill, 1930, Index, p. 517). Sometimes, perhaps, the intention is little more than to stress that at every stage of the mystical way one needs to overcome emotional attachments such as pride, envy, self-seeking, self-justification, scorn, resentment, impatience, excitability, rage, intolerance, falsehood and complacency. The uncompromising language of these mystics suggests, however, that what they had in mind chiefly was the *total* transcending of attachment (of the wrong kind) that comes with disclosure of the transformed *real being* of the mystic on entering the third path. As Suso writes of the mystic in the later stages of the way:

His being remains, though in a different form, in a different glory, and in a different power. . . . And thus it is, as has been said, a man comes forth from his selfhood. (Ibid., pp. 424f)

Though the term self points, in the mystical view, to a counterfeiting of our "real being," one may accept that in every counterfeit there is hidden a more or less unacknowledged germ of the real, which in this case can be taken to be the I AM of the Godhead, individualized somehow by the divine potentiality. It seems therefore permissible, if the description of a mystical experience is to be made to appear vividly real, that one should use the pronouns and pronominal adjectives of the first person (I, me, myself, my)—on the strict understanding that the *selfless real being,* patterned on the divine Obedience and Faith, is being referred to and not anything patterned on or limited by things in the physical life.

On the other hand, there seems no justification for using the word "Self," with a capital S, for the transcendent God (Divine Source) or the archetypal Divine Humanity. That practice would seem to have arisen from the fact that nonmystical translators of the Upanishads avoided the word "Spirit" as a translation of *ātma,* and thus opened the door to confusion between Archetypal Man (*Puruṣa*), the Godhead (*Akṣara;* the Unchanging), the

Transcendent God (*Īśa;* the Lord), God in general (*Brahma;* Godhead, the potentialities of Archetypal Man, and transcendence, all in One), and Spirit (*Ātma*), divine and universal, or individualized.

Associating the word self, which so strongly suggests counterfeits, with divinity in all its functions, is unhelpful, to say the least, and will be avoided here.

Before The Second Path

From the abundant testimonies in *The Original Vision* (Robinson, 1977) it appears that many people, perhaps most, have had in childhood (often in the first two or three years) at least one experience of the kind in which a preparatory glimpse of higher values or realities sets the life firmly and confidently in the *first stage* of the mystical way—though naturally admitting short or long periods of apparent lapsing in the years that follow. For instance:

> My childhood experiences were extremely vivid and significant and authentic. . . . (Ibid., p. 51)

> . . . In the years from eighteen months of age to five or six all the foundations of my future life were laid. . . . (Ibid., p. 50)

> I should say I had a sense of right and wrong not determined by anyone else; I feel sure of this. But I don't know that it was ever in conflict with my socially-induced conscience. It was different from rather than in conflict with [that]. Also, when different, I had no hesitation in trusting in my innate sense: I trusted it above everything. . . . (Ibid., p. 142)

Many other people, however, seem to go through life with little sense of deeper realities, aiming at what is pleasurable or advantageous from a material point of view, and following conventional patterns of morality so far as seems convenient. They never attain to the first path.

The enormous variety of individual approaches up to the third path makes it difficult to discover general principles. A close study of available autobiographies of mystics may nevertheless enable us to see sufficiently clearly what some of the qualifications, adjustments, or shifting phases are that may occur within the broad scheme of four paths and a more primitive stage of subjection to pleasure and self-advantage. Specially illuminating is the account by St. Augustine in his *Confessions* (1912), from which the following facts may be usefully summarized.

It appears that he was the only child of a well-off family, his mother being a baptized Christian, unusually devout, and his father a catechumen, "newly converted" (II.3) but not baptized. It is hard to believe that Augustine did not know the affectionate and sensitive responses of a well-brought up and gifted child, subject also to strong but probably wise discipline at school. The "sins" that he condemns so much in himself would be seen today as normal reactions of a well-brought-up boy of high spirits, joining with others in a few escapades, except only for a year after leaving school at the age of fifteen, when he seems to have become somewhat promiscuous—seeking "to love and be loved" (II.2). It does appear, however, that at that stage he had no particular aim in life except to be successful in rhetoric, and otherwise to enjoy himself.

His *first conversion* came abruptly, from reading an "exhortation to philosophy" by Cicero (the essay *Hortensius,* now lost). "With an incredible heat of spirit I thirsted after the immortality of wisdom," he writes. "How did I burn then, my God, . . . to fly from earthly delights toward thee" (III.4). This was after a period of somewhat reckless exploration of new interests in Carthage (140 miles away), whither he had been sent for further training in rhetoric, with the idea of his becoming a lawyer.

In the *first path,* following this "conversion"—a period of more dedicated exploration and outer stabilization—instead of joining in with the Christians (whose books he found repellingly unphilosophical) he was drawn to the Manichaeans, and remained with them until the age of twenty-nine. When later, as a Christian, he wrote the *Confessions* (at the age of about forty-five), he mercilessly condemned the sect. But it is clear that this period was of immense value to him in consolidating his character. He was greatly influenced for good by their strict code of morals and symbolic teaching concerning "light" and "darkness" (with God over all); his sexual obsession was brought under control in loyalty to a single mistress, by whom he had a much-loved son; and he earned his living as a respected teacher of rhetoric. But the gnostic or mystical symbolism of the Manichaeans (which he later called *fabulae*) could have meant little to him, since his world-conception was still very materialistic.

An approach to the *second path* came with his disappointment in the visiting Manichaean bishop, named Faustus, whose "gracefulness" of manner and eloquence he admired, but whom he considered inferior in philosophy and unable to solve his difficulties. He therefore decided to continue his studies in Rome, whither he went at the age of twenty-nine, with his mistress and son. Soon afterward, following a severe fever, the second path may be said to have begun (as will be shown presently).

The Second Path

We take the second path as characterized by discovery of the validity of a *nonphysical existence,* as shown by a new eagerness to engage in mental practices (especially "recollective" ones) that are felt to bring problems of good and evil, the meaning of life, and individual identity or fulfillment, to the brink of solution.

In my case, I remember the exact moment when I realized that everything seen or heard physically must have an intelligible pattern or original, by discovery of which I would be liberated from subjection to a kind of materialistic blindness or inadequacy of perception. The Recollection practices that I was then led to adopt have been set forth in ML.9f. I am not aware that anyone has thought them worth taking seriously. It may be helpful, therefore, to mention that about this time I was persuaded by my mother (having left school nine months before going to the university) to enroll for the Pelman course of mind-training. There I found, in Book II, pp. 44–46, an exercise that I carried out in slightly modified form, and which I believe was a major factor in helping me to build a secure foundation for the mystical way. The exercise (my own modification) is as follows:

> Choose a time when you have no pressing work of any kind to do, make sure you are otherwise wholly carefree and relaxed, and decide on the route for a 15-minute walk. Resolve to take keen visual note of what you see, carefully avoiding any sort of theorizing, explaining, or admitting of associated ideas or images, and dwelling purely on the visual appearance of details or wholes—not superficially, however, but as expressive of significant life, so that it sticks effortlessly in the memory. See everything as new, as a child might see it, "all eyes," without thinking. Make sure (by momentarily glancing back in time, as it were) that you can recall each detail or whole that is looked at; and then allow yourself to be carried, without imposing any reasoned choice, to another detail or whole, just as it comes. Then, having completed the walk, sit down in a chair, with eyes shut, and go over the whole from beginning to end.

In this exercise it seems to me very important, for mystical development, not to ask any question as to meaning, and not to try to recall things backward, from the end to the beginning. The object is to cultivate the power to allow contemplation of a changing scene to occur in normal sequence, without interference by directed thinking on the basis of wishes deriving from a more materialistic level. One must aim to see parts in the whole, connectedly, without being caught up in "thinking," subjectively imposed and shiftingly out of control. One must develop a "blank slate" attitude to sense, or there can be no spiritual stability. Afterward, a *higher*, obedient insight and reflection will be awakened and will provide intelligence without imposing itself disturbingly on what is seen.

It is vital that in attempting such practice one should not merely encourage a flow of images, without intelligible content. The effect should be, when each detail or whole is seen or recalled, as if *time stops;* and one is then able to go backward or forward from one thing to the next, freely, as if one were contemplating a map. A full vividness of color is not to be looked for; instead, the intelligible quality should be so distinctly grasped that one could recognize the exact shaping or shade of color if one encountered it again.

When the recalling of all visual details and forms has become easy and almost habitual, a similar exercise should be practiced with sounds (sitting in one place, with eyes shut, for two minutes). The free recollection of bodily postures and movements is cultivated in musical performance, dancing, and sports, but special exercises can be devised for making the power more reliable and habitual. As soon as seems advisable, intensive endeavors should be made to maintain, freely and constantly for all senses, a recollected attitude in which all is experienced as if detached from materiality and intelligibly free ("in the world but not of it"). But the least sign of stress, or failure of relaxation, must be corrected at once, or all one's endeavors may be vitiated.

Continuity of Recollection, in all that one observes or does, is a prime requisite. Ten minutes of canalized endeavor, thereafter slipping back with relief into the state of normal attachment to physical things, in oblivion of intelligible release, is almost useless. Say to oneself, continually, "Make Recollection continuous." In such ways Continuous Recollection will take root, and one will find one's repose in "spirit" instead of "matter" (cf. the parable of the wise and foolish virgins, Matt. 25:1-13).

The first stage of release developed by such practice occurs when any sequence of details or wholes is recallable without effort—whether it is seen, heard, smelled, felt, or known as a spatial positioning or conformation (this is Active Recollection). In the second stage, one is as if settled in a free nonphysical world of consciousness and life, loosed from the outer life (this is Continuous Recollection).

St. Augustine, and the Second Path

It is clear that to carry out intensively such practices as have just been described, one needs to have obtained already (in the first path) a sufficient development of faculties of equanimity, perseverance, idealism, and insight, along with freedom from obsessive or neurotic influences of all kinds. If security in such ways has not been attained, an adequate knowledge of recollective release may have to wait until the obstacles have been removed by some transcending illumination.

Augustine makes it clear that for about three years after arriving in Rome (at the age of twenty-nine) he was grievously bound by rigid positivistic beliefs, unable to conceive of anything not materialistically located in the physical world, unless it were a "corporeal image" (VII:1, IV:1, VI:3,4). Coupled with this, he was "tortured" by his inability to understand the meaning of evil (VI:3–7), and by anxiety over his uncontrollable sexual impulsions, though still loyal to his mistress.

After about a year in Rome he obtained appointment as a teacher of rhetoric at Milan, where the Christian bishop, Ambrose, was already famous. As he felt that help might be at hand, his anxious seeking became even more intense, but he obtained some relief by discovering that "evil" was something in his own attitude (fixation?), and that from the "corruptible" (corporeally limited?) one could proceed to an "incorruptible" knowledge (VII:4). "These thoughts I tossed up and down in my miserable heart. . . . " But "every day" he felt he was nearer the truth (VII:5), having realized that there was a kind of "attention" that itself was not a "corporeal substance" (VII:1).

Two events precipitated solution of all these problems. One was the forced abandonment of his mistress, after thirteen years. She left for Carthage after his mother, who had come to Milan, arranged for him a marriage with a girl still two years short of marriageable age (in those days, it seems, a wife gave social status, while a mistress was thought only to satisfy lust). Unable to control his bodily demands, he took another mistress. The other event, of crucial importance, was his discovery of the works of Plotinus, and his realization that the writings of St. Paul made sense in the same way. His great vision of "the unchangeable light of the Lord," continually echoed in his later writings and providing the basis for his later understanding of Christianity, occurred very soon afterward, thus initiating for him the *third path* with a "second conversion."

Other "Conversions"

William James, in his chapters on "The Sick Soul," "The Divided Self," and "Conversion" (VRE, Chaps., 6–10), discusses at some length the cases of Tolstoy, Bunyan, Henry Alline, Stephen Bradley, David Brainerd, Charles Finney, and a few others. At first sight these accounts may seem to give a picture of "conversion" incompatible with what has been said, or at least not identifiable with either a first or a second conversion, as defined. The common characteristic (except perhaps for the case of Finney) is a severe state of *contest,* as shown by what may be called an intense and sustained "philosophic" depression and anxiety, suddenly and as if completely removed by an intellectual illumination (sometimes with visual or aural accompaniments). Lapses may occur afterward. The problem is to "place" these experiences at some point in the mystical way.

The contest, colored as it is by frustration, despair, anxiety, and often also guilt feelings, is clearly centered around *subjectivizings* of stress, which means blunting the edge of stress by a kind of attachment. Possibly through deficiencies in early life, the individual in question has not sufficiently learned to face stresses with obedience and faith; and potential reactions of a neurotic kind have taken root.

The mystical means for a permanent overcoming or rooting out of such reactions is Continuous Recollection, which totally cuts off the subjectivizing and lays a foundation in the face of whose "expansiveness" and non-attachment all tendencies to attachment (of the wrong kind) fall away. Such release, if sudden, intense, and surprising, may give the impression of a "conversion." But Continuous Recollection will lapse and be restored many times before it is strong enough to promote a true *second conversion,* in direct knowledge of the Unchanging and the unitive transformation.

The holistic removal of subjectivized stress is plainly described in the following passages:

> Now did my chains fall off my legs indeed; I was loosed from my afflictions and irons; my temptations also fled away. (Bunyan, VRE.192)

> At that instant of time . . . the burden of guilt and condemnation was gone, darkness was expelled, my heart humbled and filled with gratitude . . . (Alline, ibid. p. 220)

> . . . . in an instant the bandage had fallen from my eyes; and not one bandage only, but the whole manifold of bandages in which I had been brought up. One after another they rapidly disappeared . . . (Ratisbonne, ibid. p. 227)

Although the burdensome reactions of these people have been described above as "neurotic" in character, we cannot suppose that the sufferers were in any usual kind of neurotic state characterized by screening (e.g., amnesias, conversion hysteria, phobias, obsessions, or compulsions). The meaning is that these individuals were temporarily stabilized in a *dissociated state* of *lower second-order*[2], while opposite *higher* second-order forces imposed a rudimentary Continuous Recollection (of objective "good sense") sufficient to prevent a complete lapse into such fixated reactions or obsessions. Under these circumstances the anguish of the contest would tend to strengthen tolerance until the secret power of Continuous Recollection could break through victoriously. Such release could then have the character of a sudden conversion (*intermediate* between the first and second conver-

---

[2]A lower second-order dissociated state is characterized by strong conditioning and anxiety (Whiteman, 1979–80, pp. 47f; 1980, pp. 26f. See also Appendix B).

sions) in which nonphysical realities come compellingly to knowledge, perhaps even in a mystical or premystical experience. This would not necessarily initiate the third path, since Continuous Recollection would not yet have been voluntarily cultivated.

The Buddhist *Samādhi*

Confirmation of these conclusions may be found in the Buddhist account of what has to be attained in the second path (named *samādhi*, literally "collection"). This begins with "guarding the door of the senses" and an introductory phase of "recollective attention" (*satisampajañña*), and then goes on at once to the overcoming of the "five obstacles" (*nīvaraṇas*, DN.2:68). These are precisely those obstacles in which the individuals mentioned above seem to have become enmeshed and which were eventually overcome in the contest, namely:

desireful attachment (*abhijjhā*); "temptations," i.e., tendencies to illdoing (*vyapāda*); rigidity of prepossessions (*thīna-middha*); agitation and worry (*uddhacca-kukucca*); perplexity and distraction (*vicikicchā*).

According to the Sutta, it is only after these obstacles have been substantially overcome that one proceeds (still in the second path) to the thoroughgoing practice of each kind of "dissociative control" (*jhāna*), including Active Recollection (the second *jhāna*), Continuous Recollection (the third), and full dissociative release (the fourth). The "intermediate" kind of conversion may therefore be presumed to happen only when the obstacles have been particularly strong and troublesome, perhaps through bad influences and wrong beliefs.

The Third Path

Our criterion for deciding whether or not the third path has begun for an individual is that, broadly speaking, there shall be no "lapsing" into the usual fixated identification with the outward personality and its worldly conditioning. This may be taken to imply that there is some continuing consciousness of an inner *real being,* different from the personality and like a "deep center" from which the personality is objectively seen and judged. There should be no more lapsing into the older identification and beliefs than might occur in a moment of distraction, rectified almost instantly, without effort. In other words, one has permanently changed the *ground of reality* from which one observes one's life and mental activities in this world.

It appears, however, that this ground, continuing latently and sometimes emerging into vivid awareness, can be known with any one of three degrees of fullness:

1. As a *deep center,* existing in acknowledgement of a Higher Power, which gives guidance and moral strength.
2. As both a deep center and a *transformed disposition,* created by a confirmed orientation to the Source, in Obedience and Faith.
3. As a deep center and transformed disposition, whose higher life is revealed through and in an archetypally satisfying *spiritual-bodily form,* like that which St. Paul described by saying that "the Son" was revealed "in him." One may expect such bodily form to be habitually manifested after the first disclosure. For one's *real being,* once *lived* in this way, will not easily be blocked off completely from the fulfillment which it has attained and for which it must continually yearn through Obedience.

The first of these conditions of life is not usually associated with the term "union" (in Christian mysticism) or with the third path, *paññā* (in Buddhist mysticism). The other two are distinguished as varieties of "union" by both St. John of the Cross and St. Teresa.

St. John speaks of two kinds of "permanent and total union" (AMC.II.v: 2,3), the first "with respect to the obscure habit of union," and the second a "union and transformation of the soul with God, which is "not being wrought continually, but only when there exists that likeness that comes from love." He adds that "there is naught in the one that is repugnant to the other"; that seems to mean that the second (no. 3 above) comes in periods of much fuller manifestation of *real being,* accompanied by a greatly intensified love for and in the Divine Humanity.

St. Teresa, in IC.V:1, characterizes her "fifth mansions" chiefly by the *certainty* that God is present. She also says, however, that in this state "the soul . . . can neither see nor hear nor understand," and "the period is always short." Moreover, "there are really very few who do not enter these Mansions" (pp. 51, 52, 47). These remarks could refer to a kind of knowledge coming under the first head mentioned above, or, more likely, a transient or trancelike knowledge coming under the second head. But later (V:3, pp. 58f) she refers to "another kind of union," saying "Alas that so few of us are destined to attain it!" Here there is "true union with the will of God"; one can "see oneself living a new life," having died to the former life. And a special sign that one is in these "mansions" is the intensity and completeness of our love of the neighbor (p. 63).

Mystical States in the Buddhist Way

In the account of the mystical way in DN.2 the path of *samādhi* ("collection") ends with the fourth *jhāna,* and the path of *paññā* (our third path, of nonlapsing) begins with detachment from the physical body (*ñāṇa-das-sana*) and proceeds to the cultivation of separative experience of various kinds.[3] It is not clear at what stage strictly mystical experience becomes possible. From that text, however, it seems that the path of *paññā* definitely does not begin with any strictly mystical experience; and the previous path does not end with a strictly mystical experience unless the fourth *jhāna* is interpreted as including such possibility.

These defects or confusions are repaired elsewhere in the dialogues. In DN.16:33 (Jennings, 1947, p. 400) there is an exposition of eight states or modes of "deliverance" (*vimokhā*) approaching the Changeless (*ānañja*, equivalent to the upanishadic *akṣara*). The first three accurately correspond to the first three *jhānas*. Thus in (1) we see appearances (*rūpā*) in a way as if subject to appearance; in (2) we subjectively perceive external appearances in a way beyond appearances, i.e., in Active Recollection; and in (3), saying "[it is] beautiful, good, propitious" (*subha*), we become "freed from above" (*adhimutto*), as in Continuous Recollection. The fourth *jhāna* is then expanded into no less than five possible states or characteristics of holistic release:

4. Altogether transcending consciousness of (fixated) appearance, banishing obstruction, free from the pondering attachment to multiplicity, one realizes "Space is unlimited (*ananta*)"; and having attained to unlimited space, one dwells in it [i.e., one is holistically dissociated from the limitations of physical space].
5. Altogether transcending the sphere of unlimited space, one realizes "Discernment is unlimited" . . . [i.e., all is noetically open, without any mental block].
6. Altogether transcending the sphere of unlimited discernment, one realizes "There is no-thingness (*kiñci*)" . . . [i.e., no compounding, fixation, attachment, or enclosure; all is released and interpenetrating].
7. Altogether transcending the sphere of nonattachment, one attains and dwells in the sphere of neither sense (*saññā*) nor non-sense . . . [i.e., all is nothing but "ideas"].
8. Altogether transcending the sphere of neither sense nor non-sense, one attains and dwells in the cessation (*nirodha*) of sense and feeling . . . [all is as if "time-stopped"; there is no compulsive flow].

Similar analyses are to be found in MN.26,106 (Jennings, 1947, pp. 322f, 626f).

---

[3]The term "separative experience" is applied to dissociation and the three kinds of nonphysical experience described in Appendix B as Separation (Whiteman, 1975, pp. 101f, and ML.16f and 85f).

These passages, it seems clear, imply that experience with strictly mystical characteristics can and should mark the end of the second path (*samādhi,* "collection") and thus also the beginning of the third path (*paññā,* higher knowledge and wisdom). They also demonstrate the fallaciousness of the view that Theravāda Buddhism is in these respects a speculative system and not directly evidential (Jennings, 1947, p. 624).

The Behavioral Setting

Nothing further need be said here on the *fourth* path (or unitive life), since at that stage mystical experience is already habitualized. Instead, we now look back at the earlier stages, particularly the first and second paths, and endeavour to study them in a more outward-looking way. That is, we shall consider what specific physical-world activities, practices, and regimes (besides the Recollection practices described above) may be rightly held to foster or facilitate a continual development of the powers of Recollection and Obedience, up to the stage where mystical experience becomes habitual.

So far, we have tacitly presumed that the fostering of these powers in all life is simply a matter of habitually remembering them, so that one finds oneself continually engaged in recollective watchfulness or weighing up what is good or bad in contemplated actions or in feelings and motives, by looking to the Source (the Right and Good, God, the Lord, or whatever name comes naturally). But obviously some "practices," such as taking drugs, overeating, or sexual promiscuity, habitual reactions such as "hitting out" when frustrated, or attitudes to life such as possessiveness, will make it difficult or impossible to attain habitual nonattached watchfulness and obedience, simply because in these practices or reactions an *attachment, automaticity,* or other kind of "disobedience" has already been made habitual. And contrariwise, other practices, such as the imposing of rules of life to safeguard oneself against such weaknesses, will favor advancement on the mystical way.

Motivation and "Contests": The Nature of Practice

These instances focus attention on the fact that *practice* in this physical life, and the *motivational state* in which it is performed, cannot be separated in actuality; and it would be futile to impose on ourselves certain bodily actions or regimes (e.g., breathing in and out through each nostril alternately, chanting OM, or repeating a mantra without intelligible meaning) while paying no attention to the motives behind and fulfilled in these actions. For if our motives fly against Recollection and Obedience, the acts will only confirm us in our faults.

Practice, in general, is a matter of immense subtlety, which can, however, be helpfully illuminated by considering first how one practices for mastery of technical and artistic performance on a musical instrument. For in that field of human endeavor, where "practice" has been studied for centuries, the validity of our conclusions can be immediately judged from what is seen and heard in the effects produced—here, indeed, "a tree is known by its fruits."

To be quite specific, we may refer to a number of passages from a book on *The Art of Tone-Production on the Violoncello* (Krall, 1923, pp. 17–19), and after that, "translate" them into equivalent passages in terms not of "movement" or "muscular action," but of motivation in general. It should be remarked first, however, that Krall assumes that a certain "everyday" power of individualization of movements in the lesser bodily parts—fingers, hand, and forearm—has already been obtained (just as Recollection practice presupposes a preliminary control of eyes, attention, and even words). The motivational character of practice for *specific techniques* and *effects of artistry* then comes to the forefront, and this is what Krall is here analyzing:

> All our practice is essentially the constant endeavour to find *that* form of movement which produces the most beautiful sound. . . .
>
> Every movement . . . is composed of several *part*-movements which cooperate harmoniously towards the actual finished movement.
>
> It is natural that an unpracticed movement should be stiff. The reason is, that too many muscles cooperate. . . . Appropriate movements are always graceful and they are appropriate, or have become so by practice, because that set of muscles which causes the movement works in perfect order and harmony. This is the whole secret.
>
> We must learn to distinguish between active and passive movements. . . . Active movements we have only in the upper arm . . . . it is the upper arm that leads, and the whole system of levers ust, and is bound to, follow the movement of the upper arm . . . each movement implies the cooperation of all levers, be that movement large or ever so small.

The "translation" for the purpose of mystical development is in thorough conformity with the teachings of Gotama Buddha, that the *dhamma* (rule of spiritual life) "has but one savour, the savour of release" (Woodward, 1925, p. 251). Thus:

> All our practice is essentially the constant endeavour to find *that* course of outward activity which produces the greatest sense of release and upliftment.

There is no kind of outward action which is not caused by the operation of several motivations . . . . Every motivation is composed of several part-motivations, or constituent controls, which cooperate harmoniously towards the final motivational act, if it is efficient and well-directed.

It is natural that any unsynthesised kind of outward activity should be awkward and uneaseful. The reason is that too many constituent controls cooperate . . . . Appropriate motivational acts are always full of grace, and they are appropriate, or have become so by practice, because that set of subsidiary controls which causes the act works in perfect order and harmony.

We must learn to distinguish between active and relatively passive motivations. In the active ones, *Obedience* leads. The other motivations, e.g. Recollective non-attachment and the outward adjustment to the requirements of the whole situation, are subsidiary. But, large or small, their harmonious cooperation is implied by the appropriateness of the total motivational act under Obedience.

Having recognized the overriding importance of Obedience in all acts that are undertaken in order to foster mystical development, we must look briefly at the distinction between (1) *hierophanies* ("disclosures of the sacred"; Eliade, 1958a, Chap. 1, pp. 3–9), such as the beauties and sublimities in nature, which are presentations or experiences tending to raise our level of consciousness to one that is notably released and "other-worldly" in character, without involving us in any effort, discomfort, or stress; and (2) *contests,* in which outward tendencies to attachment, fixation, discomfort and awkwardness, automaticity, or anxiety-provoking stress are countered by "higher" motivations that are secretly working for the development in us of corresponding powers or release and control (Recollection and Obedience). As St. Paul says:

It is not for us a contest (*palē*) against flesh and blood, but [one] against the [inner] dominions, authorities, and cosmic powers of the darkness of this [life], [in short] the spiritual [forces] of the stressful labour (*ponēria*) in what is over against the heavenly things. (Eph. 6:12)

Although some hierophanies (e.g., parental love or beauty in nature) provide an initiation to higher-level realities, and others (e.g., beauty in music) can be sought out and cultivated, it is easy to see that after the first few moments of initiation there will be a more or less conscious "working-out" and adjustment of outlook and ideals, in short, some degree of *contest.* An entire new field of development will have been opened up by each initiation, with involvement in corresponding contests, mild or severe. Hence it can be said that all development, mental or spiritual, depends on our subjection to contests.

It is essential, however, to realize that there are six ways in which we can approach contests and deal with the great variety of discomforts or stresses in them. In three ways (nos. 1, 2, 3, see below) the contest is *faced;* in one way (4) it is temporarily shelved by *wise digression;* in the other two ways (5, 6) it is *escaped.* Only the first three ways will directly promote the development of mystical powers, though for a particular individual in particular circumstances one of the other ways may be necessary or unavoidable. Thus:

- The contest may be *faced:*
  1. With equanimity and faith, in the certainty of a quick and easy transcendence of the discomfort or stress, by virtue of a corresponding spiritual power already developed.
  2. With a little anguish and doubt, but also strong hope, so that a sufficient degree of transcendence follows after a certain period of tolerance and incubation.
  3. With considerable anguish but also sufficient faith to prevent the anguish forcing an escape; so again a certain degree of transcendence follows eventually.
- The contest may be (4) *shelved* by wise digression, that is, by wisely choosing or working out some way to stop or block, temporarily, the drives that maintain the contest.
- The contest may be *escaped:*
  5. Involuntarily, by the personality being taken into a state of "disorganization" (e.g., impatience, anger, and "hitting back"), neurotic "screening" (e.g., amnesia, conversion hysteria), or psychotic fragmentation of reason, or fantasy, confusion of values, and loss of restraint.
  6. By the deliberate choice of some "disobedient" action constituting an escape from the stress by subjectivizing it or projecting it onto others (as in sullenness, hitting out, evasion, deceit, willfulness, revenge, profligacy, or viciousness).

These various possible outcomes in a contest are further explained and illustrated in the analysis of specific case histories, in Whiteman, 1979–1980, 1980, and LD.

We may conclude that when practices are specially undertaken for *mystical* self-discipline and enlightenment, the same background of understanding and watchfulness must be preserved, specifically by acknowledging:

1. The variety of *motivations* that proceed within one and the same outward action.
2. The *holistic* (Gestalt) character of practice for release, efficiency, beauty, or self-control, secured by "looking to the Source."
3. The various kinds of possible *outcome,* by facing the contest, or by wise digression, but not by "escape."
4. The different levels of release and illumination, up to that of a unitive and inspirational creativity, realizable through practice.

Obstacles and Negative Effects

We turn now to a consideration of what may be called "inner" obstacles, which are wrong motivations, or habits of "disobedience," somehow set up and confirmed with the help of "practices" or "regimes" that to that extent can be described as "outwardly" obstructive. Among those persons who apply themselves to practices that they believe will favor mystical development, the following wrong motivations appear to be particularly prevalent today:

1. *Desire* for personal prestige or worldly advantages, instead of the well-considered impulsion of a genuine *need.*
2. Rigid *attachment* to methods whose nature, inadequacies, and possible dangers are not understood.
3. Gullible or idolatrous dependence on some particular teacher, so that *inner* reflection and assessment are habitually pushed into the background or treated as quite secondary in importance.
4. Fixated adherence to a single system of teachings to which one has become narrowly and perhaps fanatically "loyal," so that all other evidence is regarded as untrustworthy, or at least unhelpful.
5. A confirmed belief that shortcuts or easier ways to "higher knowledge" exist, and these are what a sensible or sophisticated person should seek out.

Adoption of these motivational attitudes is likely to lead to strong negative effects, a contest being providentially required to overcome them. It could be a build-up of anxiety or other kinds of mental disorder (Epstein and Lieff, 1981), obsessive behavior patterns, a complacent lack of realism (Needleman, 1972, pp. 212f, 223f), or the confirming of "worldly" or self-centred attitudes in other ways, as remarked on by a well-informed Swiss psychiatrist, Dr. Medard Boss:

In India itself I met altogether eight European and American people who had entered upon one of the Indian ways of salvation . . . . with one exception, however, they had remained in the depths of their hearts self-willed, envious and intolerant Occidentals. They had merely inflated their very limited egos with Indian formulas of wisdom instead of with large bank accounts or other means to power. (Boss, 1965, p. 186)

If, on the other hand, one follows what may be called the regular mystical way, grounded in Recollection practices and watching obediently for inner instruction and assessments, from the Source, in all life, one is not likely to need guidance from without as to what behavioral patterns may be appropriate and when or how to practice particular techniques of self-discipline and release. The "inner voice" will give all the guidance that one needs; as classical mystical teachings declare:

Blessed indeed are those ears which listen not after the voice which is sounding without, but for the Truth teaching inwardly. (Thomas à Kempis, 1912, Book III.1)

Those who suffer the "negative effects" mentioned appear therefore to be people who have not yet learned to stop the current of time and listen to the "inner voice" of Obedience. They have perhaps grown up in a climate of opinion in which inner self-analysis is feared or scorned, and a visible teacher from the "mystic East" is depended on to save them from the disquiet that has built up in them.

It is all too easy for many people to obey the injunctions of an "outside" teacher, thus relieving themselves of the more stressful (and less showy) endeavors needed to rectify their adverse motivations through perseverance in *inner* contests, with trust in the *inner* teaching.

"Outward" Aids, Adjustments, Regimens

An obedient "looking to the Source," on the basis of "letting go" and Recollection, should be sufficient to tell us whether contemplated acts do not conform to the Right and Good; and it may also be expected to intimate to us, in due course if not at once, what actions we could rightly make when faced with a problem of any kind. Nevertheless, it is usually considered helpful to specify certain kinds of outward activity, or ways of conducting our life, that need to be carefully "adjusted" or worked at if our spiritual growth is to be facilitated or actively promoted. The study of such outward activities, regulations of behavior, or "adjustments" to circumstances, traditionally called in Sanskrit *kriyā-yoga* ("practical method"), is purportedly the subject of Book II of Patanjali's Yoga Sutras. But it will be best to present first an independent survey appropriate for our times.

An important preliminary distinction to make is between two *modes* in which any such activity can be performed—a mode of approach (to Obedience) and a mode of attainment—distinguished by St. John of the Cross as *active* and *passive*, respectively (AMC.I.13:1). These can be well illustrated in the case of breath-control (*prāṇāyāma*), where, if tightness or other constraint is marked and obsessive, one may force a kind of regularity by slow counting during inhalation and exhalation (say 5 while inhaling, and 4 exhaling). But when Obedience is fairly well established, one merely observes the constraint, faces the stress, and allows the obedient orientation to bring release.

We may next classify the activities, adjustments, or regulatings under five heads, corresponding to the four creative functions of classical mysticism[4] and a central control, thus: Regimens (3rd function), Letting-go (4th function), Creative energy and inspirational ideas (1st function), Obedience of feeling and judgment in the perfecting of socially creative life and its fruits (2nd function), and Word-power. Thus:

- *Regimens:* The right ordering of one's outer life for health, exercise, eating and drinking, social activity, study, professional work or employment, periods for the special cultivation of Recollection and separative experience of various kinds, holidays, and sleep.
- *Letting-go:* Relaxation (of all discomforts in the body), untensing of the facial muscles particularly, ease of posture and grace of movement, easy and natural response of breathing at all times, specific practices for Active or Continuous Recollection (of both outer and inner sense, also of thoughts, feelings, and incentives), attaining and maintaining dissociated or other separative states (e.g., waiting for inspirational ideas or guidance, for "hypnagogic images," psychical disclosures as in "object-reading," or mystical disclosures in secondary separation), and preparing for sleep.
- *Creative energy and insight:* Cultivation of arts and skills (in descriptive and other creative writing, music, visual arts, games, dancing, etc.) and of intuitive and discursive reason (in mathematics, language structure, symbolism, and levels of meaning).
- *Obedience: right feeling—response and judgment:* Consideration of the right and good in all one's actions, as a whole and at the same time in every detail, "grace" in all deeds and social relations, "going out" to others in loving empathy, caring and helpfulness (according to wisdom), the disciplines of sex and marriage (most powerful of all hierophanies or sacraments), and the facing up to one's moral deficiencies and adopting of special resolves or methods to correct them.

---

[4]In the terminology of this chapter, these are: Faith, Obedience, Application, and Nonattachment (Whiteman, 1979–80, pp. 34f; 1980, pp. 19–26).

- *Word-power:* Use of meaningful mantras or "key-words" (e.g., Relax, Let go, Recollect, make Obedience continuous), verbal prayer to help orientation to the Source, noting down outline-descriptions of vivid nonphysical experiences (dreams, hypnagogic images, openings, separative experiences of all kinds), noting down teachings or "points of wisdom" intuitively received in answer to problems of life (when one "listens for guidance"), copying out illuminating quotations from scriptural and mystical or other writings, listing one's faults still not conquered and opposite virtues to be "collected" in admiration of other people (whether adult or child, male or female).

It would be possible to enlarge greatly on all these suggested practices or aids, especially on the deep and many-sided illuminations and other benefits provided by music and mastery of musical performance on voice or instrument, and on the essentiality of a cultivated skill in the use of language for the recording of descriptions of nonphysical experience, the setting-out of teachings in appropriate words, and the realizing of subtle distinctions in psychological or mystical awareness. Such skills connect immediately with powers of recognition and control in separative experience, and should therefore on no account be neglected by the potential mystic.

On the whole, however, it seems best for each individual to work out each of these practices or aids in ways suited to his or her present needs. (But the intimate bearing of music on initiation to higher states of release may be further illuminated by the many quotations or references given in my paper on "The Angelic Choirs," 1954.)

Kriyā-yoga in the Yoga Sutras

It would be out of place here to try to establish the mystical authenticity, in our sense of the term, of major portions of the collection of aphorisms attributed (mistakenly, about A.D. 1000) to Patanjali the grammarian (c. 100 B.C.). What concerns us is the possible value, today, of the various traditions of *kriyā-yoga* ("practical method") embodied in Book II of the Sutras. None of these ranks as authentic mystical testimony.

The first aphorism declares that the "practical method" consists of *tapas* (stress-tolerance, ardor), *svādhyāya* (study of sacred books), and *īśvara-praṇidhāna* (obedience or prayerful approach to the Lord). The placing of this last alongside "study" as a "practical method" shows that the author of this aphorism, or the editor of the Book, either had no experience of the absolute priority of the Divine Source (as dealt with in Book I.23–29) or is using the term *praṇidhāna* in a different and altogether more superficial way. The five aphorisms on *samyoga* ("fusion", II.23–27) present the genuine mystical teaching on attachment in a new language, but this is not itself *kriyā-yoga*.

The latter half of the Book (28–55) is an exposition of eight "limbs" (*aṅgas*) of yoga, including three that are mental controls, following sensory Recollection (here called *pratyāhāra*), and leading to *samādhi* ("collectedness," or unspecified kind).

The other "limbs" are: *yama* (ordinary morality), *niyama* (the three practices of *kriyā-yoga* mentioned above, plus purity and contentment), *āsana* (sitting-posture), and *prāṇāyāma* (breath-control). It may be noted that relaxation is mentioned only once, in passing (47), and there is no mention of grace of movement and posture in general, cultivation of arts or skills, or the use of words and other aids to discernment and control.

This summary of traditional teachings, however, correct and useful it may have been at one time in India, seems to be in some ways obstructive to mystical development today. For instead of fostering rocollective watchfulness and obedience to the Source in all life, continually, it implants an image of the secluded ascetic, in a conventionally fixed sitting position, closing his eyes and engaged in self-directed breathing practices (e.g., "intercepting" the breath. II.49), that is, in the *samprajñāta* practices (self-directed and discursive ones, identifiable with the *first jhāna* in Buddhism) referred to in I.17 as an initial kind of mind-activity that it is the aim of yoga to transcend.

A discussion of the dating of the Yoga Sutras and of the commentaries by Vyāsa and Vācaspatimiśra will be found in Woods (1966, pp. xiii–xxiii), who also includes translations of these commentaries, on which all later commentators depend. Another English translation of these commentaries is by Rāma Prasāda (1924). For the Sanskrit text, see Dvivedi (1934). A scholarly and well-documented survey of yoga teachings, superstitions, practices, and magical acts in India from primitive times is provided by Eliade (1958).

No attempt is made in any of the translations mentioned to correlate the aphorisms with authentic mystical evidence, and extreme liberties are sometimes taken with the text in an attempt to make sense of it according to behavioristic ideas on psychology. The two commentaries mentioned (written some hundreds of years after the Sutras) also reveal ignorance of separative experience and other mystical evidences (see particularly III.18,21,27,39,40,43).

The Habitualization of Separative Experience

For scientific purposes it would seem most desirable that effective means should be discovered for the voluntary production, by any person of normal intelligence, of separative experiences, dissociative, primary, secondary, or tertiary in type.[5] Then it would seem impossible for open-minded scientists to become lost in puzzles about the nature and validity of "out of the body experience" (OBE, Separation).

A survey of the extensive literature of recorded OBE, nearly all of it primary in type, shows that this kind of experience can occur in a great variety of ways, some of them reasonably described as voluntary. But this is not to say that "any person of normal intelligence" could use these methods with success, or that the state attained would transcend the levels of fantasy and immersion in "duplicate" phenomena. If we are especially concerned (as here) with the voluntary habitualization of separative experiences of a mystical character, the most helpful observation seems to be that made in Patanjali III.39:

> By relaxation of the cause of bondage [to the physical body] and full understanding of the [manner of] going forth, the mind takes on another bodily form. (Literally: there is an other-body-of-the-mind entering)

In other words, if one reads, very receptively, thoroughly authentic descriptions of primary separation, and settles into an eagerly confident but fully relaxed and expansive frame of mind, it is quite likely that very soon, perhaps that very night, one will experience spontaneously a separation of that type. Many instances of this happening could be adduced from the literature. Moreover, when one has thus learned in direct experience "the manner of going forth" and the characteristics of the separative state in question, there is some likelihood that separation will occur on other occasions.

There is another difficulty, however, in the voluntary inducing of primary separations. Besides the difficulty in inducing the wakening to a nonphysical "world" and "body," there is the difficulty in having to *stabilize* the state for more than a few moments, beyond the "undeveloped" or "borderline" levels of consciousness, where fantasy takes charge and there is a powerful tendency to lapse into a dream-state or to waken. Such stabilizing, and still more so the raising of the level to that of a fully-attained separation (of first or second degree, or even mystical) is obtained by the imposing of Recollection, as habitually practiced in the physical life, so as to remove the obstacles one after the other until release is obtained. This process is well illustrated by a number of experiences recorded in ML, especially nos. 117, 587, 233, 1224, 1352 (pp. 57, 72, 175, 193, 201).

Because this removal of obstacles (which can be represented by a sinking

---

[5]See Appendix B.

through water or the earth, being caught in thorns, or tied up in one's clothing) is the first necessity in stabilizing a fully attained separation, it is very logical, and good evidence for authenticity, that the next aphorism in Patanjali, III.49, reads as follows:

By command of the "upward spirit" (udāna) [there results] dissociation from [such obstacles as] water, mud, thorns, etc., and a stepping up or out (utkrānti) [of such obstacles].

The context makes it quite clear to anyone familiar with separative experience that the "water, mud, thorns, etc." are out-of-the-body obstacles and not physical ones, and that the "stepping out" or "rising" is not death, as the commentators suppose (Woods, 1966, p. 267). The commentators also propound a quasi-physiological, mechanistic interpretation of udāna, apparently not realizing that the five prānas of the Upanishads are "functions" controlling nonattachment and consequent "raising of the level of engagement" (Freud, 1958 p. 221).

Still dealing with primary separation, it may be added that the easiest and most natural way (if one is not already stabilized in a strong state of continuous Obedience) to "awakening" in a nonphysical "world" is by the habitual practice of Recollection causing some degree of nonattached reflection to become active in the course of a dream. Muldoon calls this the "dream-control" method of "projection" (1968, Chap. 8). If Recollection is sufficiently habitual, however, or the mystical transformation is established (in recognition of one's *real being,* as opposed to physical or fantasy conceptions of oneself), dream-consciousness virtually ceases because Recollection either stops the dream from taking hold of consciousness or converts it into a separation. A fuller consideration of primary separation and its initiation is presented in LD.I Chap. 2. Muldoon's remarks concerning the "passive will method of projection" (1968, pp. 234–240) are also important.

Secondary Separation (S2)

In the third path, after the Divine Source has become known, secondary separation will have a GIR of at least nine points (i.e., second-degree or mystical in character), on account of the latent Obedience and recognition of *real being* behind the manifestations of "personality." The development of S2 may begin, however, from a cultivated facility in the experiencing of Openings, as through practice with hypnagogic images. While wholly relaxed, with eyes shut, one waits confidently and patiently in a "half-sleep" state, as if preparing one's eyes (and/or ears) for something objectively nonphysical to appear; and when it does appear, one endeavors to stabilize the state by focusing on intelligible characteristics or symbolical content and naming it (if words are heard, the endeavor to grasp them before they escape the memory may be almost painful, but provides a salutary discipline). Alternatively, one can begin with the practice of scrying (crystal gazing, or similar practices), as did Kate Wingfield (Miss A.; Myers, 1892), object-reading (Grant, 1975), or automatic writing ("Mrs. Willett"; Balfour, 1935; Betty White; White, 1948). On these matters, see also ML, pp. 80–98.

What may be, at first, one-dimensional and perhaps without color, may soon be developed by means of such practices into three-dimensional scenes in color, containing moving objects or people. The next stage is then to find oneself "in the scene," located there in an appropriate nonphysical body, with appropriate perception by the nonphysical senses (touch, hearing, perhaps smelling), and also open empathically to the feelings, the thoughts, and sometimes the memories of other beings present. Meanwhile, one is aware that the physical body is still under normal control in essential ways, and one can even speak without losing hold of one's life in the nonphysical scene. A number of novelists and play-writers also have developed the power of entering the nonphysical scenes and *living* the events that unfold for them and which they subsequently describe (ML, pp. 100–103).

Mystical grades of S2 and their many varieties will become open to development as one advances, through Recollection, further along the mystical way.

Tertiary Separation (S3)

Nonmystical varieties of tertiary separation have been recorded many times in cases of apparitional vision; and a similar kind of incompatibility between the form, placing or posture of one's "body-image" and the physical body may occur in *persona-acting,* as well as in less healthful ways. Another kind occurs at the stage of *erotic transcendence* in the development of a young woman (De Beauvoir, 1969, pp. 78f), when "her [transfigured] body enchants her like that of another." A more "normal" transfiguration of similar kind occurs when two people "fall in love."

What has to be specially noted here is that the more radical premystical and mystical "transformations," which provide an ultimately healthy fulfillment or "self-realization," can be *voluntarily* cultivated by recalling one's orientation to the Source. But these states being tertiary in type, the vividness of what is disclosed in them may vary from that of a faint suggestiveness (unmistakable, nevertheless) to a full vividness and reality that entirely blots out the physical body from consciousness, while still controlling it in intelligence and wisdom. In such a way we can have something of the fullness of a higher life while "in this world but not of it." The same teaching is to be found in the East under the term *bhāvamukha* (Nikhilananda, 1951, Glossary, p. 370).

The ideal of voluntarily disposing oneself for the mystical transformation is central in St. Paul's injunction that we should "put on the new man" (Eph. 4:24, Col. 3:10, Rom. 13:4, Gal. 2:20, 2 Cor. 5:17) and so "be conformed to the image of the Son . . . " (Rom. 8:29). C. S. Lewis puts this teaching strongly, in modern language, when he advocates:

"dressing up" as a son of God in order that you may finally become a real son. What I want to make clear is that this is not one of many jobs a Christian has to do, and it is not a sort of special exercise for the top class. It is the whole of Christianity. (1960, p. 162)

[For] very often the only way to get a quality in reality is to start behaving as if you had it already. (Ibid., p. 157)

This method of cultivating, or at least providing a sure ground for, the mystical transformation, requires some kind of reminder—"prayer" or mantra—to recall or confirm in us our orientation to the Source, as being the power that is able to conform us, at first in small ways but later completely, to the pattern of perfect humanity (under the name of "the Son" for those who are mystically male). The reminder could be simply a "name of God," or a prayer of petitionary type such as the "Jesus prayer" used by the monks of Mount Athos (Spencer, 1963, p. 228).

Since the wording of the "reminder" should spring up genuinely and intensely from the heart, it seems best, if the prayer is to remind us of our real human nature in the sight of God, that each individual should choose his own prayer or mantra. And anyone mystically female must choose a prayer that confirms identity with the Divine Womanhood—Daughter, Bride, or Mother. It would not be possible to do otherwise.

Rituals and *sacraments* can be conditionally justified in a similar way— namely, as "reminders" making use of certain powerful hierophanies for the purpose of opening up and confirming people (corporately in this case) in a state of unitive release transcending this normal physical life, so far as the individuals present can respond to such hierophanies at the time. If the whole circumstances for an individual in respect of the rituals and sacraments in question were favorable, the state of release brought about would be generally a higher dissociation, but could be exceptionally a separative state of tertiary type revealing something more definite of "the Son" or "the Bride."

Side Issues

"Meditation"

In a chapter on the habituation of mystical experiences, only three questions concerning "meditation" seem to call for an answer:

1. What do people do when they say they are "meditating"?
2. Can what they do be identified with practices that we have found specially helpful or necessary for fostering the capacity to enter mystical states?
3. Are the millions of people who regularly "meditate" doing something wrong, that fruits of strictly mystical attainment among them are so hard to find?

So far as Catholic mysticism is concerned, the answers to the first two questions seem clear enough. Meditation, in Catholic mysticism, is defined by Poulain (1950) as the second of four stages of "ordinary" prayer, and is "also called *methodical* or discursive prayer" (p. 7). He continues, "This last term indicates a chain of quite distinct reflections and arguments"; and a vocal prayer "accompanied by some reflections which help us to penetrate its meaning" also comes under this head.

This kind of practice is clearly demanded at every level of attainment, by the mere fact that one must study in order to progress, and study of any kind requires reflection on the meaning of words. While not itself a "mystical state," it is necessary for the development of mystical states. It amounts to the first *jhāna* of Theravada Buddhism, with its *vitakka* (directed thinking, deliberation, reasoning, speculation) and *vicāra* (discursive thinking, consideration), and is what is usually understood by the English word *concentration,* or perhaps when one speaks of *thinking* as being purposive.

What may be called "popular meditation" today does not seem concerned with this stage of "ordinary prayer," or, explicitly, with the third stage, which is called *affective.* But it seems on the whole to come very close to the fourth stage, called the prayer (i.e., dedicated practice in mind or spirit) of *simplicity* or *simple regard.* These alternative titles indicate two chief aspects or aims that appear also in the "popular" varieties: (1) "the persistence of one principal idea" or "dominant thought," this being "really only a slow sequence of single glances upon one and the same object" (Poulain, 1950, p. 8); and (2) the aim to replace reasoning and discursive thinking "in a great measure" by intuition, while manifesting "little variety" of affections and making use of "few words" if any.

Thus the "popular" kinds of "meditation technique" used today have been classified by some recent investigators (Naranjo and Ornstein, 1971; Goleman 1977; Kornfield, 1978, 1979) as of two chief types: (1) concentrative or absorptive; and (2) negative, distraction-removing, letting-go, seeking for "no-mind," that is, the "blank slate", no-thinking state, sometimes called *awareness* or *insight* meditation, and given the Pali name of *vipassanā* (adopted from Buddhaghosha, 1964, but given a different meaning). A similar division into *cognitive* and *relaxation* techniques has also been adopted (Boals, 1978). Some confusion results from the fact that "awareness" is often associated with "concentration" or strong emotional effects, instead of "letting go" and "no-mind" (Kornfield, 1979, pp. 46f).

The implicit dependence of the two extreme attitudes (focusing and letting-go) on each other, if a genuine approach to Active and Continuous Recollection is to be made, can be judged from the following characterizations of the two basic varieties of Recollection-practice: identifiable with the second and third *jhānas* respectively, as we have seen:

2. Active Recollection: focus, plus letting-go, and passage to the "time-stopped" purely conceptual (as distinct from the supposedly mindless objectivities of the "worldly" life).
3. Continuous Recollection: letting-go, plus expansion, and effortless removal of conditioning (fixed habits of thought, etc.); stabilizing of the ground for unconditioned observation at all levels of life. This is the state of "release" par excellence; but a pinpointing of cognitive details (*not* to be called Active Recollection here) accompanies and distinguishes each state, the whole and its parts being known with an interconnectedness that transcends ordinary space and time as known in the "worldly" life.

That these are not fantastically difficult practices, known only to experts in the mystical life, can be judged from the fact that every well-trained musician will understand what is meant; and also from the extensive writings of Husserl and his followers on *phenomenological insight* (or "essential insight"), proceeding from the *epoché* (stoppage) to "pure consciousness" and "primordial object-giving" (see Whiteman, 1967, pp. 107f, 404f).

Two chief causes may be suggested accordingly for the ineffectiveness of most present-day "meditation systems" in regard to strictly mystical development. One is the unbalanced emphasis on *either* focusing *or* "negative" processes (i.e., on *either* application *or* nonattachment), so that in every practice the meditator remains conditioned, floundering in obstacles. The other cause is the fashionable rendering of technical terms in Sanskrit or Pali by English terms habitually associated with "everyday" (conditioned) mental states and activities.

For instance, the rendering of *samādhi* as "concentration" (Woods, 1966; Nyanaponika Thera, 1962; and Ñyānamoli, 1964, in his translation of Buddhaghosha), as "absorption" (Epstein and Lieff, 1981), or as "trance" (Conze, 1956; Dvivedi, 1934) could build up huge misconceptions. For in Buddhism, *samādhi* (literally "collection") is that phase of development (the second path) in which motivational hindrances are removed and the various functional levels of Recollection (the four *jhānas*) are stabilized; while in Patanjali the term is used for states of recollective release, of many kinds and degrees (Active, Continuous, sensory, interior, etc.). It is worthy of note that Tenzin Gyatsho, the 14th Dalai Lama, renders the word *samādhi* as "collectedness" (1972, pp. 71f).

Among other English renderings that can be criticized as seriously misleading, special mention may be made of "mindfulness" for *sati* (Recollection, usually Active), and "absorption" for *jhāna*. The implication in all these renderings is that familiar ideas in Western establishment-psychology provide all that is needed for understanding the mind, so the mystical or premystical practices must be explained in those terms. But in fact a radical departure from the prevalent "one-level naturalistic" and "time-bound" world-view in the West is needed.

Irregular and Deviant Methods

The long and celebrated dialogue of the Buddha on the "setting up" of *sati* (Recollection), the Mahā Satipaṭṭhāna Suttanta (DN.22), begins:

This is the one direct path (*ekāyano ayaṃ maggo*) for the purification of beings . . . for the realization of *nibbāna* (the ultimate Release), namely the four ways of establishing Recollection (*sati*).

It is not very clear what should distinguish a path as *indirect* or *irregular*. For present purposes we may take it that an indirect or irregular path is one in which the strong sense of need (to see more meaning or purpose in life) that begins the second path leads very soon not to the systematic practice of nonattachment (through some kind of Recollection or "simple regard"), but to further attachments. These could be to some exclusive system of authoritarian teaching, or to some charismatic teacher, in the belief that "salvation" will come through trust and submission to such channel. Sometimes, perhaps, the initial "escape" into such attachments may be a means for realizing eventually, through minor elements in the teaching or a build-up of further anxieties or distaste, that an inner dedication to *release through nonattachment,* with an "inner" obedience, is "the one direct path." If the "escape" is into beliefs and practices that prove to be a far more serious obstacle (e.g., into drug abuse), we may describe the path as *deviant.*

There are some "irregular" methods that could count almost as "normal" and "healthy," and even necessary for the person in question. For example:

1. The practice of automatic (or "guided") writing. This was the beginning of Betty White's path to mystical experience (White, 1937, 1948).
2. Subjection to hypnosis. This was the beginning of A. J. Davis's development up to mystical levels (Davis, 1873).
3. Development of mediumistic or other psychical powers (Garrett, 1939).

Without venturing on any assessment of the abundant "New Religions," many of which are very competently surveyed by Needleman (1972), the following may be mentioned as of special interest on account of the practices advocated, all of which seem to put the "religion" concerned more or less in the category of the "irregular" or "deviant":

4. Sant Mat: A system centred chiefly on the "sound current," called Shabd, but also on the "third eye" (Fripp, 1964, Chaps. 1, 12, and 17–19, especially).
5. "Transcendental Meditation": A system centred on the repetition, for a short period every day, of a certain vocal sound allocated to the individual, with the idea to rid oneself of the "wandering mind." The process is said to be "automatic" (Needleman, 1970, Chap. 5).
6. Subud: A system centred on the *latihan,* which is a completely uninhibited "letting go," by people in groups, men and women separately (Needleman, 1970, Chap. 4; Bennett, 1958).
7. Rinzai Zen: A system centred on "just sitting" (zazen) and being faced with insoluble paradoxes (koans) in the hope of a sudden breakthrough (satori) to a transcendental release, or momentary enlightenment (Needleman, 1972, pp. 58f).
8. Kundalini Yoga: A system based on the idea of what is thought to be an "upward flow of the reproductive essences into the cranium," for the purpose of inducing mystical phenomena, especially a "luminosity in the head." The induction is attempted by long hours of concentration on the image of a lotus at the top of the head (or elsewhere on the spine). The practice may lead to agonizingly psychotic disturbances (Gopi Krishna, 1974, pp. 137f, 1976, pp. 5f, 36–44, 49–54, 146–154). In the modification called siddha-yoga, introduced by Muktananda (1972), the phenomena are said to be induced primarily by

the disciple's devotion to his guru. In due time, an "inner guru" may appear.

It does not seem that any authentic accounts of mystical experiences credited to the above systems of teaching and practice are available; and indeed, mystical experience (as strictly defined here) is not to be expected so long as Recollection and Obedience to the Source are not systematically inculcated and practiced habitually by the followers of such systems (for the V, H, I, ahd P ratings would be small).[6] The goal seems to be, rather, a higher dissociated state of release, with some visual or audible phenomena.

Nevertheless, it may be accepted that there are numbers of people whose present capacity and needs are suited by one of these or other systems of collective spiritual endeavor, helped by a certain dedication so as to break their rigid conditioning or otherwise to provide a certain faith in nonmaterialistic powers.

"Ultimate Contests": Regular and Irregular

Our concluding topic is one of great complexity and abstruseness, being concerned with (1) the O.T. "Oracles of the Kingdom" declared by the prophets, and similar N.T. teachings on the *synteleia tou aiōnos* (conjunct fulfilment of the aeon, or eternal power; Matt. 24:3) and the "day of the Lord" (1 Th. 5:2); (2) first-hand evidence from mystics on the experiencing of inner "world-upheavals" or "judgments"; (3) accounts of exceptional kinds of "contest" experienced by mystics immediately before the first disclosure of the Divine Source and/or mystical transformation, after such disclosure, or both before and after, in different ways; (4) the widespread myths concerning "world-destructions" by fire, earthquakes, wind, or water; and (5) numerous first-hand accounts of psychotic-type "breakdowns," following periods of intense stress.

In all this evidence there seems to be reference to the mental conditions and observed nonphysical phenomena typical of a *third-order dissociated state* of contest for the development of a genuine mystical Faith and Obedience from the Source, against counterfeit persuasions or compulsions of "self" and "the world." Such state can be predominantly of a higher, lower, or mixed kind, and the character of the mental state and phenomena (sublimely objective, or obsessive and "infernal") varies accordingly. Contests of first or second order—for the development of Active Recollection as against automaticity, and distinguished by "disorganization," or of Continuous Recollection as against conditioning, and characterized by neurotic

---

[6]See Appendix C.

"anxiety"—are not in question here, since they have no "ultimate" or end-of-the-world quality.

That the "oracles of the Kingdom," "day of the Lord," and "last times" in the Hebrew prophetic books refer to an "inner contest" leading to disclosure of the Divine Source and mystical transformation may be judged from numerous passages, especially in the book of Isaiah; for example:

> . . . the crooked shall be made straight, and the rough places plain; and the glory of the Lord shall be revealed. (Is. 40:4)

> Darkness shall cover the earth, and gross darkness the people; but the Lord shall arise upon thee, and his glory shall be seen upon thee. (Is. 60:2)

The term "people," in the prophets, is a technical term of mysticism, equivalent to the Greek *ktisis* (literally "colony"), and standing for the *personality* regarded as a confluence of spiritual entities,[7] especially those with a "worldly" orientation, cut off from the Source. These are left in darkness "below," as in St. Augustine's vision of the Unchangeable Light of the Lord (cf. Col. 1:15; Rom. 8:19).

The "Little Apocalypse" (Matt. 24:3–44) plainly describes a period of chaos before the disclosure of the Divine Source. It begins with a "horror of desolation," when one is advised to "flee into the mountains" (put one's trust in the higher values?). Startling phenomena ("great signs and wonders") could deceive even those destined to come through the ordeal; and "tribulations" will be greater than ever experienced before. But no mistake can be made regarding "the appearing of the Son of Man in heaven"; for it is like the dawn, spreading light from the east to the west. Everyone should "watch therefore" and "be ready"; for "the Son of Man comes at an hour you do not expect."

Phenomena of "world-upheaval," if mystical, will be perceived in some state of primary or secondary separation; for although the groundwork of the state can be described as third-order dissociation, the phenomena in no way resemble the physical ones around, and yet (as the accounts imply) one is immersed in them, in the same "world" or above it. Brief mention is made of such an experience in George Fox's long account of his period of "contest," 1643–51:

---

[7]Called *contributory minds, co-minds,* or CMs, in Whiteman, 1979–80, pp. 48f, and 1980, pp. 17, 32. In ML they are called *monads* (pp. 80f, 224 n.).

I saw also the mountains burning up, and the rubbish; and the rough and crooked ways and places made smooth and plain . . . (Fox, 1924, p. 10)

Various experiences, in secondary separation, of crowds of people driven by some kind of desire to escape, are recorded in ML or in the author's diaries. In one dated October 20, 1948 (ML, p. 214, no. 1780) the people were very vividly seen, and the idea of *fire* was strongly conveyed. Later, the "idea of water" was so strong and sudden as to upset my equilibrium and partly change the experience into fantasy. Another experience (Jan. 6, 1950) came at the beginning of convalescence from an attack of gastric influenza, and is recorded as follows:

[1878] Masses of people escaping in various directions because of heat; the scene surveyed from a higher vantage point, the people seem packed close together, crouching with heads down, like a procession of wood-lice, all with an equal urgency to escape. Something of the dramatic character of a "last judgement" conveyed. The scene watched for about half a minute.

Swedenborg provides many long and elaborate descriptions of "world-destructions," some with drawings, in his Spiritual Diary. The following is an example:

[5324–25, 5332; Jan. 6, 1757] . . . The vastation commenced by an east wind . . . and it carried away the mountain above . . . to such an extent that, first, the underside of the mountain appeared uncovered, and there was exhibited the character of that subterranean region, that, namely, it was full of palaces and monasteries. Round about the chasm above mentioned appeared nothing but a certain gloom . . . . Next, all the heaps between the palaces and monasteries were carried away by east and west winds . . . . Afterwards I saw a certain atmosphere fall down from heaven, which completely devastated all those tracts so that they became a desert.

Several mystics have given clear indications as to periods of "tribulation" before or adjustment after the disclosure of the Divine Source and/or mystical transformation. It seems suitable to call *regular* the kind of development in which a third-order dissociated state becomes stabilized for possibly six months or more *after* the disclosure (because then it is well under control, through higher affiliations being recognised and lower influences having no obsessive power). Presumably Gotama Buddha's development was "regular" in this respect, since there is no suggestion that he was so dissociated before his enlightenment.

St. Paul's development also seems to have been "regular." For he says that "when it pleased God . . . to reveal his Son in me . . . immediately I conferred not with flesh and blood . . . but I went into Arabia" (Gal. 1:15–17). This strongly suggests that he felt the need to work out a period of contest and adjustment, in withdrawal from his ordinary associates, *after* the revelation.

Swedenborg's "ultimate contest" (in London) seems to have begun two days before a powerful vision of "the Son," with "tremblings and noise" and some messianic identification, and to have continued then for possibly more than a year (White, 1868, pp. 121f, 129f; entry in the *Journal of Dreams* for 6 x 7 April 1744). The *Journal* ends about seven months afterward; then, at the beginning of July 1745, he left London for Sweden, and we read that "during the voyage his visions ceased" (White, 1868, p. 141).

A characteristic of many, if not all, ultimate contests is the receiving of "instructions," as by "the word of the Lord," to perform certain representative acts, in the manner of a ritual, and for the intensifying of Obedience. So Swedenborg, it is recorded, rolled himself in deep mud in a gutter and then distributed money to the crowd that had gathered around (ibid., p. 121). Ezekiel records how "the word of the Lord" came that he should bake some barley cakes with human dung and eat them (4:11), to symbolize the ordained admixture of "Israel" (the potential mystic) with "the nations" (worldly influences). On his protesting, he was allowed to use cow dung instead.

George Fox records being "taken up in the love of God" several times in 1647 (1924, p. 9) and thereafter undergoing great tribulations and miseries, as well as receiving frequent interior disclosures, evidently in a higher or mixed dissociated state. The last of such series of disclosures was at Lichfield where, he says, the three spires of the cathedral "struck at my life." He was commanded by the Lord to take off his shoes and walk up and down the streets crying "Woe to the bloody city of Lichfield"; and "the market place appeared like a pool of blood" to him (ibid., pp. 39–40). Subsequently he heard of the tradition that 1000 Christians had been martyred there about A.D. 286.

In ML (pp. 13f) there is a much abbreviated account of an ultimate contest of *regular* type, following a first disclosure of the Divine Source and the mystical transformation, which themselves followed nearly a year of continual Recollection practices. The Obedience and transformation remained stabilized, intense and unceasing, in varying degrees of tertiary separation, for about seven months. During the latter part of this period, dissociated phenomena of mixed type continued for long periods in the day, and secondary separations for long periods during the nights. The stabilizing of the transformation (in mystical tertiary separation) preserved objectivity and prevented the influences from becoming obsessive. After the seven months, the *mixed* third-order dissociation abruptly ended (in accord with Obedience). A mystical tertiary state of higher and wholly *unmixed* type, Obedience being still strong, then continued for another six months, after which normal employment was resumed, and primary separations, many of mystical grade, became habitual.

We now consider evidence indicating what is likely to happen when an ultimate contest (third-order dissociation of mixed type) is entered into *irregularly,* not from the strength of a developed proficiency in Recollection but from weakness due to overwork or some kind of psychological trauma. We are not supposing, however, that the people in question (usually young) are necessarily deficient in intelligence or moral sense compared with "normal" people. For the contest is being waged in a state of *mixed* type; otherwise, if of lower type, with counterfeits dominant, there would be manifestations of "disobedience" in such forms as paranoid delusion or violence. So there is an opening to higher powers working partly in secret; and this implies some opening to true Obedience and thus an insight that may be in some ways *beyond* what is "normal."

It may be observed that almost all cases of "breakdown" or acute schizophrenia have strong "religious" overtones. If doubt is felt about this statement, reference can be made to the conclusions of Anton Boisen, who, at the age of forty-four, was diagnosed as suffering from catatonic schizophrenia, following an unhappy love affair. While in hospital, and afterward, he studied 173 hospitalized male schizophrenics. He writes:

> Those strange ideas that came to me, ideas of world catastrophe, of death, of rebirth, of cosmic importance and mission, are found in case after case. They tend to occur in conjunction with one another. Where we find one we are apt to find the others also, and the presence of one of these ideas, in so far as it is autochthonous and not derived from other persons, is sufficient to establish the presumption that the individual concerned has made his grim journey to the lower regions and has stood face to face with the great realities of death and life. (Boisen, 1936, p. 53)

Such views are supported by numerous other cases reported autobiographically. One of the most detailed, and in some ways most fantastic, is that of Judge Daniel Schreber (1903; Freud, 1979), who, like Boisen, also experienced sex-changes with religious connotation, "miraculous apparitions" (as Schreber called them), as well as the other phenomena mentioned above, along with other effects such as "holy music."

From Schreber's long account one can see how the desperate need to make sense of the perplexing phenomena (especially the female and other "changed body-images"), while being completely ignorant of mysticism and fixated in an absurdly conventional idea of God, led him to fantastic delusional beliefs. These included the destruction of his (physical) stomach and intestines, his being forcibly made into a woman (physically) for sexual abuse by Dr. Flechsig (or alternatively because he, as coming Redeemer, must first be born as woman), and his later transvestism, explicable, as with other cases of female body-image in men, in terms of male woman-envy or the fixated need to know something of both sexes (Zilboorg, 1974, pp. 115, 127; Fromm-Reichmann and Gunst, 1974, p. 92).

Reference may also be helpfully made to cases very briefly summarized by Bowers and Freedman (1969, pp. 464–467), a number of cases in Kaplan (1964) and Landis and Mettler (1964), and the cases of "James" and "Julie" studied in much detail by Laing (1965). A few other cases are summarized in Raymond Prince's study of "Religious Experience and Psychosis" (1979–80). And on the basis of a comparison between descriptions by fifteen patients and superficially similar descriptions by mystics, Lenz (1979) has presented a table of seven effects of "delusion," described as "irrational" in the sense of Rudolf Otto (i.e., numinous; 1959). Included, beside the characteristics mentioned above—sense of mission, polarity of moods, suspension of feeling for time and space, and so on—is the very commonly reported "influence of rays," which, the patient says, "affect me or radiate from me" and put me "under the spell" of other people.

In the light of mystically objective and controlled experience of the phenomena, facing them without succumbing to delusional beliefs, we can set down the following conclusions and principles for their scientific study:

1. The state in which such phenomena are presented is a *mixed dissociated* one of third order. There is a loosening from the physical, in such a way that *both* lower and higher forces acting in the depths of the personality can manifest themselves in representative forms, for the building of knowledge and control at the highest level.
2. The phenomena can be observed or reacted to in two ways, either (a) in a controlled and objective way, from a standpoint of security through understanding and Obedience, in which case they are to be accepted as *genuine* and *real* in a nonphysical way; or (b) in a partly obsessive way, from a standpoint of perplexity, fear, hopelessness, or anguish of self-devaluation, in which case the phenomena take on a *counterfeit* but nevertheless objectively powerful quality, and may be

falsely supposed real in a *physical* way (e.g., interpreted as due to "rays").

3. The *counterfeit* is accordingly to be explained as the nonphysical manifesting of inadequacy to perceive and conform oneself to what is genuine. It is not to be explained as the senseless imaginings of someone who has lost his power of reason.

The *genuine* phenomena commonly observed in a mixed dissociated state of third order need to be recognized, and their genuine significance needs to be understood:

(a) *"Voices"* make assertions, express feelings, and very commonly try to insinuate intentions (nearly always unwise ones, even if at first they appear to be the fulfilling of an inescapable duty). The entities responsible (intermediate or lower "contributory minds") have a certain clearly recognizable moral character (sometimes mistaken for that of a physically living person), but from a higher point of view are inadequately informed about the situation and so make continual misjudgments. The communicated judgments and persuasions can have a convincing and powerful effect if one is not protected by the "upward-looking" of Obedience and the objectivizing of Recollection. But explanation, if it imparts true understanding and faith, can initiate release and control.

(b) Unusual *lighting* varies with the character of the state and degree of immersion in it, or, contrariwise, nonattached observation of it. Thus it may be vibrant, numinous, flamy, artificial, garish, gloomy, or "infernal" in character. If the physical light is artificial (as from electric lighting), in the dissociated state the character may be that of a conflagration.

(c) *Sounds* may have the character of being "changed in pitch," or may suggest that a Last Judgement or end of the world is taking place. The impression of a fateful, providentially ordered procession of events, aptly described as an "end of the world," can also come without sound, being then somehow present in the events themselves.

(d) Related to this last effect is the impression that everything is *symbolic* of something deeper and more real, so that one tends to think, and even speak, in symbolic terms or will seem to other people to speak in nothing but metaphors.

(e) It is clear that the ordinary "person," who has grown up anchored in the world, has been partly or wholly done away with, or transcended, and a new and *real being* is either in charge (through Obedience) or is hoping and trying to get known, against forces aimed at destroying it. Such forces, while not themselves physical, are associated with people in the physical world because the attachments natural to them are now seen to be subtly inimical, and indeed can make them uncomprehending and antagonistic, if not demonic. But it is essential neither to withdraw nor to resist, whatever happens, but instead, to look on all other people with love and sympathy. Then one's real being grows from the universality of one's sacrificial Obedience.

The "real being" is fully *intersubjective* or *universally empathic,* but is not thereby God, the Messiah, the Redeemer, or the Virgin Mary, in any "popular" individualistic sense of these terms. Identification with any such figure individualistically means absorption in lower contributory minds; and, as in the cases of Schreber or Charles Manson (Wilson, 1975, pp. 174–206), one acts then in a correspondingly irrational or demonic way.

Guidance for Those Undergoing the Contest

The big problem that presents itself here is that of how to deal with the untold thousands of people today, mostly young, who seem to be making an *irregular* approach to ultimate contests, in what takes the outward form of "breakdown" through mental strain, overwork, or trauma.

What might be called the therapy of Sharing has proved to be almost immediately effective in five cases of "breakdown" where close personal contact was possible and asked for. The essentials of this method (as practiced by the author) could be described as loving rapport, respect, dismissal of fears, authentic explanation, and sharing of first-hand knowledge of dissociative or other nonphysical phenomena. The method has also proved effective in other cases, for instance, with persons who are in doubt or anguish over developing psychic powers.

The first step is to banish any suggestion of superiority (of the therapist over the "mentally ill") or aloofness; the more strongly an empathic contact of love and friendly confidence can be maintained, the quicker the recovery of faith and the surer the fruits of insight. In this respect the method is the opposite of older methods (and some still practiced) in which the "patient" is made to feel a failure, and is subjected to mind-deadening drugs, depersonalizing routines, and "uninterested (even sadistic) personnel" (Kleinmuntz, 1974, pp. 530f).

Friendly and interested questioning will bring to light the particular phenomena experienced and beliefs associated with them: voices, lights and lighting, presences, influences interpreted as rays, fateful "end-of-the-world" phenomena or intimations (not on any account to be dismissed as *fantasies*). "Voices," also, are not on any account to be spoken of as imagined or fantasied. It should be explained that they come from *real nonphysical entities* in the "lower parts" of one's personality, and the inquirer or seeker (not to be thought of as a "patient," but rather as a fellow-student, brother, or sister) should be encouraged to talk to the entities (in thought or aloud) and perhaps tell them that they are not seeing straight and must not behave in a malicious way.

During this initial conversation one will be in a position to assure the inquirer that *there is nothing whatever to fear.* All that seems unpleasant, uncontrollable, or frightening is so only because an irrational fear has been allowed to take hold. He or she is in fact a *pioneer* in the first-hand exploration of deeply instructive *altered states of consciousness* and *other worlds* of conscious existence; and this is a privilege granted to very few psychiatrists or other students of the mind.

If there is little trust in a higher Wisdom (the word God having been associated with absurdities, naive pseudo-scientific dogmas, or distaste), one must explain something about Obedience and the healing power of the Source, as matters of direct experience, abundantly testified in the most explicit terms.

Anyone visiting a mental hospital or neuroclinic who sees groups of people sitting or standing about, wearing on their faces a uniform mask of hopelessness and self-devaluation, must find it inexpressibly gratifiying to take one of these young people aside and in no more than a few minutes see the mask fall, to reveal an interested and alert human being, full of hope.

Then one must try to arrange that drugs, whether medically prescribed or voluntarily taken, be entirely given up. For if certain symptoms are removed by drugs, the contest must work itself out another way (in "side-effects"), which may be more damaging. Moreover, most of the drugs that are used today, even minor tranquilizers, seem to produce, very often, anxiety-creating amnesias or other obvious losses of mental power. Recollective control (which these inquirers may also need to be taught) is seriously obstructed by these abnormal, uncontrollable, and depressing effects.

It would be beyond the scope of this chapter to investigate kinds of disorder, called "psychotic," that do not have an obvious bearing on the development of potentialities for mystical experience.

"Myths" of World-Destruction

In the light of all the preceding evidence it seems reasonable to suggest that the main source of the very widely distributed myths of world-destruction is likely to be experiences of *ultimate contest* of one or more of the kinds detailed here. Mystical knowledge seems to be specially indicated in some of the myths, by an attempt to coordinate four kinds of destruction (by fire, water, etc.) with the fourfold cycle of creative functions (cf. Stith

Thompson, 1955, section on "World Catastrophes," vol. I, A1000–1099; also Jung and Kerényi, 1951).

Conclusion

Development toward the habitualization of mystical experience and the establishing of the unitive transformation (the ultimate of "self-realization") passes through many different phases, and varies considerably from person to person. In this chapter we have been concerned chiefly with *regular* processes, in which Recollection practice leads fairly easily to a disclosure of the Divine Source and the establishment of *real being* in Obedience and Faith.

It has been felt necessary also, however, to give some study to cases where the course of development involves a period of "great tribulation" *before* such disclosure, or where the tribulation seems to have led some way toward such disclosure without actually attaining it in its fullness. Some of these, as in the cases of Bunyan and Tolstoy, seem to derive from peculiarities of thinking or circumstances in early life. Others are "reactive" cases, precipitated by mental strain or trauma (Kantor et al., 1953).

The further possibility remains, that all or most "process" cases may have been "manufactured" by unsuitable environment or treatment (Szasz, 1974, Chap. 2; 1973). Perhaps these also should be classified as *irregular* approaches to mystical development, but ones that through frustration have borne no fruits in the outer life. The alternative would be to believe that some of the worst tribulations in life have no purpose.

No one who has experienced a real disclosure of the Divine Source and mystical transformation can doubt that this is the goal, purpose, and meaning of all life. Nor can one doubt that if this goal is not attained in the present life, it lies ahead as an effective purpose for the hidden real being of each individual (when the outer parts of the personality have partly or wholly fallen away).

Our conclusion is therefore that everyone can develop that essential core of mystical experience (in an incipient "tertiary state") by habitually restoring an orientation to the Source—for the replenishment of inspirational energy, the lifting of attachments to self, and the imparting of wisdom in every predicament of life; not forgetting practices of Recollection for the "loosening from time." And the mystic who knows the goal here and now more fully can be understood to have merely anticipated (by a kind of preliminary "dying") some of the fruits that normally may be expected to follow physical death.

AC	*Arcana coelestia.* Swedenborg, 1885–1926.
AMC	*Ascent of Mount Carmel.* St. John of the Cross, 1947.
DN	*The Dīgha Nikāya.* Gotama Buddha, 1949–1960.
GIP	*The graces of interior prayer.* Poulain, 1957.
IC	*The interior castle.* St. Teresa, 1974.
LD	*Light in darkness.* Whiteman (awaiting publication)
ML	*The mystical life.* Whiteman, 1961
MN	*The Majjhima Nikāya.* Gotama Buddha, 1977–1979.
VRE	*The varieties of religious experience.* William James, 1960.
YS	*The Yoga-Sūtras of Patañjali,* Dvivedi, 1934.

(Figures following give the relevant page number)

APPENDIX B. CLASSIFICATION OF NON-PHYSICAL STATES
with extensive NP space-phenomena
[NP = non-physical; P = physical]

1) OPENING:
   (a) NP phenomena are perceived focally *as from the physical body*;
   (b) P phenomena are also perceived, but *not focally.*

2) DISSOCIATION:
   (a) NP phenomena constitute or colour the *whole field of perception*;
   (b) There is no impression of having a NP bodily organism, or of being *normally* in the physical body.

3) PRIMARY SEPARATION (S1):
   (a) NP phenomena are perceived *as from a NP bodily organism* located in the same NP space;
   (b) There is no impression of being at the same time in the P body;
   (c) The physical body is asleep or fully entranced.

4) SECONDARY SEPARATION (S2):
   (a) NP phenomena are perceived focally *as from a NP bodily organism* located in the same NP space;
   (b) There are at the same time definite impressions of being in the P body, but the *two bodies are quite independent*;
   (c) The physical body is quiet and under some degree of conscious control.

5) TERTIARY SEPARATION (S3):
   (a) NP phenomena are perceived focally *as from a NP bodily organism* located in the same space;
   (b) There are at the same time definite impressions of being in the P body in such a way that *the locations of the two bodies seem the same*, in spite of differences in their form and/or size and possibly also in their surroundings.
   (c) The "intensity" of the NP perceptions fluctuates somewhat, so that a degree of non-focal attention is also occasionally being directed to the P body and its circumstances.
   (d) The physical body is normally under full control.

(The above is reproduced from *Light in Darkness,* page 10)

SYNOPSIS OF METHOD OF ASSESSMENT

Factor	Rating Scheme
R: *Intrinsic Reality* Sense of ultimates, logical priority, life-fullness, substance, tangibility, vivid participation.	0. no objective control or reflection. 1. some dreamlike or imaginative quality, reflection and attempts at control. 2. more "real" than the physical, as regards participation and substance; free observation. 3. strong participation, sense of substance and pin-pointed objectivity.
V: *Vertical Recollection* Openness to higher direction, including moral choice, guidance, and higher significance; "obedience".	0. complete lack. 1. some awareness of moral choice or guidance. 2. continuity of latent obedience. 3. manifest obedience to the Source.
H: *Horizontal Recollection* Openness to rational continuity, including memory of and comparisons with the physical state.	0. severe lack. 1. fairly good. 2. complete openness to comparisons.
I: *Integration* Integration and joy; transformation; poise, transcendence of emotionality, excitement and fear.	0. unpleasant or indifferent. 1. beginnings of a higher freedom. 2. a first integration and release from physical habits of thought; distinct improvement in bodily form. 3. transformation to "proper form".
P: *Personal Communion* Intercommunication of thought, feeling and impression of character; openness to instruction; selfless and loving identification.	0. no person seen, or only dreamlike or "lay" figures. 1. beginnings of objective knowledge of other minds, with communication of thought and feeling. 2. clear and direct intelligible communication. 3. communion in loving identification and interchange of wisdom.
M: *Continuity of Memory*	0. no memory on return (only comes later). 1. no complete break, but some difficulty or vagueness of recall. 2. memory continues vividly, as by perpetuation of the interior state, in detail and without a break.

Total 0– 3 points: *Undeveloped* types.
      4– 5 points: *Borderline* types.
      6– 8 points: First-degree or *psychical* separations.
      9–11 points: Second-degree or *pre-mystical* separations.
      12–16 points: Third-degree or *mystical* separations.
Intermediate ratings are to be shown by a + sign, e.g + (between and).

(Reproduced from Whiteman, 1975, p. 107, and LD.40)

REFERENCES

Augustine of Hippo. *St. Augustine's confessions,* William Watts (transl.) London: William Heinemann, 1912.

Balfour, G. W., Earl of. A study of the psychological aspects of Mrs. Willett's mediumship and the statements of the communicators concerning process. *Proceedings of the Society for Psychical Research,* 1935, *43,* 43–318.

Bennett, J. G. *Concerning Subud.* London: Hodder and Stoughton, 1958.

Boals, Gordon F. Toward a cognitive reconceptualization of meditation. *Journal of Transpersonal Psychology,* 1978, *10,* 143–182.

Boisen, Anton. *The exploration of the inner world.* New York: Harper & Row, 1936.

Boss, Medard. *A psychiatrist discovers India,* Henry A. Frey (transl.). London: Oswald Wolff, 1965.

Bowers, M. B. and Freedman, D. X. Psychedelic experiences in acute psychoses. In C. T. Tart (Ed.), *Altered States of Consciousness.* New York: Wiley, 1969, pp. 463–476.

Buddha, Gotama. *The Dīgha Nikāya, Pali Text, T. W. Rhys Davids and J. Estlin Carpenter* (Eds.), 3 vols. London: Luzac (Pali Text Society, 1949, 1966, 1960.

Buddha, Gotama. *The Majjhima Nikāya,* Pali Text, V. Trenckner and R. Chalmers (Eds.), 3 vols. London: Luzac (Pali Text Society), 1977–1979.

Buddhaghosha, B. *The path of purification (Visuddhimagga),* Bhikkhu Ñyāṇamoli (transl.). Colombo: Semage, 1964.

Conze, E. *Buddhist meditation.* London: George Allen and Unwin, 1956.

Davis, A. J. *The magic staff.* Boston: William White, 1873.

De Beauvoir, Simone. *The second sex,* H. M. Parshley (transl.). London: New English Library, 1969.

Dvivedī, M. N. *The Yoga-Sūtras of Patañjali,* Sanskrit text and translation. Adyar: Theosophical Publishing House, 1934.

Eliade, Mircea. *Patterns in comparative religion,* Rosemary Sheed (transl.). London: Sheed and Ward, 1958(a).

Eliade, Mircea. *Yoga, immortality and freedom,* Willard R. Trask (transl.). New York: Pantheon, 1958b.

Epstein, M. D. and Lieff, J. Psychiatric complications of meditation practice. *Journal of Transpersonal Psychology,* 1981, *13,* 137–147.

Farges, Albert. *Mystical phenomena.* London: Burns, Oates and Washbourne, 1926.

Fox, George. *The journal of George Fox.* London: Dent, 1924.

Freud, Sigmund. Formulations on the two principles of mental functioning. *Complete Works of Sigmund Freud.* London: Hogarth, 1958, *12,* 215–226.

Freud, Sigmund. Psychoanalytic notes on an autobiographical account of a case of paranoia (Dementia Paranoides). In *Case Histories II,* Pelican Freud Library, vol. 9. Harmondsworth: Penguin Books, 1979, pp. 129–223.

Fripp, Peter. *The mystic philosophy of Sant Mat.* London: Spearman, 1964.

Fromm-Reichmann, F. and Gunst, V. On the denial of women's sexual pleasure: discussion of Dr. Thompson's paper. In J. B. Miller, *Psychoanalysis and women.* Harmondsworth: Penguin Books, 1974, pp. 85–93.

Garrett, Eileen J. *My life as a search for the meaning of mediumship.* London: Rider, 1939.

Goleman, Daniel. The Buddha on meditation and states of consciousness, part II: a typology of meditation techniques. *Journal of Transpersonal Psychology,* 1972, *2,* 151–210.

Gopi Krishna. *Higher consciousness.* New York: Julian Press, 1974.

Gopi Krishna. *Kundalini.* New Delhi: Orient, 1976.

Govinda, Anagarika. *Foundations of Tibetan mysticism.* London: Rider, 1969.

Grant, Joan. *Far memory.* London: Corgi Books, 1975.

James, William. *The varieties of religious experience.* London: Fontana, 1960.

Jennings, J. G. *The Vedantic Buddhism of the Buddha.* London: Oxford University Press, 1947.

John of the Cross, St. Ascent of Mount Carmel. In E. Allison Peers (Transl. and Ed.), *The Complete Works of St. John of the Cross,* volume I. London: Burns, Oates and Washbourne, 1947.

Jung, C. G. and Kerényi, C. *Introduction to a science of mythology,* R. F. C. Hull (transl.). London: Routledge and Kegan Paul, 1951.

Kantor, R. E., Wallner, J. M., and Winder, C. L. Process and reactive schizophrenia. *Journal of Consulting Psychology,* 1953, *17,* 157–162.

Kaplan, B. *The inner world of mental illness.* New York: Harper & Row, 1964.

Kempis, Thomas à. *Of the imitation of Christ.* London: Ward, Lock, 1912.

Kleinmuntz, Benjamin. *Essentials of abnormal psychology.* New York: Harper, 1974.

Kornfield, Jack. Contribution to a discussion on meditation. *Journal of Transpersonal Psychology,* 1978, 10, 120–126.

Kornfield, Jack. Intensive insight meditation: A phenomenological study. *Journal of Transpersonal Psychology,* 1979, *11,* 11–58.

Krall, Emil. *The art of tone-production on the violoncello.* London: Horace Marshall, 1923.

Laing, R. D. *The divided self.* Harmondsworth: Penguin Books, 1965.

Landis, C. and Mettler, F. A. (Eds.) *Varieties of psychopathological experience.* New York: Holt, Rinehart & Winston, 1964.

Laufer, Moses. *Adolescent disturbance and breakdown.* Harmondsworth: Penguin Books, 1975.

Lenz, Hermann. The element of the irrational at the beginning and during the course of delusion. *Confinia Psychiatria,* 1979, *22,* 183–190.

Lewis, C. S. *Mere Christianity.* London: Fontana, 1960.

Miller, Jean Baker. *Psychoanalysis and women.* Harmondsworth: Penguin Books, 1974.

Muktananda, Paramahansa. *Guru.* New York: Harper & Row, 1972.

Muldoon, Sylvan and Carrington, Hereward. *The projection of the astral body* (4th ed.). London: Rider, 1968.

Myers, F. W. H. The subliminal consciousness, V. *Proceedings of the Society for Psychical Research,* 1892, *8,* 466–535.

Naranjo, C. and Ornstein, R. E. *On the psychology of meditation.* New York: Viking, 1971.

Needleman, Jacob. *The new religions.* London: Allen Lane, 1972.

Nikhilananda, Swami (Transl.). *Ramakrishna: prophet of new India.* London: Rider, 1951.

Ñāṇamoli (see Buddhaghosha).

Nyanaponika Thera. *The heart of Buddhist meditation.* London: Rider, 1962.

Otto, Rudolf. *The idea of the holy,* John Harvey (transl.). Harmondsworth: Penguin Books, 1959.

Patanjali (see Dvivedī, Rāma Prasāda, Woods).

Pelman Institute. *Pelmanism,* 12 Lessons. London: The Pelman Institute, 4 Bloomsbury Street, n.d.

Poulain, A. *The graces of interior prayer,* trs. L. L. Yorke Smith. London: Routledge and Kegan Paul, 1950.

Prince, Raymond. Religious experience and psychosis. *Journal of Altered States of Consciousness,* 1979–80, *5,* 167–181.

Rāma Prasāda (transl.) *Patañjali's Yoga Sūtras, with the commentary of Vyāsa and the gloss of Vācaspatimiśra.* Allahabad: Sacred Books of the Hindus IV, 1924.

Robinson, Edward. *The original vision.* Oxford: The Religious Experience Research Unit, Manchester College, 1977.

Schreber, Daniel. *Denkwürdigkeiten eines Nervenkranken.* Leipzig: Oswald Mutze, 1903.
Spencer, Sidney. *Mysticism in World Religion.* Harmondsworth: Penguin Books, 1963.
Swedenborg, Emanuel. *The spiritual diary,* 5 vols. London: Swedenborg Society, 1846–1902.
Swedenborg, Emanuel. *Journal of dreams.* Bryn Athyn, Penn.: Academy Book Room, 1918.
Swedenborg, Emanuel. *Arcana coelestia,* 12 vols and Index. London: Swedenborg Society, 1885–1926.
Szasz, Thomas. *The manufacture of madness.* London: Granada, 1973.
Szasz, Thomas. *Ideology and insanity.* Harmondsworth: Penguin Books, 1974.
Tenzin Gyatsho, 14th Dalai Lama. *The opening of the wisdom-eye.* Wheaton: Theosophical Publishing House, 1972.
Teresa of Avila, St. *The interior castle,* E. Allison Peers (transl.). London: Sheed and Ward, 1974.
Thompson, Stith. *Motif-index of folk-literature,* 6 volumes (revised ed.). Indiana: Indiana University Press, Bloomington, 1955.
Underhill, Evelyn. *Mysticism.* London: Methuen, 1930.
White, Steward Edward. *The road I know.* New York: Dutton, 1948.
White, William. *Life of Emanuel Swedenborg.* Glasgow: Bell, 1868.
Whiteman, J. H. M. The angelic choirs. *The Hibbert Journal,* 1954, *52,* 262–277.
Whiteman, J. H. M. *The mystical life.* London: Faber and Faber, 1961.
Whiteman, J. H. M. *Philosophy of space and time.* London: George Allen and Unwin, 1967.
Whiteman, J. H. M. The scientific evaluation of out-of-the-body experience. In J. C. Poynton (Ed.) *Parapsychology in South African.* Johannesburg: South Africa Society for Psychical Research, 1975, pp. 95–106.
Whiteman, J. H. M. An introduction to the mystical model for psychopathology. *Journal of Altered States of Consciousness,* 1979–1980, *5,* 31–53.
Whiteman, J. H. M. The mystical model for psychopathology, and applications. *Parapsychological Journal of South Africa,* 1980, *1(2),* 14–44.
Whiteman, J. H. M. *Light in darkness, Vol. I; Foundations of Scientific Mysticism* (awaiting publication).
Wilson, Colin. *Order of assassins.* London: Granada, 1975.
Woods, J. H. *The Yoga-system of Patañjali.* Delhi: Motilal Banarsidass, 1966.
Woodward, F. L. *Some sayings of the Buddha.* Oxford: Oxford University Press, 1925.
Zilboorg, Gregory. Masculine and feminine. In J. B. Miller, *Psychoanalysis and women.* Harmondsworth: Penguin Books, 1974, pp. 96–131.

Indices

Name Index

Abbot, E. A., 70
Abruzzi, W., 404
Ackernecht, E. H., 302
Adamec, R. E., 213
Adler, A., 58
Adler, T., 603
Ahmed, S. H., 303
Alberti, G., 319, 343
Allport, G., 212
Andrews, G., 380
Appelle, S., 497
Arieti, S., 319, 326
Arkin, A. M., 32, 33, 39
Armitage, R., 119
Arnold-Forster, M., 592,
  602, 606
Arzumanov, J., 453
Ashby, W. R., 7, 13
Assagioli, R., 32, 557, 573
Attneave, F., 4
Augustine, St., 619, 622,
  646
Aurobindo, 556, 573, 577
Ax, A. F., 563
Azerinsky, E., 465
Azima, H., 503

Bader, 6, 18, 27
Bahr, D. M., 303
Baird, J. C., 10

Bakan, P., 63
Baldridge, B. J., 463
Balis, G. U., 390
Bandler, R., 33, 449
Bannerjii, G., 289, 299
Banquet, J. P., 164, 512
Barber, T. X., 105, 134,
  140, 348, 366, 373, 377,
  431, 572
Baril, L. L., 399
Barnett, E. A., 451
Baroja, J. C., 293
Barthes, R., 415
Basmajian, J. V., 556
Basser, L., 59
Bastide, R., 52
Bateson, G., 43, 45, 49, 50,
  62, 266, 269, 272
Baudelaire, P. C., 391
Baylor, G. W., 41
Beckett, S., 399
Beer, S., 7
Belick, D. A., 167, 179, 600
Bellak, L., 229
Belo, J., 448
Beloff, J., 333
Ben-Ari, Y., 213
Bennet, G., 259, 644
Benson, H., 15, 492, 498,
  564

Berger, R., 62, 180, 463
Bergmann, P., 73
Bernheim, H., 133, 136
Bertini, M., 354, 433
Bertschinger, H., 418
Bettelheim, B., 201
Bexton, W., 500, 501
Bilo, J., 303
Binswanger, L., 57
Birge, W. R., 333
Birkhoff, G., 89
Bjerre, P., 525
Blackmore, S. J., 175, 176,
  177, 178, 179, 343
Blake, W., 81, 83
Blanchard, E. B., 562
Bloom, H., 22, 23, 24, 25
Blum, G. S., 34, 137, 139
Blumstein, S., 437
Boals, G. F., 642
Bochner, S., 92
Bogen, A., 59
Bogen, J. E., 59
Bokert, E., 339
Bonkalo, A., 477
Borges, J. L., 406, 419
Boss, M., 57, 632, 633
Bourguignon, E., 290, 403
Bramwell, J. M., 133
Brand, L., 338

Brand, W. G., 338, 343, 350, 351, 352, 353, 355
Brenman, M., 31, 136, 139
Bresler, D. E., 451, 452
Bridgman, P. W., 92
Broad, C. D., 352
Brooks, Gunn, J., 202
Broughton, R., 161, 461–484
Brown, B. 437, 444
Brown, A. E., 162
Brownfield, C., 259, 502, 503, 504
Brunelle, A., 400
Bruner, J. S., 33
Bryden, M. P., 449
Bucke, R. M., 88, 97, 121
Buddhaghosha, B., 614, 615, 642
Budzynski, T. H., 428–460, 570, 572, 574
Bulka, R. P., 302
Burkert, W., 70
Burnham, D., 418
Burr, D., 76
Butler, F., 564
Bykov, K. M., 312

Callaway, E., 19
Campbell, J., 418, 600
Cannon, W. B., 470
Capek, M., 93
Capra, F., 584
Carrington, P., 314, 487–523, 557, 605
Carstairs, G. M., 291
Cartwright, R. D., 32
Castaldo, V., 464
Castenada, C., 288, 605
Cattell, R. B., 174, 177
Chakroborty, A., 289, 299
Chayefsky, P., 260
Clarke, J., 114, 117, 118
Cleckley, H. M., 141
Coe, W., 105, 134
Cohen, D. B., 59, 62, 188, 605
Cohen, G., 62
Cohen, S. I., 259, 371
Coleridge, S.T., 16
Conn, J. H., 134, 135

Conze, E., 490, 643
Cooper, L. F., 39
Corbalis, M. C., 60, 61
Cousins, N., 583
Cox, R., 290
Cramer, R. J., 503
Crapanzano, V., 290
Crasilneck, H. B., 133

Dallimore, N., 115
Dane, J., 165, 179, 602
Daudet, L., 32
Davidow, J., 606
Davidson, R. J., 212, 566
Davis, W., 297
Davis, A. J., 644
De Beauvoir, S., 639
Deglin, V. L., 437, 438
Deikman, A., 349, 513, 514, 606
Delaney, G., 525
DeManaceine, M., 432
Dement, W., 53, 181, 183, 189, 190, 192, 463, 465, 469
Dennet, D. C., 200
Deslauriers, D., 41
Desoille, R., 32
Devereux, G., 334
Dickman, S., 436, 453
Dimond, S. J., 441, 444, 448
Dixon, N. F., 453, 454
Douglas, M., 290
Doane, K. B., 502
Donahoe, J. J., 600, 607
Drettner, B., 115
Dreyfus, H. L., 45, 62
Drucker-Colin, R., 32
Durham, F., 25, 26

Eccles, J., 114, 115, 117, 437, 443
Edelman, G., 12
Edington, G., 488
Efron, K., 395
Ehrenwald, J., 301, 313, 319, 344
Eiblmayr, K., 135, 138

Einstein, A., 25, 70, 73, 92, 93, 250
Eisenbud, J., 313
Eliade, M., 345, 416, 636
Ellis, H., 470
Eliot, T. S., 401
Emde, N. R., 212, 229
Engel, G. L., 212
Ephron, H. S., 499
Epstein, M. D., 632, 643
Epstein, S., 202
Erickson, G., 259
Erickson, M. H., 39, 98, 99, 100, 102, 103, 104, 105, 111, 112, 349, 442, 448, 449
Esterson, H., 377
Evans, C. R., 54, 597
Evans, F. J., 136, 164
Evans, H. S., 407
Evans-Wentz, W. Y., 164, 556, 580, 583, 609
Evarts, E. V., 4
Eysenck, H., 358

Faraday, A., 160, 171, 525, 599
Farges, A., 613
Federn, P., 143–147
Fehmi, L. G., 570
Feinberg, I., 4
Felipe, A., 431
Fenichel, O., 315
Fenton, W. S., 344
Fenwick, P. B., 191
Ferenczi, S., 446
Fessard, A., 280
Fingarette, H., 200, 224
Firth, R., 293
Fischer, C., 51, 465, 476
Fischer, R., 3–30, 84, 88, 89, 111, 120, 251, 255, 256, 257, 258, 271, 272, 276, 277, 279, 280, 281, 312, 380, 395–427
Fischman, L. G., 344, 348, 391
Flattery, D., 385, 387, 388
Fletcher, R., 224
Flook, J., 13

Flor-Henry, P., 121
Fluent, J., 602
Foerster, H. von, 5, 11, 254, 263, 264, 265, 269, 272, 274, 279
Fosshage, J. L., 55
Foster, G. M., 302
Foulkes, D., 342, 354, 430, 462, 465, 473, 597, 607
Fort, A., 477
Fox, G., 646, 647, 648
Fox, O., 160, 161, 171, 604
Fourie, D. P., 337, 338
Frank, J., 439, 565
Frankel, B. L, 562
Freedman, S. J., 259
Freeman, W. J., 12, 14
Frétigny, R., 32, 46
Freud, S., 18, 44, 45, 47, 50, 52, 114, 143, 199, 201, 293, 311, 312, 334, 418, 429, 442, 464, 524, 572, 638
Friedman, A., 112, 113
Fripp, P., 644
Froeschels, E., 430
Fromm, E., 52, 55, 407, 542, 572
Frumkin, K., 562
Frumkin, L. R., 442
Funk, F., 114, 117

Gabbard, G. O., 577
Gackenbach, J., 159–198, 598, 600, 606
Galdston, I., 301
Gahn, D., 442, 443, 444, 445, 446, 447, 569
Garfield, P. L., 164, 165, 168, 169, 187, 192, 591, 592, 598, 599, 600, 602, 603, 604, 605, 606
Garrett, E., 644
Garrison, V., 288
Gastaut, H., 476, 477, 478
Gaviria, M., 289
Gazzaniga, M., 436, 444
Gebser, J., 417
George, L., 332–364
Geschwind, N., 60, 399

Gibson, J., 8
Giesler, P. V., 345
Gill, M. M., 136, 139
Gillespie, G., 591, 607
Gladman, A. E., 559
Glaserfeld, E. von, 265
Glasser, W., 264
Glassman, R. B., 9
Globus, G. G., 202, 205, 216
Gloor, P., 212
Glueck, B. C., 512
Goldberger, L., 314
Goldfarb, W., 325
Goleman, D., 100, 497, 519, 642
Goldstein, L., 14, 473
Goodenough, D. R., 186
Goodman, F., 290
Gopi, K., 97, 121, 313, 644
Gordon, G., 8
Gordon, H., 119
Gorges, D., 450
Gorer, G., 345
Govinda, L., 68, 615
Grace, W. I., 16
Graef, J. R., 137, 139, 314
Graham, D. T., 16
Grant, J., 639
Graves, R., 381
Greely, A., 580
Green, A. M., 553–589
Green, C., 162, 168, 171, 172, 180, 354, 594, 609
Green, E. E., 553–589
Greimas, A. J., 419
Grela, J. J., 337
Greyson, B., 176
Griffin, M. L., 607
Grinder, J., 33
Grindley, G. C., 260
Grof., S., 366, 367, 372, 373, 378, 379, 418
Gross, M. M., 479
Grossman, S. P., 213
Grotstein, J. S., 50
Grünbaum, A., 80
Guilleminault, C., 478
Guillen, J., 409
Gwynne, P. H., 14, 406, 414

Haan, N., 200
Haber, R. N., 8
Hackstian, J., 174, 177
Hadfield, J., 47, 52, 53
Hägg, T., 21
Haight, J., 354
Hall, C., 43, 48, 524
Hall, J. A., 133, 180
Hall, M. M., 443
Halliday, G., 599
Hamilton, W., 461
Handelman, D., 345
Harley, A. T., 336
Harman, W. W., 378
Harris, A., 503
Harrison, R., 93
Hartmann, E., 180, 313, 321
Harwood, A., 288, 303
Hasegawa M., 117
Hauri, P., 467
Havelock, E., 23
Head, H., 478
Hearne, K. M. T., 162, 165, 170, 171, 172, 175, 177, 179, 181, 184, 189, 190, 598, 600, 603, 604, 607
Hebb, D. O., 139
Heetderks, D., 114
Heidegger, M., 57
Heike, G., 400
Heisenberg, W., 279
Helm-Estabrooks, N., 437
Hendlin, S. J., 557
Heron, W., 259
Hevoh, W., 342, 357
Hey, E., 117
Hiatt, J. F., 474
Hildum, D. C., 411
Hilgard, E. R., 133, 134, 135, 139, 140, 141, 155, 354
Hilgard, J. R., 140
Hill, R. M., 14
Hillard, J. R., 300
Hines, M., 497
Hinton, C. I., 68
Hippler, A. E., 292
Hirai, T., 496
Hobson, A., 51, 53, 57, 61

Hoch, E. M., 292
Hoffman, E. L., 172, 201, 598
Hofmann, A., 371
Hofstadter, D. R., 11, 200
Holton, G., 24, 25
Honorton, C., 336, 337, 338, 339, 342, 343, 350, 352, 355
Horowitz, M. J., 321
Houston, J., 340, 354, 365, 374
Hufford, D. J., 286
Hunt, H. T., 167, 179, 180, 187, 605, 606
Hurd, G. S., 286–310
Husserl, E., 48
Huxley, A., 83, 366, 367, 370, 377

Inhelder, B., 33
Irwin, H. J., 174
Iyengar, B. K. S., 113, 118
Izard, E. C., 201

Jackson, J. H., 479
Jacobson, A., 313, 327
Jahn, R. G., 584
Jakobson, R., 400, 409, 477
James, W., 77, 87, 88, 200, 202, 453, 462, 623
Janet, P., 136
Jantsch, E., 266
Jasper, H., 268
Jaynes, J., 442, 443
Jeffrey, F., 249–285
Jennings, J. G., 614, 627, 628
John of the Cross, St., 616, 626
Johnson, R. J., 146, 148, 151, 153
Jones, C. G., 61
Jones, R. T., 414
Jonté, D., 591, 598, 606
Jouvet, M., 464
Julien, R. M., 390
Jung, C. G., 47, 52, 268, 374, 378

Kaada, B. R., 213
Kafka, F., 582
Kahan, J., 199–245, 286–310
Kales, A., 181, 185, 313, 327
Kamiya, J., 121, 189, 428
Kane, S., 288
Kanthamani, B. K., 355
Kantor, R. E., 654
Kaplan, B., 33
Kaplan, H., 520
Kaplan, S., 201
Kapur, R. L., 291
Karacan, I., 465
Kasamatsu, A., 496
Katz, R., 440, 448
Keats, J., 18
Kekule, F. A., 469
Kellogg, R., 23
Kelly, E. F., 332
Kelman, H., 57
Kiev, A., 29
Klein, R., 119
Kleinmuntz, B., 630
Kleitman, N., 98, 105, 465, 471, 473
Klinger, A., 262
Klinger, E., 32, 51
Kline, M. V., 135
Kling, A., 212
Klüver, H., 372, 373, 375
Knox, R. A., 290
Koestler, A., 47, 429, 430, 469, 470
Köhler, I., 13
Kohr, R. L., 175, 176, 178
Konorski, J., 4
Kornfield, J., 354, 642
Kosslyn, S., 33, 34, 35
Kostandov, E., 452
Koulack, D., 463
Krall, E., 629
Kramer, J. C., 404
Kranz, H., 418
Kreiger, D., 584
Kripke, D., 109, 123, 474, 507
Krippner, S., 332–364, 378, 440

Kroger, W. S., 133, 134
Kroll, J. A., 293
Krystal, J., 213
Kuba, M., 292
Kubie, L. S., 430, 572
Kuper, A., 53

LaBerge, S. P., 159–198, 313, 591, 592, 600, 602, 605, 606, 608
Lacan, J., 201, 242
Lacey, J. I., 467
Ladd, G., 461
Laguerre, M. S., 297
Laing, R. D., 377, 650
Lambert, W., 297
Laing, R. D., 377, 650
Lambert, W., 297
Landon, G. M., 403
Landy, D., 290
Langer, S., 408
Langness, L. L., 289
Lasaga, A., 432, 464
Lasaga, J., 432, 464
Lashley, K. S., 10
Lasky, E. Z., 439
Laubscher, B., 345
Laurendeau, M., 597
Lavie, P., 474, 477
Law-Whyte, L., 26
Layton, B. D., 356
LeDoux, W., 436, 444
Lefebvre, A., 180, 183
Lehman, M. N., 213
LeShan, L., 70, 584, 592
Leuba, C., 432
Leuner, H., 32
Levi-Strauss, C., 302, 396, 419
Levisky, W., 60
Levy, J., 436, 437
Levy, L., 18
Lewis, M., 202, 290
Lewis, R. W. B., 24
Liebeault, A., 136
Lieff, J., 632, 643
Lillie, H., 114
Lilly, J. C., 252, 253, 256, 258, 260, 264, 271, 280, 281, 500, 569

Llinás, R., 11
Lin, T. Y., 303
Lindenbaum, S., 304
Lipowski, Z., 479
Locke, J., 16, 404
Locke, R. G., 332
Loevinger, J., 201, 203, 205, 216, 228, 229
Lourie, R., 508
Loew, C. A., 55
Loewi, O., 470
Logue, A. W., 397
London, P., 301
Long, J., 345
Loudon, J. B., 290, 302
Lovitts, B. E., 356
Luce, G., 109
Lucid, D. P., 419
Ludlow, F., 391
Ludwig, A. M., 140, 141, 505
Lull, R., 3
Luria, A., 201
Luthe, W., 354, 570
Lynch, M. D., 202

Magoun, H. W., 16
Mahler, M. S., 218
Mahnke, D., 20
Mahoney, M. F., 524
Mahrer, A., 202
Mair, L., 290
Malamud, J. R., 164, 167, 590-612
Malatesta, V., 13
Malm, L., 115
Mandelbrot, B., 74, 75, 76
Mandell, A. J., 280
Mann, P., de, 3
Margenau, H., 70
Markowitz, J., 510
Marty, M. E., 302
Maslow, A. J., 61, 488, 496
Masserman, J., 561
Masters, R. E. L., 340, 354, 365, 374
Matefy, R. E., 414
Mathews, A. M., 356
Maturana, H., 5, 6, 7, 281

Maupin, E. W., 493
Maury, A. 463
May, E., 339
May, R., 58
McCarley, R., 51, 53, 61
McConnell, R. A., 315
McCreery, C., 162, 604, 605, 606
McDonald, G., 402, 464
McDougall, W., 333
McGough, J., 111
McGlothlin, W. H., 391
McGonigle, B. O., 13
McGuigan, F. J., 4
MacKay, D. M., 260
McLaughlin, S. C., 68-96
Maclean, P., 258, 262, 561
Mcleod, B., 164, 606
McVittie, G. C., 70
Mead, G. H., 221
Meany, J., 559
Meares, A., 133
Melnechuk, T., 280
Merrell-Wolff, F., 100
Métraux, A., 345
Metzner, R., 271
Mikaelian, H. H., 13
Meyer, L. B., 416
Michaux, H., 377
Minkowski, H., 70, 80, 92, 93
Mintz, I., 325
Mishra, R., 338, 352
Miskiman, D. E., 499
Mitchell, J., 341
Mockenhaupt, S., 351
Moers-Messmer, H., 162, 173
Molfese, D., 59
Morf, A., 4
Morley, P., 288, 303
Morris, R. L., 313, 339, 340, 351, 352
Morrow, G., 74
Moruzzi, G., 16
Moser, U., 41, 54
Mountcastle, V. B., 12
Mouret, J. R., 479
Muldoon, S., 577, 638
Murphy, G., 342, 350, 358

Nagel, T., 465
Naitosh, P., 109
Narajana, R., 164
Naranjo, C., 365-394, 642
Nash, C. B., 358
Natapoff, A., 399
Nebes, R. D., 60, 61
Needleman, J., 554, 632, 644
Neisser, U., 35, 163
Nelsen, J. M., 14
Ness, R. C., 295
Neugebauer, R., 293
Neutra, R., 303
Newland, C. A., 368
Newman, E., 54
Neuman, J., von, 12
Nicholis, G., 7
Nicolescu, B., 279
Nicoll, M., 68
Nisbett, R., 453
Noll, R., 344
Noma, E., 10
Norwich, K. E., 13, 24
Nottenbohm, F., 275
Noton, D. A., 277
Nowlis, D. P., 560

Obeyesekere, G., 293
Oesterreich, T. K., 290
Ogilvie, R. D., 180, 181, 184, 185, 186, 187, 591, 598, 603, 605
Oliver, G. W., 571
Onetto-Bachler, B., 341
Ong, W. J., 11, 23
Onions, C. T., 16
Orne, M. T., 135, 136, 137, 142, 432, 577
Ornstein, R., 436, 515, 516, 569
Orr, W. C., 474
Osgood, C. E., 56
Osis, K., 339, 577
Oswald, I., 464
Oswald, L. E., 497
Otani, S., 355
Ouspensky, P. D., 68, 73, 87, 100, 164, 168, 169, 606, 607

Pahnke, A. R., 88
Pahnke, W. N., 382
Paivio, A., 35
Palmer, J., 175, 176, 178, 179, 337, 341, 356, 357
Panton, Y., 411
Papez, J. W., 561
Parker, A., 334, 335, 340, 342, 350, 358
Passouant, P., 121
Patel, C. H., 563
Patton, J., 258, 275
Pattison, E. M., 199–245, 286–310
Pavlov, I. P., 62, 136
Paz, O., 395
Pears, A., 92
Pelletier, K. R., 499, 557
Pellionisz, A., 11
Penfield, A., 8
Penfield, W., 268
Peper, E., 580
Perls, F., 43, 54, 449
Persinger, M., 358
Piaget, J., 4, 33, 34, 43, 45, 46, 212, 265, 597
Pierce C. R., 4
Pirot, M., 497
Pisano, M., 464
Pivik, R. T., 465, 467
Plutanick, R., 174
Podmore, F., 290
Podvoll, E. M., 259
Poincaré, H., 92
Poirel, C., 112
Poitras, R., 464
Pope, A., 409
Pope, K. S., 200
Popper, K., 61, 437
Potdar, A., 114, 118
Poulain, A., 615, 616
Poulet, G., 22
Poulet, G., 396, 399, 417
Powers, W. T., 256, 257, 277, 415
Prasad, J., 354
Pratt, J. G., 313, 333
Pribram, K. H., 213, 214
Price, R., 605
Prince, R. 290, 650

Prirogine, I., 7, 588
Proust, M., 395, 398, 419
Purce, J., 395
Purrington, R. D., 25
Putnam, W. H., 135

Quine, W. V., 70

Raimy, V., 200
Rajneesh, B. S., 164, 491
Rao, K. R., 355
Rao, S., 114, 118
Rapport, N., 164
Ray, W. J., 562
Razran, G., 312
Rechtschaffen, A., 63, 181, 185, 356, 462, 465, 467, 597
Reed, H., 606
Reichel-Dolmatoff, G., 388
Reik, T., 144
Reynolds, D. K., 295
Rhine, J. B., 313, 333, 334, 336, 340, 354
Rhine, L. E., 333, 334
Richet, C., 336, 337
Rickles, W. H., 559
Ricoeur, P., 407
Riggs, L. A., 260
Riley, R. L., 399
Rivers, W. H. R., 302
Robinson, E., 619
Robinson, J., 212, 229
Roffwarg, H., 32, 34, 189
Rogers, C., 202
Rogers, S. L., 297
Rogo, D. S., 341, 344, 357, 590, 600, 604
Roland, P. E., 5
Rosen, G., 293
Rosekind, M. R., 473
Rosenthal, B. G., 301
Rosenthal, F., 392
Rossi, E. L., 97–132, 442, 599
Roth, B., 477
Rubin, F., 432, 433
Rucker, R., 68
Rush, J. A., 290

Russell, J. B., 290, 294
Rycroft, C. S., 524

Saint-Denys, H.de, 600, 601, 605, 607
Saler, B., 302
Salk, L., 509
Sanford, J., 525
Sangree, W. H., 289
Sannwald, G., 354
Sapir, E., 400
Sarbin, T., 105, 134
Sargent, C. L., 336, 337
Sartre, J. P., 35, 36, 37, 38, 43, 46, 52
Schacter, D. L., 432
Schaefer, T., 259
Schafer, R., 200, 201, 229, 608
Schaffer, J. H., 404, 405
Shafii, M., 498
Schane, S. A., 400
Schatzman, M., 599
Schechter, E. I., 338
Scheff, T. J., 297
Schillig, B., 170, 171, 172
Schlitz, M., 341
Schmeidler, G. R., 338, 339, 356
Schmidt, H., 351
Schneck, J. M., 136
Schmell, H., 439
Scholes, R., 23
Schreiber, F. R., 141, 146
Schubert, H., 68
Schultz, J., 563, 570
Schuman, M., 348
Schwartz, B. A., 180, 183
Schwartz, M., 385, 387, 388
Scott, J., 477
Seer, P., 562
Seligman, M. E. P., 397, 399
Shack, W., 289
Shallice, T., 9
Shands, H., 43
Shannon, C. E., 254, 269
Shapiro, A. P., 562
Shapiro, D. H., 356
Sharcoff, J., 598

Shealy, C. N., 557
Sheldrake, R. A., 584
Shepard, R. N., 60
Shevrin, H., 436, 453, 464
Shor, R. E., 133, 136, 494
Shulgin, A. T., 383
Shurley, J. T., 252, 253
Silver, B. V., 562
Silverman, J., 344
Silverman, L. H., 454
Simon, C., 432
Simonton, O. C., 600
Singer, J. L., 200
Skinner, B. F., 555
Skjerrheim, H., 48
Skultans, V., 293
Slade, R. D., 354
Snow, C. P., 85
Snyder, F., 173, 465
Solomon, P., 259
Sparrow, G. S., 598, 599, 603, 604, 605, 606, 608
Spence, D. P., 241
Spencer-Brown, G., 266, 267, 417
Sperry, R., 435, 442
Spiegelberg, H., 200
Sroufe, L. A., 212, 218, 229
Stace, W., 88
Stampfl, T., 432
Stanford, R., 339, 342, 343, 350, 351
Stapledon, O., 16
Stark, L., 255, 277
Stechler, G., 201
Starker, S., 473
Steiner, S. S., 563
Stekel, W., 407
Stevens, S. S., 405
Stevenson, J., 320
Sternbach, L. H., 4
Stewart, K., 599
Stoyva, J., 189
Strange, J. R., 200
Stroebel, C. F., 314
Stroud, J. M., 76
Sturm, C., 135
Stuss, D., 474
Suedfeld, P., 448
Sullivan, H. S., 202, 323

Sutherland, J. D., 201
Swedenborg, E., 577, 617, 648
Sutich, A. J., 557
Svyandoshch, A., 432

Taimni, I. K., 566
Tanimoto, S. I., 262
Tart, C. T., 97, 122, 133, 137, 165, 181, 193, 223, 341, 349, 577, 591, 592
Taylor, G. R., 200
Taylor, N., 391
Thalbourne, M. A., 356
Thatcher, K., 7
Thigpen, C. H., 141
Tholey, P., 164, 165, 599, 604, 606, 607
Thomas, K., 290
Timmons, B., 121
Tiryakian, E. A., 290
Tolaas, J., 31–67, 335, 535
Toralin, N., 259
Towe, A. L., 8
Townsend, V., 260
Trevarthen, C., 9
Trosman, H., 53
Trungpa, L. C., 268
Tsuang, M. T., 344
Tucker, D. M., 443
Tulku, T., 164
Turner, V. W., 293
Turner, W. J., 384
Twenlow, S. W., 577

Ullman, M., 41, 51, 52, 55, 319, 320, 335, 336, 344, 524–552, 600
Underhill, E., 609, 614, 616
Uzzell, D., 289, 291

Valéry, P., 408
Valle, R. S., 205
Van DeCastle, R. L., 43, 48, 336, 345
Van Eeden, F., 187, 591, 600
Varela, F. J., 11
Vaughn, F., 557
Vaysse, J., 606

Vernon, J. A., 259
Villoldo, A., 440
Vives, J. L., 397, 399
Vinekar, S., 114
Virel, A., 32, 46
Vishnudevananda, S., 517
Vogel, G., 430, 431, 477

Wade, J. A., 60
Wadden, T., 354
Wall, P. D., 415
Wallis, R., 288
Walsh, R. N., 205, 223, 553
Watkins, H. H., 133–158
Watkins, J. G., 133–158
Watson, J. C., 289, 299
Watts, A. W., 382
Webb, W. B., 313, 327
Weber, M., 48
Wehr, T., 112
Weidman, H. H., 300
Weingartner, H., 403
Weitzenhofer, A., 124, 133
Welwood, J., 557
Werntz, D., 113, 114, 117, 118, 121, 123
West, L. J., 259
Westermeyer, J., 289
Wever, R., 97
Werner, H., 33
Wheeler, J. A., 16, 23
Wheelis, A., 301
White, J., 120
White, R., 338, 342, 495
Whitehead, A. N., 78
Whiteman, J. H. M., 613–659
Wijesinghe, C. P., 291
Wilden, A., 8
Wilkinson, R. T., 474
Will, O. A., Jr., 319, 320, 323
Williams, H. L., 464
Williams, J. M., 400
Wilmes, F., 173
Wilson, C., 652
Wilson, H., 114
Wilson, M., 291
Wilson, T., 8, 453
Winkelman, M., 345

Winston, P. H., 54
Wintrob, R.M., 297, 303
Wittgenstein, L., 266
Wittkower, E. D., 300
Wolman, B. B., 32, 39,
    311–331
Wolpe, J., 150
Wolpert, E., 53
Woodroffe, J., 392
Woods, J. M., 306, 636,
    638, 643

Woodward, F. L., 629
Woolfolk, R. L., 499
Wordsworth, W., 401
Worsley, A., 170, 173, 181,
    184, 190, 191, 607
Wortz, E., 560
Wuthnow, R., 288

Yap, R. M., 290, 292
Young, A., 289, 299
Young, J. G., 212

Zachner, R. C., 382
Zaidel, E., 436
Zajonc, R. B., 441
Zamarra, J. W., 498
Zangwill, O. L., 60
Zilboorg, G., 650
Zimmerman, N., 51, 55, 525
Zubek, J. P., 259
Zukav, G., 589

Subject Index

Access to dreams, 524–552
  group dream work, 529–535
  role playing, 537–539
  therapy 546–549
Alkaloids, 384
Altered states of consciousness, 97–132,
    133–158, 188–193, 349, 365–394,
    402–405, 428–457, 475–480, 487–521,
    553–583
American Society of Clinical Hypnosis, 105
Amnesia, 403, 405
Animal imagery, 386
Autogenic shift, 571
Ayahuasca, 389

Basic Rest Activity Cycle (BRAC), 98,
    106–113
Bateson's loop, 269
Behavioral Medicine Associates, 451
Biofeedback, 433, 437, 553–583
  emotional consciousness, 566–569
  extrapersonal consciousness, 577–579
  mental consciousness, 569–573
  transpersonal consciousness, 580–583
  unconscious, 573–577
Biofeedback Society of America, 554
Biopsychosocial model of human action,
    203–219
Blank-out in meditation, 515–518

Body system, 224–228
Brain laterization model, 429, 435–436

Cannabis, 390–392
Capgras syndrome, 239
Catalepsy, 311
Cataplexy, 311
Catatonic reaction, 371
Circadian sleep rhythms, 461, 471, 472
CODA, 418–420
COEX Systems, 376
Cognitive functions, 138, 139, 511–513
Comprehensive abilities battery, 177
Connecting orientation, 237
Consciousness, 68–94, 141, 199–242,
    249–282, 461–480
Consensus: shared consciousness, 251
Creativity in sleep, 468–470

Death-rebirth experiences, 380
Defense Language Institute, 259
Delusions, 320, 321
Demonology, 291, 388
Depressive disorders, 327–329, 379, 407
Desensitization, 518–519
Dimensions of states of consciousness,
    68–96
  dimension theory, 91–94
  levels of awareness, 79

Dimensions of States of Consciousness, (cont.)
range of consciousness, 89–91
time integration of sense-impressions,
77–79, 80, 83
Double consciousness, 479
Double hallucination test, 136–139
Dreaming in waking life, 593–594
Dreams, 6, 7, 31, 33, 40–58, 325, 407, 465,
467, 524–552, 592
lucid, 159–197, 312, 313, 590–609
and Psi, 334–336
and schizophrenia, 324–325
Drug-induced states of consciousness,
365–394, 402–405
Dying-to-self, 617

Ego-death, 373
Ego deposition in meditation, 513–515
Ego operation system, 224–231
Ego psychology, 143–145
Ego states, 145–149
Ego-state theory, 152
Ego-state therapy, 149
Eigen-theory, 278–282
Expansion of consciousness, 376, 377, 378

First Degree World Logic, 268, 269
Flashback, 395–420
communication, 408–411
drug-induced flashbacks, 402–405,
415–416
interindividual flashbacks, 416–418
poetry, 401, 409
synaesthesias, 398–401
Free will, 9

Hallucinations, 16, 256, 320, 321, 365, 503
Hallucinogenic drugs, 365–394, 415
Haoma, 387
Harmaline, 385
Harvard Hypnotic Susceptibility Scale, 137
Hypersuggestibility, 431–433
Hypersynchrony, 512
Hypnagogic phenomena, 286, 477, 478, 572
Hypnosis, 31, 98–100, 105, 106, 133–158,
333, 336–338, 431, 441, 442, 451,
494–496
Hypnopaedia, 429
Hypnotherapy, 98–100, 133, 134, 451–572

"I" concept, 21
"I" experience, 216–218
Image consciousness, 35–38, 43
Imagery in lucid dreams, 175–177
Imagery, mental, 33, 34–35, 353–355
Impact-Coupling-Constraints (ICC), 257
Inertia theory, 250
Information, 49–50
International Association for Near Death
Studies (IANDS), 17
Intrapsychic experience, 294–295
Isolation research, 249–282
neurological aspects of, 261–265
profound isolation (PI), 253–275, 281
social communication, 270–275
Istigkeit, 370

Klüver's illusions, 255
Koan, 489
Kundalini, 376, 379

Language, 33, 55, 201, 438, 439
Learning, 123–125
Librium, 4
Life preservation principles, 225–228
Light of conscious awareness, 79–80
LSD, 365, 366, 367, 368, 369, 380, 381,
383, 385, 388, 389, 404
Lucid dreaming, 159–197, 312, 313,
590–609
content of, 168–173, 175–177, 591–592
control of, 607–609
inducing, 165–167, 597–599
neurophysiology of, 173–175, 180–187,
193–194
terminating of, 167–168
time of, 187–188
types of, 184
Lucidity in dreams and in waking life,
590–609

Mandala, 374
Mantra meditation, 511, 515
Marijuana, 390–302, 404, 405
MDA, MMDA, 382–384
Meditation, 19, 20, 219, 238, 313, 338–340,
487–521, 641–643
Melodic intonation therapy, 429
Memory, 123, 240–242, 395–420

Mental imagery, 33–35
Mental health, 231–235, 314
Mind-body isomorphism, 53
Mnemonic method for induction of lucid
    dreams (MILD), 165, 181, 602
Moving experience, 3–5
Modes of consciousness, 199–242
Motor deprivation (MD), 259
Multiple personality, 140–143, 239
Mystical states, 613–654
    Buddhist states, 626–628
    contest, 628–632, 645–653
    meditation, 641–643
    stages, 613–626
    world destruction myths, 653–654

Nasal cycle, 113–122
    history of, 113–114
    measurement of, 117–118
    neuro-physiology of, 114–116, 119–120
Near-death experience (NDE), 176
Neurophysiology of the transformatory
    framework: Pictorial to verbal, 59–63
Neurobiology and neuropsychology,
    213–215, 274, 435–457, 511–513
Neuro-interoceptive sensations (NI), 261,
    270, 272, 273
Neuroscience of self-experience, 3–30
    closed system, 7–8
    interpreting interpretations, 15–25
    self-knowledge, 24–26
    self-reflectivity, 8–10
    sensory-motor closure, 5–7
    socio-biological model, 10–12
Nightmares, 162, 163, 475–476
Non-drug induced states of consciousness,
    428–457

Out-of-body experience (OBE), 637
Overstimulation, 505–507

Parapsychological Association, 332
Parapsychology, 175, 176, 212, 316–325,
    332–358, 637
Personal experience and consciousness,
    199–242
Pictorial narrative, 47–58
Possession States (PS), 286–306
    modes of consciousness, 304–306

possession behavior, 298–301
    psychodynamics of, 292–295
    trance, 296–297
Prana, 517
Prayers, 493
Protoconsciousness, 311–329
    depressive disorders, 327–329
    schizophrenia, 316–327
    sociocultural influences, 315–316
Psi-phenomena, 175, 176, 332–358
Psychoanalysis, 143–145, 199, 201
Psychopathology, 4, 142, 231–235, 289,
    303, 311–329, 366
Psychotherapy, 316–327, 447–457

Raven Progressive matrices, 177
Reality testing, 238–239
Real-World Dimensions, 69–77
Remembering, 395–420
Repression, 445–447
Russian sleep learning (hypnopaedia), 420

Samadhi, 625
Schizophrenia, 4, 142, 316–327, 343–344,
    371
    in childhood, 325–326
Self as "Being," 519–520
Self, concept of, 21, 202, 203, 219, 221
Self-hypnosis, 494–496
Self-memory System, 228–231
Self-regulation training (biofeedback), 555
Sensory deprivation (SD), 259–260,
    341–343, 500–505
Shamanism, 345–346
Sleep, 6, 33, 265, 420, 429–433, 461–480
Sleep and consciousness, 462–475
Sleep-dream cycle, 122–123
Sleep research, 429–433, 461–480
Sleep terrors, 475–476
Sleep-waking rhythms, 461–480
Society of Clinical and Experimental Hyp-
    nosis, 105
Somnambulism, 327, 476–477
Stress reduction, 497
Subliminal processes, 453–455

Tao, 379
Time distortion, 39–40

Time integration of sense impressions,
    77–79
Trance, 99, 100–105, 133, 134, 286–306, 494
Transcendental meditation (TM), 313, 512
Transformatory framework: Pictorial to
    verbal, 31–63
Transitions, transients and transformations
    (TTT theory), 277–278
Transpersonal States, 120–121
Twilight learning, 429–435

Ultradian rhythms, 97–132, 472–474
Unconscious phenomena, 268, 274–277,
    311, 429, 438–445, 573–577
Uncoupling, 255

Valium, 4
Verbal reports of mental imagery, 33
Visual experience, 32–33
Visual experience and verbal report, 39–43

Waking consciousness, 474–475, 591
Waking lucidity, 590
Witch hunting, 293–294

Yage experience, 385, 386, 387, 389
Yoga, 113, 517, 563, 635

Zen, 219, 517